International Symposium on Global Navigation Satellite System (ISGNSS 2018)

E3S Web of Conferences Volume 94 (2019)

Bali, Indonesia
21 - 23 November 2018

Editor:

Dudy Darmawan Wijaya

ISBN: 978-1-5108-8619-3

Printed from e-media with permission by:

Curran Associates, Inc.
57 Morehouse Lane
Red Hook, NY 12571

Some format issues inherent in the e-media version may also appear in this print version.

For additional information, please contact EDP Sciences – Web of Conferences at the address below.

EDP Sciences – Web of Conferences
17, Avenue du Hoggar
Parc d'Activité de Courtabœuf
BP 112
F-91944 Les Ulis Cedex A
France

Phone: +33 (0) 1 69 18 75 75
Fax: +33 (0) 1 69 28 84 91

contact-edps@webofconferences.org

Additional copies of this publication are available from:

Curran Associates, Inc.
57 Morehouse Lane
Red Hook, NY 12571 USA
Phone: 845-758-0400
Fax: 845-758-2633
Email: curran@proceedings.com
Web: www.proceedings.com

TABLE OF CONTENTS

Fast and continuous developments of Global Navigation Satellite Systems (GNSS) technology during the last few decades have raised the maturity level of this technology. These developments eventually make GNSS as an attracting and useful tool and, hence, it is not difficult to believe that GNSS has been playing important roles not only in the field of surveying and geodesy, but also in different numerous fields, such as geosciences, engineering, environmental sciences, and regional planning.

Recently, further and diverse developments of GNSS in many various aspects have been being massively and extensively accomplished by many people around the world. The primary goal of the International Symposium on GNSS is therefore to consolidate these diverse developments by bringing together GNSS researchers and practitioners in one joint meeting. It is expected that this symposium can provide an enjoyable place where sharing innovative-ideas and experiences as well as promoting future opportunities can fruitfully be realized.

The International Symposium on GNSS has been annually held in a number of attractive and tradition-rich places around the Asia Pacific region. This year, as for the first time, the symposium takes place in the beautiful island of Bali, Indonesia, from 21 to 23 November, 2018. Like many other places in Indonesia, Bali may kindly offer you many wonderful natural sites to explore with unique local traditional wisdoms. We do believe that God was smiling, when He created Bali Island.

On behalf of the organizing committee of the International Symposium on GNSS 2018, I would like to congratulate all participants whose papers are finally accepted in this symposium. I do hope that you would have a successful presentation and fruitful discussions during the symposium. I also wish you to have nice and pleasant stays in Bali, Indonesia.

General Conference Chair
Dr. techn. Dudy D. Wijaya

edp sciences

E3S Web of Conferences

Statement of Peer review

In submitting conference proceedings to E3S Web of Conferences, I certify to the Publisher that I adhere to the **Policy on Publishing Integrity** of the journal in order to safeguard good scientific practice in publishing.

1. All articles have been subjected to peer review administered by the proceedings editors.
2. Reviews have been conducted by expert referees, who have been requested to provide unbiased and constructive comments aimed, whenever possible, at improving the work.
3. Proceedings editors have taken all reasonable steps to ensure the quality of the materials they publish and their decision to accept or reject a paper for publication has been based only on the merits of the work and the relevance to the journal.

Title, date and place of the conference

International Symposium on Global Navigation Satellite System 2018 (ISGNSS 2018)

Proceedings editor(s):

Dr. techn. Dudy Darmawan Wijaya

Date and editor's signature

10 April 2018

Seven days in Chile: Impact of the 2011 Puyehue-Cordon Caulle volcanic eruption on GPS ionospheric delay

Oliver Jukić[1,*], *Nenad* Sikirica[2,3], *Ivan* Rumora[3], and *Mia* Filić[4]

[1]College for Management in Tourism and Informatics, Virovitica, Croatia
[2]University College of Applied Sciences Hrvatsko Zagorje Krapina, Krapina, Croatia
[3]PhD Student, Faculty of Maritime Studies, University of Rijeka, Rijeka, Croatia
[2]Independent satellite navigation, statistical learning, and space weather researcher, Zagreb, Croatia

Abstract. Satellite navigation is a global utility and an essential component of national infrastructure. Disruptions of GNSS PNT services may be considered a threat to society and civilisation in general. Natural hazards may cause the conditions that disrupt or temporarily deny GNSS PNT services. As a contributor to ionospheric dynamics, volcanic activity is considered a source of GNSS positioning performance degradation. Here we studied the 2011 Puyehue-Cordon Caulle event, the largest 21st century volcanic eruption so far, in terms of its contribution to formation of Total Electron Content (TEC), the source of ionosphere-caused GNSS positioning error, and the effects the event made on GPS positioning accuracy. TEC values were derived from dual-frequency GPS observations collected experimentally at the International GNSS Service Network reference stations in Santiago, central Chile closest to the Puyehue-Cordon Caulle volcano. We identified considerable anomalous behaviour of TEC dynamics prior to, during and after the volcanic eruption, and examined the extent to which it affected GPS positioning accuracy. The research presented here will continue with the aim of characterisation of TEC anomalous dynamics around the eruption, and its effects on GNSS positioning performance.

1 Introduction

Proliferation of satellite navigation technology requires stable and robust Global Navigation Satellite System (GNSS) positioning performance for numerous GNSS-based technology and socio-economic systems and services. Ionospheric effects are the most prominent single cause of GNSS positioning performance degradation and even disruptions of GNSS Positioning, Navigation, and Timing (PNT) services [1]. Usually resulting from much wider space weather disturbances [2], [3], the ionospheric effects on GNSS positioning performance may be caused by the other terrestrial natural sources of additional ionisation in the Earth's atmosphere, including earthquakes and volcanic eruptions [4], [5], [6].

We studied the problem through examination of ionospheric conditions deterioration, and GNSS positioning performance degradation during the 2011 Puyehue-Cordon Caulle volcanic eruption, the largest volcanic eruption in the XXI. Century. Our study was based on post-processing of experimental data [7] taken at the International GNSS Service (IGS) network reference stations close to volcano immediately prior, during, and after its eruption in 2011, with statistical analysis of obtained position estimation error samples, and TEC estimation

The manuscript reads as follows. This Section outlines the motivation, and provide the overview of the study Section 2 presents the methodology applied, including a brief description of the software tools utilised, and outlines research results. Section 3 discusses results and outlines our contribution to the problem understanding and mitigation.

Fig. 1. Puyehue-Cordon Caulle volcano and the neighbouring stationary IGS reference station in Santiago, Chile

* Corresponding author: oliver.jukic@vsmti.hr

 https://doi.org/10.1051/e3sconf/20199401001

2 Methodology and study results

Puyehue-Cordon Caulle volcano is situated in Central Chile (Fig. 1.). It began to erupt on 4th June, 2011 (DOY 155). The IGS Network stationary reference GPS station at Santiago, Chile collected continuously raw GPS pseudorange measurements, which have been available since then to scientific community from the IGS web-site (http://www.igs.org/). We examined the TEC and GPS positioning error components time series [2], [7] for a selected period around the day or eruption, between 31 May, 2011 and 6 June, 2011.

We processed dual GPS pseudorange observations to obtain Total Electron Content (TEC) time series, as an index of ionospheric conditions [2]. An open-source software (http://seemala.blogspot.com) developed by Dr Gopi Seemala, than at Boston College, Chestnut Hill, MA, was used for derivation of TEC time series from dual-frequency GPS pseudorange observations. Time series of TEC observed at Santiago, Chile, and Coyahaique, Chile are presented in Figs 2. and 3., respectively.

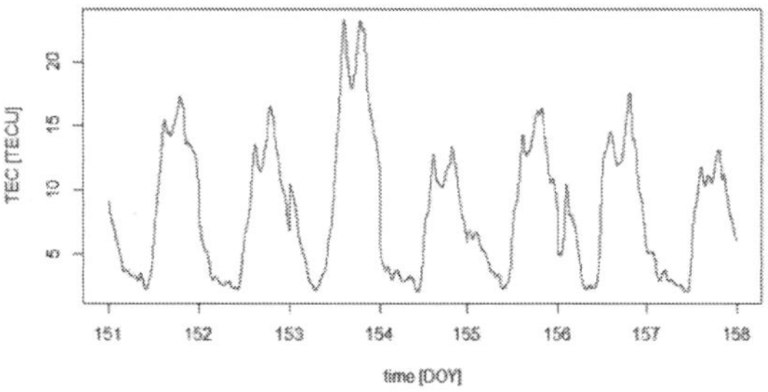

Fig. 2. TEC time series derived from dual-frequency GPS pseudorange observations at Santiago, Chile (30 s sampling period) around the time of volcanic eruption.

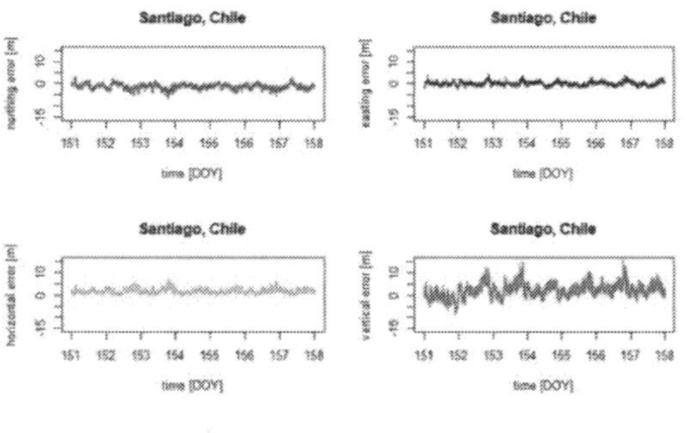

Fig. 3. Santiago, Chile RINEX-derived GPS positioning error components around the time of volcanic eruption

Additionally, we utilised single-frequency GPS pseudorange observations to simulate positioning performance of a commercial-grade single-frequency GPS receiver that utilises regularly provided parameters of correction models (satellite clock corrections, Saastamoinen tropospheric corrections, and Klobuchar ionospheric correction with broadcast parameters) during the time of eruption [7]. Simulation was conducted using RTKLIB (http://www.rtklib.com/), an open-source GNSS Software-Defined Radio receiver, in post-processing mode. RTKLIB was configured to operate as a commercial-grade single-frequency GPS receiver that utilise broadcast parameters of pseudorange error correction models [7]. It was deriving position estimate and positioning error samples using real observations of single-frequency GPS pseudoranges (RINEX o files) and broadcast navigation messages (RINEX n files), both archived on IGS.

We developed a bespoke framework for GNSS positioning error time series statistical analysis. Modelling and forecasting in the open-source R programming environment for statistical computing (https://www.r-project.org). Using the framework developed, we generate time series of northing, easting and vertical components of positioning error vector, through comparison of observed position samples with the actual (true) position of an IGS stationary reference station. Horizontal GPS positioning error was derived using (1).

$$\epsilon_H = \sqrt{\epsilon_N^2 + \epsilon_E^2} \quad (1),$$

Where:

εH … denotes horizontal GPS positioning error [m]

εN … denotes northing component of positioning error [m]

εE … denotes easting component of positioning error [m]

Time series of GPS positioning error components are depicted in Fig. 3., respectively.

Histograms of TEC, and the GPS positioning error components are presented in Figs 4. and 5., respectively.

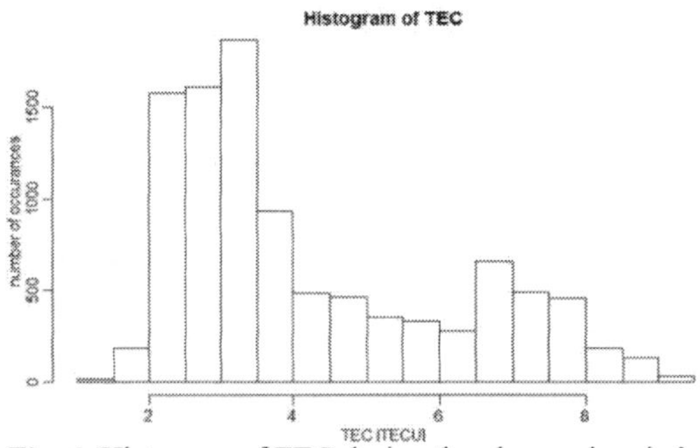

Fig. 4. Histogram of TEC during the observed period around the volcanic eruption

The Q-Q (normality) plot of TEC in the observed period of the volcanic eruption is presented in Fig. 6.

Finally, we examined the histograms of the TEC index derived from the Santiago, Chile observation site for a selected period (day 27 in 2017) when a mild ionospheric disturbance (Kp <= 4) occurred, as the reference for comparison. Histogram of TEC fr the controlled experiment on DOY27, 2017 is depicted in Fig. 7

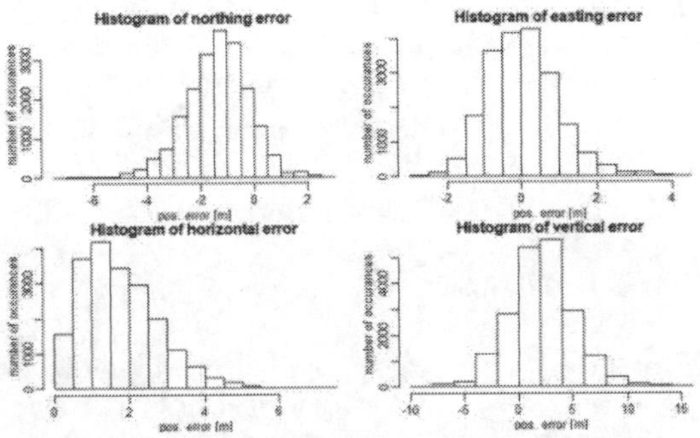

Fig. 5. Histograms of the respective components of GPS positioning error during the observed period around the volcanic eruption

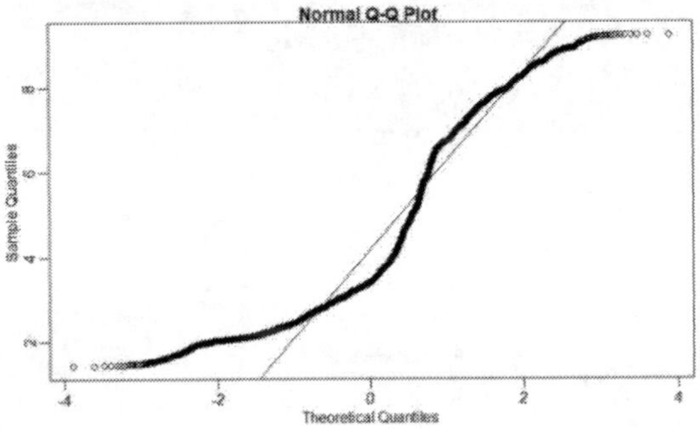

Fig. 6. TEC Q-Q plot

Histograms of TEC, and GPS positioning error components are depicted in Figs 7 and 8, respectively.

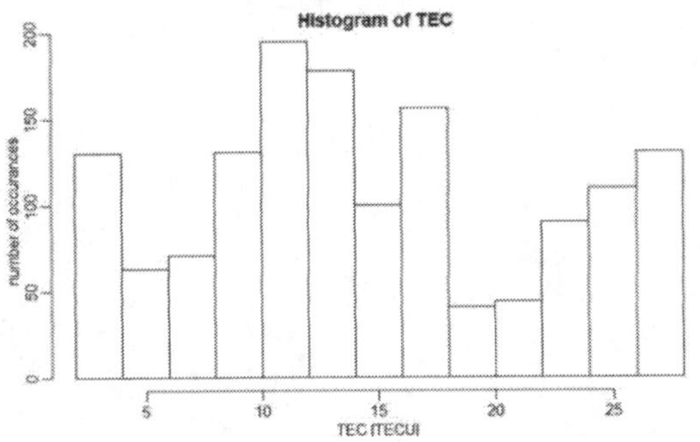

Fig. 7. Histogram of TEC during controlled period (Day 27 in 2017).

3 Discussion

Study results revealed several findings, as follows: (1) TEC daily dynamics extend two local maxima, instead of one, usually assumed as a pattern for Klobuchar ionospheric correction model; (2) TEC time series shows unusual waveform for DOYs 152, 153, 154, and 155, respectively; (3) TEC histogram for the observed period did not follow normal distribution. Further examination of geomagnetic and solar data revealed brief and moderate space weather-caused geomagnetic disturbance in the evening of DOY 155 (Kp up to 5+ level, the day eruption started, lasting for 6 hours, until midnight), and in the early morning of DOY 156 (Kp at 6+ level, lasting three hours). The event coincided with development of volcanic eruption, mimicking partially the effects of the latter on ionisation processes and GPS positioning performance. The occurrence of a moderate geomagnetic disturbance in combination with volcanic eruption that went underway at the same time may explain the rise in TEC in late hours of DOY 155 in 2011. However, disturbed waveforms of DOYs 152, 153 , and 154, and the considerable enlargement of TEC on 153 cannot be explained by any geomagnetic and/or space weather event. We believe the anomalies were correlated with volcanic activity before the main eruption on DOY 155.

Descriptive statistical analysis of the GPS positioning performance revealed the respective range of positioning error components: (1) for northing error component: between -7.02 m and 2.68 m; (2) for easting error component: between -2.72 m and 4.20 m; (3) for horizontal error component: between 0.05 m and 7.15 m; and (4) for vertical error component: between 8.38 m and 15. 51 m. Vertical and easting error components followed normal distribution fairly well, while the histogram of northing error component (and therefore the one of horizontal error, as well) shows skewed and translated distribution, compared with the normal one.

The same analysis performed on control experiment (DOY27 in 2017) observations revealed the following range of error components: (1) for northing error component: between -3.86 m and 2.34 m; (2) for easting error component: between -3.14 m and 1.65 m; (3) for horizontal error component: between 0. 06 m and 3.99 m; and (4) for vertical error component: between -3.05 m and 9.71 m.

Results show that a mild geomagnetic disturbance (Kp up to 4+ level) caused milder deterioration of GPS positioning performance then combined (at worst) effects of volcanic eruption and moderate geomagnetic disturbance. It should be noted that volcanic eruption, as well as a geomagnetic disturbance, modifies the statistical character of events, calling for cautious approach in attempts to model the events in question.

GPS position degradation we observed around the time of the 2011 Puyehue-Cordon Caulle volcanic eruption may affect usual daily GPS-related services, but to affect disaster relief activities as well. Emergency services and autonomous rovers may suffer from enlarged GPS position estimation errors. The fact calls for advanced TEC and GNSS performance monitoring and modelling [2], implementation of advanced position estimation methods [8], utilisation of network-supported satellite position estimation, and sensor data fusion to assure reliability, resilience and robustness of satellite-based position estimation.

Development of models describing TEC and GPS positioning error components dynamics is still not impossible, although it remains a challenging task. As one us has shown, careful examination of statistical properties of data, with utilisation of advanced forecasting model development methods based on statistical learning, may provide unexpectedly good results. We intend to continue our research activity on examination of various cases of GNSS positioning performance degradation due to space weather and terrestrial natural causes, as well as those caused by artificial threats, in order to contribute to GNSS resilience development, and sub-sequently to assist in stable technology development for the benefit of modern civilisation.

References

1. P. Cannon et al, *Extreme space weather : impacts on engineered systems and infrastructure* (Royal Academy of Engineering, London, UK, 2013)
2. M. Filić, R. Filjar, *Forecasting model of space weather-driven GNSS positioning performance* (LAMBERT Academic Publishing, Riga, 2018)
3. R. Filjar, J of Nav, **61**, 115-128 (2008)
4. S. Pullinets, K. Boyarchuk, Ionospheric precursors of earthquakes (Springer, Berlin, 2005)
5. G. S. Tsolis, T. D. Xenos, Nat Haz Earth Sys Sci, 10, 133-137
6. R. Filjar, S. Kos, D. Brčić, Pomorstvo, **25**(2), 287-306 (2011)
7. M. Filić, R. Filjar, L. Ruotsalainen, Transnav, **10**(3), 395-400 (2016)
8. M. Filić, L. Grubišić, R. Filjar, Improvement of standard GPS position estimation algorithm through utilization of Weighted Least-Square Approach, in *Proc 11th Ann Baška GNSS Conf* (RIN, Baška, 2018)

A New On-The-Move Integer Ambiguity Determination Method for Precise Positioning of Highly Maneuvering Ground Vehicles

Jong-Hwa Jeon[1], Sang-Hoon Yoo[2], Jeung-Won Choi[1], Tae-Kyung Sung[3*]

[1]Agency for Defense Development, 34186 Daejeon, Korea

[2]Wifive Co. Ltd, 34183 Daejeon, Korea

[3]Department of Radio Sciences and Information Communications Engineering, Chungnam National University, 34140 Daejeon, Korea

Abstract. In the conventional RTK (Real Time Kinematics), carrier phase measurements should be collected for several minutes in stationary state in order to determine the IA (Integer Ambiguity) in carrier phase to get the precise position. To determine the IA in motion, several OTM-RTK (On-The-Move RTK) methods have been proposed using vehicle dynamics or augmenting additional sensors. This paper presents a new OTM-RTK technique to determine the IA without aids of external sensors for precise positioning of highly maneuvering ground vehicles. In the proposed technique, the initial IA is determined fast by estimating precise position change during epochs using dual frequency carrier phase measurements. Therefore, IA determination of the proposed method is not influence by vehicle dynamics. By field experiment, performance of the proposed technique is analyzed including IA determination time according to vehicle dynamics and the number of visible SV.

1 Introduction

The accurate position and speed information of the car navigation is needed to control the vehicle precisely. When the precise position associated with road image and road information would be applied to vehicle autonomous control systems such as lane-keeping, robustness of longitudinal/lateral control can be greatly improved. In general, to obtain a high-precision position with an accuracy of several cms using a Global Positioning System (GPS), carrier phase measurements should be used along with code measurements [1]. For precise positioning using carrier phase measurements, the integer ambiguity included in the carrier phase measurement should be determined. The integer ambiguity can be obtained through searching and evaluating integer ambiguity candidates since there is no analytical solution, and many studies have been performed in the past to reduce time and computation of resolving the integer ambiguity such as reducing search range. Among them, Least squares AMBiguity Decorrelation Adjustment (LAMBDA) and Ambiguity Resolution with Constraint Equation (ARCE) are the typical methods [2]. Fundamentally, LAMBDA is a method of obtaining a solution of Integer Least Squares (ILS), which has the condition of an integer and has excellent computational advantages in addition to systematic theories, and is applied to various high-precision positioning systems such as Real Time Kinematics (RTK) [2]. In order to resolve the integer ambiguity in RTK, the stationary state must be maintained for a long time because the integer ambiguity should be determined by collecting measurements for several tens to hundreds of epochs in the stationary state. In addition, it is difficult to apply the conventional method of resolving the integer ambiguity in the stationary state to precision navigation systems of unmanned vehicles because the integer ambiguity must be retrieved again if the satellite signal is disconnected and re-received while the vehicle is moving or if a cycle slip occurs. Therefore, studies on new integer ambiguity resolution techniques are necessary for On-The-Move RTK (OTM-RTK) of moving vehicle.

This study proposed an OTM-RTK technique to resolve integer ambiguity using only Global Navigation Satellite System (GNSS) measurements on the move in order to perform fast and precise positioning of high maneuvering ground vehicles on the move based on low-cost GNSS receivers that can be installed in vehicle navigation systems.

2 Floating Ambiguity Estimation

Conventional RTK studies collected measurements for several tens to hundreds of epochs in the stationary state to determine the integer ambiguity included in the carrier phase measurements. Assuming that m satellites are observed in one epoch, the double differenced code and carrier phase measurements, measured during the n epoch at the stationary state are as shown in (1) [3].

* Corresponding author: tksaint@cnu.ac.kr

$$\delta\rho=\begin{bmatrix}\delta\rho_1\\ \delta\rho_2\\ \vdots\\ \delta\rho_n\end{bmatrix}=H\delta x+\varepsilon=\begin{bmatrix}H_1\\ H_2\\ \vdots\\ H_n\end{bmatrix}\delta x+\begin{bmatrix}\varepsilon_1\\ \varepsilon_2\\ \vdots\\ \varepsilon_n\end{bmatrix}$$

$$\delta l=\begin{bmatrix}\delta l_1\\ \delta l_2\\ \vdots\\ \delta l_n\end{bmatrix}=H\delta x+\lambda N+w=\begin{bmatrix}H_1\\ H_2\\ \vdots\\ H_n\end{bmatrix}\delta x+\lambda N+\begin{bmatrix}w_1\\ w_2\\ \vdots\\ w_n\end{bmatrix} \quad (1)$$

Where, $\delta\rho_i,\delta l_i (i=1\sim n)$ is a linearized double differenced code and a carrier phase measurement, respectively, and the vector of $(m-1)\times 1$, $H_i (i=1\sim n)$ is the line-of-sight differenced vector between the satellites of $(m-1)\times 3$, δx is the base line vector between the base station of 3×1 and the vehicle, λ is the length of the carrier wave, N is the integer ambiguity vector of $(m-1)\times 1$, and $\varepsilon_i, w_i (i=1\sim n)$ is the double differenced code and carrier phase measurement noise, respectively, and the vector of $(m-1)\times 1$. Assuming that measurements are collected at the stationary state and there is no change in the satellites, δx and N are constant values regardless of the change in epoch, it is assumed that the measurement errors such as ionospheric delay and tropospheric delay are removed by double differencing because the distance between the two receivers is not too far (within 10km) and there is no multipath. The measurement noise ε, w is a White Gaussian noise, which is independent from each other, and is assumed to have the characteristics of $\varepsilon: N(0,Q_\rho), Q_\rho=(DD^T)^{-1}\sigma_\rho^2$ and $w: N(0,Q_l), Q_l=(DD^T)^{-1}\sigma_l^2$, respectively. Where, D is a differentiation matrix.

In order to solve (1), (1) is arranged as (2).

$$\delta y=Aa+Bb+e=\begin{bmatrix}A & B\end{bmatrix}\begin{bmatrix}a\\ b\end{bmatrix}+e=M\tilde{x}+e \quad (2)$$

Where $\delta y=[\delta\rho \ \ \delta l]^T$, $A=[H \ \ H]^T$, $a=\delta x$, $B=[0 \ \ \lambda I]^T$, $b=N$, $e=[\varepsilon \ \ w]^T$, $M=[A \ \ B]$, and $\tilde{x}=[a \ \ b]^T$ are represented.

By applying the least squares method to (2), unknown $\tilde{x}$ can be estimated as shown in (3).

$$\hat{\tilde{x}}=(M^TM)^{-1}M^T\delta y \quad (3)$$

It is possible to resolve the integer ambiguity by applying techniques such as LAMBDA and ARCE using the floating ambiguity $\hat{N}$ estimated from (3) and the covariance of the integer ambiguity, which is a search range of the integer ambiguity, and a high precision positioning is possible using the carrier measurements by obtaining the integer ambiguity [2, 3]. Applying the Wide Lane measurement to the carrier measurement of (1) allows rapid determination of the integer ambiguity [4].

3 The proposed OTM-RTK technique

This paper proposes an OTM-RTK technique to determine the integer ambiguity on the move. The state diagram of OTM-RTK proposed in this study to resolve the integer ambiguity on the move is as shown in Fig. 1.

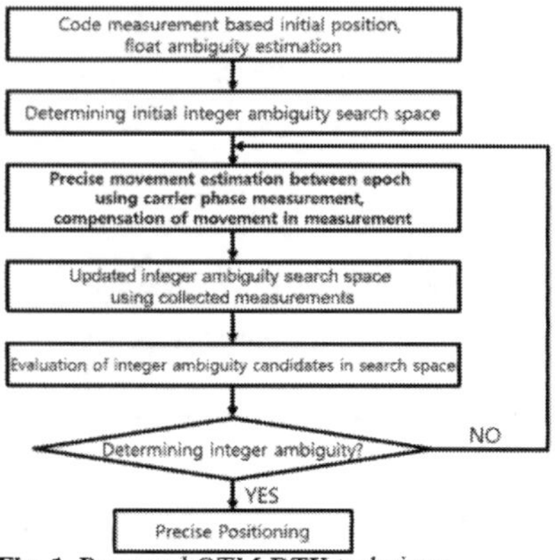

Fig. 1. Proposed OTM-RTK technique

3.1. Code-based Initial Position Calculation, Floating Ambiguity Estimation and Integer Ambiguity Search Range Configuration

The linearized double difference code and carrier phase measurements in the stationary state (0 epoch) are shown in (4).

$$\delta\rho_0=H_0\delta x_0+\varepsilon_0$$
$$\delta l_0=H_0\delta x_0+\lambda N_0+w_0 \quad (4)$$

The initial code-based position can be estimated from the code measurements in (4), consisting of a single epoch or several multiple epochs. In the case of a single epoch, code-based estimate of the floating ambiguity is obtained as shown in (5) by substituting the code-based estimated initial position into the carrier phase measurement [1].

$$\hat{N}_0=\frac{\delta l_0-H_0\delta\hat{x}_0}{\lambda} \quad (5)$$

The search range of the integer ambiguity estimated based on the code of a single epoch is expressed as a covariance matrix as shown in (6) [3, 4].

$$\mathrm{cov}(\hat{N}_0)=E\left[\hat{N}_0\hat{N}_0^T\right]\approx\frac{I}{\lambda^2}\left(\sigma_\rho^2+\sigma_l^2\right) \quad (6)$$

3.2. Position Movement Estimation between Epochs and Carrier Measurement Position Movement Compensation

In LAMBDA, δx is fixed as (3×1) in (1), because measurements are collected in a stationary state, but δx is updated every epoch in a moving state, δx becomes $(3n\times 1)$ if the measurements are collected during n epochs as shown in (7) thus, it is difficult to apply the conventional integer ambiguity resolution technique to measurements of moving vehicles.

$$\begin{bmatrix}\delta\rho_1\\ \delta\rho_2\\ \vdots\\ \delta\rho_n\\ \delta l_1\\ \delta l_2\\ \vdots\\ \delta l_n\end{bmatrix}=\begin{bmatrix}H_1\\ H_2\\ \vdots\\ H_n\\ H_1\\ H_2\\ \vdots\\ H_n\end{bmatrix}\begin{bmatrix}\delta x_1\\ \delta x_2\\ \vdots\\ \delta x_n\end{bmatrix}+\begin{bmatrix}0\\ 0\\ \vdots\\ 0\\ \lambda IN\\ \lambda IN\\ \vdots\\ \lambda IN\end{bmatrix}+\begin{bmatrix}\varepsilon_1\\ \varepsilon_2\\ \vdots\\ \varepsilon_n\\ w_1\\ w_2\\ \vdots\\ w_n\end{bmatrix}$$
(7)

In this step, the precise position movement between epochs is calculated using double differenced Integrated Carrier Phase (ICP) variation between epochs, and this is compensated in the carrier measurement. Estimating the position movement between epochs using ICP variation between epochs is shown in (8) [4].

$$\delta\hat{x}_i=\left(H_i^T\left(DD^T\right)^{-1}H_i\right)^{-1}H_i^T\left(DD^T\right)^{-1}\lambda\delta\Theta_i(i=1,2,\cdots,n) \quad (8)$$

Where, $\delta\Theta_i$ is ICP variation between epochs.

By updating $\delta\hat{x}_i$ from 1 epoch to n epoch, the measurements can be collected and summarized as shown in (9).

$$\begin{bmatrix}\delta l_1\\ \delta l_2\\ \vdots\\ \delta l_n\end{bmatrix}=\begin{bmatrix}H_1\\ H_2\\ \vdots\\ H_n\end{bmatrix}\delta\hat{x}_0+\begin{bmatrix}H_1\delta\hat{x}_1\\ H_1\delta\hat{x}_1+H_2\delta\hat{x}_2\\ \vdots\\ H_1\delta\hat{x}_1+H_2\delta\hat{x}_2+\cdots+H_n\delta\hat{x}_n\end{bmatrix}+\lambda\begin{bmatrix}N\\ N\\ \vdots\\ N\end{bmatrix}+\begin{bmatrix}w_1\\ w_2\\ \vdots\\ w_n\end{bmatrix}$$
(9)

Although (9) contains the initial position bias $\delta\hat{x}_0$, the error between $\delta\hat{x}_i$ and true value is very small and $H_i\delta\hat{x}_i(i=1\sim n)$ becomes the precise ICP correction value between epochs since the subsequent position movement between epochs $\delta\hat{x}_i$ is continuously estimated from ICP variation between epochs. If accumulated movement of the vehicle is calculated using (8) and then compensated in the carrier measurement, (9) may be rewritten as (10).

$$\begin{bmatrix}\delta l_1\\ \delta l_2\\ \vdots\\ \delta l_n\end{bmatrix}-\begin{bmatrix}H_1\delta\hat{x}_1\\ H_1\delta\hat{x}_1+H_2\delta\hat{x}_2\\ \vdots\\ H_1\delta\hat{x}_1+H_2\delta\hat{x}_2+\cdots+H_n\delta\hat{x}_n\end{bmatrix}=\begin{bmatrix}H_1\\ H_2\\ \vdots\\ H_n\end{bmatrix}\delta\hat{x}_0+\lambda\begin{bmatrix}N\\ N\\ \vdots\\ N\end{bmatrix}+\begin{bmatrix}w_1\\ w_2\\ \vdots\\ w_n\end{bmatrix}$$
(10)

If the left side of (10) is defined as $\delta\tilde{l}$, (10) is expressed in the same form as the carrier phase measurement of (1), and by applying the process in (2) and (3) to the following steps, it is possible to estimate the integer ambiguity of the moving vehicle. The integer ambiguity of the moving vehicle can be resolved by applying LAMBDA method using the estimated floating ambiguity and covariance of the integer ambiguity error, which is the search range of the integer ambiguity.

4 Experiment Results

The performance of proposed OTM-RTK technique was analyzed using filed driving experiment. The driving test was conducted at a vacant place next to Mokwon University located in Daejeon in March 2018, and compared the results of the navigation solution of proposed OTM-RTK technique and the navigation solution of Virtual Reference System (VRS)/IMU integrated equipment (Novatel SPAN-CPT) for the reference trajectory. In this experiment, a wide lane measurement was used for rapid integer ambiguity determination. The experimental trajectory is shown in Fig. 2.

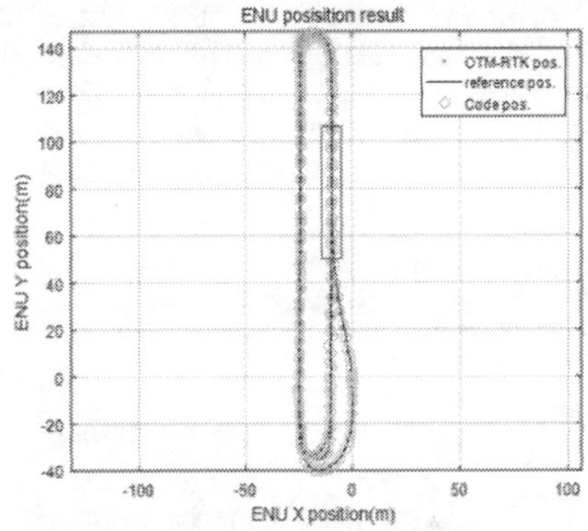

Fig. 2. Result of field driving experiment.

In order to compare the accuracy of the positioning results of proposed OTM-RTK technique, positioning error with the reference position is shown in Fig. 3, and RMS of the positioning error with respect to the reference position is shown in Table 1 in order to compare the accuracy.

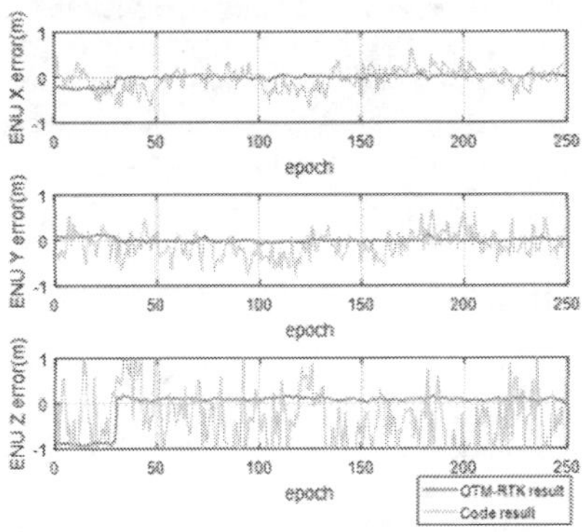

Fig. 3. Position error with reference position.

Table 1. RMS result of positioning error with reference position (unit: m).

[m]	Code result	OTM-RTK result
x	0.2426	0.0271
y	0.3062	0.0308
z	0.7805	0.0926

As a result of the experiment, although OTM-RTK contains an initial position bias before integer ambiguity determination, continuity of the trajectory was ensured by calculating the precise position movement between epochs using ICP variation between epochs, and accurate positioning was possible as the position bias was corrected after determining the integer ambiguity. In OTM-RTK results of Table 1, RMS results were confirmed to be about 12 times better than RMS results of the code measurement positioning.

Finally, in order to analyze the integer ambiguity resolution performance of proposed OTM-RTK technique, the number of residual integer ambiguities per epoch was compared according to the number of measurements as in the stationary state experiment. Although six measurements were used in the current experiment, elevation angle was adjusted to compare with cases of five and four measurements. The number of residual integer ambiguities per epoch according to the number of measurements is as shown in Fig. 4.

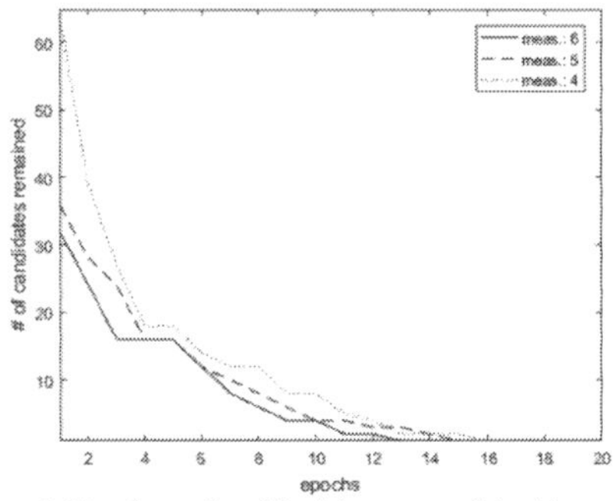

Fig. 4. Number of residual integer ambiguities per epoch by number of measurements

The DOP is large if the number of measurements is small, which increases the number of initial ambiguities to be searched as the initial ambiguity search range increases. In the case of four measurements, there were about twice as many initial integer ambiguity candidates than that of six measurements, and it took about 1.2 times longer to determine the integer ambiguity

5 Conclusion

This paper proposed an OTM-RTK technique to determine the integer ambiguity in a moving vehicle. The initial code-based measurements were used to resolve floating ambiguity, and the precise movement between epochs was calculated using the carrier phase measurements to correct the measurements, showing that the integer ambiguity can be determined in a moving vehicle. As a result of the experiment, although proposed OTM-RTK technique contains an initial position bias before integer ambiguity determination, the precise trajectory can be obtained by calculating the precise movement between epochs, and accurate position and trajectory with corrected position biases can be obtained after determining the integer ambiguity. In addition, this study compared the integer ambiguity resolution performance according to the number of measurements. As the number of measurements is influenced by DOP, there was a performance difference in the number of integer ambiguity candidates and integer ambiguity resolution time. Therefore, the proposed OTM-RTK technique can be applied to various vehicle navigation systems such as unmanned vehicles and autonomous vehicles by complementing the RTK constraints.

Acknowledgements

This work has been supported by the National GNSS Research Center program of Defense Acquisition Program Administration and Agency for Defense Development

References

1. S. H. Yoo, J. M. Lim, J. H. Jeon, T. K. Sung, Development of 3D CSGNSS/DR Integrated System for Precise Ground-Vehicle Trajectory Estimation, Journal of Institute of Control, Robotics and Systems, **22** (2016)
2. P. Jonge, C. Tiberius, The LAMBDA method for integer ambiguity estimation: implementation aspects (TU Delft, 1996)
3. S. B. Son, C. S. Park, S. J. Lee, An Effective Real-Time Integer Ambiguity Resolution Method Using GPS Dual Frequency, Journal of Control, Automation and Systems Engineering, **6** (2000)
4. J. H. Jeon, A Study on OTM-RTK Technique for High Precision Positioning in Unmanned Vehicle, Master's Thesis (Chungnam National University, 2018)

E3S Web of Conferences **94**, 01003 (2019) https://doi.org/10.1051/e3sconf/20199401003
ISGNSS 2018

Tracking of geodetic height of sea level in the west of Java Sea, Indonesia: A preliminary assessment

Poerbandono[*], *Kosasih Prijatna*, and *Irwan Gumilar*

Geodesy and Geomatics Engineering, Faculty of Earth Sciences and Technology, Institut Teknologi Bandung, Indonesia

Abstract. This paper assesses the agreement between observed heights of sea level from Global Navigation Satellite System (GNSS) and a global model of Mean Sea Surface (MSS). The assessment of the agreement is carried out according to the direct comparison between the height of MSS model and the geodetic height of actual sea level. Here, MSS is generated according to Gravity Recovery And Climate Experiment (GRACE) Gravity Model (GGM) and Mean Dynamic Ocean Topography (MDOT). The tracking of geodetic heights of actual sea level are done by Wide Area Differential (WA D) and Real Time Precise Point Positioning (RTPPP) Global Navigation Satellite System (GNSS) along an approximately 180 Nm SW-NE transect of away-return ship track in the west of the Java Sea, Indonesia. It is found that the overall agreement between geodetic height of sea level and MSS observed by WA DGNSS is 7.5 cm (away tracking), while those observed by RTPPP GNSS is 39.5 cm (away tracking) and 36.0 cm (return tracking). This work recommends selection of the best-fit tide model and careful examination on the dynamics of antenna offset due to vessel attitude.

1 Introduction

Mean Sea Level (MSL) is an essential element of a National Spatial Reference System (NSRS), which is a part of a National Spatial Data Infrastructure (NSDI) [1, 2]. Along with the other standard tidal datum, such as Highest Astronomical Tide (HAT) and Lowest Astronomical Tide (LAT), MSL defines coastlines from which various rights of ownership of dry lands across supra-, inter-, and sub-tidal areas are delineated [3, 4]. Navigation and offshore construction also demand MSL, respectively to determine the vertical separation to chart datum [5] and as a reference plane for design criteria [6]. Within an NSRS, all of these datums are compiled in the so-called hydrographic separation model [7].

This work is actually a milestone of a roadmap towards the construction of a hydrographic separation model for the domain presented here. A hydrographic separation model defines direct transformation among various vertical datum, primarily between the ellipsoid and the required tidal datum (i.e. LAT, MSL), as well as the geoid and/or another Chart Datum [8, 9]. Earlier work in the same working area on the construction of such a model discusses the spatial distribution of LAT with respect to MSL [10]. For the model to be constructed, a definition of MSL above ellipsoid must be made available. Traditionally, MSL refers to zero-gauge. Here, the term MSS is used as the height of MSL with respect to reference ellipsoid, i.e. World Geodetic System 1984 (WGS84).

It is the intention of this paper in investigating how global MSS might be used for the development of the hydrographic separation model. The work presented in this paper aims at quantifying the discrepancy of a global MSS model with respect to geodetically observed sea level. As advised by The International Federation of Surveyors [11], knowing the errors of such model is one of key factors in understanding the accuracy the data. Here, we investigate an MSS model for the west of Java Sea, Indonesia and compare it with geodetic height of sea level along the survey track (Figure 1).

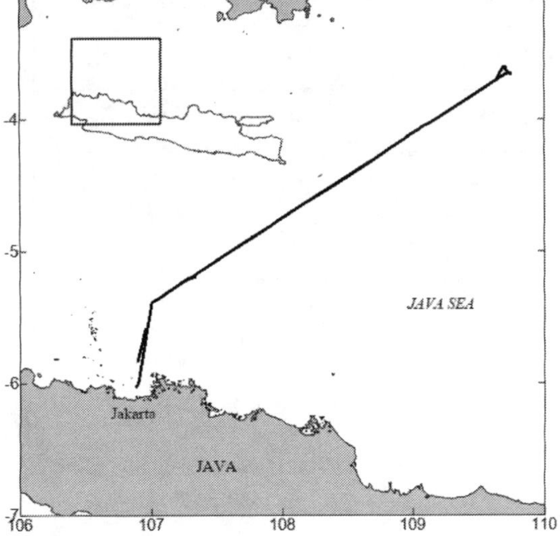

Fig. 1. Study location with track of SW-NE survey transect.

[*]Corresponding author: poerbandono@itb.ac.id

2 Materials and methods

The comparison between the MSS model and the geodetic height of sea level is carried out by tracking of actual height of sea surface. The tracking of the actual height of sea surface is carried out during a cruise of Survey Vessel (SV) Explora Nusantara. It is actually an additional mission to the cruise, which make use of vessel's transit away from Jakarta (Tanjung Priok) port to two survey sites NW of Jakarta and return. The away transect occupies a transit length of about 337 km long (including tracks of survey routes), while the return one occupies roughly 189 km in length of transit only.

During the tracking, actual height of sea surface is observed by Wide Area Differential (WA D) and Real Time Precise Point Positioning (RTPPP) Global Navigation Satellite System (GNSS). Here, we use standard position output of WA DGNSS C-Nav and RTPPP GNSS Trimble NetR9 systems, i.e. date, time, latitude, longitude, height. C-Nav is a commercial positioning service developed according to a proprietary differential GNSS. It utilizes corrections from several base stations to fix carrier phase ambiguities. Trimble NetR9 is a single GNSS receiver facilitated by real time corrections due to satellite's orbit, clock, and phase centre offset.

C-Nav is used only along the away transit, while Trimble NetR9 is used along the away and return transits. Antenna heights of both systems with respect to the sea surface are known as they are measured once upon the installation. Table 1 shows the deployment setting of the both systems. In Figure 2, sketch of installation diagram of the WA DGNSS and RTPPP GNSS onboard SV Explora Nusantara is shown. The heights of the antenna of the WA DGNSS and RTPPP GNSS receivers are respectively 3.59 m and 6.80 m.

Table 1. Deployment setting of the WA DGNSS and RTPPP GNSS devices

Method	WA DGNSS	RTPPP GNSS
Device	C-Nav	Trimble NetR9
Antenna height	3.59 m	6.80 m
Date	1-3 April 2016	1-6 April 2016
Acquisition interval	10 s	2 s

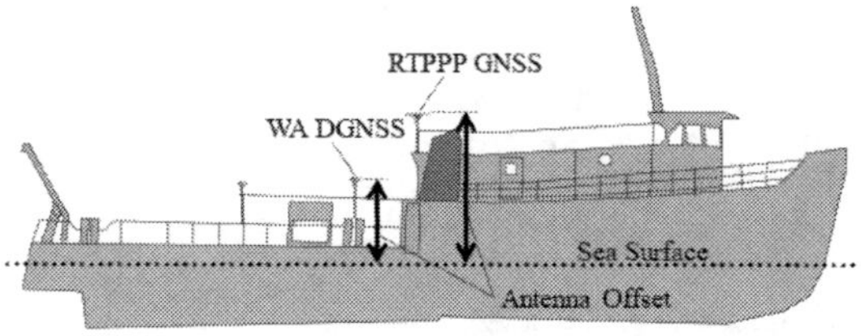

Fig. 2. Installation diagram of WA DGNSS and RTPPP GNSS antennas onboard of SV Explora Nusantara.

For the generation the MSS model, we combine Gravity Recovery And Climate Experiment (GRACE) Gravity Model (GGM) 02C geoid undulation (N) from the International Centre for Global Earth Models (ICGEM) [12, 13] extracted at 0.25 arc-degree spatial resolution. Mean Dynamic Ocean Topography (MDOT) data published by the Asia-Pacific Data Research Centre [14] is combined with the geoid undulation. The MSS model is hence obtained by [15]:

$$\mathrm{MSS} = N + \mathrm{MDOT} \tag{1}$$

with MSS = Mean Sea Surface, N = geoid undulation, and MDOT = Mean Dynamic Ocean Topography. The model of MSS is compared with the observed geodetic height of actual sea level (h_{SL}) in which a deviation (Δh) is expected, so that:

$$\Delta h(\lambda,\varphi) = h_{\mathrm{SL}}(\lambda,\varphi) - \mathrm{MSS}(\lambda,\varphi) \tag{2}$$

with $\Delta h(\lambda,\varphi)$ = the deviation between observed height of sea level and MSS at a given position, φ = latitude, λ = longitude, $h_{SL}(\lambda,\varphi)$ = height of sea level at a given position, and $\mathrm{MSS}(\lambda,\varphi)$ = MSS at a given position. We then consider the overall deviation between observed heights of sea level and MSS ($\dot{h}$) as a systematic vertical offset between both surfaces along the track:

$$\dot{h} = \frac{1}{S}\int_0^S \Delta h(s)ds \tag{3}$$

with $\dot{h}$ = the overall deviation between observed height of sea level and MSS along the track, S = the total length of the track, and s = a single track element between two consecutive positions.

Subtracting h_{SL} by Δh shall hence fit both surfaces. However, tide is still presence. We therefore subtract tide from the fitted sea level. For the purpose of the subtraction, tide is obtained from TOPEX/Poseidon crossover solution (TPXO 7.0) global ocean tide model [16]. TPXO 7.0 provides model of sea level oscillation due to tide according to eight primary (M2, S2, N2, K2, K1, O1, P1, Q1), two long period (Mf, Mm), and three non-linear (M4, MS4, MN4) harmonic constituents. From this, a vertical residual at each position and time is obtained by the following relationship:

$$\Delta R(\lambda,\varphi,t) = h_{\mathrm{SL}}(\lambda,\varphi,t) - \mathrm{MSS}(\lambda,\varphi) - \dot{h} - T(\lambda,\varphi,t) \tag{4}$$

with $\Delta R(\lambda,\varphi,t)$ = vertical residual at a given position and time, t = time, and $T(\lambda,\varphi,t)$ = tidal correction at a given position and time. The overall vertical residual along the track $\dot{R}$ is calculated as:

$$\dot{R} = \frac{1}{S}\int_0^S R(s)ds \tag{5}$$

with $\dot{R}$ = the overall vertical residual.

3 Results and discussions

Figure 3 shows model of GGM 02C geoid undulation *N* in meter above WGS84 reference ellipsoid across the area in question. Figure 4 shows model of MDOT in meter above geoid. Both combines to construct MSS investigated here. One would observe that geoid undulation varies from 17 to 31 m in the west of Java Sea. Here, MDOT varies only within 0.14 m, from 1.01 to 1.15 m.

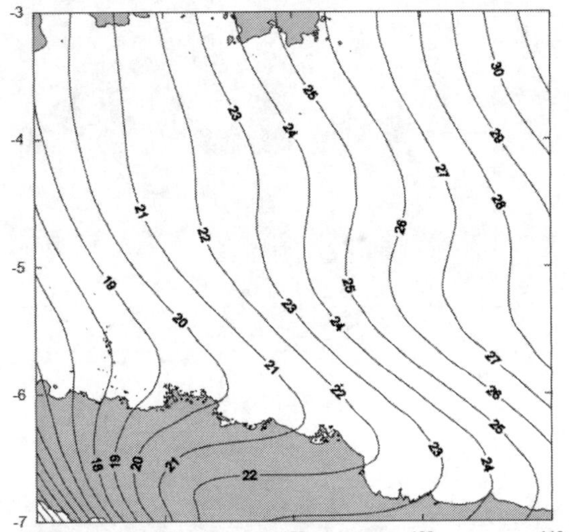

Fig. 3. Geoid undulation (*N*) generated from 1' × 1' Gravity Recovery And Climate Experiment (GRACE) Gravity Model (GGM) 02C dataset

The interpolation of geoid undulation (*N*) and MDOT for the presentation of isolines in Figure 3 and Figure 4 is carried out according to gridding of the respective datasets by using radial basis function [17].

Figure 5 shows the comparison between observed heights of sea level from the GNSS and a global MSS model projected along the longitude. It can be observed that GNSS's sea level is lined up with the trend of the MSS model. With the progressing latitude, GNSS's sea level increases above ellipsoid the way the MSS model does.

In addition to the ellipsoid heights of actual sea level and MSS model, the deviation between GNSS's sea level and the MSS model is also shown in Figure 5. One would see that the deviation vibrates much at short period in the order of decimetre. This might correspond to the uncertainty in GNSS-heighting. In addition to that, it indicates oscillation at a longer period. This longer oscillation has an approximate vertical range of about several decimetres and just less than 1 m, which is typical for the range of tide in the region. We then subtract the deviation with the tide model and expect to obtain non-systematic residual. However, the tide model used here does not seem to fit well with the deviation.

In Figure 6, we show temporal evolution of the fitted sea level, the tide model, and the residual. The fitted sea level is obtained by averaging all sea level height (Equation 5). In Table 2, the mean deviation between the GNSS's sea level and the MSS is shown as an overall vertical offset ($\dot{h}$). One would see that in general, the mean height of sea level is somewhat higher than the MSS, by less than 1 dm for C-Nav WA-DGNSS and several decimetres for Trimble NetR9 RTPPP-GNSS.

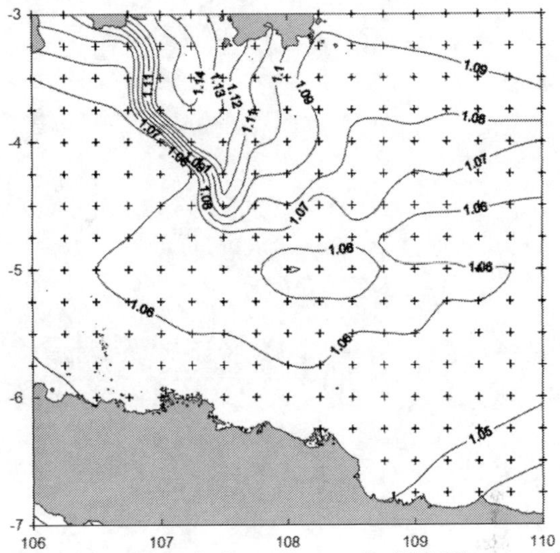

Fig. 4. Mean Dynamic Ocean Topography (MDOT) generated from 0.25° × 0.25° resolution Asia-Pacific Data Research Centre's dataset

Table 2. Overall vertical offset ($\dot{h}$) between observed sea level and MSS with the corresponding overall residual ($\dot{R}$) and the linear slope of the residual ($a_{\dot{r}}$)

Method	WA-DGNSS	RTPPP-GNSS	
Device	C-Nav	Trimble NetR9	
Transit	Away	Away	Return
$\dot{h}$ (m)	0.075	0.395	0.36
$\dot{R}$ (m)	0.002	0.032	0.039
$a_{\dot{r}}$ (m/day)	0.089	0.085	0.109

It can be seen in Figure 6 that the tide model does not fit the observed sea level. Such an indication can be observed from the disagreement between the tide model and the moving average trend of the observed sea level in terms of in their amplitude and phase-lag. As the consequence, the resulting residual still indicate cyclic oscillation due to the inaccurate tidal model subtraction, although their mean values ($\dot{R}$) are quite small, i.e. several mm for C-Nav WA-DGNSS, several cm for NetR9 RTPPP-GNSS (see Table 2).

At this present stage, no further effort could be made in looking at a better option of the tidal model. We would formulate this as one of the future work's list.

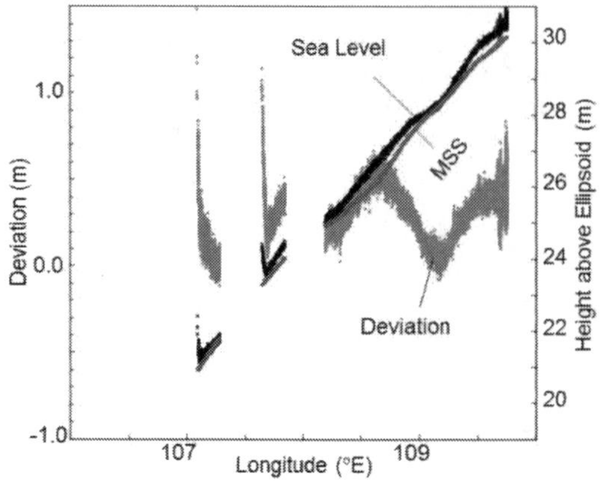

(a) Trimble NetR9 away

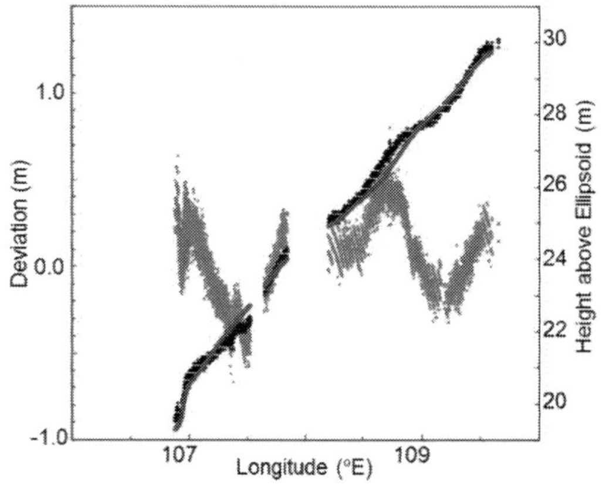

(b) C-Nav away

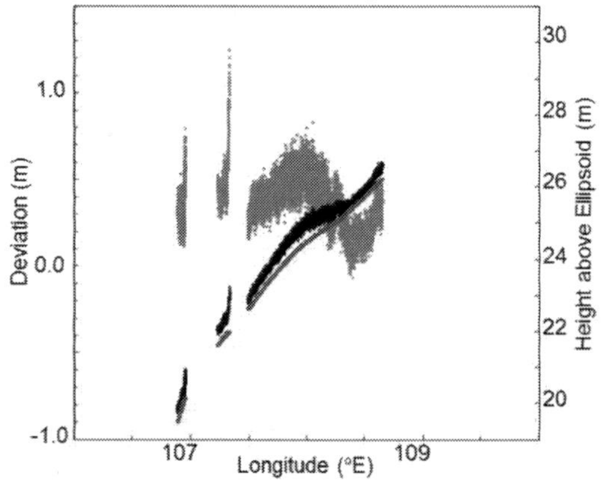

(c) Trimble NetR9 return

Fig. 5. Geodetic height of sea level and Mean Sea Surface (MSS), as well as their vertical deviation over time throughout the cruise projected along the longitude

We also look at the linear trend of the residual as an early attempt to understand its behaviour (see Figure 6). We find out that the residual rises through time by about 8.5 to 11.0 cm/day. Linear slopes of the residuals are shown in Table 2. This means that within our 5-day mission the corresponding total of vertical rise of residual height can be about close to half of meter. Such a rise could suspiciously be related to the change in the antenna offset, i.e. the vertical separation between antenna level and the sea surface, as we neither provide post-survey check nor regular monitoring (throughout the cruise) of the antenna offset. Such an increase might probably be resulted from the vessel's settlement as it continuously looses weight from fuel and water consumptions.

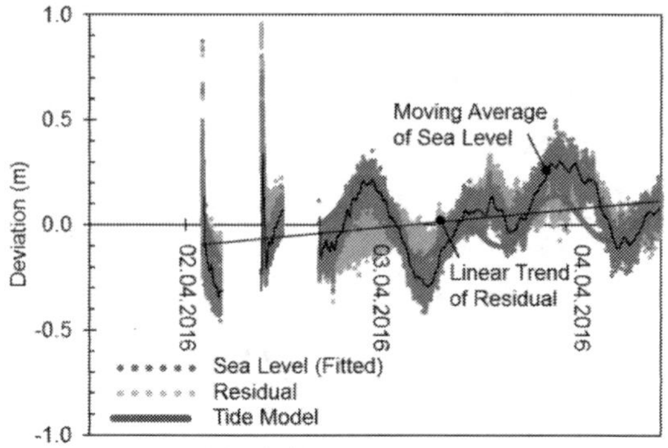

(a) Trimble NetR9 away

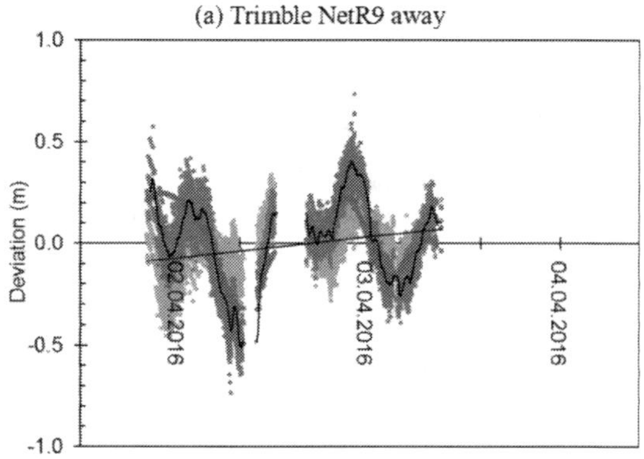

(b) C-Nav away

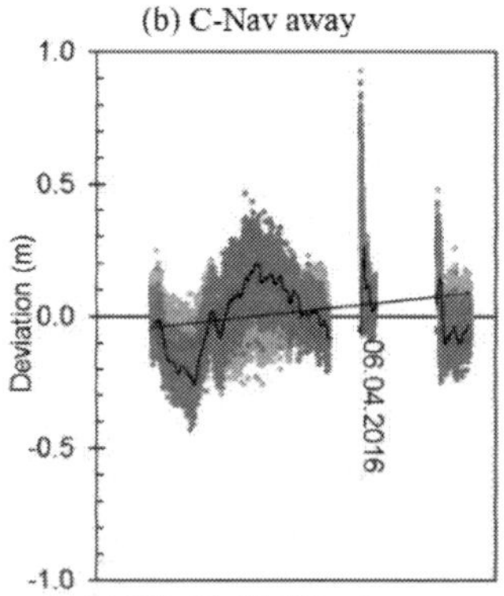

(c) Trimble NetR9 return

Fig. 6. Fitted sea level, tide, and residual across time

However, unless data from regular check of antenna offset or continuous detection of vessel motion is made available, no certain identification of such rises of residual could be elaborated. Because of this, we have to leave it as one essential subject for further improvement of the work. In addition to this, we shall look into the accuracy of the tide model. The improvement of the comparison must hence consider a more appropriate study of the tidal oscillation.

4 Conclusion and recommendation

GGM 02c and MDOT have enabled the construction of a MSS model for the west of the Java Sea, Indonesia. With this, we have shown the agreement between the MSS model and observed heights of sea level from GNSS according to the direct comparison between them by tracking of geodetic heights of actual sea level using WA D and RTPPP system across about 180 Nm SW-NE transect. According to the work presented here, the overall agreement between the geodetic height of sea level observed by WA DGNSS and the MSS is 7.5 cm. RTPPP GNSS gives 39.5 cm and 36.0 cm overall agreement from away and return tracking.

However, it should be bear in mind that the tide model used here does not fit the oscillated sea level throughout the period of the tracking. This is seen from the disagreement in amplitude and phase-lag between the tide model and the moving average trend of the observed sea level. Hence, the resulting residual contains systematic oscillation due to the application of the tide model. In addition to that, we have noticed that there has been vertical rise of residual height within the time of the tracking. It is thought that the increasing range of GNSS antenna from the sea surface could be one of the contributing reasons. Therefore, selection of the best-fit tide model and careful examination on the dynamics of antenna offset due to vessel attitude are recommended for further studies. Yet, the work exhibits the potential of the use of global model of MSS for the construction of a hydrographic separation model.

Data used in this publication is collected within the framework of a "Collaborative Research on Shallow Sub Seafloor Layers" entitled "Hydroacoustic Profiling for Reconstruction of the Late Pleistocene Landscape in the Java Sea and Spatial Modelling of Sub-tidal Terrain" funded by Amazoko. The authors acknowledged the contribution of Ms Gabriella Alodia, Ms Ajeng Salmayarista, and PT Mahakarya Geo Survey, as well as Surveying and Mapping Laboratory of the Faculty of Earth Sciences and Engineering at the Institute of Technology, Bandung during the fieldwork.

References

1. J.P. Guyer. *An introduction to geodetic reference systems for land surveys*. The Clubhouse Press, CreateSpace Independent Publishing Platform, El Macero, California, 54pp (2015).
2. J.D. Bossler, J.B. Campbell, R.B. McMaster, C. Rizos. *Manual of geospatial science and technology, Second Edition*. CRC Press, 854pp (2010).
3. A.M. Muslim, G.M. Foody. International Journal of Remote Sensing **29**(15), 4515-4536 (2008).
4. R. Li, R. Ma, K. Di. Marine Geodesy **25**, 27-36 (2002).
5. J.C. Iliffe, M.K. Ziebart, J.F. Turner. The Hydrographic Journal **125**, 3-8 (2007).
6. ISO 19901-1. *Petroleum and natural gas industries - Specific requirements for offshore structures - Part 1: Metocean design and operating considerations* (2015).
7. D. Dodd, J. Mills. International Hydrographic Review, 19-30 (2011).
8. J. Mills, D. Dodd. *Ellipsoidally Referenced Surveying for Hydrography*. Publication 62. International Federation of Surveyors (2014).
9. D.C. Slobbe, R. Klees, M. Verlaan, L.L. Dorst, H. Gerritsen. Marine Geodesy **36**(1) 31-71 (2012).
10. Poerbandono. *Assessing risk of navigational hazard from sea-level-related datum in the South West of Java Sea, Indonesia*. AIP Conference Proceedings 1857(1) (2017).
11. FIG. *FIG guide on the development of a vertical reference surface for hydrography*. Guide no. 37. International Federation of Surveyors (2006).
12. B.D. Tapley, S. Bettadpur, M. Watkins, C. Reigber. Geophysical Research Letter **31** (2004).
13. B.D. Tapley, F. Flechtner, M. Watkins, S. Bettadpur. *GRACE mission: status and prospects*. The GRACE Science Team Meeting (2015).
14. N. Maximenko, P. Knudsen, L. Centurioni, O. Andersen, J. Hafner, O. Melnichenko. *New Mean Dynamic Ocean Topography Derived from a Synthesis of Satellite Altimeter, Gravity, and Scatterometer Data and Trajectories of Lagrangian Drifters*. Ocean Surface Topography Science Team Meeting (2014).
15. D. Pugh, P. Woodworth. *Sea level science: Understanding tides, surges, tsunamis, and mean sea level changes*. Cambridge University Press (2014).
16. G.D. Egbert, S.Y. Erofeeva. Journal of Atmospheric and Oceanic Technology **19**(2) 183-204 (2002).
17. R.E. Carlson, T.A. Foley. Computers and Mathematics with Applications **21**(9) 29-42 (1991).

The Study of Position Accuracy Using Precise Point Positioning (PPP) In Perspective of Indonesian National Standard of Horizontal Reference Network

Rasyad A. Azis[1], *Hendy* F. Suhandri[2], and *Dudy* D. Wijaya[3]

[1]Geodetic Engineering Department, Faculty of Civil Engineering and Planning, Institut Teknologi Nasional, Indonesia
[2]Coastal, Ocean and Maritime Engineering Research Group, Faculty of Earth Sciences & Technology, Institut Teknologi Bandung, Indonesia
[3]Geodesy Research Group, Faculty of Earth Sciences & Technology, Institut Teknologi Bandung, Indonesia

Abstract. Precise point positioning is a GNSS based positioning method that is known to regaining more precise information about major systematical errors in its functional model. This method is seen as an advanced version of the conventional absolute positioning method that is able to offer higher accuracy of the estimate parameter. Contrarily, the relative positioning method is able to achieve high precise of the estimated parameters by using two or more receiver. Consequently, it utilizes more resources in performing observation. Hence, this contribution attempts to explore some considerable aspects that can make the PPP method has a comparable precision of the National Standard of Horizontal Reference Network (SNI JKH). Based on the experiments, with data rate of 0.03 Hz for GPS and GLONASS observation shown that result of the PPP method is comparable to the relative method, whenever the observation is performed in minimum duration of six hours. Moreover, the 3th order of accuracy can be achieved after a demanding observation period, depends on processing strategy.
Index Terms – GNSS, Precise point positioning (PPP), Relative Positioning, SNI JKH

1. Introduction

Precise point positioning (PPP) is an advanced version of the conventional GNSS-based absolute positioning. The method regains more precise information about systematical errors in its functional model, so that it can offer higher accuracy of the estimate parameter more than the absolute positioning. The quality of PPP method depends on its ability to eliminate the observation related errors. This contribution focuses on the minimum observational duration that is required to fulfill a certain level of accuracy standard. Consequently, the accuracy standard demands particular information about specific orbit products.

Relative positioning method requires more effort by using two or more receivers with one of receiver acting as a reference station. This method eliminates the observation errors with double difference technique. Relative positioning method quality depends on the distance between receivers. In case of PPP, direct usage of reference station is no longer needed, so that the spatial operating range limit is no longer exist, hence the coverage is global [6].

The experiments expect to fulfill the 3th order of the Indonesia National Standard of horizontal reference network (SNI JKH). Furthermore, this contribution attempts to investigate some considerable aspects that can make accuracy of the PPP method is comparable to the accuracy of relative positioning method.

2. Precise Point Positioning versus relative positioning

PPP method uses only one receiver without respecting to reference station. It makes common mode errors do not cancel in PPP [3], such as orbital error, tropospheric delay, ionospheric delay, multipath, satellite clock error and receiver clock error. The absolute observation model using pseudorange and phase range data, expressed by the following equations: [2, 3, and 4]

$$P^s_{r,f}(t) = \rho^s_{r,f}(t) + d\rho^s_{,f}(t) + dT^s_r(t) + dI^s_{r,f}(t) + dm^s_{r,f}(t) + c\left[\delta t_{r,f}(t) - \delta t^s_{,f}(t)\right] + e^s_{r,f}(t) \quad (1)$$

$$\varphi^s_{r,f}(t) = \rho^s_{r,f}(t) + d\rho^s_{,f}(t) + dT^s_r(t) - dI^s_{r,f}(t) + dm^s_{r,f}(t) + c\left[\delta t_{r,f}(t) - \delta t^s_{,f}(t)\right] + \lambda_f\left[\phi_{r,f}(t_0) + \phi^s_{,f}(t_0)\right] + \lambda_f N^s_{r,f} + \varepsilon^s_{r,f}(t) \quad (2)$$

Where $*^s$ is the superscript identifying satellite s, $*_r$ is the subscript identifying receiver r, $*_{,f}$ is the *subscript* identifying the L1 or L2 frequency, $d\rho^s_{,f}(t)$ is the orbital error (m), $dT^s_r(t)$ is the tropospheric delay (m), $dI^s_{r,f}(t)$ is the ionospheric delay (m), $dm^s_{r,f}(t)$ is the *multipath* (m), $\phi_{r,f}(t_0)$ is the receiver initial phase at t_0 (*cycle*), $\phi^s_{,f}(t_0)$ is the satellite initial phase at t_0 (*cycle*), $e^s_{r,f}(t)$ is the Pseudorange noise (cycle), and $\varepsilon^s_{r,f}(t)$ is the Phase noise (cycle)

* Corresponding author : alazisrasyad@gmail.com

In PPP method, utilizing precise product from IGS can eliminate the observational error. Moreover, the duration of observation can affect the result. In this contribution we assume that the observations are multipath free. Ionospheric delay can be eliminated by utilizing the ionospheric-free linear, while tropospheric delay can be eliminated by using troposphere model like saastamoinen. Utilizing precise clock product from IGS can eliminate of satellite and receiver clock errors, and using precise orbit from IGS can reduce the orbital error.

On the other side, the relative positioning method uses two or more receivers. This method requires simultaneous observations at both receivers to determine the coordinates of an unknown point with respect to a known point [2]. Assuming such simultaneous observation at the two points A and B to satellites j and k, linear combination can be formed leading to single difference, double difference, and triple difference. For example, the double difference model can be expressed with [2]:

$$P^{jk}_{AB,f}(t) = \rho^{jk}_{AB,f}(t) + dm^{jk}_{AB,f}(t) + e^{jk}_{AB,f}(t) \quad (3)$$

$$\varphi^{jk}_{AB,f}(t) = \rho^{jk}_{AB,f}(t) + dm^{jk}_{AB,f}(t) + \lambda_f M^{jk}_{AB,f} + \varepsilon^{jk}_{AB,f}(t) \quad (4)$$

By using the double difference technique, common errors can be eliminated. However, quality of the result of relative method depends on the distance between receivers. Based on SNI JKH, relative method can be performed with a maximum distance of 20 km length (short baseline) between receivers, with the absence of the tropospheric and ionospheric influences.

3. The experiment of PPP

The observation was using two points with the approximately distance of 8.5 kilometers length; which is short baseline. The reason to use short baseline is for good quality result of the relative method. Therefore, this study attempts to investigate some aspects that can make accuracy of the PPP method is comparable to the relative method.

One station is acting as reference station, CLBG, which is located at Lembang. Another station is acting as rover, ITN1, which is located at Itenas. The CLBG station is a CORS maintained by *Badan Informasi Geospasial*. Observation was held for 48 hours duration. Station position was obtained using goGPS and RTKLIB. Accuracy of position of each method is based on the standard deviation and the error ellipse parameters. The order of position is defined by horizontal error ellipse parameters. To define the PPP method order, it has to do some procedure.

The order of relative method must be defined by defining the 3rd order position based on SNI JKH from the relative error ellipse perspective, and its corresponding absolute error ellipse. The PPP method order can be achieved by comparing the absolute error ellipse of PPP method and relative method. This procedure purposes to define the quality of position accuracy from PPP process by referring to the absolute error ellipse, which corresponds to the SNI standard.

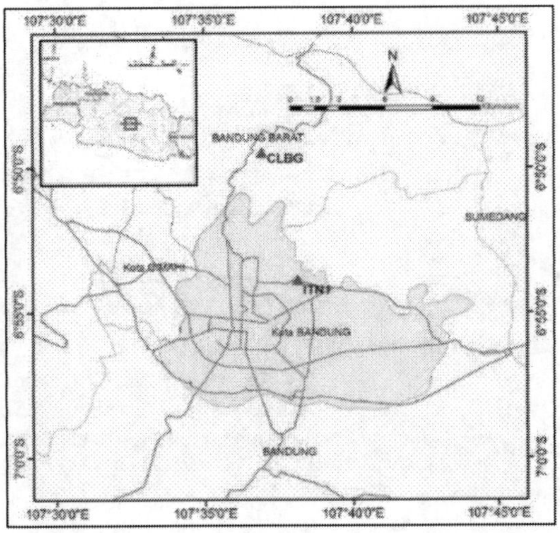

Fig 1. Location of two CORS used in the experiment

The observation was held in two days with phase and pseudorange data. Technical specification of each station is shown in Table 1.

Table 1. Technical Specification

Station	CLBG	ITN1
Location	Bosch-Lembang, Bandung	Gedung 18 Itenas, Bandung
Latitude	6° 49' 27.98" S	6° 53' 51.06" S
Latitude	107° 36' 56.16" E	107° 38' 9.32" E
Height above ellipsoid	1329.737 m	742.212 m
Receiver	Leica GRX1200GGPRO	Hi Target VNet6
Antenna	LEIAT504GG	HITAT35101CR
Antenna height	0.008 m	1.428 m
Mask Angle	10°	10°
Observation Interval	30 s	30 s
GPS Week	19750 dan 19751	19750 dan 19751

From the observation with 10 degree of mask angle and 0.03Hz of data rate, obtained the number of satellite, PDOP, and GDOP that is shown in Fig. 2. From Nsat graphic in Fig. 2 shown that station of ITN1 receive more satellite signal than CLBG station. It makes each of stations have different value of PDOP and GDOP, where the lowest value of GDOP is 1.1 and the highest value is 2.2 at ITN1, while the CLBG has the lowest value of GDOP is 1.2 and the highest value is 4.0. Each stations are on acceptable condition as the average of GDOP value is smaller than 5 [5].

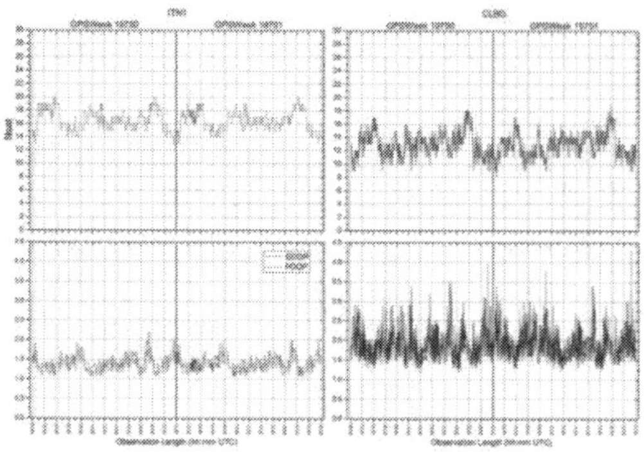

Fig 2. Nsat, PDOP, and GDOP Graphics

3.1. Residuals

Based on one-day observation and data rate of 0.03Hz for GPS and GLONASS observations, the residual value of carrier phase and pseudorange observations, respectively, can be seen at Fig. 3 (ITN1) and Fig. 4 (CLBG).

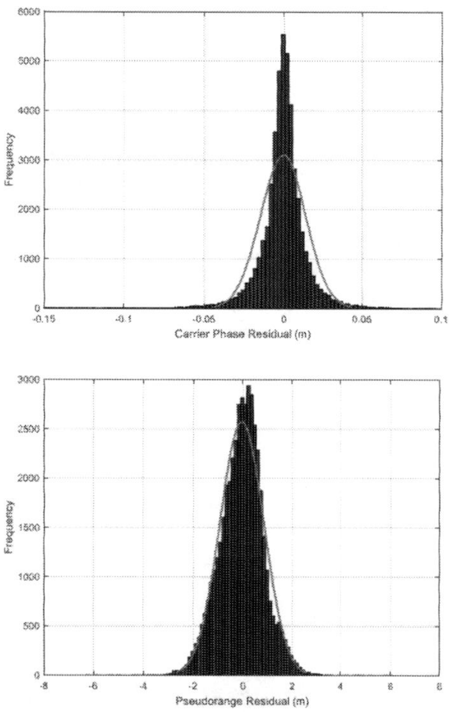

Fig. 3 ITN1 Observation Residual

Fig. 3 shown that the observation at ITN1 station is normally distributed. The observation with carrier phase is more accurate than pseudorange, it can be seen from the class interval of carrier phase is every 5 cm and pseudorange is 2 m.

The observation at CLBG station is also normally distributed. It is similar with ITN1 station that carrier phase observation is more accurate than pseudorange. The class interval of carrier phase observation is 5 cm while at pseudorange observation is 5 m. This also shows that the observation on ITN1 is better than CLBG.

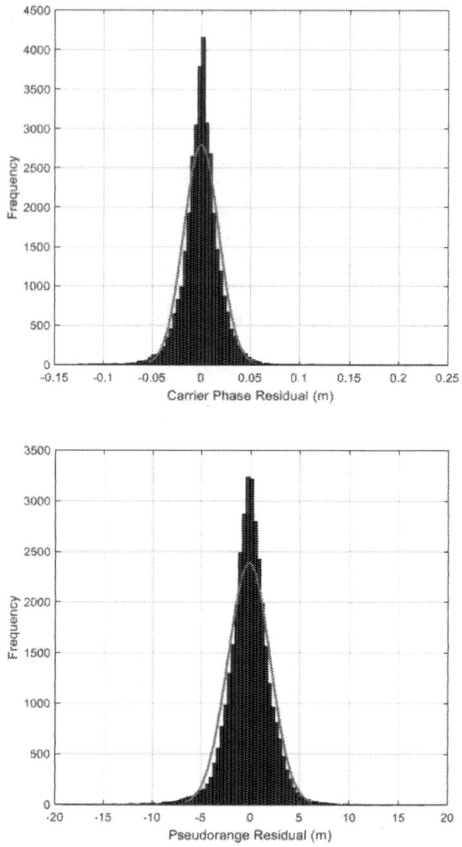

Fig. 4 CLBG Observation Residual

3.2. Coordinates difference

Fig. 5 shows the result of PPP method by utilizing IGS Final orbit. CLBG is used as the reference station of relative positioning to determine the coordinate of ITN1. The coordinates on Fig. 5 are expressed in local ENU coordinates system.

Fig. 5 Shows the result of PPP method by 48 hours duration of observation. The results are settled in 3-4 cm to the known point by using IGS final or IGS rapid product for both softwares. The difference between RTKLIB and goGPS result is only at the level of 1.1 cm, where the result from RTKLIB processing is 3.4 cm deviated to the known point, and the result from goGPS processing is 4.3 cm deviated to the known point. On the other side, the use of IGS Ultra product for both softwares is deviated by 6 up to 9 cm to the known point.

 https://doi.org/10.1051/e3sconf/20199401004

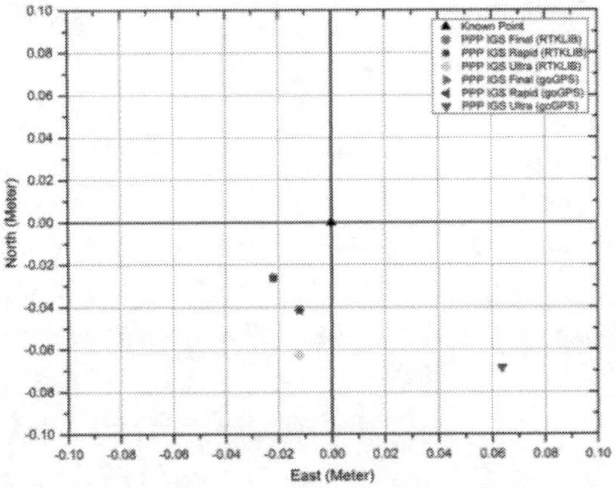

Fig. 5 Horizontal position of CLBG station

Similar to the CLBG station, the observation at ITN1 station use data rate of 0.033 Hz and IGS final orbit. In this point, the method that used to processed observation data are both of PPP method and relative positioning method. The coordinates variation is illustrated by Fig.6.

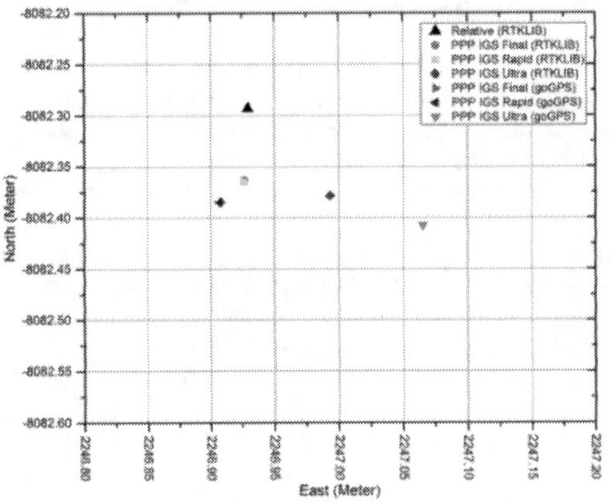

Fig. 6 Variations of ITN1 Station

Fig.7 shows the result from 48 hours duration of observation. The difference between RTKLIB and goGPS result are 2 cm, where RTKLIB and goGPS result are deviated 7.1 and 9.4 cm to the known point, respectively. Further, the using of IGS Ultra product gives bigger deviations for both processing, which is around 10 cm and 17 cm to the known point, respectively.

The coordinates differences between the product from PPP processing method and the known point can be seen at CLBG station. The known point of CLBG station refers to report from BIG. In this case, PPP method has three different results by utilizing three precise orbit products (IGS final, IGS rapid, and IGS ultra-rapid). Fig.7 shows the coordinates difference between PPP product and known point that using RTKLIB software. It shows that the using of IGS final and IGS rapid product gives more convergence than the IGS ultra products by 6 hours duration of observation.

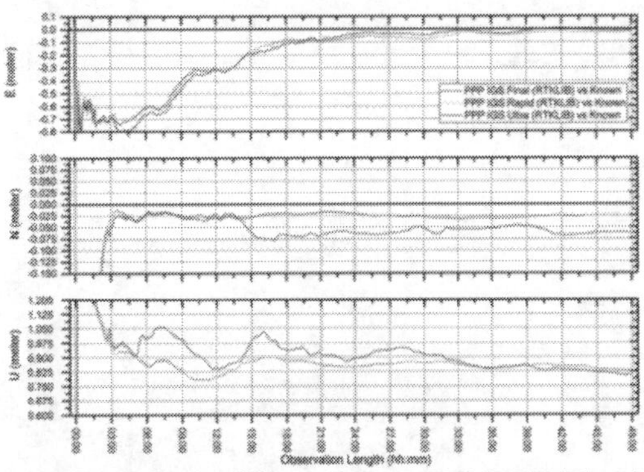

Fig.7 Coordinates difference between PPP (RTKLIB) and known point

In this case, the difference of North component is convergent after 3 hours observation, on the other side the difference of East and Up components is convergent after 15 hours duration of observation. Coordinates difference between PPP and the known point using goGPS is shown in Fig.8.

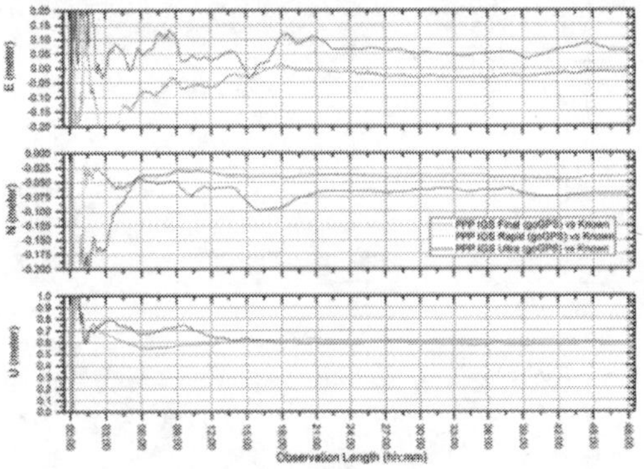

Fig.8 Coordinates difference between PPP (goGPS) and known point

By using goGPS software, the average coordinates difference between PPP and known point is convergent after 6 hours duration of observation. The utilization of the IGS final and IGS rapid product is more accurate than the IGS ultra product. The difference of North component is convergence after 6 hours duration of observation in 2-5 cm scale. On the other side, the East component is convergent after 15 hours of observation in 5 cm scale, and the Up component is convergent after 15 hours of observation in 7 dm scale. The coordinates difference figure shows that the vertical position difference is less convergent than horizontal [2].

Coordinates difference between PPP and relative positioning method can be seen at ITN1 station. The result of relative positioning on ITN1 station is referring to CLBG station.

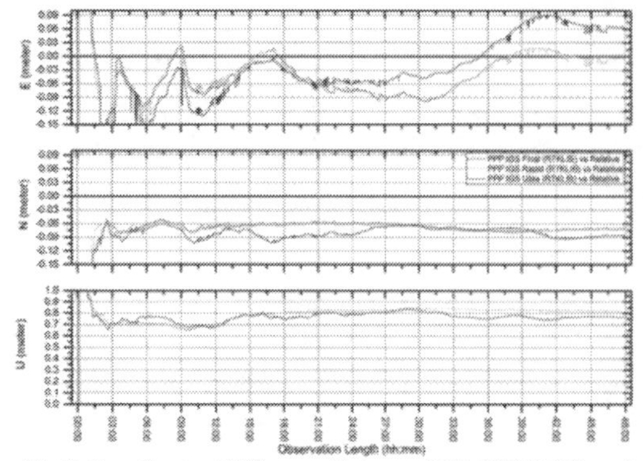

Fig.9 Coordinates Difference Between PPP (RTKLIB) and Relative Method

Fig.9 shows that coordinate difference between the PPP against the relative method is going to be convergent after 2 hours duration of observation for North component. Coordinates difference for East and Up components is not good as North component.

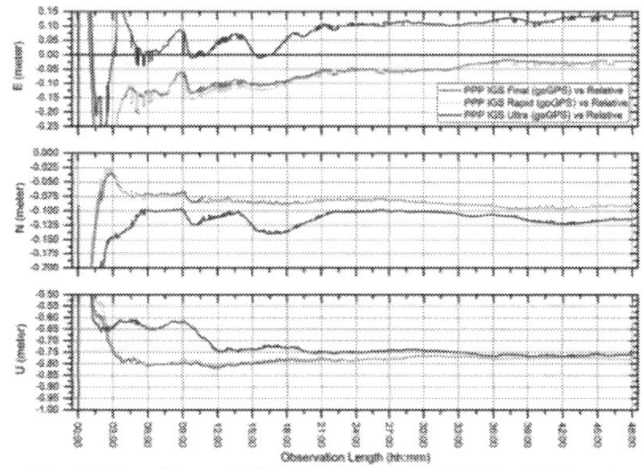

Fig.10 Coordinate Difference Between PPP (goGPS) and Relative method

Fig.10 is the coordinates difference between PPP and relative positioning using goGPS software. The coordinates difference for North component is convergent after 3 hours observation for IGS final and IGS rapid product. On the other side, coordinate difference for East component is convergent after 6 hours of observation, and Up component is convergent after 12 hours of observation. The average of absolute coordinates difference for East, North, and Up components are 18 cm, 15 cm, and 85 cm, respectively.

3.3 Standard deviations

Standard deviations of precise products are also can be seen in this station. Standard deviation comparisons between IGS Final, IGS Rapid, and IGS Ultra-rapid products are shown in Fig.10.

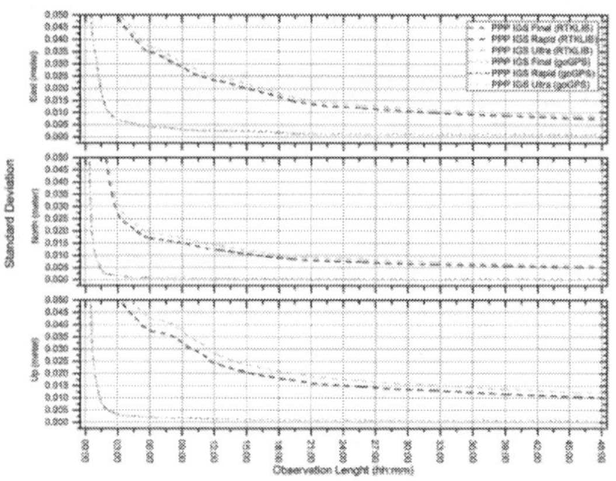

Fig.11 Standard deviation of precise product on CLBG station

Fig.10 shows that the using of goGPS is more accurate than RTKLIB. Standard deviation from goGPS software is in millimeter level after 3 hours duration of observation, yet the standard deviation from RTKLIB is still in centimeter level. The Standard deviation of RTKLIB is in millimeter level after 36 hours duration of observation. The difference between goGPS and RTKLIB standard deviation after convergence is 7 mm for East and North components, and 10 mm for Up component. The using of precise product IGS final and IGS rapid gives a very small difference of standard deviation for both softwares.

Comparison of standard deviation between PPP and relative positioning method can be seen on ITN1 station. The relative positioning method is computed for ITN1 by taking CLBG as the master station.

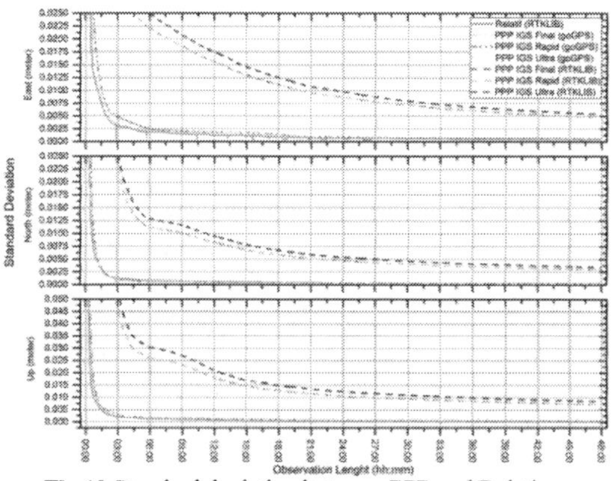

Fig.12 Standard deviation between PPP and Relative positioning method

Fig.12 shows that the standard deviation of the relative positioning method and the PPP using goGPS is convergent faster than the PPP from RTKLIB. Standard deviation of relative positioning reaches decimeter scale by minimum 0.5 hours duration of observation, and it reaches millimeter level after 1.5 hours observation. On the other side, PPP method using goGPS reaches millimeter scale after 2 hours duration of observation, and PPP method using RTKLIB reaches millimeter scale after 22 hours duration of observation. The smallest standard deviation value of PPP method can be reached by using goGPS for 48 hours duration of observation with 0.6 mm for East component, 0.2 mm for North component, and 0.6 mm for Up component. Standard deviation of relative method by 48 hours of observation is 0.5 mm for East component, 0.2 mm for North component, and 0.4 mm for Up component. The result of PPP method on ITN1 station is more accurate than CLBG station because of field condition in ITN1 is widely open than CLBG.

4. Classification of horizontal reference point network

The classification depends on the relative error ellipse. Relative error ellipse can be obtained only in relative positioning method. Hence, the horizontal position order of PPP method is assumed by regarding absolute error ellipse from relative positioning that has been accepted in 3rd order of horizontal position.

Based on SNI JKH, the 3rd order of horizontal position can be achieve by regarding on empiric value of 30 ppm. By the distance between CLBG and ITN1 station of 8.41 km length and 30 ppm of empiric value, the maximum semi-major axis (r) can be achieved by

$$
\begin{aligned}
r &= c\,(d + 0.2) \\
r &= 30\,(8.41 + 0.2) \qquad (5) \\
r &= 258.291 \text{ mm} = 25.83 \text{ cm}
\end{aligned}
$$

Calculating of equation 5, maximum value of semi-major axis is 25.83 cm, then the 3rd order of horizontal position can be achieved after value of semi major-axis of relative error ellipse is less than 25.83 cm. The semi-major axis value of relative error ellipse is shown at Table.2

Table.2 Relative error ellipse parameter between CLBG and ITN1

Duration of Observation (hours)	Relative error ellipse parameter			r (cm)
	a (cm)	b (cm)	θ	
0.5	1.95668	1.27017	34.49512°	25.38
0.75	1.16718	0.66352	35.31097°	
1	0.98798	0.46677	35.36272°	
2	0.46668	0.23134	35.23794°	
4	0.31005	0.20154	35.20035°	
6	0.26550	0.19512	35.21533°	
12	0.23503	0.19242	35.22364°	

By referring to SNI JKH and technical specification, the 3rd order can be reached after 1 hours duration of observation. The absolute error ellipse parameters of relative positioning method after 1 hours duration of observation are a = 0.0116 m, b = 0.0043 m, and θ = 17° 40' 55.55". If the absolute error ellipse of PPP method is lower than the value above, it means that the PPP method reaches the 3rd order of horizontal position.

The semi major axis value of absolute error ellipse for PPP method with 1 hour observation of relative positioning method is shown by Fig.13.

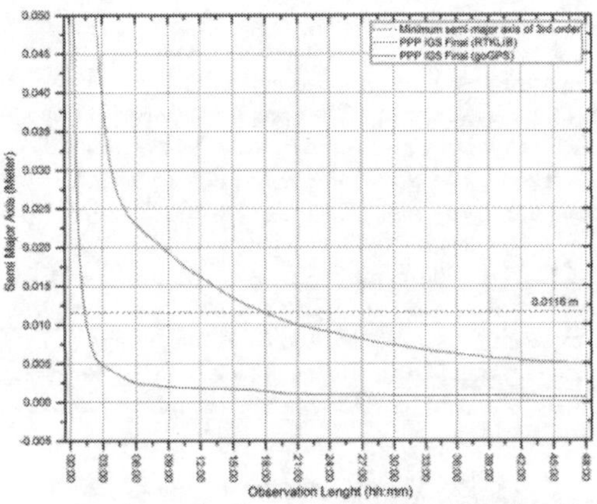

Fig.13 Semi major axis of absolute error ellipse

Fig.13 implies that longer observation period causes the absolute error ellipse is getting smaller. By assuming the position of absolute error ellipses is at the same position, the comparison of both methods can be seen (Fig.14).

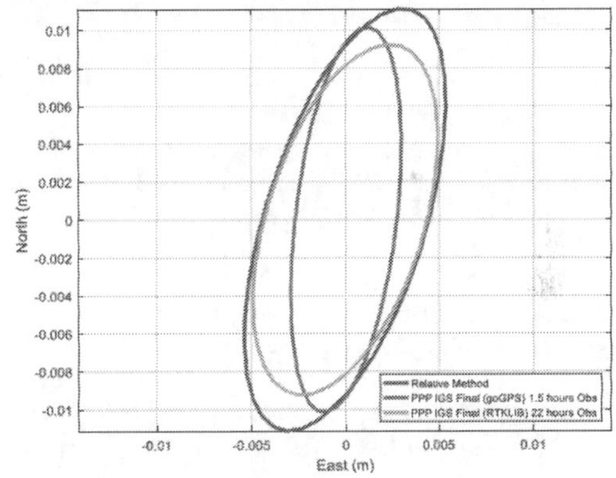

Fig.14 Comparison of PPP and relative method error ellipse

Based on the experiments, the 3rd order of horizontal position accuracy for PPP method can be achieved by using goGPS within 1.5 hours duration of observation, or by using RTKLIB within 22 hours duration of observation. In the case of time efficiency, the usage of goGPS gives more effective time than RTKLIB. It is possible to have different result for using other softwares. The value of absolute error ellipse parameters by using goGPS is 0.0102 m for semi-major axis, 0.0026 m for semi-minor axis, and 13°54'58.86" for azimuth angle. The value of absolute error ellipse parameters by using RTKLIB is 0.0102 m for semi-major axis, 0.0026 m for semi-minor axis, and 13°54'58.86" for azimuth angle.

8. Summary

Based on the result of the experiment, PPP method can reach the 3rd order classification by utilizing the IGS final product after 1.5 hours duration of observation, which is performed by using goGPS software. The RTKLIB software needs more time to reach 3rd order classification.

The difference of standard deviations of the PPP and the relative method is around 0.1 - 0.3 mm for each of East, North, and Up components, respectively. GoGPS software gives more excellent result than RTKLIB by looking at the standard deviation and error ellipse parameter.

The result on ITN1 station is more accurate than CLBG station because of field condition at ITN1 station widely open than CLBG station. Therefore, in this experiment shows that the PPP can be applied to some positioning to fulfill the 3rd order of Indonesian National Standard of Horizontal Reference Network (SNI JKH).

Reference

1. Badan Standarisasi Nasional, *Indonesian National Standar of Horizontal Reference Network (SNI JKH)*, SNI 19-6724-2002 (2002).
2. B. Hofmann-Wellenhof, H. Lichtenegger, and E. Wasle, *GNSS – Global Navigation Satellite System GPS, GLONASS, Galileo & more,* SpringerWienNewYork, Austria, (2008).
3. B. Witchayangkoon, *Elements of GPS Precise Point Positioning,* PhD dissertation, University of Maine, Orono, Maine. (2000).
4. H. F. Suhandri, *Instantaneous Estimation of Attitude from GNSS,* Institute of Navigation, University of Stuttgart, Germany. (2017).
5. H. Z. Abidin, J. Andrew, and J. Kahar, *Survei dengan GPS*, Institut of Technology Bandung, Indonesia, ISBN 978-602-905-01-3, (2011).
6. J. Kalita, Z. Rzepecka, and I. Szuman-Kalita, *The Application of Precise Point Positioning in Geosciences*, eISSN 2029-7092 / eISBN 978-609-457-640-9 (2014).

Feature coordinate estimation by time differenced vision/GPS/INS

Yu dam Lee[1], *Kwang Ho* Choi[1], *Won Jae* Yoo[1], *La Woo* Kim[1], and *Hyung Keun* Lee[2,*]

[1]Department of Electronics and Information Engineering, Korea Aerospace University, 10540 Gyeonggi-do, South Korea
[2]School of Electronics, Telecommunication and Computer Engineering, Korea Aerospace University, 10540 Gyeonggi-do, South Korea

Abstract. This paper proposes a multi-baseline method to estimate absolute coordinates of point clouds and the camera attitude parameter utilizing feature points in successive images. Conventionally, 3D map generation methodologies have been based on images acquired by aerial or land vehicles. Pixels corresponding to known landmarks are manually identified at first. Next, the coordinates are directly geo-referenced and automatically allocated to pixels with high-quality Global Positioning System (GPS) and Inertial Navigation System (INS). However, it is difficult to obtain accurate coordinates by the conventional methodology with low-cost GPS and INS. With camera positions and attitude parameters, image-based point clouds can be compensated accurately. A simulation was carried out to evaluate the performance of the proposed method.

1 Introduction

3D map generation methodologies have been studied for decades. They are generally based on images acquired by aerial or land vehicles. In the conventional methods, pixels corresponding to exact locations of landmarks appeared in images are identified manually to allocate them. Their coordinates can be directly geo-referenced and automatically processed with high-quality Global Positioning System (GPS) and Inertial Navigation System (INS). However, due to insufficient accuracy, it is hard to obtain their accurate coordinates [1, 2, 3, 5].

This paper proposes a method to estimate three-dimensional (3-D) coordinates of point clouds and attitude parameters simultaneously by two-dimensional (2-D) matched feature points in two successive images. To extract feature points and to match them in the two successive images, Speeded-Up Robust Feature (SURF) algorithm is utilized [4]. A loosely-coupled Kalman filter is applied to estimate absolute coordinates of the camera and its attitude parameters. With these parameters and error of them, image-based point clouds are compensated and converted to absolute coordinates of them.

Moreover, comparing to the conventional stereo method with static baseline, the proposed method can make it to time differenced multi-baseline; this makes depth estimation more accurate.

This paper is organized as follows. Firstly, overall system flow is explained. Then the proposed method to estimate absolute coordinates of point clouds and to compensate error of attitude parameters is briefly explained by pictures. Finally, a simulation result is analysed.

2 Absolute coordinates of point clouds with attitude error compensation

Fig .1 shows the diagram of the proposed system. In the proposed system, error of attitude parameters from GPS/INS Kalman outputs can be compensated by 2-D feature points extracted from the images.

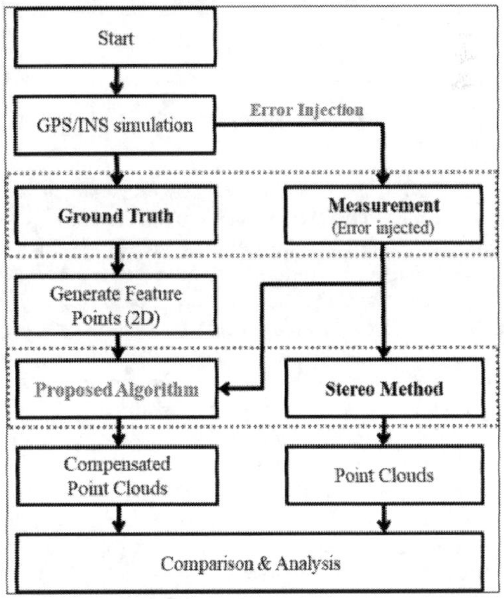

Fig. 1. Diagram of the proposed system.

* Corresponding author: hyknlee@kau.kr

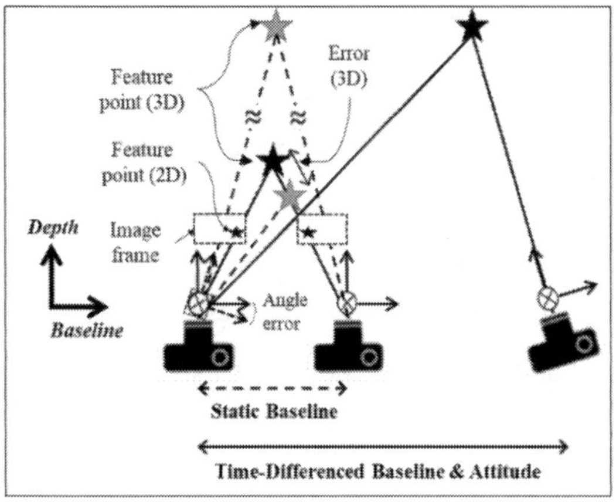

Fig. 2. Comparison between the conventional stereo method and the proposed method.

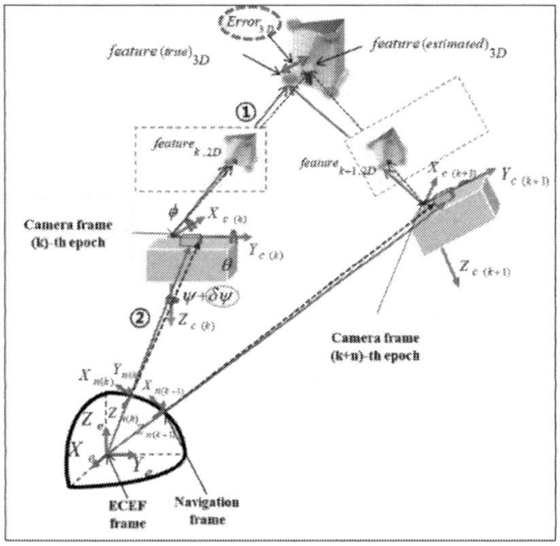

Fig. 3. Geometric relationship between different epochs in the proposed method.

In Fig. 2, the conventional and proposed methods are compared. In the figure, star symbols indicate feature points in 2-D and 3-D. The grey stars indicate 3-D feature points with errors. The direction to them are depicted in dotted lines. The estimation errors are partly due to the limitation of the stereo method for distant depth estimation and partly due to the insufficient accuracy when utilizing low-cost GPS and Inertial Measurement Unit (IMU) modules. On the other hand, the black stars indicate 3-D feature with reduced errors. The direction to them are depicted in solid lines.

The proposed method utilizes GPS and INS not only to overcome its limitation on static baseline but also to be applicable for different attitudes between cameras. Since the camera motion is directly geo-referenced at each epoch with GPS/INS, various baselines and attitude parameters can be calculated time-differentially.

Fig. 3 shows the geometric relationship between feature points extracted at different epochs. In the figure, yaw angle is only considered for the compensation due to the fact that roll and pitch angles of GPS/INS Kalman outputs are fairly accurate enough to utilize.

In Fig. 3, the line ① can be considered by the translation and transformation matrix from the Earth-Centered Earth-Fixed (ECEF) frame to the camera frame. The line ② can be considered by the relative coordinates of point clouds in the camera frame. If it is assumed that all of modules are aligned, the relative coordinates are converted to the absolute coordinates [5].

3 Simulation

To evaluate the accuracy of the proposed method, a systematic simulation was carried out. For the system inputs, no error was added to provide the ground truth data. Then, errors were added to the measurements for simulation. 2-D feature points were generated with the ground truth data only. The 2-D feature points were generated for even distribution. Depths for the system input were set as 2, 5, 7, 10 m. To evaluate how accurate yaw angles can be compensated, large initial yaw errors were injected in measurements at the (k)-th and (k+n)-th epochs, respectively (n=1, 2, 3, ...). The effect of time-differenced baselines was also considered in this simulation. The main purpose of this simulation is to analyse the relationship between depth, length of baseline and injected yaw error.

Fig. 4 shows the relationship between the compensated yaw error, the length of baseline and the depth accuracy. In general, the longer the baselines are, the smaller the yaw errors are. It can be seen that, though the initial yaw error was set as 4 degree when length of baseline is more than 2 m, it was compensated below 1 degree by the proposed method.

In Fig. 5, the errors of the point clouds by the two methods are compared. It can be seen that errors increase when depth and injected yaw error increase. However, the errors are significantly larger by the conventional method than by the proposed method when the length of baseline is short. They are relatively small around cm-level in the proposed method.

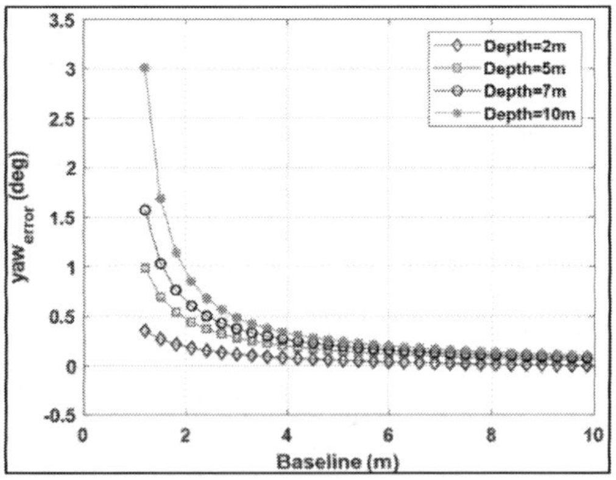

Fig. 4. Characteristics of compensated yaw error with respect to time-differenced baselines and various depths (Injected yaw error: 4 degree).

https://doi.org/10.1051/e3sconf/20199401005

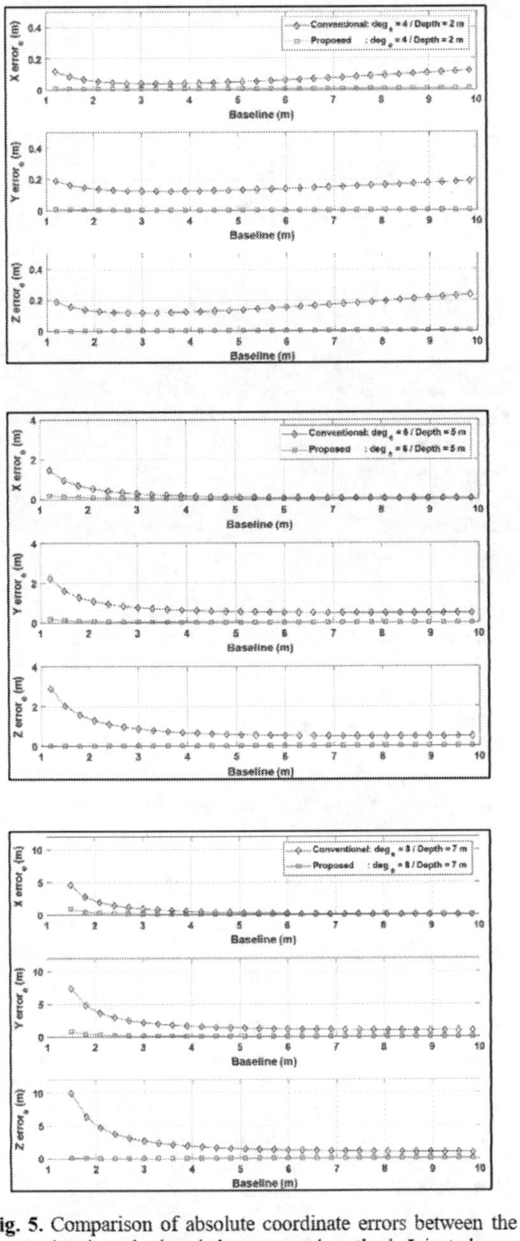

Fig. 5. Comparison of absolute coordinate errors between the conventional method and the proposed method. Injected yaw errors are (4/6/8) degrees and depth setting: (2/5/7) m.

In summary, the simulation results show that the proposed method improves accuracy compared with the conventional stereo method. In more detail, the depth accuracy is similar by both methods if the length of baseline is long. However, the accuracy in Y-axis and Z-axis are considerably larger by the conventional method than the proposed method.

4 Conclusion

This paper proposed a multi-baseline method to estimate absolute coordinates of point clouds and the camera attitude parameters simultaneously by 2-D matched feature points in two successive images. A simulation was carried out to evaluate its performance compared with the conventional stereo method. By the simulation, it was confirmed that the proposed method properly compensates important yaw error and improves the accuracy of the absolute coordinates of point clouds.

This research was supported by Basic Science Research Program (2016R1D1A1B01009881) through the National Research Foundation of Korea (NRF) funded by the Ministry of Education, Science and Technology, Korea.

References

1. G. Zhou, C. Song, J. Simmers, P. Cheong, "Urban 3D GIS from LiDAR and digital aerial images," C & G, **30**, 345-353 (2004)
2. Y. Song, S. Nuske, S. Scherer, "A multi-sensor fusion MAV state estimation from long-range stereo, IMU, GPS and barometric sensors," Sensors, **17**, 1-26 (2017)
3. Y. B. Park, J. G. Lee, C. G. Park, "Performance analysis of INS/GPS integration system," *KIEE*, 2433-2435 (2000)
4. K. Mikolajczyk, C. Schmid, "A performance evaluation of local descriptors," IEEE transactions on pattern analysis and machine intelligence, **27**, 1615-1630 (2005)
5. Y. D. Lee, K. H. Choi, J. H. Lim, W. J. Yoo, L. W. Kim, H. K. Lee, "A System for Generating Spatial Information utilizing RTK GPS/INS/Stereo Camera for 3D Map-Based Hybrid Navigation, " JICRS, **28**, 757-766 (2018)

https://doi.org/10.1051/e3sconf/20199401006

Network-based RTK Performance for Drone Navigation

Tae-Suk Bae[1,*]

[1]Sejong University Seoul Korea

Abstract. The Real-time Kinematic (RTK) was predominantly used for the positioning of the ground applications including moving vehicles. Due to the limited baseline lengths, the Network-based RTK (NRTK) was introduced since late-1990s, and successfully applied to the high precision surveying purposes for more than a decade. We conducted the experiments to analyze the performance of the single-baseline RTK (SRTK) as well as the NRTK using one of the operational NRTK systems of Korea, which is the Virtual Reference Stations (VRS) technique. A total of 46 Continuously Operating Reference Stations (CORS) are used for both SRTK and NRTK to secure the redundancy of the baseline lengths. Since the CORS are quite evenly located at an average of 50-60 km, the analysis of error behavior is restricted in terms of seamless variation of baseline length. Therefore, on top of the existing CORS, we simulated the GNSS RINEX data of the rover (that is, the drone position) at a specific location to get the uniform distribution to the reference stations. Furthermore, the rover was generated for different altitude to evaluate the performance of vertical component of the NRTK system. The CORS GNSS data were obtained at 1 Hz in RINEX format, and the low-cost receiver (ublox) was used for the rover with same interval, single-frequency capability. The correction information from the NRTK server was simultaneously logged for post-processing using the open source software RTKLIB. The percentage of ambiguity resolution was quite reasonable up to 50 km, and drastically drops down as the baseline gets longer. The generated VRS was located with an offset of a few meters in a certain direction, and the horizontal errors also showed a similar pattern. The vertical error behavior due to the tropospheric model deficiency should also be analyzed further.

1 Introduction

The conventional Global Navigation Satellite System (GNSS) surveying was conducted by either the absolute positioning based on C/A code for low accuracy navigation purpose or the Real-time Kinematic (RTK) technique for surveying and/or geodetic purposes. The RTK has been successfully applied to many applications of precision positioning, especially the real-time applications of moving objects. However, the weakness of RTK is that the accuracy is closely dependent on the distance between the rover and the reference station. This is because the common receiving environment of two receiver positions tends to be spatially decorrelated for longer baseline. Therefore, the accuracy declines beyond a certain limit in the baseline length.

The Network-based RTK (NRTK) was proposed to overcome the drawback of the traditional RTK technique [1,2,3]. It was successfully applied to many applications, mostly on the real-time surveying or the moving rover. The accuracy of operational NRTK was compared to that of a single-baseline RTK (SRTK) in terms of baseline lengths. In addition, the characteristics of the positioning accuracy were analyzed as well with respect to the actual RTKs in this study.

2 The GNSS reference network

The Continuously Operating Reference Station (CORS) network is configured in the southern area of the Korean peninsula. Figure 1 shows the distribution of the CORS network that is being operated by the National Geographic Information Institute (NGII) of Korea. The baseline length is about 60 km on average to the neighboring CORS. All reference stations are equipped with a geodetic grade GNSS receiver, and the antenna is installed on a pillar that meets the International GNSS Service (IGS) standard specification [4].

The collected data is transferred to the NGII server via Networked Transport of RTCM via Internet Protocol (NTRIP) data stream in real time [5]. The GNSS observations can be downloaded as either daily or hourly observation files at later times. The rover antenna was installed on the rooftop of a building in Seoul which is located in the northwestern part of Korea. The data was logged at 1-second interval (1 Hz) with an elevation angle cutoff of 15 degrees.

* Corresponding author: author@e-mail.org

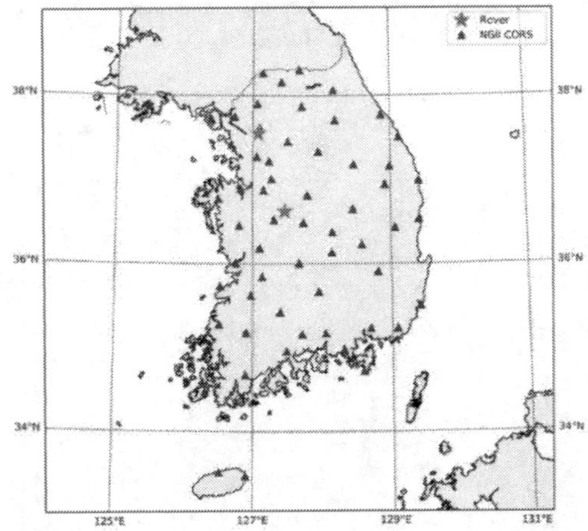

Fig. 1. The configuration of the reference network in Korea.

3 The Network RTK (NRTK) positioning

Currently, two NRTK systems are operational by NGII of Korea, that is, Virtual Reference Station (VRS) [6] and Flächen Korrektur Parameter (FKP).

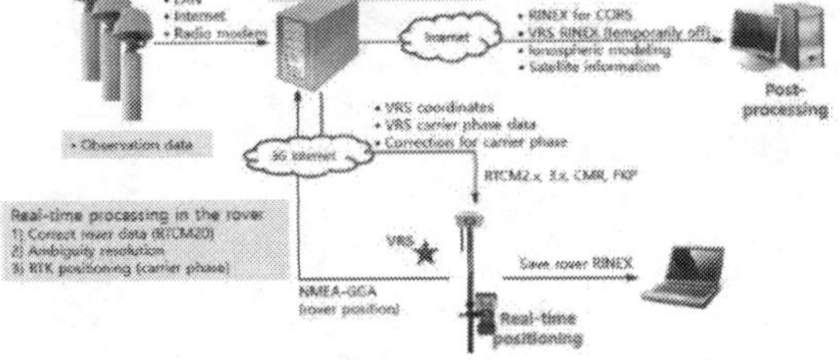

Fig. 2. The system architecture of network-based RTK.

Two systems are designed with a similar concept and provide an equivalent performance in terms of positioning accuracy and ambiguity fixing rates.

Figure 2 shows the system architecture of the NRTK system. All GNSS measurements transferred to the server are converted into RINEX files, and the data quality is instantly evaluated. Once the rover sends its approximate coordinates to the server in an NMEA message, the server generates the virtual reference near the rover position. The correction message in RTCM format (or an equivalently proprietary message such as CMR/CMR+) includes all information for RTK positioning at the rover [7]. The messages are transmitted back and forth through the internet with cellular communication (3G/4G).

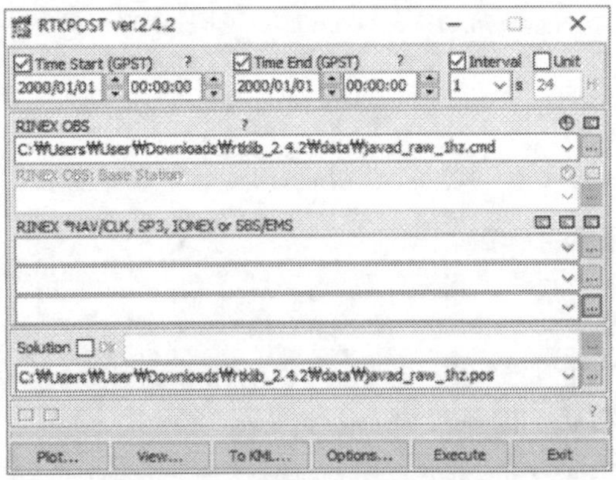

Fig. 3. GNSS positioning software RTKPOST.

The RTK positioning, including the NRTK, was conducted in post-processing mode. The open source software package RTKLIB [8] was used for logging the correction information as well as processing the baselines. Either the RINEX file or the logged correction information was input to the processing software as can be seen in Figure 3. The broadcasting navigation message was used for the satellite orbit and the clock information. The positioning results can be simultaneously stored with the same time interval (1 Hz). The output can be expressed in global Cartesian coordinates or the local plane at the rover position. Only the ambiguity fixed solutions were considered to calculate the statistics in this study.

The estimated coordinates and the variance-covariance matrix are given in the global Cartesian coordinates system. These need to be transformed into the local frame to analyze the characteristics of the solution. Eq. (1) represents the rotation matrix from the global coordinates system to local (planar) frame. The variance-covariance matrix, Q, should also be transformed according to the relationship as given in Eq. (2).

$$R = \begin{bmatrix} -\sin\varphi\cos\lambda & -\sin\varphi\sin\lambda & \cos\varphi \\ -\sin\lambda & \cos\lambda & 0 \\ \cos\varphi\cos\lambda & \cos\varphi\sin\lambda & \sin\varphi \end{bmatrix} \quad (1)$$

$$Q_{neu} = R \cdot Q_{XYZ} \cdot R^T \quad (2)$$

where φ and λ are the geodetic latitude and longitude, respectively.

4 Experiments of long baseline RTK

As discussed above, both SRTK and NRTK was accomplished using the package software of RTKLIB (see Table 1) where the processing is done with dual-frequency measurements. Although multi-GNSS signals can be obtained, only the GPS signals were used in this study. The Saastamoinen model was applied for tropospheric delay correction. For the maximum

https://doi.org/10.1051/e3sconf/20199401006

redundancy of the analysis, the elevation cutoff angle was set to 15 degrees, and both a Kalman forward filter and backward smoothing were applied for consistent solutions.

Table 1. The specification of the GNSS RTK positioning.

	Model
Receiver/antenna	Geodetic grade
Satellites	GPS
Frequency	Dual frequency
Ephemeris	Broadcast message
Tropospheric model	Saastamoinen model
Elevation cutoff	15°
Filter	Forward / backward

Two kinds of experiments were conducted to analyze the effect of the baseline lengths on the positioning accuracy. The SRTK was carried out for the rover in Seoul to all CORS in Korea. In addition, the same procedure was applied for one of CORS to increase the test cases. The NRTK was performed based on VRS that is generated near CORS (same procedure as SRTK).

5 Test results

Figure 4 shows the output of SRTK and NRTK positioning. The VRS generated from the server was plotted on the left side, and the horizontal errors from both RTKs are plotted together on the right side. As can be seen in the figure, VRS locations are biased to northeastern direction, and can be classified into two groups.

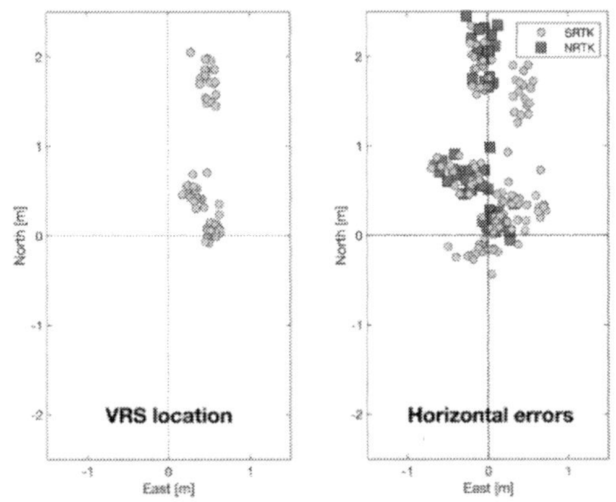

Fig. 4. Error ellipses of RTK solutions.

The average offsets of the VRS are 76 cm and 45 cm for the north and east component, respectively. One thing to be noticed is that the error behavior for the NRTK as well as the SRTK solutions is very close to the VRS locations. The accuracy performance of two RTKs is almost comparable in this experiment. This attributes to the fact that most of the RTK processing was conducted for the baselines longer than 50 km. The statistics of the SRTK and NRTK solutions are summarized in Table 2.

The Root Mean Squared Error (RMSE) of NRTK seems slightly worse than that of SRTK.

Table 2. The overall statistics of single-baseline RTK and the Network-based RTK.

	Single-baseline			Network-based		
	N	E	U	N	E	U
Mean [m]	0.7	0.1	1.9	1.0	-0.1	1.8
Std. Dev. [m]	0.8	0.3	1.2	0.8	0.2	1.4
RMSE [m]	1.1	0.3	2.3	1.3	0.2	2.3

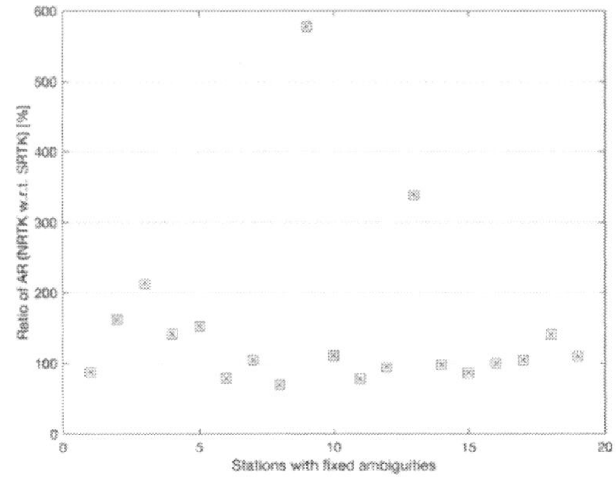

Fig. 5. The ratio of ambiguity resolution for two RTKs.

Figure 5 represents the ratio of ambiguity resolution for two RTK solutions, which is the key success factor. The NRTK shows an improvement in ambiguity resolution (about 150% on average), although some of the stations show a similar or slightly worse performance. Therefore, the NRTK has an equivalent or better performance in the ambiguity resolution under the same experimental conditions.

As can be seen in Figure 6, most of the baselines are longer than 100 km since the rover is located in the upper left corner of the (southern) Korean peninsula. The ambiguities are sufficiently resolved for short baselines. However, the success rate rapidly drops down for longer baselines of 50 km. Furthermore, it was almost impossible to resolve the ambiguities over 100 km, except one exceptional station near 100 km. For stations with baselines shorter than 50 km, the NRTK has better performance in resolving the ambiguities.

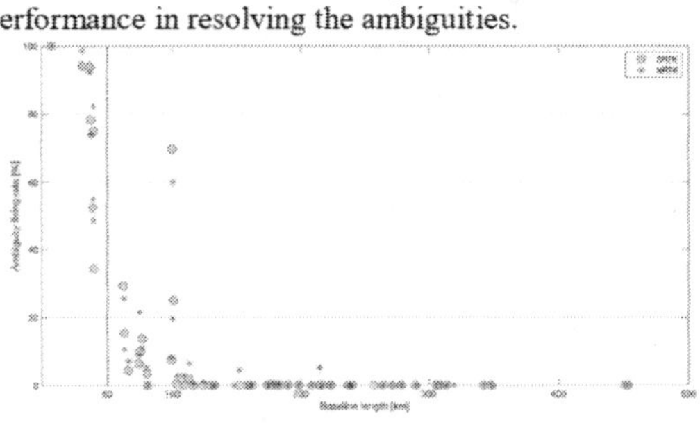

Figure 6: Error ellipses of RTK solutions

6 Conclusion

https://doi.org/10.1051/e3sconf/20199401006

The experiment was conducted to precisely determine the dependency of the baseline lengths of the RTKs. The performance of the SRTK as well as the NRTK generally degrades as the baseline gets longer. The NRTK shows a better performance in terms of success rate of ambiguity resolution. Especially, the ambiguities are reasonably resolved up to 50 km of baselines while it sharply drops down to the marginal state over 100 km.

The horizontal errors of the RTK solution show that the slope of the north component is larger than that of the east component, which is possibly due to the geometric configuration of the RTK processing. The actual VRS is generated within about 2 m from each CORS, and the amount of horizontal error corresponds to the bias of VRS locations.

The NRTK positioning assumes the rover to be located within the reference network. Therefore, it needs to be investigated further to apply the NRTK for the extrapolated cases.

This research was supported by the project "Development of soil moisture based on GNSS reflective signals (KMI2018-05710)."

References

[1] W. Tang, X. Meng, C. Shi, and J. Liu, "Algorithms for sparse network-based RTK GPS positioning and performance assessment," *The Journal of Navigation*, vol. 66, pp. 335–348 (2013)

[2] U. Vollath, A. Buecherl, H. Landau, C. Pagels, and B. Wagner, "Multi-base RTK positioning using virtual reference stations," *Proceedings of ION GPS 2000*, Salt Lake City, UT, pp. 123-131 (2000)

[3] G. Wubbena, A. Bagge, and M. Schmitz, "Network-based techniques for RTK applications," *GPS JIN 2001* (2001)

[4] M. Kim, *Algorithm Development of Integrated Navigation System for Ground Vehicle Using Network-RTK*, Sejong University, Master's thesis, 134p (2015)

[5] M. H. Kim and T. S. Bae, "Preliminary analysis of network-RTK for navigation," *Journal of the Korean Society of Surveying, Geodesy, Photogrammetry and Cartography*, vol. 33, no. 5, pp. 343-351 (2015)

[6] G. R. Hu, H. S. Khoo, P. C. Goh, and C. L. Law, "Development and assessment of GPS virtual reference stations for RTK positioning," *Journal of Geodesy*, vol. 77, pp. 292-302 (2003)

[7] N. Talbot, G. Lu, T. Allison, and U. Vollath, "Broadcast network RTK-transmission standards and results," *Proceedings of the Proceedings of the 15th International Technical Meeting of the Satellite Division of The Institute of Navigation (ION GPS 2002)* (2002)

[8] T. Takasu, *RTKLIB: An open source program package for GNSS positioning*, http://www.rtklib.com (2018)

[9] T. Takasu and A. Yasuda, "Development of the low-cost RTK-GPS receiver with an open source program package RTKLIB," *International Symposium on GPS/GNSS* (2009)

Comparison of Sea Surface Variation Derived from Global Navigation Satellite System (GNSS) and Co-tidal in Java Sea

Danar Guruh Pratomo[1,*], *Khomsin*[1], and *Khariz* Syaputra[1]

[1]Geomatics Engineering, Institut Teknologi Sepuluh Nopember, Surabaya, Indonesia

Abstract. Tide represents the vertical variation of sea surface. This parameter plays important rules in bathymetric survey. The conventional method to observe the sea surface variation is by using tide pole. Nowdays, a Global Navigation Satellite System (GNSS) can be used as a means to measure the variation of sea surface as it provides high accuracy coordinates. In this research, the vertical component of GNSS was utilized to analyze the variation of sea surface. The distance between tidal stations and the survey area can be a constrain to the depth reduction because its tidal zoning.The traditional tidal zoning is a discrete model. This can be minimalized using a co-tidal chart. In this research, the vertical variation of sea surface from GNSS and co-tidal chart approachs were examined and compared to the conventional method. The comparative analysis was performed with Root Mean Square Error (RMSE). The maximum and minimum RMSE during 3 days period between the GNSS and conventional approach are 0.246 m and 0.051 m, respectively. Whereas, the maximum and minimum RMSE between the co-tidal chart model and the conventional approach at the same time are 0.286 m and 0.109 m.

1 Introductions

Tide is a natural phenomenon of water surface's periodic rise and fall as the result of celestial objects' gravity, especially the moon and sun. Influence of other astronomical objects can be excepted since the distance and size are relatively smaller than the moon and sun. Tide on quasi-closed area like bay is affected by non-astronomical factors, such as coastal forms and basic topography [1].

Tidal observations are generally carried out on the beach or dock / harbor using tide pole or other tide gauge equipment. Tidal characteristics observed at the beach or dock / port are only valid for areas within a certain radius from the observation point. Outside of the area, as offshore, the tidal characteristics are usually determined indirectly by prediction using co-tidal charts.

Tidal observations are carried out with the aim to record vertical sea level movements that occur periodically. Results of tidal observations can be used as a correction to the depth surveyed. Sometimes, tidal observation conducted quite far from the survey location. So there's a possibility that the tide data is invalid for correction. This situation happened because the characteristics of the tides can differ from one region to another [2].

Global Positioning System (GPS) can be used to overcome tidal characteristics differences in different places. GPS can be used on a boat along with the sounding. Observations using GPS aims to position both horizontally and vertically with millimeters accuracy. To achieve high accuracy using GPS, differential kinematic methods can be used both real-time kinematic (RTK) and post-processed kinematic (PPK). In some cases, Differential GPS (DGPS) used [3].

This research was conducted with the aim to determine the differences found in sea level height results from tidal observation data using GPS and the results of co-tidal data. To find out the difference between these two data, this research must be done in the same place with relatively in the same time period. Knowing the differences in sea level height results from tidal observations using GPS and the results of co-tidal data on tide pole observation, conclusions can be drawn in which observational data has the smallest accuracy error.

2 Methods

2.1. Location

The location of this research took a case study of the Java Sea in the coordinates of 2°27'35,21" – 8°23'0,26" LS dan 105°49'9,76" – 119°41'44" BT.

* Corresponding author: dg.pratomo@gmail.com

Fig. 1. Research Location

2.2 Data and Tools

Data used in this research are both primary and secondary data, specified as below:

a. GPS tide observation data using moving ship on Java Sea, April 26th to April 28th 2018.
b. Tide observation data using tide pole April 26th to April 28th 2018.
c. Geoid model data (EGM2008).
d. Coastline data of Java Sea (GSHHG).
e. Observation data from 25 tidal stations on Java Sea waters February 1st to March 1st, 2018.

As for equipments used in this research are software for data processing, such as:

a. RTKLIB for GPS data processing.
b. Alltrans EGM2008 Calculator 1.2 for EGM2008 data processing.
c. Matlab R2014a for tidal data processing.
d. PydroGIS 18.4 for tidal and co-tidal modelling.
e. ArcGIS 10.3 for layouting the data results.

2.3 Data Processing

Steps on data processing are explained as below:

a. GPS Tide Data Processing
GPS tide observation data used to obtain sea level. Sea level generated from this data is still refers to ellipsoid. Geoid EGM2008 model data then used to correct sea level which still refers to ellipsoid, becoming sea level refers to geoid (assumed its coincide with MSL).
b. Tide and Co-Tidal Modellling
Data from 25 tidal stations and coastline are used to make tidal models. Method for making the tide model is the triangulation interpolation method. Results of the tidal model are then exported to be processed into co-tidal and to obtain sea level height values that have MSL reference.
c. Comparative Analysis of GPS Tide Observation Data and Co-tidal toward Tide Pole Observation Data.
Tide pole observation data are used as comparative data on GPS and co-tidal sea level value. Analysis is done by comparing the accuracy level from the comparison of 2 sea level height values (GPS compared to tide pole and co-tidal compared to tide pole). Root Mean Square Error (RMSE) was calculated to test the accuracy level between these two.

3 Result

3.1 Result of GPS Tide Observations

The results of GPS tide observations show GPS observation date and time, ellipsoid height, undulation, and orthometric height. The time of GPS observation varies for each day. This is due to the condition of a conditional measurement schedule. The average GPS observation time for each day is 5-6 hours with interval every 10 seconds.

Orthometric height is the final result of GPS observation which refers to geoid. Where, the height of the geoid is assumed to coincide with the mean sea level (MSL). The height is obtained by correcting the ellipsoid height value with undulation and the height value of the GPS antenna against sea level. Thus, the final value of orthometric height is the sea level that refers to geoid (coincides with MSL). The sea level height of the GPS observation results is shown in the GPS tide chart as in Figure 2, 3 and 4.

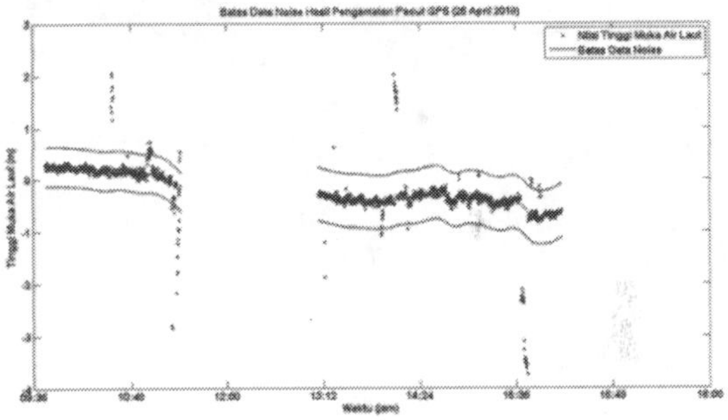

Fig. 2. Noise GPS Tide (26 April 2018)

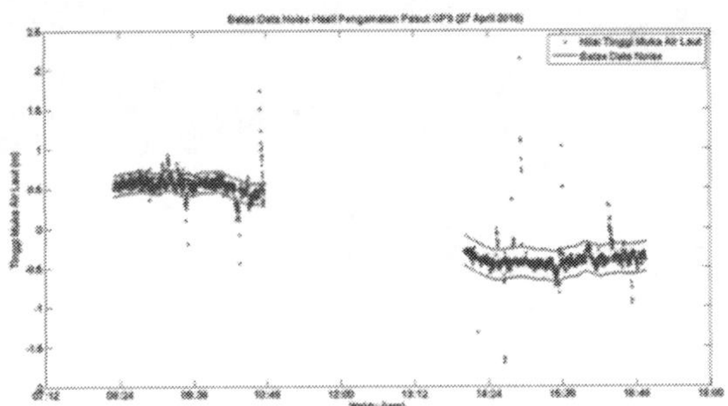

Fig. 3. Noise GPS Tide (27 April 2018)

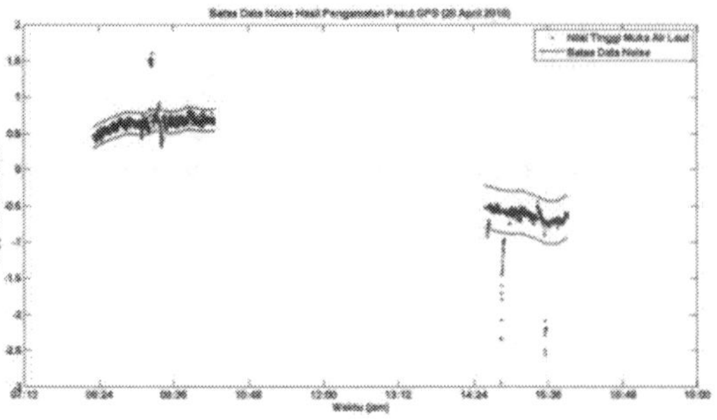

Fig. 4. Noise GPS Tide (28 April 2018)

Figure 2, 3 and 4 shows the graph of sea level on 26th, 27th and 28th April 2018. The sea level is already referring to geoid (coinciding with MSL) in meter unit. The graph shows there is noise data that is outside the upper and lower limits of the data. Data that is outside the upper and lower limit will need to be cleaned to obtain a smooth GPS observation graph. The results of cleaning and smoothing of GPS sea level data are shown in the graph in Figure 5, 6 and 7.

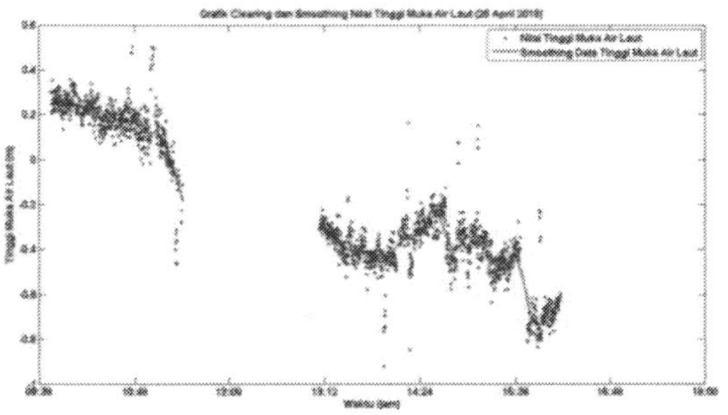

Fig. 5. Smoothing GPS Tide (26 April 2018)

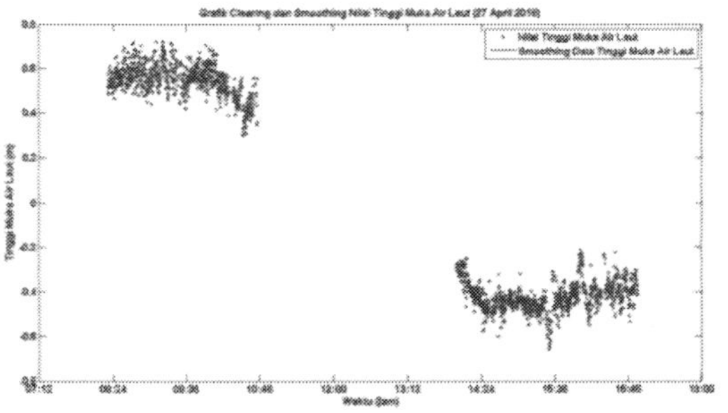

Fig. 6. Smoothing GPS Tide (27 April 2018)

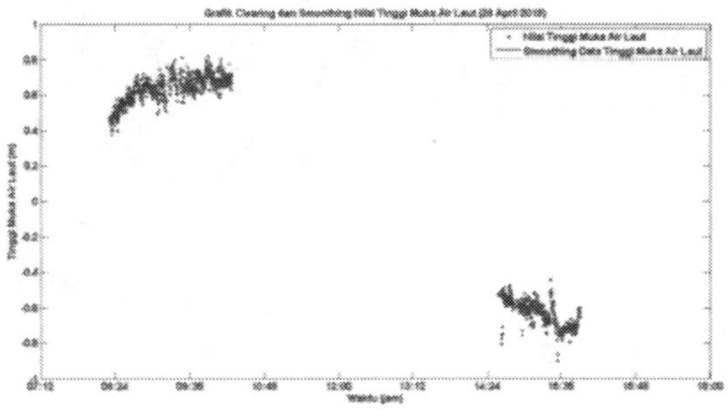

Fig. 7. Smoothing GPS Tide (28 April 2018)

Figure 5, 6 and 7 show the smoothing observations of GPS tides on April 26th, 27th and 28th 2018. The smoothing results are obtained from the results of GPS tide data that have been cleared from noise. The method used to perform data noise clearing and data smoothing is the moving average filtering method. The process is carried out to minimize the effects of vessel / boat movements that cause data noise. The data of GPS tide observations of this smoothing result will be compared to the co-tidal data and observation of tide pole.

3.2 Result of Tide and Co-tidal Modeling

The results of the tide model that is processed using Pydro 18.4 are in the form of contours of the amplitude and phase values of each constant (M2, S2, N2, K1, and O1). The values of each amplitude and phase are obtained by using the least square method on the Matlab R2014a. The data used is the observation data of 25 tidal stations.

The amplitude that generated at each constant indicate the values variation at 25 tidal stations. The largest amplitude for the K1 constant is at the Bangka tidal station with a value of 0.811 meters. The largest amplitude for M2 constant is at Ketapang station with a value of 0.477 meters. The largest amplitude for the N2 constant is at the Ketapang tidal station with a value of 0.094 meters. The largest amplitude for the O1 constant is at the Bangka tidal station with a value of 0.521 meters. The amplitude for S2 constant is at Kotabaru tidal station with a value of 0.497 meters.

The resulting phase value shows the direction and magnitude of the constant wave propagation in degrees. The phase in each harmonic constant is the tidal phase against equilibrium tides in Greenwich. Variations in the value and direction of propagation that show differences at each tidal location against the tidal force. To see the differences more clearly, variations in values and directions in the amplitude and phase in each tidal station are processed into a mesh (domain model) of the tidal model which is then exported to co-tidal charts.

Mesh of tide model is obtained from the interpolation process of tidal observation data, tidal constituent and phase data, and vertical datum data as a reference for sea level height. The interpolation method used is the triangulation method. Figure 8 shows the results of the tide mesh model.

Fig. 8. Result of Tide Mesh Model

This triangulation method works by making triangles that do not intersect. Where, for each interconnected triangles have different weights. The weighting value generated in the interpolation process is represented by the midpoints of the triangles at each coordinate of the interpolation result.

Besides being able to export the amplitude and phase contour values which are then processed into co-tidal charts, the tide model which is processed from the mesh making process (domain model) from the observation data of 25 tidal stations can also be exported to determine the sea level height value. The resulting sea level can be exported at certain coordinates as needed. The vertical datum that is used can also be set according to the required needs. In Figure 9, 10 and 11 are shown the graphical pattern of co-tidal sea level height.

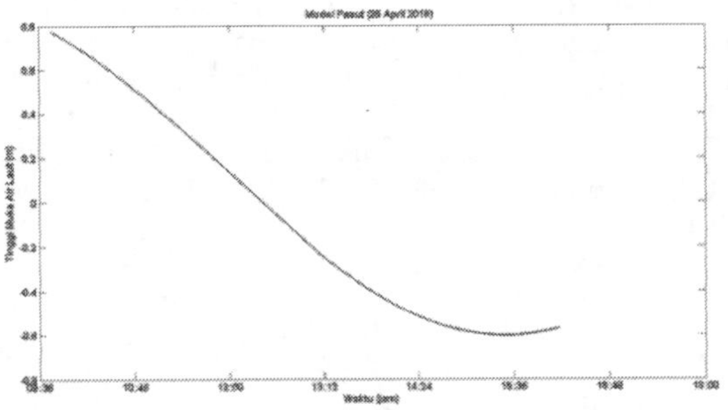

Fig. 9. Sea Level Height from Co-tidal (26 April 2018)

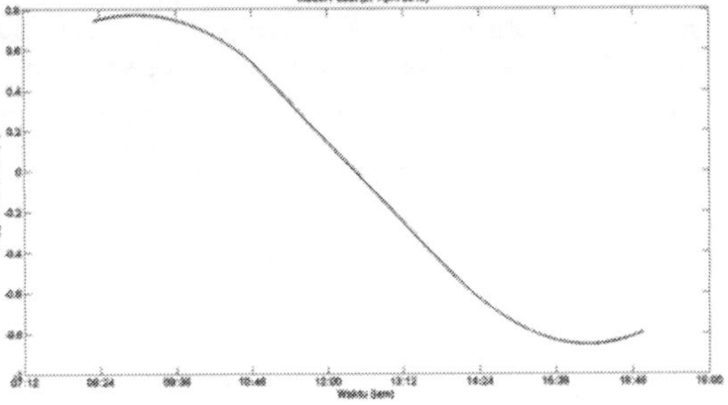

Fig. 10. Sea Level Height from Co-tidal (27 April 2018)

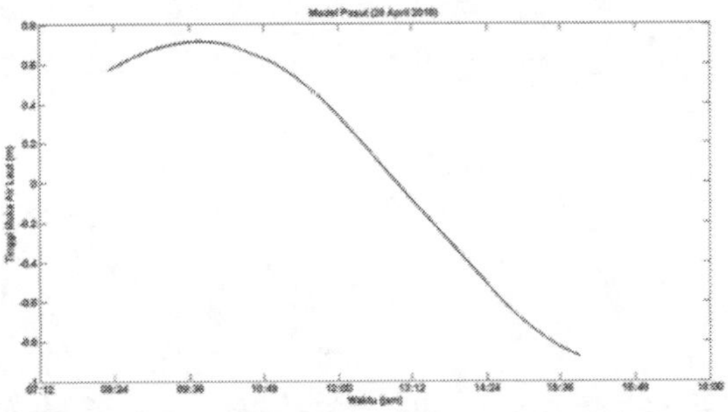

Fig. 11. Sea Level Height from Co-tidal (28 April 2018)

Figure 9, 10 and 11 show the chart pattern of co-tidal water level on the 26th, 27th and 28th April 2018. The graph shown has a pattern that is relatively the same as the sea level height chart of the GPS smoothing results shown in the previous section. Comparison of graph patterns between sea level highs of GPS smoothing results and co-tidal to sea level height observations of tide pole will be explained in the next section.

3.3 Comparison of GPS Tide and Co-tidal to Observation of Tide Pole

In this research, a comparison of sea surface variation data from the results of 2 observations of sea level height was carried out by observing tide pole. Whereas, the sea level height values of these observations are assumed to be correct data. The first, is the comparison of the sea level height of the results of GPS observations on sea level height values observed by tide pole. The second, is the comparison of the value of co-tidal sea level (tidal model) to the sea level height observed by tide pole.

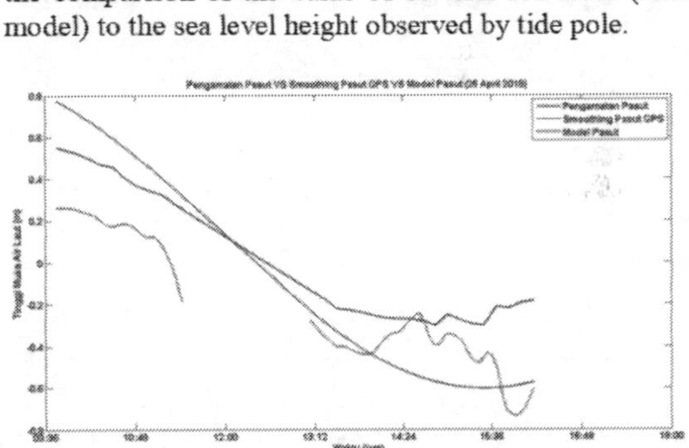

Fig. 12. Comparison of Sea Level Height (26 April 2018)

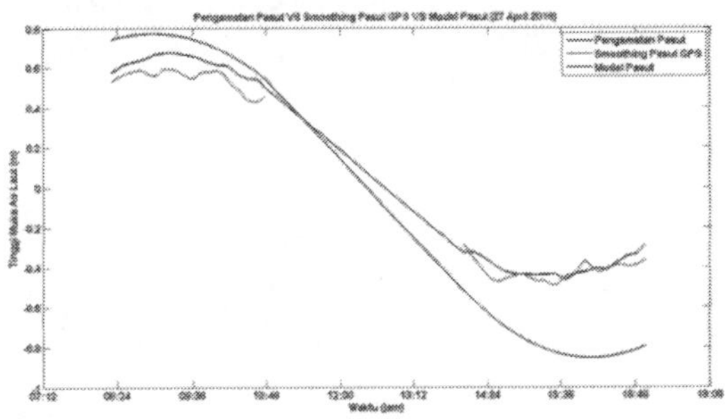

Fig. 13. Comparison of Sea Level Height (27 April 2018)

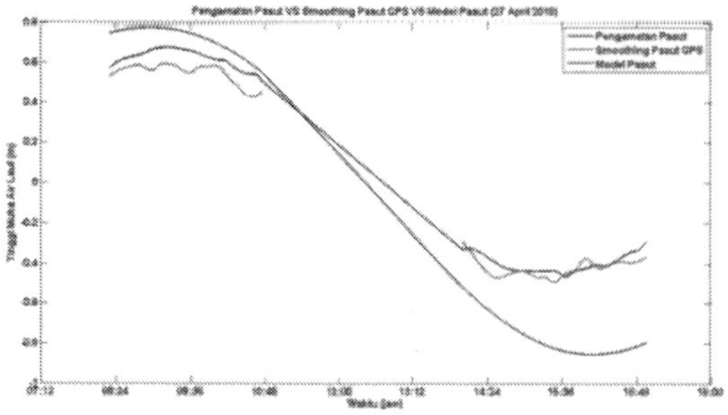

Fig. 14. Comparison of Sea Level Height (28 April 2018)

Figure 12, 13 and 14 show a comparison graph of sea level height on April 26th, 27th and 28th 2018. The sea level height graph from GPS observations is shown with a red graph. Graph of sea level co-tidal results (tidal model) is shown with a blue graph. Charts of sea level height observed by tide pole are shown with a black graph. Overall, the chart pattern of the three sea level height values produced is relatively the same but has a difference in sea level height. In this research, analysis of sea level height which was carried out from GPS, co-tidal, and tide pole is by looking for sea level height values that are closest to sea level height values observed by tide pole which are considered correct data.

The analysis carried out is by calculating the level of accuracy on the value of the sea level of GPS results and cotidal results on sea level as a result of observations of tide pole. Accuracy test is done by calculating the RMSE (Root Mean Square Error) value at each observation time (26, 27, and 28 April 2018). RMSE calculations can be done using the following formula [4].

$$RMSE = \sqrt{\frac{\sum_{i=1}^{n}(y_i - \hat{y}_i)^2}{n}} \quad (1)$$

Where $\sum_{i=1}^{n}(y_i - \hat{y}_i)^2$ is the sum of the squares of the size minus the value that is considered true, and n is the length of the data. From these calculations, the RMSE values are shown in Table 1 below.

Table 1. RMSE Values.

Date	Comparison	RMSE
26/4/2018	Tide Pole – GPS Tide	0,246
	Tide Pole – Co-tidal	0,237
27/4/2018	Tide Pole – GPS Tide	0,061
	Tide Pole – Co-tidal	0,286
28/4/2018	Tide Pole – GPS Tide	0,051
	Tide Pole – Co-tidal	0,109

In the comparison of sea level height values from tide pole and GPS tidal results, the largest RMSE value was on April 26th 2018 with a value of 0.246 meters. Meanwhile, on the next 2 days, on 27th and 28th April 2018, the resulting RMSE value was smaller with a value of 0.061 and 0.051 meters. The difference between the height of the sea level of the tide pole and the results of the GPS tide does not always provide a solution at the centimeter (cm) level. There are times, the difference in the value of the sea level generated will reach the level of decimeters (dm) up to meters (m). This can occur due to several factors as follows [5]:

a. Error on base station height measurement
b. Error in measuring the height of the rover antenna
c. Error in the separation model.

Meanwhile, in the comparison of sea level height values from tide pole and co-tidal results, the largest RMSE value was on April 27, 2018 with a value of 0.286 meters. Meanwhile, on April 26 and 28 the resulting RMSE values were 0.237 and 0.109 meters. From the comparison of sea level height values, both between the results of the tide pole with GPS and between the results of the tide pole with co-tidal it can be seen that on April 27 and 28 2018 the average error value on the sea level of GPS results is smaller than co-tidal average error results. It can be interpreted that the value of the sea level of the GPS results is closer to the sea level height of the tide pole.

4 Conclusion

The sea level height value generated from GPS observation data is referenced to the ellipsoid which is then corrected so that it refers to the geoid (assumed to coincide with MSL). Meanwhile, sea level height results from co-tidal and observation of tide pole refer to the mean sea level (MSL). The sea level height results from GPS observation data and the results of co-tidal have a relatively similar pattern to sea level height results from observations of tide pole at each observation time (26th, 27th, and 28th April 2018). Based on the resulting graph, the closest pattern is on the third day on 28th April 2018.

Comparison of sea level height of tide pole and GPS tides, the RMSE values obtained on April 26th was 0.246 meters, April 27th was 0.061 meters, and on April 28th was 0.051 meters. Whereas, in the comparison of sea level height of tide pole and co-tidal results, the RMSE value on April 26th was 0.237 meters, April 27th was 0.286 meters, and on April 28th the resulting RMSE value was 0.109 meters. From the comparison of sea level height, both between the results of the tide pole with GPS and between the results of the tide pole with co-tidal it can be seen that on 27th and 28th April 2018 the average error value on the sea level of GPS results is smaller than co-tidal average error results. It can be interpreted that the value of the sea level height of the GPS is closer to the sea level height of the tide pole.

5 References

1. R. H. Stewart. Intoductioan to Physical Oceanography. Am. J. Phys. (2008)
2. S. Haryono, Narni. Karakteristik Pasang Surut di Pulau Jawa. Forum Tek, **28** (2004)

https://doi.org/10.1051/e3sconf/20199401007

3. H. Z. Abidin. Penentuan Posisi dengan GPS dan Aplikasinya. (2007)
4. C. D. Ghilani, P. R. Wolf. Adjusment Computations: Spatial Data Analysis. (2011)
5. D. J. Mills, Dodd. Ellipsoidally Refenced Surveying for Hydrography. (2014)
6. S. R. Deloach. GPS Tide: A Project to Determine Tidal Datums with The Global Positioning System. (1995)
7. M. Cisternelli, Gill. Implementation of TCARI into NOS Hydrographic Survey Operation. (2014)

Performance Evaluation of Multi Radio Integrated Navigation System under Navigation Warfare in M&S Software

Heyone Kim [1], *Jae Hoon* Son[1], *Sang Heon* Oh[2], *Hyoungmin* So[3], and *Dong-Hwan* Hwang[1,*]

[1] Chungnam National University, Department of Electronics Engineering, 34134 Daejeon, Korea
[2] Navcours Co., Ltd, Integrated Navigation Division, 34014 Daejeon, Korea
[3] Agency for Defense Development, 34186 Daejeon, Korea

Abstract. In this paper, a modelling and simulation software is designed in order to evaluate the performance of a multi radio integrated navigation system and the performance evaluation results are presented. The modelling and simulation software is divided into navigation algorithm module, navigation environment generation module, and graphic user interface module with performance evaluation algorithm. In order to show the validity of the design, the modelling and simulation software for GPS, KNSS, Loran-C, eLoran, and DME/VOR is implemented in C++ under Windows OS environment. Accuracy, integrity, continuity and availability are evaluated for the multi radio integrated navigation system in the modelling and simulation software. The performance evaluation results show that the designed modelling and simulation software can be effectively used for the performance evaluation of multi radio integrated navigation systems.

1 Introduction

The NAVWAR (NAVigation WARfare) is defined as the deliberate defensive and offensive action to assure and prevent positioning, navigation and timing information [1]. GNSS (Global Navigation Satellite System) is vulnerable to jamming and spoofing since the received signal power is very small and signal structure is open to the public [2-3]. In recent years, many research results on the alternative navigation system and anti-jamming and/or anti-spoofing receivers have been introduced to cope with these threat [4-6]. By integrating GNSS with other radio navigation system in the alternative navigation system, continuous navigation outputs can be provided in NAVWAR environments [3, 6]. As examples of these systems, integration of GPS (Global Positioning System) and ground based navigation system in U.S. (United Station) and GPS/eLoran in U.K. (United Kingdom) have been planned and carried out [7-9]. In Korea, a research on a multi radio integrated navigation system, in which GPS, KNSS (Korean Navigation Satellite System) and ground based navigation systems are integrated, have been being carried out for the outage of GPS [11-15].

Lots of tests and performance evaluations are required before the multi radio integrated navigation system is deployed for real-time navigation. For the performance evaluation, much time and cost can be saved if an M&S S/W (Modelling and Simulation SoftWare) is used [10].

Generally, the performance of the radio navigation system is evaluated through four indices, accuracy, integrity, continuity and availability [1, 17, 18], and relation between these four indices has pyramid scheme with the accuracy as base [18].

In this paper, the M&S S/W for performance evaluation of a multi radio integrated navigation system is designed and the results of the performance evaluation are presented. The M&S S/W is divided into navigation algorithm part, navigation environment generation part, performance evaluation part and GUI (Graphic User Interface). The designed M&S S/W is implemented in C under Windows environment. The navigation algorithm in the M&S S/W is run for a motion of a vehicle in a normal situation, and then the performance evaluation part in the M&S S/W is run for the outputs of the navigation algorithm, in which the performance evaluation method recommended by IMO (International Maritime Organization) is adopted. The NAVWAR effect is reflected in the navigation environment generation part and performance evaluation for the navigation algorithm in this situation is performed. The performance evaluation results are compared for two situations.

In the sequel, in section II, requirements of the M&S S/W for performance evaluation and M&S S/W design result to satisfy the requirements are presented. In section III, the designed M&S S/W is implemented and performance evaluation results are presented. Finally, in section IV, concluding remarks and further studies are presented.

* Corresponding author: dhhwang@ cnu.ac.kr.

https://doi.org/10.1051/e3sconf/20199401008

2 M&S S/W requirement and design

2.1. M&S S/W requirements for performance evaluation

In order to evaluate the performance of the multi radio integrated navigation system under NAVWAR in the M&S S/W, the M&S S/W should satisfy the following requirements.

- The multi radio integrated navigaiton algorithms to evaluate should be prepared.

- Measurements for the multi radio integrated navigation algorithm should be prepared.

- In the measurements, motion of the vehicle should be reflected. The characteristics of the signal transmission process from signal sources to the measurments should be reflected in the measutements. The characteristics of the signal transmission can be modelled as measurements error.

- The effect of NAVWAR environment should be reflected in the M&S S/W. Due to the NAVWAR, measurements errors becomes larger. In order to reflect the effect of NAVWAR, another measurement error is added to the generated measurements.

- The performance evaluation algorithms should be prepared in the M&S S/W.

- In order for the user to easily set parameters of the multi radio navigaiton algorithm, measurement generation and performance evaluation and check the results of navigation algorithm and performance evalution, a GUI (Graphic User Interface) should be prepared.

2.2. M&S S/W design

An M&S S/W configuraion satisfying the requirements given above is shown in figure 1. The M&S S/W consists of navigation algorithm part, navigation environment generation part, performance evaluation part and GUI part. As shown in figure 1, the multi radio integrated navigation system is an integrated navigation system in which, GPS, a local satellite navigation system KNSS(Korean Navigation Satellite System) and ground based radio navigaiton systems such as Loran-C (Long range navigation), e-Loran (enhanced Loran), DME (Distance Measuring Equipment) and VOR (Very high frequency Omnidirectional Radio range). In the navigaiton environment generation part, motion of the vehicle, signal transmission characteristics and effect of NAVWAR environment are reflected.

When the M&S S/W is implemented in a platform, the S/W is divided into function modules as shown in figure 2. For data exchange between function modules, the message broker is included in the M&S S/W. Due to this message broker, each function module can be independently operated. Since the functions modules are operated independently, each function module can easily modify and expand its function. The navigation algorithm module will run in a real-time multi radio integrated navigation system. Since the M&S S/W is run based on the M&S message broker, the navigation algorithm can be ported in the real-time multi radio integrated navigation system without little modification.

In order to perform evaluation of navigaiton algorithms, the whole outputs of the navigation algorithm for one trajectory are needed, there is no data exchange of performance evaluation part with other function module. For this reason, the performnce evaluation part is included in the GUI module in the M&S S/W.

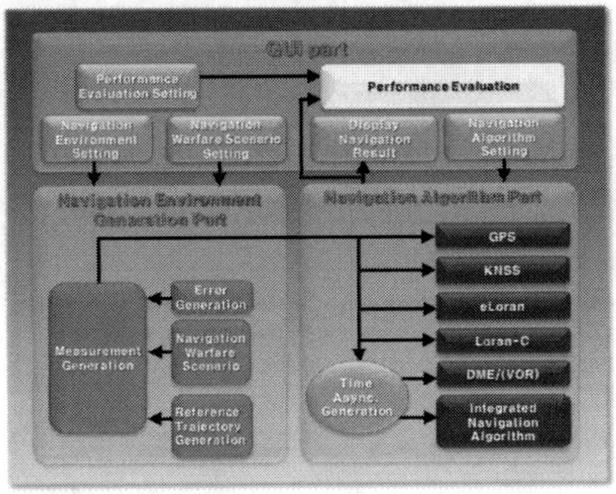

Fig. 1. M&S S/W configuration

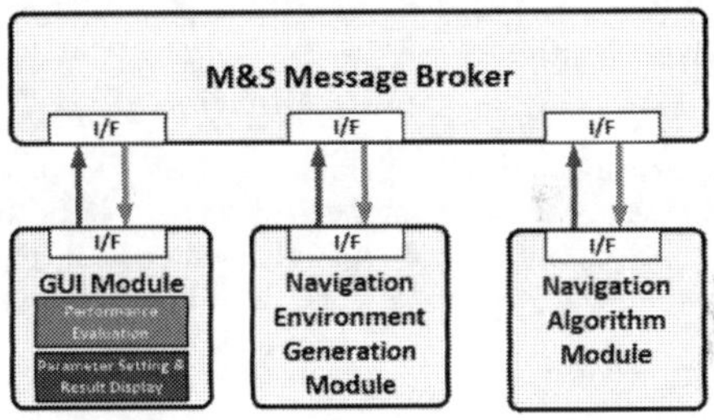

Fig. 2. Multi radio integrated navigation system M&S S/W with message broker

2.2.1. Navigation algorithm module

The multi radio navigation algorithm module is shown in figure 3. Outputs of each navigation system and integrated navigation systems are calculated from the measurements. The weighted least square method and Kalman filter can be used.

2.2.2. Navigation environment generation module

The navigaiton environment generation module is shown in figure 4. The navigation genertation module generates measurements for the navigaiton algorithms. It can be seen from figure 4 that motion of the vehicle, signal transmission characteristics and effect of NAVWAR environment are reflected in the navigation environment generation module. The visibility of the navigaiton signal sources is determined from geographic information, locations of the navigaiton signal sources and characteristics of the navigation signals.

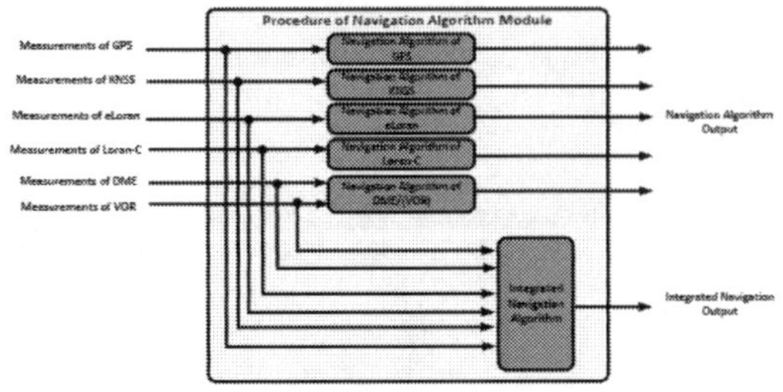

Fig. 3. Multi radio integrated navigation algorithm module

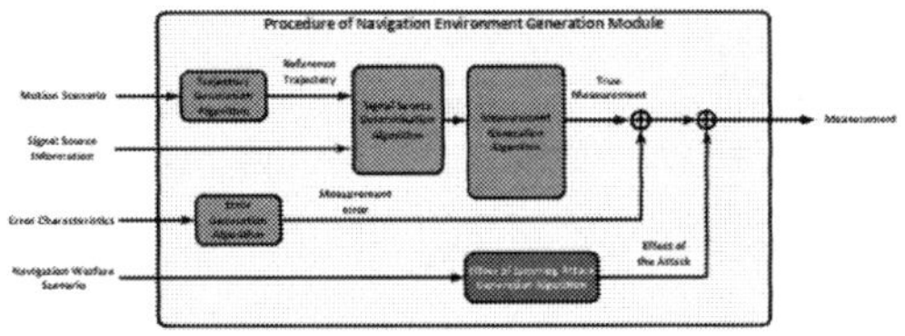

Fig. 4. Navigation environment generation module

2.2.3. GUI module

As shown in figure 5, GUI module receives parameters for navigation environment module, navigation algorithm module and performance evaluation module and gives navigation output display and performance evaluation result.

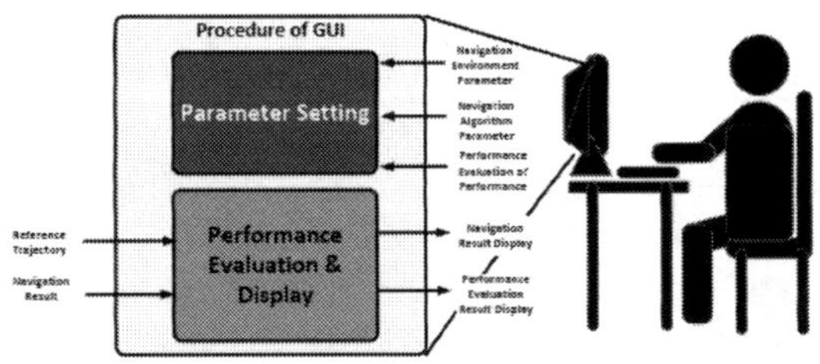

Fig. 5. GUI in the M&S S/W

2.2.4. Performance evaluation module

The performance of radio navigation systems is evaluated through four indices, accuracy, integrity, continuity and availability. Relation between these four indices has pyramid scheme with the accuracy as base as shown in figure 6 [17-20].

Performacne evaluation module in the M&S S/W is shown in figure 7. The accuracy is evaluated from reference trajectory and navigation result. The integrity is from alarm limit and navigaion error which is result of the accuracy evaluation. The continuity is from CTI (Continuous Time Interval) and MTBF (Mean Time Between Failure) which is integrity evaluation result. The availability is from MTBF and MTTR (Mean Time To Repair) which are result of the integrity evaluation.

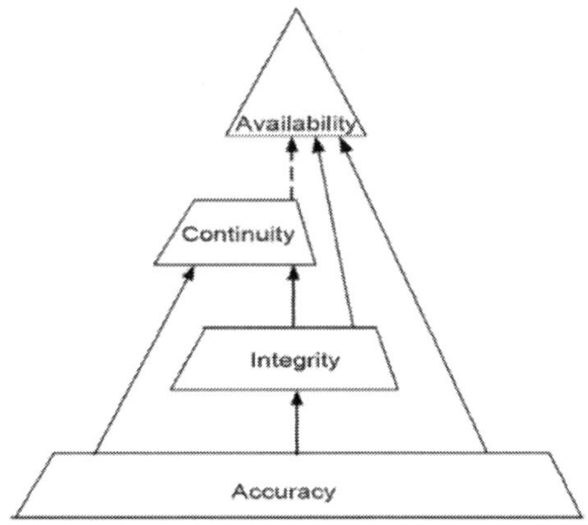

Fig. 6. Relation between four indices for performance evaluation with pyramid scheme

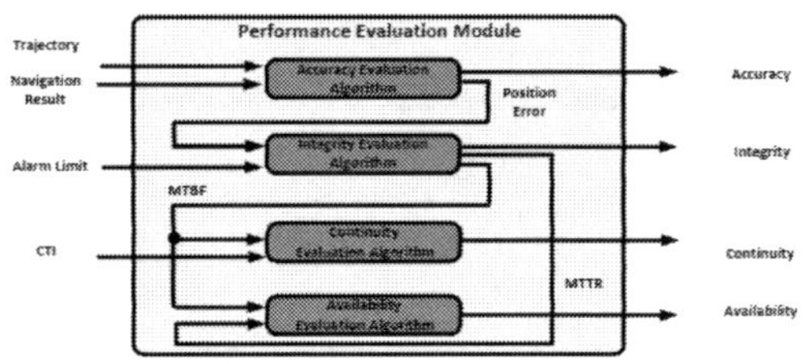

Fig. 7. Performance evaluation module

2.2.4.1. Accuracy index

The accuraccy index is the radius of distance in which navigation errors are located in 95% probabilty. The distance is obtained from equation (1).

$$(Accuracy\ index) = 1.96 \times RMSE \tag{1}$$

where *RMSE* denotes Root Mean Square Error.

2.2.4.2 Integrity index

The integrity is evaluated from navigation result, Alarm Limit (AL) and Protection Level (PL). The AL is the error limit required in the navigaiton system. The PL is the estimate of error limit which is obtained from navigation output. The integrity index is given in equation (2).

$$(Integrity\ Index) = \frac{N_{PE<AL\&PE<PL}}{N_{total} - N_{Unavailable}} \times 100 \qquad (2)$$

where $N_{PE<AL\&PE<PL}$ denotes the number of cases when PE (Position Error) is less than AL and PE less than PL. N_{total} denotes all the number of cases. $N_{Unavailable}$ denotes number of cases the when the system is not operated. In this case, PL is greater than AL.

2.2.4.3. Continuity index

The continuity index is given in equation (3).

$$(Contiuity\ index) = e^{-\frac{CTI}{MTBF}} \times 100 \qquad (3)$$

In order to calculate MTBF, failure should be determined. Failure is determined to occur when PL is greater than AL and PE is greater than PL.

2.2.4.4 Availability index

The availability index is given in equation (4).

$$(Availability\ index) = \frac{MTBF}{MTBF + MTTR} \times 100 \qquad (4)$$

The repair to calculate the MTTR is determined when AL is greater than PL and PE is less than PL.

3 Performance evaluation

The M&S S/W was implemented in visual C++ under Windows Operating System in PC. GDI(Graphic Device Interface) API(Application Programming Interface) was used for display for GUI. Performance evaluation was performed for a multi radio integrated navigation system of GPS, KNSS, eLoran, Loran-C, DME and VOR in the M&S S/W.

3.1. Motion of the vehicle

Trajectory of the vehicle is shown in figure 8. The vehicle is moving for 2500s. Initial position of the vehicle is 35.34 ° of latitude, 126.19° of longitude and 100m of altitude. After the vehicle goes up to 8km of altitude, it carries 8-shaped motion and descends.

3.2. Navigation warfare environment

In order to evaluate the performance of the navigaiton sytem in a NAVWAR environment, a jammer is located in 35.34° of latitude, 125.74° of longitude and 500m of altitude. The effect of the jammer reflected in the navigation enenvironment generation module in the M&S S/W. The jammer is operated during 0s to 2500s and power of the jammer is 30W. For this case, GPS signal cannot be received if the vehicle is located within 280km from the jammer.

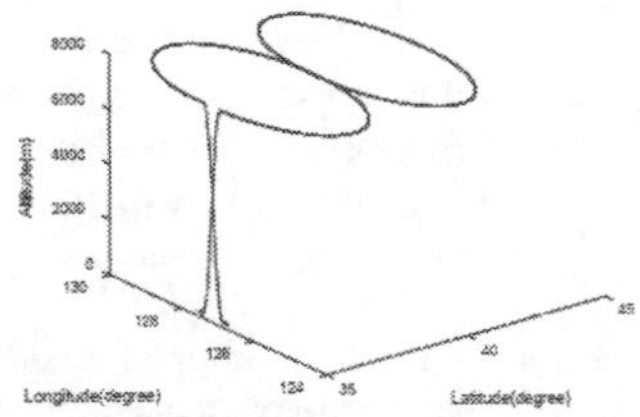

Fig. 8. Trajectory of the vehicle

3.3. Performance evaluation result

The performance evaluation results for the navigation algorithms is shown in table 1 when there is no jammer.

Table 1. Performance evaluation results with no jammer

Algorithm	Accuracy [m]	Integrity [%]	Continuity [%/15s]	Availability [%]
GPS	North: 2.815534 East : 2.379671 Down: 3.111354	99.99	99.99	99.99
Multi-radio Integrated Navigation System (GPS, KNSS, eLoran, Loran-C, DME/VOR)	North: 2.585857 East : 2.278709 Down: 3.047878	99.99	99.99	99.99

The performance evaluation results for the navigation algorithms is shown in table 2 in the NAVWAR environment. It can be seen from table 2 that the accuracy indices are very large values in the NAVWAR environmnent since there is intervals in which GPS signals are available. It can also seen from table 2 that the performance indes of the integrated navigation algorithms are larger than GPS navigaiton algorithm in the NAVWAR environment. Since the integrated navigaiton algorithm can provide navigation outputs even though GPS cannot. Altitude errors of output of navigation algorithms are shown in figure 8 and 9. It can also observed from figure 8 and 10 that altitude error of the integrated navigation algorithm are much less than that of GPS navigation algorithm.

4 Concluding remarks and further studies

In this paper, a modelling and simulation software has been designed in order to evaluate the performance of a multi radio integrated navigation system and the performance evaluation results have been presented. In order to show the validity of the design, the modelling and simulation software for GPS, KNSS, Loran-C, eLoran, and DME/VOR has been implemented in C++ under Windows OS environment. Accuracy, integrity, continuity and availability have been evaluated for the multi radio integrated navigation system in a NAVWAR environment in the modelling and simulation software. The performance evaluation results showed that the designed modelling and simulation software can be effectively used for the performance evaluation of multi radio integrated navigation systems in the NAVWAR environment.

As further studies, research on integrated navigation system with an optimal performance and performance evaluation for various operation of vehicles will be performed.

This work has been supported by the National GNSS Research Center Program of Defense Acquisition Program Administration and Agency for Defense Development.

Table 2. . Performance evaluation results with a jammer

Algorithm	Accuracy [m]	Integrity [%]	Continuity [%/15s]	Availability [%]
GPS	North: ∞ East : ∞ Down: ∞	84.65	92.21	78.61
Multi-radio Integrated Navigation System (GPS, KNSS, eLoran, Loran-C, DME/VOR)	North: 10.09799 East : 6.587799 Down: 11.48838	99.99	99.99	99.99

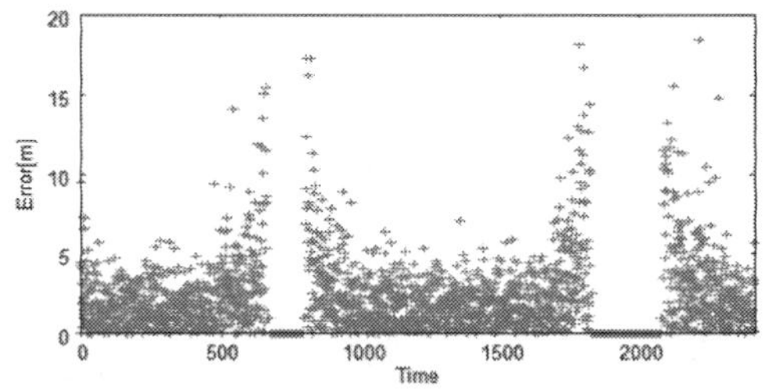

Fig. 8. Altitude error of GPS navigation algorithm

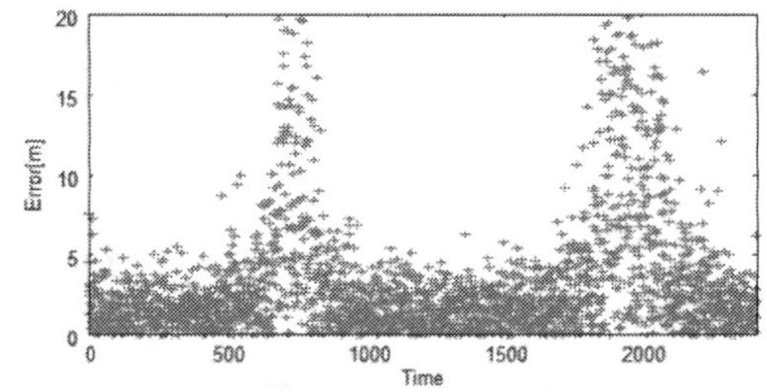

Fig. 9. Altitude error of the integrated navigation algorithm

References

1. Department of Defense, Department of Homeland Security and Department of Transportation, *Federal Radio Navigation Plan 2017*, pp.56-57 (2017)
2. E. D. Kaplan and C. J. Hegarty, *Understanding GPS : Principles and Applications*, 2nd ed. (Artech House, Norwood, MA 2006)
3. Department of Transportation, National PNT Architecture Workshop at Volpe, The Volpe Center, (2007)
4. L. Eldredge, P. Enge, M. Harrison, R. Kenagy, S. Lo, R. Loh, R. Lilly, M. Narins and R. Niles, Alternative positioning, navigation & timing (PNT) study, *Proc. of International Civil Aviation Organization Navigation Systems Panel*, pp.1-19 (2010)
5. N. A. White, P. S. Maybeck and S. L. DeVilbiss, Detection of Interference/Jamming and Spoofing in a DGPS-aided Inertial System, IEEE Trans. on AES, **34**, 4, pp.1208-1217 (1998)
6. S. Lo, P. Enge, F. Niles, R. Loh, L. Eldredge and M. Narins, Preliminary Assessment of Alternative Navigation Means for Civil Aviation, *Proc. of ION ITM 2010*, pp. 314-322 (2010)
7. P. Williams, S. Basker and N. Ward, e-Navigation and the Case for eLoran, The Journal of Navigation, **61**, 3, pp. 473-484 (2008)
8. M. Koo, Y. Kim, H. So, S.H. Oh, S.C. Kim and D.-H. Hwang, Modeling & Simulation Software Design for Coverage Analysis of Multiple Radio Positioning Integration System, JPNT, **5**, 2, pp. 47-57 (2016)
9. J. Lee, H. Kim, D.-H. Hwang, S. H. Oh and H. So, Multi-radio Integrated Navigation System M&S Software Design for GNSS Back-up, *Proc. of 2018 IEEE/ION PLANS*, pp. 1026-1033 (2018)
10. A. Maria, Introduction to Modeling and Simulation, *Proc. of 1997 Winter Simulation Conference*, pp.7-13 (1997)
11. H. Kim, J. Lee, S. H. Oh, H. So, D.-H. Hwang, Design of Navigation Environment Generation Module of M&S Software for Integrated Navigation System Performance Evaluation, JPNT, **7**, 2, pp.73-90 (2018)
12. C.-M. Choi, K.-S. Ko, A Study on Development Direction of Navigation System for NAVWAR, JKIICE (in Korean), **19**, 3, pp. 756-763 (2015)
13. H. Kim, J. Lee, W. J. Yoo, S. H. Oh, H. K. Lee, H. So, D.-H. Hwang, Design of Navigation Environment Generation Module of Multi-radio Integrated Navigation System M&S Software for Countermeasure to Navigation Warfare, *Proc. of 2018 IEIE Summer Conference (in Korean)*, pp.791-794 (2018)
14. S. K. Jeong, T. H. Kim, C. S. Sin and S. U. Lee, Technical trends of smart jamming for GPS signal, ETRI Electronics and Telecommunications Trends (in Korean), **27**, 6, pp. 75-82 (2012)

https://doi.org/10.1051/e3sconf/20199401008

15. S. P. Song, M. Y. Shin, S. B. Son, Y.-B. Kim, S. J. Lee and C. Park, The Integrated eLoran/GPS Navigation Algorithm for Reduced Calculational Complexity and High Accuracy, Trans. of KIEE (in Korean), **60**, 3, pp.612-619 (2011)
16. Y.-K. Lee, C.-B. Lee, S.-H. Yang, J.-K. Lee and H.-D. Kong, Diurnal Effect Compensation Algorithm for a Backup and Substitute Navigation System of GPS, JKICS (in Korean), **33**, 12, pp. 1225-1232 (2008)
17. H.-W. Bernhard, L. Herbert and W. Elmar, *GNSS – Global Navigation Satellite Systems GPS, GLONASS, Galileo, and more*, (Springer, Wien, 2008)
18. European Commission 2003, *World Wide Radionavigation System - Evaluation of the Galileo Performance Against Maritime GNSS Requirements*, (IMO, 2003)
19. M. Tossaint, J. Samson, F. Toran and J. Ventura-Traveset, The Stanford - ESA Integrity Diagram: A New tool for the user domain SBAS integrity assessment, JIN. **54**, 2, pp.1-17 (2007)
20. Annual of navigation, *Availability, Reliability and Continuity Model of Differential GPS Transmission*, (Gdańsk Branch of the Polish Academy of Sciences, 2003)

Multi-Thread Based Design of Navigation Algorithm Module in Multi Radio Integrated Navigation System M&S Software

Jae Hoon Son[1], *Heyone* Kim [1], *Sang Heon* Oh[2], *Hyoungmin* So[3], and *Dong-Hwan* Hwang[1,*]

[1] Chungnam National University, Department of Electronics Engineering, 34134 Daejeon, Korea
[2] Navcours Co., Ltd, Integrated Navigation Division, 34014 Daejeon, Korea
[3] Agency for Defense Development, 34186 Daejeon, Korea

Abstract. A multi-thread based navigation algorithm module is designed in a multi radio integrated navigation system modeling and simulation software in order to efficiently use resources in the software platform of the modeling and simulation software. By adopting the multi-thread architecture, features of navigation algorithms and concurrency of the algorisms can be easily included in the navigation algorithm module. In order to show the usefulness of the multi thread based navigation algorithm module design, a navigation algorithm module in the multi-radio integrated navigation system for GPS, KNSS, Loran-C, eLoran and DME/VOR is implemented in C++ under the Windows operating system. The implementation results show that the thread based design can be useful in the development of multi radio integrated navigation systems.

1 Introduction

Navigation outputs can be provided by combining GNSS (Global Navigation Satellite System) with other radio navigation systems even for the outage of GNSS [1-5]. Before a multi radio integrated navigation system, in which GNSS is combined with other radio navigation systems, is operated in real-time, performance evaluations and tests should be performed. Much time and cost can be saved in the evaluation if the M&S S/W (Modeling and Simulation S/W) is used [6].

The can be divided into function modules in order to add new functions and modify the module easily. In M&S S/W, the navigation algorithms should be in an independent module since the navigation algorithms will be running in a real-time multi radio integrated navigation system [1]. The navigation algorithm should contain features of radio navigation algorithm units and integrated navigation algorithms of GNSS and radio navigation systems. In addition to this, the navigation algorithms should be concurrently run.

By using the thread in the operation system, features of the unit navigation system can be included in the navigation algorithm module and concurrency of the algorithms can be easily implemented in the M&S S/W [8-9].

In this paper, a multi thread based navigation algorithm module is designed in a multi radio integrated navigation system M&S S/W. In the navigation algorithm module, a navigation algorithm corresponds to a thread. By doing this, features of navigation algorithms can be independently included in the navigation algorithm module. When a new navigation algorithm needs to be added to the navigation algorithm module, a new thread can be easily generated without modifying other navigation algorithms [7-8].

In the sequel, in section II, the multi thread based navigation algorithm module design is presented. In section III, implementation results of the multi thread based navigation algorithm for GPS, KNSS(Korean Navigation Satellite System), Loran-C (Long range navigation), e-Loran (Enhanced Loran), DME (Distance Measuring Equipment) and VOR (Very high frequency Omnidirectional Radio range) are presented. Finally, in section VI, concluding remark and further studies are presented.

2 Multi thread based navigation algorithm module design

2.1 M&S S/W

M&S S/W configuration is shown in figure 1. The M&S S/W is divided into navigation algorithm part and GUI (Graphic User Interface) part and navigation environment generation part. Unit navigation algorithm and integrated navigation algorithms are in the navigation algorithm part. The navigation environment generation part generates measurements to the parameter set by the GUI part. The generated measurements are an input of the navigation algorithm part. Through GUI, parameters to send the navigation algorithm part and the navigation environment

* Corresponding author: dhhwang@ cnu.ac.kr.

generation part can be set by the user and navigation results can be displayed.

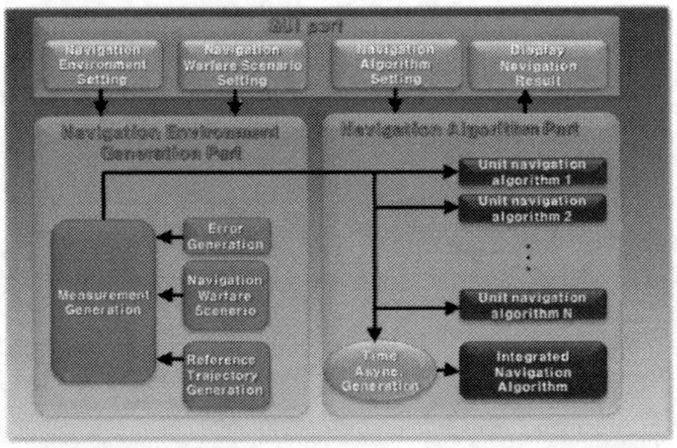

Fig. 1. M&S S/W configuration

Since the M&S S/W has many functions and algorithms, the S/W is modularized as shown in figure 2. By doing this, the M&S S/W can be easily modified and more functions can be easily added into the S/W. The navigation algorithm module would be ported into a real-time integrated navigation system without little modification. The M&S S/W in figure 2 consists three function modules and M&S message broker. Each function module does not directly exchange data with other function modules. Instead of sending data to another function module, the function module sends the data to the M&S message broker. The message broker sends the data to another function module. Due to the M&S message broker, each function module does not need to all I/Fs (InterFaces) to exchange with other function modules.

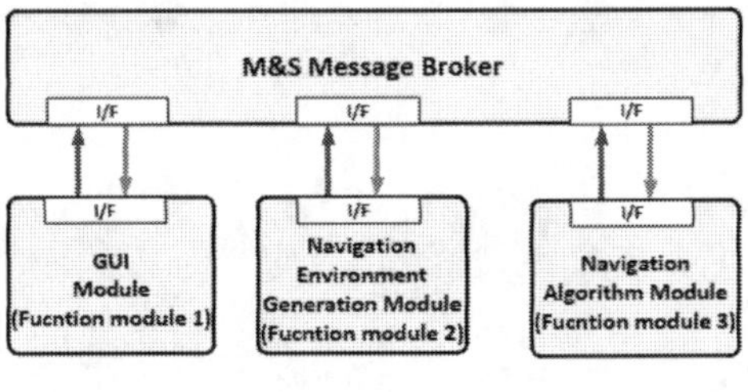

Fig. 2. Message broker based M&S S/W

The structure of the function modules is shown in figure 3. The navigation algorithm module has this structure. The broker is composed of an I/F, an encoder, a decoder, and a procedure. The decoder converts the binary data in the received M&S messages into internal variables for the procedure. The encoder converts the internal variables processed by the procedure into the binary data in the M&S message to transmit. The procedure is a combination of subroutines to carry out functions of the M&S software. Due to the encoder and decoder, variables in the procedure need not be shared with other function modules, i.e., each function module can be independently operated. Programs which have already been developed in other platforms can be reused or easily ported in a function module in the M&S software. In this case, the only thing for the operators and/or developers of the M&S software to do is updating the encoder and decoder.

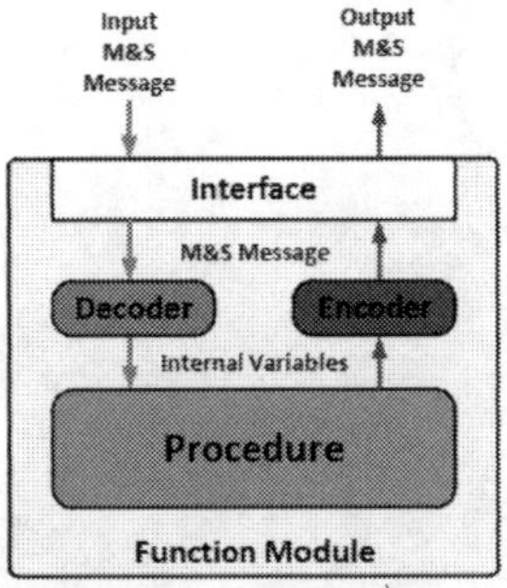

Fig. 3. Function module structure of M&S S/W

2.2. Multi thread based navigation algorithm module

The navigation algorithm module based on the multi thread is designed for the structure shown in figure 3. It is well known that the thread provides many useful characteristics to the program developers [7-10]. Among the useful characteristics, the scalability, concurrency, and economy are used in the design of the navigation algorithm module. Due to the scalability, a new navigation algorithm can be easily added to the navigation algorithm module by generation a new thread. The threads are to be seen to the user that they are run concurrently. Even though actual thread programs are run in time-sharing mode in a CPU (Central Processing Unit), the operation of the S/W has no problem as long as the running time is short enough. In the navigation algorithm module, a program is included in a thread if it is running independently or its function is clearly different from other program. Due to the scheduler of threads, the program developer can give more throughput.

As mentioned previously, the navigation algorithm module is composed of an I/F, a decoder, an encoder and procedure. The navigation algorithms are in the procedure. The I/F, decoder and encoder are designed in separate threads. Navigation algorithms are also designed in a separate threads as shown in figure 4.

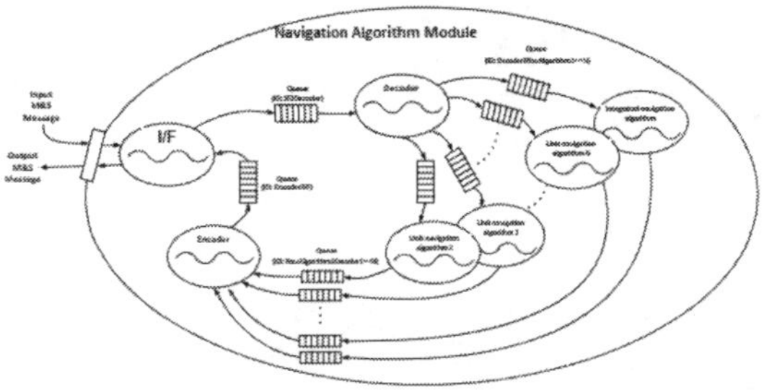

Fig. 4. Multi thread based navigation algorithm module

 https://doi.org/10.1051/e3sconf/20199401009

3 Implementation result

3.1 M&S S/W

The M&S S/W for GPS, KNSS, Loran-C, e-Loran, DME and VOR shown in figure 5 was implemented to show the validity of the design of the multi thread based navigation algorithm module.

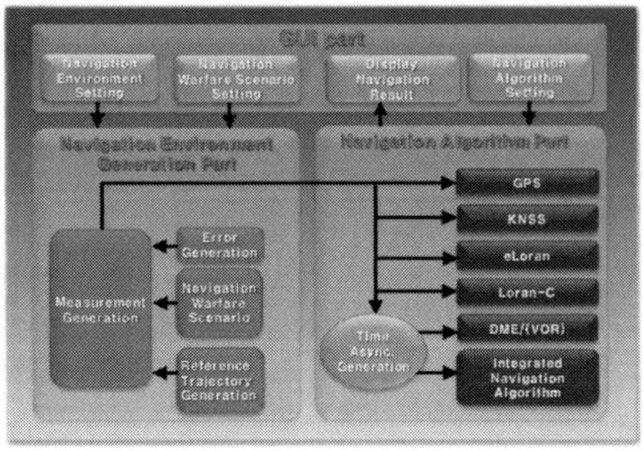

Fig. 5. Implemented M&S S/W

3.2 Navigation algorithm module

If the design method described in section II. 2 is applied to this navigation algorithm module with GPS, KNSS, Loran-C, e-Loran, DME and VOR, the navigation algorithm module has 9 threads and 14 queues as shown in figure 6.

The M&S S/W with the multi thread based navigation algorithm module was implemented in visual C++ under Windows operating system.

The weighted least method was used to estimate navigation results.

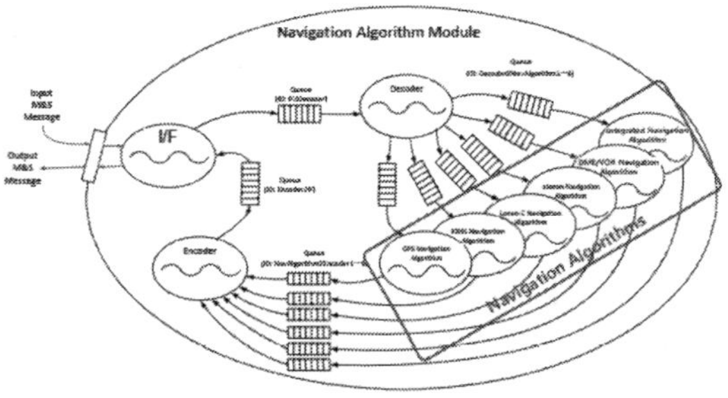

Fig. 6. Implemented thread based structure of the navigation algorithm module

3.3 Result

For the trajectory of a vehicle shown in figure 7, the M&S S/W was implemented. It can be seen that the vehicle is moving for 2500s. Initial position of the vehicle is 35.34° of latitude, 126.19° of longitude and 100m of altitude. It also can be observed that the vehicle carries 8-shaped motion and descends after it goes up to 8km of altitude.

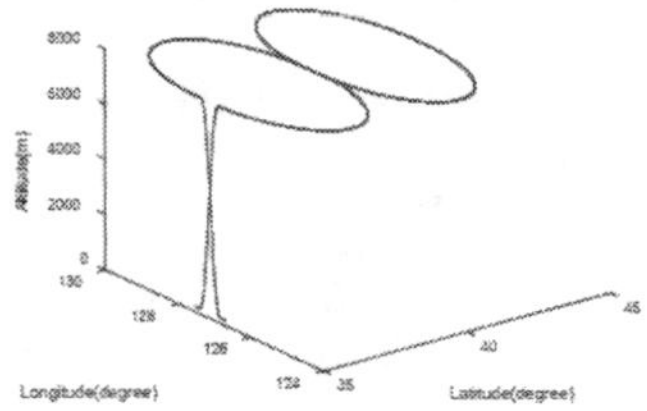

Fig. 7. Motion of the vehicle

A result of the integrated navigation algorithm with GPS, KNSS, eLoran, Loran-C, DME, and VOR is shown in figure 8 and figure 9. Numerical values for the navigation result are shown in table 1. The values in table1 are absolute values of errors in 95% probability. For comparison, results for unit navigation algorithms are listed in table1. The results show that the navigation algorithm module designed in multi thread in the M&S S/W is well operated.

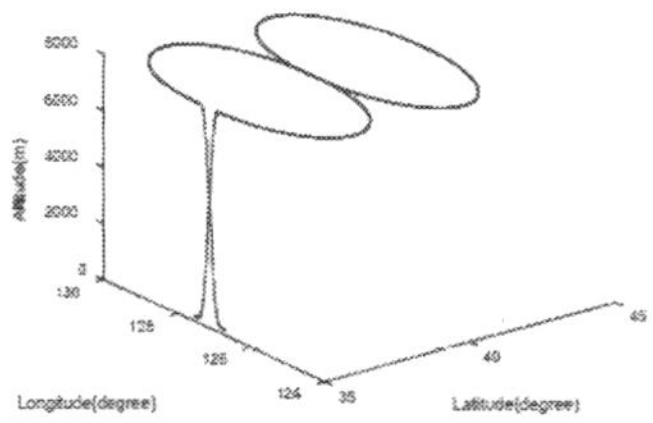

Fig. 8. Navigation result

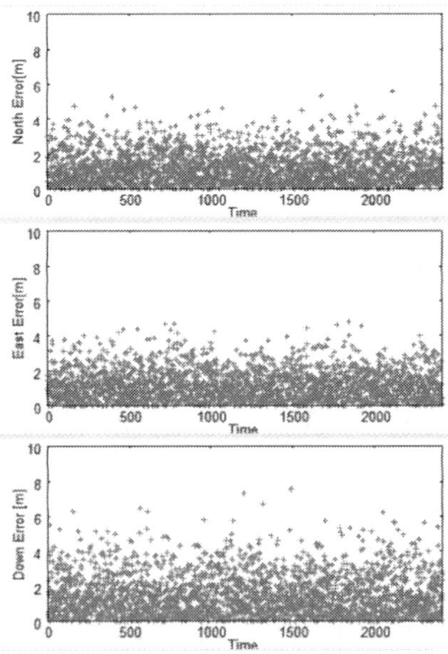

Fig. 9. Navigation error

 https://doi.org/10.1051/e3sconf/20199401009

Table 1. Navigation result

Navigation algorithm	North [m]	East [m]	Down [m]
GPS	2.82	2.38	3.11
KNSS	23.79	13.31	25.5
Loran-C	162.43	130.51	1957.08
eLoran	142.58	71.67	1438.11
DME/VOR	1262.76	985.60	29395.47
Multi Radio Integrated Navigation System	2.59	2.28	3.05

4 Concluding remarks and further studies

In this paper, a multi thread based navigation algorithm module was designed in a multi radio integrated navigation system M&S S/W. In order to show usefulness of the multi thread based navigation algorithm module design, a navigation algorithm module in the multi-radio integrated navigation system for GPS, KNSS, Loran-C, eLoran, and DME/VOR was implemented in C++ under the Windows Operating System. The implementation results showed that the thread based design could be useful in the development of multi radio integrated navigation systems.

As further study, results on the multi thread based approach and addition of fixed and moving pseudolite navigaion system in the navigation module.

This work has been supported by the National GNSS Research Center Program of Defense Acquisition Program Administration and Agency for Defense Development.

References

1. J. Lee, H. Kim, D.-H. Hwang, S. H. Oh and H. So, Multi-radio Integrated Navigation System M&S Software Design for GNSS Back-up, *Proc. of 2018 IEEE/ION PLANS*, pp. 1026-1033 (2018)
2. H. Kim, J. Lee, S. H. Oh, H. So, D.-H. Hwang, Design of Navigation Environment Generation Module of M&S Software for Integrated Navigation System Performance Evaluation, JPNT, **7**, 2, pp.73-90 (2018)
3. C.-M. Choi, K.-S. Ko, A Study on Development Direction of Navigation System for NAVWAR, JKIICE (in Korean), **19**, 3, pp. 756-763 (2015)
4. H. Kim, J. Lee, W. J. Yoo, S. H. Oh, H. K. Lee, H. So, D.-H. Hwang, Design of Navigation Environment Generation Module of Multi-radio Integrated Navigation System M&S Software for Countermeasure to Navigation Warfare, *Proc. of 2018 IEIE Summer Conference (in Korean)*, pp.791-794 (2018)
5. S. K. Jeong, T. H. Kim, C. S. Sin and S. U. Lee, Technical trends of smart jamming for GPS signal, ETRI Electronics and Telecommunications Trends (in Korean), **27**, 6, pp. 75-82 (2012)
6. A. Maria, Introduction to Modeling and Simulation, *Proc. of 1997 Winter Simulation Conference*, pp.7-13 (1997)
7. W. Stallings, *Operating Systems : Internals and Design Principles*, 4th ed. (Pearson Education International, Upper Saddle River, 2005)
8. A. Silberschatz, P. B. Galvin and G. Gagne, *Operating System Concepts*, 9th ed. (Wiley, River Street Hoboken, 2012)
9. U. K. Park, Development and Performance Evaluation of Dynamic Memory Management Methodology in Multithreaded System, The Journal of Applied Science Technology (in Korean), **11**, 1, pp. 55-76 (2002)
10. J. H. Lee, H. K. Song and T. G. Kim, Analysis and Application of Performance Improvement of a Real-time Simulation Visualization based on Multi-thread Pipelining Parallel Processing, JKSS (in Korean), **26**, 3, pp. 13-22 (2017)

Development of GNSS Receiver for Mobile CORS with RTK Correction Services Using Cloud Server

Parluhutan Manurung[1], *Hari* Pramujo[2], *Joshua* BP Manurung[2]

[1] Badan Informasi Geospasial (BIG)
[2] PT Luwes Inovasi Mandiri

Abstract. Requirements for precise Real Time Kinematic (RTK) positioning have been significantly growing in Indonesia since early 2010, resulting from the national programs on village mapping, land cadastre certification, infrastructure developments, and one map policy. The activities require a sub-decimetre level of positioning accuracy to produce detail maps to the scale of 1:500. RTK positioning with CORS should be the most reliable technique to meet the accuracy level. However, the existing distribution of Indonesia CORS Network, consisting of 150 active stations, is still far from adequate since the inter-station distances are of around 500 km while an ideal range should be less than 50 km. This paper related to an initiative for the development of a GNSS receiver that can be transportable and easily set up in the field as a base station to provide RTK CORS correction services with local contents. The initiative supports national efforts on the densification of Indonesia CORS Network to better distribution. The development was started using the Tersus OEM GNSS board series BX305, including the integration of the board to a mini PC. Further developments have been made covering the following, namely: i) to add a long-term stable power supply in the receiver, ii) customization of receiver command settings, iii) to add a GSM modem and internet protocol for data communication from the receiver to a cloud server, iv) installation of SNIP software in a cloud server to provide CORS corrections with NTRIP caster, and v) testing the NTRIP client performance in the rover receiver. Results from the land cadastre surveys carried out in Bandung, Padang and Tangerang Cities show that the length of time for the fixed positioning with resolved ambiguities could be obtained within less than 5-7 seconds with the rover locations less than 10 km from the base station. A longer time to obtain fixed solutions required for the distance at the range of 10 to 20 km, and it is becoming more difficult to get fixed solutions over 20 km. Further developments would be carried out using affordable price GNSS OEM boards provided by different manufacturers.

1. INTRODUCTION

Indonesia Continuously Operating Reference Station (CORS) Network consists of 150 stations, as of November 2018, is still inadequate to provide centimeter-level accuracy with *Real Time Kinematic* (RTK) positioning across the Archipelago since the average inter-station distance is of about 500 km. The distance is far from 50 km idealistic distribution that can provide fixed ambiguity resolution in ionospheric distribution (Chen et al. 2001; Wielgosz et al. 2005; Grejner-Brzezinska et al. 2007), resulting in the users of the Indonesian CORS limited in numbers, namely of about 1,906 users (BIG Outlook, 2017). The number of users would be growing significantly in the future as the CORS distribution is improving and costs of geodetic GNSS receivers could be significantly declining to an affordable price in the future.

Efforts on the development of geodetic GNSS receiver with local content are highly encouraged. The opportunity is growing since many re-known GNSS receivers producers are now shifting to produce OEM boards which can be further developed by third parties to their applications. Access to develop the OEM boards has highly reduced cost and more possibility to provide customization of products to specific applications.

The motivation of the research is to develop CORS-enabled GNSS receiver with local contents and affordable price. By providing an affordable CORS base receiver, this strongly supports the acceleration of the Indonesia CORS network densification leading to speed up the utilization of GNSS positioning techniques supporting national program on large-scale mapping from cities to village level. The research is inlined with Indonesia national program on technology independence.

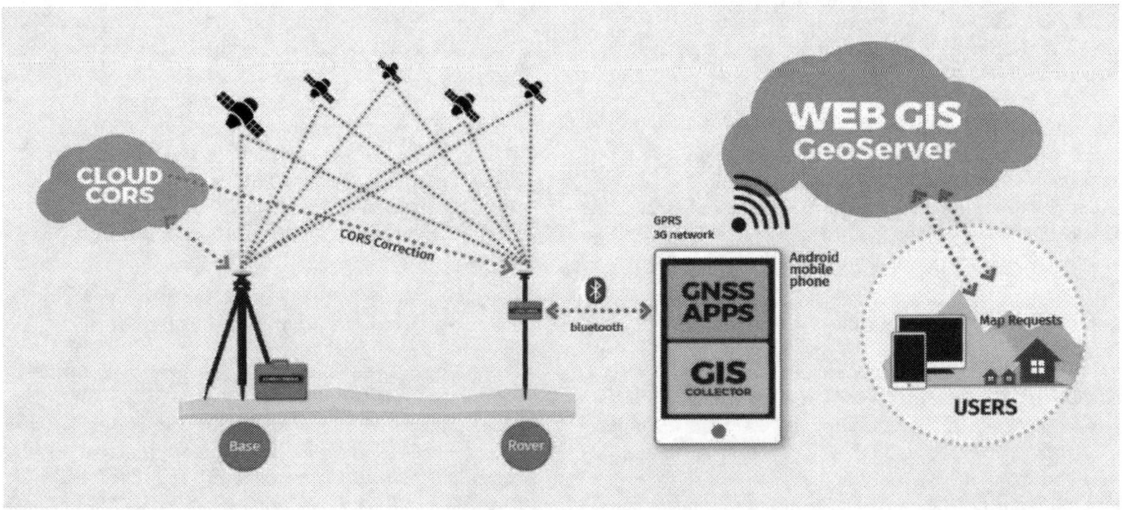

Figure 1 Online Survey Concept

2. GNSS RECEIVER DEVELOPMENT FOR ONLINE SURVEY

2.1 System Design

An online survey with CORS technique is possible by integrating GNSS positioning with GIS software to the internet of things (IOT) using cellular data communication. The whole system consists of 5 components, namely: i) GNSS Base Receiver, ii) Cloud-based CORS Service, iii) GNSS Rover Receiver, iv) Android Smartphone controller, v) Web GIS Cloud Server. The flow of operation can be described as the following, Figure 1. The base station sends the data to the cloud server which provide service for positioning corrections to the rover via NTRIP Caster. The Android Smartphone controller equipped with NTRIP Client application receives the corrections to compute the point coordinates. The position is stored and displayed using GIS Software in the smartphone. To make the data survey online to internet and access to other partners, the surveyor with the smartphone could send the shapefile periodically to the Web GIS Cloud with GeoServer engine.

2.2 Base GNSS Receiver

The OEM board for the base receiver is designed to provide efficient algorithm enabling fast ambiguity resolution within a few seconds. A key element supporting an RTK survey is to select multi-channel receiver which can receive multi-satellite signals namely GPS, BEIDOU, GLONASS and GALILEO. The PCB design should accommodate high quality of electronic components consisting of GNSS OEM boards, cellular modem for data communication, mini PC, power supply system including the electronic casing for protection.

The OEM board selection was carried out based on the data sheet provided by several manufacturers available in the market, namely Tersus, Novatel, Trimble, and CHC. The main criteria that we sought for are the following, namely: i) supporting RTK switch base and rover, ii) option to use Bluetooth connection to Android smartphone, iii) RTK accuracy better than 5 cm, iv) affordable pricing, and v) strong support from the manufacturers for data protocol. Based on the working paper data analysis, it was decided to use the OEM Board Tersus serial BX305.

The GNSS OEM board is integrated with the following components, namely: i) a mini PC for an internal controller, ii) power supply electronic circuit system and UPS, iii) firmware controller and embedded processing, iv) Cellular (GSM) modem dan Bluetooth for data communication. A standard survey grade antenna used is series AX3702. The antenna could be replaced with that of choke ring type registered in International GNSS Service (IGS), if high precision applications are required, as such as monitoring crustal deformation and survey constructions.

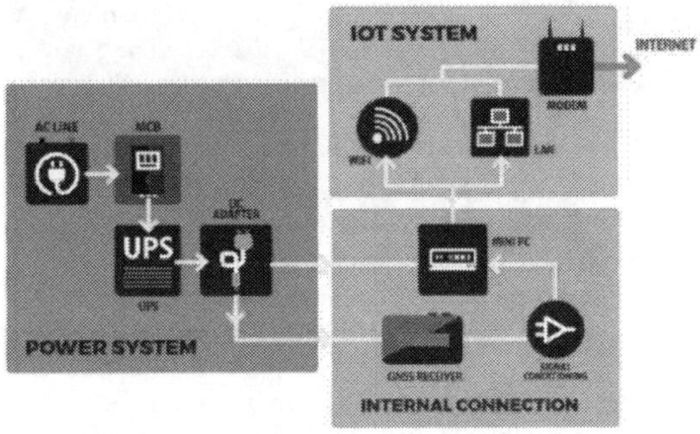

Figure 2 Power System and IOT Feature controlled by mini PC

A mini PC unit is the system controller embedded to the GNSS OEM board. The conditioning signal is needed to change the GNSS board output data in the form of LVTTL converted into data in the form of USB so that the mini PC can read it. A Mini PC link with a unit power system (UPS) with the capacity of 650KVA for 30 minutes power back up, as shown in Figure 2. A smart power system is highly required to provide control for extreme power flow and to maintain a long time operation and permanent monitoring.

2.3 Cloud NTRIP Caster

We decided to use a commercial software namely SNIP, an NTRIP Caster that allows multiple types of data streams, typically containing RTCM corrections messages, to be repeated and sent to various end users over the internet. The advantage of SNIP, it follows multiple industry standards for its message process and connection protocols, allowing any serial port data, any NTRIP Server and client to connect to it. SNIP is now widely used to extend the CORS networks coverage in places not yet served by those of national networks, Figure 3. SNIP provide options to users either using a public NTRIP Caster server namely RTK to Go or a dedicated private server, requiring an extra charge for the service.

Figure 3 NTRIP System Diagram

2.4 Rover GNSS Receiver

The basic design for a rover receiver is to provide a user-friendly receiver that can be easily understood and operated by users with common knowledge on positioning and mapping. The integration of the receiver controller with a GIS collector together in an Android smartphone is a significant step to provide users with a controller of which the users are more familiar than that of a dedicated controller. Mapit GIS software is a simplified GIS command operation that can handle data acquisition with an Android smartphone.

Criteria to measure performance metrics of rover receiver is based on four factors, U.S Department of Defense (2008), namely i) accuracy, ii) time to first fix, iii) continuity, and iv) availability. The accuracy is defined as the difference of the calculated position solution and the true position. Time to First Fix (TTFF) refers to a receiver's state when it has derived and is reporting a valid position solution after being powered. TTFF is a performance metric of receiver initialization. It is the amount of time that it takes to report a solution from a cold start. Continuity is the likelihood of a detected, but unscheduled navigation function interruption after an operation has been initiated. A loss of RTK lock is a loss of continuity. The RTK availability is defined as the total amount of time as a percentage that a receiver spends in an RTK position solution. An ideal receiver will have an RTK availability close to 100%.

2.5 Android Smartphone Controller

Technological development has been significantly turned the Android smartphone as a GNSS controller. This standard feature available in the market is more reliable and even more affordable than that of the controller made specifically to the receiver. Smartphones are becoming more potent with reinforced processors, larger storage capacities, and more data communication methods. An open-source platform Android is commonly used in smartphones, equipped with software package consisting of an operating system, middleware layer, and core applications, Yan and Shi (2013). Bluetooth facilitates data communication between the smartphone and the GNSS Receiver. Bluetooth technology and other similar techniques, with a dramatic increase in Smartphone users, smartphones have gradually turned into an all-purpose portable device.

A smartphone is treated as the external brain of GNSS receiver by adding three main functions as the following: i) Controlling the receiver, ii) Connecting the receiver with CORS Service using NTRIP Client, iii) collecting data and display with GIS Collector. The smartphone device enables the system connected to the external world by facilitating the smartphone to send GIS shapefiles to Web-GIS server allowing multiple users to access data from the field. This achievement is a new state of the art survey with online mode.

2.6 Web GIS Cloud: GeoServer

GeoServer is a Java-based software server that allows users to view and edit geospatial data and allows for great flexibility in map creation and data sharing. This uses the Web Feature Service (WFS) standard, which permits the actual sharing and editing of the data that is used to generate the maps, Henderson (2014). GeoServer comes with a WMS that can fit into other Java applications like OpenLayers and can create maps of different formats. GeoServer can display data on any popular modern map applications as such as Google, Yahoo, and Bing. It can also connect to the traditional desktop GIS tools like ESRI ArcGIS.

3. RESULT

There are four testing schemes conducted to measure the performance of the solutions starting from testing the base and rover receivers to the cloud GIS GeoServer.

Figure 4 Mobile CORS base station & Antenna located in the University of Indonesia Campus.

First, testing the mobile GNSS base receiver was carried out by deploying the instrument located in the rooftop of Multidisciplinary Building at the University of Indonesia Campus in Depok City, Figure 4. Data communication between the base station to the cloud CORS service is carried out using a broadband cellular modem. A survey grade antenna with a serial type of AX3702 is installed on the top of the building wall. The performance of the base station has shown a significant improvement to provide CORS service for high precision RTK solution in the surrounding area around the radius of 20 km.

Figure 5 Testing the GNSS Rover Receiver with an antenna pole

Second, testing the performance of rover receiver, as shown in Figure 5, and the NTRIP Caster was carried out in every 5 km radius from the base station to the maximum distance which can be possible for the rover to resolve ambiguities, as shown in Figure 6. The Table shows that time for fixing ambiguities increases as the location of the rover to the base station is more significant. However, the result shows that time to fixed ambiguities on average is less than 5 seconds within the maximum distance of 20 km. Resolving ambiguities for more than 20 km is becoming harder and uncertain since the model in the SNIP Caster does not take into account a complicated situation of atmospheric condition.

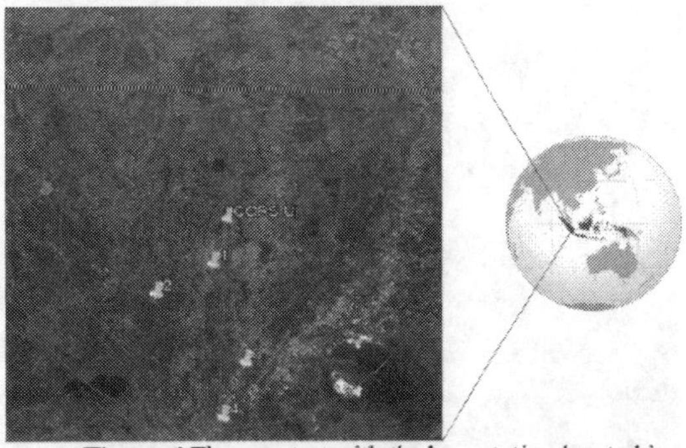

Figure 6 The area test with the base station located in the University of Indonesia Campus. The red circles show the rover distance from the base with 5 km radius interval.

Third, testing the system by making the distance between the base and rover receivers closer at a distance between 15 km, it has shown a significant improvement to resolve ambiguity to less than 5 seconds. Results from the land cadastre surveys carried out in three big cities, namely Bandung (West Java Province), Padang (West Sumatra Province), and Tangerang (Banten Province), these show that the length of time for the fixed positioning with resolved ambiguities could be obtained within less than 5 seconds with the rover locations less than 10 km from the base station.

Table 1 Time to acquire for a fixed solution using a base station located in the University of Indonesia

Point		1	2	3	4
Distance to the base station (km)		5	10	15	20
Time for a fixed solution (second)	P1	2	3	5	5
	P2	2	2	4	4
	P3	2	2	4	4
	P4	1	2	2	5
	P5	1	2	3	2
	P6	1	1	1	4
	P7	1	2	2	5
	P8	2	2	1	2
	P9	1	2	1	3
	P10	2	2	3	2
	P11	1	2	2	3
Average Time		1,45	2	2,55	3,55

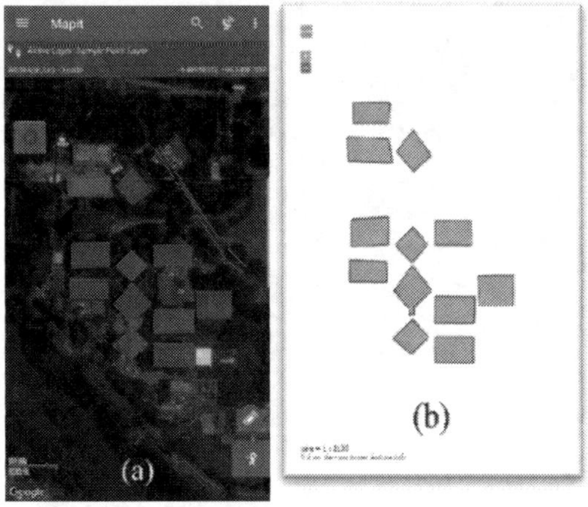

Figure 7 The measured area displayed in the Smartphone collector (a) and presented data in web GIS (b).

Finally, testing for the sending of the GIS data layers collected in the Android smartphone to the web GIS GeoServer was carried out by doing field data collections in the University of Indonesia Campus. The survey target is to map around 11 buildings in the campus as shown in the Mapit GIS Collector, Figure 7 (a). The time for data collecting was completed around two hours only. Then the shapefile of the sampling was sent via cell phone to the Web GIS and displayed by GeoServer as shown in Figure 7 (b).

4. CONCLUSION

The objective of the paper is to develop a GNSS CORS receiver which is easy to deploy in the field as a base station and to provide RTK correction services to rover receivers using a cloud server. The system has been successfully developed to make possible an online survey by combining high precision RTK CORS positioning with a web GIS cloud. This technique was tested resulting in less than 5 seconds for ambiguity resolution with inter-station distances of maximum 20 km and the accuracy level between 2-5 cm. There are four essential elements to improve the CORS positioning technique into online mode, namely: i) a base GNSS receiver connected to the cloud server caster, ii) a rover GNSS receiver equipped with an Android smartphones controller of which the GIS collector is installed, iii) the cellular coverage for strong data connection to IOT, and iv) a web GIS cloud with GeoServer for online map creation and data sharing. The online survey solution demonstrates a significant improvement to a faster field data acquisition and GIS data sharing.

5. ACKNOWLEDGMENT

This development was financed by PT Luwes Inovasi Mandiri; a start-up company focused on solution development for precise GNSS positioning. Support provided by the Department of Geoscience of University of Indonesia and Badan Informasi Geospasial (BIG) during the project is gratefully acknowledged.

6. REFERENCES

Badan Informasi Geospasial (BIG) (2017). *Outlook Pusat Jaring Kontrol Geodesi dan Geodinamika* 2017. Cibinong.

Chen W, Hu C, Chen Y, Ding X (2001) *Rapid static and kinematic positioning with HongKong GPS active network*. In: ION GPS 2001, Salt Lake City, UT, pp **346–352**

Grejner-Brzezinska D, Kashani I, Wielgosz P, Smith D, Spencer P, Robertson D, Mader G (2007) *Efficiency and reliability of ambiguity resolution in network-based real-time kinematic GPS*. J Surv Eng 133(2):**56–65**

Henderson, Colin (2014). *Mastering Geoserver*. Birmingham, UK.

Herring, T. A., R. W. King, M. A. Floyd, S. C. McClusky (2015). *Introduction to GAMIT/GLOBK*. Department of Earth, Atmospheric, and Planetary Sciences Massachusetts Institute of Technology, Cambridge, MA 02139, USA.

Schwieger, V., Lilje, M., & Sarib, R. (2009). *GNSS CORS Reference Frames and Services*. In 7th FIG Regional Conference, Hanoi, Vietnam (Vol. 19, No. 22.10, p. 2009).

Snay, R. A., & Soler, T. (2008). *Continuously operating reference station (CORS): history, applications, and future enhancements*. Journal of Surveying Engineering, 134(4), **95-104**.

SNIP. (2018). *About SNIP*. Cited in https://www.use-snip.com/ [14 Agustus 2018]

Takasu, T., & Yasuda, A. (2009). *Development of the low-cost RTK-GPS receiver with an open source program package RTKLIB*. In International Symposium on GPS/GNSS (pp. **4-6**). International Convention Center Jeju Korea.

Tersus GNSS Inc, (2016). *User Manual Precis BX305 Precise GNSS RTK Board*. Cited in https://www.tersus-gnss.com/ [8 December 2018]

U.S. Department of Defence. (2008). *Global Positioning System Standard Positioning Service*. Retrieved from http://www.gps.gov/technical/ps/2008-SPS-performance-standard.pdf

Wielgosz P., Kashani I, Grejner-Brzezinska D (2005) *Analysis of long-range network RTK during severe ionospheric storm*. Journal of Geodesy 79(9):524531

Yan, M., and Shi, H (2013). *Smart Living Using Bluetooth Based Android Smartphone*. International Journal of Wireless & Mobile Networks (IJWMN) Vol. 5, No. 1, February 2013

https://doi.org/10.1051/e3sconf/20199401011

Multi-GNSS Induced Performance Enhancements in Constrained Environments

Wenzhe Wang[1,*], *Fengyu* Chu[2], and *Ming* Yang[3]

[1]Department of Geomatics, National Cheng Kung University, Tainan, Taiwan
[2] Department of Geomatics, National Cheng Kung University, Tainan, Taiwan
[3] Department of Geomatics, National Cheng Kung University, Tainan, Taiwan

Abstract. Nowadays, three global navigation satellite systems (GNSS), namely GPS, GLONASS and China's BeiDou System (BDS), are fully-operational in the Asia-Pacific region. Furthermore, the European Galileo system and the Japanese Quasi Zenith Satellite System (QZSS), which is a regional navigation satellite system (RNSS), jointly provide 4 to 8 additional visible satellites in the region. Thus, it is expected that a combination of the above five systems will improve positioning performance as a result of enhanced satellite availability provided by multi-GNSS. In this research, we develop a method to combine GPS, GLONASS, BDS, Galileo, and QZSS pseudorange and carrier phase observations, and investigate positioning performance improvements brought by multi-GNSS. Experimental data were collected in Southern Taiwan to perform pseudorange-based, meter-level absolute (point) positioning as well as carrier phase-based, centimeter-level relative positioning. Test results indicate that (1) using multi-GNSS can effectively improve the accuracy of absolute (single point) and relative positioning, particularly in highly-masked, constrained environments, such as urban areas; (2) combining the five constellations can significantly shorten the Time-To-First-Fix (TTFF) for rapid ambiguity resolution required by Real-Time Kinematic (RTK) applications in constrained environments.

1 Introduction

Since its full operation, GPS (global positioning system) has been the most widely used navigation satellite system ([1,2]). Other satellite positioning systems, e.g., the Russian GLONASS system, the European Galileo system, the Chinese Beidou system (BDS), and the Japanese Quasi Zenith Satellite System (QZSS) are also in rapid development nowadays. It is advantageous to utilize multiple GNSS constellations (Multi-GNSS) to provide more continuous and accurate positioning services for user ends compared with using a single GNSS system alone ([3-7]).

As satellite positioning usually requires an open-sky environment, positioning in constrained environments (such as dense urban districts) has always been difficult when using single GNSS system since only limited number of visible satellites can be used in these areas. Thus it is expected that combining multi-GNSS systems may improve the positioning performance when environments are highly-masked.

In this research, a multi-GNSS positioning model was developed by combining observations from GPS, GLONASS, Galileo, BDS, and QZSS systems. Based on this model, we perform pseudorange-based single point positioning and carrier phase-based, relative positioning in order to analysis the performance improvements induced by using multi-GNSS for positioning in constrained environments.

2 Multi-GNSS Positioning

Considering the number and health condition of on-orbit satellites, we use five GNSS constellations for multi-GNSS positioning. Measurements (psuedoranges and carrier phases) from GPS, GLONASS, Galileo, BDS, and QZSS are adopted to establish multi-GNSS single point positioning model and relative positioning model. The flow of data processing is shown in **Figure 1**.

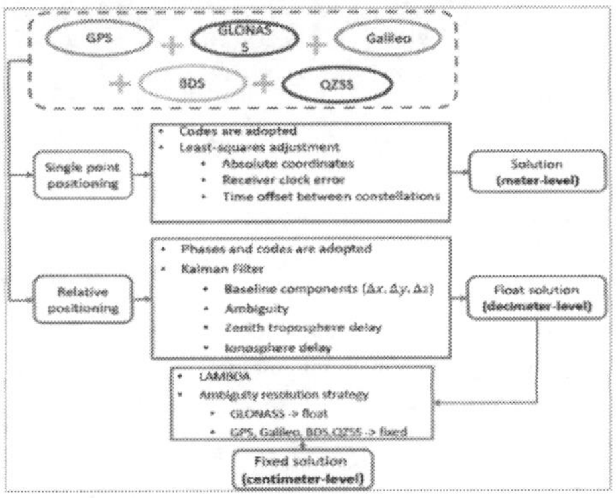

Fig. 1. Date Process Flow

* Corresponding author: myang@mail.ncku.edu.tw

https://doi.org/10.1051/e3sconf/20199401011

2.1. Single Point Positioning

In multi-GNSS single point positioning, pseudorange measurements from GPS, GLONASS, Galileo, BDS, and QZSS are used. At one epoch, the pseudorange measurements can be expressed as:

$$\begin{cases} \rho_{GPS} = \sqrt{(x_u - X^G)^2 + (y_u - Y^G)^2 + (z_u - Z^G)^2} \\ \qquad + c \cdot dt_{GPS} + \varepsilon \\ \rho_{GLO} = \sqrt{(x_u - X^L)^2 + (y_u - Y^L)^2 + (z_u - Z^L)^2} \\ \qquad + c \cdot dt_{GPS} + GGTO + \varepsilon \\ \rho_{GAL} = \sqrt{(x_u - X^A)^2 + (y_u - Y^A)^2 + (z_u - Z^A)^2} \\ \qquad + c \cdot dt_{GPS} + GETO + \varepsilon \\ \rho_{BDS} = \sqrt{(x_u - X^B)^2 + (y_u - Y^B)^2 + (z_u - Z^B)^2} \\ \qquad + c \cdot dt_{GPS} + GBTO + \varepsilon \\ \rho_{QZS} = \sqrt{(x_u - X^Q)^2 + (y_u - Y^Q)^2 + (z_u - Z^Q)^2} \\ \qquad + c \cdot dt_{GPS} + GQTO + \varepsilon \end{cases} \tag{1}$$

In (1), ρ_{GPS} , ρ_{GLO} , ρ_{GAL} , ρ_{BDS} , ρ_{QZS} are the pseudorange measurements (with satellite clock offset, ionospheric and tropospheric delay removed) from GPS, GLONASS, Galileo, BDS, and QZSS system; (x_u, y_u, z_u) is the user position; $(X^G,Y^G,Z^G),(X^L,Y^L,Z^L),(X^A,Y^A,Z^A)$, $(X^B,Y^B,Z^B),(X^Q,Y^Q,Z^Q)$ are positions of GPS, GLONASS, Galileo, BDS, and QZSS satellites; dt_{GPS} is receiver clock error with respect to GPS time; GGTO,GETO,GBTO,GQTO are the between-system-biases of GLONASS, Galileo, BDS and QZSS with respect to GPS; ε is random noise error in pseudorange observation; c is the speed of light. By linearizing equation (1), the multi-GNSS single point positioning model can be expressed in a linear form:

$$\Delta\boldsymbol{\rho}_{n\times1} = \boldsymbol{H}_{n\times8}\boldsymbol{x}_{8\times1} + \boldsymbol{\varepsilon}_{8\times1} \tag{2}$$

In (2), $\Delta\boldsymbol{\rho}_{n\times1} = \boldsymbol{\rho}_{n\times1} - \boldsymbol{\rho}^0_{n\times1}$, $\boldsymbol{\rho}_{n\times1}$ are the n pseudorange measurements at the epoch, $\boldsymbol{\rho}^0_{n\times1}$ are the corresponding computed values of pseodoranges, $\boldsymbol{\rho}^0_{i\times1} = \sqrt{(x^0_{user} - X^i)^2 + (y^0_{user} - Y^i)^2 + (z^0_{user} - Z^i)^2}$ ($1 \le i \le n$, while i is an integer), where $(x^0_{user}, y^0_{user}, z^0_{user})$ is the approximate user position and (X^i, Y^i, Z^i) is the position of the *i-th* satellite, $\boldsymbol{H}_{n\times8}$ is the coefficient matrix that can be written as:

$$\boldsymbol{H}_{n\times8} = \begin{vmatrix} \boldsymbol{G}_{n_{GPS}\times3} & \boldsymbol{I}_{n_{GPS}\times1} & 0 & 0 & 0 & 0 \\ \boldsymbol{G}_{n_{GLO}\times3} & \boldsymbol{I}_{n_{GLO}\times1} & \boldsymbol{I}_{n_{GLO}\times1} & 0 & 0 & 0 \\ \boldsymbol{G}_{n_{GAL}\times3} & \boldsymbol{I}_{n_{GAL}\times1} & 0 & \boldsymbol{I}_{n_{GAL}\times1} & 0 & 0 \\ \boldsymbol{G}_{n_{BDS}\times3} & \boldsymbol{I}_{n_{BDS}\times1} & 0 & 0 & \boldsymbol{I}_{n_{BDS}\times1} & 0 \\ \boldsymbol{G}_{n_{QZS}\times3} & \boldsymbol{I}_{n_{QZS}\times1} & 0 & 0 & 0 & \boldsymbol{I}_{n_{QZS}\times1} \end{vmatrix}$$

$\boldsymbol{G}$ is the geometry matrix between satellite and receiver, $\boldsymbol{G}_{i\times3} = \begin{vmatrix} \frac{x^0_{user} - X^i}{\rho^0_i} & \frac{y^0_{user} - Y^i}{\rho^0_i} & \frac{z^0_{user} - Z^i}{\rho^0_i} \end{vmatrix}$ ($1 \le i \le n$, while i is an integer), $n_{GPS}, n_{GLO}, n_{GAL}, n_{BDS}, n_{QZS}$ are the number of pseudorange measurements from GPS, GLONASS, Galileo, BDS and QZSS system $\boldsymbol{x}_{8\times1} = |\Delta x_u \quad \Delta y_u \quad \Delta z_u \quad c \cdot dt_{GPS} \quad GGTO \quad GETO \quad GBTO \quad GQTO|^T$. Applying least-squares estimation to (2) yields:

$$\hat{\boldsymbol{x}}_{8\times1} = (\boldsymbol{H}^T{}_{n\times8}\boldsymbol{H}_{n\times8})^{-1}\boldsymbol{H}^T{}_{n\times8}\Delta\boldsymbol{\rho}_{n\times1} \tag{3}$$

In multi-GNSS single point positioning, the parameters to be estimated include user position (x_u, y_u, z_u), receiver clock error with respect to GPS time (dt_{GPS}), between-system-biases (GGTO,GETO,GBTO,GQTO).

2.2 Relative Positioning

In multi-GNSS relative positioning, pseudorange measurements from GPS, GLONASS, Galileo, BDS and QZSS, along with carrier phase measurements from GPS, Galileo, BDS and QZSS are adopted. Because the FDMA (Frequency Division Multiple Access) technique used to transmit GLONASS signals may bring difficulties to ambiguity resolution ([8,9]), carrier phase measurements from GLONASS system are excluded here when establishing relative positioning model for multi-GNSS. At one epoch, the double-differenced pseudorange measurements and carrier phase measurements can be expressed as:

$$\begin{cases} \Delta\nabla P^S = \Delta\nabla\rho^S + \Delta\nabla T^S + \Delta\nabla I^S + \Delta\nabla\varepsilon^S_P \\ \Delta\nabla\Phi^S = \Delta\nabla\rho^S + \lambda^S\Delta\nabla N^S + \Delta\nabla T^S - \Delta\nabla I^S + \Delta\nabla\varepsilon^S_\Phi \end{cases} \tag{4}$$

In (4), S indicates system type (GPS, GLONASS, Galileo, BDS, QZSS), P and Φ are pseudorange and carrier phase (in meters) measurements, ρ is the geometric distance between user and satellite, N is the number of integer cycles of carrier phase measurement, T and I are tropospheric and ionospheric delays, respectively, ε_P and ε_Φ are noise errors in pseudorange and carrier phase measurements. A simplified linearized multi-GNSS positioning model in relative positioning can be given as:

$$\boldsymbol{y} = \boldsymbol{A}\boldsymbol{a} + \boldsymbol{B}\boldsymbol{b} + \boldsymbol{\varepsilon} \tag{4}$$

In (4), $\boldsymbol{a}$ denotes the parameter vector of double-differenced integer ambiguity, $\boldsymbol{b}$ denotes the parameter vector including baseline components (Δ*x*,Δ*y*,Δ*z*), ionospheric delay and zenith tropospheric delay (**ZTD**), $\boldsymbol{A}$ and $\boldsymbol{B}$ are the coefficient matrices corresponding to vector $\boldsymbol{a}$ and $\boldsymbol{b}$, $\boldsymbol{y}$ is the observation vector that includes double-differenced pseudorange observations and carrier phase observations. $\boldsymbol{\varepsilon}$ is the vector that denotes random noise error.

According to (4), in relative positioning, pseudorange and carrier phase measurements from multi-GNSS systems are adopted. By using Kalman filtering, unknown parameters including baseline components (Δ*x*,Δ*y*,Δ*z*), float-value carrier phase ambiguities, zenith tropospheric delay (**ZTD**) and ionospheric delay can be estimated at each epoch. It should be mentioned that the float-value carrier phase ambiguities need be correctly fixed, so LAMBDA method ([10]) is applied to deccorelate the carrier phase ambiguities. Once correct integer ambiguities of carrier phase measurements from GPS, Galileo, Beidou and QZSS systems are found, centimeter-level accuracy can be achieved in relation positioning.

3 Experiments and Results

Currently in Taiwan, dual-constellation (GPS/GLONASS) combination are commonly used in positioning ([11]). To investigate the improvements (especially in constrained environments) in positioning performance induced by combining multi-GNSS constellations, experimental data were collected to perform pseudorange-based, meter-level absolute (point) positioning as well as carrier phase-based, centimetre-level relative positioning. The two experiments were performed in southern Taiwan, on November 15th ,2017. Static data were collected for one hour at two stations SPSI and HHLA equipped with Zephyr geodetic antennas and Trimble NetR9 receivers. Precise positions of SPSI and HHLA stations were obtained using GIPSY software in a Precise Point Positioning mode over one-month observation data. Dual-frequency signals collected in this research include GPS L1 and L2C, GLONASS L1 and L2, Galileo E1 and E5, BDS B1 and B2, QZSS L1 and L2. **Figure 2** and **Figure 3** show satellite the constellations and the number of visible satellites during the test period.

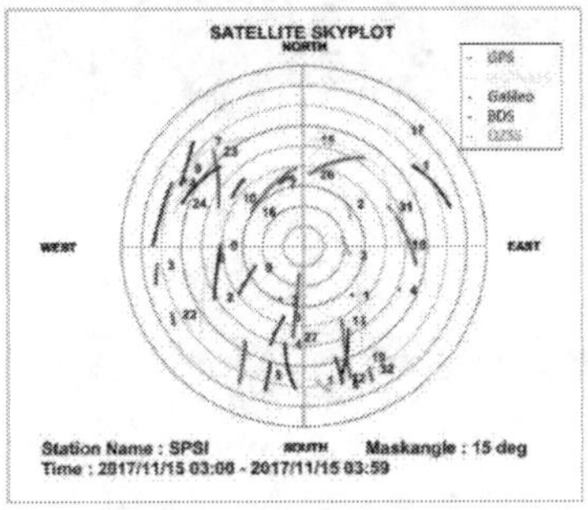

Figure 2. Satellite constellation (Nov 15th, 2017)

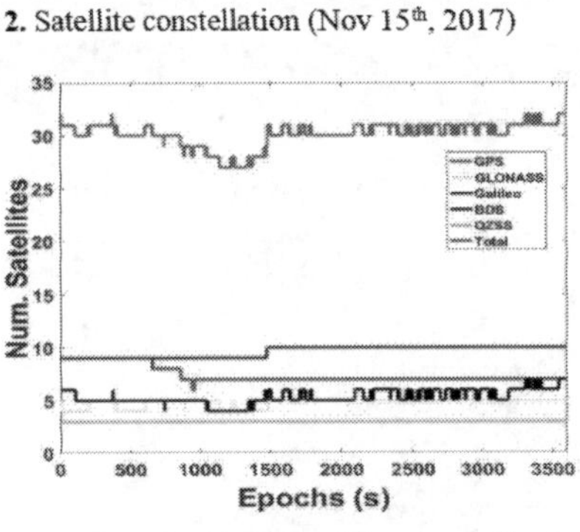

Figure 3. Number of available satellites (cut-off=15°)

3.1. Single Point Positioning Results

Single point positioning is often used in navigation. In this experiment, one-hour static data was collected in station SPSI to perform multi-GNSS single point positioning. The sampling rate was 1Hz.

Table 1. Horizontal(H) and vertical(V) mean error/RMS value, single point positioning (in meters)

	15°		35°	
	H	V	H	V
GPS/GLONASS	0.71/1.38	0.89/1.98	1.23/7.50	4.67/42.08
Multi-GNSS	0.53/0.98	0.59/1.10	0.78/1.93	1.42/2.36

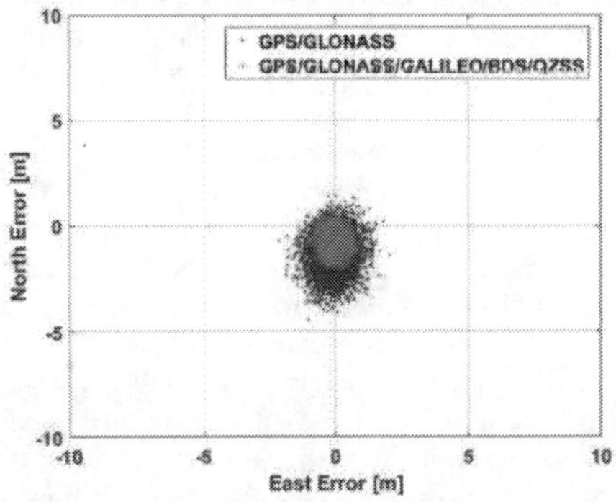

(a) Cut-off =15°, Horizontal

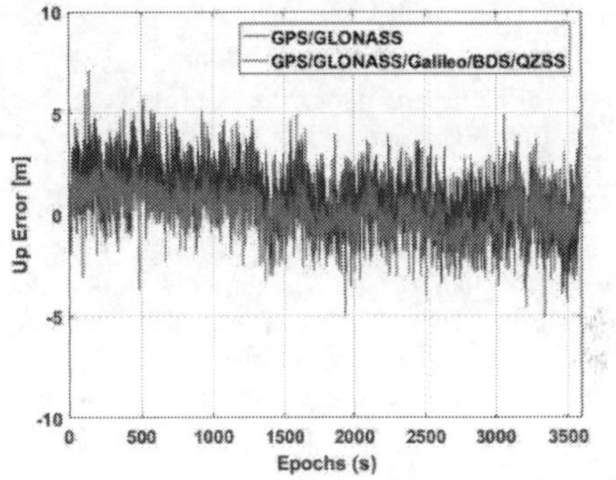

(b) Cut-off =15°, Vertical

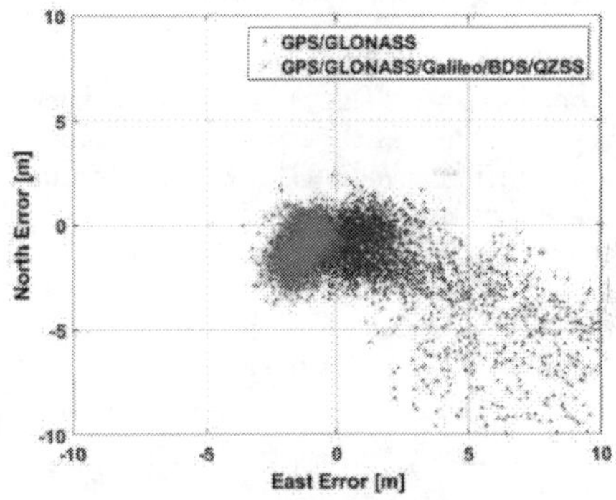

(d) Cut-off =35°, Horizontal

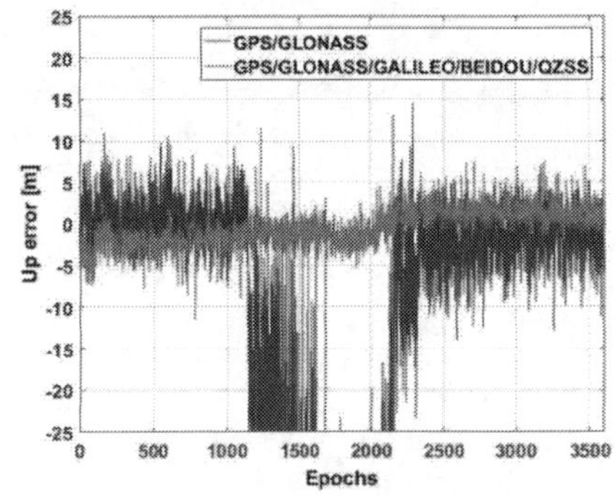

(d) Cut-off =35°, Vertical

Fig. 4. Single Point Positioning Errors.

To investigate and compare the positioning performance in normal and constrained environments, positioning results under 15° and 35° cut-off angles are analysed in this section. In **Table 1**, horizontal (H) and vertical (V) mean errors and root mean square (RMS) errors of single point positioning are given for 15° and 35° cut-off angle. The result indicates that, mean error and RMS values (in horizontal and vertical directions) are both decreased by using multi-GNSS constellations in single point positioning. It should be mentioned that under 35° cut-off angle, the positioning accuracy for dual-constellation combination is only 7.50m and 42.08m in horizontal and vertical directions, while corresponding results of the multi-GNSS combination are 1.93m and 2.36m. The positioning results under 35° cut-off angle indicate that, using multi-GNSS combination can greatly improve the positioning performance (particularly in the vertical direction) in constrained environments.

In support of better understanding the results of Table 1, the results of single point positioning error are graphically present in **Figure 4**. This figure consists of 2 × 2 subfigures, **Figure 4(a)** and **Figure 4(b)** indicate the positioning results under 15° cut-off angles, **Figure 4(c)** and **Figure 4(d)** indicate the positioning results under 35° cut-off angles. The blue dots and line indicate the horizontal and vertical errors using GPS/GLONASS combination while the red dots and line indicate the horizontal and vertical errors using multi-GNSS combination.

3.2. Relative Positioning Results

Relative positioning is often applied in researches on geodesy or earth science and so on. In this experiment, one-hour static data was collected in two stations SPSI and HHLA to perform multi-GNSS relative positioning. The distance between two stations is about 11Km and the sampling rate was 1Hz. To investigate and compare the positioning performance in normal and constrained environments, positioning results under 15° and 35° cut-off angles are analysed in this section.

Table 2. Horizontal(H) and vertical(V) mean error/RMS value, relative positioning (in meters)

	15°		35°	
	H	V	H	V
GPS/GLONASS	0.014/0.013	0.009/0.024	0.011/0.018	0.017/0.131
Multi-GNSS	0.013/0.010	0.004/0.017	0.008/0.011	0.016/0.026

In **Table 2**, horizontal (H) and vertical (V) mean errors and root mean square (RMS) errors of 11Km relative positioning are given for 15° and 35° cut-off angles. Similar to the results of single point positioning, in relative positioning, mean errors and RMS values (horizontal and vertical directions) are decreased by using multi-GNSS constellations. When under 35° cut-off angle, the horizontal and vertical RMS values of GPS/GLONASS combination are 0.018m and 0.131m, respectively, while corresponding values of multi-GNSS combination are 0.011m and 0.026m. The results indicate that in relative positioning, centimetre-level accuracy can still be achievable by using multi-GNSS even in high cut-off angle.

The results of relative positioning error are graphically

(a) Cut-off =15°, Horizontal

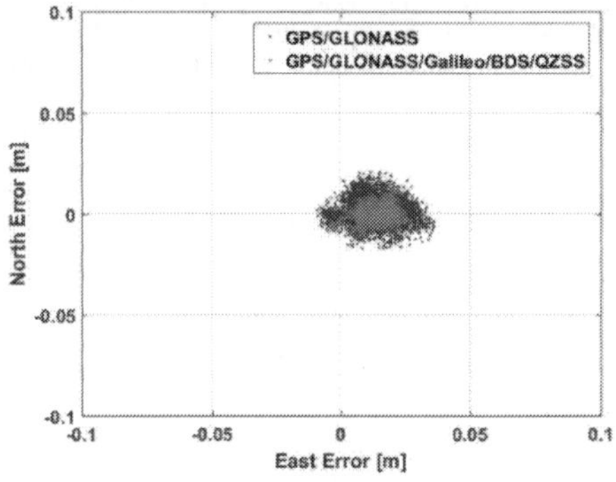

(b) Cut-off =15°, Vertical

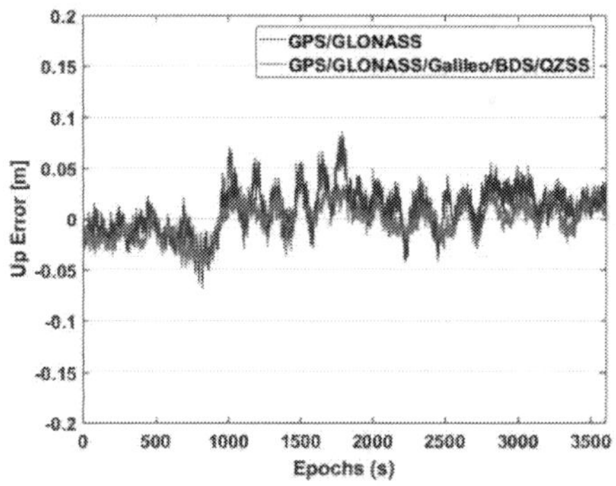

(c) Cut-off =35°, Horizontal

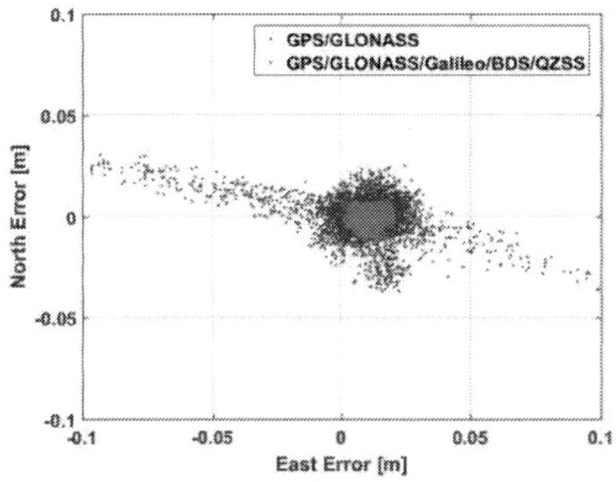

(d) Cut-off =35°, Vertical

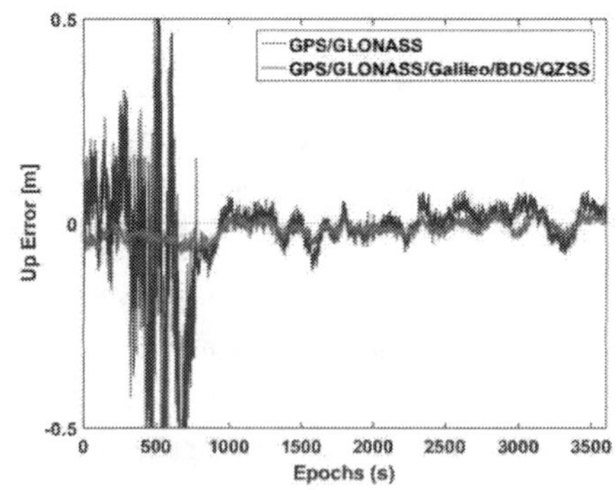

Fig. 5. Relative Positioning Errors.

present in **Figure 5**. **Figure 5** consists of 2×2 subfigures, **Figure 5(a)** and **Figure 5(b)** indicate the positioning results under 15° cut-off angles, **Figure 5(c)** and **Figure 5(d)** indicate the positioning results under 35° cut-off angles. The blue dots and line indicate the horizontal and vertical errors using GPS/GLONASS combination while the red dots and line indicate the horizontal and vertical errors using multi-GNSS combination.

In relative positioning, Time-To-First-Fix (TTFF) is an important issue as TTFF value indicates the time for rapid ambiguity resolution required by high-accuracy relative positioning applications, such as Real-Time Kinematic (RTK) in constrained environments. **Figure 6** shows the TTFF values in relative positioning, the TTFF values for using GPS/GLONASS combination under 15° and 35° cut-off angle are 15 seconds and 25 seconds, while for multi-GNSS, the TTFF values are 4 seconds and 5 seconds, respectively. The result shows that with multi-GNSS system, when using multi-GNSS, less time are required to perform centimetre-level positioning. This may benefit some filed works that are in urban area where sky-view is limited.

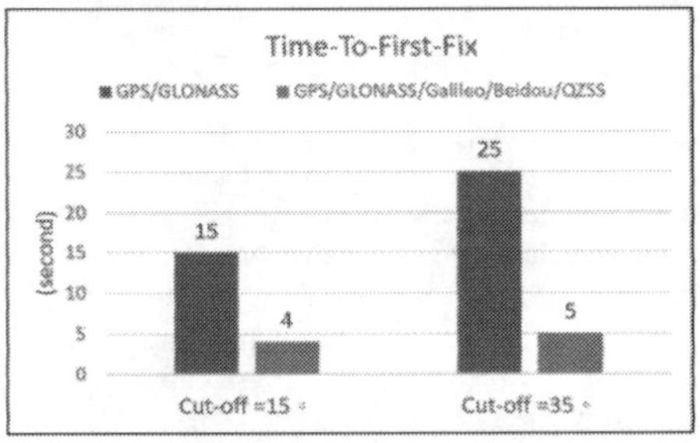

Fig. 6. Time-To-First-Fixing Values.

4 Conclusions

In this research, we have adopted a method to fully combine GPS, GLONASS, BDS, Galileo, and QZSS pseudorange and carrier phase observations, and perform single point positioning as well as relative positioning to further investigate positioning performance improvements brought by multi-GNSS. The conclusions are: (1) using multi-GNSS can effectively improve the accuracy of single point and relative positioning, particularly in highly-masked, constrained environments, such as urban areas; (2) combining the five constellations can significantly shorten the Time-To-First-Fix (TTFF) for rapid ambiguity resolution required by Real-Time Kinematic (RTK) applications in constrained environments.

References

1. E. Kaplan, C J. Hegarty, *Understanding GPS: Principles and Applications* (2nd Edition. Boston : Artech House, 2006)
2. G. Xie, *Principle of GPS and Receiver Design* (Beijing : Publishing House of Electronics Industry, 2009)
3. A. Angrisano, S. Gaglione, C. Gioia, Performance Assessment of GPS/GLONASS Single Point Positioning in an Urban Environment[J]. Acta. Geod. Geophys. **48**, 148-161 (2013)
4. C. Weng, C. Chen, W. Ting, Statiostical Characterization of BEIDOU Navigation Errors with a Consumer Multi-constellation GNSS receiver[C]. *ION GNSS*, Tennessee, (2013)
5. A. Angrisano, S. Gaglione, C. Gioia, Performance A ssessment of Aided Global Navigation Satellite System for Land Navigation[J]. IET Radar, Sonar and Navigation. 671-680(2012)
6. R. Winit, K. O'Keefe, Four-constellation Reliability in challenging GNSS Signal Environments and the Estimation of Inter-system Time-offsets[C]. *ION GNSS*, Nashivelle, TN, (2013)
7. C. Cai. Y. Gao, A combined GPS/GLONASS Navigation Algorithm for Use with Limited Satellite Visiability[J]. Journal of Navigation. E **62**, 671-685 (2009)
8. R.B. Ong, M.G. Petovello, G. Lachapelle, Assessment of GPS/GLONASS RTK under Various Operational Conditions[C]. *ION GNSS*, Savannah, GA, (2009)
9. L. Wanninger, S. Wallstab-Freitag, Combined Processing of GPS,GLONASS, and SBAS Code Phase and Carrier Phase Measurements[C]. *ION GNSS*, Fort Worth, TX, (2007)
10. P. J. G. Tuenissen, The Least-squares Ambiguity Deccorrelation Adjustment : A Method for Fast GPS Inter Ambiguity Estimation[J]. Journal of Geodesy. E **72**, 606-612 (1998)
11. Tsai, M. L., K. W. Chiang, M. Yang, and H. C. Chen, The accuracy and reliability analysis for future GNSS in Taiwan region, Journal of Photogrammetry and Remote Sensing, **13**, 57-64 (2008)

Variability and Performance of Short to Long-Range Single Baseline RTK GNSS Positioning in Indonesia

Irwan Gumilar[1,*], *Brian* Bramanto[1], *Fuad* F. Rahman[1] and *I Made* D. A. Hermawan[2]

[1]Geodesy Research Group, Institut Teknologi Bandung, Indonesia
[2]General Technology Indonesia

Abstract. As the modernized Global Navigation Satellite System (GNSS) method, Real Time Kinematic (RTK) ensures high accuracy of position (within several centimeters). This method uses Ultra High Frequency (UHF) radio to transmit the correction data, however, due to gain and power issues, Networked Transport of RTCM via Internet Protocol (RTCM) is used to transmit the correction data for a longer baseline. This Research aims to investigate the performance of short to long-range single baseline RTK GNSS (Up to 80 KM) by applying modified LAMBDA method to resolve the ambiguity in carrier phase. The RTK solution then compared with the differential GNSS network solution. The results indicate that the differences are within RTK accuracy up to 80 km are several centimeter for horizontal solution and three times higher for vertical solution.

1 Introduction

Global Navigation Satellite System or commonly abbreviated as GNSS is a satellite based point or moving object positioning system. In simplified, GNSS determines the user position by measuring at least four distance from known satellites position simultaneously. Point position can be determined by either using absolute or relative point positioning. Absolute point positioning uses stand-alone receiver GNSS while relative point positioning use two receivers GNSS on the same time observation as base and rover, which can also be referred as differential positioning. There are various other methods that can be used in GNSS point positioning, such as static and kinematic method. Static is such condition when the object is not moving, while kinematic is when the object is moving. The position of those condition can be determine by using either absolute or differential positioning. The point position can also be determine either real time or post-processing.

Real Time Kinematic (RTK) has been widely used is several application [1-4]. Moreover, with the existence of CORS (Continuously Operating Reference System), the RTK can be done easier. CORS is a reference system that works continuously as a base station in differential GNSS positioning. CORS send various kind of correction data needed in GNSS measurement using a specific data transfer system, such as RTCM (Radio Technical Commission for Maritime Services). CORS can provide a position with an accuracy of ± 20 mm, however, it should be noted that the optimum distance between CORS station and rover is about 15-20 km [5-6]. This is due to various types of errors that will increase with increasing baseline distance.

In RTK GNSS measurements, the distance between base station and rover might varies from several kilometers to hundreds of kilometers. Along with the greater baseline, the greater error also occurred on the observation data, such as ionospheric bias, tropospheric bias and orbital error bias, which lead to unresolved ambiguity integer.

In this study a new algorithm [7] is used to improve the RTK performance in long baseline condition. The new algorithm determine the atmospheric bias and correct the orbital error by using precise orbit that obtained from Starfire™ network and further process in resolving ambiguity integer.

2 Research Methodology

2.1 Tropospheric Bias Determination

In general, atmospheric bias (Ionospheric and Tropospheric) is estimated through the Kalmam Filter process along with the position, velocity and ambiguity parameters. Tropospheric bias thus can be overcome using a variety models such as UNB, Hopfield or Saastomoinen Models [8-10]. Dry components of the troposphere can be easily modeled, however, the wet components are relatively hard to modeled.

Various tropospheric condition can be overcome by using a scale factor for the Zenith delay value. After removing the tropospheric delay with the model from the observed data, the Relative Tropospheric Zenith Delay (RTZD) can be approximate properly.

* Corresponding author: igumilar@gd.itb.ac.id

2.2 Ionospheric Bias Determination

Having implemented the broadcast model and Double Difference (DD) process to minimize the ionospheric delay, the residual ionospheric delay are then estimated on the Kalman filter calculation. Empirically, the residual ionospheric delay can be modeled as 1st order Gauss Markov. Ionospheric correction derived from global and regional ionospheric model (for example WAAS) can be considered as virtual measurements and included in the Kalman filter estimation. However, the accuracy obtained from both of broadcast and WASS models are still not enough. This is because the model can only handle some part of the ionosphere delay.

In recent year, the concepts of using a network reference station for GNSS RTK have been developed by several academic institutions and several GNSS manufacturers. The development of these concepts resulted new correction for atmospheric bias and orbital errors for GNSS measurements. This correction can be used to overcome errors which are influenced by the length of baseline. The developed ionosphere model will improve the performance and reliability of determining ambiguity and reduce the time to get fix solutions on RTK GNSS.

2.3 Orbital Error

Navigation message broadcast by satellites contain orbit keplerian elements and time elements. These message is estimated from network GNSS observation station and control segment of GNSS that is updated every two hours. Several test have proven that the error results obtained from orbital errors might vary from 2 to 5 meters [11]. In general, orbital error is the biggest source of error in RTK GNSS point positioning after removing the atmospheric error.

Some of the differential GNSS systems have been able to provide the orbital correction, such as HA-ND GPS (High Accuracy Nationwide Differential GPS). HA-ND GPS is a differential correction broadcasting system that developed by several US government organization. John Deer also has developed the Starfire^{tm} system. This system sends orbital corrections in a global scale via communication satellites.

2.3 Ambiguity Fixing

In theory, ambiguity is a constant value, however, float ambiguity uncertainty values that is estimated through the Kalman filter may contain multipath and systematic bias errors that are not modeled, such as orbital errors and atmospheric bias residual. Based on these considerations, before the ambiguity value is fixed, the ambiguity for the L1/L2 signal and its variance were first converted into L1/Wide Lane (WL) form which is then returned to L1/L2 after fulfilling the ambiguity criteria test. This process can be called as a Partial Search and Fix process. This process determined the "true" ambiguity value. This process is carried out when the conventional ambiguity search process does not meet the criteria.

In ambiguity fixing process, a minimum of five satellites is needed. When there are six or more satellites observed, some ambiguity values from the satellite can be removed in the search process. By calculating all the five satellite combinations needed, the value of ambiguity that has the biggest bias can be seen and eliminated so as to facilitate the process of determining ambiguity. This process increases the success rate of determining ambiguity, but this process takes a lot of time and it will be very difficult to determine all satellite combinations with limited tool processing capabilities.

Therefore, the Partial Search and Fix process is used. After the DD calculation process for both frequencies is carried out, the ambiguity values and its variances can be obtained through the Kalman filter process. Although the parameters used in the process of ambiguity resolution are ambiguities of L1 and L2, the search process using the Lambda method can be different. So that the forms L1 and L2 can be changed into L1 and (WL). WL is used because it has a longer wavelength (0.86 cm) so it will be easier to determine its ambiguity. From the search process using the Lambda method, the best and second best ambiguity candidate values are obtained. If the value meets the ambiguity validation test, the best value is used in the calculation of fixed solutions. But if it does not meet the validation test, the Partial Search and Fix process can be done by eliminating the satellite with the value of ambiguity outside the best and second best value.

2.4 Data acquisition

Nine point were observed using GNSS RTK in this research. The number of points is adjusted to the needs of the baseline distance interval to be observed and then adjusted to the availability of reference points in the field. The baseline length varies from 5 km to 85 km with an interval for approximately every 10 km. The observation point and its baseline length can be seen on **Table 1.** and **Fig. 1.**

Table 1. Point ID and its baseline length

Point ID	Baseline length
BDG066	5.00 km
BDG073	10.00 km
ITB01	17.70 km
TTG698	21.45 km
KM30	30.00 km
TTG693	36.34 km
TTB	47.85 km
J681A	59.78 km
N1.0304	72.57 km
J670	83.51 km

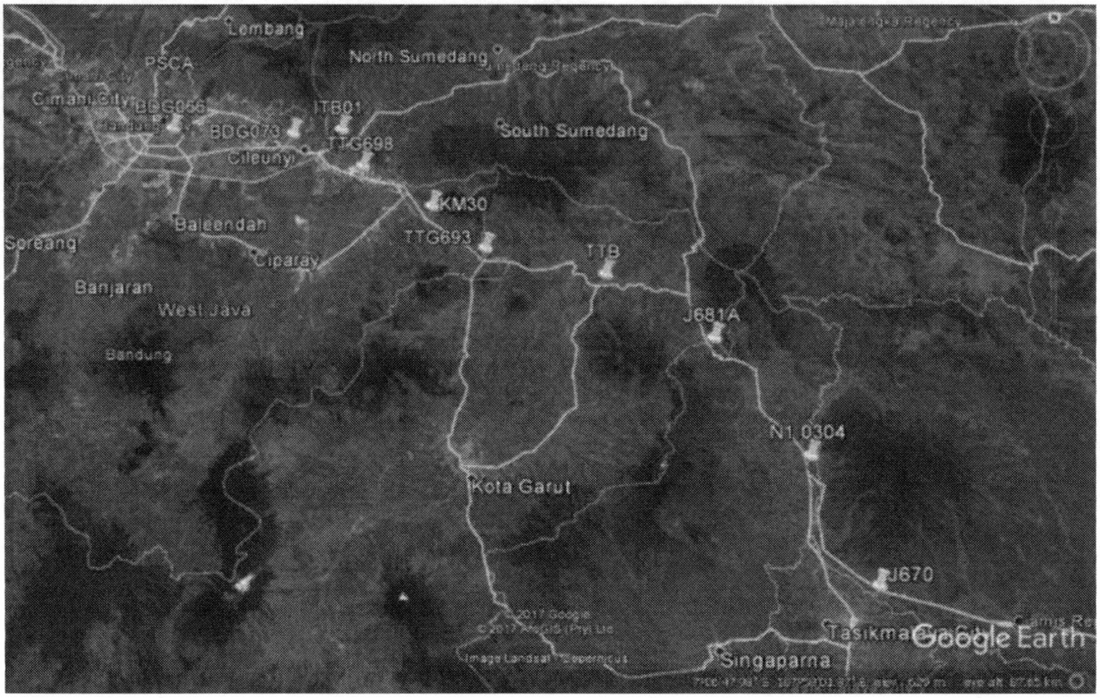

Fig. 1. Location of the observed point

3 Results and Discussions

3.1 Accuracy and Precision

To assess the accuracy of point positioning, the estimated point position from RTK GNSS were compared to reference coordinate. The reference coordinate were derived from static differential method. The precision is derived from RTK GNSS position deviation from its mean position. Three selected observation points will be discussed further in this section. Three selected observation points are ITB01, TTB and J670.

The maximum error of ITB01 for easting and northing components are about 24 cm and 10 respectively, while maximum error for height component is 28 cm. The precision for easting, northing and the elevation components are about 3 cm, 2.6 cm and 12 cm.

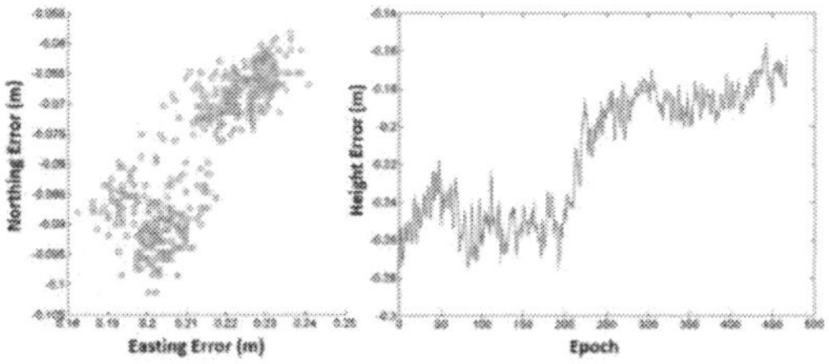

Fig. 2. Position error of ITB01

The high value of error likely due to the geometry of the satellite. To illustrate the different condition, a comparison observation point is needed. BDG066 is chosen because BDG066 has relatively good obstruction compared with ITB01. **Fig. 3.** shows the skyplot of BDG066 and ITB01. There is no observed data in the direction of 30^0 to 120^0 from the North of ITB01, while BDG066 has a good skyview for all of the direction.

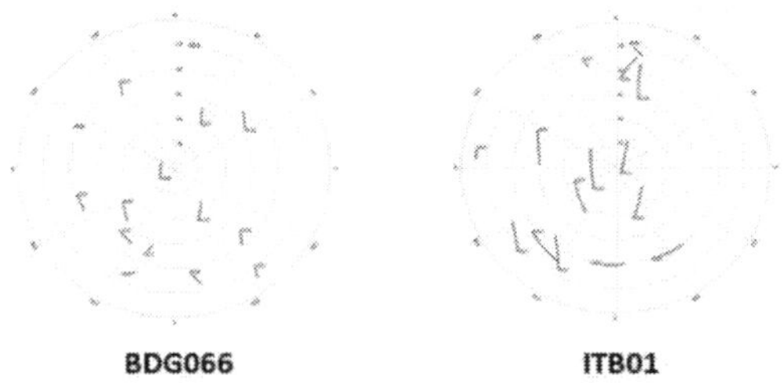

Fig. 3. Skyplot of BDG066 and ITB01

Fig. 4. ITB01 observation point

The maximum error of TTB for easting and northing components are no more than 6.5 cm and 5.5 respectively, while for height component is vary from 5 cm to 26 cm. The precision for easting, northing and the elevation components are about 3 cm, 5.8 cm and 13 cm.

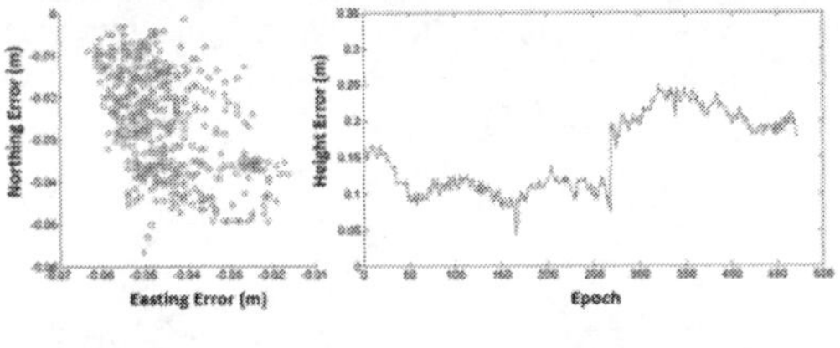

Fig. 3. Position error of TTB

With the baseline length for about 83.51 km, J670 was the farthest observation point. The maximum error of ITB01 for easting and northing components are about 8 cm and 5 respectively, while maximum error for height component is 18 cm. The precision for easting, northing and the elevation components are about 3.7 cm, 3.7 cm and 15 cm.

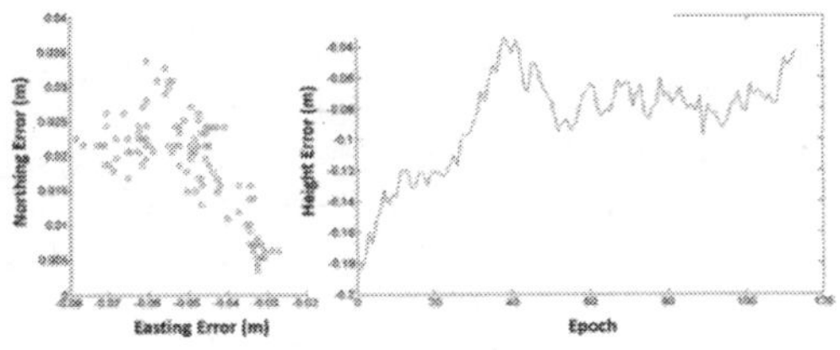

Fig. 3. Position error of J670

3.2 Overal Accuracy

Fig.4. and **Fig. 5.** show the overall accuracy both of horizontal and vertical estimated position. The accuracy for horizontal varies from 2 cm to 45 cm while the accuracy of vertical varies from 10 cm to 70 cm. The huge error mostly due to the unresolved bias.

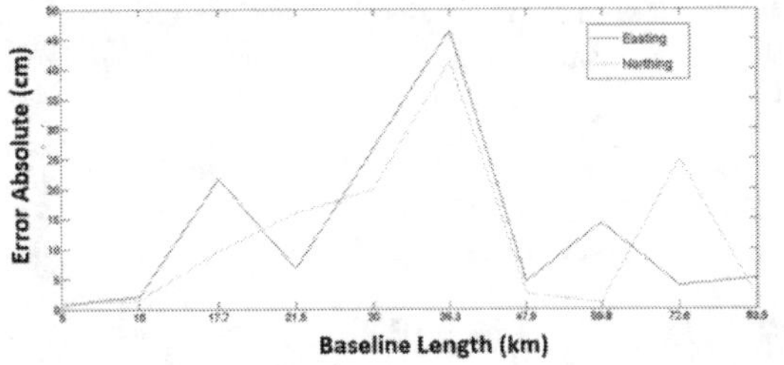

Fig. 4. Overall horizontal accuracy

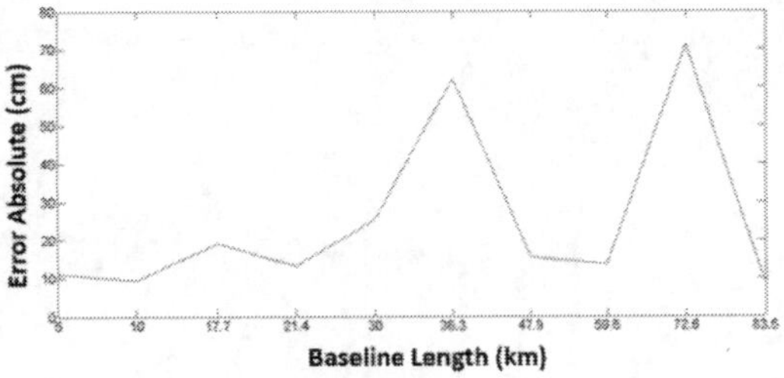

Fig. 4. Overall vertical accuracy

In GNSS data acquisition, there are numerous factors that can affect the estimated position. One of them is field condition. In accordance with previous explanation in Section 2, that error on the GNSS RTK observation will increase along with the increase of the baseline length. With a greater baseline length, there will be spatial and temporal variation in the atmospheric bias. Therefore, in order to be able to analyze the effects of spatial and temporal variations, the weather conditions and the observation time are needed.

Table 2. Point ID and its weather condition

Point ID	Time observation		Weather Condition
	Start	End	
BDG066	10:30	11:15	Drizzle
BDG073	20:05	21:15	Daylight
ITB01	12:10	13:15	Daylight
TTG698	14:50	15:25	Daylight
KM30	18:42	19:00	Daylight
TTG693	16:35	16:55	Drizzle
TTB	18:40	19:05	Daylight
J861A	09:35	10:15	Drizzle
N1.0304	11:00	12:00	Daylight
J670	13:55	15:30	Daylight

The huge error on ITB01 (17.7 km), TTG693 (36.34 km) and J861A (59.78 km) are due to the unresolved atmospheric bias and ionosphere bias. As seen on **Table 2**, the observation time of ITB01 was on the noon, the high activity on the ionosphere and with the error addition from the poor geometry satellites, lead into a worse estimation coordinate. TTG693 and J861A suffer a variation on the atmospheric condition, combined with the baseline length, the estimated position is going worse.

3.3 Reliability Analysis

Reliability means how consistent the method produces fixed solutions. In this case, the reliability value is obtained from the comparison of the RTK Fixed (Dual) solution with all solutions obtained during the observation time of each baseline. The percentage results of each baseline can be seen in **Fig. 5**.

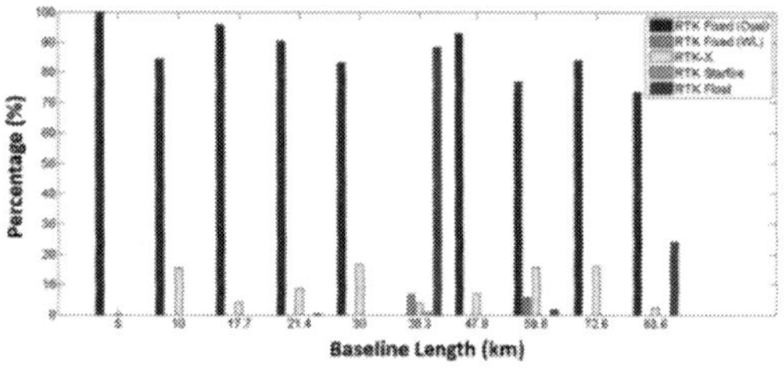

Fig. 5. Percentage for each solution

TTG693 has the lowest percentage of fixed dual solution compared to the others. TTG693 suffer a bad obstruction condition. It has a lot of vegetation. In this condition, ambiguity fixing is very difficult to obtain so that it takes time to the first ambiguity fixing. Overall, the ambiguity fixing percentage is decreasing along with the increasing of the baseline length as seen on **Fig. 6**.

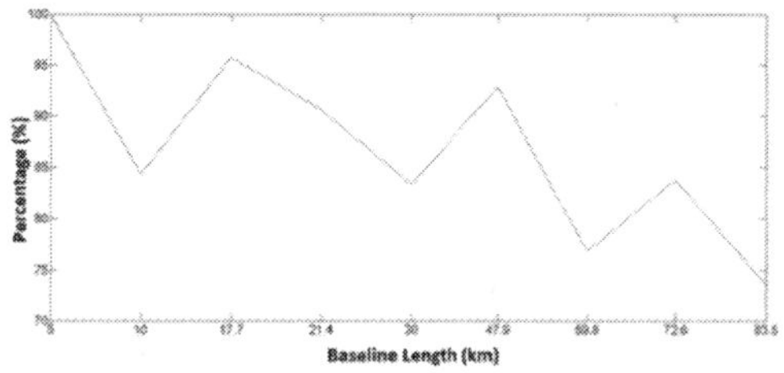

Fig. 6. Ambiguity fixing percentage over baseline length

4 Conclussions

The GNSS RTK measurement results show the error position and precision for each baseline length. The error accuracy for easting components vary from 0.8 cm to 46.6 cm, while for northing components vary from 0.8 cm to 41.3 cm. Error accuracy for height components vary from 8.6 cm to 62.1 cm. The results also indicate that rate of ambiguity fixing depends on the baseline length and the site obstruction..

References

1. Tae-Suk Bae and Minho Kim, "Performance Analysis of Network-RTK Techniques for Drone Navigation considering Ionospheric Conditions," Journal of Sensors, vol. 2018, Article ID 5154697, 8 pages, 2018. https://doi.org/10.1155/2018/5154697
2. W. Stempfhuber and M. Buchholz, "A Precise, Low-Cost RTK GNSS System For UAV Applications" International Archives of the Photogrammetry, Remote Sensing and Spatial Information Sciences, Volume XXXVIII-1/C22, 2011
3. S. R. Saghravani, Sa'ari bin Mustapha and S. F. Saghravani "Accuracy Comparison of RTK-GPS and Automatic Level for Height Determination in Land Surveying" Journal Of Reviews and Surveys, Volume 1 Issue 1, 2009
4. Ahmed EL-MOWAFY "Surveying with GPS for Construction Works Using the National RTK Reference Network and Precise Geoid Models" 1st FIG International Symposium on Engineering Surveys for Construction Works and Structural Engineering, 2004
5. Yanmin Feng and Jinling Wang "GPS RTK Performance Characteristics and Analysis" Journal of Global Positioning Systems 2008 Vol. 7, No. 1 : 1-8, 2008
6. R. M. Alkan, İ. M. Ozulu and V.İlÇi "Comparison of Single Baseline RTK and Network RTK GNSS Methods" International Symposium On Modern Technologies, Education And Professional Practice In Geodesy And Related Fields, 2017
7. Liwen Dai, Dan Eslinger and Tenny Sharpe "Innovative Algorithms tp Improve Long Range RTK Reliability and Availability" ION NTM 2007
8. S. Katsougiannopoulos, C. Pikridas, D. Rossikopoulos, I. M. Ifadis and A. Fotiou "Tropospheric Refraction Estimation Using Various Models, Radiosonde Measurements and Permanent GPS Data" FIG Congress XXIII, 2006
9. Chalermchon Satirapod and Prapod Chalermwattanachai "Impact of Different Tropospheric Models on GPS Baseline Accuracy: Case Study in Thailand" Journal of Global Positioning Systems (2005) Vol. 4, No. 1-2: 36-40, 2005
10. Langley, R.B. "Propagation of the GPS Signals, In: Kleusberg, A. and Teunissen, P.J.G. (eds), GPS for Geodesy (2nd edition)", Springer-Verlag, Berlin Heidelberg New York, 111-150, 1998
11. Janusz Zielinski and Ryszard Zdunek "GPS orbit accuracy and its influence on large network solutions" Advances in Space Research 23(4):665-665 DOI: 10.1016/S0273-1177(99)00149-0, 1999

Integration of Inertial Navigation System with EM-log Using H-infinity Filter

Jaehyuck Cha[1,2], *Hojin* Ju[2], *Chan Gook* Park[1,2*], *Kijeong* Yoo[3], and *Chanju* Park[3]

[1]Department of Mechanical and Aerospace Engineering, Seoul National University, 08826 Seoul, Korea
[2]Automoation and Systems Research Institute, Seoul National University, 08826 Seoul, Korea
[3]Agency for Defense Development, 34186 Daejeon, Korea

Abstract. This paper presents the integration of inertial navigation system (INS) with electromagnetic-log (EM-log) as an underwater navigation system using H-infinity filter for robustness from the uncertainty of the sea current model. In underwater environments, the electromagnetic signals are attenuated rapidly, so that the global navigation satellite system is not available in general. Thus, INS is usually chosen for underwater navigation, and other aiding sensors are also used to complement its accumulative errors, one of which is EM-log. Since an EM-log provides the relative velocity to seawater, the integrated navigation cannot be performed accurately unless the sea current speed is compensated properly. Generally, the INS and EM-log can be integrated using extended Kalman filter (EKF). However, EKF guarantees its performance when the stochastic properties of the system's process and measurement noises are perfectly known. In other words, in the presence of sea current modelling errors, the integration using the EKF is not expected to show good performance. On the other hand, H-infinity filter is a robust filter which can tolerate such uncertainties. In this paper, the integration of INS and EM-log using H-infinity filter is studied. The performance is compared with that of the EKF case by proper computer simulation.

1 Introduction

Autonomous underwater vehicles (AUVs) have been developed since 1970s, they are being operated to carry out their own missions. To achieve a successful operation, the vehicles need their position or attitude information, so called navigation solutions. Global navigation satellite system (GNSS) is one of the most popular navigation system on the ground. In water, however, the signals transmitted from the GNSS satellites are attenuated rapidly, hence, the system is seldom chosen for underwater navigation.

On the other hand, inertial navigation system (INS) is self-consistent, so that it is usually chosen for underwater navigation system. Nevertheless, it has a critical limitation of cumulatively increasing positioning error with time [1]. Therefore, in most cases, INS is integrated with other sensors or systems to overcome this advantage. Long baseline (LBL), short baseline (SBL), and ultrashort baseline (USBL) have been adopted as such systems [2]. But in order to operate those baseline systems, their own infrastructure must be already constructed. Doppler velocity log can be another choice [3-5], which provides the vehicle's velocity information the device mounted on. Owing to the depth range of the sensor, however, it is also not versatile enough.

To the point of this view, even though it is not popular as other sensors, electromagnetic log (EM-log) can appeal its advantage of self-consistency. EM-log is a sensor that provides velocity information, but unlike that of DVL, the output is relative velocity to water rather than absolute velocity, since the principle of EM-log is based on Faraday's law which states electromagnetic induction.

Vaisgant et al. [6] proposed a method verifying EM-log measurements and further, if need, excluding them to improve INS/EM-log integration. They focused on the effect of the low-pass filter employed in the EM-log which is for the purpose of reducing measurement noise. The integration was conducted by means of Kalman filter, which requires accurate stochastic characteristics of process and measurement noises to be known [7]. In other words, the integration of INS and EM-log is optimal only when the stochastic dynamic model of sea current is perfectly known. Unfortunately, it is very hard to model the dynamics of sea current accurately.

In this paper, the integration of INS and EM-log using H-infinity filter is presented. H-infinity filter, also called the minimax filter, is one of the basic robust filters which can tolerate such uncertainties, that is, the influence of uncertainty in sea current model which can be severe to performance of the EKF is reduced.

The remaining parts are organized as follows; the system model including sea current model and measurement model are presented in section 2. Then, section 3 develops H-infinity filter for INS/EM-log integration. The performances of EKF and H-infinity filter are compared via computer simulation and discussed in section 4, and the last section concludes this paper.

* Corresponding author: chanpark@snu.ac.kr

2 System and measurement model

2.1. System model

In this subsection, the system model including INS model and sea current model is presented.

2.1.1 INS error model

It is well-known that the vertical channel is very weakly coupled with the horizontal channels. Hence, we separated down-axis velocity and height states from general 15th order INS model and constitutes 3rd order damping loop in conjunction with depth gauge [8]. Since we used NED navigation frame, INS state vector is

$$\mathbf{x}_{INS} = \left[L,\ l,\ v_N,\ v_E,\ \phi,\ \theta,\ \psi, \nabla_x, \nabla_y, \nabla_z,\ \varepsilon_x,\ \varepsilon_y,\ \varepsilon_z \right]^T \tag{1}$$

where L and l denotes latitude and longitude, v is velocity along the subscripted direction, north and east, ϕ, θ, ψ are Euler angles, roll, pitch, and yaw in order, and ∇, ε are accelerometer and gyro bias, respectively. We assumed that these biases are all random constant.

Eventually, we can define the corresponding system matrix INS error dynamic model F_{INS} and process noise covariance Q_{INS} which are 13×13 matrices [1].

2.1.2 Sea current model

As mentioned above, EM-log measures the relative velocity of the vehicle to the sea water, so that it is required to augment sea current velocities as states. They will be denoted by

$$\mathbf{x}_C = \begin{bmatrix} v_{C_N} & v_{C_E} \end{bmatrix}^T \tag{2}$$

In general, sea current is modelled by 1st order Markov-model [9], that is,

$$\dot{v}_{C_{N,E}} = -\frac{1}{T_C} v_{C_{N,E}} + \sigma_C \sqrt{\frac{2}{T_C}} \xi \tag{3}$$

where v_C is sea current along the subscripted direction, north and east, σ_C is root mean square (RMS) current speed, T_C is the correlation interval of current speed, and ξ is white noise following standard normal distribution. Hence, the system matrix F_C and process noise covariance Q_C for sea current can be determined.

To add a comment, T_C is related to the tendency of the sea current, so that if T_C is large, the speed of sea current varies slowly, and vice versa. On the other hand, σ_C is related to the roughness of the sea current, so that if σ_C is large, the sea current becomes more rough, and vice versa. Figure 1 shows the example of sea current created by Eq. (3).

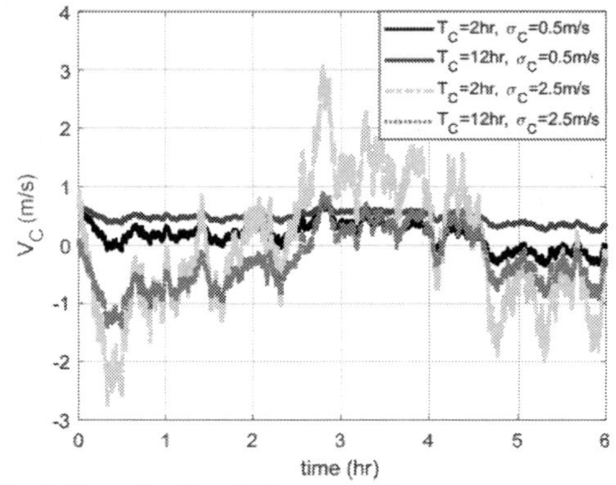

Fig. 1. Example of created sea current.

2.1.3 Total system model

There are no correlation between INS states and the sea current states, so that the total state vector, system matrix and process covariance matrix are difined as

$$\mathbf{x} = \left[\delta\mathbf{x}_{INS}^T \quad \delta\mathbf{x}_C^T \right]^T \tag{4}$$

$$F = \begin{bmatrix} F_{INS} & 0_{13\times2} \\ 0_{2\times13} & F_C \end{bmatrix} \tag{5}$$

$$Q = \begin{bmatrix} Q_{INS} & 0_{13\times2} \\ 0_{2\times13} & Q_C \end{bmatrix} \tag{6}$$

where $0_{m\times n}$ means zero matrix in $m \times n$ dimension.

2.2. Measurement model

The measurement of EM-log is not only the relative velocity of the vehicle to the water, but also that in body frame $\{B\}$. In our research, we only used longitudinal direction measurement, which is on the x-axis of forward-right-down body frame we used. Hence, coordinate transformation matrix is used in order to mediate the state and the measurement. Therefore, considering the perturbation of attitude, the observation matrix for total states is obtained by

$$H = \begin{bmatrix} 0_{1\times2} & H_{12} & H_{13} & 0_{1\times6} & H_{15} \end{bmatrix} \tag{7}$$

where

$$H_{12} = \begin{bmatrix} 1 & 0 & 0 \end{bmatrix} \times C_n^b \times \begin{bmatrix} 1 & 0 \\ 0 & 1 \\ 0 & 0 \end{bmatrix} \tag{8}$$

$$H_{13} = -\begin{bmatrix} 1 & 0 & 0 \end{bmatrix} \times C_n^b \left[\left(v^n - v_C^n \right) \times \right] \tag{9}$$

$$H_{15} = -\begin{bmatrix} 1 & 0 & 0 \end{bmatrix} \times C_n^b \times \begin{bmatrix} 1 & 0 \\ 0 & 1 \\ 0 & 0 \end{bmatrix} \tag{10}$$

3 H-infinity filter for INS/EM-log

3.1. Basic formulation of H-infinity filter

The formulation of H-infinity filter is summarized as [7]

$$\mathbf{z}_k = L_k \mathbf{x}_k \tag{11}$$

$$\overline{S}_k = L_k^T S_k L_k \tag{12}$$

$$K_k = P_k \left(I - \theta \overline{S}_k P_k + H_k^T R_k^{-1} H_k P_k\right)^{-1} H_k^T R_k^{-1} \tag{13}$$

$$\hat{\mathbf{x}}_{k+1} = F_k \hat{\mathbf{x}}_k + F_k K_k \left(\mathbf{y}_k - H_k \hat{\mathbf{x}}_k\right) \tag{14}$$

$$P_{k+1} = F_k P_k \left(I - \theta \overline{S}_k P_k + H_k^T R_k^{-1} H_k P_k\right)^{-1} F_k^{-1} + Q_k \tag{15}$$

where $\mathbf{z}_k$ is our interest, S_k is a weight matrix for $\mathbf{z}_k$, and θ is the user-specified performance bound. In addition, $\mathbf{y}_k$ is a measurement, and $\hat{\mathbf{a}}$ denotes the estimate of $\mathbf{a}$.

Here, we should be careful that if we set θ too large, it will broke a positive-definiteness of P_{k+1} in Eq. (15), which violates the peroperty of covariance matrix.

3.2. INS/EM-log integration

We used Eqs. (5-10) for Eqs. (13-15). In our system and measurement models, the most uncertain parameters are related to the sea current velocities, so that we chose L_k as

$$L_k = \begin{bmatrix} 0_{2\times 13} & I_2 \end{bmatrix} \tag{16}$$

where I_n denotes identity matrix of dimension $n \times n$. And then, we set S_k as large as possible fixing the value of θ, which means increasing the robustness of P_{k+1} in Eq. (15).

4 Simulation

4.1. Simulation condition

In order to verify the performance of H-infinity filter, it is compared to the optimal and suboptimal EKF. As mentioned in the introduction, it is hard to accurately parameterize the sea current model. In this simulation we used $T_C = 2\text{hr}$ and $\sigma_C = 0.5\text{m/s}$ for the true sea current model, and the optimal filter was adopted with the same parameters while $\sigma_C = 0.2\text{m/s}$ was used in the suboptimal filter. For a fair comparison, we also used $\sigma_C = 0.2\text{m/s}$ in H-infinity filter.

The navigation trajectory was generated as shown in Figure 2, which is 24 hours long and contains stop in place motion, acceleration and deceleration, and pitching and turning maneuvers. Then, Monte-Carlo simulation with 32 runs were performed to consider random conditions.

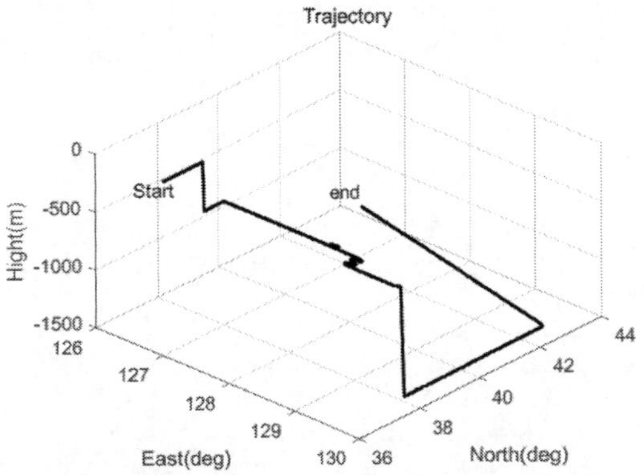

Fig. 2. 3D trajectory of simulation.

4.2. Simulation result

Figure 3 shows normalized latitude and longitude errors of each filter. The reason why the errors are normalized is that our interest is only in their relative magnitude. As shown in the figure, the performance of the optimal EKF is the best, which is natural result. In the suboptimal EKF case, which is conducted with inaccurate process noise model of sea current, the position estimation errors were found to increase more since 4 hours after the start of navigation. It is because using inaccurate sea current model, the filter cannot reflect its true speed, hence, the sea current estimation errors are propagated to the position estimation errors through the observation matrix. Likewise, the H-infinity filter also performs worse in position estimation than the optimal filter. Nevertheless, it shows better results than suboptimal filter, since the designed H-infinity filter considers the uncertainty in the stochastics of the sea current model.

Figure 4 shows further obvious difference among filter performance. The error metric presented in the figure is normalized time circular error probability (TCEP), which is defined as

$$\text{TCEP}(k) = \frac{0.589}{k} \sum_{i=1}^{k} \left[\sigma_N(i) + \sigma_E(i)\right] \tag{17}$$

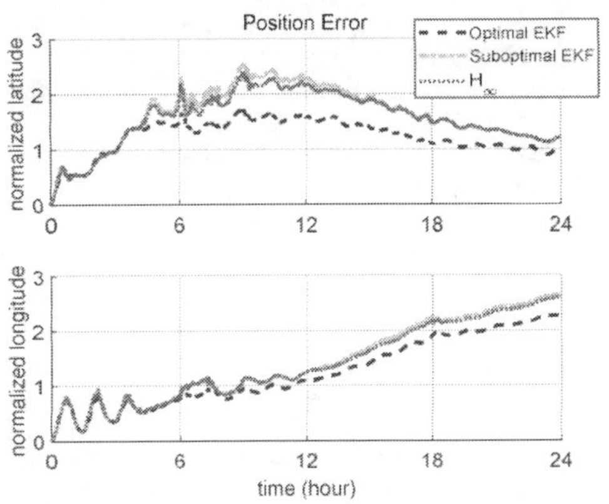

Fig. 3. Normalized latitude and longitude errors of optimal EKF, suboptimal EKF, and H-infinity filter.

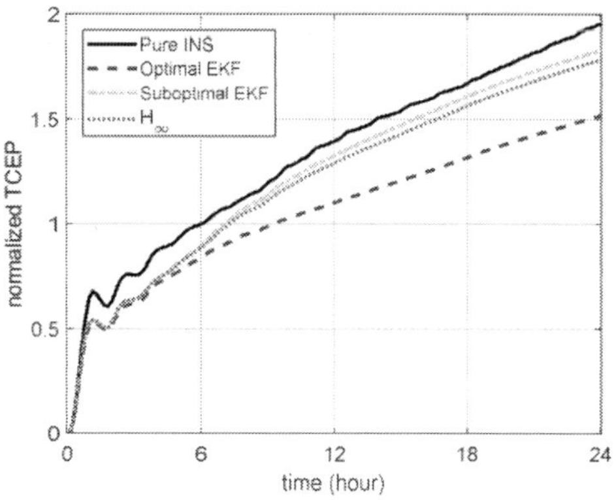

Fig. 4. Normalized time circular error probability of pure INS, optimal EKF, suboptimal EKF, and H-infinity filter.

where $\sigma_N(i)$, $\sigma_E(i)$ are the root mean squared error of north and east position estimates at time step i, respectively. Since high-grade INS has several error oscillations such as Schuler oscillation of 84.4 minutes and earth loop oscillation of 24 hours, the position errors at the final point are not always the worst. Therefore, an error metric that takes this effect into account is needed, of which TCEP is one.

The normalized TCEP and its accuracy rate of increase compared to the pure navigation of each filter at 6, 12, 18, and 24 hours from the start are shown in table 1. The optimal EKF steadily improves the TCEP compared to the pure navigation over time, which is due to the fact that the biases of the inertial sensors are properly estimated by the EM-log measurement. On the other hand, those of the suboptimal filters do not so owing to the uncertain sea current model. Still, in all time domains, H-infinity is found to outperform the suboptimal EKF.

5 Conclusion

In this paper, the integration of INS and EM-log using H-infinity filter has been studied. In the presence of uncertainty in the process and measurement noise stochastics, the EKF does not guarantee the performance as desired. Since EM-log measures not the absolute velocity but the relative of the vehicle to the sea water, the estimation errors of north and east sea current velocities are augmented to the filter states. Nonetheless, the system model of the sea current states is not easy to design. That is, the inaccurate system model of the sea current degrades the performance of EKF. Therefore, H-infinity filter, one of the most popular robust filter, has been adopted to integrate those two systems. In our research, we have designed the filter to focus on the estimation of sea current, and the required parameters are proposed in this paper. A proper computer simulation has been conducted and shown that even though the robust filter is not good as the optimal filter naturally, it outperforms the suboptimal EKF during all navigation time. The positioning errors are compared by using TCEP metric. The designed filter needs to be verified using real data as a future work.

Table 1. Normalized TCEP and accuracy rate of increase compared to the pure navigation of each filter

Time step	Pure INS	EKF-opt	EKF-sub	H-infinity
6 hr	1	0.8403	0.8968	0.8862
	-	15.97%	10.32%	11.38%
12 hr	1.3950	1.1029	1.3256	1.2905
	-	20.94%	4.96%	7.5%
18 hr	1.6734	1.3171	1.6094	1.5632
	-	21.29%	3.82%	6.58%
24 hr	1.9561	1.5181	1.8333	1.7877
	-	22.40%	6.28%	8.61%

This study was supported by the research project "A Study on Multi Sensors Aided Navigation for Underwater Environment" of Agency for Defense Development.

References

1. D. Titterton, J. L. Weston, J. Weston, *Strapdown inertial navigation technology* (IET, 2004)
2. L. Paull, S. Saeedi, M. Seto, H. Li, IEEE J. Ocean. Eng., **39**, 1 (2014)
3. D. Rudolph, T. A. Wilson, *Southeastcon, 2012 Proceedings of IEEE,* pp. 1-7 (2012)
4. P. A. Miller, J. A. Farrell, Y. Zhao, V. Djapic, IEEE J. Ocean. Eng. **35**, 3 (2010)
5. A. Tal, I. Klein, R. Katz, Sensors, **17**, 2 (2017)
6. I. B. Vaisgant, Y. A. Litvinenko, V. A. Tupysev, Gyroscopy and Navig., **2**, 1 (2011)
7. D. Simon, *Optimal state estimation: Kalman H infinity, and nonlinear approaches* (John Wiley & Sons, 2006)
8. J. Seo, J. G. Lee, C. G. Park, 16th IFAC Symposium on Automatic Control in Aerospace, pp. 14-18 (2004)
9. S. P. Dmitriev, V. M. Zinenko, Y. A. Litvinenko, Gyroscopy and Navig., **3**, 4 (2012)

ANALYSIS OF THE VOLUME COMPARATION OF 3'S (TS, GNSS and TLS)

Khomsin[1,*], *Danar* Guruh Pratomo[1], and *Ira* Mutiara Anjasmara[1], *Faizzuddin* Ahmad[1]

[1]Geomatic Engineering Department, ITS Surabaya, Indonesia

Abstract. Recently, technological developments in the field of surveys and mapping are growing very rapidly such as total station, navigation satellite (Global Navigation Satellite System), drones and laser scanners. One application of this technology is to measure a stockpile area quickly and accurately. This research will measure two stockpiles (coal warehouses) using total station (TS), GNSS and terrestrial laser scanner (TLS). This research will compare the results of volume calculations with the data generated by 3'S (TS, GNSS and TLS). Research is conducted at Coal Yard PT. Barkalin Surabaya in Benowo District, Surabaya, East City with geographically located at 112°39'11" E and 7°07'13" S. The first step is to make 3D model of Laser Scanner data by TLS Faro 3D 120 and to do regristrastion and filltering using Faro Scene. After that the data export to be 3D model from Faro Scene format to Recap 2016 (.rcp) to present and get coordinates. The next step is to compare the coordinates from TLS, TS and GNSS RTK. Finally, the accuracy of volume calculation from TS and GNSS RTK can be compared to TLS. The volume differences between TS and TLS data are -7.31 m^3 (-0.45%) for the 1st location and -6.89 m^3 (-0.24%) for the 2nd location. While the volume differences between GNSS RTK and TLS are -10.34 m^3 (-0.63%) and -9.05 m^3 (-0.31%) for the 1st location and the 2nd location respectively. Generally, the volume differences between TLS, TS and GNSS RTK are not significant. Therefore, 3'S can be used to measure a volume of stockpile.

1 Introduction

Surveying or land surveying is a science that aims to determine the relative positions of points above, on, or beneath the Earth's surface. Surveying has a very important role in measuring and marking boundaries of property ownership since the beginning of civilization [1]. The last few decades its importance has steadily increased with the growing demand for many applications, not only making a map but also other spatially related types of information.

Volume of earthwork is an important matter in many type of engineering project such as to determine the capacities of bins, tanks, reservoirs and buildings, to check stockpile of coal, gravel and other materials, to compute cut and fill landfill and landclearing for road and drainage engineering and construction. There are several methods for estimate the stockpile of coal volumes [1]. In the traditional method the data is obtained from a theodolite or a digital theodolite or a total station (TS).

The survey technique using total station provides horizontal and vertical coordinates, and three-dimensional coordinates (x,y,z). This technique has been widely used for volume determination due to its high accuracy result [2][3]. In this method you need to hold a staff, a prism pole and occupy areas of a large pile of material, this method can be time consuming and dangerous in some cases. To overcome this problem, we can use the reflectorless (without prism) total station. However, the range (distance) is limited and if the field is open pit and during the day, the laser beam is not visible

There are other methods for obtain data to estimate the stockpile volumes with different technologies like GNSS RTK and Lidar (Terrestrial Laser Scanner). GNSS RTK survey technique requires at least two receivers. One was located on the precisely known ground coordinate, as Base Station and another receiver moves between position to be determined, as Rover Station [4]. Moreover, both receivers must receive navigation satellite signals from at least four mutual satellites and be able to connect with radio link or internet to provide a coordinate correction.

Terrestrial Laser scanning called TLS [5] is a new method to obtain geometric data easily and quickly from detail situation such as buildings, trees, roads, objects etc. Each point is determined by the position (x, y, z) and the intensity (i) of the returning signal. Thus this method can also be used to measure coal stockpile volume very fast, very detail and very accurate [6].

This research aims to compare the results of the calculation of the volume of coal raw materials using the 3's (TS, TLS and GNSS RTK) in two different locations. In addition, this research also aims to find out the

* Corresponding author: khomsin95@yahoo.com

https://doi.org/10.1051/e3sconf/20199401014

efficiency of survey time and costs by using 3'S for stockpile volume calculation.

2 Data and Method

2.1. Data

Locating a suitable area for conducting this study is the coal stockpile yard of PT. Barkalin, Benowo, Surabaya, East Java with geographically located at 112°39'11" E and 7°07'13" S

Figure 1. Survey Location

2.2 Instruments

The study used Total Station Topcon GTS 235, TLS Faro Focus 3D 120, and Topcon HiperPro to measure the surface area for volume determination. The instrument specifications are shown in Table 1 to Table 3 respectively.

Table 1. Total Station GTS 235 [7] Specification

Accuracy Horizontal and Vertical Angle	5"
Distance Measurement	3000 m with 1 prism
Distance Accuracy	± (2mm + 2ppm×D)
Measuring Time	0.3 s

Total Station GTS 235 has 5" for horizontal and angle accuracy and ± 2 mm + 2ppmxD for distance accuracy. In addition, the measuring time is 0.3 s.

From Table 2, it can be seen that GNSS RTK Topcon HiPer Pro has 10 mm + 1.0 ppm for horizontal accuracy and 15 mm + 1.0 ppm for vertical accuracy. These accuracies are very enough to conduct volume measurement of coal stockpile.

Table 2. GNSS RTK Topcon HiPer Pro [8] Specification

Static Accuracy of Horizontal	3mm + 0.5 ppm
Static Accuracy of Vertical	5mm + 0.5 ppm
RTK Accuracy of Horizontal	10 mm + 1.0 ppm
RTK Accuracy of Vertical	15 mm + 1.0 ppm

Table 3. TLS Faro 3D 120 [9] Specification

Integrated digital camera	70 megapixel color
Maximum range	120 m
Minimum range	0.6 m
Range accuracy	2mm

Finally, TLS Faro 3D 120 has range between 0.6 m and 120 m and its range accuracy is 2mm. This TLS is enough to conduct measurement coal stockpile in these locations where these areas are less than 1 ha.

2.3 Method

The first procedure of this research is to measure the coal stockpile surface using 3'S (TS, TLS and GNSS RTK). To get x, y and z coordinates of coal stockpile surface, TS measurements used tachymetric method as follow [7]:

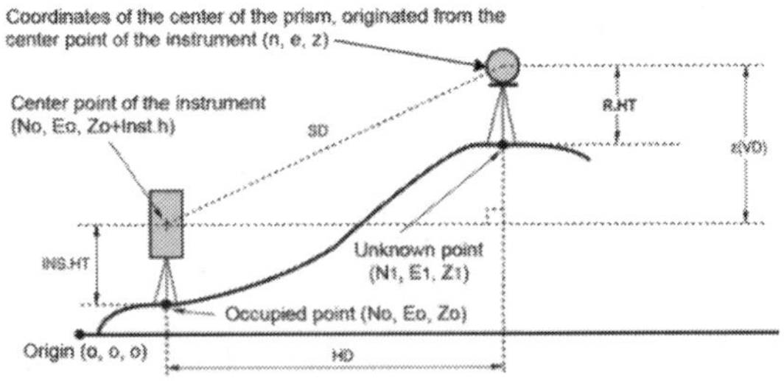

Figure 2. Tachymetric Method [7]

$$N_1 = N_0 + n \quad (1)$$
$$E_1 = E_0 + e \quad (2)$$
$$Z_1 = Z_0 + Ins.HT + z - R.HT \quad (3)$$

where:

N_1 = northing coordinate of object
E_1 = easting coordinate of object

https://doi.org/10.1051/e3sconf/20199401014

Z_1 = elevation of object
N_0 = northing coordinate of origin
E_0 = easting coordinate of origin
Z_0 = elevation of origin
SD = slope distance
VD = vertical Distance
Inst.h = height of instrument
R.HT = height of reflector (prism height)
n = HD sin Az
e = HD cos Az
z = HD tan VA
HD = horizontal distance
Az = azimuth
VA = vertical angle

Basically, TS is an equipment used to measure distance (slope distance) and angle (horizontal and vertical). From slope distance and vertical angle can be used to compute horizontal distance and vertical distance. In addition, horizontal angle and horizontal distance can be used to compute abscissa and ordinate difference (dx,dy). Finally, these data can be processed to get x, y, z coordinates.

Furthermore, at the same time with TS measurements, GNSS RTK measures points that are the same point measured by TS. One receiver as a base station that sends corrections by radio link and another receiver as a rover that measures the surface points of coal stockpile. The principles used in RTK GNSS [10] is as follows:

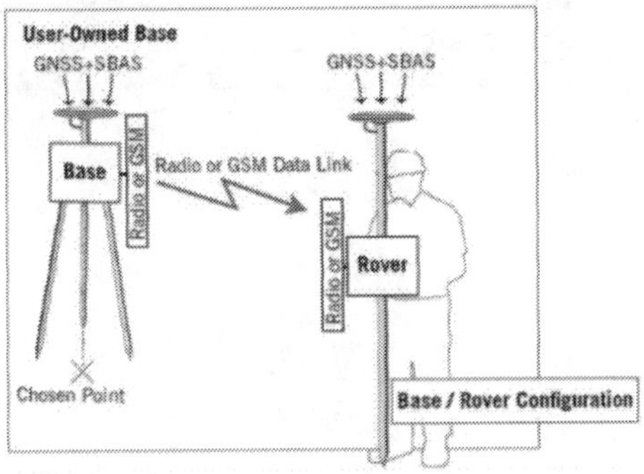

Figure 3. GNSS RTK Principle [10]

GNSS RTK measurement takes 5s - 10s to get fix coordinates. The advantage of GNSS RTK compared to TS and TLS is that there is no need for post processing to obtain x, y, and z coordinates.

The next step is Terrestrial Laser Scanning (TLS) can be defined as the scanning of a surface by the means of Electromagnetic pulses of energy and then creates three dimensional (3D) points of data. Data is achieved by remotely sensing horizontal & vertical angles and reflected distances [11]. This data can then be used to represent the real world in the form of coordinates for the analysis of information and design on a computer display. The TLS principle can be seen Figure 4 as follow:

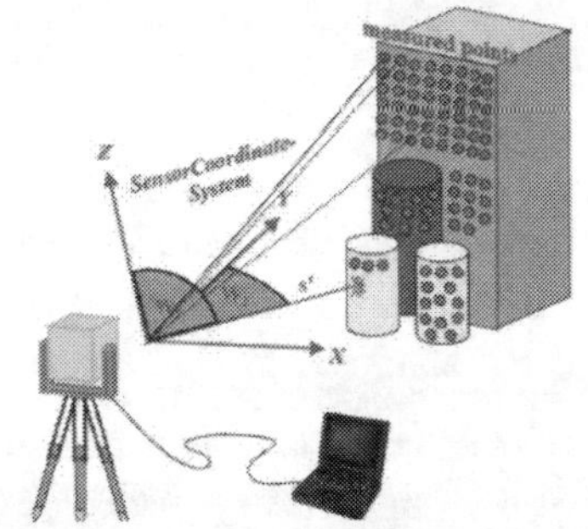

Figure 4. Principle of Terrestrial Laser Scanning [5]

Each TLS measurement will generate thousands of data points in 10 minutes. Therefore TLS measurement will record point cloud at the location. The amount of data points is very dense and massive.

The next step is comparing of some points elevation of TS and GNSS RTK to TLS. Because the TLS data points are very massive and dense, we can assume that the TLS elevations are true value. Furtheremore we can calculate the accuracy of TS and GNSS RTK elevations to TLS elevations by formula as follow [12] :

$$RMS = \sqrt{\frac{1}{n}\sum_{i}^{n}(x_i - a_i)^2} \quad (4)$$

where a_i refers to accepted elevations value from TLS, x_i refers to TS and GNSS RTK elevations and n is number of point elevations.

The results of the 3'S measurement are in the x, y and z coordinates in the same coordinate system. When creating a stockpile object, the user draws the base surface of the stockpile. This base surface is computed by applying a constrained Delaunay Triangulation on its vertices. Volume is calculated from surface 3D models formed from the Triangulated Irregular Network (TIN). TIN forms a prism geometry from two surfaces. These two surfaces are design surface and base surface. Design surface (actual surface) is the surface whose volume is calculated while the base surface (existing surface) is the surface that is used as a base. The calculation of the volume method is visualized in Figure 5 [13] and volume of a prism is determined using the Equation (5).

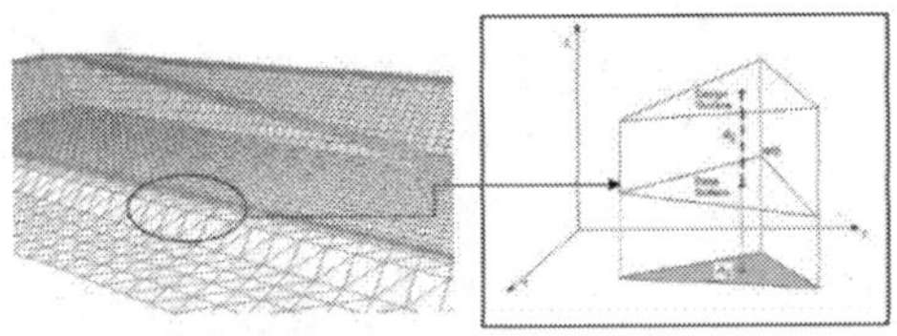

Figure 5. Illustration of TIN and Triangular prism

$$V_i = P\frac{\sum_{i=1}^{3} H_i}{3}. \quad (5)$$

where V is volume, H_i is elevation and P is area of triangle prism.

Then the volume of TS and GNSS RTK is compared with the volume of TLS. Since TLS data is very dense and massive, the TLS volume calculation results are assumed to be the most accurate (true value).

This study will also compare the measurement time of each measuring instrument ie TS, GNSS RTK and TLS. We will observe that which instrument will produce an effective and efficient measurement time in these cases.

3 Result and Discussion

3.1 3D Model

The number of data points for each TS, GNSS RTK and TLS measurement can be seen on Table 4 below.

Table 4. Amount of Points Data 3'S Survey

Equipment	Amount of Points	
	1st Location	2nd Location
TS	253	218
GNSS RTK	253	218
TLS	22,770,961	24,541,952

TS and GNSS RTK have the same points in both of locations 253 and 218 points respectively. TLS has 22 millions points in the 1st location and 24 million points in the 2nd location. However TLS data points must be filtered with the aim of removing spikes and the outside of area. After filtering the amount of TLS data in the first location is 2.2 millions of points andn the 2nd points is 2.8 millions of points.

Each TS, GNSS RTK and TLS points of coordinate data can be presented in 3D models as in the following Figure 5 and Figure 6.

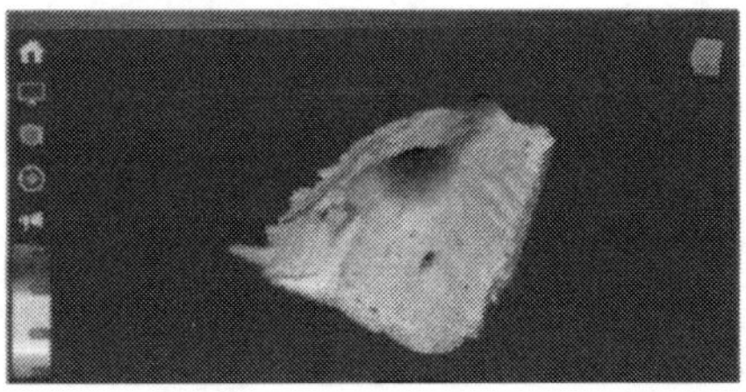

(a)

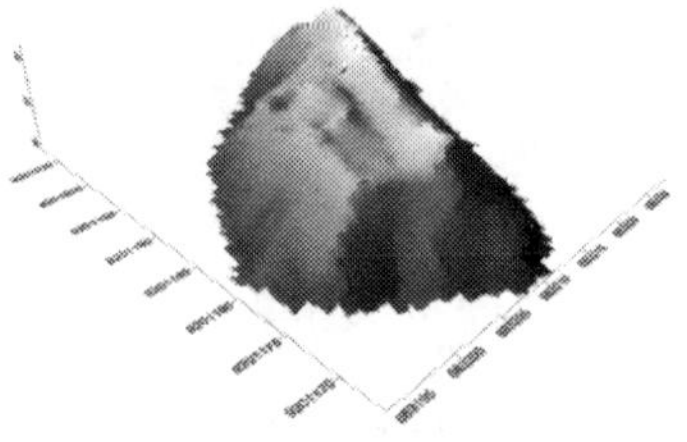

(b)

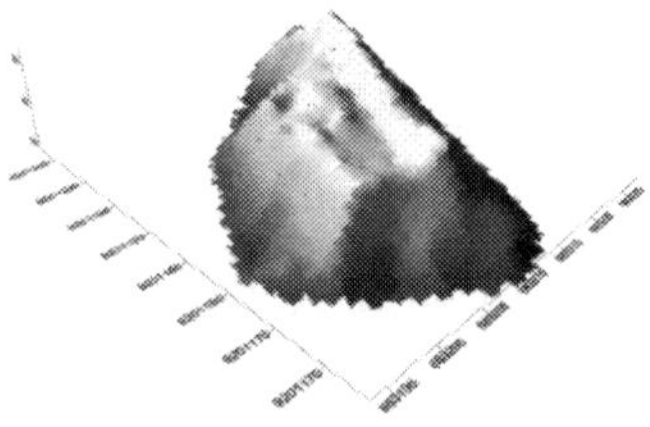

(c)

Figure 5. 3D model TLS (a), TS (b) and GNSS RTK (c) for the 1st location

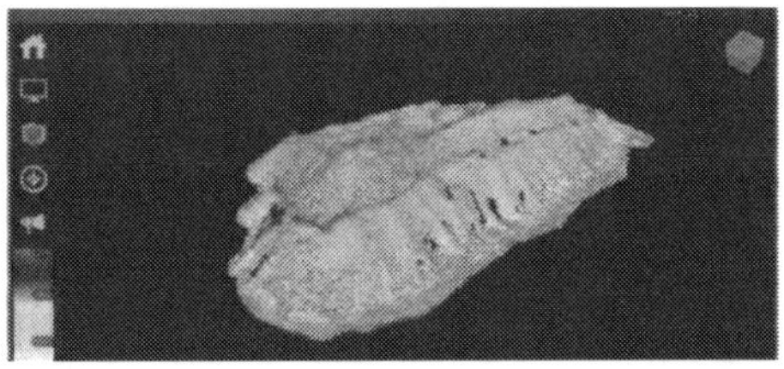

(a)

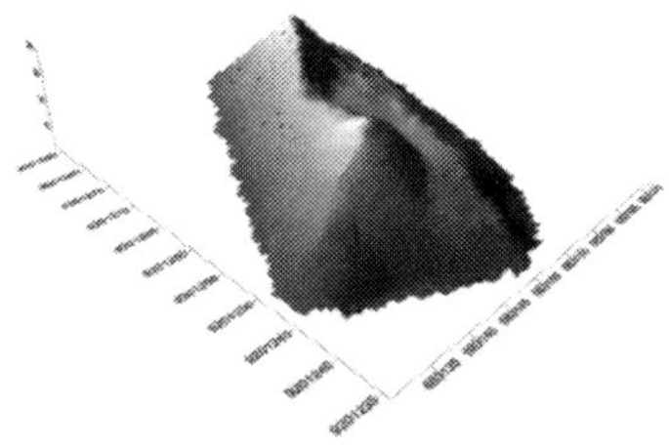

(b)

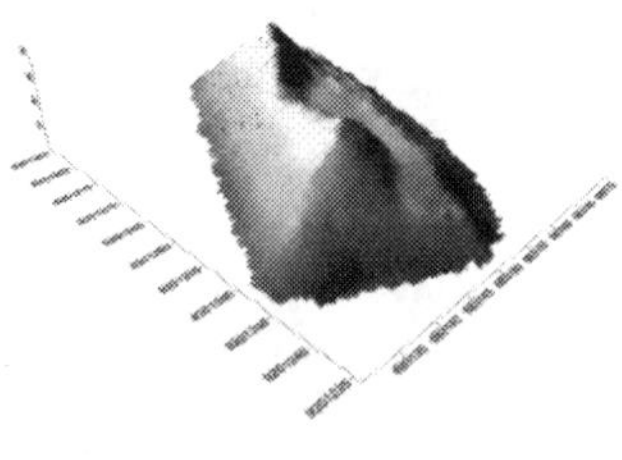

(c)

Figure 6. 3D model TLS (a), TS (b) and GNSS RTK (c) for the 2nd location

Both of locations show that 3D model of TLS are the finenest and TS and GNSS RTK have similar 3D models. These are caused by the amount of data where TLS have millions data compared TS and GNSS have only hundreds of data. Therefore data interpolation in TS and GNSS RTK will produce rough data models.

3.2 Accuracy Elevation

Position measurement using TS, GNSS RTK and TLS in this study was carried out in two places with each location area is 822.04 m^2 and 1289.91 m^2. The conditions of the measured location (coal stockpile) are open space and there are no significant obstacles. Therefore it was easy to conduct measurements with TS, GNSS RTK and TLS.

Figure 7. Condition of the area during the survey

In this case study, we assume that TLS elevations data are the true value, because the amount of data in TLS are millions of points. Thus we can calculate the TS and RTK elavations accuracies to TLS elevations. The accuracy of TS and GNSS RTK elevations to TLS elevations can be seen on Table 5. Based on the Equation 4, the accuracy of TS to TLS elevation is 0.46 and 0.71 cm for GNSS RTK in the 1st location. In addition, the 2nd location, the accuracy of TS elevations is 0.36 cm and GNSS RTK elevation is 0.51 cm. These accuracies ar very small and less than 1 cm. It means that TS, GNSS RTK and TLS data have the same elevation accuracy, therefore their data can be used to compute volume of coal stockpile.

Table 5. RMSE of TS and GNSS RTK point elevations to TLS elevations

Equipment	RMSE	
	1st Location	2nd Location
TS	0.46 cm	0.36 cm
GNSS RTK	0.71 cm	0.51 cm

3.3 Volume Comparation

Coordinate points (x,y,z) of 3'S measurement is computed by composite method to get volume of coal stockpile in both locations. From the calculation of the volume below (Table 6), the difference between volume of TS and TLS is -7.31 m^3 (-0.45%) and GNSS RTK and TLS is -10.34 m^3 (-0.63%) for the 1st location. In the 2nd location, the volume difference of TS and TLS is -6.89 m^3 (-0.24%) and GNSS RTK and TLS is -9.05 m^3 (0.31%). In general, it can be concluded that the difference of TS, GNSS RTK and TLS can be ignored. In other word, the volume calculation of TS, GNSS RTK and TLS has the same results.

Table 6. Volume Computation Results of 3'S elevations

Equipment	Volume (m^3)	
	1st Location	2nd Location
TS	1632.55	2904.74
GNSS RTK	1629.52	2902.58
TLS	1639.86	2911.63

3.4 Time Measurements

In this research, there are two places of coal stockpile to data measurement using TS, GNSS RTK and TLS equipment. Field measurements at the 1st location need time 5.15 hours for TS, 4.20 hours for GNSS RTK and 1.25 hours for TLS. In the 2nd location, the field measurement of TS, GNSS RTK and TLS need time 5.45 hours, 4.50 hours and 1.45 hours respectively. Measurement with TLS is 4.12 times faster than TS and 3.36 times faster than GNSS RTK for the 1st location. For 2nd location, TLS measurement is 3.75 times faster than TS and 3.10 times faster than GNSS RTK.

Table 7. Time of 3'S Measurement

Equipment	Time (hours)	
	1st Location	2nd Location
TS	5.15	5.45
GNSS RTK	4.20	4.50
TLS	1.25	1.45

Although TLS is the fastest measurement, TLS data processing will take a long time compared to TS. GNSS RTK does not need data processing to produce x, y and z coordinates because this method can directly get coordinates within 5s – 10s. TS processing requires a little time to convert distance and angle x, y, and z coordinates.

4 Conclusion

In this research, the measurement method with TS and GNSS RTK to estimate volumes of stockpile were compared with TLS from the same site were taken and the post processing was done with a TIN model. After comparing the results, it was found that there was -7.31 m^3 (-0.45%) difference between the volume calculated with the TS and the TLS volume in the 1st location and -10.34 m^3 (−0,63%) and -6.89 m^3 (-0.24%) and -9.05 m^3 (-0.31%) for the 2nd location. The volume difference between TS, RTK GNSS and TLS are not significant, therefore they have the same accuracy for two locations with 0.8 ha in the 1st location and 1.3 ha in the 2nd location. Additionally, we compare the time taken to get the data for the three methods, in this comparison, it was concluded that the TLS is the fastest measurement with four times faster than TS and three times faster than GNSS RTK.

5 Acknowledgment

We wish to acknowledge PT. Berkalin for the contributions of the locations and PT. Geosolution Pratama Nusantara and Geodesy and Surveying Laboratory, Geomatic Department ITS Surabaya, for the Total Station GTS 235, GNSS RTK HiPer Pro and TLS Faro 3D 120, thus we can complete this research quickly and accurately

References

1. C.D. Ghilani and P.R. Wolf. Elementary Surveying. An introduction to Geomatics. 13th edition. Prentice Hall. 2012
2. B. Keawaram, P. Dumrongchai. Comparisons of Surveying with Terrestrial Laser Scanner and Total Station for Volume Determination of Overburden and Coal Excavations in Large Open-Pit Mine. World Academy of Science, Engineering and Technology International Journal of Geological and Environmental Engineering Vol:11, No:12, 2017
3. L.P. Rahayu. Studi Perbandingan Volume dengan menggunakan Total Station dengan Prisma dan Non Prisma. Tugas Akhir. Institut Teknologi Sepuluh Nopember Surabaya 2014.
4. I.M. Elhassan, Testing RTK GPS Horizontal Positioning Accuracy within an Urban Area., Journal of Engineering and Technology. e-ISSN:2319-9873
5. R. Staiger., Terrestrial Laser Scanning Technology, Systems and Applications, 2nd FIG Regional Conference Marrakech, Morocco, December 2-5, 2003
6. E. Prasetyo. Penggunaan Terrestrial Laser Scanner untuk pengukuran volumetric Stock Opname Batubara. TA. Universitas Gajah Mada. 2016
7. JSIMA. Instruction Manual Electronic Total Station. GTS 230N Series. Topcon Corporation. Japan. 2008
8. Topcon. HiPer Pro Operator Manual. Topcon Positioning System. December, 2004.
9. FARO Focus3D Features, Benefits & Technical Specifications
10. R. Supply. RTK (Real Time Kinematic) Basics for Surveying. Resource Supply, LLC 11607 SW Winter Lake. 2008.
11. J.F. Jones. Comparison of Robotic Total Stations for Scanning of Volumes or Structures. Faculty of Engineering and Surveying. University of Southern Queensland. 29 October 2009.
12. R.E.Deakin, D.G.Kildea,. A Note on Standard Deviation and RMS. The Australian Surveyor Vol. 44 No. 1. June 1999.
13. S. Labant, H. Stankova, R. Weiss., Geodetic Determining of Stockpile Volume of Mineral Excavated in Open Pit Mine. GeoScience Engineering. Volume LIX (2013), No.1. p. 30-40, ISSN 1802-5420

Analyze Angle of the Camera Payload LSU-02 in Mission of Aerial Photo

Sunar[1,*], *Ari Sugeng* Budiyanta[2],*Prasepvianto* Estu Broto[3], *Agus Bayu* Utama[4]

[1,2,3,4]LAPAN, Aeronautics Technology Center, Indonesia

Abstract. In carrying out its mission, LAPAN Surveillance UAV version 2 (LSU-02) was equipped with a camera payload sensor mounted on a gimbal system. When taking upright aerial photos according to photogrammetric requirements, the axis of the aerial camera must be aligned with the direction of gravity with a slope tolerance less than 3 degrees (< 3°), so that the shooting results meet the map to the desired standard. The camera payload was equipped with a 3-axis gimbal system which pitch and roll directions installed by the gyro sensor to measure the camera's tilt angle. Gimbal camera payload with dimensions (160x170x155) mm are designed to be installed on a casing (190x190x180) mm according to the available space in the LSU-02 payload space, which was the length x width x height (190x190x180) mm. Testing was done by flying LSU-02 on Rumpin and Pamengpeuk runway. From the test results, it was obtained the deviation of roll and pitch angle less than 3degree, which the gimbal angle oscillation when the payload camera shooting was only ± 1 degree with the respon time until it reaches a stable condition of approximately 35 to 55 seconds, and the offset value for roll and pitch approximately -1 degree, which it has met the standard for making aerial photo maps according to photogrammetric requirements.

***Keywords**: gimbal, payload, upright aerial photo, pitch angle, roll angle, LSU-02*

1. INTRODUCTION

The aerial mapping technique with photogrammetric approach using UAVs with low cost spatial data collection has been carried out (Muneza J. Maurice, *et al*) [1]. Several aerial photography techniques have been used by using UAV technology and some applications: UAV stabilization techniques during flight by maintenance of a constant speed, maintenance of a straight line of flight and the reduction of tilt (Volodymyr Hlotov *et al*., 2015)[2]; Oblique photogrammetric system by integrating a cheap double-camera imaging system designed to acquire images with ground resolutions better than 3 cm has been conducted by San Jiang *et al*., 2017 [3],[9]; the methodology for the determination of mapping costs is developed and the example of efficiency evaluation is presented which is based on the photogrammetric data gained by UAV technology using an experimental object has been developed by Lina Kukliene *et al*., 2017 [4]; Mingxing Gao and his colleagues have conducted high-resolution UAV data use research with digital elevation models (DEM) to identify the shift of the earth's plates to assess seismic hazards (Mingxing Gao *et al*., 2017) [5]; use of aerial photographs using uav to produce orthophoto maps (D. Wierzbicki *et al*., 2015) [6]; use of multi-rotor uavs with high resolution camera to produce aerial photographs with a spatial resolution of 2 inches / pixels (Wenang Anurogo et al., 2017) [7]; UAVs used for a wide variety of applications in plant ecology, including mapping vegetation over small-to medium-sized regions (Mitchell B. Cruzan et al., 2016) [10].

Aerial photography is a photograph taken from the air using an air camera mounted on an airplane from a certain height. Aerial photography can be divided into: 1). Upright aerial photography (vertical aerial photography), which is an aerial photograph produced from shooting aerial photographs upright, meaning that the execution of shooting with the optical axis of the camera is really upright or almost upright (in this paper slope tolerance < 3 degrees), 2). Slanted aerial photos, which are aerial photographs generated from the result of skewed aerial photography, meaning that it is carried out with the optical axis of an aerial camera that forms an angle with a vertical line. There are two types of oblique aerial photography, namely: 1. Angled shooting, which done with the camera forming a small angle towards the vertical direction, 2. Very oblique shooting, which shooting with a camera that forms a very large angle towards the vertical direction. In other words, tilting when the photo is visible. Aerial photography shall not be undertaken when the angle is less than thirty (30) degrees above the horizon [8]. In general, the photos used for maps are upright photos (Wolf, 1974).

One of the variants of the LAPAN Surveillance UAV (LSU) is LSU-02, which is a type of variant that is the mainstay of the survey mission, aerial photography and mapping. In carrying out its mission, UAV Surveillance LAPAN version 2 (LSU-02) was equipped with a camera sensor mounted on a gimbal system. When taking upright aerial photos according to photogrammetric requirements, the axis of the aerial

*Corresponding author: sunar.st@gmail.com

camera must be aligned with the direction of gravity with a slope tolerance of less than 3 degrees so that the shooting results meet the map to the desired standard. In this paper discusses the use of gimbal systems for mounting the camera sensor at LSU-02 to get a pitch and roll angle deviation of no more than 3 degrees when performing aerial photo operations, so that it meets the photogrammetric requirements for creating aerial photo maps.

2. METHOD

2.1. UAV used

LSU-02 used in this research shown in figure 1, with the gimbal specifications and camera payload shown in Table 1.

Fig. 1. LSU-02

Table 1.LSU-02 specifications and camera payload installed.

Element	Specifications
LSU-02	o Wing span = 2.400 mm (2,4 m) o Length of fuselage = 1.700 mm (1,7 m) o MTOW = 15 kg o Weight of payload = 3 kg o Engine power = 10 Hp (5 ltr gasoline fuel capacity) o Max. cruise speed = 100 km/h o Endurance = 5 jam o Telecomunication: 900 MHz, 1 watt for telemetry,
Gimbal system	DYS 3 axis Alexmos gimbal controller
Payload Camera	Sony Alpha 6000

2.2. Gimbal and Payload System

2.2.1. Gimbal controller

Gimbal controller used DYS 3 Axis Brushless gimbal controller which has the following specifications and features:

Specifications:

- Size: Approx. 52x55mm/ 2.05×2.17"
- Mounting Hole Diameter: 3mm/ 0.12"
- Power Supply Voltage: 8–25 V
- Maximum Motor Current: 1.5 A
- 5V Output Current to Power External Devices: Up to 1 A

Features:

- Upgradeable 32Bit BGC V3.0, with a protection case
- 32bit MCU–ARM Cortex M4. Effectively calculates the complex tasks for 3-axes stabilization
- Allows camera control with the RC or analog joystick
- Use several switchable profiles for different modes of operation
- Supports variety of RC protocols: PWM, Sum-PPM, spektrum and s-bus
- Battery voltage monitoring, compensating voltage drop in the PID-regulator
- Low battery alarm (output to 5V active buzzer)
- Increased number of inputs for controlling signals + 3 additional reserved input/output AUX1-AUX3
- Can supply up to 1A current for external devices on the 5V power line
- Reverse-polarity protection, overheat and overcurrent protection
- USB interface for the PC connection, to configure, control and upgrade firmware
- Control through the Serial-protocol using dedicated API
- Optional second IMU, that will increase the short-term precision of the stabilization 10x-30x times and will make stable work in any frame position

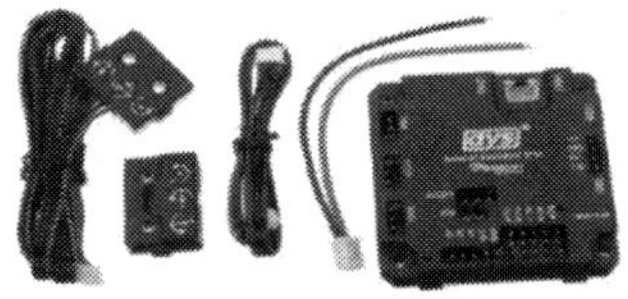

Fig. 2. DYS 3 Axis Brushless Gimbal Controller

This gimbal controller has a feature to control the 3-axis, but in this study it was only used to control the direction of the 2 axis, the direction of pitch and roll, so that the yaw axis of the gimbal was removed, and the direction of the yaw gimbal follows the direction of the yaw plane.

2.2.2. Gimbal Mounting and Actuators

Gimbal mounting and actuators used DYS BLG3SN 3-Axis Brushless Gimbal with 3pcs BGM4108-130 Brushless Motors for Sony NEX.

Fig. 3. DYS BLG3SN 3-Axis Brushless Gimbal with 3pcs BGM4108-130 Brushless Motors

Specifications:

- Material: Aluminum alloy & carbon fiber on the top.
- Camera: Support Sony NEX / Lumix GH or equivalent weight and size (Alpha 6000)
- Gimbal Weight: 328g(not included motors)
- Gimbal Motor: BGM4108-130 x3
- Wire Weight: 150g
- Ω Ri :17.0ohm

- Motor Weight: 93g

2.2.3. Integration Gimbal System in LSU-02

Gimbal controller, gimbal mounting along with a brushless motor, and the camera sensor was placed on the casing as the mounting, then it placed into the casing placement chamber in the fuselage so that it was integrated in the LSU-02 aircraft as shown in figure 4.

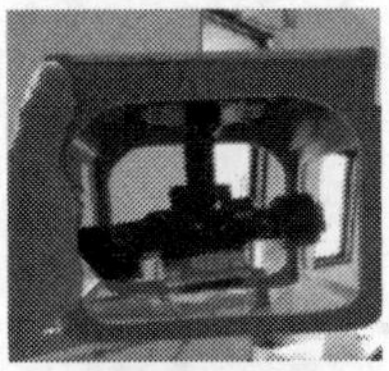

4(a) : Casing, Gimbal and camera

4(b) : Gimbal casing placement space in fuselage

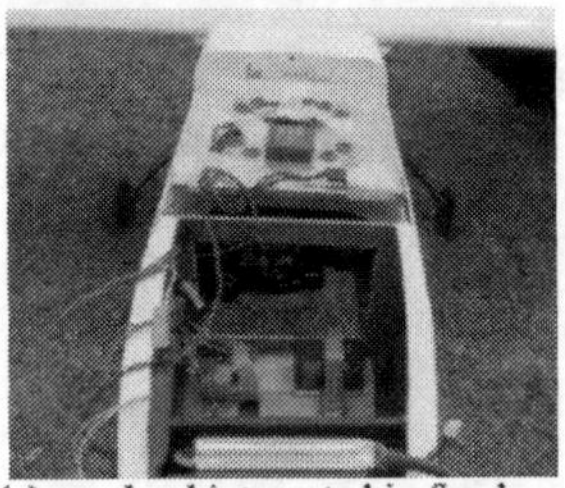

(c): payload integrated in fuselage

Fig. 4. Integration of camera payload system into fuselage LSU-02

2.3 Data Processing

To plan the flyway using mission planner software [11]. Data processing was done by according steps;first, storing data pitch and roll of camera angle behavior during flight operation (in logfile in memory), second, downloading data into *.xls files, then plotting in graphical be interpreted until conclusions were obtained.

3.RESULTS AND DISCUSSION

The LSU-02 aircraft was flown 500 m altitude from the ground surface with a programmed waypoint trajectory with an average cruising distance of 1.5 km per track for testing on the Rumpin runway as shown in figure 5 and tested with an average cruising distance 10 km trajectory for each track for testing on the Pamengpeuk runway as shown in figure 9. Analysis was done when the cruising flight position, because at this position the best shooting results were produced and in accordance with the conditions of taking aerial photography data carried out by the aircraft while carrying out aerial photo missions.

3.1Test Results on Rumpin Runway

Tests on the Rumpin runway, carried out 2 times the flight. From the results of the logfile data and plotting into the graph, the pitch and roll angle data are obtained. The first test results of gimbal payload can be seen in Figure 6.

Fig. 5. Flyway test of payload gimbal on Rumpin runway

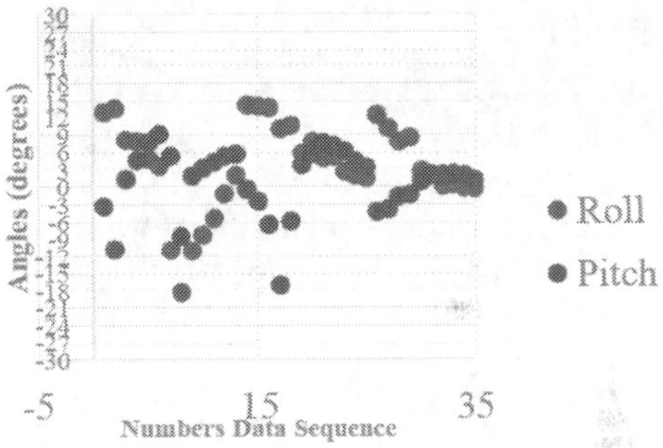

Fig. 6. Angles position of the Roll and Pitch of the payload gimbal when flown

It can be seen from figure 6 that the roll and pitch deviation was still large, which can be up to ± 12 degrees. Itwas because the engine vibration and installation of the center of gravity (CG) camera affect the stability of the camera angle. Therefore, before being flown back, it was necessary to test the effect of engine vibration on the performance of gimbal. The LSU-02 engine was turned on and then the angle of the camera gimbal deviation was measured at various engine speeds. Engine speed was monitored on the remote controller's Pulse Width Modulation (PWM) scale. The engine speed was increased from PWM values 1000 to 1400. It seen that the measurement of gimbal angle rises up to a maximum of 1150 PWM and decreases at equal and more than 1300 PWM as can be seen in Figure 7 (a), (b), (c), (d). From the graph, it can be seen that pitch stability (blue line) was better than roll (red line). This was presumably because CG roll was less good than CG pitch. For this reason, changes in the mounting arm of the gimbal was made so that the CG roll can be adjusted better. After CG roll was repaired the second flight test was carried out.

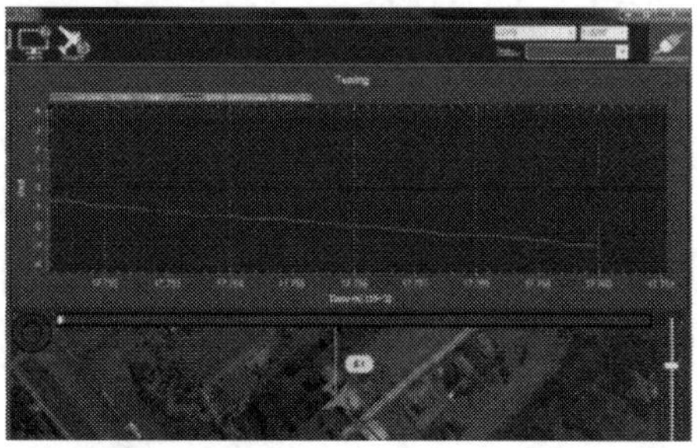

(a) the range of PWM values increased from 1000 to 1150

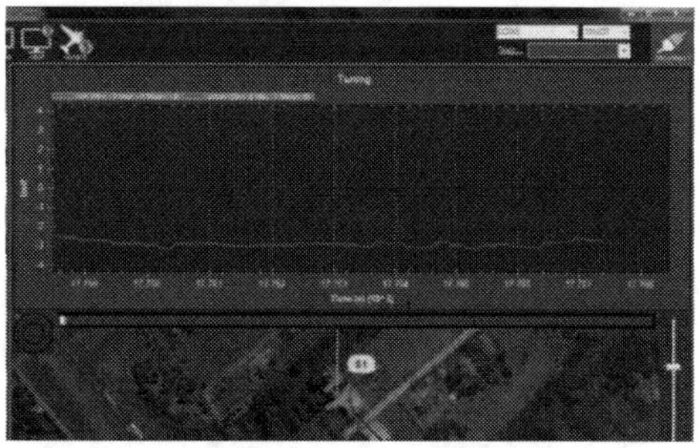

(b) the PWM engine value remains at 1150

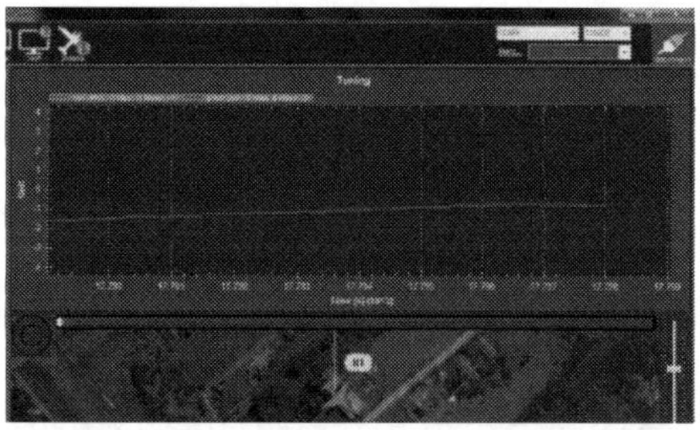

(c) the range of PWM values is increased from 1150 to 1300

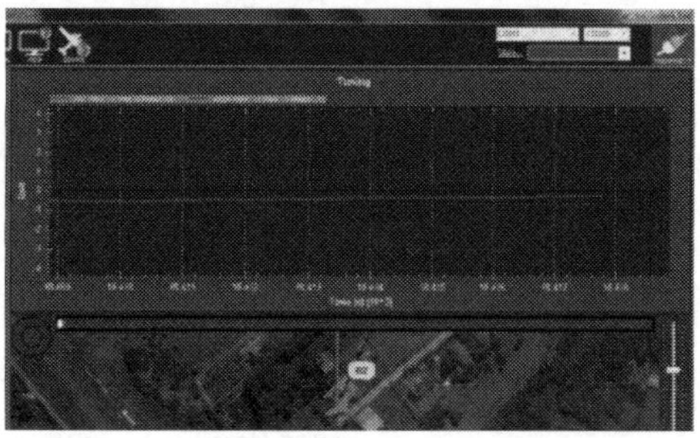

(d) the PWM engine value remains at 1300

Fig.7. Effect of the PWM engine value due to camera gimbal stability

The second test, the plane was flown at an altitude of 500 m from the ground surface with the same trajectory as the first test. The second test results can be seen in Figure 8. It can be seen from Figure 8 that the roll and pitch deviation is still relatively large, which can be up to ± 12 degrees when the initial data sequence, but when the data sequence is more than 30 the roll and pitch deviation is less than ± 3 degrees.

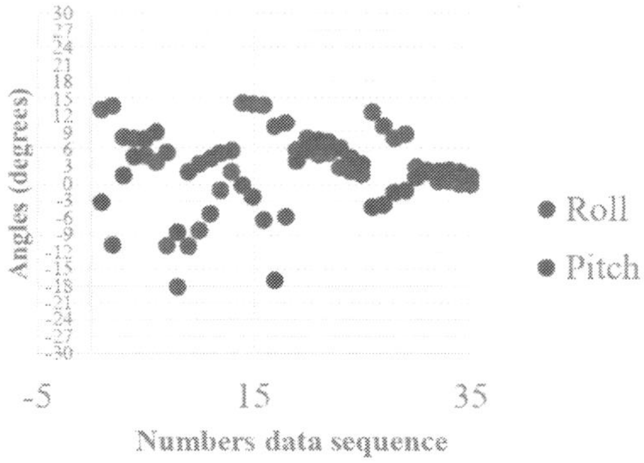

Fig. 8. Angle position of Roll and Pitch of Gimbal

3.2. Test Results on Pemengpeuk Runway, Garut

Before flying test, the flight path was programmed as shown in figure 9. The test was carried out 3 times. The test results were expected to show the performance of the gimbal in adjusting so that the camera was always facing down with an angle less than 3 degrees.

Fig. 9. Flyway testing gimbal-payload LSU-02 in Pamengpeuk

Payload gimbal test on the first day used 2 axis gimbal for roll and pitch directions, so it was expected that aircraft movements in these two directions can be controlled by gimbal to always face down. The test results could be seen in figure 10. When the Yaw angle of the plane showed a constant value, the value of Roll and Pitch of gimbal showed stability in 10 to 15 camera data retrieval. Data is taken every 100 meters, with an average aircraft speed of 100 km / hour. Camera gimbal reaction to a stable condition of approximately 35 to 55 seconds. While the Roll and Pitch angle oscillations range from ± 1.5 to 2 degrees and the offset of each Roll and Pitch angle was 6.5 and 3 degrees. To overcome the rsults above, then the test will be carried out on one axis gimbal, namely the gimbal that moves on the roll direction only. The results of camera recording on gimbal concluded that the gimbal vibration still looked quite large.

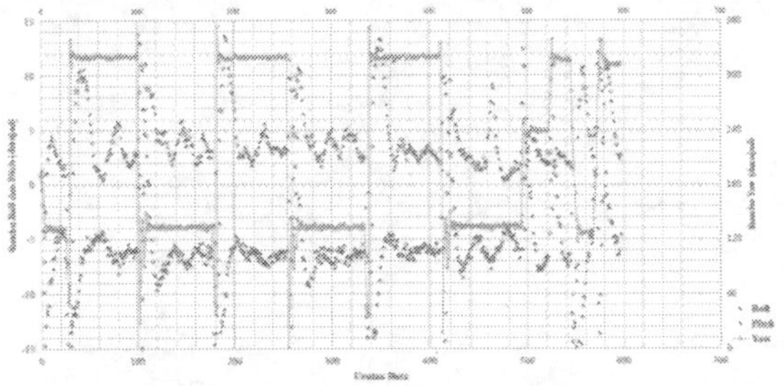

Fig. 10. Results of the first flying gimbal test

The second day test used the same trajectory but used gimbal with one axis in roll direction, while the pitch axis is turned off, so that the payload gimbal pitch axis was the same as the plane's pitch axis. This was done because from the test data the motion of the plane in the direction of the pitch axis showed good results. Figure 11 showed a graph of aircraft movements during cruising. The roll and pitch values each oscillate with a maximum amplitude of 12 and 7 degrees. From the test results, one axis gimbal vibration observed using a relative camera shows a decrease in vibration. Data on camera roll and pitch position when cruising recorded by pixhawk when taking pictures shows oscillations around ± 1 degree, see figure 12. It showed good enough results because the requirement of photogrammetric mapping was ± 3 degrees. However, the graph still shows an offset of data of approximately 4 degrees on the roll and 2 degrees on the pitch. While when taking photo data on the first day, when LSU-02 before take off, the plane observed at the level position was 0.49 degrees in the direction of roll, -0.39 degrees in the direction of pitch. So that it can be concluded when the cruise shifts or offset the gimbal direction of several degrees. To overcome this, an attempt was made to check and improve so that the camera's payload mounts on the gimbal precisely at the center of gravity (CG) position of the aircraft.

In addition to monitoring the gimbal payload angle position, monitoring of the angle behavior of the LSU-02 aircraft when cruising was shown in Figure 11.

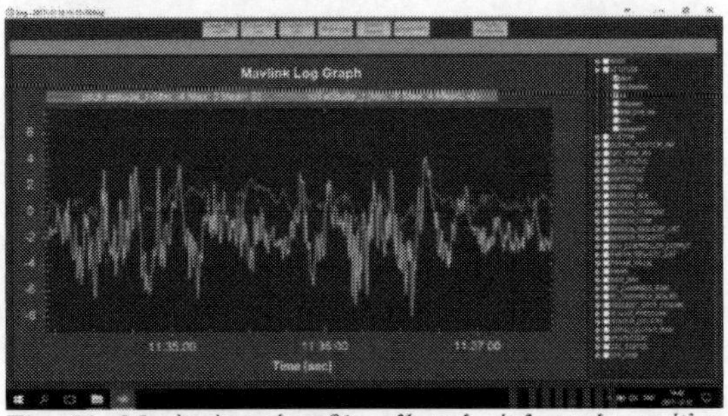

Fig. 11. Monitoring aircraft's roll and pitch angle position during the second flight cruising

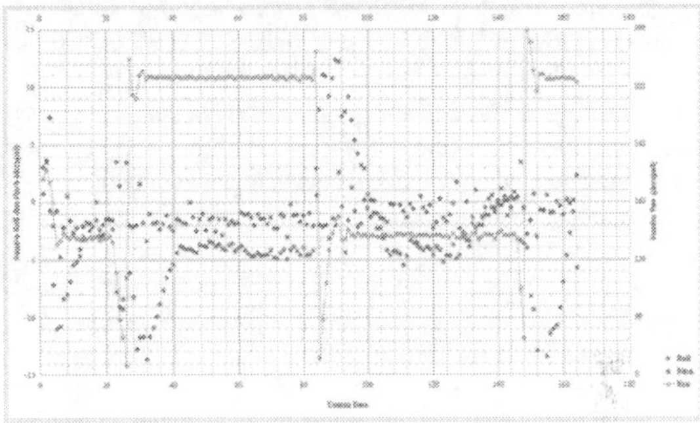

Fig. 12. Results of the second flying payload gimbal test

The results of the third day's test was shown in figure 13. From the graph it can be seen that the position of the camera when shooting has shown a smaller offset value than the results of the second previous test. The offset value for roll and pitch was approximately -1 degree. While the initial value for roll and pitch when each level was 0.12 and 0.00 degrees. For the gimbal oscillation value when shooting was only ± 1 degree. However, the position adjustment of the gimbal in the direction of the roll still looks slow until the condition reached stable, approximately 35 to 55 seconds (there was a time delay response).

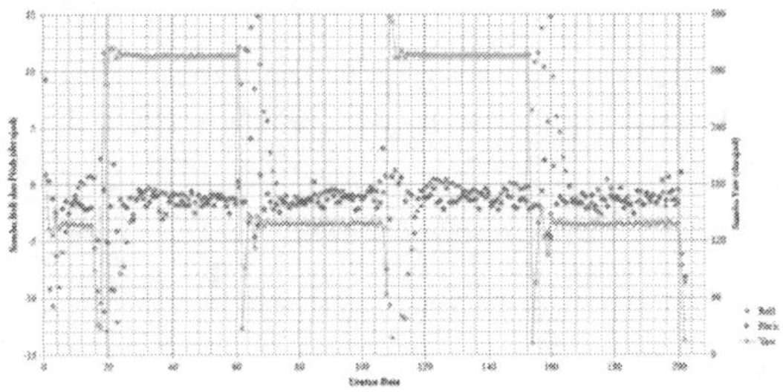

Fig. 13. Results of the third day payload gimbal test

4. CONCLUSION

Analysis of camera payload gimbal stability has been carried out at LSU-02 when in Mission of Aerial Photo Operation by analyzing camera angular deviation to gravitational upright lines. Tests were carried out in 2 places, first on the Rumpin runway and second on the

Pamengpeuk runway. The aircraft was flown at an altitude of 500 m with a flying route following the programmed waypoint, which is a horizontal route length of 1.5 km per track in Rumpin, while the length of the track is 10 km per track in Pamengpeuk. Tests at Rumpin were carried out in 2 flights, the result of the first flight the roll and pitch angle deviation was still large, which could be up to ± 12 degrees due to engine vibration and the improper installation of center of gravity (CG) cameras, while the second test results after adjusting the PWM engine deviation value roll and pitch anglewere smaller than ± 3 degree range. To get more valid results, testing was done in Pamengpeuk. Testing in Pamengpeuk is carried out with 3 flights; The results of the first flight of Roll and Pitch angle oscillations ranged from ± 1.5 to 2 degrees, offset by Roll and Pitch angles of 6.5 degrees and 3 degrees respectively. To overcome the above, then the test will be carried out on one axis gimbal, namely the gimbal that moves on the roll direction only. The second flight was carried out with a one-axis roll gimbal, where the pitch axisof the payload gimbal was same as the plane's pitch axis. The result of the second flight was the camera's roll and pitch angle oscillation when taking a picture of about ± 1 degree, however the data offset was still about 4 degrees on the roll and 2 degrees on the pitch. To overcome the offset, an attempt was made to check and fix the mounting of the camera's payload gimbal so that it was right in the center of gravity (CG) position of the aircraft, then the third flight test continued. The result of the third flight of gimbal angle oscillation when shooting was only ± 1 degree, with response time until it reaches a stable condition of approximately 35 to 55 seconds, and the offset value for roll and pitch was approximately -1 degrees. It can be concluded that the stability of the payload gimbal camera of LSU-02 when performing aerial photo missions can meet the photogrammetry requirement.

5. ACKOWLEDGMENT

I would like to thank you to Head of the Aeronautical Technology Center and the dissemination team who provided the opportunity in the LSU-02 payload research. Thanks alot of also for the INSINAS Ristekdikti 2018 fiscal year program which has provided financial support in this study.

References

1. Muneza J. Maurice, Mila N. Koeva, Markus Gerke , Francesco Nex ,Caroline Gevaert, A photogrammetric approach for map updating using UAV in Rwanda, GeoTechRwanda 2015 – Kigali (2015)

2. Volodymyr Hlotov, Zbigniew Siejka, Vadym Kolesnichenko, Oleksandr Prokhorchuk, Anatoliy Tserklevych, Lyubov Babiy, The Analysis of The Results of Aerial Photography Experiments on The Basis of a Developed UAV Model, Nr IV/3/2015, POLSKA AKADEMIA NAUK, Oddział w Krakowie, s. 1329–1350, Komisja Technicznej Infrastruktury Wsi (2015).

3. San Jiang, Wanshou Jiang, Wei Huang and Liang Yang, UAV-Based Oblique Photogrammetry for Outdoor Data Acquisition and Offsite Visual Inspection of Transmission Line, Remote Sens., **9**, 278 (2017)

4. Lina Kukliene, Dainora Jankauskiene, Indrius Kuklys, Birutė Ruzgiene, Requirements for Aerial Mapping Using UAV-photogrammetry Technology: Baltic Sea Coast Measurement, International Scientific Conference "RESEARCH FOR ENVIRONMENT AND CIVIL ENGINEERING DEVELOPMENT 17" Proceedings "CIVIL ENGINEERING`17" (2017).

5. Mingxing Gao, Xiwei Xu, Yann Klinger, Jerome van der Woerd & Paul Tapponnier, High-resolution mapping based on an Unmanned Aerial Vehicle (UAV) to capture paleoseismic offsets along the Altyn-Tagh fault, China, Scientific Reports, www.nature.com/scientificreports (2017)

6. D. Wierzbicki, M. Kedzierski, A. Fryskowska, Assesment of the Influence of UAV Image Quality on the Orthophoto Production, The International Archives of the Photogrammetry, Remote Sensing and Spatial Information Sciences, Volume **XL-1/W4**, 2015

7. Wenang Anurogo *et al.*, A Simple Aerial Photogrammetric Mapping System Overview and Image Acquisition Using Unmanned Aerial Vehicles (UAVs), Journal of Applied Geospatial Information, **Vol 1 No 1**, 2017

8. Department of Transportation The State of New Jersey, Minimum Guidelines for Aerial Photogrammetric Mapping, **p. 1-1**

9. I. Aicardi, F. Chiabrando, N. Grasso, A.M. Lingua, F. Noardo, A. Spano, UAV Photogrammetry with Oblique Images: First Analysis on Data Acquisition and Processing, The International Archives of the Photogrammetry, Remote Sensing and Spatial Information Sciences, **Volume XLI-B1**, Prague, Czech Republic, 2016

10. Mitchell B. Cruzan, Ben G. Weinstein, Monica R. Grasty, Brendan F. Kohrn, Elizabeth C. Hendrickson, Tina M. Arredondo, and Pamela G. Thompson, Small unmanned aerial vehicles (micro-

https://doi.org/10.1051/e3sconf/20199401015

UAVs, drones) in plant ecology, Applications in Plan Sciences, http://www.bioone.org/loi/apps , Botanical Society of America, 2016

11. ___, Mission Planner Home, http://ardupilot.org/planner/ (accessed Oktober 2018)

GNSS RTK Application to Determine Coastline Case Study at Northen Area of Sulawesi and Gorontalo

Wahyudi Nugraha[1], *Andri Daniel* Parapat[2], *Dewi Sekar* Arum[3], and *Fatichatus* Istighfarini[4]

[1,2,3,4] Geospatial Information Agency, 16911 Cibinong West Java, Indonesia

Abstract. Article 12 of Indonesia Government Regulation No.4-year 2011 about Geospatial Information [5], coastline is an element of base map. Article 13 subsection 1 states that the boundary form between the land and the ocean were affected by the tides. In subsection 2, coastline is divided into three types, namely lowest, highest, and mean sea level tides. Studies about coastline is important to support many maritime activities such as to determine administrative area (such as province, etc.), determine the length of coastline, coastal and marine management, also inland and marine spatial planning. Due to the importance of coastline, data with good accuracy is needed. Coastline mapping technology has developed rapidly. Previous method of coastline mapping is to trace marine debris carried by wave to the coast. At present time, because of needs of coastline data with higher accuracy and in the bigger scales, the GNSS RTK technology is starting to be used. GNSS technology generated coordinates and elevation and use tides values as reference datum. After the above, Digital Elevation Model generated from those points are combined with bathymetry and land elevation data resulting three types of coastline in accordance with the Indonesia Government Regulation about Geospatial Information Article 13 Subsection 2.

1 Introduction

As a maritime nation, coastline determination in Indonesia is necessary to support many maritime activities such as to determine administrative area (such as province, etc.), determine the length of coastline, coastal and marine management, also inland and marine spatial planning.

Previously, coastline mapping is to trace marine debris carried by wave to the coast, using GPS handheld. As states on Indonesia Government Regulation No.4-year 2011 about Geospatial Information [5], article 12 states that coastline is one of the elements of base map. Article 13 subsection 1 states that the boundary form between the land and the ocean were affected by the tides. In subsection 2, coastline is divided into three types, namely lowest, highest, and mean sea level coastline. After the regulation has been legalized, the GNSS handheld is no longer relevant to be used because the three types of coastline cannot be generated.

Coastline determination has been described in many studies with different methods. Khomsin [6] used rectified SPOT 7 Imagery to determine coastline in high water level by interpreting the visual appearance of objects natural color composite as the firm boundaries between sea and land. in term of the advantage of using the GNSS technology, Gonclaves [3] described that GNSS-based method offers a quicker, all-weather, highly accurate and continuously updatable shoreline positional time series relevant for monitoring and management task. Mendonça [8] used kinematic GNSS for shoreline monitoring as it has advantages of being able to produce consistent data for temporal analysis. the result shows that for temporal analysis of five years, the shoreline constantly changes in different periods.

We organize the study as follows: section 2 explains about method used in the study, area, and data collection. Section 3 explains about the results from the study and analysis. The study is concluded in section 4.

2 Method

Data needed in the study are:

- Tidal measurement data,
- Bathymetry data,
- Benchmark (BM) measurement data,
- Levelling measurement from BM to tide station,
- Coastline data tracking using GNSS RTK.

Flowchart of the study can be seen on **Fig. 1.**

* Corresponding author: wahyudi.nugraha@big.go.id

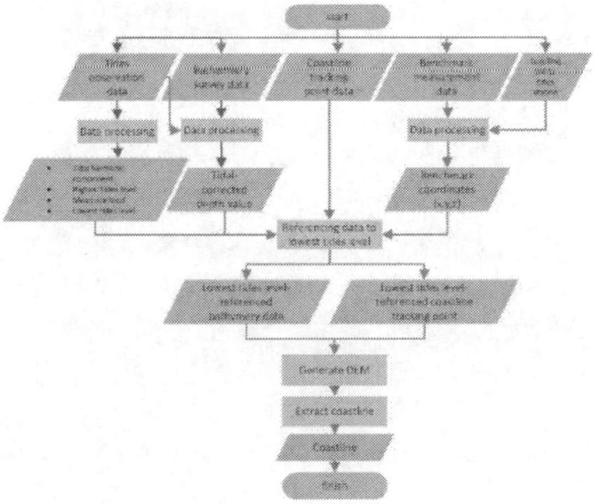

Fig. 1. Flowchart of the Study

2.1. Study Area

The study area for this paper is located in the Northern area of Sulawesi Island, that included to North Sulawesi and Gorontalo Province of Indonesia, see **Fig. 2.** Area of study is along the coastline of the study area with approximately 750 kilometres in length. Data acquisition for this study retrieved in 2017.

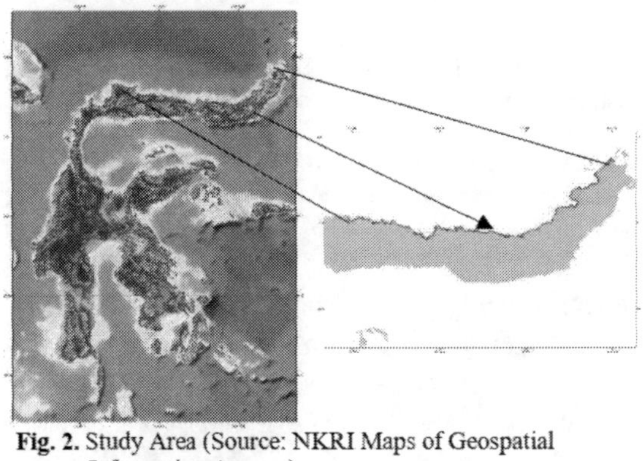

Fig. 2. Study Area (Source: NKRI Maps of Geospatial Information Agency)

2.2. Data Collection

Data collection for this study contains several activities. Those are tidal observation, levelling from BM to tide station, bathymetry survey, and coastline tracking. **Fig.3** represented the process to determine coastline using GNSS RTK.

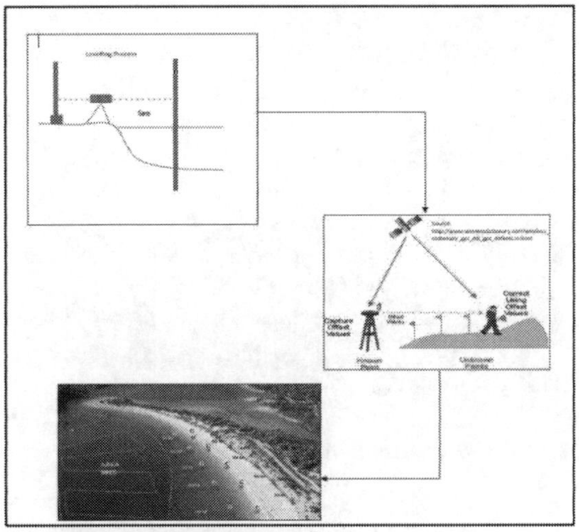

Fig. 3. Schema to determine coastline

2.2.1. Tides and Levelling

Tidal observation needs to be done at least 30 days of observation. This observation can be done using AWLR (Automatic Water Level Recorder) with an observation interval every 5 minutes. The observation can be assisted with manual tide observation, which has observation interval every hour. Along with this observation, levelling process needs to be done to determine the value of highest, lowest, and mean sea level according to BM. For tracking measurement using RTK, the final result of tides values is used as a reference. In the survey area, 19 tides station are built to find out the characteristics of tides. Because of the device and environmental factor, the data which can be used only from 15 tides stations. The tides station installation will be depending on the characteristics of the area, therefore there are some terms and conditions refers to the national standard of Indonesia about tides station installation (SNI 7924:2013). Those are: must not be placed in estuary, must be placed in stable position which is not affected by direct wave but still have a direct access to the sea in both conditions (high and low), can be accessed in every weather and conditions, the depth value around that area is homogeny. The area of this study is using two types of tides station, port and temporary tide building, see **Fig. 4**.

 https://doi.org/10.1051/e3sconf/20199401016

Fig. 4. Installation tide stations.

2.2.2. Bathymetry Data

Depth values of survey area generated from bathymetry survey using single beam echosounder. Bathymetry survey focused on shallow area, which depth is 5 metres or less. The survey was done near to the coast, as near as it can be, and also on the high tide during the survey time.

The collected depth values were later referenced to defined datum, which in this study, lowest tide is used. This data is used as a complement for tracking data inshore to intertidal zone. Bathymetry data acquisition will start after lowest tide zone. Both of the data will be combined to form elevation profile for coastal area up to shallow area. See **Fig 5**.

Fig. 5 Acquisition bathymetry data

2.2.3. GNSS RTK Tracking Data

For coastline tracking data acquisition using differential method of radio RTK. Every point must be bounded to Benchmark which already attached to tides station. Illustration of data tracking acquisition can be seen in **Fig 6.**

Fig. 6 Illustration RTK tracking

Figure explanation:

Point a = This point located in land that can be indicated it never affected by highest water level and can be noted by vegetation

Point b = This point can be indicated as mean sea level. This point marked by the wet condition of sand beach and have a contrast color with sand area in land.

Point c = This point is intersection between land and waters sea level at that time.

Point d = This point is considered to have lowest tide elevation

If in the field there are areas cannot be surveyed and reached because of natural conditions in that area, such as cliff or dense mangrove forest, secondary data like satellite imagery can be used. Tracking documentation can be seen in **Fig 7**. Three until four months were the time needed to measure all RTK point along North Sulawesi and Gorontalo Province.

Fig. 7 Documentation tracking RTK

https://doi.org/10.1051/e3sconf/20199401016

3 Results and Analysis

3.1. Tidal Data Processing

Table 1 Result of tidal processing

	PS_01	PS_03	PS_04	PS_06	PS_07	PS_09	PS_10	PS_11	PS_12	PS_13	PS_14	PS_15	PS_16	PS_17	PS_19
MSL	1,60	1,71	1,58	1,83	1,91	2,06	1,71	2,05	3,09	2,21	1,77	1,69	1,68	1,32	1,61
Lowest	0,43	0,51	0,43	0,65	0,72	0,82	0,43	0,80	1,86	0,94	0,49	0,38	0,42	0,11	0,43
Highest	3,02	3,08	3,05	3,25	3,28	3,40	3,09	3,37	4,39	3,46	3,23	3,07	3,04	2,62	2,88
Z0	1,17	1,20	1,15	1,19	1,19	1,25	1,28	1,25	1,23	1,28	1,27	1,30	1,27	1,22	1,18
Range	2,58	2,58	2,62	2,60	2,56	2,59	2,66	2,58	2,53	2,52	2,74	2,69	2,62	2,51	2,45

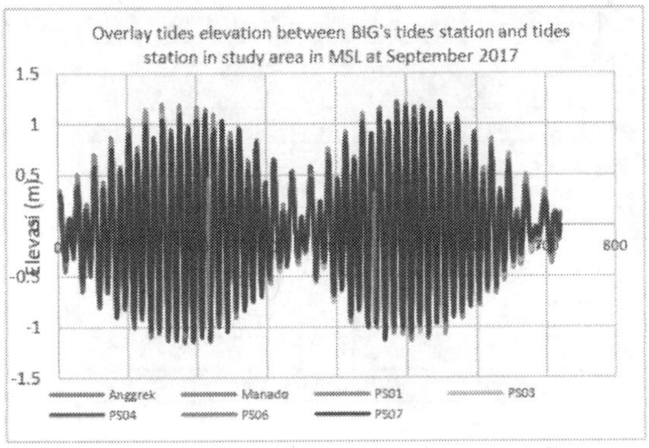

Fig. 8 Graphic comparison tide data between BIG station with several tidal processing.

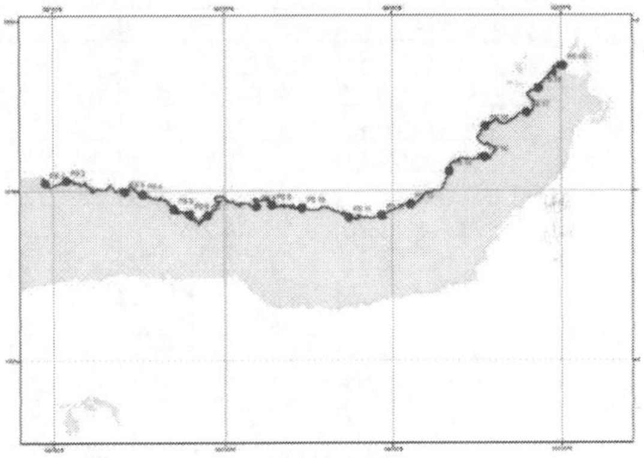

Fig. 9 Tides station location at survey area

Tidal data processing has a purpose to get the value of highest, lowest, and mean sea level elevation. Tidal data processed by least square method with the help of UTide MATLAB program [2]. UTide processed tidal data to produce tidal harmonic constituents. Tidal harmonic constituents are needed to generate tidal prediction data in one year after time of tides measurement. Value of highest, lowest, and mean sea level elevation are derived from this tidal prediction data. The results of tidal processing data in 15 from 19 tides station at survey area can be seen in **Table.1** The value of highest, lowest, and mean sea level elevation still referenced to each local tides station, and location tides station can be seen in **Fig.9.**

We also processed tides data from BIG tides station in Anggrek and Manado to compare with several tidal processing data results from tides station survey area. The results can be seen in **Fig.8** We chose one value of highest, lowest, and mean sea level elevation from 15 results of tidal processed data as a reference to generate coastline vector from DEM interpolation. We did this because the coastline vector elevation must be in one value and seamless line. Lowest sea level elevation from tide station was chosen as a reference elevation for all data.

3.2. Bathymetry and RTK Tracking Data Processing

First, bathymetric data that obtained from bathymetric survey using Singlebeam Echosounder needs to be cleaned from spike or outlier data. Then, cleaned data needs barcheck correction and tidal correction to get final bathymetric data with good accuracy. To make sure that the data has a good accuracy is to compare bathymetric data from main sounding survey line and cross sounding survey line. In this research, we use Orde 1b IHO SP 44 standard [4] to check the data. The result is we got 95,02% confidence level that indicated the data are good. The last step is to reference bathymetric data to lowest sea level.

GNSS RTK tracking data consists of horizontal coordinates and height value that referenced to benchmark point. GNSS RTK tracking data precision level is under 1 meter in order to fulfil level of accuracy in large-scale mapping. GNSS RTK tracking data processing only reference height value of RTK tracking data to lowest sea level. The method is reference height value of benchmark point to lowest sea level using height difference from benchmark point to tidal station.

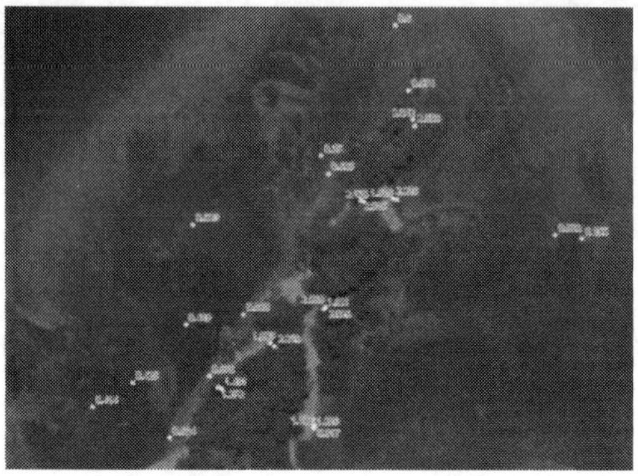

Fig. 10 Sample of referenced RTK Tracking Data

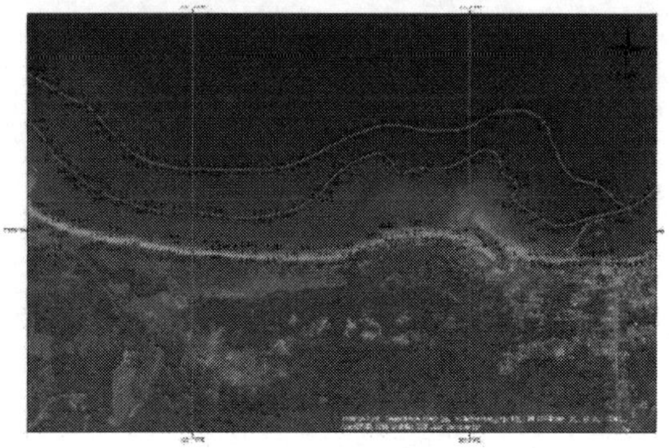

Fig. 11 Sample of referenced Bathymetric data

Table 2 Check confidence level bathymetry data

ID_CROSS	DATE	TIME	X	Y	Z	FORMULA	DEVIATION	ANNOTATION
4	12/06/2017	15:21:21	558399.3	98179.81	6.005556	0.5060586	0.222	ENTER TOLERANCE
4	11/03/2017	10:38:13	558400.1	98180.05	5.783556	X	X	X
5	12/06/2017	15:12:11	559488.7	98179.63	4.860556	0.5039768	0.142	ENTER TOLERANCE
5	11/03/2017	10:31:12	559487.5	98180.48	4.718556	X	X	X
9	12/06/2017	15:23:56	558105.3	98204.75	6.388556	0.5068506	0.222	ENTER TOLERANCE
9	11/03/2017	10:40:07	558106.6	98205.41	6.166556	X	X	X
10	12/06/2017	15:24:25	558043.8	98211.84	6.469556	0.5070242	0.319	ENTER TOLERANCE
10	11/03/2017	10:40:32	558042.6	98212.81	6.150556	X	X	X
13	12/06/2017	15:26:55	557776	98240.48	6.820556	0.507801	0.357	ENTER TOLERANCE
13	11/03/2017	10:42:15	557776.4	98240.5	6.463556	X	X	X
19	12/06/2017	14:58:08	561190.5	98333.47	5.875556	0.5058006	0.451	ENTER TOLERANCE
19	11/03/2017	10:20:24	561190.2	98333.64	5.424556	X	X	X
22	12/06/2017	14:53:02	561614	98366.71	4.024556	0.5027298	0.257	ENTER TOLERANCE
22	11/03/2017	10:17:43	561614.3	98367.11	3.767556	X	X	X
24	12/06/2017	15:37:14	556389.5	98375.09	6.395556	0.5068655	0.335	ENTER TOLERANCE
24	11/03/2017	10:51:07	556391.2	98377.44	6.060556	X	X	X
25	11/03/2017	10:16:29	561812	98390.38	3.612556	0.5022007	-0.128	ENTER TOLERANCE
25	12/06/2017	14:51:27	561813.7	98391.26	3.740556	X	X	X
27	11/03/2017	10:15:48	561922.5	98408.3	3.437556	0.5019931	-0.34	ENTER TOLERANCE
27	12/06/2017	14:50:39	561922.9	98409.17	3.777556	X	X	X
28	12/06/2017	15:39:27	556100.1	98414.99	5.193556	0.5045378	0.359	ENTER TOLERANCE
28	11/03/2017	10:53:00	556100	98418.21	4.834556	X	X	X
32	30/10/2017	10:52:05	555656.4	98446.46	1.122556	0.5002129	-0.269	ENTER TOLERANCE
32	12/06/2017	15:42:22	555657.7	98446.75	1.391556	X	X	X
33	11/03/2017	10:14:33	562121.9	98448.69	3.059556	0.5015795	-0.261	ENTER TOLERANCE
33	12/06/2017	14:48:54	562121.1	98449.51	3.320556	X	X	X
34	12/06/2017	14:48:30	562183	98461.32	3.113556	0.5016356	0.216	ENTER TOLERANCE
34	11/03/2017	10:14:10	562182.6	98461.61	2.897556	X	X	X
36	12/06/2017	15:45:48	555169.3	98504.95	2.159556	0.5007875	0.1875	ENTER TOLERANCE
36	30/10/2017	10:47:37	555170.2	98505.17	1.972056	X	X	X
37	30/10/2017	10:46:54	555090	98507.59	1.853056	0.50058	-0.0475	ENTER TOLERANCE
37	12/06/2017	15:46:23	555089.4	98507.9	1.900556	X	X	X
38	30/10/2017	10:50:05	555440.8	98509.4	1.216056	0.5002499	-0.1955	ENTER TOLERANCE
38	12/06/2017	15:43:52	555440.5	98510.18	1.411556	X	X	X
39	12/06/2017	15:44:27	555356.4	98510.56	1.650556	0.5004602	0.1465	ENTER TOLERANCE
39	30/10/2017	10:49:20	555357	98512.07	1.504056	X	X	X
40	30/10/2017	10:44:03	554762.2	98510.27	1.305056	0.5002878	-0.5195	ENTER TOLERANCE
40	12/06/2017	15:48:40	554762.9	98510.47	1.824556	X	X	X

3.4. Generating DEM and Coastline

Bathymetric data and RTK tracking data point that referenced to lowest sea level are used to generating DEM that used to extract coastline data. In this paper, we use Natural Neighbor method in ArcGIS to create the DEM after considered distribution of the data that spread not evenly and with the least consume time to create. The Natural Neighbors interpolation method was introduced by Sibson [9]. The model works by finding the nearest subset of samples for a given cell without a measured value, and then applies weights to the samples based on the proportional area they occupy [9]. This method is well known for its ability to interpolate scattered and unevenly distributed data [7, 10]. The result can be seen in **Fig. 12**

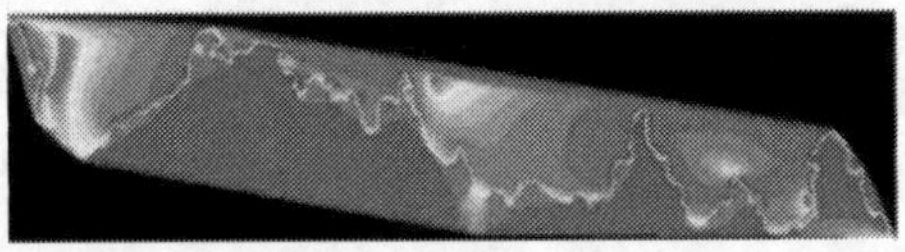

Fig. 12 DEM interpolation result

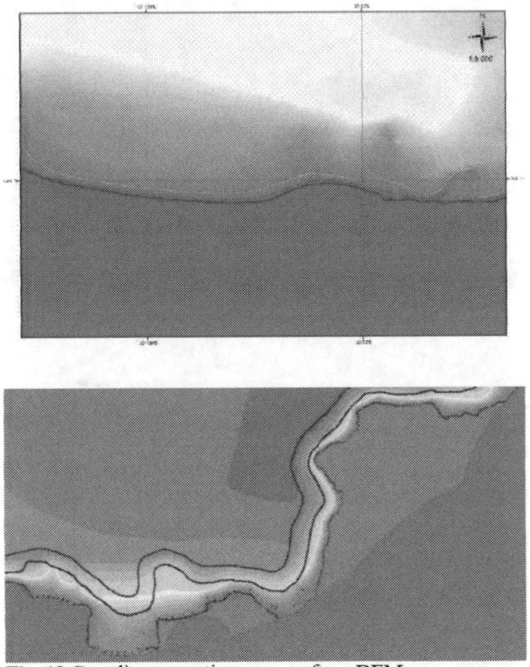

Fig. 13 Coastline extraction process from DEM

We extract coastline data from DEM with the value of highest, lowest, and mean sea level that we choose from tidal processing data that referenced to lowest sea level value. The result can be seen in **Fig.13**

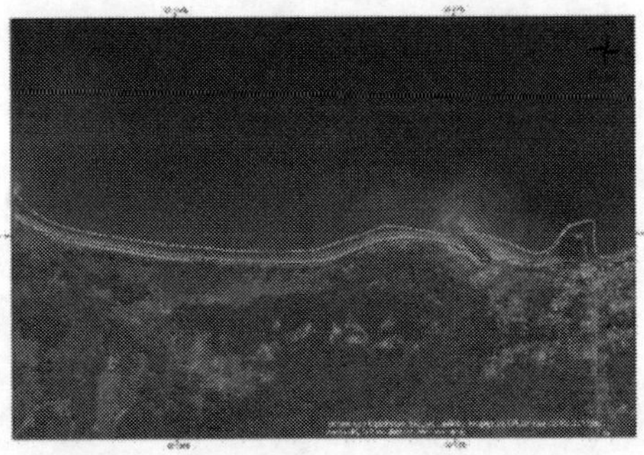

Fig. 14 Final result 3 coastline

4 Conclusions

GNSS Real Time Kinematic (RTK) method can be used as a method to determine highest, lowest, and mean sea level coastline. In order to extract three coastline vector data needs DEM that created from RTK tracking point and bathymetric data that referenced to lowest sea level. We use Natural Neighbor method to creates DEM then to extract coastline data. This method create DEM with less time than Kriging method. But, in the next research, we will try to use Kriging method to create DEM and compared the result with Natural Neighbor method.

Advantage of this method is accuracy level of coastline data that can be used in large-scale mapping especially in 1:10.000. This is because the coastline data that generated from DEM that formed from RTK tracking data and bathymetric data were good and met the required criteria for large-scale mapping. To make sure, validation of coastline data still needed in the future. Another advantage is if the area measured not to large has a low budget operation compared to another method such as LiDAR or photogrammetry.

Disadvantage of this method is the time taken to complete the measurement of RTK tracking data will be long. In this paper, RTK tracking measurement needed three until four months to completed. Another shortcoming is we can measure RTK tracking data only in the sandy coast area. Coast which has cliff or mangrove characteristic cannot be measured. In this area, we need referenced topographic data that obtained from LiDAR or photogrammetry method.

However, GNSS RTK method to determine coastline is still applicable in most area in Indonesia and with the need of large-scale mapping of coastline data.

References

1. H. Z. Abidin, *GPS Positioning and Application*. Jakarta: Pradnya Paramita (2007)
2. D.L. Codiga, *Unified Tidal Analysis and Prediction Using the UTide Matlab Functions. Technical Report 2011-01*. Graduate School of Oceanography,

* Corresponding author: wahyudi.nugraha@big.go.id

University of Rhode Island, Narragansett, RI. 59pp (2011)

3. Goncalves, Awange and Krueger. *GNSS-based monitoring and mapping of shoreline position in support of planning and management of Matinhos/PR* (Brazil) (2012)
4. International Hydrographic Organization, *IHO Standard for Hydrographic Surveys 5th Edition, February 2008 – Special Publication No. 44.* Monaco: International Hydrographic Bureau (2008)
5. Indonesia Government Regulation No.4-year 2011 about Geospatial Information.
6. Khomsin and S Intan Ary Prayogi, *IOP Conf. Ser.: Earth Environ. Sci.* **135** 012019 (2018)
7. Ledoux, H.; Gold, C. *An Efficient Natural Neighbour Interpolation Algorithm for Geoscientific Modelling;* Springer: Berlin/Heidelberg, Germany; pp. 97–108 (2005)
8. Mendonça, F. J. B. et al. *Temporal Shoreline Series Analysis Using GNSS.* BCG - Boletim de Ciências Geodésicas - On-Line version, p. 701-719 (2014)
9. Sibson, R. *A brief description of natural neighbor interpolation. In Interpreting Multivariate Data;* John Wiley & Sons: Hoboken, NJ, USA; pp. 21–36 (1981)
10. S. Salekin; J.H. Burgess; J. Morgenroth; E.G. Mason; D.F. Mason. ISPRS International Journal of Geo-Information. *A Comparative Study of Three Non-Geostatistical Methods for Optimising Digital Elevation Model Interpolation*. **7**, 300. (2018)

The Effect of Highway Vibration to The Hills Slope Stability by an Integrated GPS-Vibration Data Processing

Achmad Ruchlihadiana Tisnasendjaja[1], *Hasanuddin Z.* Abidin[2], *Dina A.* Sarsito[2], *Imam A.* Sadisun[3], and *Irwan* Gumilar[2]

[1]Geodesy Department, Faculty of Technic, Winaya Mukti University, Pahlawan St. no. 69 Bandung 40123, West Java, Indonesia
[2]Geodesy Research Group, Faculty of Earth Sciences and Technology, Bandung Institute of Technology, Ganesha St. 10, Bandung 40132, West Java, Indonesia
[3]Applied Geology Research Group, Faculty of Earth Sciences and Technology, Bandung Institute of Technology, Ganesha St. 10, Bandung 40132, West Java, Indonesia

Abstract. Bandung-Jakarta, Indonesia highway have high density vehicles pass even often jammed. High activity of vehicles cause repeated vibrations and occur continuously. In case, the highway that divides the hills. The passing vehicles give rise repeatedly vibration and indicated disturbance of hillside slope stability. Vehicles vibration depend on speed, weight, number of vehicles and road construction materials. A method in question is counting a vehicle volume and determine the volume pattern of the vehicle. The magnitude of vibration is function of the object distance from the sources. The magnitude of the vibration effect is very dependent on the geological structure of hills formation. Hilly slope stability indicates experiencing interference if the object or material slope changes position or displacement. GPS observation give position changes and its displacement. The effect of Toll road vibration to slope stability is known by GPS and Vibration simultaneous measurement. Data acquisition used six unit GPS receivers and six unit vibration sensor which is installed on the hillside beside the highway. Integrated data processing techniques using Empirical Mode Decomposition (EMD). Integrated GPS-Vibration data are implemented to find actual displacement which are caused by highway vibration.

1 Introduction

Cipularang toll road is toll roads on Java, Indonesia. Opened on 2005, this road connects the Jakarta–Cikampek Toll Road and the Padaleunyi Toll Road. The toll road is operated by PT Jasa Marga Tbk. The names come from abbreviation of Cikampek - Purwakarta - Padalarang. This toll road stretches along the mountains so the track is going up and downhill and many bends and bridges. Using the toll road can save up to half the time because a shortcut between Bandung and Jakarta.

The volume of various types and weights of vehicles crossing the road, even on weekends and holidays there is a traffic jam. December 2015 data the average vehicle that passes is 40 thousand per day and each year has increased [2]. Mid-2018, the number of vehicles examined is 259 units, 39% of the average daily traffic volume, see below Figure 1. Of that number, the vehicles that were proven to be overloaded 153 units (59.07%), over dimensions of 33 units (12.74%), and normal 73 units (28.19%). This road is the most populated toll road in Indonesia. In such conditions, the vehicle creates vibrations that take place continuously and repeatedly. This situation can trigger a disturbance in the surrounding slope stability. The volume of vehicles of the Cipularang toll road has increased steadily, see Figure 2. So monitoring the impact of vehicle vibrations on the slopes needs to be done.

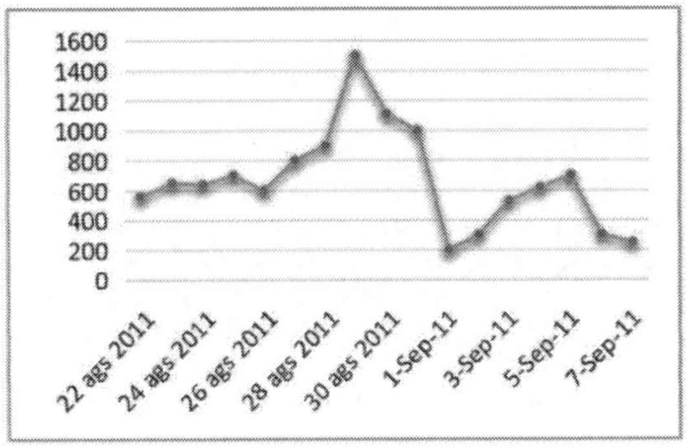

Fig. 1. Average Daily Traffic in 17 days at 2011 [1]

* Corresponding author: achmadrt87@gmail.com

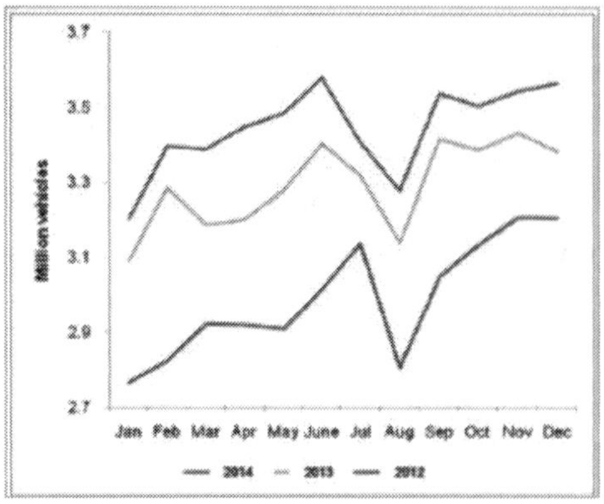

Fig. 2. Average Daily Traffic Increase [2]

Therefore, to determine the effect of vehicle loads passing through the toll road on slope stability, GPS observations and vibration measurements were carried out simultaneously.

2 Data Acquisition

The monitoring points are installed on the slopes around the toll road, see Figure 3. GNSS observations are carried out simultaneously with vibration measurements. Data acquisition is done simultaneously so that time synchronization can be done well.

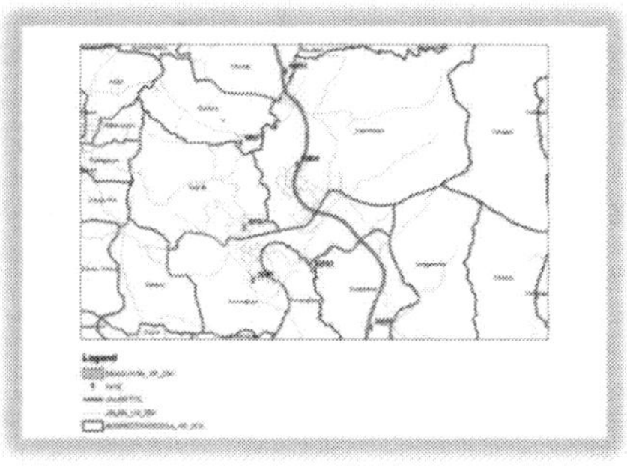

Fig. 3. Monitoring Points Distribution

First Period data acquisition was carried out at 6 monitoring points. Furthermore, the monitoring point is added to get a better distribution. The research area is between the Cipularang toll road (north) and the Darangdan Purwakarta highway (south). So the research area gets the vibrational influence of both.

2.1. GNSS Observation

GNSS observation used specification as follow:

Table 1. GNSS Observation Specification

Satellite Visibilty (GPS)	: min 6
Elevation Mask	: 15
PDoP / GDoP	: < 8
Interval Data	: 5
Observation Method	: Static
Duration	: 4 hours
Receiver Type	: Dual Frequency

2.2 Vibration Measurement

The instrument used is a triaxial vibration sensor. Vibration sensor measurement where placed at the ground of monitoring point use specification as follow:

Table 2. Vibration Measurement Specification

Frequency	: 1 Hz in high frequency mode 0.1 Hz in low frequency mode
Duration	: 10 - 100 (duration is adjusted to the duration of GPS observation)
Interval	: 0.1
Type -unit	: LSM6DS3 Accelerometer – m/s^2
Resolution	: 5.950928E-04
Range	: max 78.4532
Power	: 0.9 mW

3 Empirical Mode Decomposition (EMD)

A new nonlinear technique, referred to as Empirical Mode Decomposition (EMD), has recently been pioneered by N.E. Huang et al. for adaptively representing nonstationary signals as sums of zero-mean Amplitude Modulation (AM) - Frequency modulation (FM) components [3].

All real processes that must be faced in practice are complex, as a rule, which consists of a large number of components. A chart of this type is therefore quite difficult to be analyzed as its components, when interacting with each other, mask and distort the regularities we would like to identify. This gives rise to a rightful desire to break down the process under consideration into individual components and analyze each of the components separately [7]. Analysis of individual components and consideration of contributions made in the existing process will help to better understand the processes that are running, as well as, can improve the reliability of estimates.

The term "decomposition" formally means the breaking down of a compound process or a composite material into separate constituent components. But in many areas related to analysis of different processes, signal analysis, analysis of various sorts of sequences. These functions are sort of artificially formed in the process of data decomposition but despite their "artificial" origin they allow for a deeper analysis of data helping to identify hidden patterns. There is a lot of various decomposition methods that can be applied in practice to a given sequence under consideration. These methods may have different underlying mathematical or empirical approaches, different degree of complexity and different areas of application [7].

The algorithm as proposed by Huang is based on producing smooth envelopes defined by local maxima and minima of a sequence and subsequent subtraction of the mean of these envelopes from the initial sequence. This requires the identification of all local extrema that are further connected by cubic spline lines to produce the upper and the lower envelopes. The procedure of plotting the envelopes is shown in Figure 4.

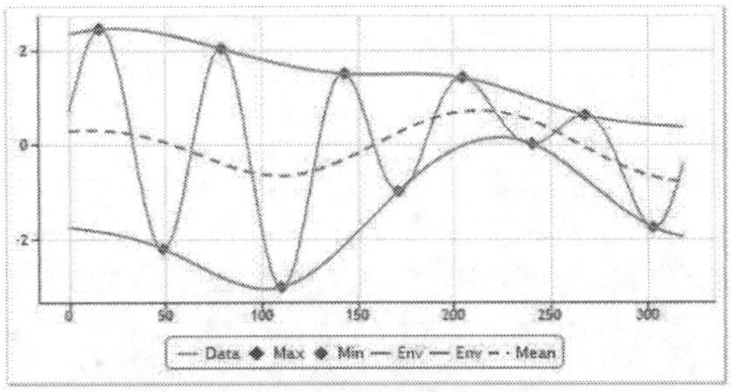

Fig. 4. Plotting the envelopes and their mean [7]

Emd decomposes a signal X(t) into k number of intrinsic mode functions (IMF), and residual rk(t) using the sifting process. A brief overview of the sifting process, listed in [3] and [4], is as follows [8]:

1. Find local maxima and minima for signal $X(t)$ to construct an upper envelope $s_+(t)$, and a lower envelope $s_-(t)$.
2. Compute mean envelope for i^{th} iteration, $m_{k,i}(t)$,

$$m_{k,i}(t)=\frac{1}{2}[s_+(t)+s_-(t)] \quad (1)$$

3. With $c_k(t) = X(t)$ for the first iteration, subtract mean envelope from residual signal,

$$c_k(t)=c_k(t)-m_{k,i}(t) \quad (2)$$

If $c_k(t)$ does not match the criteria of an IMF, steps 4 and 5 are skipped. The procedure is iterated again at step 1 with the new value of $c_k(t)$.

4. If $c_k(t)$ matches the criteria of an IMF, a new residual is computed. To update the residual signal, subtract the kth IMF from the previous residual signal,

$$r_k(t)=r_{k-1}(t)-c_k(t) \quad (3)$$

5. Then begin from step 1, using the residual obtained as a new signal $r_k(t)$, and store $c_k(t)$ as an Intrinsic Mode Function (IMF).

For N intrinsic mode functions, the original signal is represented as [8],

$$X(t)=\sum_{i=1}^{N} c_i(t) + r_N(t) \quad (4)$$

Sift Relative Tolerance is a Cauchy type stop criterion proposed in [6]. Sifting stops when current relative tolerance is less than SiftRelativeTolerance. The current relative tolerance is defined as [8],

$$RelativeTolerance \triangleq \frac{\|c(t)previous-c(t)current\|^2}{\|c(t)current\|^2} \quad (5)$$

Energy ratio is the ratio of the energy of the signal at the beginning of sifting and the average envelope energy [4]. Decomposition stops when current energy ratio is larger than MaxEnergyRatio. For k IMFs, EnergyRatio is defined as [8],

$$EnergyRatio \triangleq 10\log_{10}\left(\frac{\|X(t)\|^2}{\|r_k(t)\|^2}\right) \quad (6)$$

3.1 GNSS Data Processing

GNSS data processing uses a kinematic method. GNSS survey data for 30-60 minutes is processed as initiation. after that data processing is done by kinematic algorithm. the goal is that we can get positions every 5 seconds. Among the 6 monitoring points, one is used as a reference point. By considering the stability of the point position against vehicle vibrations on the toll/highway road, the point above the construction of the km97 bridge is used as a reference. From the distribution of the position of the monitoring point, two points were chosen as the focus of the analysis, namely the point on the edge of the km95 toll road ('msjd97') and the point in the center of the research area, which has a distance of 1.4 km. The point in question is the 'kbn1' point installed in the middle of the cropland.

The results of GNSS processing use a topocentric coordinate system (east, north, up) and find accelerations to match the vibration measurement system. In order for the analysis to be carried out, the suitability of GNSS observation and vibration time must be the same, following the intended time suitability.

Table 4. Time Suitability GNSS and Vibration Measurement

	kbn1		msjd97	
	Start	End	Start	End
GNSS OBSV	11:20:38	12:33:08	11:21:03	13:58:23
VIBRATION MEAS	11:42:21	12:33:08	11:43:49	12:52:06

Field data acquisition begins and ends with the same time. because there is a problem with the instrument, then time synchronization obtained as listed in table 3. So the analysis of the results of kbn1 and msjd97 points can only be done with signal decomposition patterns. The following are sequentially presented by processing result at point kbn1.

Plotting of kbn1 GNSS data (a_e, a_n, a_u)

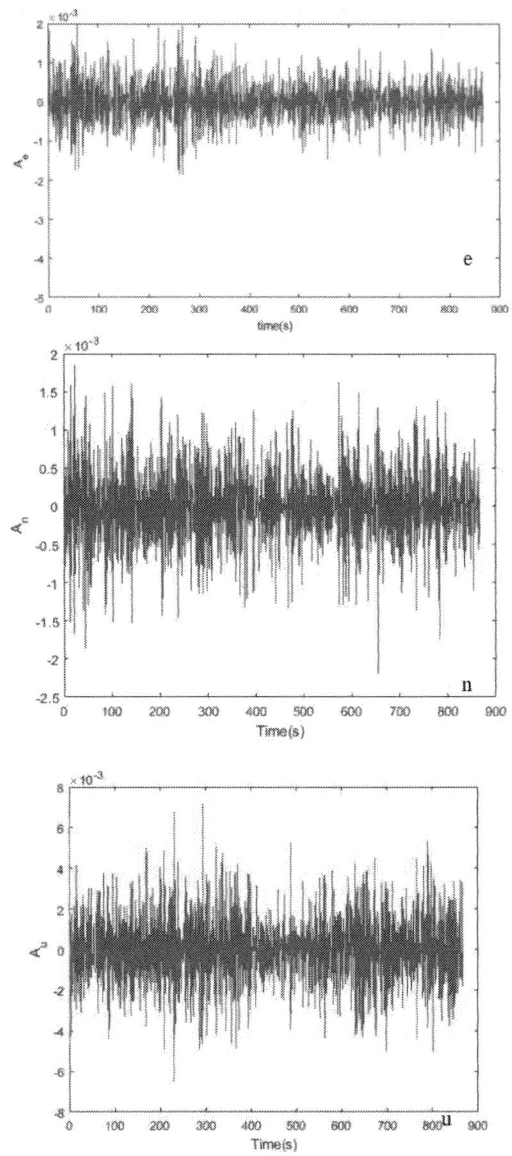

Fig. 5. Time vs Amplitude (e, n, u) GNSS Data of 'kbn1'

Plotting of kbn1 Emd-Imf (e, n, u)

Current IMF	#Sift Iter	Relative Tol	Stop Criterion Hit
1	1	0.063515	SiftMaxRelativeTolerance
2	1	0.19525	SiftMaxRelativeTolerance
3	2	0.040539	SiftMaxRelativeTolerance
4	2	0.062387	SiftMaxRelativeTolerance
5	3	0.023439	SiftMaxRelativeTolerance
6	2	0.029548	SiftMaxRelativeTolerance
7	2	0.068727	SiftMaxRelativeTolerance
8	1	0.14283	SiftMaxRelativeTolerance

The decomposition stopped because the current energy ratio is greater than 'MaxEnergyRatio'

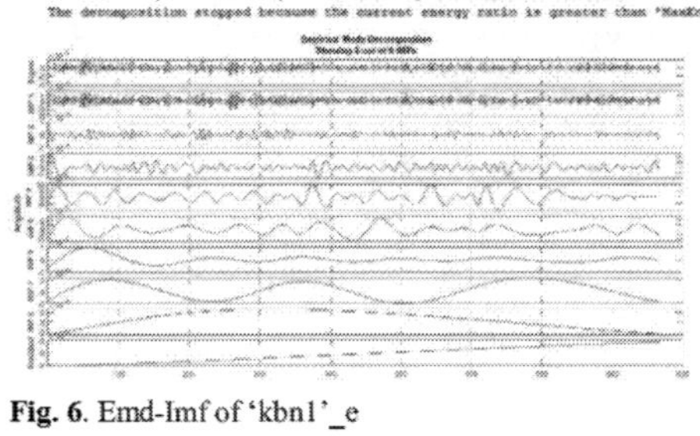

Fig. 6. Emd-Imf of 'kbn1'_e

Current IMF	#Sift Iter	Relative Tol	Stop Criterion Hit
1	3	0.11873	SiftMaxRelativeTolerance
2	2	0.065702	SiftMaxRelativeTolerance
3	2	0.072546	SiftMaxRelativeTolerance
4	2	0.18312	SiftMaxRelativeTolerance
5	2	0.08782	SiftMaxRelativeTolerance
6	2	0.058376	SiftMaxRelativeTolerance
7	2	0.1815	SiftMaxRelativeTolerance
8	2	0.14007	SiftMaxRelativeTolerance
9	2	0.048995	SiftMaxRelativeTolerance
10	2	0.18746	SiftMaxRelativeTolerance

The decomposition stopped because 'MaxNumIMF' was reached.

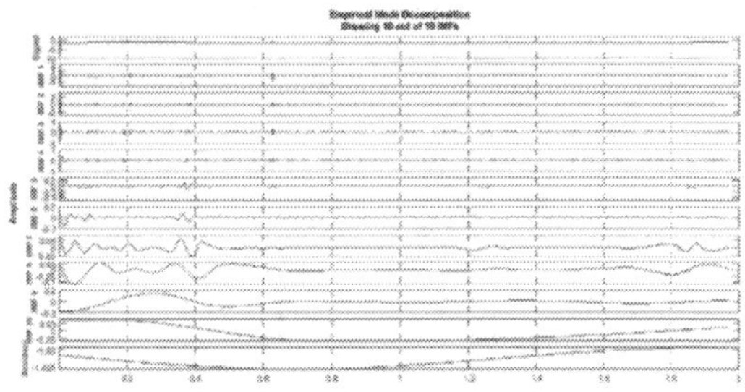

Fig. 7. Emd-Imf of 'kbn1'_n

Current IMF	#Sift Iter	Relative Tol	Stop Criterion Hit
1	1	0.06489	SiftMaxRelativeTolerance
2	2	0.02561	SiftMaxRelativeTolerance
3	2	0.083944	SiftMaxRelativeTolerance
4	2	0.04099	SiftMaxRelativeTolerance
5	2	0.11508	SiftMaxRelativeTolerance
6	2	0.14021	SiftMaxRelativeTolerance
7	2	0.1453	SiftMaxRelativeTolerance
8	1	0.19296	SiftMaxRelativeTolerance

The decomposition stopped because the current energy ratio is greater than 'MaxEnergyRatio'

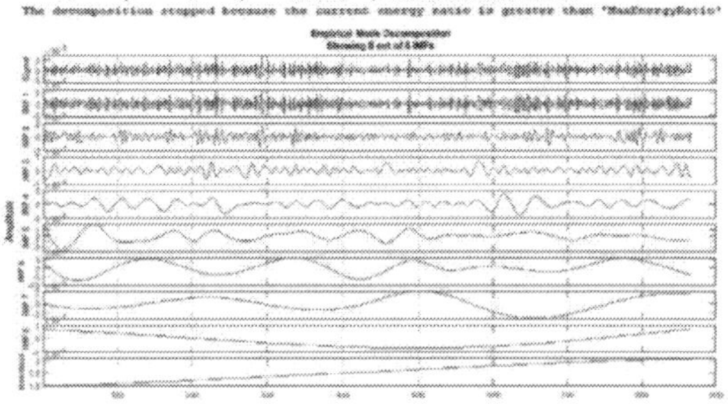

Fig. 8. Emd-Imf of 'kbn1'_u

Further point is msjd97:

Plotting of msjd97 GNSS data (a_e, a_n, a_u)

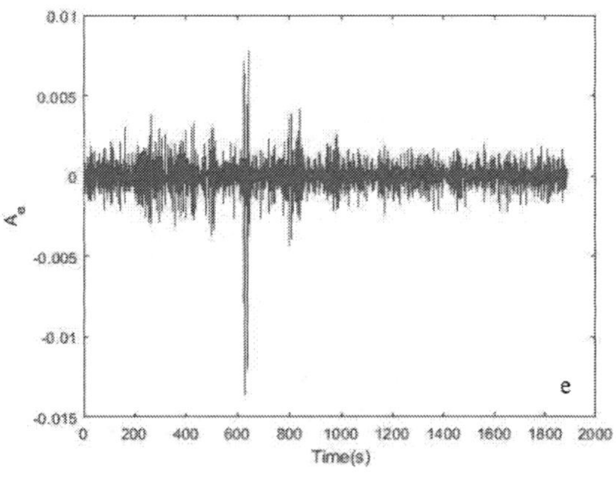

https://doi.org/10.1051/e3sconf/20199401017

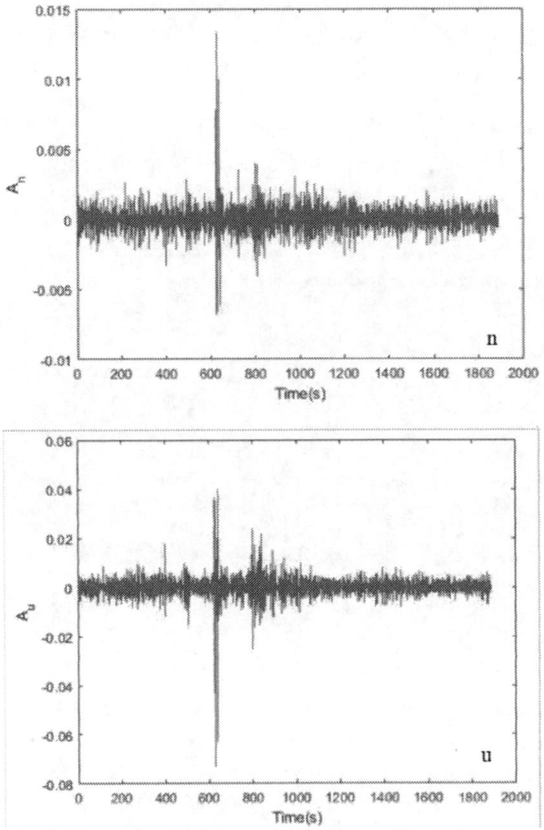

Fig. 9. Time vs Amplitude (e, n, u) GNSS Data of 'msjd97'

Plotting of msjd97 Emd-Imf (e, n, u)

Current IMF	#Sift Iter	Relative Tol	Stop Criterion Hit
1	1	0.873438	SiftMaxRelativeTolerance
2	1	0.15556	SiftMaxRelativeTolerance
3	2	0.049147	SiftMaxRelativeTolerance
4	2	0.022228	SiftMaxRelativeTolerance
5	2	0.043944	SiftMaxRelativeTolerance
6	2	0.031531	SiftMaxRelativeTolerance
7	2	0.029504	SiftMaxRelativeTolerance
8	2	0.10193	SiftMaxRelativeTolerance
9	3	0.053562	SiftMaxRelativeTolerance

The decomposition stopped because the number of extrema of the residual signal is less than

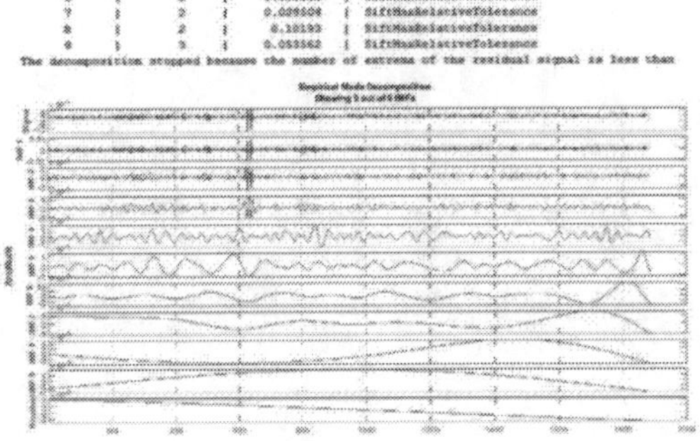

Fig. 10. Emd-Imf of 'msjd97'_e

Current IMF	#Sift Iter	Relative Tol	Stop Criterion Hit
1	1	0.084257	SiftMaxRelativeTolerance
2	1	0.15591	SiftMaxRelativeTolerance
3	2	0.027039	SiftMaxRelativeTolerance
4	2	0.05314	SiftMaxRelativeTolerance
5	2	0.035297	SiftMaxRelativeTolerance
6	2	0.013331	SiftMaxRelativeTolerance
7	3	0.059382	SiftMaxRelativeTolerance
8	4	0.17005	SiftMaxRelativeTolerance
9	2	0.081471	SiftMaxRelativeTolerance

The decomposition stopped because the number of extrema of the residual signal is less than

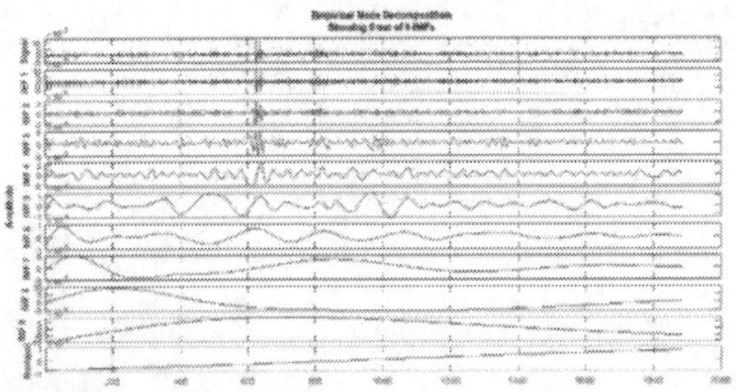

Fig. 11. Emd-Imf of 'msjd97'_n

Current IMF	#Sift Iter	Relative Tol	Stop Criterion Hit
1	1	0.098373	SiftMaxRelativeTolerance
2	2	0.063771	SiftMaxRelativeTolerance
3	2	0.020333	SiftMaxRelativeTolerance
4	2	0.036663	SiftMaxRelativeTolerance
5	2	0.014311	SiftMaxRelativeTolerance
6	2	0.014884	SiftMaxRelativeTolerance
7	2	0.0113	SiftMaxRelativeTolerance
8	2	0.033324	SiftMaxRelativeTolerance
9	2	0.070579	SiftMaxRelativeTolerance

The decomposition stopped because the number of extrema of the residual signal is less than

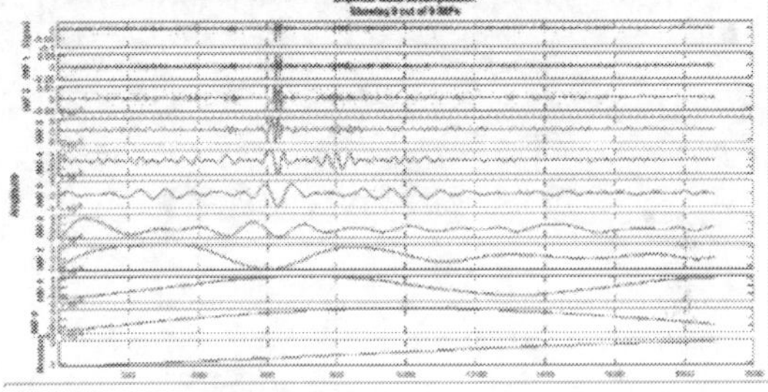

Fig. 12. Emd-Imf of 'msjd97'_u

3.2 Vibration Data Processing

Vibration measurement uses a triaxial vibration sensor so that the acceleration data has a value of 3 axes (x, y, z). The unit is m/s2. For analysis, the data process is carried out for each axis, as well as gnss data. The following are the results of processing for vibrations data at kbn1 and msjd97 point.

Plotting of kbn1 vibrations data (x, y, z)

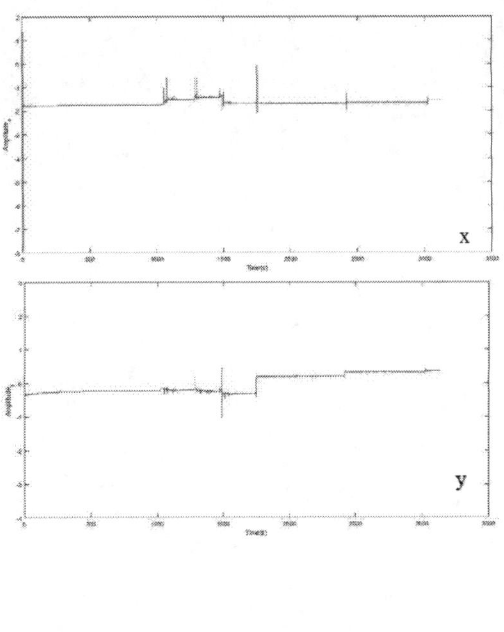

https://doi.org/10.1051/e3sconf/20199401017

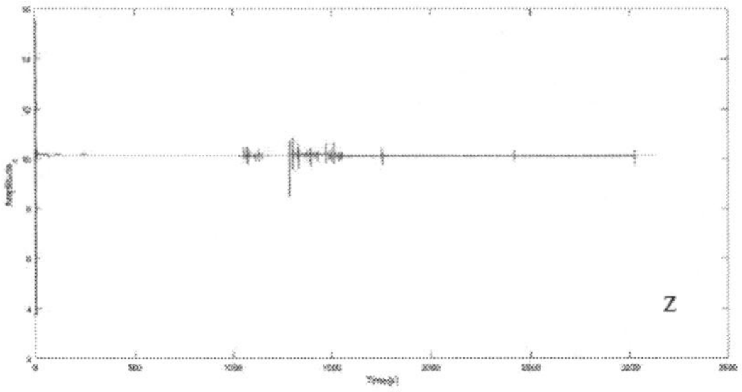

Fig. 13. Time vs Amplitude (x,y, z) Vibration Data of 'kbn1'

Plotting of kbn1 Emd-Imf (x,y, z)

Current IMF	#Sift Iter	Relative Tol	Stop Criterion Hit
1	3	0.11873	SiftMaxRelativeTolerance
2	2	0.065702	SiftMaxRelativeTolerance
3	2	0.072546	SiftMaxRelativeTolerance
4	2	0.18312	SiftMaxRelativeTolerance
5	2	0.08782	SiftMaxRelativeTolerance
6	2	0.058376	SiftMaxRelativeTolerance
7	2	0.1815	SiftMaxRelativeTolerance
8	2	0.14007	SiftMaxRelativeTolerance
9	2	0.048995	SiftMaxRelativeTolerance
10	2	0.18746	SiftMaxRelativeTolerance

The decomposition stopped because 'MaxNumIMF' was reached.

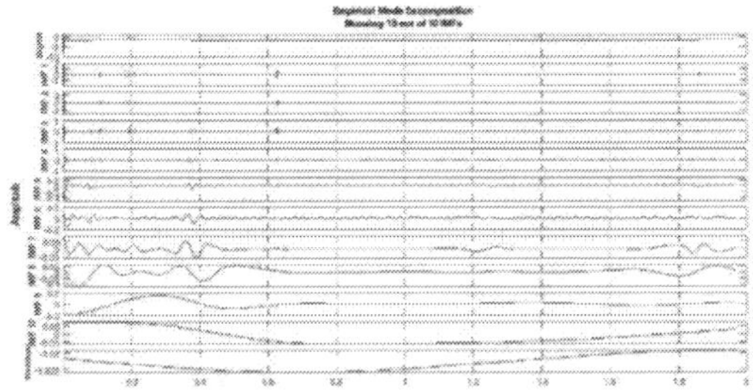

Fig. 14. Emd-Imf of 'kbn1'_x

Current IMF	#Sift Iter	Relative Tol	Stop Criterion Hit
1	3	0.021554	SiftMaxRelativeTolerance
2	2	0.056268	SiftMaxRelativeTolerance
3	2	0.012425	SiftMaxRelativeTolerance
4	2	0.17403	SiftMaxRelativeTolerance
5	2	0.19242	SiftMaxRelativeTolerance
6	2	0.12744	SiftMaxRelativeTolerance
7	2	0.13632	SiftMaxRelativeTolerance
8	3	0.035678	SiftMaxRelativeTolerance
9	2	0.02482	SiftMaxRelativeTolerance
10	3	0.072143	SiftMaxRelativeTolerance

The decomposition stopped because 'MaxNumIMF' was reached.

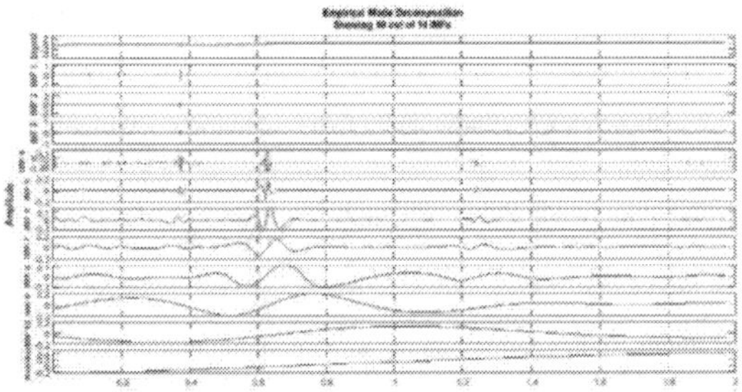

Fig. 15. Emd-Imf of 'kbn1'_y

Current IMF	#Sift Iter	Relative Tol	Stop Criterion Hit
1	2	0.021549	SiftMaxRelativeTolerance
2	3	0.077109	SiftMaxRelativeTolerance
3	2	0.079921	SiftMaxRelativeTolerance
4	2	0.013867	SiftMaxRelativeTolerance
5	2	0.12156	SiftMaxRelativeTolerance
6	3	0.053871	SiftMaxRelativeTolerance
7	2	0.014933	SiftMaxRelativeTolerance
8	3	0.09138	SiftMaxRelativeTolerance
9	3	0.15757	SiftMaxRelativeTolerance
10	3	0.018011	SiftMaxRelativeTolerance

The decomposition stopped because 'MaxNumIMF' was reached.

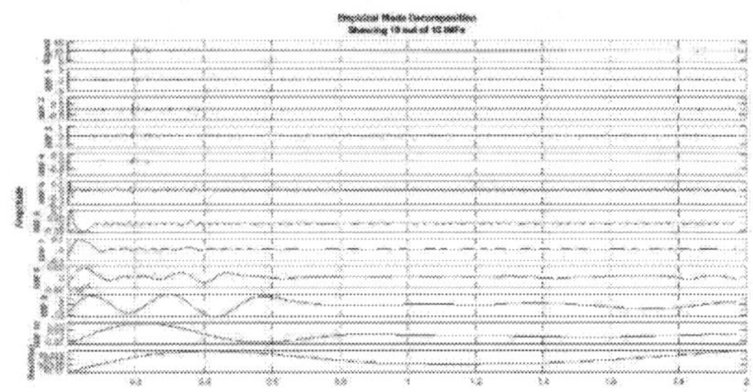

Fig. 16. Emd-Imf of 'kbn1'_z

The next point:
Plotting of msjd97 vibrations data (x, y, z)

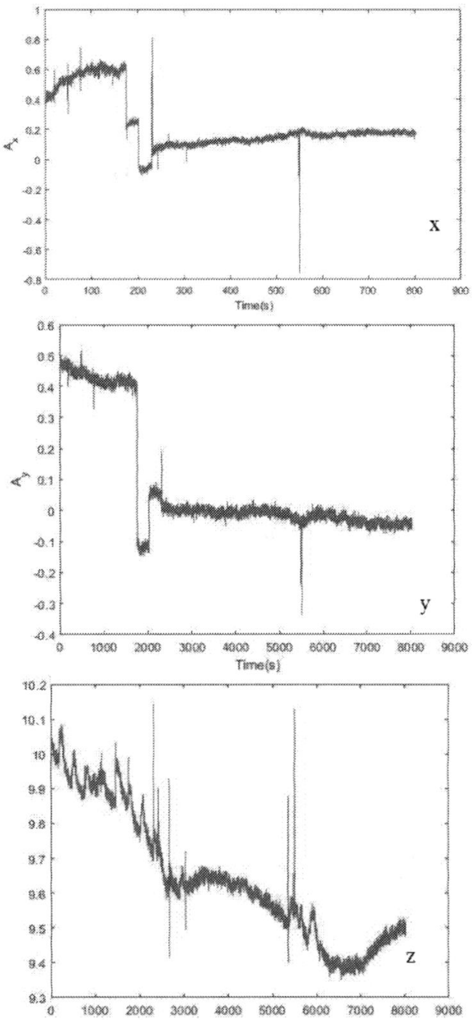

Fig. 17. Time vs Amplitude (x,y, z) Vibration Data of 'msjd97'

Plotting of msjd97 Emd-Imf (x, y, z)

https://doi.org/10.1051/e3sconf/20199401017

Current IMF	#Sift Iter	Relative Tol	Stop Criterion Hit
1	2	0.081795	SiftMaxRelativeTolerance
2	2	0.066402	SiftMaxRelativeTolerance
3	2	0.14802	SiftMaxRelativeTolerance
4	3	[illegible]	SiftMaxRelativeTolerance
5	2	0.13124	SiftMaxRelativeTolerance
6	2	0.016485	SiftMaxRelativeTolerance
7	3	0.012879	SiftMaxRelativeTolerance
8	2	0.13958	SiftMaxRelativeTolerance
9	2	0.079971	SiftMaxRelativeTolerance

The decomposition stopped because the number of extrema of the residual signal is less than

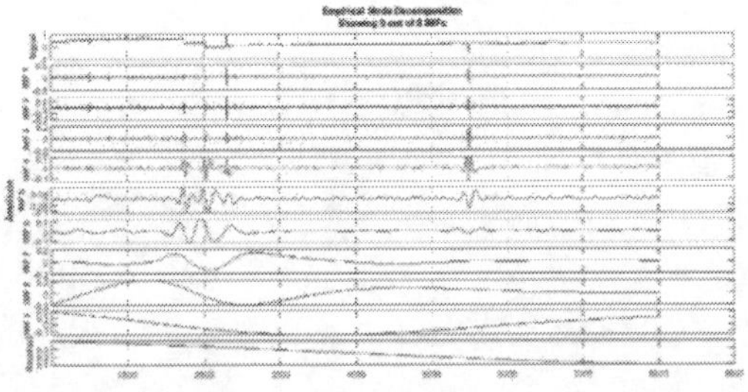

Fig. 18. Emd-Imf of 'msjd97'_x

Current IMF	#Sift Iter	Relative Tol	Stop Criterion Hit
1	2	0.052629	SiftMaxRelativeTolerance
2	2	0.05246	SiftMaxRelativeTolerance
3	2	0.086083	SiftMaxRelativeTolerance
4	2	0.15481	SiftMaxRelativeTolerance
5	2	0.19946	SiftMaxRelativeTolerance
6	2	0.068236	SiftMaxRelativeTolerance
7	2	0.10976	SiftMaxRelativeTolerance
8	2	0.10553	SiftMaxRelativeTolerance
9	2	0.11999	SiftMaxRelativeTolerance
10	3	0.19824	SiftMaxRelativeTolerance

The decomposition stopped because 'MaxNumIMF' was reached.

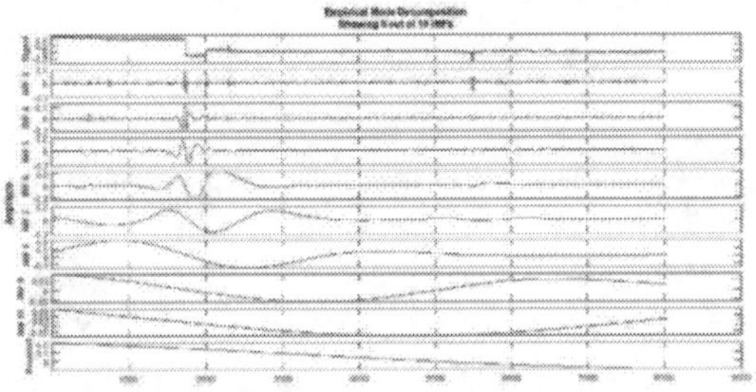

Fig. 19. Emd-Imf of 'msjd97'_y

Current IMF	#Sift Iter	Relative Tol	Stop Criterion Hit
1	2	0.12336	SiftMaxRelativeTolerance
2	2	0.10393	SiftMaxRelativeTolerance
3	3	0.029896	SiftMaxRelativeTolerance
4	3	0.097468	SiftMaxRelativeTolerance
5	4	0.047501	SiftMaxRelativeTolerance
6	3	0.01337	SiftMaxRelativeTolerance
7	3	0.14346	SiftMaxRelativeTolerance
8	3	0.1468	SiftMaxRelativeTolerance
9	3	0.034243	SiftMaxRelativeTolerance

The decomposition stopped because the number of extrema of the residual signal is less than

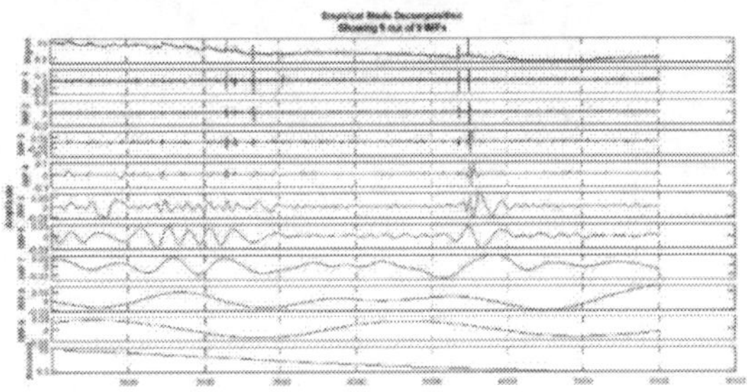

Fig. 20. Emd-Imf of 'msjd97'_z

3.2 Indication of Vibration Effect of on Slope Stability

The figure below is presented with vector changes resulting from periodic GNSS observations from 1 September 2018 to 6 October 2018.

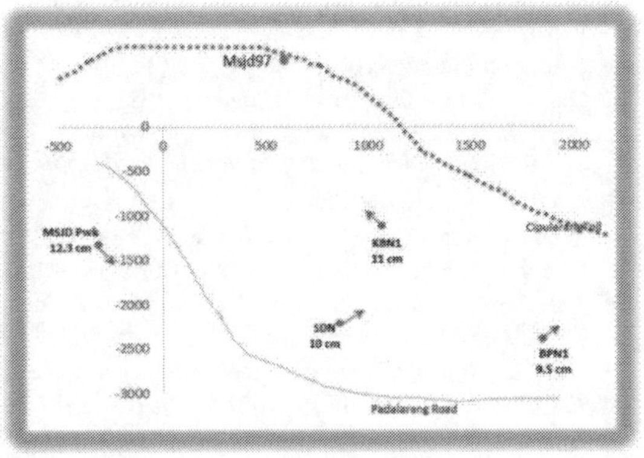

Fig. 21. Average Daily Traffic Increase [2]

4 Discussion and Conclusion

The following conclusions are based on the assumption that the observations of GNSS and Vibration are carried out for 2 periods and at the same time.

1. Figures 5 to 12 show changes in acceleration resulting from variations in GNSS position during observation. That variation can be indicated as the influence of vibrations on the road.
2. Figures 13 to 20 show changes in acceleration resulting from variations in vibration during observation. That variation can be indicated as the influence of vehicle activity on the road
3. That indeed at points observed both the observations of GNSS and the vibrations of material slope movements occur.

For further studies, indications of the conclusions above will be examined further.

References

1. Manggala G., *Kecelakaan di Tol Cipularang: Human Error atau Kondisi Jalan? Sebuah Tool Statistik Sederhana Bisa Membantu*, https://gdmanggala.wordpress.com/2011/09/18/ (2011).
2. JSMR, *Investor Summit and Capital Market Expo 2015*, Jasa Marga Indonesia Highway Corp, **19** (2015).

3. N.E. Huang, Z. Shen, S.R. Long, M.L. Wu, H.H. Shih, Q. Zheng, N.C. Yen, C.C. Tung and H.H. Liu, The empirical mode decomposition and the Hilbert spectrum for nonlinear and non-stationary time series analysis. *Proceedings of the Royal Society of London.* **Series A**: Mathematical, Physical and Engineering Sciences, (1998).
4. G. Rilling, Flandrin, P. Flandrin and P. Gonçalves, On empirical mode decomposition and its algorithms. *IEEE-EURASIP workshop on nonlinear signal and image* processing, p.8-11, (2003).
5. Rato, R.T., Ortigueira, Manuel, Batista, and Arnaldo, On the HHT, its problems, and some solutions, *Mechanical Systems and Signal Processing*, p.1374-1394, (2008).
6. Wang, Gang, Chen, Xianyao, Qiao, Fang-Li, Wu, Zhaohua, Huang, Norden. On Intrinsic Mode Function, *Advances in Adaptive Data Analysis*, p. 277-293, (2010).
7. Victor, Introduction to the Empirical Mode Decomposition Method, *MQL5 Articles*, p.1-13, (2012).
8. https://www.mathworks.com/help/signal/ref/emd.html#mw_01f39430-58d5-4b1f-b2f7-285ffeeca163
9. S.Maheswari and A.Kumar, Empirical Mode Decomposition : Theory & Applications, *International Journal of Electronic Engineering*, **Vol. 7**, p. 873-878, (2014)

Study on Search and Rescue System for Military and Civil use by using COSPAS SARSAT and Terrestrial Communication Network

Sanguk Lee[1], Incheol Jeong[1], Woo-Geun Ahn[2]
Satellite Research Department, ETRI[1], Agency for Defense Development[2]

[1]Satellite Research Department, ETRI, Daejeon 34129, Korea
[2]Agency for Defence Development Daejeon, Korea

Abstract. We propose search and rescue system for the both military and civil uses with minimizing burden to COSPAS SARSAT by using terrestrial communication network like LTE as an example in the paper. The terrestrial network may not be limited to LTE but extended to 5G, SigFox, LoRa, etc, later on. For security, special encryption mechanism is applied to the both COSPAS SARSAT and Terrestrial links. Also, operation concept for critical and normal situation. Implementation result and enhancing positioning accuracy by using rescue signal itself from ground signal processing is presented too.

1 Introduction

COSPAS SARSAT is very famous and popular system and cooperation organization for rescuing people from distress. Tens of thousands of people has been rescued by the system since it started service in 1979. In critical situation like war or normal situation like peace, if military forces and air, terrestrial and maritime military equipment like armoury vehicle, fighter and cargo aircraft, vessels are in trouble like distress or lost, we may need special search and rescue system. In the operational sense, if distress beacon is allowed to personal use, then limited number of simultaneous burst signals some support communication links such as satellite communication link like thuraya, orbcomm, GMPCS and so on or ground links like TRS and LTE. We determined the LTE as assisting communication link and did not choose satellite links due to highly expensive costs to use. In the sense of security, we employed cryptography for guarantee user security. Cosmitscheskaja Sistema Poiska Awarinitsch Sudow (Russian: space system for search of vessels in distress) Search and Rescue Satellite-Aided Tracking (COSPAS SARSAT) system allows utilization of national use field for each member states as described in COSPAS SARSAT(2017). But it has limitation on number of distress signals that can be accommodated at the same time as the limited channel allocation. The burden due to the limitation may be mitigated by additional encrypted satellite link and/or terrestrial link.

2 COSPAS SARSAT

The COSPAS-SARSAT system, which is an international search and rescue system, can be divided into distress beacon, satellite system, and ground facilities. Satellite systems have three different system such as Low Earth Orbit SAR(LEOSAR) and Geostationary Earth Orbit SAR(GEOSAR) as the first generation and Medium Earth Orbit SAR(MEOSAR) as the second generation[1]. The ground facilities are consisted of Local User Terminal, Mission Control Center, and Rescue Control Center). Automatically or manually search and rescue beacon in the event of a vessel / airplane or personal distress as shown in Fig. 1.

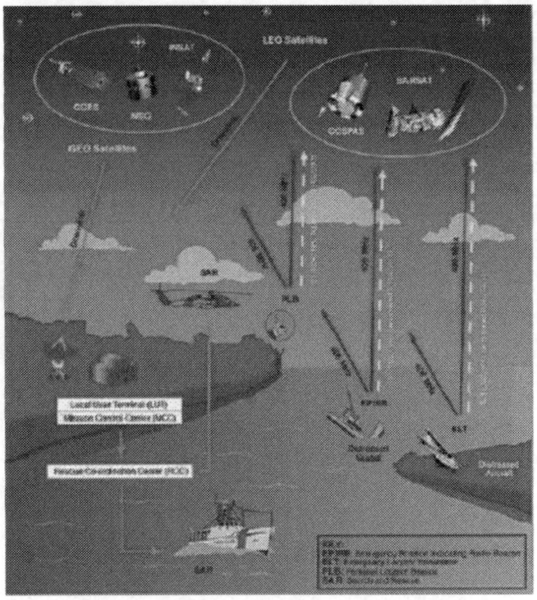

Fig. 1. COSPAS SARSAT configuration and operation

When a distress alert signal on search and rescue beacon is busted out to satellites, it is received by the satellite and relayed to the LUT of the ground system. The LUT

* Corresponding author: slee@etri.re.kr

computes or acquires the position of search and rescue beacon and transmits the information on the result to the RCC (Rescue Control Center) through the MCC to provide information necessary for expanding the area search and rescue activities. The search and rescue beacon is mounted on a moving object such as a ship or an aircraft including a personal portable device for military and civil uses, and automatically or manually transmits an alarm signal using a wireless communication links when an individual, a ship or an aircraft is in distress or missing, It is a device to help identify a distress situation including localization. .

GPS such as GNSS tells users location to themselves but COSPAS SARSAT such as search and rescue system tells someone else users' location and urgent situation for fast rescue activity possible.

The good news to COSPAS SARSAT is that GNSS system like GPS, GLONASS, Galileo will equip COSPAS SARSAT transponders to their system. Especially, Galileo system already equipped the transponder including return link service which is very good tool for providing the fact that distress signal is acknowledged to distressed person and for control search and rescue beacon to prevent over loading distress signals after it is acknowledged when mass disaster situation.

3 Military & Civil Search and Rescue System

3.1. Top-level Requirements

The Military & Civil Search and Rescue System that is proposed in this paper may be harmonized between military and civil uses. Most of countries employ the COSPAS SARSAT as military use and some counties use dedicated satellite system for the purpose [2]. For the harmonization of them, we made some top level requirements as follows;

- Functional requirements
  - Military and civil services should be supported simultaneously but mechanical requirement may be comply application areas and their purposes
  - The services starts from the first generation COSPAS SARSAT based and should be expanded to the second generation such as Galileo/SAR, GPS/SAR, and GLONASS/SAR
  - Encryption mechanism should be applied for the security and privacy
  - Two-way link(or return rink) service should be provided for relieving distressed people and reducing false alerts and increasing capacity of the search and rescue system by burst distress signal control after their recognition.
  - Distress signal should be transmitted automatically, manually, and by interrogate signal.
  - The alternative communication link(s) should be available to prevent distress signal loss due to tremendous distress signals in mass disaster or critical situation like war.

- Performance requirements
  - Most performance requirements on communication links including data link should be comply those of COSPAS SARSAT.
  - Positioning accuracies are 50 m or better with GNSS signal and 1 km or better without GNSS signal as generic performance
  - Recognition and localization of distressed people or equipment should be done 5 minutes in the defined service area.

3.2. Operation Concept

A threat level and burden to COSPAS SARSAT in the sense of limitation on channel allocation and assigned frequency band. The operation concept for military and civil search and rescue system is that LTE link is primary for minimizing burden to COSPAS SATSAT and taking benefit (large capacity) of LTE(or PS-LTE) in less threat or peace but COSPAS SARSAT is primary for taking stability of satellite communication of COSPAS SARSAT and preventing vulnerability of LTE that is weak from ground attack in critical situation like a war[3].

LTE(or PS-LTE) is used as distress signal and its return link and COSPAS SARSAT link is used when terrestrial LTE link is not available after pre-defined number of watch-dog timer counts without any acknowledgement from MCC in less threat or peace. For a critical situation like a war, COSPAS SARSAT link may be primary link and its return link and terrestrial LTE link will be the secondary link and its return link when return link does not provide acknowledgement from MCC of COSPAS SARSAT. The terrestrial link is not limited to LTE or PS-LTE but can be extended 5G, SigFox, LoRa, NB-IOT, etc. Especially terrestrial IOT network is very useful for the alternatives for the ground cost effective link.

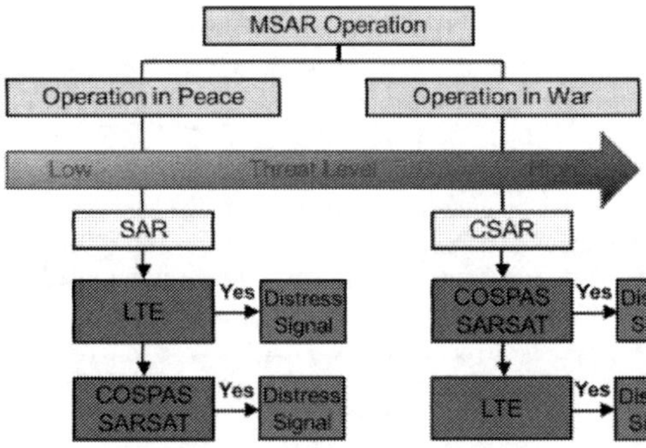

Fig. 2. Operation Concept of military and civil SAR

4 Military & Civil Search and Rescue System Prototype and Its Results

4.1. SW Modelling & Simulation Tool

Modelling and Simulation (M&S) tool for prototyping of Military & Civil Search and Rescue System has been developed and its feasibility was checked. Initially, prototyping was made in full software as shown in Fig. 3. We take into account GPS jamming which gives impact on positioning of search and rescue beacon that is equipped with GPS chipset in it. This situation activated positioning of people in distress in alternative way by using distress beacon signal itself.

Fig. 3. SW M&S tool Military & Civil Search and Rescue System[3].

4.1.1 Cross Ambiguity Function

Even though positioning accuracy is not accurate as much as GPS, it gives reasonable accuracy without GNSS signal like GNSS jamming situation. A cross ambiguity function (CAF) method was used to localize the distress signal sources. This methodology provide locations of multiple distress signal sources at the same time by post processing.

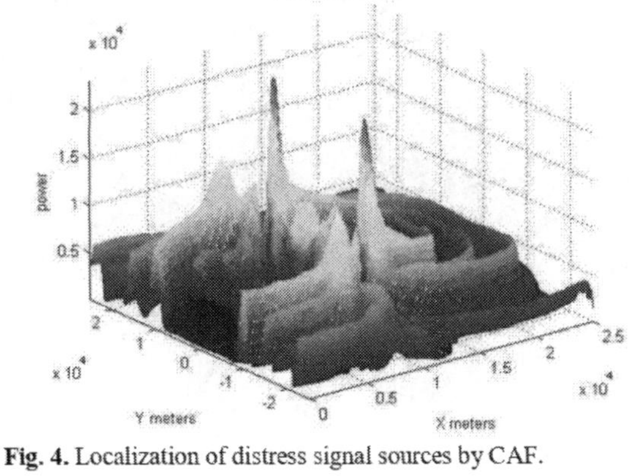

Fig. 4. Localization of distress signal sources by CAF.

4.1.2 Multi- CAF

In order to improve localization accuracy, multiple CAF method was used. It provided positioning accuracy about 1 km.

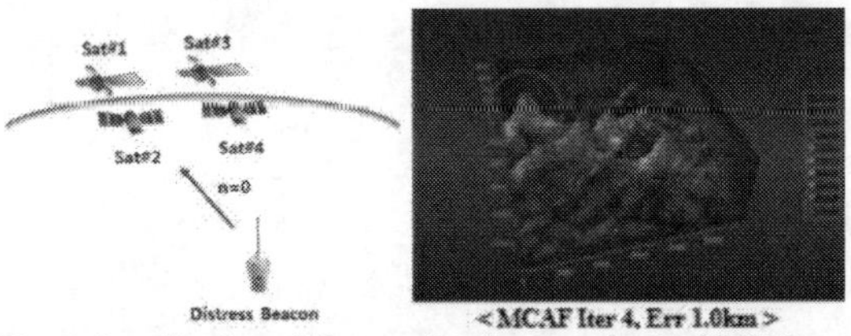

Fig. 5. Localization of distress signal sources by Multi-CAF.

4.2. Hybrid Modelling & Simulation Tool

An LTE communication link were replaced with hardware module as LTE modem with COSPAS SARSAT in SW emulation in data level. It has been merged into hybrid system to check its feasibility with more realistic environment as shown in Fig. 6.

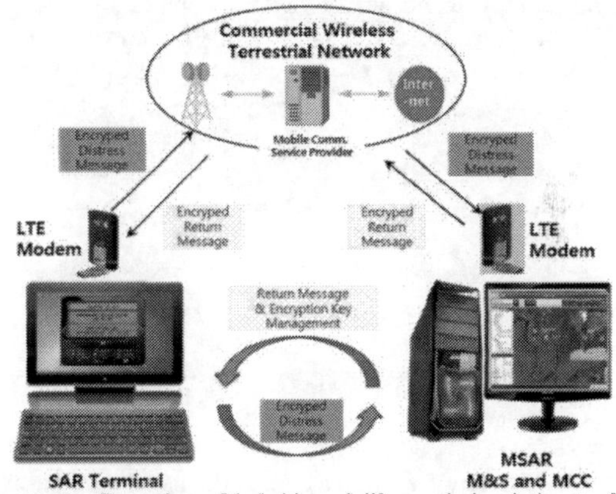

Fig. 6. Configuration of hybrid modelling and simulation tool for Military & Civil Search and Rescue System

For providing security on the user information including location, encryption scheme was employed to the both LTE and COSPAS SARSAT message protocols. Encryption by 128 bits AES/CFB & Key management[3][4][5][6] was utilized for COSPAS SARSAT messages by using National User Protocol message format and data fields as shown in figures 7 and 8.

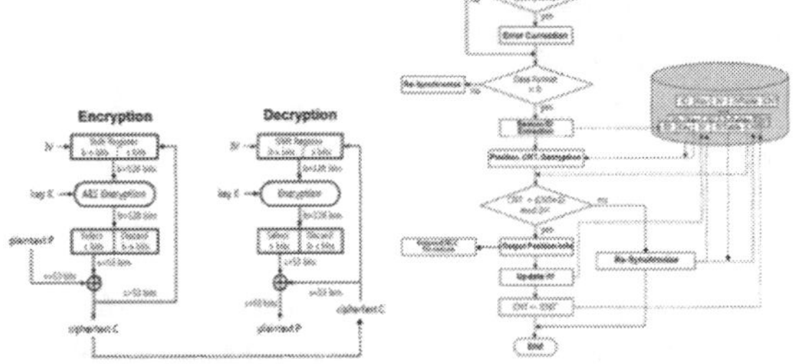

Fig. 7. Encryption by 128 bits AES/CFB & Key management

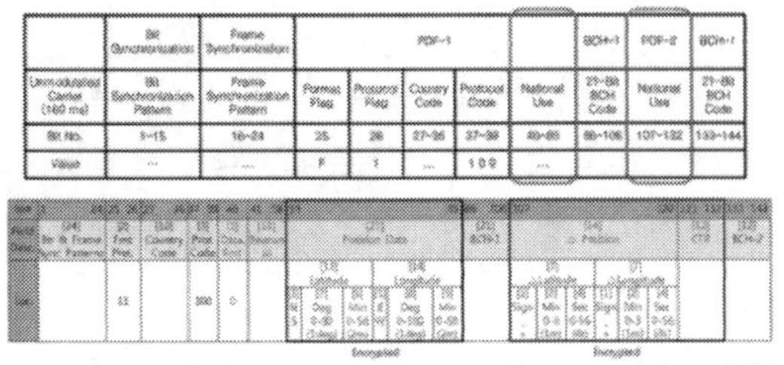

Fig. 8. National User Protocol message format and data fields from COSPAS SARSAT message structure[7].

LTE link provides its own security mechanism and additional security mechanism by using AES 256 bits for LTE was used. Encryption algorithm with IPSec protocol was applied including LTE user terminal control through return link, MCC encryption message processing, and encryption key management through return link.
Additionally, COSPAS SARSAT link based on USRP in RF was utilized to check its feasibility as shown in Fig. 9.

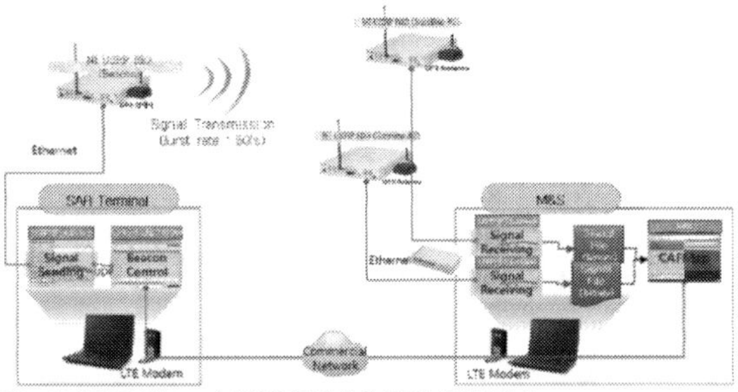

Fig. 9. USRP based CCOSPAS SARSAT M&S.

Also, signal by taking into account dynamics of satellite and relative motion of the satellite [8] were applied to the hybrid system as shown in Fig. 10. We, also, applied new COSPAS SARSAT signal scheme in spread spectrum was applied to the system.

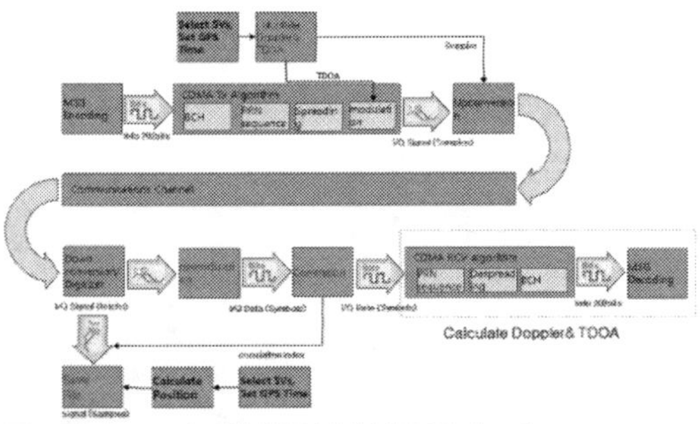

Fig. 10. Dynamic CCOSPAS SARSAT signals

5 Conclusions

Results of the study on Search and Rescue System for Military and Civil use by using COSPAS SARSAT and Terrestrial Communication Network was described. The study has been made to show the feasibility of the system under consideration of prompt implementation. System was designed by considering less burden to conventional COSPAS SARSAT, employ encryption for security and privacy, alternative positioning with distress signal itself, and RF level signal feasibility check. Based on the study, commercialization and mass production of the beacon including system is proposed as future work.

This work has been supported by National GNSS Research Center program of Defence Acquisition Program Administration and Agency for Defence Development.

References

1. COSPAS SARSAT(2017), https://www.cospas-sarsat.int/en/system-overview/cospas-sarsat-system
2. Kim, J. H., Lee, S. U., Kim, J. H., Ahn, W. G. 2014, Development Status of Military Search and Rescue System M&S Software, The Journal of Korea Society of Communication and Space Technology, Vol 9 No 3, 121-126
3. Sanguk Lee, I. C. Jeong, Jaehyun Kim, and Woo-Geun Ahn, " Security enhanced Search and Rescue System by using LTE and COSPAS SARSAT, " 11th Annual Baska GNSS Conference, Baska, Kirk Island, Croatia. 5. 7-9, 2017
4. FIPS(2001), FIPS-197, Advanced encryption standard (AES).
5. IEEE(2007), "Standard for cryptographic protection of data on block-oriented storage services," IEEE P1619/D16.
6. Stallings, W. (2011), Cryptography and Network Security, 5th Ed., Pearson.
7. COSPAS SARSAT(2012A), JC-26/Inf.27, SAR/GALILEO Return Link System Message Specification
8. Jeong, I. C., Kim, D. W., Ahn, W. G., & Lee, S. U., 2017, Development of Search and Rescue System with Dynamic Model by RF Signal Based LTE, Journal of Satellite, information and Communications, Vol 12 No.4, 120-124

ACCURACY ANALYSIS OF GNSS (GPS, GLONASS AND BEIDOU) OBSEVATION FOR POSITIONING

Khomsin[1,*], *Ira* Mutiara Anjasmara[1], *Danar* Guruh Pratomo[1], and *Wahyu* Ristanto[1]

[1]Geomatic Engineering Department, ITS Surabaya, Indonesia

Abstract. Global Navigation Satellite System called GNSS is a term used for the entire global navigation that already operate or are in the planning for the future. Some of the satellite that can be used are GPS (Global Positioning System) operated by USA, GLONASS (Global Navigation Satellite System) operated by Rusia and BeiDou/Compass operated by China. Many errors and biases that occur when measuring with GNSS in the field. Theoritically, there are some errors and biases that can be eliminated or subtracted by strength of satellite geometric. One factor to get a good satellite geometric is to increase the number of satellites received by receiver. In general, the more number of satellites received, the better the geometric satellites received by receivers. The development of receiver technology is currently able to capture GPS, GLONASS and BeiDou signals at one time. Thus the receiver can receive many satellites and finally the shape of geometric satellite becomes better. HiTarget V30 is one of the latest GNSS technology on the market today. This receiver is capable of receiving GPS signals, GLONASS and BeiDou at one time of observation. This research will compare the accuracy of positioning using GPS, GLONASS and BeiDou satellite.

1 Introduction

Recently, the technology of satellite navigation is continuously increasing in number of new applications. A few decades ago, many applications that were just a dream are becoming reality today and the potential applications coverages has grown significantly over the last few years. The unprecedented social, economic, technological and environmental benefits to be gained through these applications are becoming very clear [1].

Global Navigation Satellite System called GNSS is a term used for the entire global navigation satellite system that already operate or are in the planning [2]. Some of which are GPS, GLONASS, Galileo, BeiDou, IRNSS, dan QZSS satellite system. The use of GNSS make the extraterrestrial survey easier and will give better precision. GNSS can not only be used world-wide, all weather and all times but also can be used to determine precise position to all manner of user especially for surveying and geodetic applications [3].

A GNSS receiver calculates position based on data received from satellites. However, there are many sources of errors that, if left uncorrected, cause the position calculation to be inaccurate. Some of these errors, such as those caused by the refraction of the satellite signal as it passes through the ionosphere and troposphere, multipath, cycle slip, orbit, satellite clock and receiver noise [4]. The accuracy of positioning from a GNSS survey will generally depend on 4 (four) factors, namely: the accuracy of the data used, the observation geometry, the observation strategy used, and the data processing strategy. The accuracy of the data used will basically depend on three factors, namely: data type (pseudo range or phase), the quality of the receiver, and the level of error and bias affecting the observation data [5].

The observation geometry includes the observer geometry (network) and satellite geometry that depends on the number of satellites, locations, and distribution of satellites received. Theoretically, the more satellites received, the better satellite geometry [2][6]. The evolving receiver technology can overcome the error of less satellite geometry when retrieving data.

According to [7], GNSS signal combination which is between BeiDou signals (B1 and B2) and GPS signals (L1 and L2) has produced x, y, and z coordinates with better accuracy and precision. The combination of GPS signals and GLONASS signals [6] can increase accuracy up to millimeter order for short baselines and order centimeters for long baselines. In this research we will analyze the use of three combinations of GPS, GLONASS and BeiDou satellites using Hi-Target V30 receiver. With the use of more satellites it will get more data which expected to increase the accuracy of GNSS surveys.

* Corresponding author: khomsin95@yahoo.com

2 Data and Method

2.1. Data

Locating a suitable area for conducting this research is Surabaya City, East Java. The survey location and the design of baseline survey can be seen in Figure 1 below.

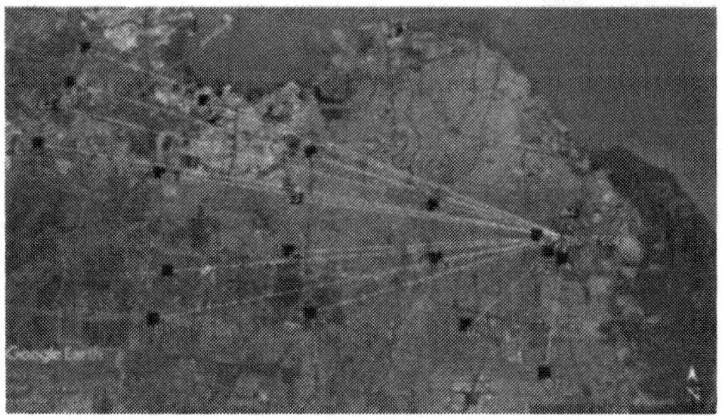

Figure 1. Survey Location and baseline survey plan

2.2 Instruments

The study used GNSS receiver Hi-Target V30 to observe the baseline from base to other points (rovers). The instrument specifications and visualizations can be seen in Table 1 and Figure 2.

Table 1. GNSS receiver Hi-Target V30 Specification [8]

Measurement	220 channels
Satellite signal tracked simultaneously	GPS (L1C/A, L2C, L2E, L5)
	Glonass (L1C/A, L1P, L2C/A)
	BeiDou (B1 and B2)
Static and Fast Static	H: 2.5 mm x 0.5 ppm D
	V: 5.0 mm x 0.5 ppm D
RTK Surveying	H: 8.0 mm x 1.0 ppm D
	V: 15.0 mm x 1.0 ppm D

Figure 2. GNSS receiver Hi-Target V30

2.3 Method

The first step taken in this research is planning a survey that includes the baseline design and field orientation. In this case, we plan some baselines with distance of 1 km, 5 km, 10 km 15 km and 20 km from a base station. In addition, each baseline distance categories have four baselines (points), so that total observations in this case are twenty baselines. After that is the field orientation to check the location of the points to be measured whether the location meets the requirements or not by looking at multipath and other obstacles.

The next step is the GNSS survey was carried out in accordance with the designs previously made using two V30 Hi-Target GNSS Receivers where one receiver as a base and another as a rover. The observation method used is static with an hour observation and only radial observation with BM ITS-01 as a base and other points as rovers.

After the all of observations are complete, the observation data are downloaded and then to be processed with 6 strategies:

- 1st strategy is GPS, GLONASS and BeiDou signals are processed simultaneously
- 2nd strategy is both of GPS and GLONASS signal are processed simultaneously
- 3rd strategy is both of GPS and BeiDou signals are processed simultaneously
- 4th strategy is both of GLONASS and BeiDou signals are processed simultaneously
- 5th strategy is only GPS signal is processed
- 6th strategy is only GLONASS satellite signal is processed

We could not process only BeiDou signal because the GNSS receiver Hi-Target V30 just received two satellite of BeiDou, namely B1 and B2. Finally, this research will compare coordinate results between one strategy and other strategies.

 https://doi.org/10.1051/e3sconf/20199401019

3 Result and Discussion

3.1 BM Referenced

The GNSS observation in this case was carried out by static positioning and radial methods which were tied at the BM ITS – 01 as referenced point. This BM is located in front of the ITS Rectorat building in Sukolilo Campus – Eastern of Surabaya (Figure 3). The coordinates of BM ITS-01 can be seen at Table 2.

Figure 3. BM ITS – 01 and its location

Table 2. BM ITS-01 coordinate as referenced point

Coordinate	
Easting (m)	698.076.449
Northing (m)	9194686.012
Latitude (S)	7°16'55.123"
Longitude (E)	112°47'38.956"
Ellipsoid Height (m)	36.056

The condition of BM ITS - 01 is relatively still strong and sturdy, and generally the location is free from multipath and other obstacles. Even though there is a little multipath from the surrounding trees, but it can still be reduced by 15^0 mask angle observation.

3.2 Length of baseline observation

In this research, the GNSS observation is divided to five categories of length of baselines: 1 km (A), 5 km (B), 10 km (C), 15 km (D) and 20 km (E) from the base station. Each category has four measured points, so that a total of twenty points are measured (Table 3). The Table 3 below shows that the baseline distance at each point. The length of the baseline obtained cannot be fixed with the planning carried out, because only estimates and location conditions do not make it possible to take measurements so that it must be shifted. However, in general the conditions of GNSS observations are still the same as the planned.

3.3 Coordinate accuracy analysis of baseline processing

This GNSS data processing used Hi-Target Geomatics Office (HGO) software to convert format data from Hi-Target format to RINEX (Receiver Independence Exchange) format and Topcon Tools 8.2.3 software to perform a baseline (differential positioning) processing. Table 4 to Table 9 shows the accuracy of coordinate results for category A, B, C, D, and E with 1st strategy to 6th strategy. There are two accuracies, namely horizontal accuracy and vertical accuracy.

Table 3. Length of Baseline observation

Base	Category	Point	Distance (m)
BM ITS - 01	1 km	A1	915.584
		A2	1123.152
		A3	960.171
		A4	968.860
	5 km	B1	5022.564
		B2	4957.415
		B3	6518.977
		B4	5561.453
	10 km	C1	10061.730
		C2	10096.420
		C3	10513.090
		C4	9778.561
	15 km	D1	14847.860
		D2	14648.180
		D3	14597.480
		D4	14242.440
	20 km	E1	20628.960
		E2	20492.890
		E3	20848.130
		E4	20860.360

Table 4 shows that the 1st strategy processing using GPS + GLONASS + BeiDou signals together produce horizontal and vertical accuracy less than 1 cm for length of baseline ≤ 5 km. For the length of baseline from 10 km to 20 km, this strategy resulted less than 2 cm for horizontal accuracy and 2.5 cm for vertical accuracy. These accuracies can be used as ground control point measurements for high resolution satellite image, airborne photogrammetry and complete land registration.

In the 2nd strategy used GPS + GLONASS signals together to process the data, it can be seen in Table 5 that all baselines have the same horizontal and vertical accuracy with the 1st strategy. It means that BeiDou satellite signals namely B1 and B2 has no significant to improve GPS + GLONASS accuracy. Therefore, all the 2nd strategy coordinates accuracies can be used as ground control point and independent check point measurements for high resolution satellite image and airborne Lidar and photogrammetry rectification and orthorectification process. In addition to these accuracies can also be used as control points for surveying and mapping and complete land registration project.

Table 4. Coordinate accuracy from GPS + GLONASS + BeiDou processing (1st Strategy)

Category	Point	Horizontal RMS (m)	Vertical RMS (m)
1 km	A1	0.2	0.5
	A2	0.3	0.6
	A3	0.5	0.8
	A4	0.3	0.4
5 km	B1	0.3	0.5
	B2	0.3	0.4
	B3	0.4	0.8
	B4	0.3	0.5
10 km	C1	1.1	2.0
	C2	1.4	2.3
	C3	1.9	1.4
	C4	0.7	1.2
15 km	D1	0.8	1.1
	D2	0.7	1.2
	D3	0.8	1.3
	D4	0.8	1.3
20 km	E1	1.3	1.5
	E2	1.0	2.3
	E3	1.5	1.5
	E4	1.3	2.0

GPS + BeiDou signal processing in the 3rd strategy can be seen in Table 6. This table describes that in general, the horizontal accuracies for all baselines have almost the same accuracy with the 1st and 2nd accuracies but C3 and E3 have accuracy more than 1.5 cm that is 3.3 cm and 1.7 cm for C3 and E3 respectively. The vertical accuracies for length of baselines ≤ 5 km has the same value with the 1st and 2nd strategies, however many baselines have more 2 cm accuracies for 10 – 20 km baselines.

Coordinate accuracy obtained from the 4th strategy, ie GLONASS + BeiDou Satellite signal processing can be seen in the Table 7. Horizontal accuracies for 1 – 5 km baseline length are less than 1 cm and vertical accuracies are less than 1.5 cm. Generally, the horizontal accuracies for 10 – 20 km baseline are less than 20 cm, although some points have more than 20 cm such as C1 (44.5 cm) and E3 (30.4 cm). Vertical accuracies in these baselines almost have similar accuracy with horizontal accuracies. Some points have accuracy more than 20 cm, namely C1 (38.0 cm), E2 (25.4 cm) and E3 (28.3 cm).

Table 5. Coordinate accuracy from GPS + GLONASS processing (2nd Strategy)

Category	Point	Horizontal RMS (m)	Vertical RMS (m)
1 km	A1	0.2	0.5
	A2	0.3	0.6
	A3	0.5	0.8
	A4	0.3	0.4
5 km	B1	0.3	0.5
	B2	0.3	0.4
	B3	0.4	0.8
	B4	0.3	0.5
10 km	C1	1.1	2.0
	C2	1.4	2.3
	C3	1.9	1.4
	C4	0.7	1.2
15 km	D1	0.8	1.1
	D2	0.7	1.2
	D3	0.8	1.3
	D4	0.8	1.3
20 km	E1	1.3	1.5
	E2	1.0	2.3
	E3	1.5	1.5
	E4	1.3	2.0

Table 8 shows that the accuracy of the 5th strategy (only GPS processing). It can be seen that the horizontal accuracies for the baseline length less than or equal 5 km are ≤ 1.0 cm and baseline between 10 km and 20 km have accuracies less than 2.0 cm. Except A3, the vertical accuracies for baseline 1 – 5 km are ≤ 1.0 cm and for baseline 10 – 20 km have accuracies less than 6.0 cm.

Finally, the 6th strategy used only GLONASS satellite signal describes that the horizontal accuracies for less than or equal 5 km baseline have ≤ 1.0 cm and their vertical accuracies are less than 1.5 cm. Some points in the baseline length between 10 and 20 km have accuracies more than 30 cm both horizontally and vertically. Therefore, GLONASS data cannot be used to observe ground control point for high resolution satellite image, lidar and airborne photogrammetry. In addition, this strategy also cannot be used to observe ground control points for land surveying and mapping.

Table 6. Coordinate accuracy from GPS + BeiDou processing (3rd Strategy)

Category	Point	Horizontal RMS (cm)	Vertical RMS (cm)
1 km	A1	0.2	0.4
	A2	0.4	0.7
	A3	1.0	1.9
	A4	0.5	0.9
5 km	B1	0.3	0.5
	B2	0.4	0.5
	B3	0.5	1.0
	B4	0.3	0.5
10 km	C1	1.0	2.4
	C2	1.5	2.3
	C3	3.3	5.3
	C4	0.6	1.1
15 km	D1	0.8	1.2
	D2	0.8	1.6
	D3	0.9	1.3
	D4	0.9	1.9
20 km	E1	1.3	1.6
	E2	1.1	2.8
	E3	1.7	2.7
	E4	1.4	1.8

Table 7. Coordinate accuracy from GLONASS + BeiDou processing (4th Strategy)

Category	Point	Horizontal RMS (cm)	Vertical RMS (cm)
1 km	A1	1.0	1.4
	A2	0.5	1.0
	A3	0.6	0.8
	A4	0.4	0.4
5 km	B1	0.6	1.0
	B2	0.5	0.5
	B3	0.5	1.0
	B4	0.7	1.2
10 km	C1	44.5	38.0
	C2	8.8	17.8
	C3	1.6	1.1
	C4	1.8	4.6
15 km	D1	1.3	1.8
	D2	1.7	1.9
	D3	1.3	2.1
	D4	5.1	6.4
Category	Point	Horizontal RMS (cm)	Vertical RMS (cm)
20 km	E1	5.6	11.3
	E2	17.8	25.4
	E3	30.4	28.3
	E4	2.2	2.5

Table 8. Coordinate accuracy from only GPS processing (5th Strategy)

Category	Point	Horizontal RMS (cm)	Vertical RMS (cm)
1 km	A1	2.0	4.0
	A2	4.0	7.0
	A3	1.0	1.9
	A4	0.5	0.9
5 km	B1	0.3	0.5
	B2	0.4	0.5
	B3	0.5	1.0
	B4	0.3	0.5
10 km	C1	1.0	2.4
	C2	1.5	2.3
	C3	3.3	5.3
	C4	0.6	1.1
15 km	D1	0.8	1.2
	D2	0.8	1.2
	D3	0.9	1.3
	D4	0.9	1.9
20 km	E1	1.3	1.6
	E2	1.1	2.8
	E3	1.7	2.7
	E4	1.4	1.8

Table 9. Coordinate accuracy from only GLONASS processing (6th Strategy)

Category	Point	Horizontal RMS (cm)	Vertical RMS (cm)
1 km	A1	1.0	1.4
	A2	0.5	1.0
	A3	0.6	0.8
	A4	0.4	0.4
5 km	B1	0.6	1.0
	B2	0.5	1.0
	B3	0.5	1.0
	B4	0.7	1.2
10 km	C1	36.3	62.4
	C2	58.5	35.9
	C3	1.6	1.1
	C4	1.8	4.5

 https://doi.org/10.1051/e3sconf/20199401019

15 km	D1	1.3	1.8
	D2	1.8	1.9
	D3	1.3	2.1
	D4	5.6	6.8
20 km	E1	5.3	11.1
	E2	1.8	25.4
	E3	33.8	30.1
	E4	2.2	2.5

3.3 Coordinate accuracy analysis of baseline processing

The coordinates accuracies of the data processing with the six strategies mentioned above can be categorized based on the length of the baseline. The accuracy of coordinates of each category from A (1 km) to E (20 km) can be seen in Tables 10 to Table 14.

Table 10 shows that all strategies resulted horizontal accuracy for category A (1 km baseline) ≤ 1 cm. However only the 1st strategy and the 2nd strategy produced vertical accuracies less than or equal 1 cm and other strategies have accuracy almost 2 cm for some points.

Table 10. Coordinate accuracy category A (length of baseline 1 km)

Strategy	Accuracy	A1 (cm)	A2 (cm)	A3 (cm)	A4 (cm)
1st	Horizontal	0.2	0.3	0.5	0.3
	Vertical	0.5	0.6	0.8	0.4
2nd	Horizontal	0.2	0.3	0.5	0.3
	Vertical	0.5	0.6	0.8	0.4
3rd	Horizontal	0.2	0.4	1.0	0.5
	Vertical	0.4	0.7	1.9	0.9
4th	Horizontal	1.0	0.5	0.6	0.4
	Vertical	1.4	1.0	0.8	0.4
5th	Horizontal	0.2	0.4	1.0	0.5
	Vertical	0.4	0.7	1.9	0.9
6th	Horizontal	1.0	0.5	0.6	0.4
	Vertical	1.4	1.0	0.8	0.4

All coordinate accuracies for category B (5 km baseline) can be seen on Table 11. In this case all points have horizontal and vertical accuracies less than 1.25 cm. This category has better accuracy than category A.

Table 11. Coordinate accuracy category B (length of baseline 5 km)

Strategy	Accuracy	B1 (cm)	B2 (cm)	B3 (cm)	B4 (cm)
1st	Horizontal	0.3	0.3	0.4	0.3
	Vertical	0.5	0.4	0.8	0.5
2nd	Horizontal	0.3	0.3	0.4	0.3
	Vertical	0.5	0.4	0.8	0.5
3rd	Horizontal	0.3	0.4	0.5	0.3
	Vertical	0.5	0.5	1.0	0.5
4th	Horizontal	0.6	0.5	0.5	0.7
	Vertical	1.0	0.5	1.0	1.2
5th	Horizontal	0.3	0.4	0.5	0.3
	Vertical	0.5	0.5	1.0	0.5
6th	Horizontal	0.6	0.5	0.5	0.7
	Vertical	1.0	1.0	1.0	1.2

Horizontal accuracies for the 10 km length of baseline can be seen Table 12. This table shows that horizontal accuracies are less than 2 cm for the 1st and 2nd strategies, otherwise generally other strategies have more than 2 cm accuracies. Many points have more than 35 cm accuracies such as C1 for 4th and 6th strategies and C2 for 6th strategy. The 1st and the 2nd strategies have vertical accuracies less than 2.5 cm and the 4th and 6th strategies have 38 cm and 62.4 cm for C1 and 17.8 cm and 35.9 cm for C2.

Table 12. Coordinate accuracy category C (length of baseline 10 km)

Strategy	Accuracy	C1 (cm)	C2 (cm)	C3 (cm)	C4 (cm)
1st	Horizontal	1.1	1.4	1.9	0.7
	Vertical	2.0	2.3	1.4	1.2
2nd	Horizontal	1.1	1.4	1.9	0.7
	Vertical	2.0	2.3	1.4	1.2
3rd	Horizontal	1.0	1.5	3.3	0.6
	Vertical	2.4	2.3	5.3	1.1
4th	Horizontal	44.5	8.8	1.6	1.8
	Vertical	38.0	17.8	1.1	4.6
5th	Horizontal	1.0	1.5	3.3	0.6
	Vertical	2.4	2.3	5.3	1.1
6th	Horizontal	36.3	58.5	1.6	1.8
	Vertical	62.4	35.9	1.1	4.5

In general, horizontal and vertical accuracies for category D have better than category C. All accuracies in category D (Table 13) are less than or equal 2.1 cm. Some points have accuracies more than 5 cm such as D4 for 4th and 6th strategies.

Table 13. Coordinate accuracy category D (length of baseline 15 km)

Strategy	Accuracy	D1 (cm)	D2 (cm)	D3 (cm)	D4 (cm)
1st	Horizontal	0.8	0.7	0.8	0.8
	Vertical	1.1	1.2	1.3	1.3
2nd	Horizontal	0.8	0.7	0.8	0.8
	Vertical	1.1	1.2	1.3	1.3
3rd	Horizontal	0.8	0.8	0.9	0.9
	Vertical	1.2	1.6	1.3	1.9
4th	Horizontal	1.3	1.7	1.3	5.1
	Vertical	1.8	1.9	2.1	6.4
5th	Horizontal	0.8	0.8	0.9	0.9
	Vertical	1.2	1.2	1.3	1.9
6th	Horizontal	1.3	1.8	1.3	5.6
	Vertical	1.8	1.9	2.1	6.8

Finally, coordinate accuracies for category E can be seen in Table E. This table shows that horizontal and vertical accuracies are less than 3 cm for 1st, 2nd, 3rd and 4th strategies, however in the 4th and 6th strategies almost all points have accuracies more than 11 cm except all point in E4.

Table 14. Coordinate accuracy category E (length of baseline 20 km)

Strategy	Accuracy	E1 (cm)	E2 (cm)	E3 (cm)	E4 (cm)
1st	Horizontal	1.3	1.0	1.5	1.3
	Vertical	1.5	2.3	1.5	2.0
2nd	Horizontal	1.3	1.0	1.5	1.3
	Vertical	1.5	2.3	1.5	2.0
3rd	Horizontal	1.3	1.1	1.7	1.4
	Vertical	1.6	2.8	2.7	1.8
4th	Horizontal	5.6	17.8	30.4	2.2
	Vertical	11.3	25.4	28.3	2.5
5th	Horizontal	1.3	1.1	1.7	1.4
	Vertical	1.6	2.8	2.7	1.8
6th	Horizontal	5.3	18.0	33.8	2.2
	Vertical	11.1	25.4	30.1	2.5

4 Conclusion

Based on the results of this research, it can be concluded that:

1. The 1st (GPS + GLONASS + BeiDou) and 2nd (GPS + GLONASS) strategy have the same horizontal and vertical accuracies for all categories (1 – 20 km) whereas horizontal accuracies are less than 2 cm and vertical are accuracies less than 2.5 cm.
2. All strategies have horizontal accuracies less than or equal 1 cm and vertical accuracies less than 2 cm for baseline ≤ 5 km.

5 Acknowledgment

We wish to acknowledge PT. Geosolution Pratama Nusantara for the GNSS HiTarget V30 equipment thus we can complete this research

References

1. H.C. Chen, Y.S. Huang, K.W Chiang, M Yang, And R.J. Rauthe. Performance Comparison Between GPS And Beidou-2/Compass: A Perspective from Asia. Journal of The Chinese Institute of Engineers, Vol. 32, No. 5, Pp. 679-689. 2009.
2. Novatel. An Introduction to GNSS GPS, GLONASS, BeiDou, Galileo and other Global Navigation Satellite Systems. Novatel Inc. Second Edition 2015.
3. C.D. Ghilani and P.R. Wolf. Elementary Surveying. An introduction to Geomatics. 13th edition. Prentice Hall. 2012
4. G. Seeber. Satellite Geodesy 2nd Edition. Walter de Gruyter · Berlin 2003
5. H.Z. Abidin, A. Jones, dna J. Kahar. Survei Dengan GPS. Cetakan Ketiga. Jakarta: PT Pradnya Paramita. 2011.
6. B. Rudianto., Y. Izman., Analisis Komparatif Ketelitian Posisi Titik Hasil Pengukuran dari Satelit GPS dan Satelit GLONASS. Institut Teknologi Nasional. 2011.
7. I. Gumilar , A.I. Pamungkas, H.Z. Abidin, B. Bramanto, F.S. Adi. 2016. The Contribution of BeiDou Positioning System for Accuracy Improvement : A Perspective from Bandung, Indonesia. International Symposium on GNSS at Tainan, Taiwan. 2016.
8. Hi-Target. V30/50 GNSS RTK System Manual. Hi-Target. Surveying Instrument Co., Ltd. 2010

Designing Control Points in UAV-Photogrammetry Mapping Using GNSS Concept to Produce Land Use Map (Case Study: Ciwidey Village, Bandung Regency, Indonesia)

Sadikin Hendriatiningsih, *Asep* Y. Saptari, *Sudarman*, *Ratri* Widyastuti, *Putri* Rahmadani

Surveying and Cadastre Research Division, Institut Teknologi Bandung, 40132, Indonesia

Abstract. Production of orhtophoto maps from UAV-photogrammetry method depend on aerial data and control points that are measured by GNSS method. Quality control of orhtophoto maps need comparison coordinate from Check Points and orthophoto maps coordinate to calculate the Root Mean Square Error (RMSE). So that, quality of control points is important in aerial data processing. In this research, baseline length, observation time, measurement method, and area characteristics will be discussed based on the GNSS concept to fulfill the accuracy standard of control points from the American Society of Photogrammetry and Remote Sensing (ASPRS). The shorter baseline length, and the loner observation time, accuracy should be increase significantly, but it depends on the field situation and the accuracy required for the user. After all, the result of this research is to obtain control points design based on GNSS concept in Ciwidey Village, Bandung Regency

1. Introduction

Unmanned Aerial Vehicle (UAV) – Photogrammetry mapping can be used for many applications, for example to produce base map in high resolution that can be used in many purposes, such as land use map. Standard accuracy refer to the standard accuracy by American Society of Photogrammetry and Remote Sensing.

UAV-photogrammetry processing need control points where distribute evenly in the Area of Interest (AOI). One way to produce high accuracy of control points is using GNSS method. The concept of GNSS is used to determine the position of a receiver on land, at sea, or in space by means of constellation of multiple artificial satellites [1]. GNSS use many satellite such as GPS, GLONAS, GALILEO, SBAS, QZSS, and BEIDOU. These kind of GNSS satellite can be used in many applications. There are five stages of basic GNSS concept; firstly, GNSS satellites orbit the earth; secondly, GNSS regularly broadcast their ephemerides, time, and their status; thirdly, GNSS user equipment receives the signals from multiple GNSS satellites, receive information the time it takes the signals to travel from the satellite to the receiver; fourthly, GNSS user equipment uses the recovered information to compute time and position; fifthly, GNSS user equipment utilizes the position and time information in their applications [2]. Positioning with wide-area GNSS network is basically based on Differential Global Positioning System (DGPS) and Real Time Kinematic (RTK) concept [3]. It is a method to define unknown position by knowing the distance from three known points [2].

Device that uses GNSS concept is Global Positioning System (GPS) receiver. A typical non-geodetic grade GPS can estimate the user's position accuracy about 12 meters, but GPS-geodetic-grade can produce position that are accurate to sub-centimeter level [3]. Therefore, device selection in data acquisition stage must be adjusted to the research purposes. Furthermore, there are various satellite observation methods that will affect the data accuracy. This research discuss how to manage data acquisition using GNSS concept in order to fulfill required accuracy of control point.

2. Methodology

The purpose of this research is to obtain control points in certain accuracy to produce high accuracy of orhtophoto maps. Methodology of this research can be seen in Figure 1.

* Corresponding author: hningsih@gmail.com

https://doi.org/10.1051/e3sconf/20199401020

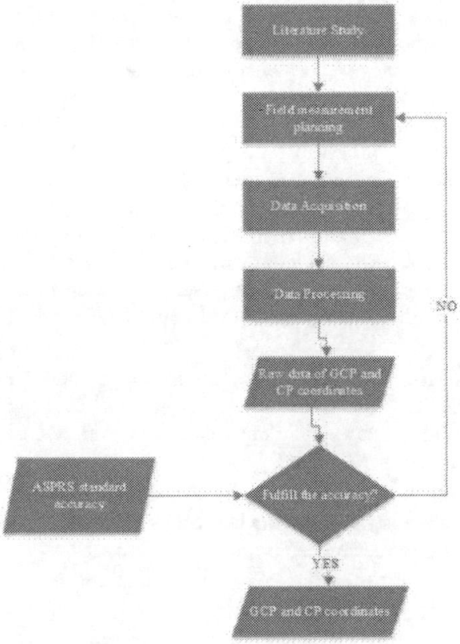

Figure 1. Methodology scheme

Figure 1 can be explained as follows:

2.1. Literature Study

There are some errors in GNSS that affect accuracy, including clock-related errors, signal propagation errors, system errors, intentional error sources, user equivalent error, and dilution of precision [4].

GPS positional accuracy can be improved by using differential correction obtained by using a technique called Differential GPS (DGPS), which has been known to provide the most accurate positioning result [5]. Differential GPS concept need two receivers: one is referred to the base station (known coordinates point) and the other one is referred to the rover (unknown point), so that the common errors such as clock synchronization errors and the atmospheric range delays can be eliminated by differential method observation [3]. There are estimated of DGPS positioning accuracy in the equation below [3]:

$$DGPS\text{-}A = \pm[0.5 \text{ cm} + 1 \text{ ppm of } BL \quad (1)$$

where:

DGPS-A: DGPS positioning accuracy

BL : baseline length

Satellite observation methods also affect the control point's accuracy. There are several methods of satellite observation, rapid static, stop and go, pseudo-kinematic, and combination methods [6]. Generally, rapid static method uses in radial mode and vulnerable to the effects of errors and bias. Stop-and-go method must be based on differential positioning methods using phase data and the determination of the correct phase ambiguity is essential from this method. As in the case of rapid static methods, this pseudo-kinematic method requires a good satellite geometry, a low level of bias and error in the data, and a relative environment that does not cause multipath effects. Basically, the selection of satellite observation methods affects the length of time observation in the field. Moreover, length of time observation and open space observation location is affected the accuracy [6].

2.2. Field Measurement Planning

There are some parameters that need to be considered to do a GPS survey, described as follows [6]:

a. equipment

The type of GPS receiver that would be used in field survey has to be planned first. Equipment selection affects the accuracy produced during the survey.

b. observation strategy

Things that are taken into consideration for the GPS observation strategy are observation methods, time and duration of observation, reference points, and observation of quality control. There are two kind of observation methods such as post processing method and real-time method. Static, rapid static, stop-and-go, pseudo-kinematic, and kinematic methods are included in post processing observation methods. Prolonged observation can lead to better randomization of the effects of orbital errors and the biased effects of the ionosphere and troposphere on distance measurement data [7]. Furthermore, number of satellite, satellite type, ionosphere activity, signal obstruction, receiver type (single or dual frequency), and point's accessibility must be considered to determine the length of time of observation. The reference point is used to bind unknown points that are measured to define the datum from the corresponding basic framework.

c. implementation mechanism

Number of personnel, job desk distribution, communication and transportation, equipment, and accommodation need to be prepared before field survey.

d. observation geometry

Condition of device location need to be considered. to avoid multipath effect and noise effect, device location need to be far away from reflective objects and elevation mask ranges from $10^0 - 15^0$. Furthermore, other condition must be considered such as the location is easy to reach, safe and has a stable soil structure.

e. data processing strategy

There are several prominent characteristic for GPS data processing, such as [8]:

- point coordinates are determined in three dimensions towards a geocentric Cartesian coordinate system defined by the 1984 WGS datum
- the estimation process of baseline vector and point coordinates refer on the least squares method
- Data processing is processed after data from several GPS receivers involved are collected
- Data processing is processed in stages, from the baseline to the baseline so that it forms a network, which is then followed by network alignment and coordinate transformation from the 1984 WGS datum to the datum used by the user

Regarding to the Standard Accuracy by American Society of Photogrammetry and Remote Sensing, horizontal accuracy standards for digital planimetric data class I = 1.25% of map scale factor. This research was planning to produce 1:5000 scale maps of landuse map. So, this research need to produce 0.625 mm horizontal accuracy of orhtophoto map, with the assumption to produce required orhtophoto map, horizontal accuracy for control points are 0.5 of required orhtophoto map. So that the horizontal accuracy of the control points is less than 0.325 m. Referred to the equation (1), maximum value of baseline length is ± 32 km. Furthermore, some parameters as explained above need to be considered.

2.3. Data Acquisition

Table 1 describe data acquisition in this research.

Table 1. Data Acquisition Information

Type	Information
Equipment	GPS Emlid Reach Rs, single frequency,
Observation Methods	Real Time Kinematic Methods for Control Point and Rapid Static methods for Check Point
Number of GPS	3 Receiver
Number of Personnel	4 persons
Mask Elevation	10^0
Baseline Length	< 25 kilometers
Time Duration of field survey	10 days

GPS device have been using in this research is GPS geodetic but using one single frequency. Number of control pints is 11 points. Because there are none reference point near Ciwidey, so one base point in Ciwidey area is being taken from Indonesian Geospatial Information Agency (BIG) benchmark in Padalarang area for four hours observation used static methods. Ten GCP observed for ±0.5 hour for each control point used *Real Time Kinematic* (RTK) method. Furthermore, 20 check points observation used static method is also conducted along with check point observation. Check point and control point observation need 10 days because of rain makes the work takes much longer than it should. Satellite observation methods are chosen based on the accuracy requirements and time available to conduct field surveys

Job desk distribution is for four persons, one person is a driver, and the other did the observation. Baseline distance from BIG benchmark as referenced point to base point in Ciwidey is ±28 km.

Control point distribution can be seen in Figure 2 and check point distribution can be seen in Figure 3.

Figure 2. Control Point Distribution

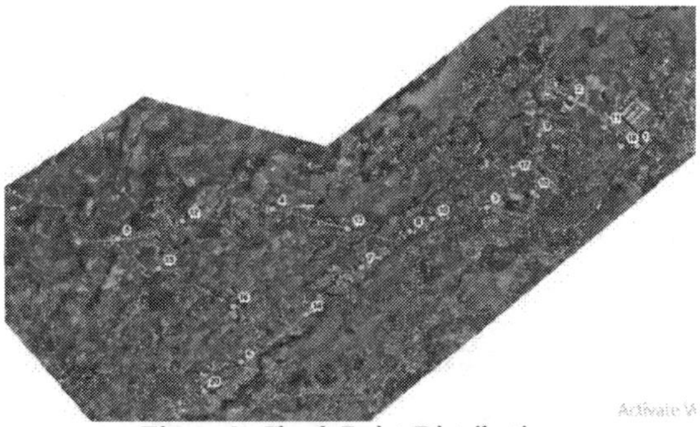

Figure 3. Check Point Distribution

2.4. Data Processing

RINEX format is received from the GPS device. Data processing in this research using open source software, RTK Lib. Because this is open source software and can processed many varies of GPS devices, there are some parameters must be defined first, such as antenna height, and approximate station coordinates. The concept of data processing can be seen in Figure 4.

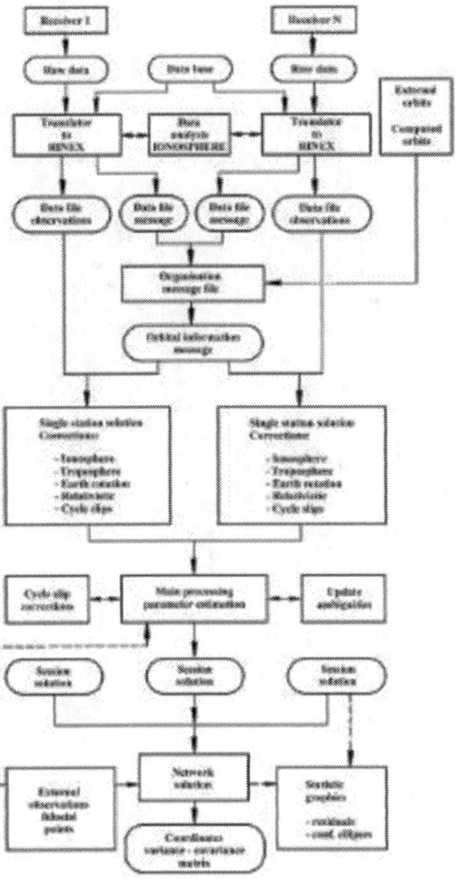

Figure 4. Simplified functional flow diagram of generic GPS software package [9]

3. Result And Discussion

Referred to equation (1) about DGPS positioning accuracy, Table 2 is a comparison between equations (1) based in the baseline length and horizontal accuracy calculation based on the observation data.

Table 2. Comparison DGPS positioning accuracy prediction and horizontal accuracy of data processing

Control Point	Horizontal accuracy (m)	DGPS-A (m)
BM CWDY	0.001	0.035
CWDY 1	0.004	0.006
CWDY 2	0.003	0.006
CWDY 3	0.004	0.005
CWDY 5	0.004	0.006
CWDY 6	0.001	0.006
CWDY 7	0.006	0.007
CWDY 8	0.003	0.007
CWDY 9	0.006	0.008
CWDY 10	0.001	0.006
CWDY 11	0.003	0.007

Table 2 indicate that the result of horizontal accuracy of this research below from the horizontal accuracy prediction from equation (1). So that, the equation (1) can be applied to plan the control points distribution based on the baseline length.

As mentioned in the sub-section 2.1, there are various variable that affect accuracy. Table 3 gives the information about horizontal accuracy, baseline length, and radius of open space.

Table 3. Control Point's information

Control Point	Horizontal Standard Deviation (m)	Baseline Length (m)	Time Duration (minute)	Radius of Open Space (m)
CWDY 1	0.004	917.751	28.700	5.319
CWDY 2	0.003	911.474	43.733	10.893
CWDY 3	0.004	464.828	31.017	11.745
CWDY 5	0.004	1127.773	40.033	5.316
CWDY 6	0.001	1447.740	86.533	28.707
CWDY 7	0.006	2301.420	64.083	15.254
CWDY 8	0.003	2129.266	80.667	1.630
CWDY 9	0.006	2645.321	35.200	2.977
CWDY 10	0.001	639.555	60.500	8.844
CWDY 11	0.003	1882.338	94.150	2.257

: Highest value

: Lowest value

Point 'CWDY 9' gives highest value of horizontal standard deviation and baseline length. It indicates that baseline length affect the horizontal accuracy in that point. Shorter baseline length increase horizontal accuracy. Point 'CWDY 6' gives the lowest value of horizontal standard deviation but gives the highest value in radius of open space. It indicates that longer radius of open space increase the horizontal accuracy. Conclusion of Table 3, indicates that the open space radius, baseline length, and duration of observation influence each other on horizontal accuracy as mentioned in the concept of satellite observation

4. Conclusion

Equation (1), prediction of horizontal accuracy can be applied to design the control point distribution for the benefit of orhtophoto processing. Location selection of control points must consider baseline length, time duration of satellite observation, radius of open space, accuracy requirements, time schedule of field survey, number of human resources, and device availability. The methodology of this research can be applied to obtain control points in UAV-Photogrammetry method.

5. Reference

[1] S. Dawoud, "GNSS principles and comparison," Postdam University.

[2] C. Jeffrey, An Introduction to GNSS, Canada: NovAtel Inc, 2010.

[3] T. A. Ali, "Positioning with Wide-Area GNSS Networks: Concept and Application," *Positioning,* pp. 1-6, 2012.

[4] M. Karaim, M. Elsheikh and A. Noureldin, "GNSS Error Sources," in *Multifuntional Operation and Application of GPS*, Intechopen, 2018.

[5] P. V. Bolstad, J. Andy and B. Jon, "A Comparison of Autonomous, WAAS, Real-Time, and Post-Processed Global Positioning Systems (GPS) Accuracies in Northern Forests," *Northern Journal of Applied Forestry,* pp. 5-11, 2005.

[6] H. Z. Abidin, Survei Dengan GPS, Bandung: Penerbit ITB, 2011.

[7] D. Wells, N. Beck, D. Delikaraoglou, A. Kleusberg, E. J. Krakiwsky, G. Lachapelle, R. B. Langley, M. Nakiboglu, K.-P. Schwarz, J. M. Tranquilla and P. Vanicek, "Guide to GPS Positioning," Geodesy and Geomatic Engineering UNB, Canada, 1999.

[8] R. C. Principles and Practice of GPS Surveying, School of Geomatic Engineering, University of New South Wales, 1997.

[9] G. Seeber, Satellite Geodesy, Berlin: Walter de Gruyter, 2003.

https://doi.org/10.1051/e3sconf/20199401021

Study the capabilities of RTK Multi GNSS under forest canopy in regions of Indonesia

Heri Andreas[1,*], *Hasanuddin* Zainal Abidin[1], *Dina* Anggreni Sarsito[1] and *Dhota* Pradipta[1]

[1]Geodesy Research Division, Faculty of Earth Science and Technology, Institute of Technology Bandung, Indonesia

Abstract. For more than two decade, the position on the earth can be precisely determined "real-time" in the order of few centimeters by Real Time Kinematic (RTK) GNSS (Global Navigation Satellite Systems) Method. Nevertheless, few limitations are still recognized such as degradation of accuracy against limited satellite visibilities (e.g. heavy satellite obstructions from forest canopy). It usually takes time to resolve the ambiguities or even in many occasion resulted in failure. Fortunately since recent years to the future seems more satellite systems beside GPS and GLONASS are being launched such as BEIDOU, GALILEO, QZSS, etc. It means that more satellite will be existed above the sky. The term GNSS has changed into Multi GNSS. This Multi GNSS is theoretically adding the value to previous GNSS System like GPS; problems of limited satellite visibilities (e.g. under forest canopy) to the position accuracy perhaps will reduce. Within this paper we try to do study the capabilities of RTK Multi GNSS under forest canopy in Indonesia. We observed by RTK in the forest areas which have canopy of 40 to 90 percent. As conclusion we found improvement in positioning result of even area of very limited satellite visibilities.

1 Introduction

Back in the early 70, the revolution in world scale positioning has begun as the satellite technology invented. Before that moment the best technique for worldwide positioning were using astronomical technique with their limitation of accuracy while after on the satellite base GNSS (Global Navigation Satellite System) technology has been played as remarkable tool for positioning and mapping with high accuracy can be achieved in the easiest way (Seeber [1], Abidin [2-3], Leick [4], Hofmann et. al [5]). In everywhere and in anytime worldwide when signals from the satellites GNSS (e.g. GPS and GLONASS) received by the receivers, in these cases the position in 3D or even 4D can be determined precisely and even with precision in the order of millimeter. Not to mention, the position can be also precisely determined "real-time" in the order of few centimeter by RTK (Real Time Kinematic) Method. The GNSS indeed become a revolution in positioning on the 20th century. Nevertheless, few limitations are still recognized such as the capability of positioning under heavy satellite obstructions (e.g. in dense urban area, and in canopy area like forest), especially for the RTK method (figure 1). Obstruction will disturb the signal connection and produce cycle slip, and un-favor fixing the ambiguity (Leick [4], Mudita et.al [6]). As for the RTK, in many cases it would give autonomous result, float solution, hardy waiting for resolved ambiguity, and or in some cases given the possibility of fixing to the wrong integer. Not to mention if we set up longer baseline, therefore the degradation in accuracy will more significant. This is the new challenge to be solved, since many applications are dealing with situation of positioning under heavy satellite obstruction such as for forest boundary surveys, rural urban parcel measurements, in between high rise building measurements, etc. Theoretically the availability of more satellites, the existence of another phase signal, and or stronger signal may answer the limitation.

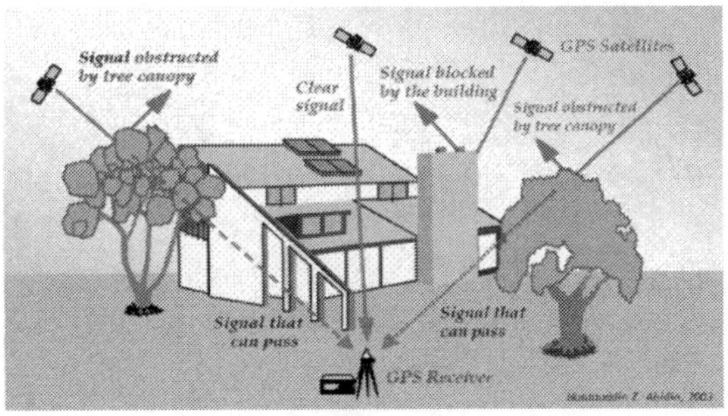

Fig. 1. Illustration of obstruction (e.g. tress canopy, building) and interference to GNSS signal

In the recent years, the GNSS BEIDOU or COMPASS has been launched by the China, the GALILEO by European Union, QZSS (Quasi Zenith Satellite System) by the Japan, and so on. This additional satellite system is theoretically adding the value to others GNSS System since more satellite can be observed (figure 2). With combination of geostationary and the moving satellites, it may improve the capability in

*Corresponding author: heriandreas49@gmail.com

positioning, especially for the RTK method. Problems of satellite obstruction perhaps will reduced by the combination of GPS, GLONASS, BEIDOU, GALILEO and others. The better result on the position is also expected. The term of GNSS has changed into Multi GNSS. Within in this paper we try to do exercise on the capability of RTK Multi GNSS under forest canopy area where we have challenge for satellite signal observation. We observed by this RTK in National Forest Park in northern Bandung, and in forest area in Jambi Indonesia Province where 40 to even 90 percent of canopy existed. This paper will highlight if there are or aren't any improvements in positioning result, especially for the area as mentioned above when many user trend in using more RTK method.

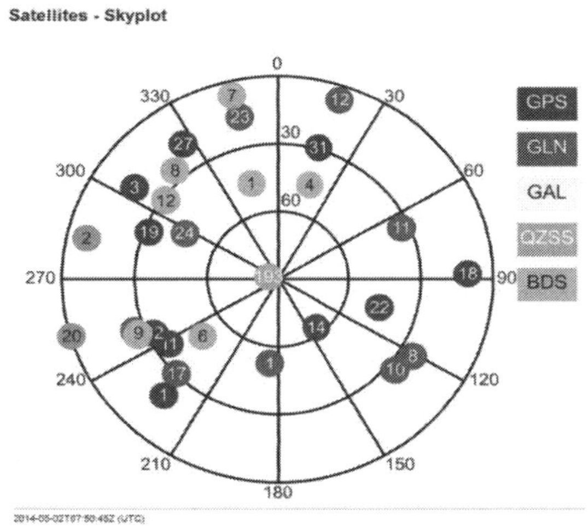

Fig.2. Constellation of Multi GNSS system (e.g. GPS, GLONASS, BEIDOU, GALILEO) allow us to observe more satellite

2 Method

As previously mention before era of Multi GNSS, degradation of precision of coordinate's position will likely to occur when we measure under heavy obstruction to the satellites like in the forest area. Troubles during measurement are typically existed such as takes time to resolve the ambiguities or even in many occasion resulted in failure. So, it is very interesting to see how multi GNSS can improve that precision and even accuracy under such situation. For the information, measuring boundary of forest (either between forest and forest with non-forest) is necessary for production, conservation, etc. So we try to do study.

We observe the boundary simulation of forest by RTK Multi GNSS in Forest Park northern Bandung and forest concession Jambi. We simulate line with several points. One line represent boundary between two forests while the other one is boundary between forest and non-forest (figure 3). In every simulation point we observe repeatedly 100 coordinates value to see the precision statistically for horizontal and vertical component.

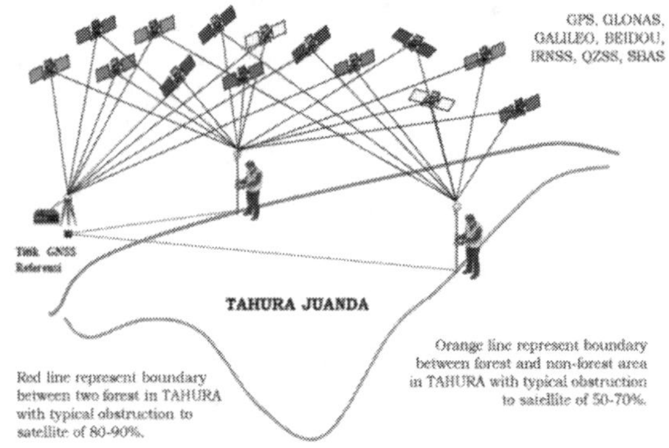

Fig.3. Illustration of measurements of simulation in the field. We measured boundary between two forests and the forest with non-forest area.

Further on we estimate the percentage of obstruction to the satellites as consequences from canopy in every measurement points. We grouped the points into 40 percent, 50, 60, 70, 80 and 90 percent of satellite signal obstruction. The estimation is simply by set up 15 degree of mask angle over 360 degree of horizon and clustered all quadrant of satellite until zenith. We see spatially the clear and the obstruction to the satellite and put them on percentage value.

Figure 4 show the illustration of satellite signal obstruction from tress canopy. With such obstruction theoretically less satellite will be observed and even chance to have cycle slip is higher. This limitation of number of satellite and many of cycle slip will be troubles for fixing the ambiguities and finally degrade the position precision and accuracy.

Fig.4. Illustration of satellite obstruction in the field due to forest canopy. The obstruction can be up to 90 percent.

In order to do the measurements we use geodetic type Multi GNSS Channel System STONEX S800 and S10. These receivers can observe well the GPS, GLONASS, BEIDOU, GALILEIO, QZSS and others GNSS available. We may observe 20 to 30 satellites simultaneously in the sky with mask angle 15 degree. So far many vendors are busy to upgrade their receivers to become Multi GNSS Channel System.

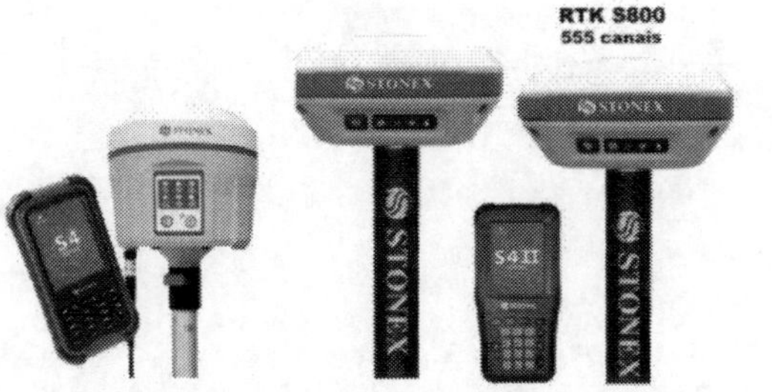

Fig.5. Geodetic multi-channel of multi GNSS STONEX S800 and S10 that are used for this research.

We set up base and rover with baseline length generally below 1 kilometer. The first reason is to make sure the correction of RTK from base to rover well received. With using only 0.5 Watt of radio communication we need to put closer the base and the rover, otherwise the radio signal might be lost. Shorter baseline will also reduce biases from atmospheric effect (e.g. Ionosphere and troposphere) and also reduce the orbital error. In this case we can focus more to the obstruction influence which relatively affect the ambiguity resolution. Off course study for the longer baseline is very interesting and even necessary as in many time it is not cost effective to put closer base.

Fig.6. Documentation of RTK Multi GNSS in National Forest Park in northern of Bandung

Figures 6 show documentation of RTK Multi GNSS measurement in National Forest Park in northern of Bandung. The time of data acquisition in this area was in March 2018 while in forest concession Jambi was around March 2017. Both of data point's acquisition were processed together and also analyze together. As mentioned earlier we grouped the points into 40 percent, 50, 60, 70, 80 and 90 percent of satellite signal obstruction.

3 Results

Figure 7 to 10 show plotted of horizontal and vertical component from 100 repeated measurements in each group of points each represent 60 percent of satellite signal obstruction due to canopy, 70, 80 and 90 percent respectively. Few of outlier was removed. The existence of outlier was probably to the resolution of ambiguity to the wrong integer. As we now with many cycle slip and few only satellite recorded as in heavy obstruction, resolving ambiguity is not easy.

Result of 60 percent (figure 7) shows average horizontal precision of 1 centimeter and average vertical precision of 1 centimeter. Average time to fix ambiguity for 60 percent obstruction is 10 second with all ambiguities was fixed. Result of 70 percent (figure 8) shows average horizontal precision of 1 centimeter and average vertical precision of 2 centimeter. Average time to fix ambiguity for 70 percent obstruction is 10 second with all ambiguities was fixed. Result of 80 percent (figure 9) shows average horizontal precision of 3 centimeter and average vertical precision of 11 centimeter. Average time to fix ambiguity for 80 percent obstruction is 13 second with several ambiguities was remains float. Result of 90 percent (figure 10) shows average horizontal precision of 3 centimeter and average vertical precision of 8 centimeter. Average time to fix ambiguity for 90 percent obstruction is 2 minutes with more than a half of ambiguities were remains float.

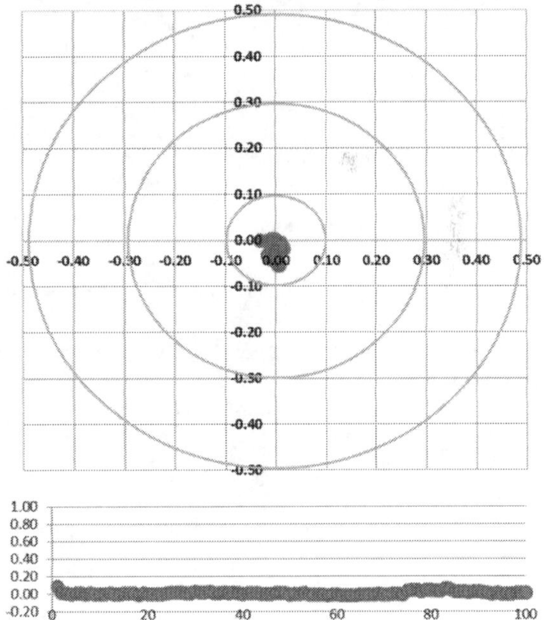

Fig.7. Plot of horizontal component and vertical component (all in meter). They figure out their precision of location with 60 percent of canopy obstruction to the satellite

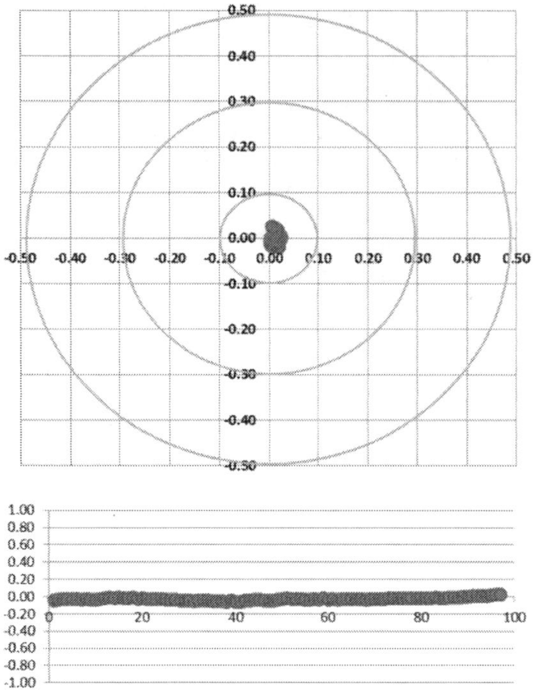

Fig.8. Plot of horizontal component and vertical component (all in meter). They figure out their precision of location with 70 percent of canopy obstruction to the satellite

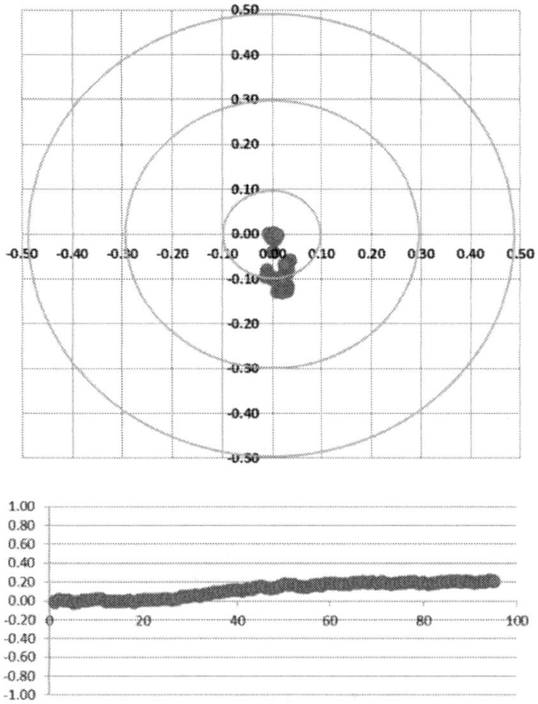

Fig.9. Plot of horizontal component and vertical component (all in meter). They figure out their precision of location with 80 percent of canopy obstruction to the satellite

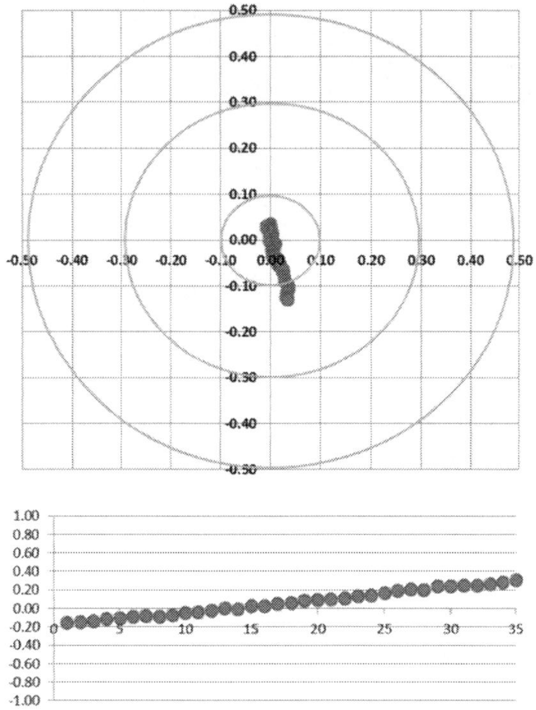

Fig.10. Plot of horizontal component and vertical component (all in meter). They figure out their precision of location with 90 percent of canopy obstruction to the satellite.

Table 1 summarize the average of horizontal and vertical precision of 100 times measurements and groups of the same typical obstruction to the satellite (e.g. 60 percent, 70, 80 and 90 percent). Degradation of precision and longer time to fix the ambiguity is clearly seen when more obstruction to satellite existed. For 80 and 90 percent of obstruction, fixing ambiguity sometimes failed. We have record of several float solution for 80 percent obstruction and even more than a half data of float solution for 90 respectively.

Table 1. Summary of average horizontal and vertical precision for different obstruction to satellite visibilities.

	Obstruction to satellite visibilities 60%	**Obstruction to satellite visibilities 70%**	**Obstruction to satellite visibilities 80%**	**Obstruction to satellite visibilities 90%**
Average horizontal precision	0.01 m	0.01 m	0.03 m	0.03 m
Average Vertical precision	0.01 m	0.02 m	0.11 m	0.08 m
Ambiguity status	All Fix	All Fix	Fix & Float	Fix & Float
Time to FIX ambiguity	10 sec	10 sec	30 sec	2 min
Baseline length	< 1 km	< 1 km	< 1 km	< 1 km

https://doi.org/10.1051/e3sconf/20199401021

Result of coordinate position from RTK Multi GNSS on forest area as studied is enough for boundary forest requirement. Indeed according to specification only sub meter accuracy is recommended for between forests and few decimeter recommended for forest and non-forest while from studied we can achieved better result of few centimeter of precision. Sub meter of accuracy generally requested also for administration boundaries such as province and districts.

Figure 11 show plotted of coordinates of measurements at National Forest Park northern of Bandung on Google Map. We noted that typical obstruction between forests is about 70-90 percent while typical for forest and non-forest is about 40-60 percent. Result of study is promising for forest boundary demarcation. To make sure the capabilities it is good to conduct study in more sample area. Perhaps each area has its own characteristic that is influence the result of measurements.

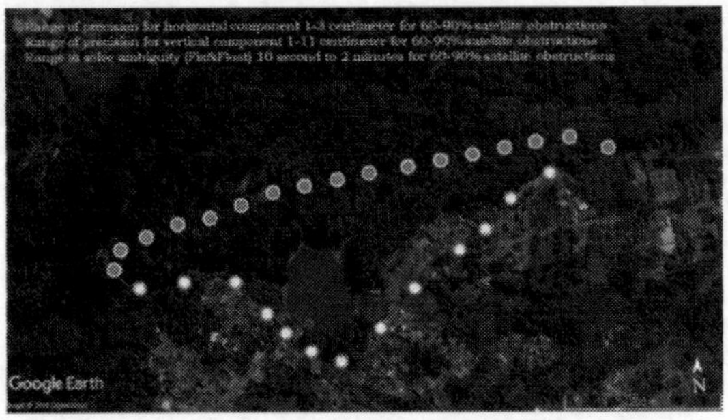

Fig.11. Plotted of results of measurements on the Google map. Result of measurements is promising for forest boundary demarcation.

4 Discussions

Problems for better result of coordinate's position on limited satellite visibilities or more obstruction to the satellite seem answered by Multi GNSS System. An easy reason is due to more satellite availability. As mentioned earlier with GPS, GLONAS, BEIDOU, GALILEIO, QZSS and others GNSS System available, 20 to 30 satellite can be measured simultaneously. Theoretically we need only 4 satellite to calculate position. Nevertheless the more is better. Another more specific reason why Multi GNSS System given better result on coordinate is the availability of geostationary satellites. As we know that several BEIDOU satellites is set up at geostationary orbit. QZSS is also typically a geostationary satellite with quasy move a bit along zenith. The existence of geostationary satellites will give more stability on the signal transmission and reduce the potency of cycle slip. In this case it would be easier on calculation of position especially when resolving the ambiguity.

On this study we still set up baseline below 1 kilometer and we only analyze precision component. Theoretically the longer baseline the more challenge on achieving good coordinate. Precision is not always accuracy while the accuracy is true indicator of good coordinates. So in the future we need to study longer baseline and take a look on accuracy instead precision only.

Indonesia has huge forest area (figure 12). It divided to conservation forest, peat land, production forest, society forest, etc. Definition on their boundary in this case is necessary. As mentioned earlier we need the boundary for management, production and for sure for conservation. We have degradation on forest area which is one factor is due to uncertainty in the boundary.

Fig.12. Map of Indonesia forest (Natural and Peat land)

Many methods and technologies have been applied for forest boundary demarcation. Firstly we use Theodolite and followed by Total Station. Several years ago we use GPS. The result of demarcation is not optimum yet. Using Total Station is time consuming while using GPS we have problem of satellite obstructions. The availability of RTK Multi GNSS again we stated it is quite promising for better forest boundary demarcation. Combination of CORS (Continuously Operating GNSS Reference Station) and RTPPP (Real Time Precise Point Positioning) is seems very interesting for further study.

5 Conclusion

Result of coordinate's position from RTK Multi GNSS on forest area as studied is enough for boundary forest requirement. This RTK Multi GNSS give better result on the coordinate position on limited satellite visibilities or more obstruction to the satellite since more satellite can be observed and there are several geostationer satellite which help more stability on the signal transmission and reduce the potency of cycle slip that are crucial parameters for deliver good coordinates position.

With such huge hectare of forest in Indonesia and others reason it makes forest boundary demarcation is very important. Many methods and technologies have been applied. The result of demarcation is not optimum yet. Using RTK Multi GNSS as in this study is promising. We found improvement in positioning result of even area of limited satellite visibilities and it is match with the forest boundary position requirements.

Further studies are still necessary off course to answer longer baseline, accuracy versus precision, and also combination method like with CORS, RTPPP and event with Total Station, etc.

Acknowledgements

Many thanks and appreciation to students and surveyors from Institute of Technology Bandung who helped the investigation in the field, and especially to the vendor PT Wisesa Berkah Bumi for kindly borrowed the STONEX Multi GNSS Receiver so we can measure in the fields.

References

1. Seeber, G., Satellite Geodesy: foundation, method, and applications, Walter de Gruyter, Berlin-New York, C7 (1993)
2. Abidin, H.Z., Penentuan Posisi dengan GPS dan Aplikasinya (PT. Pradnya Paramita, Jakarta, 1999)
3. Abidin, H.Z., Geodesi Satelit (Departemen Teknik Geodesi ITB, PT. Pradnya Paramita, Jakarta, 2001)
4. Leick A. GPS satellite surveying, 3rd edn Wiley, New York (2004)
5. Hofmann-Wellenhof, B., Lichtenegger, H. and Walse, E., GNSS Global Navigation Satellite Systems: GPS, GLONASS, Galileo, and More. (Springer Verlag, Wien, 2007)
6. Mudita, I.,GNSS-RTK Network Technology Impact Assessment for Land Surveying at Badan Pertanahan Nasional Republik Indonesia (BPN RI): Asian Geospatial Forum: 10th Annual Asian Conference & Exhibition on Geospatial Information, Technology & Applications (2011)

Long-range Single Baseline RTK GNSS Positioning for Land Cadastral Survey Mapping

Brian Bramanto[1,*], *Irwan* Gumilar[1], *Muhammad* Taufik[1] and *I Made* D. A. Hermawan[2]

[1]Geodesy Research Group, Institut Teknologi Bandung, Indonesia
[2]General Technology Indonesia

Abstract. In Indonesia, Global Navigation Satellite System (GNSS) has become one of the important tool in survey mapping, especially for cadastral purposes like land registration by using Real Time Kinematic (RTK) GNSS positioning method. The conventional RTK GNSS positioning method ensure high accuracy GNSS position solution (within several centimeters) for baseline less than 20 kilometers. The problems of resolving high accuracy position for a greater distance (more than 50 kilometers) becomes greater challenge. In longer baseline, atmospheric delays is a critical factor that influenced the positioning accuracy. In order to reduce the error, a modified LAMBDA ambiguity resolution, atmospheric correction and modified kalman filter were used in this research. Thus, this research aims to investigate the accuracy of estimated position and area in respect with short baseline RTK and differential GNSS position solution by using NAVCOM SF-3040. The results indicate that the long-range single baseline RTK accuracy vary from several centimeters to decimeters due to unresolved biases.

1 Introduction

As a breakthrough technology in position determination, Global Navigation Satellite System (GNSS) has become one of the important tool in survey mapping. GNSS term includes e.g. the GPS (Global Positioning System), GLONASS (*Globalnaya Navigazionnaya Sputnikovaya Sistema*), Galileo, BeiDou and other satellite-based positioning system. In accordance with its rapid growth, there is such a huge increase interest in GNSS position determination, but not limited to, e.g. Automatic Vehicle Location (AVL) [1, 2], tracking system [3, 4], geodynamic monitoring [5-7], atmospheric monitoring [8, 9], hazard mitigation [10-12] and so on.

In Indonesia, GNSS is mostly used in surveying and mapping purposes, especially for cadastral purposes like land registration by using Real Time Kinematic (RTK) GNSS positioning method [13-15]. RTK GNSS ensure the high accuracy in point determination, however, in conventional RTK GNSS the high accuracy can only be obtained for baseline less than 20 kilometers [16]. For medium to long baseline RTK GNSS, the atmospheric bias is considered as the dominant factor which lead into unresolved ambiguity resolution. Consider GNSS signal travelling from a satellite to two receivers that are in a distant, the signal would be subjected to a different atmospheric effects. Several approaches have been proposed to mitigate the atmospheric bias [17-18]. Network RTK is also considered to mitigate the atmospheric bias [19].

It has been found that atmospheric bias affect more error in vertical component rather than in horizontal component which up to several decimeters in RTK GNSS positioning [20, 21]. Fig. 1 shows the comparison of code absolute method positioning error using corrected pseudorange and uncorrected pseudorange. It could be seen that the deviation could vary up to 20 meters in vertical component. The corrected terms indicate the used of troposphere and ionosphere model.

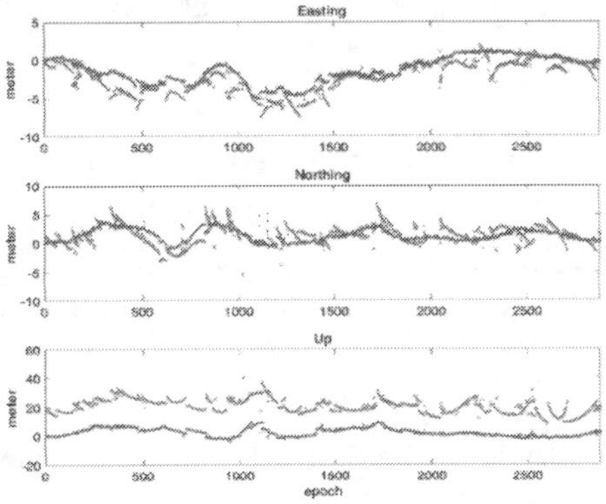

Fig. 1. Error position in absolute positioning method. Red dots indicate when no atmospheric correction was applied on the data, while blue dots indicate when atmospheric correction was applied on the data

Thus, several researches has stated that orbital error [22] and satellite clock error [23] also indicate as the problems in GNSS-based positioning system. The orbital trajectory of GNSS satellites disturbed by surrounding environments e.g. the Earth's gravity, the attraction of the

[*] Corresponding author: brian@fitb.itb.ac.id

sun and the moon and as well as solar radiation, while the satellite clocks are subject to relativistic effects. The GNSS satellite clock tends to run faster than the clocks in the receivers.

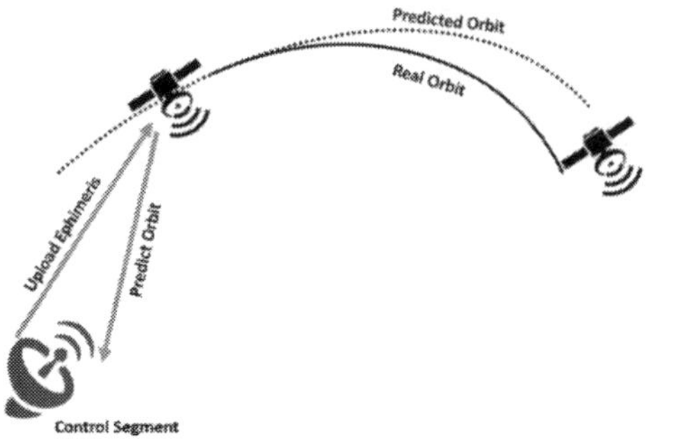

Fig. 2. GNSS orbital satellite error

In a relatively short baseline, the double difference (DD) observations could reduce and eliminate both of orbital and clock satellite error, however, for a far baseline orbital and clock satellite error still contained on the data observation. The connection between baseline length, observing time and rms accuracy were summarize in Fig. 3.

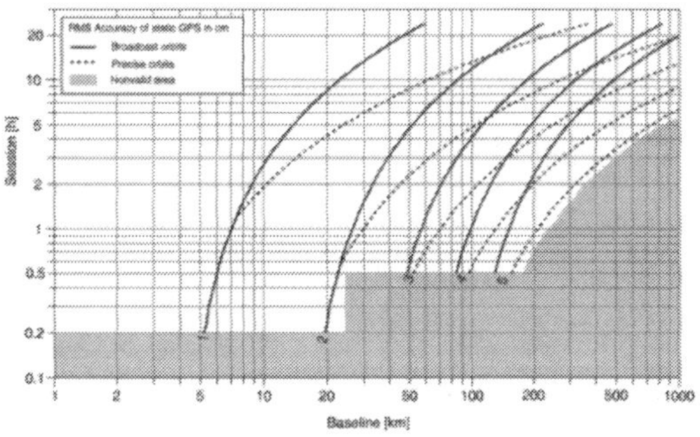

Fig. 3. Accuracy of GNSS static in cm and its correlation with the baseline length and observing time when using broadcast orbit and precise orbit [22]

In this research, a relatively new algorithm [23] was used to enhance the RTK GNSS accuracy in a long baseline for land cadastral survey mapping. This method used a modified LAMBDA method which can be separated into several aspects e.g. modified functional model to estimate the atmospheric bias, the usage of precise orbit correction from WADGPS, a modified Kalman filter and a partial search and ambiguity fixing strategies.

2 Data and Basic Concept

2.1 Data

Base station was established at the rooftop building. Bandung, Indonesia, while the land cadastral survey mapping were simulated on three land parcels in Pamengpeuk, Indonesia which located for about 85 kilometers away from the base station and has significant height differences for about 800 meters. Eight benchmarks were also used to assess the performance of the algorithm.

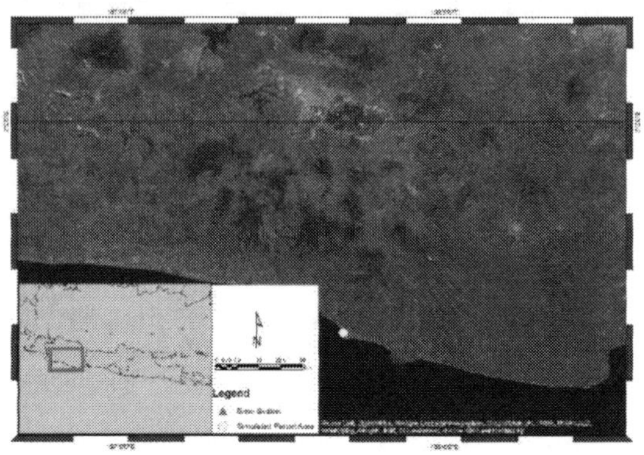

Fig. 3. The location of base station (red triangle) and simulated parcel area (yellow dot)

Fig. 4. The location of land parcels (green dot) and benchmark (yellow triangle)

Fig. 5. Shows the research methodology. In general, to assess the performance of the algorithm, the long-range RTK coordinate results were then compared with a priori coordinates. The term a priori coordinate refers to reference coordinate based on static differential observation method or shorter baseline RTK GNSS method.

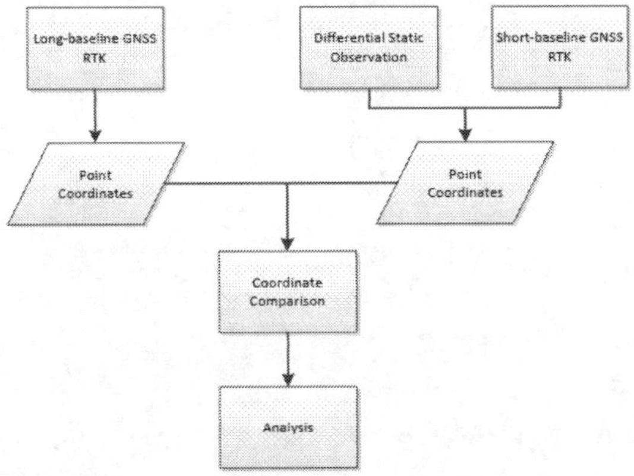

Fig. 5. Research methodology used in this research

2.2 Basic Concept

This section describe the general concept in RTK GNSS method and the Kalman filter design to enhance the accuracy of RTK GNSS in long-range baseline.

2.2.1 Observation Models in RTK

The observation model for code and carrier phase measurement are described as follows:

$$P(Li) = \rho + d_{orb} + d_{trop} + d_{ion_i} + c(dt - dT) + MPi + \varepsilon_i \quad (1)$$

$$\Phi(Li) = \rho + d_{orb} + d_{trop} - d_{ion_i} + c(dt - dT) + \lambda_i N_i + M\Phi i + \varepsilon_i \quad (2)$$

where:

$P(Li)$	is the measured pseudorange on *Li* frequency (i = 1, 2)
$\Phi(Li)$	is the measured carrier phase on *Li* frequency
ρ	is the true geometric range
d_{orb}	is the satellite orbital error
d_{trop}	is the tropospheric error
d_{ion}	is the ionospheric error
c	is the speed of light
dt	is the satellite clock error
dT	is the receiver clock error
MPi	is the multipath effect on measured code
$M\Phi i$	is the multipath effect on measured phase
ε_i	is the noise

DD then performed to eliminate the orbital error, clock error and atmospheric error in short baseline. The DD (Δ∇) observation model for code and carrier phase measurement can be described as follows:

$$\Delta\nabla\Phi(Li)_{AB}^{jk} = \Delta\rho_{AB}^{jk} + \lambda_i N_{i\,AB}^{jk} + M\Phi i_{AB}^{jk} + \varepsilon_{i\,AB}^{jk} \quad (3)$$

$$\Delta\nabla P(Li)_{AB}^{jk} = \Delta\rho_{AB}^{jk} + MPi_{AB}^{jk} + \varepsilon_{i\,AB}^{jk} \quad (4)$$

Linearization of the DD observation then can be represented as follows:

$$V = AX - L$$

where V is the residual matrix, *A* is the design matrix. *L* is the observation data and *X* is the estimated parameters containing three baseline components and ambiguities. In a longer baseline the estimated parameters including residual ionospheric bias and residual tropospheric bias.

2.2.2 General Kalman Filter System Design

Kalman filter predicts the a priori parameters using the recent estimate of the observation data. The prediction is based on some assumed model for how the parameters changes in time [24, 25]. The dynamic model on Kalman filter can be represented as follows:

$$X_{K+1} = \Phi_k X_k + w_k \quad (5)$$

which then continued along with measurement model,

$$L_k = A_k X_k + v_k \quad (6)$$

where:

Φ_k	is the transition matrix (k = epoch)
w	is the noise from the dynamic model
v	is the noise from the observation data

Kalman filter also applied recursive least square which then can be defined into two main parts as follows [26]:

- Observation model

$$K_k = P_k^- A_k^T (A_k P_k^- A + R_k)^{-1} \quad (7)$$

$$X_k = X_k^- + K_k(L_k - A_k X_k^-) \quad (8)$$

$$P_k = (I - K_k A_k) P_k^- \quad (9)$$

- Dynamic model

$$X_{k+1}^- = \Phi_k X_k \quad (10)$$

$$P_{k+1}^- = \Phi_k P_k \Phi_k^T + Q_k \quad (11)$$

where:

K	is the gain matrix
P	is the covariance matrix observation model
I	is the identity matrix
-	is the prediction from previous epoch
Q	is the covariance matrix for dynamic model
R	is the weighting matrix

The estimated parameter is summarized in Table 1.

Table 1. Parameter estimated in Kalman filter. Superscript (*) indicates the optional parameter while N is the number of satellites used

Parameter in Kalman Filter	Dimension
Position XYZ	3
Velocity XYZ*	3
Acceleration XYZ*	3
Residual troposphere*	1
Residual DD ionosphere*	N-1
L1 DD ambiguity*	N-1
L2 DD ambiguity*	N-1

2.2.3 Precise Satellite Ephemeris

As stated on the introduction, precise satellite ephemeris is needed in GNSS-based point positioning for a longer baseline. In static differential method, the precise satellite ephemeris can be easily obtained two weeks after the observation is done. However, in conventional RTK such a precise ephemeris cannot be obtained. Several researches indicate that the satellite's position error might vary up to 5 meters [22, 27]. The satellite's position error is generally the biggest error source after atmospheric bias is estimated in Kalman filter for long-range RTK.

Thus several GNSS industries have developed their own system to accommodate the use of precise satellite ephemeris. John Deere, as one of the GNSS industry has developed the StarFire™ system which transmits the needed data correction in near real-time using satellites communication.

2.2.4 Ambiguity Resolution

The ambiguities are considered as constant. However, due to remaining tropospheric and ionospheric biases, the ambiguities can be modeled as a random walk with very small dynamic noise, such as 0.001 cycle. Thus, the ambiguities are modeled as constants once the ambiguities are fixed. The use of these small dynamic noise is useful in resolving the ambiguities in several condition, such as bad site condition, excessive multipath, or the movement of receiver from a severe shading surrounding to the open sky surrounding.

In a longer baseline, the ambiguities are resolved improperly due to significant bias. [7] implemented the modified partial search technique to fixing the ambiguities. The ambiguity for the L1/L2 signal and its variance were first converted into L1/Wide Lane (WL) as described in following vector equation:

$$\begin{pmatrix} \widehat{L_1} \\ \widehat{WL} \end{pmatrix} = \begin{pmatrix} 1 & 0 \\ 1 & -1 \end{pmatrix} \begin{pmatrix} \widehat{L_1} \\ \widehat{L_2} \end{pmatrix} \quad (12)$$

$$Q_{\widehat{L_1},\widehat{WL}} = \begin{pmatrix} 1 & 0 \\ 1 & -1 \end{pmatrix} \begin{pmatrix} Q_{\widehat{L_1}} & Q_{\widehat{L_1},\widehat{L_2}} \\ Q_{\widehat{L_1},\widehat{L_2}} & Q_{\widehat{L_2}} \end{pmatrix} \begin{pmatrix} 1 & 1 \\ 0 & -1 \end{pmatrix} \quad (13)$$

The used of WL is important due to its wavelength characteristic. With 0.86 cm wavelength, WL's ambiguities are easy to resolve. If the ambiguities are resolved, the original L1 and L2 ambiguities and the variance-covariance in the Kalman filter can be recovered as follows:

$$\begin{pmatrix} \widehat{N_1} \\ \widehat{N_2} \end{pmatrix} = \begin{pmatrix} 1 & 0 \\ 1 & -1 \end{pmatrix} \begin{pmatrix} \widehat{X_1} \\ \widehat{X_{WL}} \end{pmatrix} \quad (12)$$

$$Q_{\widehat{N_1},\widehat{N_2}} = \begin{pmatrix} 1 & 0 \\ 1 & -1 \end{pmatrix} \begin{pmatrix} Q_{\widehat{N_1}} & Q_{\widehat{N_1},\widehat{N_{WL}}} \\ Q_{\widehat{N_1},\widehat{N_{WL}}} & Q_{\widehat{N_{WL}}} \end{pmatrix} \begin{pmatrix} 1 & 1 \\ 0 & -1 \end{pmatrix} \quad (13)$$

3 Result and Discussion

Over 1840 epoch were collected within 23 point observations. Only resolved ambiguities data showed and considered in further analysis. Coordinates derived from differential static method were considered as reference coordinates in bench mark point, while coordinates derived from short baseline GNSS RTK method were used as reference coordinates in land parcel point. Short baseline GNSS RTK (under 3 km) was considered because in shorter baseline and in the open-sky condition (Fig. 6) the biases were assumed reduced or eliminated [28].

Fig. 6. Condition over the simulated area

3.1 Accuracy and Precision

2.2.1 Horizontal Accuracy

Fig 7. shows the overall accuracy for benchmark point, while Fig 8. shows the overall accuracy for land parcel point. The accuracy of long-baseline GNSS RTK in benchmark points were within 3 cm and only 1 point was slightly worse than the other, however still within RTK accuracy.

The accuracy of long-baseline GNSS RTK in land parcel points were within 12 cm. It could be seen that there was a systematic compared with those for benchmark point. As mentioned before, coordinate estimated from short baseline RTK GNSS used to assess the accuracy of long baseline RTK GNSS in land parcel points. To evaluate the consistency of the used reference coordinate on all off the observation method, benchmark points were also observed using short baseline RTK GNSS.

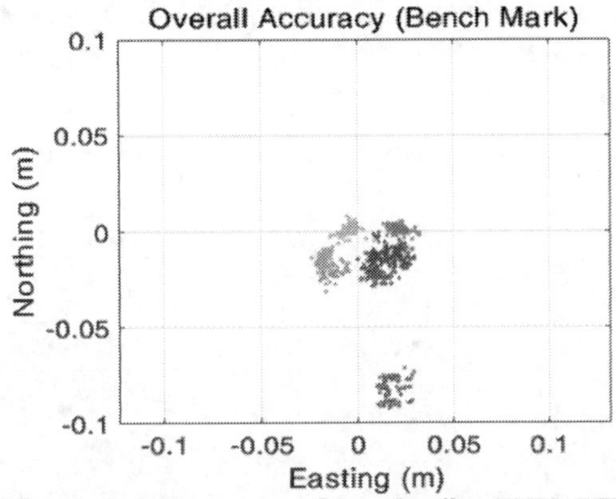

Fig. 7. Overall accuracy of long baseline GNSS RTK for benchmark points

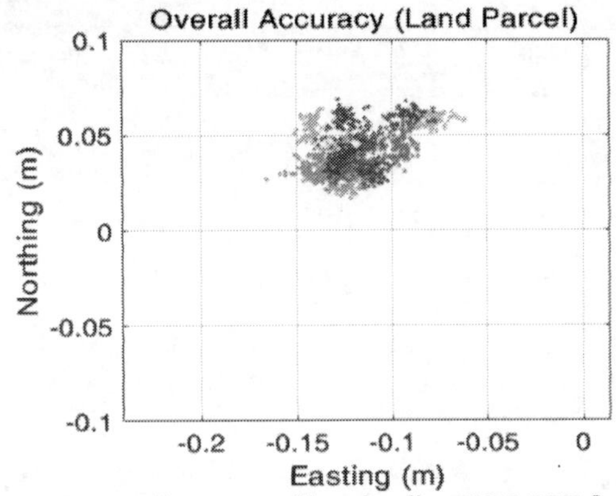

Fig. 8. Overall accuracy of long baseline GNSS RTK for land parcel points

Fig. 9. shows the overall accuracy for both short and long baseline GNSS RTK. It could be seen that there was a shift tendencies to South-East. It indicates that the system coordinate might be different.

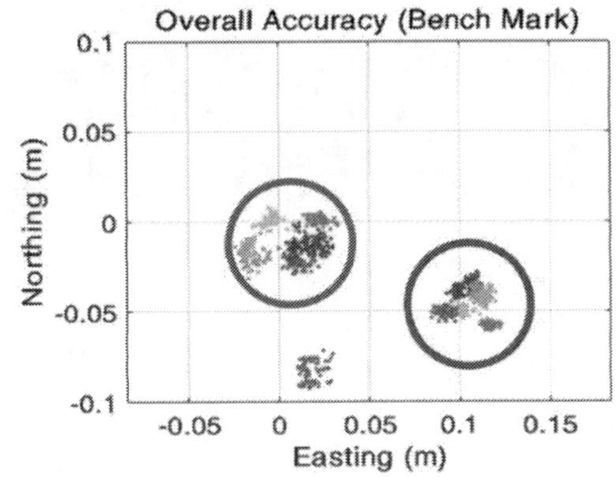

Fig. 9. Overall accuracy of short baseline (Red Circle) and long baseline (Blue Circle) GNSS RTK for benchmark points

2.2.2 Vertical Accuracy

Fig 10. shows the overall vertical accuracy for benchmark point, while Fig 11. shows the overall vertical accuracy for land parcel point. The accuracy of long-baseline GNSS RTK in benchmark points were within 15 cm and the accuracy of long-baseline GNSS RTK in land parcel points were vary from -20 cm to 15 cm. There is one point that indicates the unresolved bias. A linear trend of the up component is found on that point, there is also deviation in horizontal component as shown on Fig. 7. Further analysis is needed to explain this phenomenon.

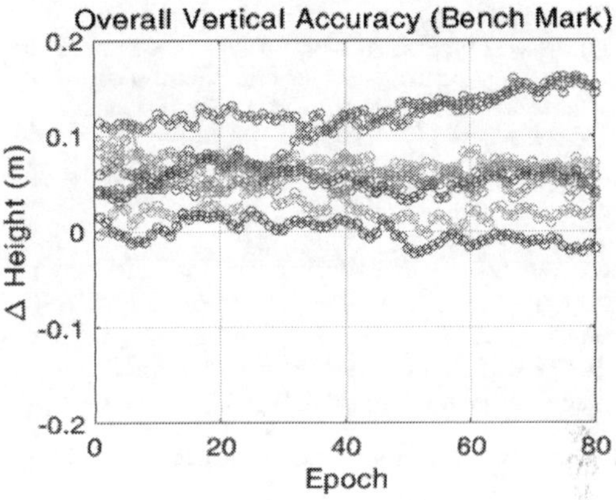

Fig. 10. Overall vertical accuracy of long baseline GNSS RTK for benchmark points

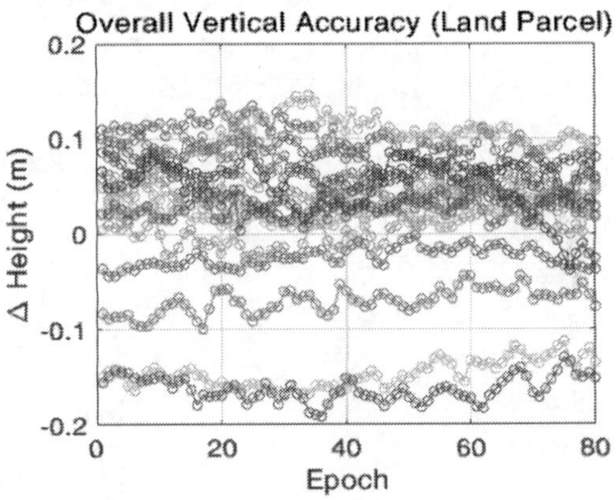

Fig. 11. Overall vertical accuracy of long baseline GNSS RTK for land parcel points

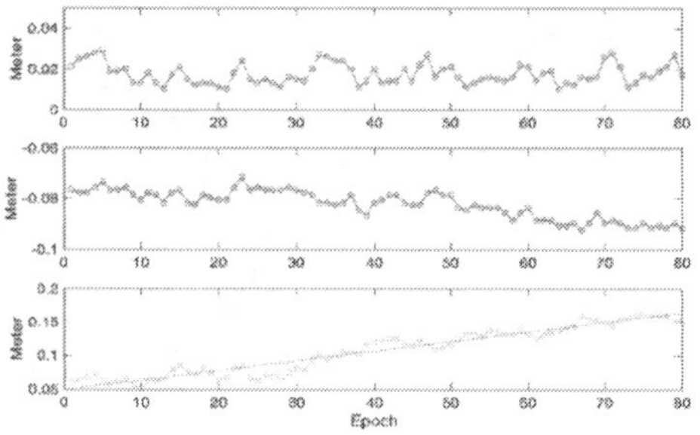

Fig. 12. Selected timeseries of Blue dot, red dot and cyan dot refer to easting, northing and up component respectively. Yellow lines indicates the linear trend of up component.

2.2.3 Overall Precision

Table 1. shows the overall precision for long baseline GNSS RTK. Precision indicated the repeatability of the estimated coordinate. Over 90% of estimated coordinate met the 95% of confidence interval as shown on Fig.13. This indicate that this algorithm is reliable to used.

Table 1. Overall precision for long baseline GNSS RTK

Easting (m)	Northing (m)	Up (m)	Note
0.0055	0.0050	0.0345	BM
0.0020	0.0044	0.0093	BM
0.0028	0.0034	0.0102	BM
0.0045	0.0031	0.0117	BM
0.0044	0.0048	0.0143	BM
0.0029	0.0018	0.0106	BM
0.0036	0.0040	0.0117	BM
0.0021	0.0040	0.0142	BM
0.0026	0.0042	0.0098	Land Parcel
0.0057	0.0083	0.0130	Land Parcel
0.0028	0.0064	0.0138	Land Parcel
0.0031	0.0064	0.0129	Land Parcel
0.0042	0.0066	0.0098	Land Parcel
0.0042	0.0056	0.0114	Land Parcel
0.0039	0.0044	0.0110	Land Parcel
0.0047	0.0046	0.0088	Land Parcel
0.0062	0.0036	0.0195	Land Parcel
0.0049	0.0030	0.0135	Land Parcel
0.0047	0.0050	0.0078	Land Parcel
0.0035	0.0058	0.0203	Land Parcel
0.0054	0.0057	0.0240	Land Parcel
0.0053	0.0050	0.0294	Land Parcel
0.0037	0.0057	0.0408	Land Parcel

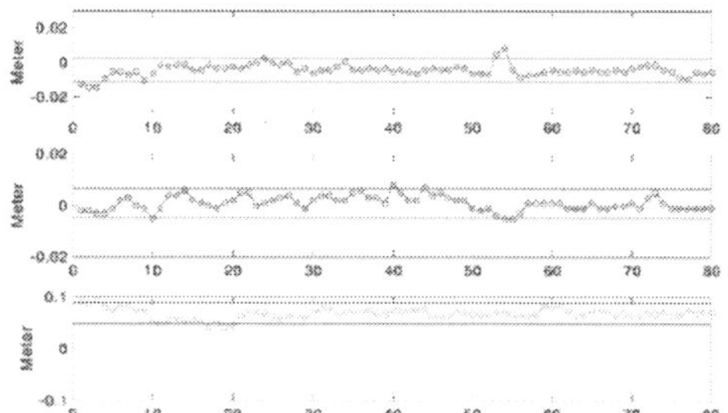

Fig. 13. Selected timeseries of estimated coordinate for long baseline GNSS RTK. Blue dot, red dot and cyan dot refer to easting, northing and up component respectively. Red lines indicates the 95% of confident interval.

2.2.1 Area Estimation

Government policy about land and building tax in Indonesia indicates that the errors tolerances is about 10%. Table.2. shows the differences in calculated area with the reference area, there is no significant differences between reference and calculated area. The deviation in under 0.05% for each area. This result indicates that the long baseline GNSS RTK algorithm can be used for land parcel mapping.

Table 2. Area differences

ID	Reference Area	observed Area	Area Differences	%
1	2490.9708	2490.1062	0.8646	0.03%
2	63787.5385	63779.2118	8.3267	0.01%
3	2111.4568	2111.1478	0.309	0.01%

Fig. 13. Formed area over simulated area. Black lines indicate the reference area while red lines indicate the observed area.

4 Conclusion

The algorithm gives significant improved in long-range single baseline GNSS RTK for up to 90 km. The accuracy vary from several centimeters to decimeters due to unresolved biases. For land cadastral purposes, the algorithm can be used as one of the method, the observed area shows no significant difference compared with the reference area.

References

1. Qing-Jie Kong, Zhipeng Li, Yukai Chen, Yuncai Liu. "An Approach to Urban Traffic State Estimation by Fusing Multisource Information" In IEEE Transactions on Intelligent Transportation System 10.3 (2009) pp. 499-511'
2. E. Mazloumi, G. Currie, and G. Rose. "Using GPS data to gain insight into public transport travel time variability". In: Journal of Transportation Engineering 136.7 (2010), pp. 623–631.
3. Sathe Pooja "Vehicle Tracking System using GPS" In: International Journal of Science and Research (IJSR), India Online ISSN: 2319-7064 (2013)
4. Matej Supej and Ivan Čuk "Comparison of Global Navigation Satellite System Devices on Speed Tracking in Road (Tran)SPORT Applications" In: Sensor 2014, 14 23490-23509 (2014)
5. M. Ben Rabha, M.F. Boujmil, M. Saadoun, B. Bessaïs, Eur. Phys. J. Appl. Phys. (to be published)
6. Luigi T. De Luca, *Propulsion physics* (EDP Sciences, Les Ulis, 2009)
7. F. De Lillo, F. Cecconi, G. Lacorata, A. Vulpiani, EPL, **84** (2008)
8. Brian Bramanto, Irwan Gumilar, Teguh P. Sidiq, Wedyanto Kuntjoro, Daniel A. Tampubolon "Sensing of the atmospheric variation using low cost GNSS receiver" IOP Conference Series Earth and Environmental Science 149(1):012073 (2018)
9. P. Xia, C. Cai, Z. Liu "GNSS troposphere tomography based on two-step reconstruction using GPS observation adn COSMIC Profiles" Ann. Geophys., 31, (2013) pp 1805-1815
10. K. M. Kafi, M. B. A. Gibril "GPS Application in Disaster Management: A Review" Asian Journal of Applied Sciences, 4:01 (2016)
11. Y. Lin, C. Huang, S. Chen, D. Doong, C. C. Kao "Development of a GNSS Buoy for Monitoring Water Surface Elevations in Estuaries and Coastal Areas" Sensors 17(1) (2017) pp 1-19
12. C. Rizos, S. Han, L. Ge, H. Chen, Y. Hatanaka, K. Abe "Low-cost densification of permanent GPS networks for natural hazard mitigation: First tests on GSI's GEONET network" Earth Planet Space, 51 (2000) pp 867-871
13. A. Priti, N. Arslan, B. Deveci, O. Aydin, H. Erkaya, R. G. Hosbas "Real-time kinematic GPS for cadastral surveying" Survey Review vol. 41(314) (2009)
14. Hasanuddin Z. Abidin, Tony S. Haroen, F. H. Adiyanto, Heri Andreas, Irwan Gumilar, Imam Mudita, I. Soemarto "On the establishment and implementation of GPS CORS for cadastral

surveying and mapping in Indonesia" Survey Review 47(340) (2015) pp 61-70

15. H. Z. Abidin, T. S. Haroen, I. Mudita, F. H. Adiyanto "Implementation of GPS CORS for Cadastral Survey and Mapping in Indonesia: Status, Constraints and Opportunities" FIG Working Week 2012 (2012)
16. Yanmin Feng and Jinling Wang "GPS RTK Performance Characteristics and Analysis" Journal of Global Positioning Systems 2008 Vol. 7, No. 1 : 1-8 (2008)
17. P. Wielgosz, I. Kashani and D. Grejner-Brzezinska "Analysis of long-range network RTK during a severe ionospheric storm" In: J. Geod. 2005:79 (2005) pp 524–531
18. Y.W. Ahn, D. Kim, P. Dare and J. Park "Estimation of troposphere decorrelation using the combined zenith-dependent parameter" In: Proceedings of the ION GNSS 2008; Savannah, GA, USA. (2008) pp. 261–270.
19. S. Han and C. Rizos "GPS network design and error mitigation for real-time continuous array monitoring system" In: Proceedings of the ION GPS 1996 (1996) pp. 1827–1836.
20. H. Guo, H. He, J. Li and A. Wang "Estimation and mitigation of the main errors for centimetre-level COMPASS RTK solutions over medium-long baselines" In: J. Navig. 2011;64 (2011) pp 113–126
21. Y. Feng and B. Li "Wide area real time kinematic decimetre positioning with multiple carrier GNSS signals" In: Sci. China Ser. D. 2010;53 (2010) pp 731–740
22. Pasi Häkli, Hannu Koivula and Jyrki Puupponen "Assessment of Practical 3-D Geodetic Accuracy for Static GPS Surveying" In: FIG Working Week 2008 (2008)
23. Bharati Bidikar, Gottapu Sasibhushana Rao, Laveti Ganesh and MNVS Santosh Kumar "Satellite Clock Error and Orbital Solution Error Estimation for Precise Navigation Applications" In: Positioning, 2014, 5 (2014) pp 22-26
24. B. Witchayangkoon "Elements of GPS Precise Point Positioning" In: Doctoral Disertation (2000)
25. M. S. Grewal and A. P. Andrews "Kalman Filtering Theory and Practices Using MATLAB" (2008)
26. R. G Brown and P. Y. C. Hwang "Introduction to Random Signals and Applied Kalman Filtering" (2012)
27. Janusz Zielinski and Ryszard Zdunek "GPS orbit accuracy and its influence on large network solutions" In: Advances in Space Research 23(4):665-665 DOI: 10.1016/S0273-1177(99)00149-0, (1999)
28. B. Bramanto, I. Gumilar, H. Z. Abidin, K. Prijatna, F. S. Adi "Assessment of the BeiDou Data Quality and the Positioning Performance: A Perspective from Bandung, Indonesia" Journal of Aeronautics, Astronautics and Aviation, Series A 49(2) (2017)

Stability Analysis of GNSS Control Point Network for Material Displacement Monitoring on the Slopes using Stability Monument Evaluation and Adjustment Data Processing Scheme: Preliminary Result

Vera Sadarviana*, *Brian* Bramanto, *Teguh* P. Sidiq, *Mohamad* Gamal, *Daniel A.* Tampubolon, *Rahmadi* Hilmafizar, *Reyhan* A. Biantoro, *Hana* Alifiyanti., *Muhammad* T. A. Faruq, *Muhammad* F Muttaqin

Geodesy Research Group, Insitut Teknologi Bandung, Indonesia

Abstract. The Global Navigation Satellite System (GNSS) has been used widely for hazards monitoring, such as landslide or material displacement on the slope due to its high accuracy and precision positioning. However, to assure its accuracy and precision, a further data quality and site assessment must be taken into account. In such a way, it is possible to determine whether the site monitoring is moved or not. Six location of GNSS observation points were established based on the geological structure and the terrain slopes. Satellite visibilities analysis, multipath analysis, and kinematic precise point positioning analysis were performed to assess the GNSS data quality and the monitoring stability. These procedures will determined the further processing scheme for each site monitoring. Some of areas experience the indication of cracks in road and building construction, which lead into an assumption of the displacement has been accumulated in a sub meter fraction. Thus, accounting all of those aspects, first adjustment data processing was implemented to achieve the preliminary results of the first observation.

1 Introduction

The Toll road is intended to shorten travel time with short and congestion-free routes. Hence, many Toll road routes pass through hills or mountains and create new slopes. Toll road vehicles are traversed by various types and weights of vehicles. The ability of vehicles to travel on toll roads is not the same because there are vehicles that carry goods with the maximum weight unable to pass the toll road with a minimum speed of 60km/hour. This situation causes vibration to the morphology of the surrounding area, including the slope. This makes the slope susceptive to landslides because there is vibration as a trigger.

The Cipularang toll road connecting Bandung and Jakarta have high vehicle density and cause congestion. These conditions give the vibrations continuously and repeatedly. Another trigger factor is rain. As a result, the Cipularang toll road experiences avalanches in several segments like km92 and km96. For mitigation, the stability of the slope material monitoring that is by putting up points on the slopes and conduct periodic position observation.

Geologically, some areas of the Cipularang toll road have clay rocks that are hard, easy to swell-shrink if it is affected by rain and heat. In addition, the physical condition of the road in the form of fill the embankment makes the toll road area easy to move. So many factors make the Cipularang toll road area vulnerable to movement. Each points monitor can move or change its position due to the influence of one or a combination of these factors.

Monitoring of ground movements is defined by the difference between two or more position observation periodic. The stability of the monitoring point used must be ascertained first so as not to misunderstand the existing position changes. On the other hand, the quality of the observation method must be ensured so that the resulting differences do not come from errors or inconsistencies of observation. In this paper, the GNSS data were first assess to ensure the quality of the data, then some proccessing scheme was accounted to estimate the first network solution as a preliminary results.

2 Data and Method

Gunung Hedjo, West Java, Indonesia is traversed by Bandung – Jakarta highly occupied toll road, however, Gunung Hedjo suffers from numerous landslides. Thus, the high accuracy and precision positioning monitoring in this area is indeed needed. Six GNSS observation sites were established to monitor the slopes stability on the research area.

* Corresponding author: vsadarviana@gmail.com

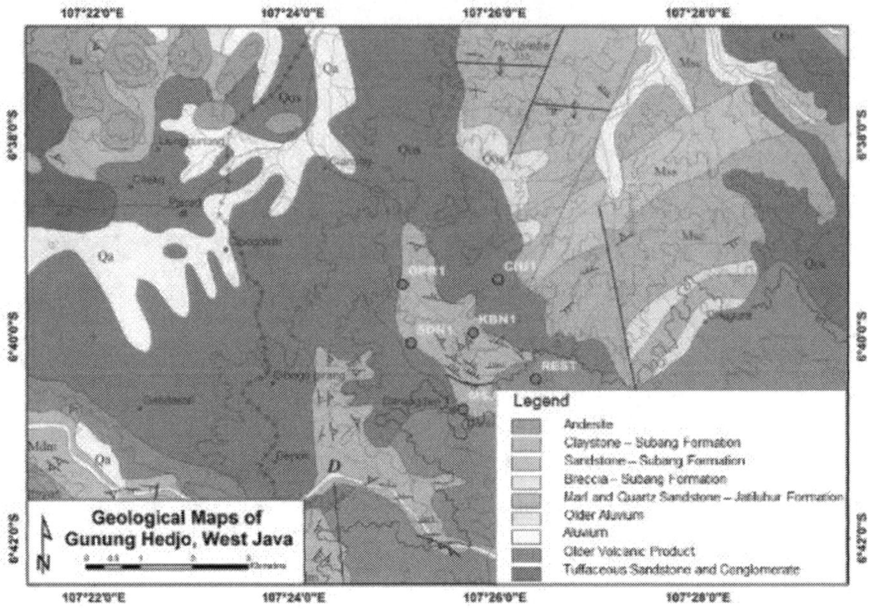

Fig. 1 Observation monitoring sites (Orange Dot) overlaid with the geological map

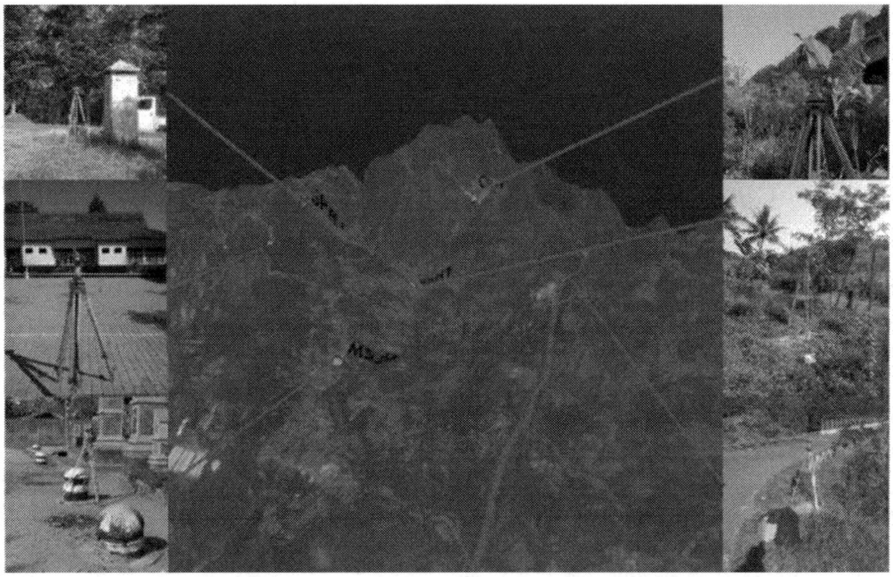

Fig. 2 3D view of observation site (orange dot) and the condition of measurement

The geological structure and the terrain slope were considered for the site monitoring placement. Fig. 1 shows the geological structure over the research area. It could be seen that the area are mostly consists of quaternary and Miocene rock. Tuffaceous sandstone, conglomerate and alluvium are commonly found on the quaternary rock, while marl, quartz sandstone and volcanic product are commonly found on the Miocene rock. The landslide are often occurred on the tuffaceous sandstone and other volcanic product [1, 2, 3]. Fig. *2* indicates the terrain over the research area. The elevation height of the research area is vary from 350 to 550 meter above sea level.

The classical geodetic campaign was carried out on July 2018 using four Topcon GR-3 GNSS receiver, Leica GS-08 and Leica GRX-1200. In the first campaign, 10 baseline observation with duration of 3 hours each and 1 baseline observation with duration of 6 hours had been held out. All of the observation were collected in 1 Hz sampling interval. One Continuous Operating Reference System (CORS) GNSS station used as a reference, it was assumed that the CORS GNSS is not affected from any mass displacement. The CORS GNSS is located for about 30 kilometers away in Bandung, West Java, Indonesia.

Before the differencing and network adjustment process is carried out, the data quality assessment must be done. The data quality assessment is consists of satellite visibilities analysis, multipath analysis, Signal to Noise Ratio (SNR) analysis and Kinematic Precise Point Positioning (KPPP) analysis.

Satellite visibilities is one way to estimate the precision of the estimated position which correlated with the geometry of the observed satellite, namely Dilution of Precision (DOP). DOP can be divided into several terms which are correlated by the position or time, such as vertical DOP (VDOP), horizontal DOP (HDOP), position DOP (PDOP) and time DOP (TDOP). Those terms can be generalize by using Geometric DOP (GDOP) term. DOP can be described as [4]:

$$GDOP = \frac{\sqrt{\sigma_{x_u}^2 + \sigma_{y_u}^2 + \sigma_{z_u}^2 + \sigma_{ctb}^2}}{\sigma_{UERE}} \quad (1)$$

$$\sqrt{\sigma_{x_u}^2 + \sigma_{y_u}^2 + \sigma_{z_u}^2} = PDOP.\sigma_{UERE} \quad (2)$$

$$\sqrt{\sigma_{x_u}^2 + \sigma_{y_u}^2} = HDOP.\sigma_{UERE} \quad (3)$$

$$\sigma_{z_u} = VDOP.\sigma_{UERE} \quad (4)$$

$$\sigma_{ct_b} = TDOP.\sigma_{UERE} \quad (5)$$

where σ_x, σ_y, σ_z is the standard deviation of the three-dimensional position and σ_{ctb} is the standard deviation of the clock timing defined in distance at the specified location ($_u$).

Multipath is one of the unavoidable source of error in GNSS signal propagation [5]. Although it is difficult to model the error, it is very necessary for us to describe the quality of the monitoring site. The multipath can be investigate by applied the Multipath Combination (MPC) algorithm. The MPC can be expressed as [6]:

$$MP1 = P_1 - \frac{f_1^2+f_2^2}{f_1^2-f_2^2}L_1 + \frac{2f_2^2}{f_1^2-f_2^2}L_2 \quad (6)$$

$$MP2 = P_2 - \frac{2f_2^2}{f_1^2-f_2^2}L_1 + \frac{f_1^2+f_2^2}{f_1^2-f_2^2}L_2 \quad (7)$$

where P and L are the GNSS pseudorange and carrier phase range respectively and f is the frequency of the carrier phase. The first order of ionospheric delay and geometric range could be eliminated by using these linear combination.

In general, KPPP refers as an absolute point positioning which adopt the linear combination and other supporting product to reduce and eliminate the huge amount of error in the GNSS signal propagation. KPPP uses ionospheric-free linear combination to eliminate the first order ionospheric error and precise orbit and clock to reduce the orbital and satellite clock error. The linear combination of KPPP can be described on the following equation [7, 8]:

$$P_{IF} = \frac{f_1^2 P_2 - f_2^2 P_2}{f_1^2 - f_2^2} \quad (8)$$

$$L_{IF} = \frac{f_1^2 L_2 - f_2^2 L_2}{f_1^2 - f_2^2} \quad (9)$$

Thus, those observation can be used to determine the unknown parameter. The unknown parameter in the KPPP method include three coordinate parameter (*X, Y, Z*), a receiver clock bias (*dt*), a wet zenith tropospheric delay and float ambiguity.

Considering all of the previous pre-process analysis, double difference (DD) positioning applied to obtain the final baseline solution. DD conducted by differencing two single difference (SD) observation. The phaserange SD between receivers can be described as follows [9]:

$$\Delta L_{AB}^j = \Delta\rho_{AB}^j + d_{tropAB}^j - d_{ionAB}^j + c(dt - dT)_{AB}^j + ML_{AB}^j + \lambda N_{AB}^j + \delta L_{AB}^j \quad (10)$$

Where Δ is the difference between receivers A and B. ρ denotes the geometric range. d_{tropAB}^j and d_{ionAB}^j denote the delay of tropospheric and ionopsheric respectively. C denotes the speed of light while dT refers to receiver clock bias. The remaining ML, λN and ϑL refer to multipath, integer ambiguity and noise. The superscript -j corresponds with the observed satellite. Thus, by subtracting two SD observation, DD can be defined as follows:

$$\Delta\nabla L_{AB}^{jk} = \Delta\rho_{AB}^{jk} + ML_{AB}^{jk} + \lambda N_{AB}^{jk} + \delta L_{AB}^{jk} \quad (11)$$

Where the superscript-j and k define the two observed satellite on the same epoch. The shorter baseline might eliminated the atmospheric bias.

3 Data Observation Assessment

3.1 Satellite Visibilities Analysis

Table 1 shows that loops formed from 3 monitor points produce a horizontal closure in easting and northing axis, a vertical closure in height element. The biggest loop closure occurs in loops 2 and 5. It directs suspicion towards the points of GPR1 and KBN1.

Selected satellite visibilities shown in Fig. 3 and Fig. 4 for GPR1 and KBN1 site respectively. GPR1 and KBN1 were chosen to emphasize the two different surrounding. GPR1 uses Leica GS08 while KBN1 uses Topcon GR3 GNSS Receiver. GPR1 located near the highway while KBN1 located in the middle of cropland as illustrated in

 https://doi.org/10.1051/e3sconf/20199401023

Fig. 5. Cycle slips then detected by the jump of observed phaserange in the data observation. GPR1 suffers a lot of cycle slip which occurred in the direction of about 30^0, 150^0, 240^0-300^0 and 330^0 from North with the low satellite elevation as indicated by the red line. Contrarily, KBN1 experiences no cycle slip for all of the observation. Closely look at the surrounding of GPR1, the cycle slips in the direction of 30^0, 150^0 and 240^0-300^0 are likely due to the obstructed trees, while in the direction of 330^0 is due to the existence of the pillar. The occurrence of cycle slips will decrease the successful rate of resolved ambiguity. Further data treatment should be applied to minimize the unresolved ambiguities, such as, repair all cycle-slips or remove the cycle slips from the observed data.

Although the data collected on the same period of the observation and the distance between each site were relatively close, the number of observed satellites might be different. Fig. 6 shows the number of observed satellite as well as the DOP. As seen on Fig. 6, the variation of number of satellite in GPR1 is slightly larger than in KBN1. The statistic over those sites indicate that the mean number of observed satellite for GPR1 and KBN1 are 17 and 18 satellite respectively, while the standard deviation are 2 and 1 satellites for each site. As mentioned before, high disturbed surrounding at the low elevation satellite. This condition interferes the GNSS signal propagation.

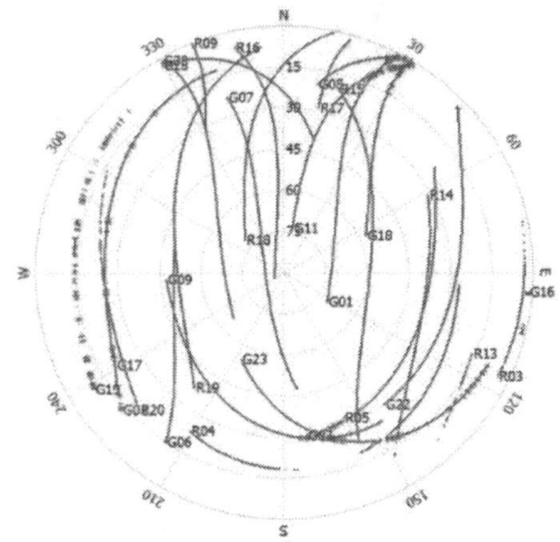

Fig. 3 The skyplot of satellite over GPR1 monitoring sites. Red lines indicate the occurred cycle slip on the observed data

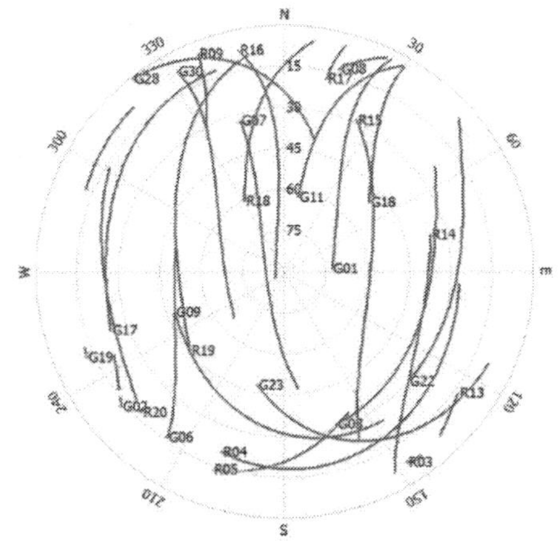

Fig. 4 The skyplot of satellite over KBN1 monitoring sites. Red lines indicate the occurred cycle slip on the observed data

Fig. 5 Surrounding of selected sites. GPR1 shown on the top of figure, while KBN1 shown on the bottom of figure. Left to the right picture indicate the North, East, South and West orientation respectively

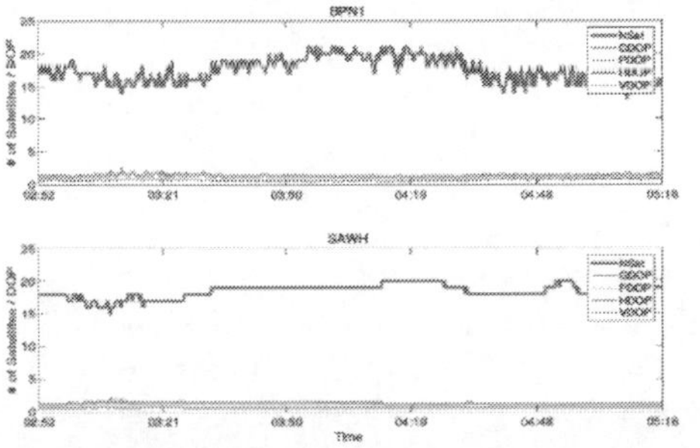

Fig. 6 Number of observed satellite and DOP for each site. GPR1 shown on the top of figure, while KBN1 shown on the bottom of figure

3.2 Multipath Analysis

Multipath is a localized effect, which depends on the local surrounding site. Fig. 7 illustrates the multipath signals. Any range measurement will severely disturbed by the multipath effect, due to the longer propagation path from the satellite to receiver.

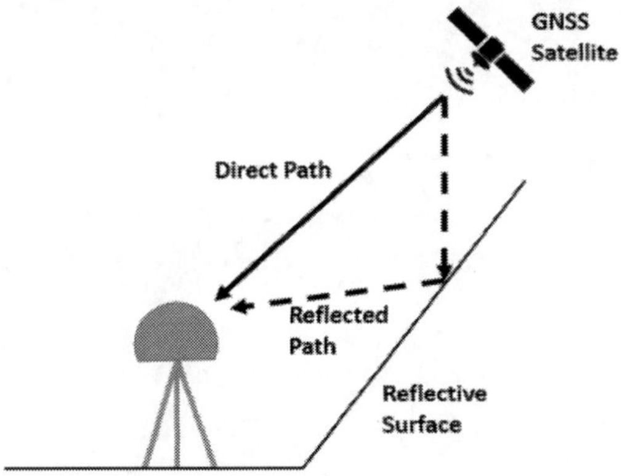

Fig. 7 Direct path and reflected path/multipath received signal

Fig. 8 and Fig. 9 show the L1 and L2 multipath for each site. In general, the multipath error variation in KBN1 relatively larger than those in GPR1. This is likely due to the typical noise from the receiver itself. All of the multipath error estimated from Topcon GR-3 show the similar pattern and variation. However, further investigation for the multipath error show that the multipath error variation tends to be more random and have significant multipath error.

Fig. 10 until Fig. 13 show the L1 and L2 skyplot of multipath for each site. Multipath usually occurred on the low elevation satellite angle, however, the significant multipath error occurred on the high elevation satellite angle on GPR1. The significant multipath error mostly occurred in the direction of about 330 degrees from North. Due to the close distant between pillar and the antenna, multipath significant error might be occurred even in the high elevation satellite angle. Differ from GPR1, multipath error which occurred in KBN1 relatively constant on all of the observation and tend to decrease on the high elevation satellite.

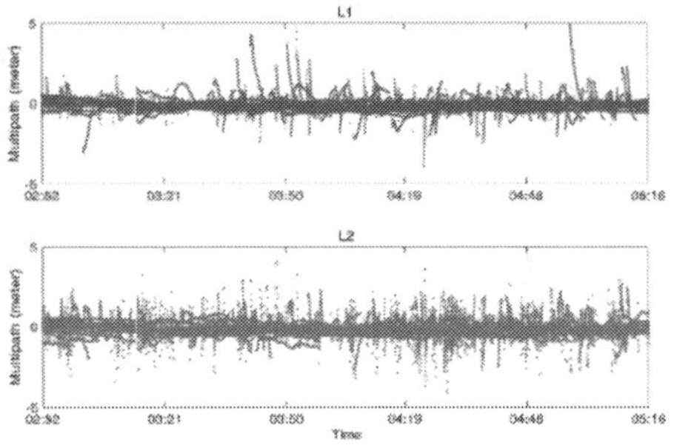

Fig. 8 Multipath error on GPR1

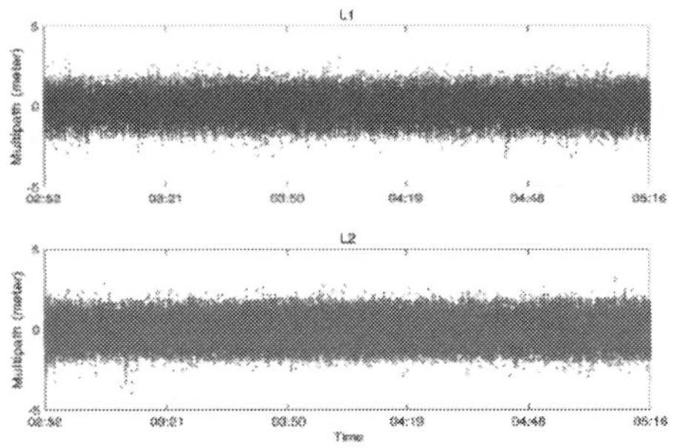

Fig. 9 Multipath error on KBN1

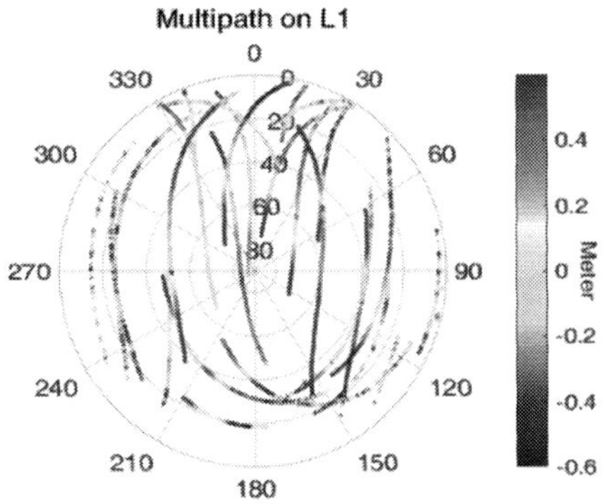

Fig. 10 Skyplot multipath L1 on GPR1

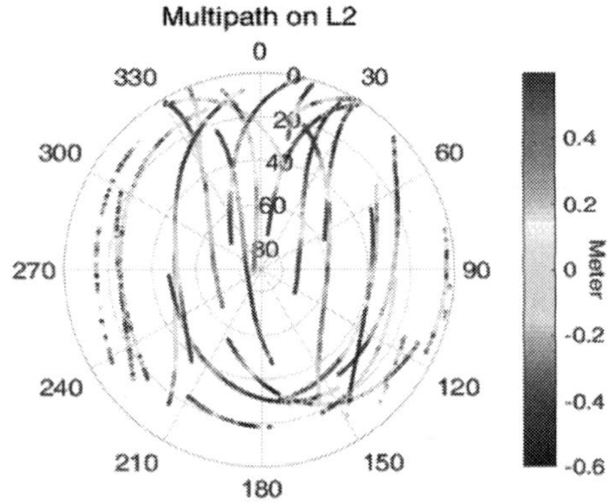

Fig. 11 Skyplot multipath L2 on GPR1

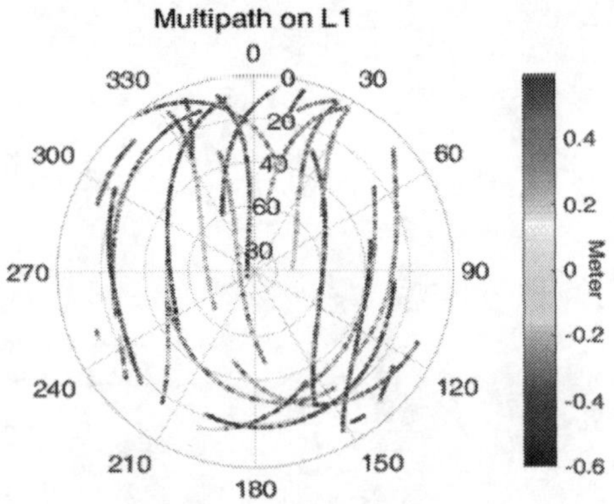

Fig. 12 Skyplot multipath L1 on KBN1

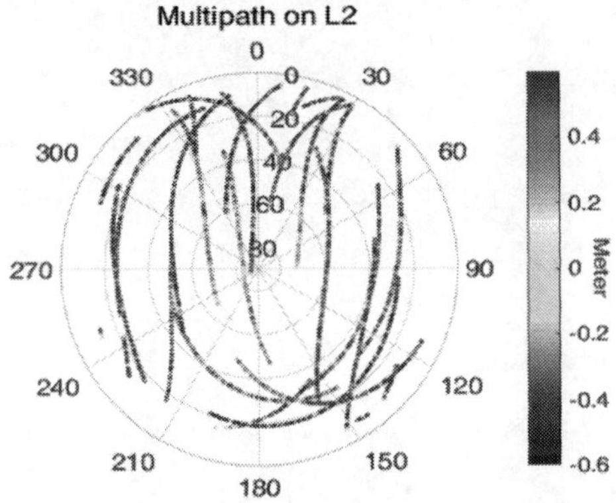

Fig. 13 Skyplot multipath L2 on KBN1

3.3 Kinematic Precise Point Positioning Analysis

KPPP was conducted to analyze the effect of observed geometry satellite and multipath. IGS final orbit and clock correction was used to eliminate the orbit and satellite clock bias. LAMBDA ambiguity resolution search was used to estimate the carrier phase ambiguities with 0^0 of elevation mask angle. Final solution used Forward and Backward filter.

Fig. 14 until Fig. 17 show the estimated position in ENU coordinate system for GPR1 and KBN1. Due to high obstructed surrounding, GPR1 estimated position tend to spread within 10 cm, while KBN1 only half of it. A tendency towards the northeast-southwest direction is indicated in GPR1, this is as a result of the reflector surface (pillar) in the direction of about 330^0. The receiver may receive both of the direct and the reflected signal from GNSS satellites [10].

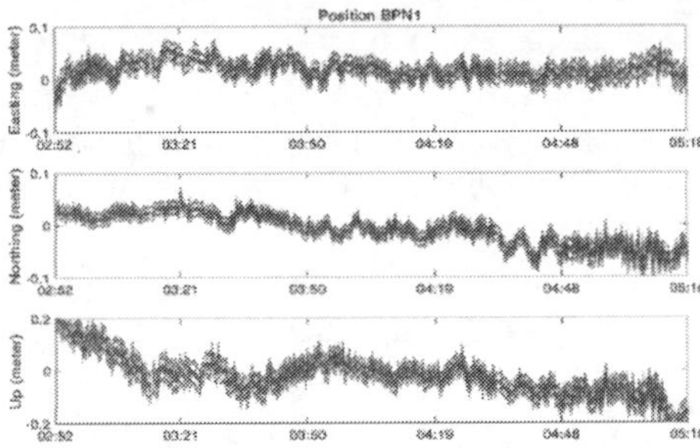

Fig. 14 GPR1 estimated position (ENU coordinate system). Blue dot and red line refer to estimated positon and its standard deviation

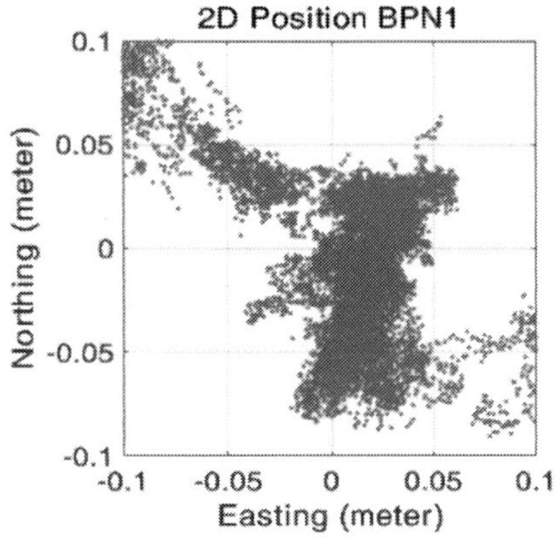

Fig. 15 GPR1 2D position

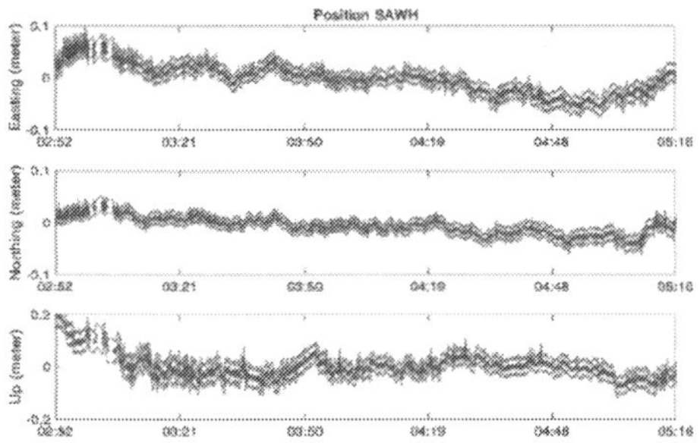

Fig. 16 KBN1 estimated position (ENU coordinate system). Blue dot and red line refer to estimated positon and its standard deviation

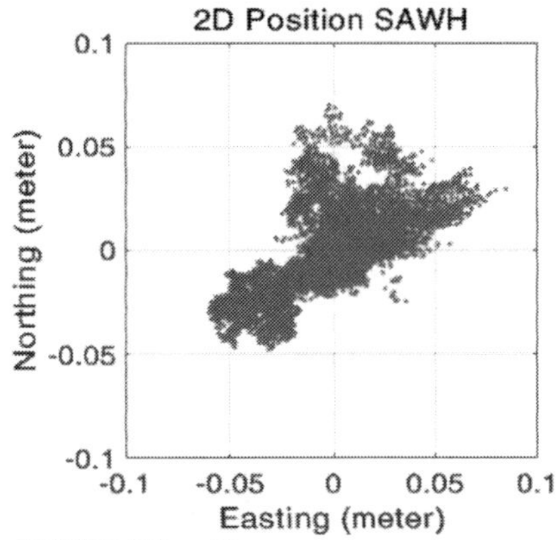

Fig. 17 KBN1 2D position

4 Network Adjustment

Accounting all of those aspects, first preliminary network adjustment is conducted. Baseline processing is done by using Leica Geo Office 8.1. The intermitted data is first removed from the observation data. Furthermore, 20^0 elevation mask angle was applied to minimize the multipath effect from low elevation satellite.

Five loops were formed for network adjustment. Loop closure are within mm level for horizontal and cm level for vertical. Further analysis revealed that loop 1, 2 and 5 slightly worse than loop 3 and 4 for vertical closure. Site condition on GPR1 and CIUJ were relatively worse than the others. Both of them were one of the observed point in loop 1, 2 and 3. Thus final network adjustment is applied.

Table *2* and Table 3 summarized the final solution.

Table 1 Loop closure for each formed loops (unit: meter)

Loop	From	To	Easting	Northing	Height

1	KBN1 RA97 CIUJ	RA97 CIUJ KBN1	-0.0012	0.0036	0.0130
2	KBN1 SDN1 GPR1	SDN1 GPR1 KBN1	-0.0055	0.0021	0.0172
3	KBN1 SDN1	SDN1 MSJD	-0.0082	0.0009	0.0072
	MSJD	KBN1			
4	MSJD KBN1 RA97	KBN1 RA97 MSJD	-0.0006	-0.0019	-0.0060
5	CIUJ KBN1 GPR1	KBN1 GPR1 CIUJ	-0.0022	0.0003	-0.0170

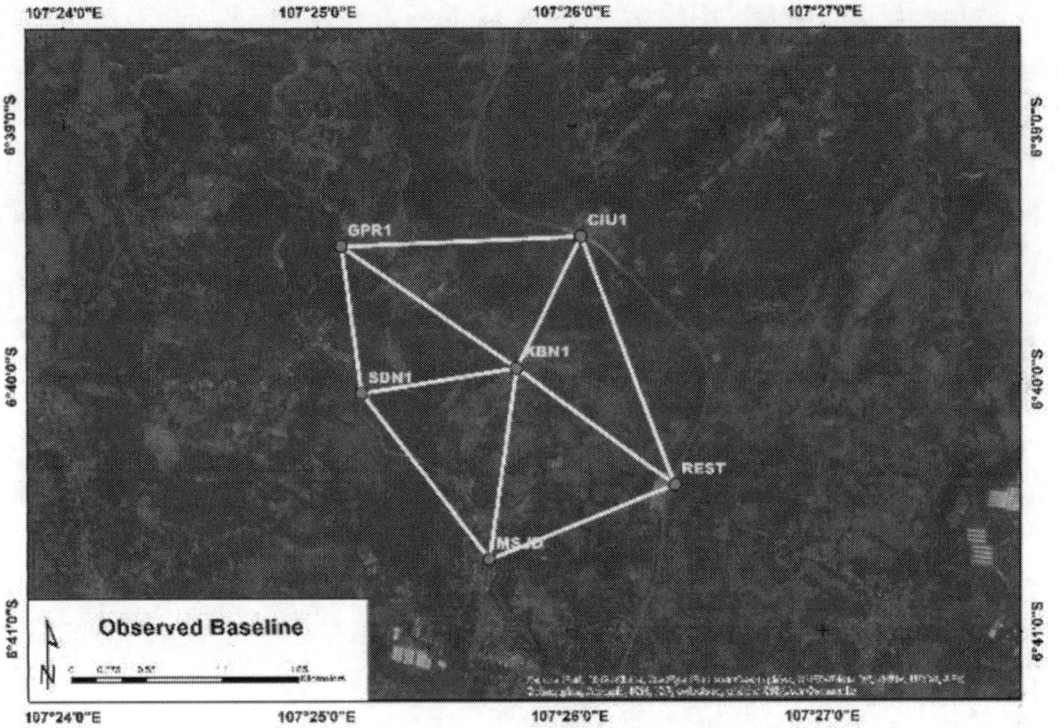

Fig. 18 Formed baseline indicated as yellow lines

Table 2 Adjusted point coordinates in UTM 48S (unit: meter)

Point	Easting	Northing	Height
GPR1	767386.1438	9263276.7253	437.1725
CIUJ	768999.8599	9263484.8570	455.5000
MSJD	768439.6020	9261119.1939	511.8749
RA97	769772.5571	9261416.1212	570.2214
KBN1	768651.2936	9262489.8261	401.3860
SDN1	767551.8261	9262292.4662	490.6122

Table 3 Standard deviation (unit: meter)

Point	Sd. E	Sd. N	Sd. H
GPR1	0.0016	0.0015	0.0044
CIUJ	0.0001	0.0001	0.0003
MSJD	0.0017	0.0015	0.0043
RA97	0.0015	0.0013	0.0038
KBN1	0.0015	0.0013	0.0038
SDN1	0.0018	0.0016	0.0046

5 Conclusion

The acquisition of reliable landslide monitoring points needs to be done by reducing the lack of observations. Observations using different types and brands must be considered the adjustment process based on the characteristics of the device. The location of GPR1 which is on the side of the road and beside the area of plantation makes more cycleslip, the recorded number of satellite changes rapidly more than KBN1 in the middle of the cropland, but KBN1 has a large multipath error. The result of the estimated position spreading of KBN1 is smaller than GPR1. Temperature at observation will cause a refractive effect and reduce the level of accuracy of the observation data, especially for points that are on the edge of the highway. For the purpose, several steps must be taken towards the results of observational data, such as an elevation mask angle of at least 15° to reduce errors due to multipath, choose satellite data with a high SNR value or remove satellite data that has many cycle slips.

References

1. Busthan, A. M. Imran, L. Samang, and M. Ramli. (2016) Engineering Geological Study of Malino-Manipi Landslide Susceptibility South Sulawesi Indonesia. *APRN Journal of Engineering and Applied Sciences*,11(15).
2. Hiromitsu Yamagishi and Yoji Ito (1994) Relationship of the landslide distribution to geology in Hokkaido, Japan. *Engineering Geology 38,* 189-203.
3. Masahiro Chigira (2002) Geologic factors contributing to landslide generation in a pyroclastic area: August 1998 Nishigo Village, Japan. *Geomophology 46*, 117-128.
4. E. D. Kaplan (1996). Understanding GPS: Principles and Applications. London: Artech House Boston.
5. G. Xu (2007) GPS Theory, Algorithms and Application. Berlin: Springer.
6. K. Yedukondalu, A. D. Sarma and V. Satya Srinivas (2011) Estimation and mitigation of GPS multipath Interference using adaptive filtering. *Progress In Electromagnetics Research M,* (21), 133-148.
7. Yang Gao and Kongzhe Chen (2004) Performance analysis of precise point positioning using rea-time orbit and clock products. *Journal of Global positioning,3(1-2)*, 95-100.
8. J. Kouba and P. Heroux (2001) GPS Precise Point Positioing Using IGS Orbit Products. *GPS Solution 5(2),* 12-28
9. B. Hofmann-Wellenhof, H. Lichtenegger and J. Collins (2001) GPS theory and practice, fifth, revised edition.
10. Tomislav Kos, Ivan Markezic and Josip Pokrjcic (2010) Effects of multipath reception on GPS Positioning Performance. *Proceedings ELMAR-2010*

A Simulation Study on Triple Frequency Ambiguity Resolution for Reference Stations Using Different Strategy Regarding Elevation angles

Sun-Kyoung Yu[1], Dong-uk Kim, June-sol Song[2], and *Changdon* Kee[1*]

[1]School of Mechanical and Aerospace Engineering and the SNU-IAMD, 08826 Seoul, Korea
[2]ENAC, France

Abstract. This paper proposes an ambiguity resolution method using triple frequency for reference stations. Using the reference coordinate information, geometry based ambiguity resolution performance is analysed. Although orbit errors and tropospheric model errors still remain, wide lane ambiguity could be fixed in several epochs. However, the narrow lane wave length of about 10cm is too short to overcome error sources by simply combining the measurement. Therefore, we have divided the elevation angle into 5 degree intervals and investigated the measurement errors and the time to fix of each section. For high elevation satellites, it is possible to determine in several epochs by integer rounding. On the other hand, if the elevation is lower than 30 degrees, the tropospheric zenith delay must be estimated with ambiguities. The proposed algorithm estimates ambiguities and tropospheric zenith delay simultaneously utilizing ambiguity free observations of high elevation satellites. Ambiguities for high elevation satellites are resolved by integer rounding in several epochs. The algorithm has been verified by generating the simulated observation data for the 'Cheon-an' and 'Boen' reference stations in the Korea.

1 INTRODUCTION

Network RTK is one of the carrier phase differential GPS system, which broadcasts correction messages to users for providing cm level precise positioning. Correction messages could be generated as soon as the station ambiguities are fixed. Therefore reference station need reduce the time to fix ambiguity.

For reducing the time to fix ambiguities, many researchers have been studied. In these days, triple frequency ambiguity resolution is one of the major topics to shorten the time to fix ambiguity. Also the modernized GNSS systems plans and already broadcasts additional frequency measurements to improve their performance. BEIDOU and GLONASS broadcasts more than 2 frequency measurements. GPS plans L5 signal full operation since 2020.[1]

Therefore many researchers have already investigated efficient coefficients. In general, two independent ambiguities, which have meter level wave lengths, could be fixed even if with integer rounding in several epochs. They are called Extra Wide Lane(EWL) and Wide Lane(WL). However, to be free from ambiguities, one more independent ambiguity must be resolved. [2]
The last ambiguity is generally called narrow lane(NL) which has about 10 cm wave length. Since the difficulty to overcome other errors for short wave length, many studies have been assumed the measurement errors for several baseline lengths. [1]

In addition to previous researches, we have investigated measurement errors regarding to elevation angles in [4]. The errors depend on elevation angle as well as the baseline length. Utilization of measurement errors regarding to elevation angle, the time to fix for each interval was studied. For high elevation satellites, it is possible to determine the ambiguity in several seconds. On the other hand, if elevation angle is lower than 30 degrees, the tropospheric zenith delay must be estimated with ambiguities. Therefore the paper proposed an algorithm which has different strategies for high and low elevation satellites. In this paper, the algorithm was assessed for several environments.

We test the algorithm for 'Cheon-an' and 'Boen' reference stations in the Korea which has about 70 km baselines and conducted in three cases. The first case is that all GPS satellites transmit triple frequency signals. Currently, however, the GPS modernization project is underway, so only BLOCK IIF satellites has triple frequencies. Therefore, a case where only a part of satellites broadcasts triple signals is also examined. Finally, a dual frequency environment is handled and compared with others.

* Corresponding author: kee@snu.ac.kr

1 ALGORITHM

1.1 Geometry Based

Pseudo range and carrier phase are composed of distance, satellite clock error, troposphere delay, ionosphere delay and user clock error. Carrier phase has one more component, which is ambiguity. By double differencing pseudo range and carrier measurements, clock errors are eliminated.

For reducing or eliminating measurement errors, many researchers have combined pseudo range(ρ_1, ρ_2, ρ_3) and carrier phase measurements(ϕ_1, ϕ_2, ϕ_3) for three different frequencies (f_1, f_2, f_3).

The following equation (1) is general triple frequency geometry based combination formula. The combination coefficients(i, j, k, l, m, n) are all integers.

$$\rho_{(l,m,n)} = \frac{l \cdot f_1 \cdot \rho_1 + m \cdot f_2 \cdot \rho_2 + n \cdot f_3 \cdot \rho_3}{l \cdot f_1 + m \cdot f_2 + n \cdot f_3} \quad \phi_{(i,j,k)} = \frac{i \cdot f_1 \cdot \phi_1 + j \cdot f_2 \cdot \phi_2 + k \cdot f_3 \cdot \phi_3}{i \cdot f_1 + j \cdot f_2 + k \cdot f_3} \tag{1}$$

Eq. (2) shows the triple frequency combination for Double Differenced (DD) measurements. The effect of L1 ionosphere delay could be expressed with $\beta_{(i,j,k)}$. $\varepsilon_{\Delta\nabla\rho_{(l,m,n)}}$, $\varepsilon_{\Delta\nabla\phi_{(i,j,k)}}$ are noise for DD pseudo range and DDCP for the combination. $\lambda_{(i,j,k)}$ is the ambiguity wave length.[5]

$$\begin{aligned} \Delta\nabla\rho_{(l,m,n)} &= \Delta\nabla d + \Delta\nabla T + \beta_{(l,m,n)}\Delta\nabla I_1 + \varepsilon_{\Delta\nabla\rho_{(l,m,n)}} \\ \Delta\nabla\phi_{(i,j,k)} &= \Delta\nabla d + \Delta\nabla T - \beta_{(i,j,k)}\Delta\nabla I_1 - \lambda_{(i,j,k)}\Delta\nabla N_{(i,j,k)} + \varepsilon_{\Delta\nabla\phi_{(i,j,k)}} \end{aligned} \tag{2}$$

In this paper, geometry based measurement, which was eliminated distance and troposphere delay with broadcast orbits and Saastamoinen model, is applied for ambiguity resolution.

1.2 Time to fix for each ambiguity

In previous research, EWL is fixed in 1 epoch. Furthermore, we have studied WL and NL geometry based combinations characteristics for solar max activity duration. [4]

For WL, the integer rounding of $\Delta\nabla\phi_{(1,-6,5)}$ is 99.7 %. It seems that the triple frequency WL could be solved in 1 epoch and the dual frequency WL is fixed in 25 epoch. However NL has low success rate for low elevation angle. Using the error analysis for elevation angle intervals, Table 1 could be calculated. The time to fix is the minimum necessary epochs which the integer rounding success rate exceeds 99.7%. It shows that elevation higher than 30 degree could be fixed with integer rounding method without estimated troposphere delay.

Table 1 The time to fix for each elevation range

Elevation range	combination				
	(4,-3,0)	(4,-1,-2)	(4,-2,-1)	(154,0,-115)	(154,-120,0)
85~90	2	2	**1**	2	2
80~85	2	2	**1**	2	2
75~80	2	2	**1**	2	2
70~75	2	2	**1**	2	2
65~70	2	**2**	**2**	2	2
60~65	2	**2**	**2**	2	2
55~60	2	**2**	**2**	2	2
45~55	2	**2**	**2**	2	3
40~45	3	**2**	**2**	2	3
35~40	5	**4**	**4**	5	7
30~35	25	**16**	17	19	33

1.3 Algorithm for low elevation satellites

Using Table 1, high elevation satellites could be resolved in several epochs. On the other hand the low elevation satellites suffer from troposphere delay due to short wave length.

Eq. (3), (4) are high elevation and low elevation measurements. For low elevation satellite ambituity resolution, ionofree measurement is selected to estimate troposphere delay. High elevation measurement could be free from ambiguity by integer rounding in several epochs. Therefore the ambiguity solved measurement would be helpful to estimate zenith troposphere delay.

$$\begin{aligned} z_{high} &= \left(\Delta\nabla\phi_{(77,-12,46)} - \Delta\nabla d_{brdc} - \Delta\nabla T_{model} - \Delta\nabla N_{(77,-12,46)} \cdot \lambda_{(77,-12,46)}\right) \\ &= \Delta\nabla\delta d + \Delta\nabla\delta T + \Delta\nabla\varepsilon_{\phi_{(77,-12,46)}} \end{aligned} \tag{3}$$

$$\begin{aligned} z_{low} &= \left(\Delta\nabla\phi_{(77,-12,-46)} - \Delta\nabla d_{brdc} - \Delta\nabla T_{model}\right) - \frac{(77 \cdot \Delta\nabla N_{WL} - 46 \cdot \Delta\nabla N_{EWL})}{(77-46)} \cdot \lambda \\ &= \Delta\nabla\delta d + \Delta\nabla\delta T + \Delta\nabla N_{(9,1,0)} \cdot \lambda + \Delta\nabla\varepsilon_{\phi_{(77,-12,-46)}} \end{aligned} \tag{4}$$

Eq. (5) is the measurement equation for low elevation ambiguities and zenith tropo delay of two stations.

$$\bar{z} = \begin{bmatrix} z_{high}^{1} \\ \vdots \\ z_{high}^{n_1} \\ z_{low}^{n_1+1} \\ \vdots \\ z_{low}^{n_1+n_2} \end{bmatrix} = \begin{bmatrix} \nabla^1 m_{ref_1} & \nabla^1 m_{ref_2} & \\ \vdots & \vdots & \underline{0}_{n_1 \times n_2} \\ \nabla^{n_1} m_{ref_1} & \nabla^{n_1} m_{ref_2} & \\ \nabla^{n_1+1} m_{ref_1} & \nabla^{n_1+1} m_{ref_2} & \\ \vdots & \vdots & \lambda \cdot I_{n_2 \times n_2} \\ \nabla^{n_1+n_2} m_{ref_1} & \nabla^{n_1+n_2} m_{ref_2} & \end{bmatrix} \begin{bmatrix} T_{ref_1} \\ T_{ref_2} \\ \Delta\nabla N^1 \\ \vdots \\ \Delta\nabla N^{n_2} \end{bmatrix} + \begin{bmatrix} \Delta\nabla\varepsilon^1 \\ \vdots \\ \Delta\nabla\varepsilon^{n_1} \\ \Delta\nabla\varepsilon^{n_1+1} \\ \vdots \\ \Delta\nabla\varepsilon^{n_1+n_2} \end{bmatrix} \tag{5}$$

2 SIMULATION

The algorithm has been assessed by generating the simulated observation data for the 'Cheon-an' and 'Boen' reference stations in the Korea which has about 70 km baselines. It is on September 1st, 2014 because the day was one of solar max activity.

Simulated data was generated using NGA precise orbits of antenna phase center, zenith tropo delay by PPP results, Neill mapping function, and IONEX data.

Three cases were conducted in three cases. CASE 1 is that all triple frequency signals are available. CASE 2 is only

BLOCK IIF triple frequency available situation and CASE 3 is dual frequency case.

The initial state of zenith tropo delay error is zero and the initial standard deviation is 30cm. The initial ambiguity for each satellite is residual of ionosphere measurement eliminated distance and troposphere delay using broadcast orbit and Saastamoinen model.

2.1. Without integer rounding for high elevation

For ionofree measurements, troposphere error should be estimated to solve the ambiguity. Fig 1 shows the NL ambiguity error and station differenced zenith troposphere delay error. The green line is plus 3 sigma for states. Table 2 show the time to fix for each satellite. It was high order sorted for mean elevation. PRN 16 is fixed in 2 seconds for all cases because the troposphere delay affects nearly zeros.

For triple frequency measurements, EWL and WL ambiguities are resolved in only 2 epochs. However dual frequency WL is fixed in 26 epochs. Therefore, the NL ambiguity of dual frequency satellites, CASE 2 except block IIF and CASE 3, could be estimated after 26 epochs. In figure 1, station differenced zenith troposphere delay error of case 3 is most fast to be estimated.

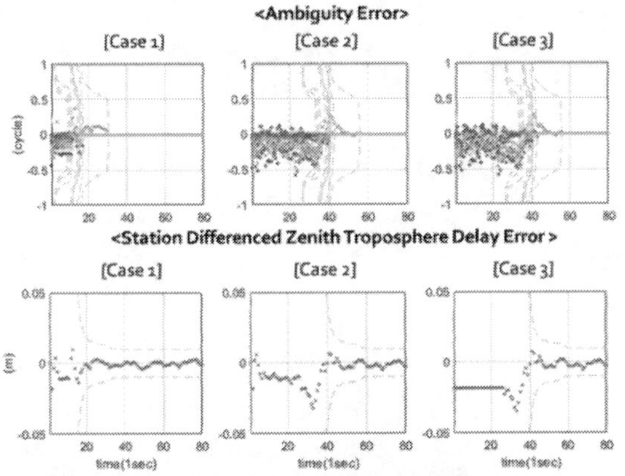

Figure 1 Ambiguity and station differenced zenith tropo sphere delay error without integer rounding for high elevation

Block IIF satellites are PRN 1, 8, 30 for this simulation. Therefore, case 1 shorten almost 20 epoch compared to case 2 and case 3. Because the dual frequency ambiguity estimation starts after 26 epochs, sum of EWL and WL ambiguity fixing time. As the result, by reducing WL ambiguity time to fix, the ambiguity resolution has shorten in table 2 and 3.

Table 2 The time to fix and elevation without integer rounding for high elevation

PRN	elevation	time to fix		
		case 1	case 2	case 3
11	69	2	2	2
4	48	10	34	34
28	46	11	35	35
30	41	12	36	36
8	32	15	39	39
32	31	17	41	41
19	29	16	41	41
7	29	16	40	40
20	24	18	43	43
17	18	31	56	56

2.2 The application of integer rounding for high elevation

Figure 2 and table 3 are the results of the proposed algorithm. Table 3 is 6-32 epoch faster than Table 2. The integer rounding for high elevation satellites helps troposphere delay error estimation and it results other ambiguity resolution to be fastened.

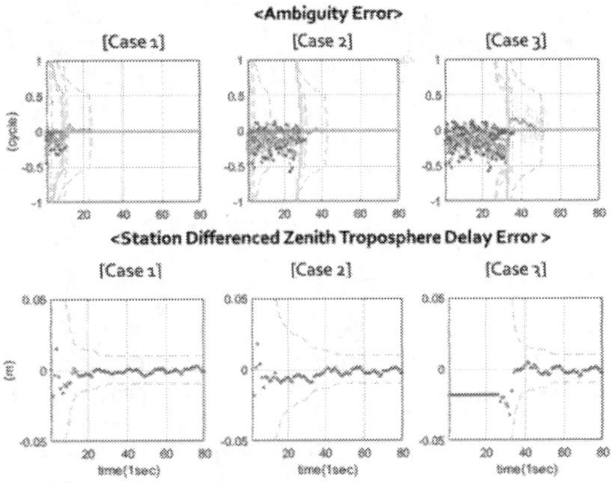

Figure 2 Ambiguity and station differenced zenith tropo sphere delay error without integer rounding for high elevation

Table 3 The time to fix and elevation with integer rounding for high elevation

PRN	elevation	time to fix		
		case 1	case 2	case 3
11	69	2	2	2
4	48	4	29	33
28	46	4	29	33
30	41	4	4	33
8	32	9	13	33
32	31	11	30	33
19	29	10	30	34
7	29	10	29	34
20	24	12	32	36
17	18	24	43	51

3 Conclusion

The proposed triple frequency ambiguity resolution algorithm, which uses integer rounding method for high elevation satellites, has been tested by simulation in three cases. Three cases are classified with the number of triple frequency broadcasting satellites. For WL ambiguity, triple frequency ambiguity resolution is 24 epochs faster than dual frequency satellites. With the integer rounding method, the time to fix for NL was shortened 6 to 32 epochs. The integer rounding for high elevation satellites helps low elevation satellite ambiguity resolution as well as zenith troposphere delay estimation.

Acknowledgement

This research was supported by a grant (18TLRP-C113269-03) from Transportation logistics research Program funded by Ministry of Land, Infrastructure and Transport of Korea government. This research was supported (in part) by the Institute of Advanced Aerospace Technology at Seoul National University. The Institute of Engineering Research at Seoul National University provided research facilities for this work.

References

1. B. Li, The Journal of Global Positioning Systems, **16**, 1 (2018).
2. X. Wang, W. Liu, G. Sun, Journal of Navigation, **69**, 1393-1408.(2016).
3. B. Li, Y. Feng, GPS solutions, **14**, 177-184 (2010).
4. S. Yu, D. Kim, J. Song, C. Kee, IPNT, (2018)
5. Y. Feng, C. Rizos, GPS Solutions, **13**, 43-56 (2009).

E3S Web of Conferences **94**, 01025 (2019) https://doi.org/10.1051/e3sconf/20199401025
ISGNSS 2018

Implementation of the modeling and simulation software of search and rescue system based Korea navigation satellite system

Incheol Jeong[1], *Sanguk* Lee[1], *Woo-Geun* Ahn[2]

[1]Satellite Research Department, ETRI
[2]Agency for Defense Development

Abstract. This paper describes the development of M&S (Modeling and Simulation) system based COSPAS-SARSAT SAR (Search and Rescue) system. SAR system transmits a distress signal to the terminal and transmits it to the satellite network or the terrestrial network. It recognized distress incident from anywhere in the world. The M&S system is designed to analyze the accuracy, reliability, and availability of the SAR (Search and Rescue) system. It is also designed to simulate the actual distress beacons of a distress situation. It was developed to enable performance analysis. We will verify the validity of the implemented results, applying the RF signal processing based on KNSS.

1 Introuction

In this paper, we investigate the accuracy, reliability, and availability of the SAR (Search and Rescue) system when constructing the M&S (Modelling and Simulation) system based on the concept of the existing military SAR and the result of analyzing the civil search structure system based on COSPAS-SARSAT (Cosmicheskaya Sistema Poiska Avariynich Sudov – Search and Rescue Satellite-Aided Tracking). SAR system can provide distress alert and location information to SAR service if land and aircraft distress incident occurs from anywhere in the world.

When the search structure terminal is activated, a distress signal of 406 MHz is emitted (1), the structure signal is received from the COSPAS-SARSAT composed of low-earth orbit satellite (2), relayed by the local receiver station (LUT) (3), the ground receiving station calculates the position of the search structure terminal and transmits it to the Rescue Coordination Centre (RCC) through the MCC (MCC) (5), and the RCC performs the rescue operation do.

The purpose of this paper is to measure the accuracy, reliability, and availability performance of the search structure system and to present the direction of the COSPAS-SARSAT search structure system by building a test bed.

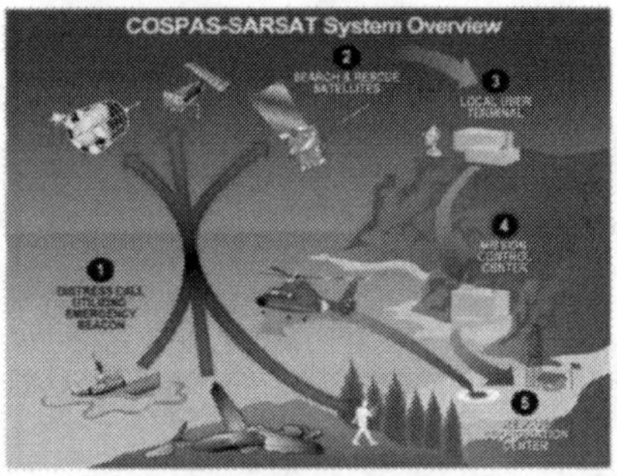

Fig. 1 Flow of the COSPAS-SARSAT SAR

We describe the results of analyzing the accuracy, reliability, and availability of the SAR system based on the M&S system of the RF signal-based military search and rescue system through COSPAS-SARSAT and applying the dynamics model to the USRP test bed.

In this paper, functional scope of the simulator, the architecture of the SAR M&S Software will be presented. It is ensured that SAR system satisfies the desired performance in KNSS environment.

2 Modelling and simulation of the search and rescue system

The USRP test bed consists of one transmitter and two receivers, as shown in Fig. 2. The military navigation system is based on the Korea Navigational Satellite System (KNSS), the LTE, and the COSPAS-SARSAT. . AES 128bit algorithm is implemented and a static signal is implemented by developing the COSPAS-SARSAT (C/S) Spread Spectrum specification and satisfying the second generation COSPAS-SARSAT standard.

The USRP system was used to implement the RF signal-based search structure system, and the accuracy, reliability, and availability performance of the COSPAS- SARSAT search structure system were measured using the on-board dynamics model.

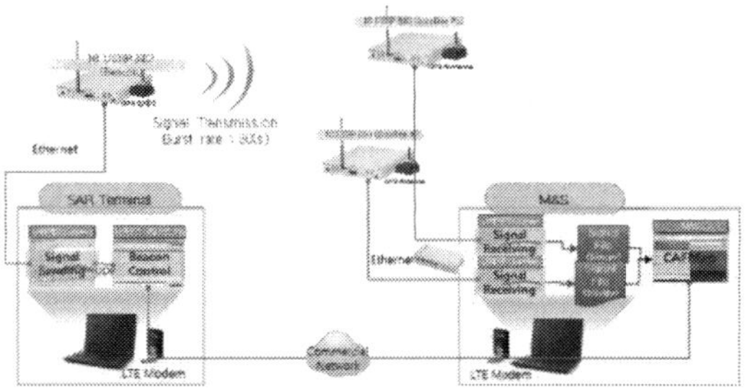

Figure 2 Search and Rescue System based USRP

M&S software of military navigation system consists of 4 main modelling domains which are user, communication link, ground station (including mission control centre) and system operating environment as shown in Figure 3.

The User model of the SAR system is a function that automatically sends a distress signal when a distress situation occurs and transmits a distress signal in response to a call signal of the ground station. The system operation environment models GIS (Geometric Information System), weather information, antenna information, and satellite information required to calculate propagation attenuation for terrestrial and satellite signals.

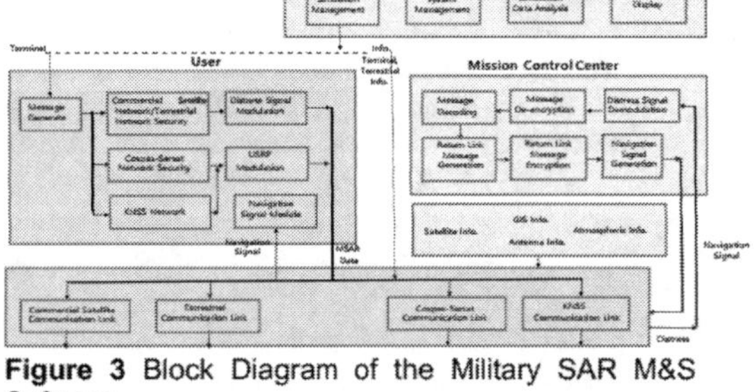

Figure 3 Block Diagram of the Military SAR M&S Software

In the communication link model, the propagation attenuation of the input transmission signal is composed of the terrestrial network and the satellite network, and the attenuation variable of the operating environment model is reflected on the distance between the terminal and the ground station. The ground station consists of a mission control center, a search and rescue team, and a ground receiving station for ground communication.

The M&S software of the military SAR system includes satellite orbital generation, availability analysis of beacon terrain and beacon satellites using terrain, analysis of rescue time and beacon operation time in distress, and terrestrial signal and satellite signal reach analysis. It is possible to simulate a military search and rescue structure similar to the actual situation using GIS information.

3 Search and rescue system and Korea Navigation Satellite System

COSPAS-SARSAT system was provided by using low-earth orbit satellite and geostationary satellite. There are same types as marine, airborne, and potable handheld navigation devices. They are installed in personal portable devices, ships or aircraft and transmit alarm signal to navigation satellite to inform distress signals.

A military SAR is a system that detects and locates distress signals by mounting them on high-speed vehicles such as satellites. Therefore, rather than loading the equipment into a satellite mobile object, the motion of the high-speed mobile object is simulated by applying a dynamic model. The military SAR system simulates Doppler frequency measurement and actual propagation environment according to satellite motion to reflect the dynamic model.

KNSS system consists of the 3 Geostationary Orbit Satellite (GEO-1, GEO-2, GEO-3) and 4 Elliptical Inclined Geosynchronous Orbit Satellite (EIGSO-1, EIGSO-2, EIGSO-3 and EIGSO-4).

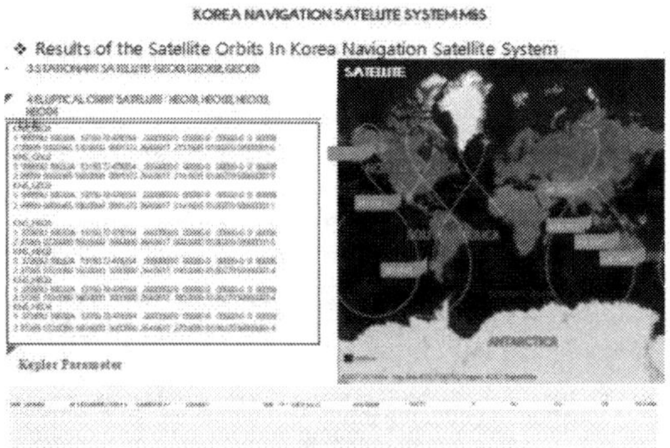

Figure 4 Satellite Orbits in KNSS

As a result of analyzing the satellite orbits of the KNSS, it continuously covers the Korean peninsula and always maintains more than 6 satellites.

Elevation angel of the GEO (Geostationary Orbit) satellites are fixed at 21 ~ 47 degrees, and

EIGSO (Elliptical Inclined Geosynchronous Orbit) satellites are 6 ~ 83 degrees depending on orbit change. The C/No for the satellite received signal strength is 36.86 ~ 37.36 dB for GEO satellites and 34.8 ~ 38.3 dB for EIGSO satellites.

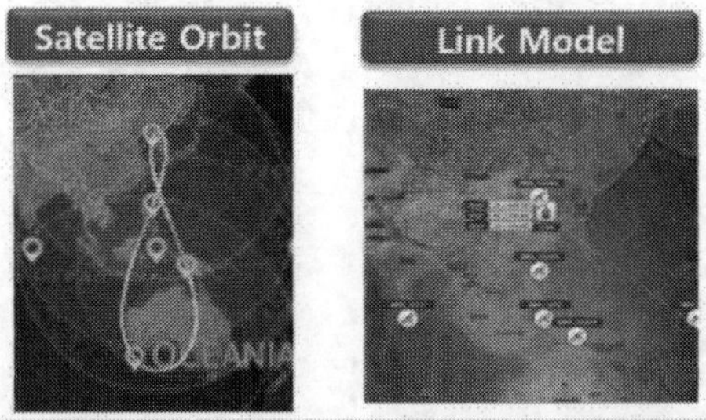

위성	Semi major axis (km)	Eccentricity	Inclination (deg)	RAAN (deg)	Arg. of Perigee (deg)	Mean Anomaly (deg)
GEO1	42165.0	0	0	0	0	179.65
GEO2	42165.0	0	0	0	0	226.65
GEO2	42165.0	0	0	0	0	279.65
EIGSO1	42165.0	0.075	41	316.633	270	0
EIGSO2	42165.0	0.075	41	226.633	270	90
EIGSO3	42165.0	0.075	41	136.633	270	180
EIGSO4	42165.0	0.075	41	46.633	270	270

Figure 5 Satellite Orbits in Korea Navigation Satellite System

4 Analysis of the M&S of the KNSS

In KNSS, the EIGSO has a large variation in position accuracy depending on the point of time since the satellite velocity is not constant, and it is difficult to form a geometry due to a lack of number of the satellites.

Therefore, as a result of the performance evaluation simulation, the peak due to the accumulation of CAF (Cross Ambiguity Function) was not formed well. The results were measured to be 1km level with ground positioning performance only by elliptical satellite orbit. We think about that it must use LEO (Low Earth Orbit) and MEO (Middle Earth Orbit) satellite same as Galileo and COSPAS-SARSAT for good geometry.

The performance of the ground positioning in a SAR system was measured to be less than 1 KM only by the combination of the KNSS. This means that the location of the distress incident has an error of about 1 KM compared to the location identified by the system. After that, ETRI will make efforts to reduce errors by developing algorithms to improve ground positioning performance.

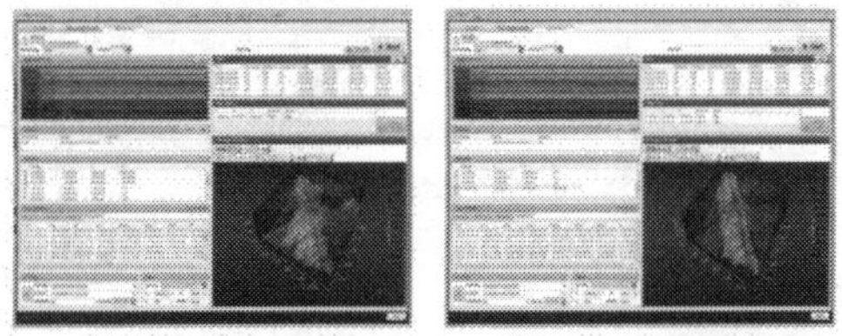

<EIGSO 4 16 times signal accumulation - location error:996m> <EIGSO 4 6 times signal accumulation - location error:1.3km>

Figure 6 Performance Evaluation of the Ground Positioning using KNSS

5 Conclusion

This paper presents validity of the implemented results about M&S, applying the RF signal processing based on KNSS and applying the dynamics model to the USRP test bed.

At the sending the distress signal, distress terminal generates and transmits a spread spectrum RF signal. At the receiving end, the possibility of the location estimation of the victim was verified based on the signal. In the next approach, ETRI will verify and extend algorithm applied to the module about ground positioning.

Reference

1. Jeong, I. C., Kim, D. W., Ahn, W. G., & Lee, S. U., (2017) Development of Search and Rescue System with Dynamic Model by RF Signal Based LTE, *Journal of Satellite, information and Communications*, Vol **12** No.4, 120-124

2. Kim, J. H., Lee, S. U., Kim, J. H., Ahn, W. G. (2014) Development Status of Military Search and Rescue System M&S Software, *The Journal of Korea Society of Communication and Space Technology*, Vol **9** No 3, 121-126

Robust Positioning Performance in Indoor Environments

Allison Kealy[1], *Guenther* Retscher[2,*], *Yan* Li[3], *Thomas* Gonzales[4], *Salil* Goel[5], *Jelena* Gabela[3]

[1]School of Science, RMIT University, City Campus, Melbourne, Australia
[2]Department of Geodesy and Geoinformation, TU Wien, Gusshausstrasse 27-29, 1040 Vienna, Austria
[3]Department of Electrical and Electronic Engineering, The University of Melbourne, Melbourne, Australia
[4]French Civil Aviation University, Toulouse, France
[5]Department of Civil Engineering, Indian Institute of Technology Kanpur, Uttar Pradesh, India

Abstract. Increasingly, safety and liability critical applications require GNSS-like positioning metrics in environments where GNSS cannot work. Indoor navigation for the vision impaired and other mobility restricted individuals, emergency responders and asset tracking in buildings demand levels of positioning accuracy and integrity that cannot be satisfied by current indoor positioning technologies and techniques. This paper presents the challenges facing positioning technologies for indoor positioning and presents innovative algorithms and approaches that aim to enhance performance in these difficult environments. The overall aim is to achieve GNSS-like performance in terms of autonomous, global, infrastructure free, portable and cost efficient. Preliminary results from a real-world experimental campaign conducted as part of the joint FIG Working Group 5.5 and IAG Sub-commission 4.1 on multi-sensor systems, demonstrate performance improvements based on differential Wi-Fi (DWi-Fi) and cooperative positioning techniques. The techniques, experimental schema and initial results will be fully documented in this paper.

1 Introduction

This paper reports about an experiment, conducted in a GNSS-denied/challenged, indoor environment at the Queen Victoria Market (QVM) located in Melbourne, Australia. The overall aim of this campaign was to assess the feasibility of achieving GNSS-like performance for ubiquitous positioning at affordable cost efficiency. In the experimental campaign, we developed a cooperative system comprising of seven pedestrian users equipped with smartphones using an integration of signals such as Wi-Fi (Wireless Fidelity) and UWB (Ultra-Wide Band) with the objective of achieving precise positioning in indoor environments. In this paper, the set-up of the experiments and their characteristics are presented, and selected results are discussed.

For Wi-Fi Received Signal Strength (RSS) based indoor positioning, fingerprinting is one of the widely-employed methods which can offer relatively high positioning accuracy. Conventional fingerprinting methods, however, normally perform a training using a site survey only once in the beginning and thereafter only if the environment changes significantly, which are not resistant to dynamic environment changes. Continuously updating the fingerprint database is a new way to enhance the achievable positioning accuracy. For that purpose, a Differential Wi-Fi (DWi-Fi) scheme by analogy to DGNSS is applied. It is a network calibration method based on reference stations realized by low-cost Raspberry Pi units which is able to derive the correction parameters in real-time. In this way, the measured RSS values at the user's side are corrected, the fingerprinting database is continuously updated, and thus an adaption to the possible changes in the dynamics of the environment is achieved.

Furthermore, in this study, the derivation and integration of UWB ranges for positioning of mobile users is investigated. These UWB ranges serve either as more precise reference for the Wi-Fi derived ranges or are integrated into the overall positioning solution. Due to a collocation of the UWB transmitters forming the anchors of the UWB positioning system with the Raspberry Pi units for Wi-Fi positioning in the test site an integration of the two system solutions is possible.

The paper is organized as follows: Firstly, key requirements and performance parameters for PNT (Position, Navigation and Timing) are identified in section 2. Section 3 presents Wi-Fi positioning based on the differential approach (termed Differential Wi-Fi, DWi-Fi) followed by the UWB positioning scheme in section 4. Then the test area is introduced in section 5 and the main results in section 6. Section 7 presents concepts for Wi-Fi signal distribution interpolation approaches – realized by so-called radio maps –and their use in the DWi-Fi scheme. Concluding remarks and an outlook are drawn in the final section 8.

* Corresponding author: guenther.retscher@tuwien.ac.at

2 Key Requirements and Performance Parameters

As stated in the 2017 GNSS market report [1] the key GNSS requirements and performance parameters are summarized in the following. It must be noted that they are also applicable for any other PNT applications not involving only GNSS but also other sensors and technologies which are additionally and independently used. The key parameters are:

- **Availability**: percentage of time over a specified time interval that a sufficient number of satellites are transmitting a usable ranging signal within view of the user. Values vary greatly according to the specific application and services used, but typically range from 95-99.9%.
- **Accuracy**: the difference between true and computed position (absolute positioning). This is expressed as the value within which a specified proportion of samples would fail if measured. Typical values for accuracy range from tens of meters to centimeters for 95% samples. Accuracy is typically stated as 2D (horizontal), 3D (horizontal and height) or time.
- **Continuity**: ability to provide the required performance during an operation without interruption once the operation has started. Continuity is usually expressed as the risk of discontinuity and depends entirely on the timeframe of the application (e.g. application that requires 10 minutes of uninterrupted service has a different continuity figure than one requiring two hours of uninterrupted service, even if using the same receiver and services). A typical value is $1x10^{-4}$ over the course of the procedure where the system is in use.
- **Integrity**: the measure of trust that can be placed in the correctness of the position or time estimate provided by the receiver. This is usually expressed as the probability of a user being exposed to an error larger than alert limits without warning.
- **Time To first Fix (TTFF)**: a measure of a receiver's performance covering the time between activation and output of position within the required accuracy bounds. Activation means subtly different things depending on the status of the data the receiver has access to.
- **Robustness**: the ability of systems or system elements to withstand a level of interference and/or jamming without significant degradation or loss of performance.
- **Authentication**: the ability of the system to assure that they are utilising signals and/or data from trustworthy source (e.g. GNSS constellation), and thus protecting sensitive applications from spoofing threats.

If these key requirements and performance parameters are applied, for instance, for Wi-Fi or UWB positioning a similar statement or meaning can be formulated. Regarding availability the number of transmitters (UWB stationary transmitters or Wi-Fi Access Points) replaces the number of satellites. Especially integrity is often neglected and not paid full attention. It can be seen as a very important key parameter. The way that integrity is ensured and assessed, and the means of delivering integrity related information to the user are highly application dependent. TTFF in the case of Wi-Fi positioning is highly correlated to the received signal strength (RSS) scan duration of a certain mobile device. This is especially important in kinematic positioning. As seen in [14] the appearing scan durations can vary significantly for different smartphones which results in a different level of achievable positioning accuracy in dependence of the walking speed in the case of pedestrian navigation. For different users robustness may have a different meaning, such as the ability of the solution to respond following a server shadowing event. Here, robustness is defined as the ability of the solution to mitigate interference.

Other requirements and performance parameters are power consumption, resiliency, connectivity, interoperability and traceability [1]. Especially in the case of mobile devices power consumption is still very critical to provide a long-term solution possibility. Resiliency is the ability to prepare for and adapt to changing conditions, such as it is the case for Wi-Fi RSS signal variations and fluctuations. To encounter for their influence a new differential scheme is developed which is briefly discussed in the following section 3.

3 Differential Wi-Fi (DWi-Fi) Scheme

In all common RSS-based Wi-Fi positioning approaches scanned absolute RSS values are used either directly in fingerprinting or for the RSS to range conversion using path loss models for trilateration. In a differential approach referred to as Differential Wi-Fi (DWi-Fi) trilateration – by analogy to the commonly employed Differential GNSS – continuous RSS measurements performed at reference stations (RSs) distributed in the area of interest are used to derive real-time corrections for the mobile users. Instead of theoretical path loss models this approach utilizes continuous RSS scans carried out during user localization to improve the positioning accuracies, its solution integrity and reliability [13, 17]. For a low-cost realization Raspberry Pi units serve as reference stations (RSs) and Access Points (APs) at the same time scanning and emitting Wi-Fi signals. Using these devices the RSS scans are recorded together with their MAC addresses of the Wi-Fi APs continuously. Furthermore, relative RSS values instead of absolute numbers either between consecutive epochs or different APs are used in addition. If different APs can be received at a certain location the RSS values can be ordered in dependence of their RSS of the AP. At a second location in the area of interest the order is usually different. Then the difference in order sequence of the AP RSS values between the different locations can be used to match the current RSS measurements to the correct location. Consider, for example, a descending order of RSS where AP1 has higher values than the other APs. On a different location this order might be reverse. If the difference is

 https://doi.org/10.1051/e3sconf/20199402001

significant then it is easier to determine where the smartphone is currently located. The difference in order results most likely from physical differences in building structures as in one room the situation is completely different than in another room. Furthermore, different consecutive epochs of RSS measurements can be considered in assignment of the correct location. Due to the significant temporal variation of RSS it is then easier to match the users' location to the correct one. If one considers long-time measurements of RSS at reference stations then in real-time the change of RSS of all visible APs can be determined. This approach results into a fusion of different localization techniques as RSS observations are performed continuously on the aforementioned RSs and used to derive dynamically changing maps of RSS distributions, the so-called radio maps, in real-time. Thus, the principle is the fusion of the location fingerprinting and trilateration techniques combining the advantages of both methods [12]. The main advantage is that no lengthy training phase requiring high workloads and frequent re-calibration as in standard fingerprinting is required [16].

4 Ultra-wide Band (UWB)

In addition to low-cost Wi-Fi technology, in this study an UWB (Ultra-wide Band) system was employed. Due to high-bandwidth communication characteristics and the high standard clock synchronization between transmitter and receiver, UWB radio technology offers strong multipath resistance capabilities and to a certain extend penetrability for building materials leading to high accuracy range measurements compared to other radio-based technologies [11]. Commercially available UWBs rely on two way TOF (time-of-flight) to realize the distance between the UWBs. This study employed the Time Domain's PulsON® OEM [2] modules that uses the coherent transmission of sequences of short duration, low duty cycle radio frequency pulses to provide high quality ranging measurements. Fig. 1 shows the Time Domain's PulsON® OEM transmitter set-up on a tripod.

5 Test Site Characteristics, Sensor Deployment and Smartphone Specifications

Fig. 2 shows impressions from the test site in a part of Queen Victoria Market (QVM) in Melbourne, Australia, indicating the sensor deployment and reference points RPs along the chosen circular trajectory. Seven smartphone users were walking along this closed-loop trajectory around the shops comprising of four corridors with 16 RPs distributed in a test grid of 4 m. Seven Raspberry Pi units were deployed to serve both as APs or RSs at the same time and six static UWBs. They were surveyed by a total station for ground truth. Both kinematic and stop-and-go measurements were carried out [15]. In the first case, a continuous recording of the RSS scans was performed and in the second case up to ten RSS scans on each of the 16 RPs were carried out. The users started at different RPs while walking behind each other along the trajectory. Moreover, the inertial sensor observations from the smartphones were recorded as well. Table 1 shows the employed smartphones specifications and their start reference points along the trajectory shown in Fig. 2.

The role of UWB system (see Fig. 1) was, firstly, to provide a high quality trajectory to serve as a ground truth for the DWi-Fi solution, and secondly to provide further location information (e.g. in the form of control points along a trajectory) for improving the DWi-Fi positioning solution. In this paper, the UWB measurements are used only to produce the range measurements between the moving user and stationary UWB nodes, as a means of quality assurance of the mobile user trajectory. A further step is a comparison with the Wi-Fi derived ranges. This is facilitated as the UWB anchors fixed on the walls were collocated with the Raspberry Pi units for Wi-Fi positioning.

Table 1. Smartphone user configuration and start reference points.

User ID	Smartphone	Start reference point
1	Sony Xperia Z1	1
2	Samsung Galaxy S3	3
3	Samsung Galaxy S3	5
4	Motorola G3 – MotoG3	9
5	Huawei Mate 7	11
6	Huawei Honor 8	13
7	Samsung Galaxy GT-S7262	15

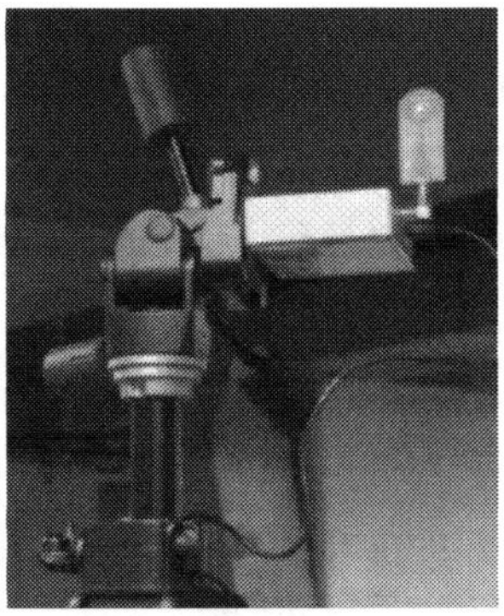

Fig. 1. Time Domain's PulsON® OEM.

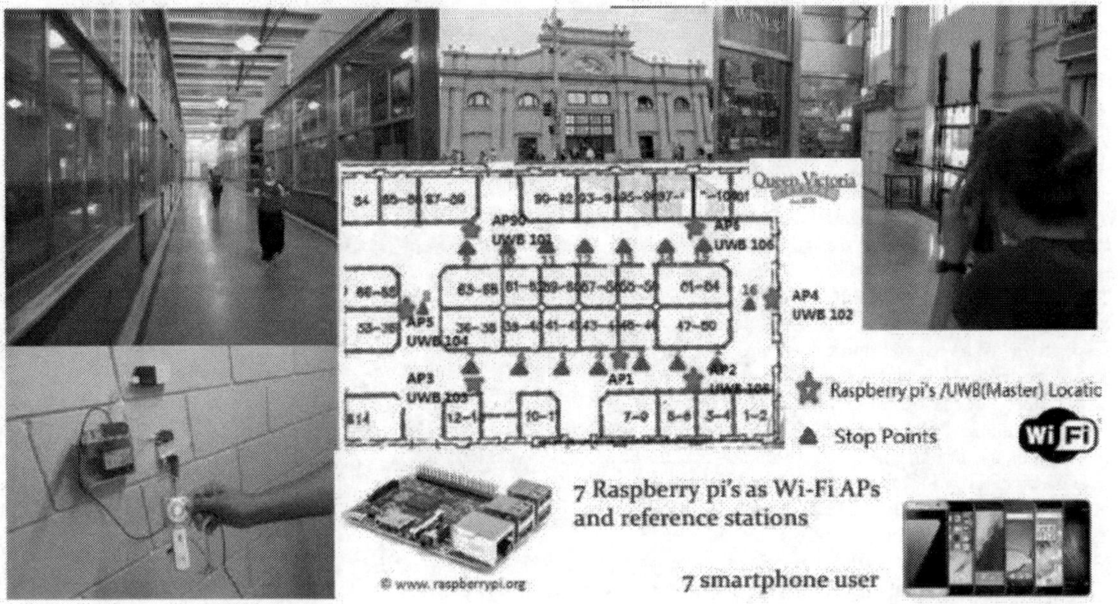

Fig. 2. Impressions from the test site in QVM showing Raspberry Pi and UWB sensor deployment and 16 reference stop points.

6 Analyses and Main Results

In outdoor environments, the positioning solution is derived as usually primarily from GNSS and relative range observations among pedestrians. In indoor and transition environments, the localization solution is estimated using relative range observations among pedestrians and Wi-Fi RSS measurements. In this section, selected results of the measurement campaign in QVM are presented.

6.1 Wi-Fi Positioning Results

Wi-Fi is nowadays kind of ubiquitous in our environments. This pervasiveness of Wi-Fi signals allows to use parameters like RSS to estimate the distance between mobile devices from which Wi-Fi signals are exchanged. In the conducted work, Raspberry Pi units (RPis) served as Wi-Fi Access Points. Using path loss models the relationship between the measured RSS and the range is derived [17] and knowing the coordinates of the respective Access Points then the position of a user can be estimated.

In the first stage of the analyses, the following properties of the RSS measurements at the Raspberry Pi units were investigated [7]:

- Mean, variance and standard deviation of the signal quality,
- Mean, variance and standard deviation of the RSS measurements, and
- The ascending ranking order of those two parameters, more particularly for RSS measurements.

The aim of checking their mean and standard deviation is to determine for each Raspberry Pi unit serving as Access Point (AP) which is the best one with the best quality and/or highest RSS. Moreover, it is interesting to know their ascending ranking order in terms of power (like in dBm or Watt for the RSS) for each time of the experiment. This gives an idea of the architecture built by the Raspberry Pi units. In a matter of fact, a high RSS means a shorter distance between the RPi units (according to path loss models). Then, a weak RSS means a longer distance between two APs. And if one RSS close to a RPi is weaker than it should be, this may indicate a connection loss, something that for instance AP2 underwent during the experiment. Mean and variance are affected by extreme values. That's why also the percentage of time of each RSS ranking order was investigated. In other words, the percentage of time where a RSS from one AP_i is higher than a RSS from a second AP_j was investigated.

From all the measured RSS data unfortunately not all Access Points recorded at once. So among those seven units, only four could be used to perform lateration, which are AP2, AP4, AP5 and AP6. For 2D lateration four APs provide at least some redundancy.

Fig. 3 shows a visualization of the RSS value distributions. The two horizontal axes in the diagrams show either the AP number or the reference points RPs with their Point ID. The absolute measured RSS values from up to 10 scans at each RP are shown on the vertical axis [16]. As it can be seen from the plots, the absolute RSS values of the seven APs vary significantly in dependence on the respective location of the user. Such a situation is favourable for positioning if the absolute RSS values are used since the match to the current location can be achieved more easily. Furthermore, a quite similar distribution for the different APs can be seen when comparing the different smartphones. The absolute RSS values, however, can differ in dependence of the smartphone.

In the following, the ascending ranking order of the Raspberry units was investigated. As can be seen from the RSS value sequences in the top Fig. 4 for AP2 in respective to the other three APs a clear order is visible. Thereby, the RSS relationship between AP2 and AP4 is depicted in blue, with AP5 in red and with AP6 in green, respectively. The ascending ranking order is very stable. The RSS order AP5 < AP6 < AP4 occurs more than 98% of the time. The reason for this is that AP5 is further away from AP2 than AP6. And that's the case as can be seen in the map of the test site in QVM shown in Fig. 2. This is also the case for AP4. In fact, if a stable RSS ranking order occurs, the position of the electronic devices can be estimated with a good precision.

A further result was that a connection loss between the Raspberry Pi units happened less than 1% of the whole time, meaning that the APs performance was excellent, almost perfect.

The result of this investigation for AP6 is shown in the lower Fig. 4. The RSS relationship between AP6 and AP2 is depicted in black, with AP4 in yellow and with AP6 in red. Here, the RSS ranking order is completely different as before as APs which are further away from AP6 do not result always in lower RSS values. Furthermore, the noise of the RSS numbers is higher.

Thus, the consistency of the ranking order was further investigated more in detail. It is defined as follows: equality between the RSS AP_i => AP_j and RSS AP_j => AP_i. Equal consistency means in other words that if a signal coming from AP_i to AP_j is the same in reverse from AP_j to AP_i. It was also verified if the RSSs were distributed according to a Gaussian law to check some properties on them like computing trust intervals. Fig. 5 shows as an example the consistency of the RSS values sequence between AP2 and AP4. Consistency could never been verified in the whole data set. There is always a significant difference between the RSS AP_i => AP_j and RSS AP_j => AP_i. In the case shown in Fig. 5 for the consistency between AP2 and AP4 a relatively constant difference of around 11 dBm occurred which can be seen as a significant bias. This bias was stable over the whole common time interval. In general, this bias occured in all AP combinations with a value of around 10 dBm on average.

To see if on the RPi data can be relied on the RSS correlation was investigated. It was tested if the signals are independent between each others or if there is a form of correlation. From the correlation matrix it was found that the correlation factors were very weak of all possible RPi couples. Thus, the hypothesis validated the independency of the signals coming from the Access Points. Table 2 is an example of the correlation matrix with AP5 as a receiver (so correlation tested here will be between AP2-AP4, AP2-AP6 and AP4-AP6).

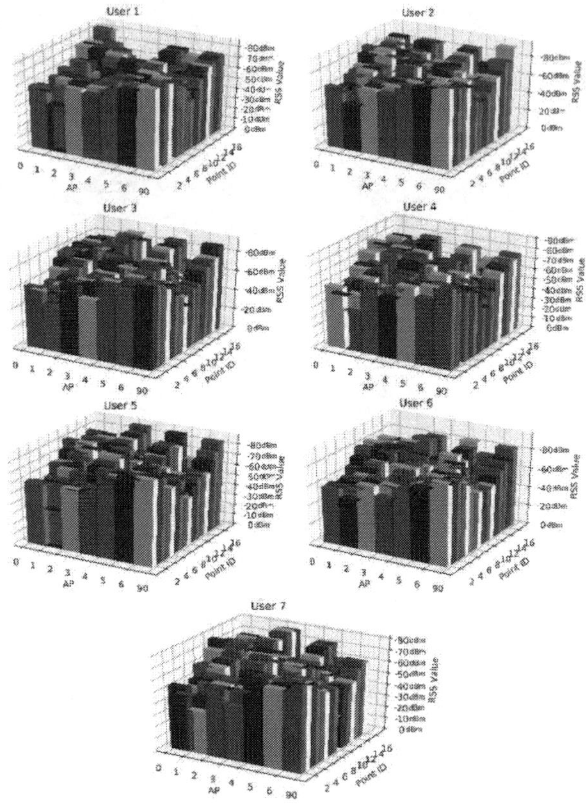

Fig. 3. Comparison of the absolute RSS values on the 16 RPs collected by seven different smartphone users (Source: [16]).

Table 2. RSS correlation matrix with AP5 recorded data, showing correlation between different signals coming to AP5

	AP2	AP4	AP6
AP2	1	-0.0267	-0.708
AP4	-0.0267	1	-0.0103
AP6	-0.0708	-0.0103	1

6.2 UWB Positioning Results

Pedestrians rely on relative UWB ranges (including ranges between pedestrians, and ranges between pedestrian and UWB anchors) and Wi-Fi measurements, for localizing all users cooperatively. Fig. 6 shows a plot of range measurements as observed by two pedestrians with respect to the UWBs as a function of time. Thereby pedestrian user 1 started at point 9 and the second user at point 1. The measurements were performed in stop-and-go manner. The two highlighted time interval windows in Fig. 6 can be seen more clearly in detail in Fig. 7 (zoomed view 1 and 2). The region where the UWB ranges are constant are the regions where the pedestrians were standing for a certain period of time. It is seen that a maximum range of 20 m was achievable in the QVM indoor environment. Significant communication drops between the pedestrians and RPi as seen in Fig. 6. For example, no communication of the pedestrian with the

 https://doi.org/10.1051/e3sconf/20199402001

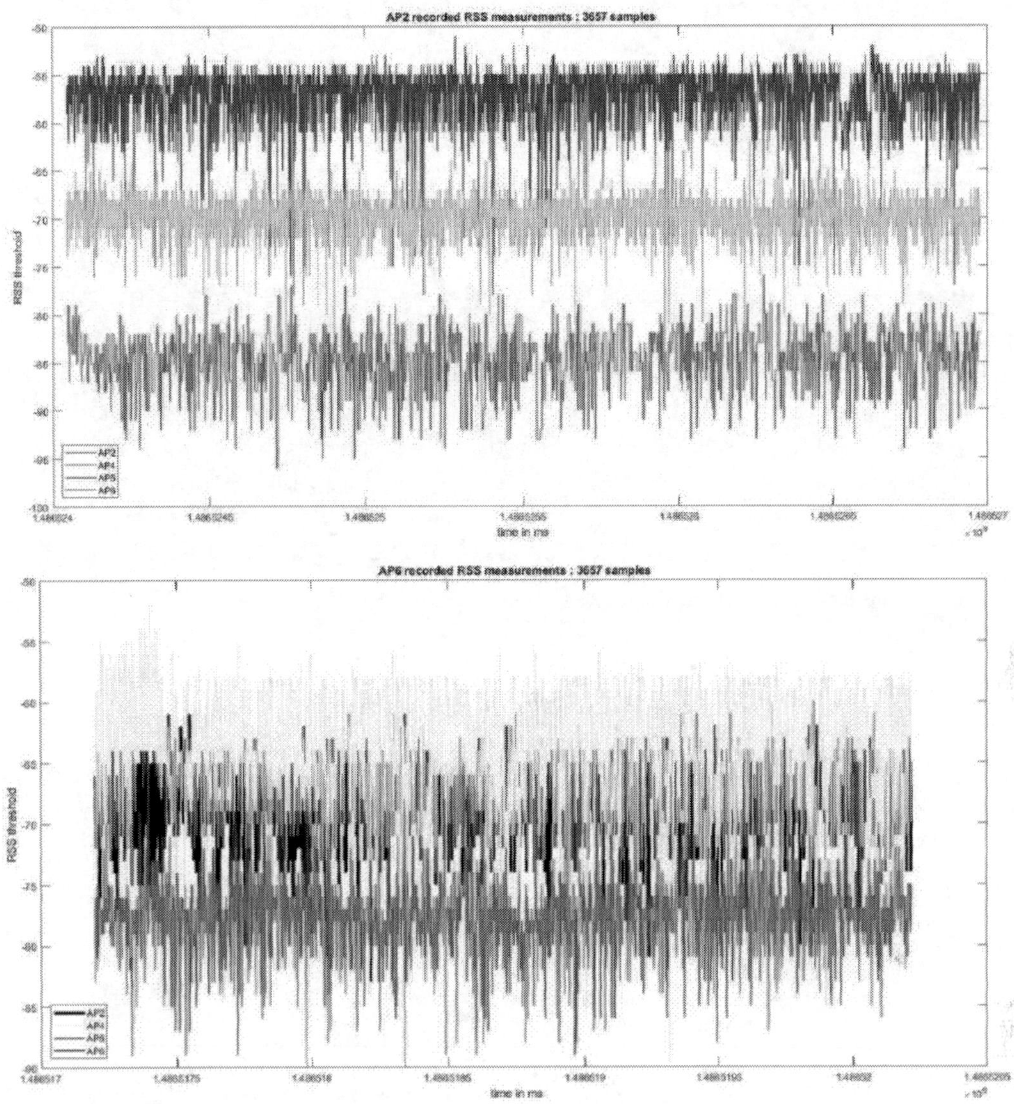

Fig. 4. RSS values sequence of AP2 (top) and AP6 (bottom) seen from the other APs.

RPi is observed between time instants 2.6×10^4 s to 2.7×10^4 s and from time instant 2.8×10^4 s to 3.1×10^4 s. This is most likely due to the complex nature of the indoor environment and non-availability of direct Line of Sight (LOS) between the pedestrian and RPi. It is obvious that non-availability of communication signals to the pedestrians will affect their indoor localization performance. One of the ways to improve communication capabilities in indoor environments is to deploy more number of reference RPi UWBs. Several interesting observations regarding the behaviour of UWBs in indoor environments can be made from Figures 6 and 7. It is observed that the points occupied by the pedestrians can be easily identified in the plots shown in Fig. 7. This is represented by the regions where the UWB range measurements are relatively constant (since the data is collected in a stop-and-go manner). Even when the pedestrian is stationary at a given location, significant sudden changes in the range observations can be observed. For example, at time instants 2.62×10^4 s and 2.8×10^4 s, sudden jumps in the range observations are visible. This is most likely because of multipath in indoor environment in the UWB observations [5]. Similar corruption by the outliers in the ranges derived from UWBs in complex environments has been previously reported by authors in [4, 5]. Such outliers should be accounted for, within the cooperative state estimation framework. One such framework for incorporating corrupted UWB range measurements in a cooperative estimation framework is presented by authors in [5]. Further, it is interesting to observe that the nature of the UWB signals observed by both the pedestrians are very similar. For example, the UWB signals as observed by pedestrian 1 in two different corridors is seen (in Fig. 7)

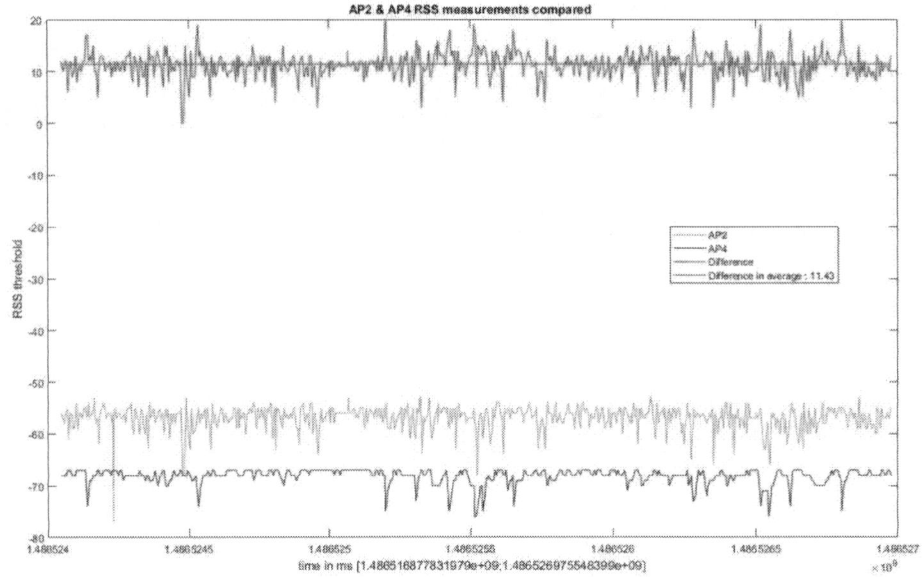

Fig. 5. Consistency of the RSS values sequence between AP2 and AP4.

between time instants 2.56 x 10^4 s to 2.58 x 10^4 s and 2.74 x 10^4 s to 2.76 x 10^4 s. Similarly, the UWB signals observed by pedestrian 2 in the same two corridors are shown between time instant 2.6 x 10^4 s to 2.63 x 10^4 s and 2.78 x 10^4 s to 2.81 x 10^4 s in Fig. 7. A careful analysis of the UWB observations between these instants reveals that the pattern of the UWB range variation as observed by two pedestrians is very similar. This is to be expected since the nature of UWB range variation is dependent on the pedestrian movement (given the location of the RPi) and one pedestrian is right behind the second pedestrian, and thus, following the same trajectory.

The position estimates of both the pedestrians can be known if at least three range observations from reference RPi UWBs are available to each pedestrian [6]. However, given the limited number of available UWB sensors, achieving at least three range observations in indoor environments for extended periods is found to be rather challenging. In the experiments described in this paper, it is found that three or more range observations are observed rarely by the pedestrians, while 1-2 UWB observations were available most of the time during the experiment. This is due to the complex indoor environment and the insufficient number of UWBs deployed during the experiment. It is because of these reasons that pedestrian locations could not be derived from UWB observations only. Some of the key observations of these experiments is that a large number of UWBs need to be deployed depending on the complexity of the indoor environment to ensure availability of at least three range observations, and that ranges derived from UWBs are corrupted by outliers, which should be accounted for, within the cooperative state estimation framework.

7 Wi-Fi Radio Map Interpolation and DWi-Fi

In analyses of the Wi-Fi measurements the next step is the creation of maps of RSS distribution for the whole test site. These maps are reffered to as radio maps. In our study, the concept of radio map estimation is based on DWi-Fi, so using two data files, one for RSS AP_i => AP_j and one for RSS AP_j => AP_i to determine one distance. The method of Voronoï Tessellation, based on geometrical theory, allows to conduct the estimation of all APs. For that purpose an interpolation method has to be applied to estimate the RSS for each point on the map. For this interpolation several methods exist, but it is necessary to achieve a good balance between the accuracy of the algorithm and its speed or efficiency. Thus, mainly two options shall be applied, i.e.:

- Linear interpolation: it is quite simple, but not so accurate. In fact, as the electromagnetic signals undergo an exponential decrease in distance the term of power evolves according to a logarithmic function. So opting for a linear interpolation is not always suitable.
- Delaunay algorithm based on Voronoï cells. Note that Delaunay and Voronoï concepts are linked because the the Delaunay triangulation is the dual problem of Voronoi diagram.

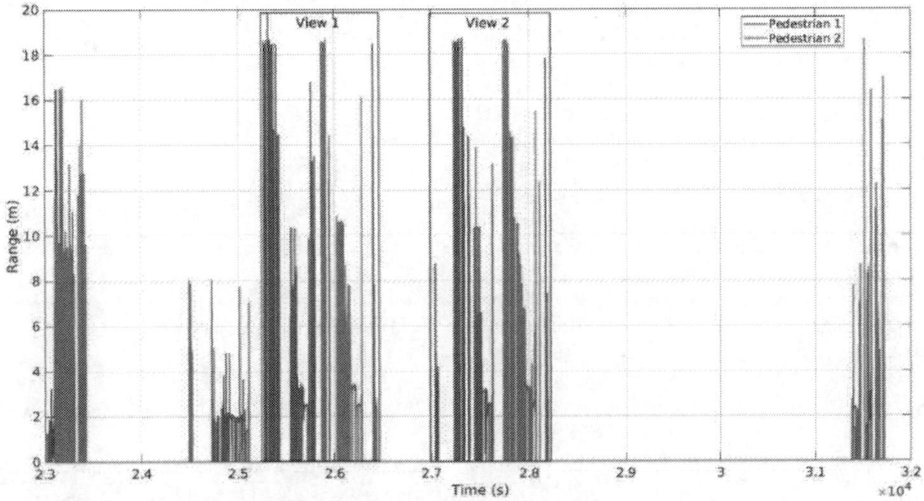

Fig. 6. Plot of range observations from the UWBs for two pedestrian users over time.

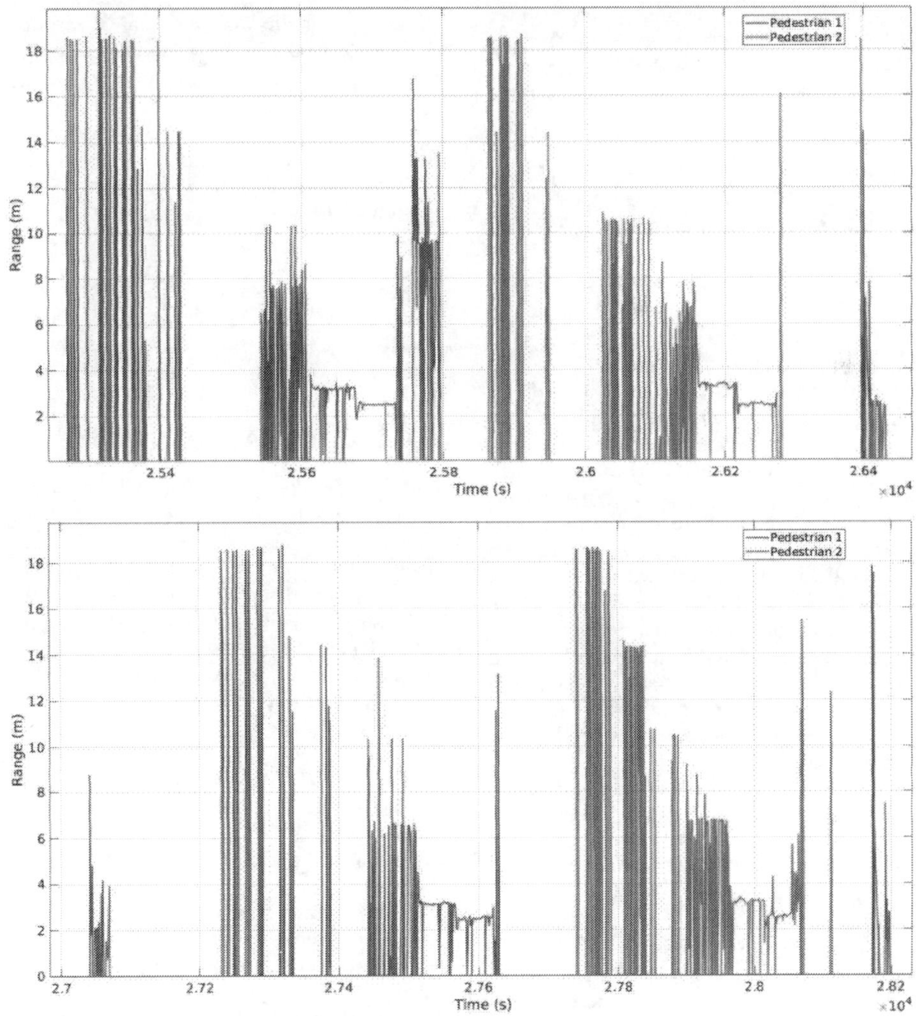

Fig. 7. Zoomed views 1 and 2 of the UWB range observations for the two pedestrians.

The principle of the second interpolation approach is that a Voronoï diagram consists of so-called from Voronoï cells which are are defined by segments drawn between two points. Starting from a cloud of points, only some points are going to be linked between each others [3, 10]. More precisely, the Voronoï/Delaunay method uses the nearest neighbour interpolation [9] giving a smooth approximation of the interpolated function. More accurate than linear interpolation, the building of the Voronoï tessellation brings advantage in the following two steps: Firstly, to quickly estimate the localization of all the Access Points, and secondly, to estimate signal fading parameters. To sum up it can be said that the Voronoï/Delaunay algorithm provides the possibility to interpolate the RSS function. In other words, it is going to perform a smooth interpolation of the function $f(x,y)$ = RSS where (x,y) represents the position coordinates of a point P located in the map (in 2D) and RSS the value of the RSS in dBm for this point. But above all, a function is needed to interpolate, or better said a base which could be used to estimate the RSS everywhere on the radio map. This can be done with the Raspberry Pi units as their true coordinates are known in the map. In addition, the RSS values they exchanged between them during the experiment are also available. So, based on those Access Points the function can be built for the interpolation.

As aforementioned, the true distance between each Raspberry Pi is known. So thanks to the relationship between the RSS values given in equation (1) the distance that signals exchanged can be covered to be received.

$$P_{received} = P_{transmitted} + 20log(\lambda/(4\pi d)) \quad (1)$$

where d is the distance covered by the signal and λ is the wavelength in this logarithmic path loss model.

But when we compare this distance d to the true distances, a difference is observed. That's totally normal, and this is wanted because even in perfect conditions, signals, when travelling in the indoor environment, will undergo some issues like noise or spontaneous fluctuations. Knowing their difference for each time epoch, a correction for each Access Point can be computed. Taking the example illustrated in Fig. 8 with four Access Points AP2, AP4, AP5 and AP6 which communicate between each other and receive Wi-Fi signals from the other Raspberry Pi units and knowing their true distances, then from the theoretical RSS (RSS_t) values which they should have obtained a RSS correction value dR can be computed in comparison with the measured RSS m easured (RSS_m).

As shows Fig. 8, the smartphone to be positioned is receiving signals from the Access Points and records their RSS values (i.e. the RSS_m). But due to noise and other influences, RSS_m will be different from the theoretical RSS (RSS_t) that the smartphone should have received. Then if the distance with this RSS is directly computed, a wrong distance will obtained. But as for the Raspberry Pi units, the RSS values can be corrected as performing an interpolation. A simple way is given in equation (2):

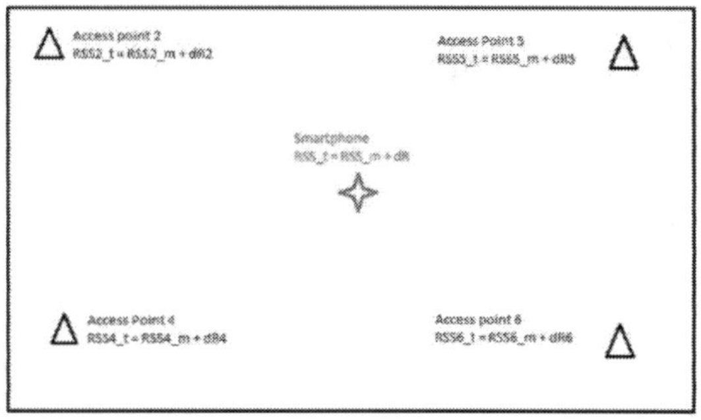

Fig. 8. DWi-Fi principle of operation.

$$dR = w_2 \times dR_2 + w_4 \times dR_4 + w_5 \times dR_5 + w_6 \times dR_6 \quad (2)$$

where w are the weights affected at the correction from a certain Access Point (i.e., AP2, AP4, AP5 and AP6).

Then different ways could be taken into account to calculate such a correction:

- Equiprobability: all weights are the same,
- Path loss impact: adapt the weight taking into account the distance covered by the signal (an Access point nearer than the others will contribute more for the correction),
- Reliability: if an Access Point has a high variance, its impact in the final smartphone correction is diminished.

To start with, the equiprobability to compute the corrections between the Raspberry Pi's and for the smartphone was opted. For further information the detailed stepwise procedure to derive the correction parameters can be found [16].

8 Conclusions and Outlook

In this paper, key parameters and requirements as given for GNSS in the market report published in 2017 [1] are identified for indoor positioning using Wi-Fi and UWB. Field tests in an indoor market scenario were carried out and are reported here. The experimental area was covered with Raspberry Pi units serving as Wi-Fi Access Points and reference stations at the same time broadcasting and scanning the Wi-Fi signals of all available Raspberry Pi's and Wi-Fi routers. At the same location UWB transmitters, the anchors, were installed. Seven smartphones were employed to test the positioning solution.

In the analyses, the main parameters were the ID of the incoming Wi-Fi signal, its RSS and quality values, and the time where it was recorded. The signals exchanged between the Raspberry Pi units undergo several issues like not being with the same level of power according to the direction where they go. In addition, noise can interfere RSS measurements. However, corrections are derived from the known bias and the current RSS measurements thanks to Differential Wi-Fi. Work still to be done, is the interpolation of the RSS function $f(x,y)$ to determine the

RSS value for each point in the radio map. This task could be done with Voronoï/Delaunay algorithms. It could be identified that especially in environments which are not suitably covered with Wi-Fi APs the use of Raspberry Pi units is economic.

A further task of future work is the integration of the UWB ranges into the overall positioning solution to increase the key parameters such as reliability and integrity.

With the solution proposed in this paper a step forward to GNSS-like positioning performance in indoor and combined transitional out-/indoor environments is achieved. Then for safety and liability critical applications, such as indoor navigation for the vision impaired and other mobility restricted individuals, emergency responders and asset tracking in buildings, a better performance is enabled.

The tests in QVM built the basis for an extensive measurement campaign conducted at the Ohio State University in October 2017 as part of the joint FIG Working Group 5.5 and IAG Sub-commission 4.1 on multi-sensor systems. A description of the experimental set-ups and characteristics of this campaign can be found in [8].

References

1. 2017 GNSS Market Report, https://www.gsa.europa.eu/2017-gnss-market-report (accessed October 2018).
2. B. Dewberry, A. Petroff, Precison Navigation with AD-HOC Autosurvey using UltraWideBand Two-Way Ranging Network, 12th IEEE Workshop on Positioning, Navigation and Communication WPNC'15, Dresden, Germany, March 11-12, 6 pgs. (2015).
3. S. Fortune, Voronoi Diagrams and Delaunay Triangulations, in: Handbook of Discrete and Computational Geometry, DOI:10.1201/ 9781420035315.ch23 (2004).
4. S. Goel, A Distributed Cooperative UAV Swarm Localization System: Development and Analysis, Proceedings of the 30th International Technical Meeting of the Satellite Division of the Institute of Navigation (ION GNSS+ 2017), Portland, Oregon, September 25-29, 2501-2518 (2017).
5. S. Goel, A. Kealy, B. Lohani, Development and Experimental Evaluation of a Low-Cost Cooperative UAV Localization Network Prototype, Journal of Sensor and Actuator Networks, 7(4), DOI: 10.3390/jsan7040042 (2018).
6. S. Goel, A. Kealy, G. Retscher, B. Lohani, Cooperative P2I Localization using UWB and Wi-Fi, Proceedings of the International Global Navigation Satellite Systems Association (IGNSS) Conference 2016, December 6-8, Sydney, Australia (2016).
7. T. Gonzales, Indoor Positioning Based on Differential Wi-Fi Measurements as well as GNSS Integrity, Internship Report, RMIt University and The University of Melbourne, 21 pgs. (2018).
8. A. Kealy, G. Retscher, J. Gabela, Y. Li, S. Goel, C. K. Toth, A. Masiero, W. Błaszczak-Bąk, V. Gikas, H. Perakis, Z. Koppanyi, D. A. Grejner-Brzezinska, A Benchmarking Measurement Campaign in GNSS-denied/challenged Indoor/Outdoor and Transitional Environments, Proceedings of the FIG Working Week, April 22-26, Hanoi, Vietnam, 15 pgs. (2019) (submitted and under review).
9. H. Ledoux, C. Gold, An Efficient Natural Neighbour Interpolation Algorithm for Geoscientific Modelling, https://pdfs.semanticscholar.org/52ca/255573eded0e4371fe2ced980b196636718d.pdf (accessed October 2018).
10. M. Lee, D. Han, Voronoi Tessellation Based Interpolation Method for Wi-Fi Radio Map Construction, IEEE Communications Letter, 16:3, 404-407 (2012).
11. R. Mautz, Indoor Positioning Technologies, Swiss Geodetic Commission, Geodetic-Geophysical Reports of Switzerland, 86, 134 pgs. (2012).
12. G. Retscher, Fusion of Location Fingerprinting and Trilateration Based on the Example of Wi-Fi Positioning. ISPRS Annals of the Photogrammetry, Remote Sensing and Spatial Information Sciences, Volume IV-2/W4, 2017, ISPRS Geospatial Week 2017, 18-22 September Wuhan, PR China, DOI 10.5194/isprs-annals-IV-2-W4-377-2017, pp. 377-384 (2017).
13. G. Retscher, H. Hofer, A. Kealy, V. Gikas, F. Obex, Cooperative Localization in Indoor Environments Using Constrained Differential Wi-Fi and UWB Measurements, Proceedings of the ION GNSS+ Conference, Institute of Navigation: Portland, Oregon, USA (2017).
14. G. Retscher, A. Leb, Influence of the RSSI Scan Duration of Smartphones in Kinematic Wi-Fi Fingerprinting, Proceedings of the FIG Working Week, April 22-26, Hanoi, Vietnam, 15 pgs. (2019) (submitted and under review).
15. G. Retscher, Y. Li, S. Williams, A. Kealy, B. Moran, S. Goel, J. Gabela, Wi-Fi Positioning Using a Network Differential Approach for Real-time Calibration, Proceedings of the IGNSS 2018 Conference, February 7-9, 2018, Sydney, Australia, 15 pgs (2018).
16. G. Retscher, Y. Li, A. Kealy, H. Hofer, J. Gabela, S. Goel, O. Qureshi, E. Smith, L. Bao, Real-time Wi-Fi RSS Variation Correction Using a Network Differential Positioning Approach, Proceedings of the 9th International Conference Indoor Positioning and Indoor Navigation IPIN, September 24-27, Nantes, France, 4 pgs. (2018).
17. G. Retscher, T. Tatschl, Indoor Positioning with Differential Wi-Fi Lateration, Journal of Applied Geodesy, ISSN 1862-9016, DOI 10.1515/jag-2017-0011, 11:4, 249-269 (2017).

E3S Web of Conferences **94**, 02002 (2019) https://doi.org/10.1051/e3sconf/20199402002
ISGNSS 2018

Trilateration Approaches for Indoor Wi-Fi Positioning

Guenther Retscher[1,*], *Jonathan* Kleine[1], and *Lisa* Whitemore[1]

[1]Department of Geodesy and Geoinformation, TU Wien, Gusshausstrasse 27-29, 1040 Vienna, Austria

Abstract. In smartphones several sensors and receivers are embedded which enable positioning in Location-based Services and other navigation applications. They include GNSS receivers and Wireless Fidelity (Wi-Fi) cards as well as inertial sensors, such as accelerometers, gyroscope and magnetometer. In this paper, indoor Wi-Fi positioning is studied based on trilateration. Three methods are investigated which are a resection, a calculation of the center of gravity point and a differential approach. The first approach is a commonly employed resection using the ranges to the Wi-Fi Access Points (APs) as radii and intersect the circles around the APs. In the second method, the center of gravity in a triangle of APs is calculated with weighting of the received signal strength (RSS) of the Wi-Fi signals. The third approach is developed by analogy to Differential GNSS (DGNSS) and therefore termed Differential Wi-Fi (DWi-Fi). Its advantage is that a real-time modeling of the temporal RSS variations and fluctuations is possible. For that purpose, reference stations realized by low-cost Raspberry Pi units are deployed which serve at the same time as APs. The experiments conducted in a laboratory and entrance of an office building showed that position deviations from the ground truth of around 2 m are achievable with the second and third method. Thereby the positioning accuracies depend mainly on the geometrical point location in the triangle of APs and reference stations and the RSS scan duration.

1 Introduction

The motivation of this study is that for indoor positioning there is still no generally valid solution. In many public buildings, infrastructures, such as Bluetooth, Wi-Fi, etc., are already available for indoor positioning [1, 2, 4, 9]. Different approaches for position determination can be distinguished, which are cell-based methods (Cell-of-Origin CoO), Time of Arrival (ToA) or Angle of Arrival (AoA) measurements, hyperbolic trilateration (Time Difference of Arrival TDoA), scene analysis with measured signal strengths (Received Signal Strength RSS) and digital images as well as fingerprinting (see e.g. [3, 4, 5, 9]]. With smartphones, however, the selection of sensors and receivers and their quality differ depending on the device, which means that the position solution can also be influenced differently. In this study, the method of trilateration with Wi-Fi signals is used. In this case, the measured RSS are usually used for positioning and they have to be converted from [dBm] into a range in [m] to the respective AP. Approaches for conversion are discussed in section 4. Firstly, the principle of operation of a differential Wi-Fi positioning approach is presented introduced in [8] which is termed Differential Wi-Fi (DWi-Fi) by analogy to Differential GNSS (DGNSS). A low-cost realization is the use of Raspberry Pi (RP or RPi) units which broadcast Wi-Fi signals and are therefore APs and scan RSS of the other units as reference stations at the same time.

2 Differential Wi-Fi Positioning

An influence that can have a significant effect on positioning and should therefore be taken into account is caused by fluctuations in the Wi-Fi network. As an example, Fig. 1 shows the Wi-Fi RSS recorded at the Raspberry Pi unit RP 31 of five other RPs indicating that they can be quite noisy. Especially at the beginning of the recording, large fluctuations can be observed. This can be attributed to the fact that the RPs did not start broadcasting Wi-Fi signals at the same time as they were sequentially started. Thus, these fluctuations can be omitted for the evaluation. It is also clearly visible that RP 31, 32, 33 and 34 were installed in the same room, as they recorded with higher stability to each other than RP 35 and 36 over the entire period of measurement.

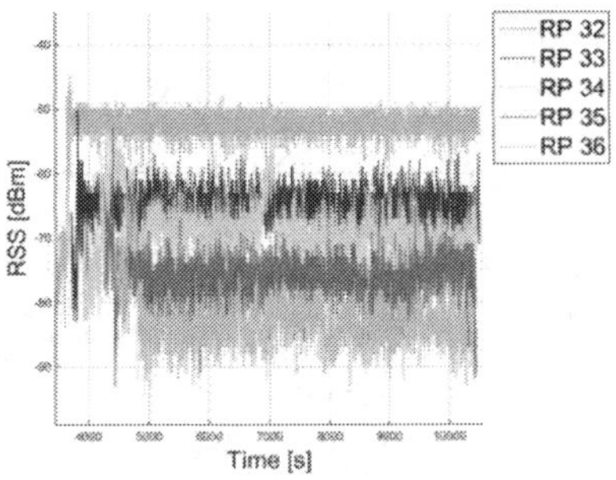

Fig. 1. Wi-Fi RSS in [dBm] recorded at Raspberry Pi unit RP 31 of the other five RPs.

* Corresponding author: guenther.retscher@tuwien.ac.at

 https://doi.org/10.1051/e3sconf/20199402002

DWi-Fi shall encounter for the following influences in the course of position determination: (1) spatial and temporal signal variations and fluctuations, (2) influences from outside, e.g. due to shielding by persons, by objects of hidden RPs, etc. and (3) no continuous transmission, e.g. due to fault hardware, interrupted power supply, etc. Therefore time-dependent correction parameters are estimated using known reference stations as it is done in DGNSS [8]. In a networked solution the correction parameters can be derived similar as in a CORS (Continuous Operating Reference Station) GNSS network. Then area correction parameters referred to as with the German term Flächenkorrekturparameter (FKP) are estimated and applied by the user [6].

3 Trilateration Approaches

Ranges must be derived from the RSS measurements of the RPs for user localization with trilateration. A triangle of RPs is formed, in which the searched position of the smartphone user is located. Then a resection can be solved by intersecting circles, where there radii are the ranges to the RPs. For cases where this resection does not lead to an unique position fix (see Fig. 2) using least squares adjustment an extended approach has been developed. A minimum and maximum range to the RPs are defined in this case, which describe thus a value range for the circle radii. For the derivation of the radii, an approximated polynomial function for the relationship between RSS and range to the RP from the empirical calibration (see Fig. 3) is used and shifted twice along the vertical axis. Two minimum and maximum radii are therefore available for each AP for determining the point of intersection of the circle. The position of the smartphone user should lie in the overlap area of all three circular rings, each formed by the minimum and maximum radii. Ideally, the resection results then in six intersecting points as depicted in Fig. 2 on the top. In the following, the center of gravity of the overlap area from these six points is calculated in order to obtain the desired location of the user. Furthermore, the RSS can be subsequently weighted where the three highest RSS values of all recorded RPs are used, since high RSS values naturally corresponds to a stronger signal. This has to be done in cases where the circles do not intersect (see the second example in Fig. 2 on the bottom).

4 Approaches for RSS to Range Conversion

A particular challenge is to deduce the range in [m] from the measured RSS in [dBm] to an AP. The conversion can be done using a signal propagation model or a device specific empirical calibration. The first strategy, however, can be very complex once there are walls between the transmitter and receiver. The influence of the resulting damping is practically impossible to model [8]. Thus, a site specific empirical calibration was performed for each employed smartphone so that the range can be deduced directly from the measured RSS in the evaluation. Fig. 3 shows the resulting RSS observations averaged over four

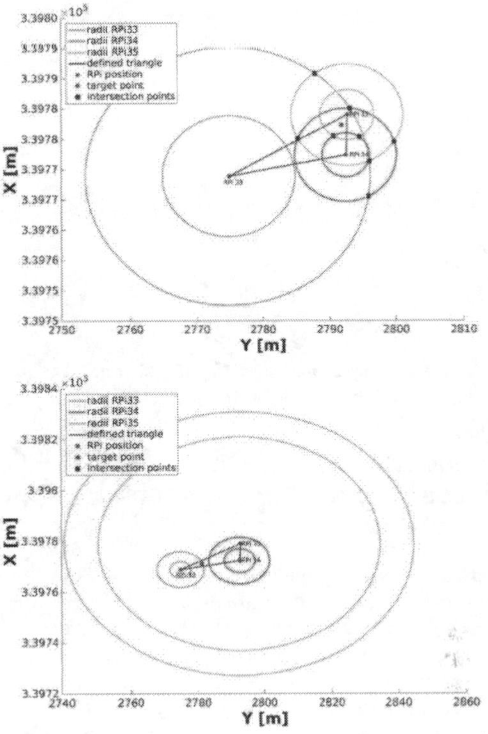

Fig. 2. Resection and determination of the center of gravity.

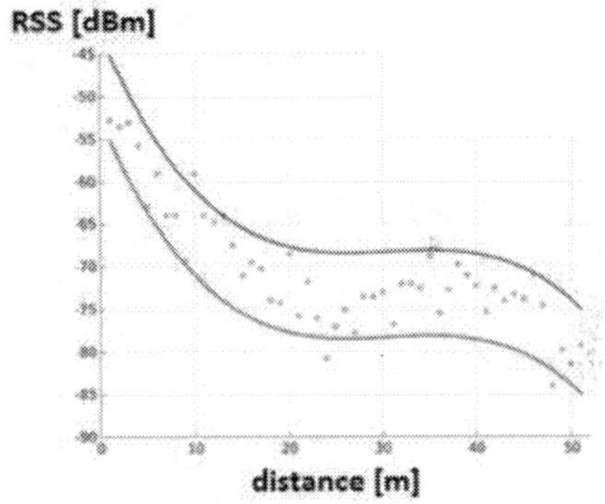

Fig. 3. Mean RSS values from all four orientations and twice shifted approximated polynomial in the laboratory.

smartphone orientations along a 52 m long baseline between two RPs where checkpoints (CPs) where measured at intervals of 1 m. The performance of measurements in four orientations is a common practice to encounter for the shielding of the Wi-Fi signals from the user. A polynomial fitting of third degree was carried out to establish the relationship between RSS and range. The values in the range of up to 15 m are of particular interest for the conversion. The polynomials show that the averaged RSS values range from -40 to -65 dBm. However, from the measurements it could be seen that many measured values occur at -35 dBm or higher. Thus, in order to improve the empirical calibration another relationship between RSS and range was derived as shown in Fig. 4. It is a linear regression independent of the used smartphone.

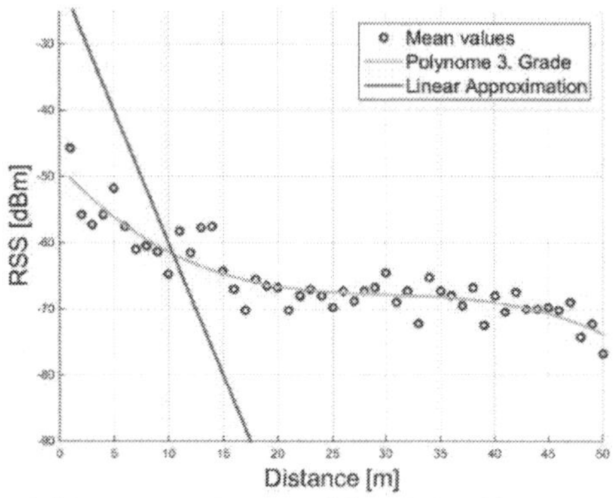

Fig. 4. Linear approximation of the relationship between RSS and range.

5 Specifications of the Used Mobile Devices and Experimental Site Characteristics

Experiments were conducted in an indoor laboratory setting and in a combined out-/indoor environment at the entrance of an office building. Table 1 summarizes the specifications of the used six smartphones and one tablet PC. Fig. 5 shows a map of the laboratory with the location of six RPs and 16 CPs. To serve as ground truth their location were surveyed with a total station from a traverse. Stop-and-go and kinematic measurements were carried out along two trajectories.

In the entrance area of the University office building a combined in-/outdoor trajectory was defined. It runs indoors from a staircase to the laboratory into the outdoor environment in front of the building and further along a road with 5- to 6-storey tall buildings. The total length of the trajectory is 86 m (see Fig. 6). All indoor RPs and CPs were surveyed with a total station using traversing. In this paper, only the indoor position solutions are considered and their results presented.

6 Results of the Stop-and-Go Measurements in the Laboratory

Tables 2 and 3 show the deviations from the ground truth of the estimated positions of the CPs along trajectory 2 for the stop-and-go measurements in the laboratory. The center of gravity was calculated using the three RPs with the highest RSS. For the other three solutions, the center of gravity is calculated using four, five and all six RPs installed in the laboratory. As can be seen from the Table the resulting deviations can differ quite significantly. Smaller deviations for several CPs occurred if they are located closer to an RP. One can also see that the calculation with three RPs seems more stable than with the addition of more of them. If the DWi-Fi positioning approach is used an improvement of the performance and the achievable positioning accuracies is expected as the calculation of the DWi-Fi corrections is carried out epoch by epoch. Thus, the observations are improved in real-time and local fluctuations are taken into account. It can be seen from Table 3 that in many CPs the resulting deviations do not differ if a different number of RPs are used for the calculation of the position solution. The reason for this is that very high RSS values (higher than -35 dBm) were measured in the area of the first CPs to the RPs, which span the triangle used for position determination. By adding more RPs the weight is only slightly changed and therefore there was no difference in the results. The other RPs thus had a minor influence on the position determination. However, compared to the results without using DWi-Fi, no uniform improvement could be observed across the entire trajectories. There are fewer differences at some CPs, but not in general. Applying the DWi-Fi corrections changes the weighting of the RPs, but it can also happen that the geometry for trilateration is changed. For example, the triangle RP 32/33/36 no longer contributes to the calculation of CP 22, but RP 32/33/36 and has therefore led to a smaller deviation. Especially, the start and end points of the trajectories are best determined. This is because the CP and RP are less than 1 m apart.

Table 1. Specifications of the employed smartphones and one tablet PC.

				Sensors			**GNSS**					
ID	**Manu-facturer**	**Model**	**System name**	accelerometers	gyroscope	magnetometer	GPS	A-GPS	Glonass	Galileo	Beidou	QZSS
1	ASUS	Zenfone 2	ASUS_Z00AD	✓	✓	✓	✓	✓	✓			✓
2	Huawei	P9 Lite	HUAWEI VNS-L21	✓		✓	✓	✓	✓			
3	BQ	Aquaris A4.5	AQUARIS_A4.5	✓	✓	✓	✓					
4	Samsung	Tab A	SMT T580	✓			✓		✓			
7	Sony	Xperia Z3	D6603				✓	✓				
8	Samsung	Galaxy S3	GT-I9300	✓	✓	✓	✓		✓			
13	Samsung	Galaxy A3	SM A310F	✓		✓	✓		✓		✓	

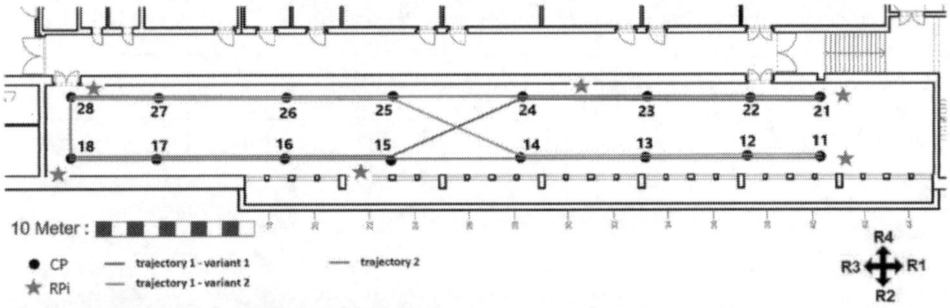

Fig. 5. Map of the laboratory showing the location of the six RPs (RPi's) and 16 CPs along two trajectories.

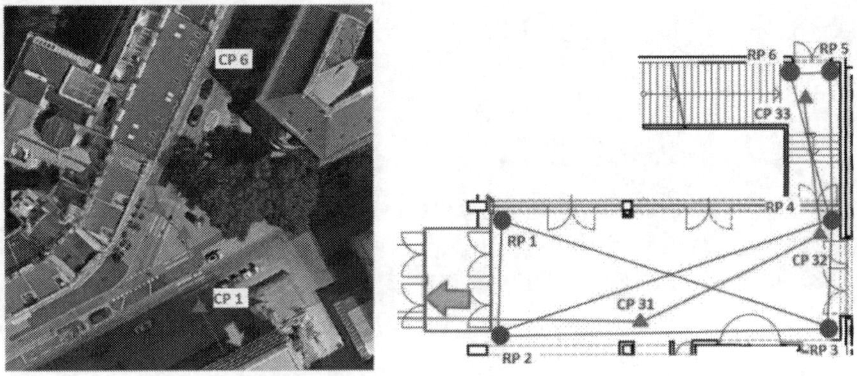

Fig. 6. Combined out-/indoor trajectory at the entrance area of the University office building.

Table 2. Deviations from ground truth in [m] for smartphone ID1 along trajectory 2.

center of gravity	CP11	CP12	CP13	CP14	CP15	CP16	CP17	CP18
3 RPi's	0.67	3.08	3.58	3.31	1.16	3.85	2.20	0.77
4 RPi's	0.69	6.17	5.26	3.16	1.32	4.23	7.08	1.62
5 RPi's	0.67	10.07	4.27	2.82	1.26	4.36	7.53	1.57
6 RPi's	0.67	12.26	3.79	2.77	1.32	3.94	8.77	1.83
center of gravity	**CP28**	**CP27**	**CP26**	**CP25**	**CP24**	**CP23**	**CP22**	**CP21**
3 RPi's	2.80	3.04	3.10	3.81	1.81	3.30	6.76	0.31
4 RPi's	4.01	2.14	2.18	4.57	1.83	2.24	4.76	0.33
5 RPi's	4.41	2.04	1.90	4.31	0.83	4.03	7.31	0.29
6 RPi's	4.22	1.84	2.01	4.59	0.43	5.64	8.99	0.28

Table 3. Deviations from ground truth in [m] for smartphone ID1 along trajectory 2 with DWi-Fi corrections.

center of gravity	CP11	CP12	CP13	CP14	CP15	CP16	CP17	CP18
3 RPi's	0.46	7.99	5.16	3.03	1.34	5.38	4.32	0.92
4 RPi's	0.46	7.99	5.16	3.03	1.34	5.38	3.83	2.49
5 RPi's	0.46	7.99	5.16	3.03	1.34	5.38	3.87	3.02
6 RPi's	0.46	7.99	5.16	3.03	1.34	5.38	3.92	2.75
center of gravity	**CP28**	**CP27**	**CP26**	**CP25**	**CP24**	**CP23**	**CP22**	**CP21**
3 RPi's	3.30	1.35	2.14	5.01	3.24	12.08	4.32	0.33
4 RPi's	4.94	4.99	2.19	4.20	3.22	11.13	4.03	0.36
5 RPi's	5.49	6.60	2.27	3.94	2.43	12.38	3.80	0.32
6 RPi's	5.23	6.42	2.25	4.22	1.89	13.13	3.81	0.31

Table 4. Comparison of the deviations in [m] without our with DWi-Fi corrections.

	CP 12	CP 23	CP 14	CP 24	CP 13	CP 22
without DWi-Fi	29.72	13.12	8.49	1.36	3.69	7.78
with DWi-Fi	5.74	3.49	6.35	18.08	4.96	6.30

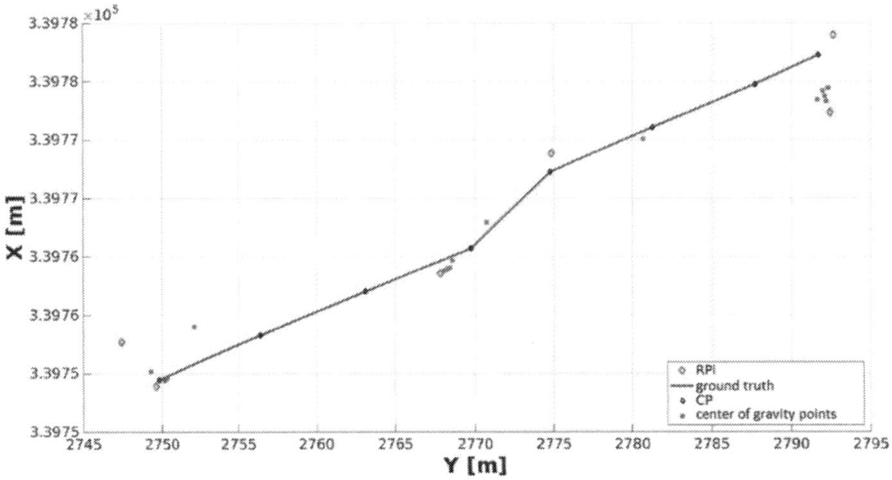

Fig. 7. Kinematic positioning solution along trajectory 1 in the laboratory.

7 Results of the Kinematic Measurements in the Laboratory

The CPs along the trajectories were passed in a specified sequence and a time stamp was set when the points were passed in the kinematic measurements. Thereby the biggest influence on the obtaining positioning results was the RSS scan duration of the different smartphones depending on the device specific Wi-Fi chip. With a longer scan time, another distance between the CPs is covered. The longest scan time of one of the smartphones had was for SP1 with 4.5 seconds. Accordingly, only eleven scans along the first trajectory were recorded, whereas with SP2 84 scans with an average scan time of only 0.5 s. In the following evaluation, only the calculation of the center of gravity was considered. Fig. 7 shows a resulting trajectory of smartphone SP2. It can clearly be seen how the user walked along the trajectory. Table 4 compares the results without and with the use of DWi-Fi for different CPs. Some improvements can be seen in the CPs, but no smartphone results can be improved over the entire trajectory. It must be noted that the shielding by other users has a significant influence on the results. The measurements of a trajectory were not performed independently for each smartphone, but by several users walked along the trajectory at the same time. Thus, the signals were possibly attenuated by other users. This would also be the case under real world conditions, such as those found in buildings with other users moving around.

8 Analysis of the RSS Behaviour in the Building Entrance Test Area

For the analysis of the use of DWi-Fi, statistical values were calculated from the observations in the first step so that the range of the variations of the RSS can be seen. For this purpose, the RSS recorded by each RP 31 was analyzed to see its emission behaviour. Fig. 8 shows the median, arithmetic mean, minimum and maximum RSS value radio maps in the building entrance test area. The spatial conditions are recognizable, the signals of RP 31 can propagate more towards RP 34 than towards RP 35. Moreover, the signals to RP 35 decrease much more than to RP 34, with large differences between the minimum and maximum RSS values. The reason for this can again be attributed to the high fluctuations of the RSS at the beginning of the measurements (compare Fig. 1). In the next step, the correction values were determined. They correspond to a value of a few dBm for all SPs. Fig. 9 shows the frequency distributions of the correction values for RP 31 to 36 for smartphone SP3 and SP7. These two, as well as the distribution of the remaining SPs, show similarities to a normal distribution. The statement is also supported by the calculation of averages and medians. The mean values for all RPs are less than 1 and the median values are 0 with the exception of individual values, which are between 0 and 1 (in maximum one per SP evaluation). Finally, the position solutions were calculated with these correction values.

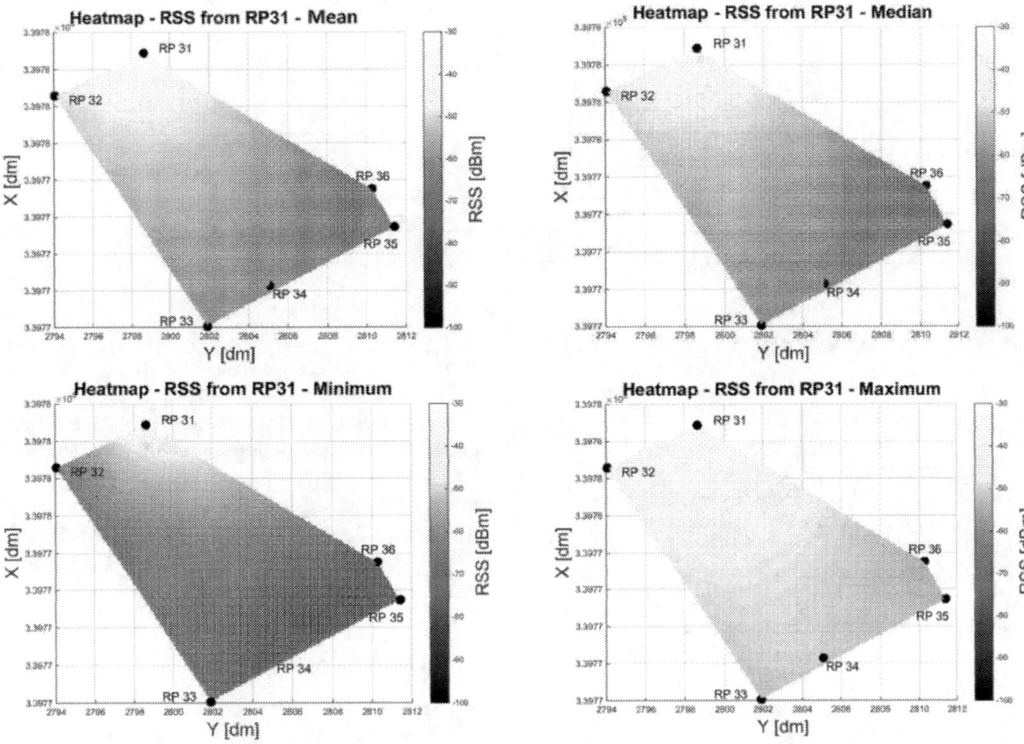

Fig. 8. Heatmaps of RSS distribution in the entrance area of the office building ((top left) arithmetic mean, (top right) median, (bottom left) minimum and (bottom right) maximum RSS of all four orientations).

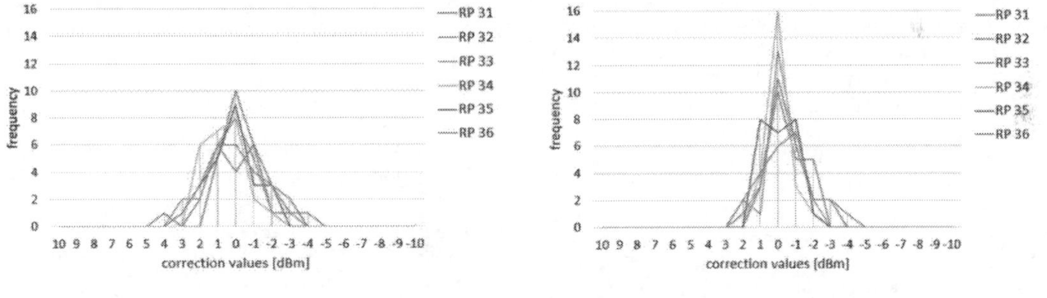

Fig. 9. Frequency distribution of RSS correction values in [dBm] of the six RPs for the two smartphones SP3 and SP7.

9 Results of the Kinematic Measurements in the Entrance Area of the Office Building

Table 5 shows a comparison of the resulting position deviations from the ground truth of seven smartphones for the three CPs in the building entrance area without and with DWi-Fi corrections. One can easily recognize that there are not significant differences if DWi-Fi corrections are applied or not. Furthermore, the results show that the deviations for CP 32 are by a factor of 2 worse than the ones for the other two CPs. The main reason for this is that CP 32 is unfavorably located in respective to geometry. CP 31 and 33 are located more centrally in the triangle spanned by the RPs which results in much smaller deviations. Thus, it can be concluded that the location of the points in the triangle has a great influence on the achievable positioning results.

Table 5. Comparison of the deviations in [m] without our with DWi-Fi corrections for the kinematic measurements.

without DWi-Fi	**SP1**	**SP2**	**SP3**	**SP4**	**SP7**	**SP8**	**SP13**
CP31	1.77	1.20	1.52	1.54	1.76	1.42	1.33
CP32	5.42	5.88	5.95	4.82	5.41	5.44	6.29
CP33	1.85	2.12	1.99	1.61	1.19	1.75	2.32
with DWi-Fi	**SP1**	**SP2**	**SP3**	**SP4**	**SP7**	**SP8**	**SP13**
CP31	1.75	1.27	1.56	1.48	1.76	1.49	1.35
CP32	5.49	6.00	6.09	4.72	5.47	5.51	6.46
CP33	1.88	2.13	1.98	1.54	1.17	1.75	2.32

10 Conclusions and Outlook

The results of the experiments show that the selection of a suitable calibration procedure for the conversion of the RSS to ranges is of great importance. The best results were achieved if a generally valid approximation for all devices of the signal propagation (variant 3) instead of a device specific calibration (variant 1) is used. In the stop-and-go measurements good position solutions were achieved at certain checkpoints. The deviations from the ground truth could be reduced by a factor of 2 from 3 to 6 m to 1 to 2 m respectively with variant 3. To achieve these results, the geometrical checkpoint location within the RPs triangle is very important. In addition, the scan duration has a significant influence on the results, especially for the kinematic measurements. As different Wi-Fi chips are installed in the smartphones, the time periods that a device needs for a RSS scan were also very different. Further investigation has been carried out regarding this influence. First results are presented in [7].

The results of the DWi-Fi evaluation showed that the deviations from the ground truth can be reduced to better than 2 m using certain evaluation methods. It is possible to locate position of the user where he is in a building. If three RPi's are not available in every area of a building, further information, such as the damping of the signals through walls, doors, etc., must be considered. Thus, in future research this extension of the method will be investigated.

The laboratory set-up is similar to a wide corridor of an office building or an underground train or metro platform. If the following key points are considered it is then possible to find either certain offices or the platform exits. Firstly, it must be taken into account that it is better to define a uniform polynomial function for a limited distance range. Then only the nearest RPs are considered because far away APs show low RSSs and therefore contribute little to position determination. Secondly, sufficient RPs have to placed in the entire area so that the user is surrounded by three RPs at any time in order to calculate the center of gravity in the AP triangle. Thirdly, the center of gravity calculation should only be used with three RPs.

References

1. Y. B. Bai, S. Wu, G. Retscher, A. Kealy, L. Holden, M. Tomko, A. Borriak, B. Hu, H. R. Wu, K. Zhang, A New Method for Improving Wi-Fi Based Indoor Positioning Accuracy, Journal of LBS, 8:3: 135-147 (2014).
2. R. Chen, L. Pei, J. Liu, H. Leppäkoski, WLAN and Bluetooth Positioning in Smart Phones, in R. Chen (ed.): Ubiquitous Positioning and Mobile Location-Based Services in Smart Phones. IGI Global, Hershey PA, USA, 44-68 (2012).
3. H. Liu, H. Darabi, P. Banerjee, J. Liu, Survey of Wireless Indoor Positioning Techniques and Systems, IEEE Transactions on Systems, Man, and Cybernetics, Part C: Applications and Reviews, 37:6: 1067-1080 (2007).
4. R. Mautz, Indoor Positioning Technologies, Swiss Geodetic Commission, Geodetic-Geophysical Reports of Switzerland, 86, 134 pgs. (2012).
5. G. Retscher, Indoor Navigation, Chapter 9-1, in: E. W. Grafarend (ed.), Encyclopedia of Geodesy, Earth Sciences Series, Springer International Publishing Switzerland, ISBN: 978-3-319-02370-0 (Online), DOI 10.1007/978-3-319-02370-0_9-1, 7 pgs. (2016).
6. G. Retscher, H. Hofer, A. Kealy, V. Gikas, F. Obex, Cooperative Localization in Indoor Environments Using Constrained Differential Wi-Fi and UWB Measurements, Proceedings of the ION GNSS+ 2017, September 25-29, Portland, Oregon, USA, 2869-2882 (2017).
7. G. Retscher, A. Leb, Influence of the RSSI Scan Duration of Smartphones in Kinematic Wi-Fi Fingerprinting, Proceedings of the FIG Working Week, April 22-26, 2019, Hanoi, Vietnam, 15 pgs (2019) (submitted and under review).
8. G. Retscher, T. Tatschl, Indoor Positioning with Differential Wi-Fi Lateration, Journal of Applied Geodesy, ISSN 1862-9016, DOI 10.1515/jag-2017-0011, 11:4, 249-269 (2017).
9. D. Stojanović, N. Stojanović, Indoor Localization and Tracking: Methods, Technologies and Research Challenges, Facta Universitatis, Series: Automatic Control and Robotics, 13:1: 57-72 (2014).

Performance evaluation on GNSS, wheel speed sensor, yaw rate sensor, and gravity sensor integrated positioning algorithm for automotive navigation system

Joong-hee Han[1,*] and *Chi-ho* Park[1]

[1]Intelligent Device and Systems Research Group, DGIST, Republic of Korea

Abstract. The Global Navigation Satellite System (GNSS) positioning technique is widely used for the automotive navigation system since it can provide the stable and accurate position and velocity in the most road environments at an affordable price. However, the performance of GNSS positioning technique is degraded in certain areas, where GNSS signals are blocked by buildings and tunnel. To overcome this problem, the GNSS positioning technique should be integrated with dead reckoning (DR) sensors such as accelerometer, gyroscope, and odometer. Recently, the most passenger cars are equipped with the Advanced Driver Assistance System (ADAS) based on numerous sensors to improve safety and convenience in driving. Among sensors for the ADAS, vehicle dynamic sensors such as wheel speed sensor (WSS), yaw rate sensor (YRS), gravity sensor (GS) can be used for the DR algorithm since those sensors measure vehicle's motions. Therefore, this paper evaluates the vehicle positioning algorithm that integrate the GNSS with a three-dimensional dead reckoning based on WSS, YRS, and GS. The vehicle positioning algorithm is implemented through the extended Kalman filter of a loosely-coupled mode. Performance was evaluated through tests carried out in real driving trajectory including various GNSS signals reception environments. It is found that the proposed algorithm can be an alternative solution to compensate the limitation of the GNSS positioning technique, without the use of a low-cost inertial measurement unit.

1 Introduction

The importance of accuracy, integrity, and continuity in a positioning technique has increasingly been emphasized in land vehicle application such as automotive navigation, advanced driver assistance systems (ADAS), intelligent transportation system (ITS) [1-2]. Nowadays, global navigation satellite system (GNSS) positioning technique is widely used for these applications since it can provide the stable and accurate position and velocity in the most road environments at an affordable price. However, the GNSS positioning technique may produce abnormal position errors mainly cause by multipath and non-line-of-sight (NLOS) signal interferences in urban canyons. Therefore, the standalone GNSS positioning technique cannot guarantee an accurate and continuous positioning in all vehicle driving environment [3]. To overcome this problem, the GNSS positioning technique should be integrated with additional sensors such as inertial measurement unit (IMU) and odometer.

Recently, to improve safety and convenience in driving, most passenger car have been equipped with various advanced driver assistance system (ADAS) applications such as anti-lock braking system (ABS), electronic stability control (ESC), and traction control system(TCS) [4]. ADAS uses data which are continuously acquired by numerous on-board vehicle sensors such as wheel speed sensor (WSS), yaw rate sensor (YRS), gravity sensor (GS), steering angle sensor (SAS). These sensors measure and provide vehicle's motions. Therefore, on-board vehicle sensors can be applied to develop for the car positioning technique. The development of car positioning technique can be used by on-board vehicle sensors following two main strategies. First, on-board vehicle sensors are applied to compensate for the INS error. Most of the previous researches are the integration of WSS with GNSS/INS to prevent INS error degradation during GNSS outages [5-7] Reference [8] developed five types of sensors integration algorithms for precise positioning, namely GPS/INS/WSS, GPS/INS/GS/YRS, GPS/INS/SAS, GPS/INS/WSS/SAS, and GPS/INS/WSS/GL/YRS/SAS. Second, on-board vehicle sensors are applied for dead reckoning (DR) to overcome the limitation of GNSS technique. Most of the related researches developed integration of GNSS with the dead-reckoning on-board vehicle sensors in two ways, GNSS/WSS as well as GNSS/WSS/YRS [9-11]. Also, GNSS/on-board vehicle sensors integration based on vehicle model was studied [12-13].

This paper proposes and evaluates an EKF (Extended Kalman Filter)-based GNSS/on-board sensors integrated vehicle positioning algorithm to overcome the limitation of GNSS based technique. This combines data from a

* Corresponding author: jhhan@dgist.ac.kr

GNSS receiver with data coming from six on-board vehicle sensors: two WSS, a YRS, a lateral GS, and a longitudinal GS. A description of the proposed algorithm is presented in Section 2. A performance evaluation of the proposed algorithm is provided in Section 3. The conclusion is given in Section 4.

2 GNSS/on-board vehicle sensors integration algorithm

Figure 1 is a block diagram of the GNSS/on-board vehicle sensors integration algorithm. The GNSS/on-board sensors integrated vehicle positioning algorithm is implemented loosely coupled integration through EKF. Three dimensional DR based on on-board vehicle sensors calculates the positions, the velocities in the navigation frame, and attitudes at an interval of 0.02s. A three dimensional DR based on on-board vehicle sensors uses data measuring from two rear WSS, a YRS, a lateral GS, and a longitudinal GS. The procedure for this DR is as follows. To define the velocity in the body frame using the vehicles speed derived from two rear WSS we applied two no holonomic constraints on the lateral and vertical directions. In additional, the center of body frame is set to the center of rear wheel axle. The velocities in the body frame are defined as follows:

$$\boldsymbol{v^b} = \begin{bmatrix} v_x \\ v_y \\ v_z \end{bmatrix} = \begin{bmatrix} (v_{rL} + v_{rR})/2 \\ 0 \\ 0 \end{bmatrix} \tag{1}$$

where v_x, v_y, and v_z are velocities in the body frame, v_{rL} and v_{rR} are the rear left and rear right WSS measurements, respectively.

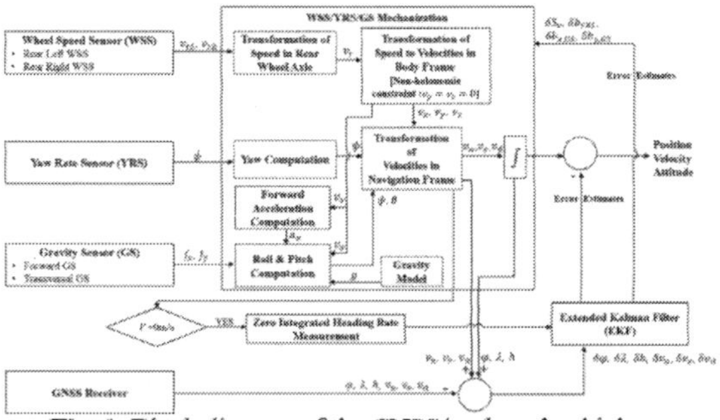

Fig. 1. Block diagram of the GNSS/on-board vehicle sensors integration algorithm.

When the forward vehicle acceleration is derived from WSS measurement, the pitch angle (θ) can be computed as shown in Equation (2) using the longitudinal GS and Earth's gravity model.

$$\theta = \sin^{-1}\left(\frac{f_x - a_x}{g}\right) \tag{2}$$

where f_x is the longitudinal GS measurement, a_x is the WSS derived foward vehicle acceleration, g is the gravity at the present location.

The roll angle (ϕ) can be calculated as shown in Equation (3) using the lateral GS, YRS, Earth's gravity model and the value for forward velocity.

$$\phi = \sin^{-1}\left(\frac{f_y - v_x\dot{\psi}}{g\cos\theta}\right) \tag{3}$$

where f_y is the lateral GS measurement, v_x is the foward velocity, $\dot{\psi}$ is the YRS measurement, and g is the gravity at the present location.

The yaw angle (ψ) can be calculated by numerical integration using the YRS, as expressed in

$$\psi(t) = \psi(t-1) + \dot{\psi}\Delta t \tag{4}$$

where ψ(t) and ψ(t − 1) are the yaw angle at time t and t − 1, respectively, $\dot{\psi}$ is the YRS measurement, and Δt is the samling time interval.

The velocities in the navigation frame can be transformed by using

$$\boldsymbol{v^n} = \begin{bmatrix} v_n \\ v_e \\ v_d \end{bmatrix} = \boldsymbol{C_b^n v^b} \tag{5}$$

where v_n, v_e, and v_d are velocities in the navigation frame, and $\boldsymbol{C_b^n}$ is the direction cosine matrix from the body frame to the navigation frame.

The velocities in the navigation frame are transformed into the rate of change of the positions in the geodetic coordinate system by using Equation (6), and then integrated over the sample interval to obtain positions in the geodetic coordinates system.

$$\dot{\boldsymbol{r}}^{\boldsymbol{n}} = \begin{bmatrix} \dot{\varphi} \\ \dot{\lambda} \\ \dot{h} \end{bmatrix} = \begin{bmatrix} \frac{1}{M+h} & 0 & 0 \\ 0 & \frac{1}{(N+h)\cos\varphi} & 0 \\ 0 & 0 & -1 \end{bmatrix} \begin{bmatrix} v_n \\ v_e \\ v_d \end{bmatrix} \tag{6}$$

where $\dot{\varphi}$, $\dot{\lambda}$, and $\dot{h}$ are the rate of change of the latitude, longitude, and ellipsoidal height, M is the radius of curvature of the meridian, N is the radius curvature of the prime vertical, h is the ellipsoidal height, φ is the geodetic latitude.

In EKF-based GNSS/on-board sensors integrated vehicle positioning algorithm, the state vector of the navigation error is composed of latitude error ($\delta\varphi$), longitude error ($\delta\lambda$), ellipsoidal height error (δh), north velocity error (δv_n), east velocity error (δv_e), down velocity error (δv_d), roll error ($\delta\phi$), pitch error ($\delta\theta$), and yaw error ($\delta\psi$). The state vector of the sensor error is composed of the average of left and right rear WSS scale factor (δs_v), the YRS bias (δb_{YRS}), the longitudinal GS bias ($\delta b_{x,GS}$), and lateral GS bias ($\delta b_{y,GS}$), defined random constants. The dynamic model of GNSS/on-board sensors integrated vehicle positioning algorithm is shown in the following Equation (7):

$$\boldsymbol{\delta\dot{x}} = \boldsymbol{F\delta x} + \boldsymbol{Gu} \tag{7}$$

where $\boldsymbol{F}$ is the dynamic matrix, $\boldsymbol{\delta x}$ is the error state vector, $\boldsymbol{G}$ is the shaping matrix, $\boldsymbol{u}$ is the white noise vector.

The error state vector ($\boldsymbol{\delta x}$) is written as follows :

$$\boldsymbol{\delta x} = [\delta\varphi\ \delta\lambda\ \delta h\ \delta v_n\ \delta v_e\ \delta v_d\ \delta\phi\ \delta\theta\ \delta\psi\ \delta s_v\ \delta b_{YRS}\ \delta b_{x,GS}\ \delta b_{y,GS}]^T \quad (8)$$

The dymamic matrix ($\boldsymbol{F}$) is written as follows :

$$\boldsymbol{F} = \begin{bmatrix} \boldsymbol{F_{11}} & \boldsymbol{F_{12}} & \boldsymbol{0_{3\times3}} & \boldsymbol{0_{3\times4}} \\ \boldsymbol{0_{3\times3}} & \boldsymbol{0_{3\times3}} & \boldsymbol{F_{23}} & \boldsymbol{F_{24}} \\ \boldsymbol{0_{3\times3}} & \boldsymbol{0_{3\times3}} & \boldsymbol{0_{3\times3}} & \boldsymbol{F_{34}} \\ \boldsymbol{0_{4\times3}} & \boldsymbol{0_{4\times3}} & \boldsymbol{0_{4\times3}} & \boldsymbol{0_{4\times4}} \end{bmatrix} \quad (9)$$

where $\boldsymbol{0_{n\times m}}$ is n x m zero matrix and $\boldsymbol{F_{11}}$, $\boldsymbol{F_{12}}$, $\boldsymbol{F_{23}}$, $\boldsymbol{F_{24}}$, and $\boldsymbol{F_{34}}$ are written as follows:

$$\boldsymbol{F_{11}} = \begin{bmatrix} 0 & 0 & \frac{-v_n}{(M+h)^2} \\ \frac{v_e \tan\varphi}{(N+h)\cos\varphi} & 0 & \frac{-v_e}{(N+h)^2\cos\varphi} \\ 0 & 0 & 0 \end{bmatrix} \quad (10)$$

$$\boldsymbol{F_{12}} = \begin{bmatrix} \frac{1}{M+h} & 0 & 0 \\ 0 & \frac{1}{(N+h)\cos\varphi} & 0 \\ 0 & 0 & -1 \end{bmatrix} \quad (11)$$

$$\boldsymbol{F_{23}} = \begin{bmatrix} 0 & -v_x \sin\theta\cos\psi & -v_x\cos\theta\sin\psi \\ 0 & -v_x\sin\theta\sin\psi & v_x\cos\theta\cos\psi \\ 0 & -v_x\cos\theta & 0 \end{bmatrix} \quad (12)$$

$$\boldsymbol{F_{24}} = \begin{bmatrix} \cos\theta\cos\psi & 0 & 0 & 0 \\ \cos\theta\sin\psi & 0 & 0 & 0 \\ -\sin\psi & 0 & 0 & 0 \end{bmatrix} \quad (13)$$

$$\boldsymbol{F_{34}} = \begin{bmatrix} 0 & 0 & 0 & 0 \\ 0 & 0 & 0 & 0 \\ 0 & 1 & 0 & 0 \end{bmatrix} \quad (14)$$

The shaping matrix $\boldsymbol{G}$ is written as follows :

$$\boldsymbol{G} = \begin{bmatrix} \boldsymbol{G_{11}} & \boldsymbol{0_{3\times1}} & \boldsymbol{0_{3\times1}} & \boldsymbol{0_{3\times1}} \\ \boldsymbol{0_{3\times1}} & \boldsymbol{0_{3\times1}} & \boldsymbol{0_{3\times1}} & \boldsymbol{0_{3\times1}} \\ \boldsymbol{0_{3\times1}} & \boldsymbol{G_{32}} & \boldsymbol{G_{33}} & \boldsymbol{G_{34}} \\ \boldsymbol{0_{4\times1}} & \boldsymbol{0_{4\times1}} & \boldsymbol{0_{4\times1}} & \boldsymbol{0_{4\times1}} \end{bmatrix} \quad (15)$$

where $\boldsymbol{G_{11}} = \begin{bmatrix} \frac{\cos\theta\cos\psi}{M+h} & \frac{\cos\theta\sin\psi}{(N+h)\cos\varphi} & -\sin\theta \end{bmatrix}^T$, $\boldsymbol{G_{32}} = [1\ \ 0\ \ 0]^T$, $\boldsymbol{G_{33}} = [0\ \ 0\ \ 1]^T$, $\boldsymbol{G_{34}} = [0\ \ 0\ \ 1]^T$

The white noise vector ($\boldsymbol{u}$) is written as follows :

$$\boldsymbol{\mu} = [w_{v_{WSS}}\ \ w_{\phi_{GS}}\ \ w_{\theta_{GS}}\ \ w_{\psi_{YRS}}]^T \quad (16)$$

where $w_{v_{WSS}}$ is the white noise of WSS derived vehicle speed, $w_{\phi_{GS}}$ is the white noise of GS derived roll, $w_{\theta_{GS}}$ is the white noise of GS derived pitch, $w_{\psi_{YRS}}$ is the white noise of YRS.

The measurement model in EKF is generally expressed as follows:

$$\boldsymbol{z} = \boldsymbol{H\delta x} + \boldsymbol{w_m} \quad (17)$$

where $\boldsymbol{z}$ is the measurement residual vector, $\boldsymbol{H}$ is the design matrix, and $\boldsymbol{w_m}$ is the measurement noise vector.

The measurement residual vector for GNSS ($\boldsymbol{z_{GNSS}}$) is the difference the position and velocity calculated by DR based on on-board vehicle sensors and the data acquired from GNSS receiver, as expressed in

$$\boldsymbol{z_{GNSS}} = \begin{bmatrix} \varphi \\ \lambda \\ h \\ v_n \\ v_e \\ v_d \end{bmatrix}_{DR} - \begin{bmatrix} \varphi \\ \lambda \\ h \\ v_n \\ v_e \\ v_d \end{bmatrix}_{GNSS} \quad (18)$$

Where the subscripts DR and GNSS denote the value calculated by DR based on on-board vehicle sensors and the data acquired from the GNSS receiver.

The design matrix for GNSS ($\boldsymbol{H_{GNSS}}$) is expressed in

$$\boldsymbol{H_{GNSS}} = \begin{bmatrix} \boldsymbol{I_{3\times3}} & \boldsymbol{0_{3\times3}} & \boldsymbol{0_{3\times3}} & \boldsymbol{0_{3\times4}} \\ \boldsymbol{0_{3\times3}} & \boldsymbol{I_{3\times3}} & \boldsymbol{0_{3\times3}} & \boldsymbol{0_{3\times4}} \end{bmatrix} \quad (19)$$

where $\boldsymbol{I_{n\times n}}$ is n x n identity matrix.

To prevent the drift error of yaw, the zero integrated heading rate (ZIHR) measurement update [14] is applied when the vehicle stationary. The measurement residual vector for ZIHR ($\boldsymbol{z_{ZIHR}}$) is given by

$$\boldsymbol{z_{ZIHR}} = \psi_k - \psi_{k-1} \quad (20)$$

where ψ_k is the yaw angle at the current epoch, ψ_{k-1} is the yaw angle at the previous epoch.

The design matrix vector for ZIHR is expressed in

$$\boldsymbol{H_{ZIHR}} = [\boldsymbol{0_{1\times3}}\ \ \boldsymbol{0_{1\times3}}\ \ \boldsymbol{0_{1\times2}}\ \ 1\ \ \boldsymbol{0_{1\times4}}] \quad (21)$$

3 Performance evaluation of GNSS/on-board vehicle sensors integration algorithm

To evaluate the performance of the proposed algorithm, a field test was conducted in a suburban of Daegu, Korea. Since the test vehicle (Figure 2) was equipped with ESC, the on-board vehicle sensors data were obtained from an in-vehicle control area network (CAN). The specifications of the on-board vehicles mounted on the test vehicle are described in Table 1. GNSS based position and velocity data were logged by the Novatel DL-V3-GENERIC receiver. The GNSS positioning method was set to the point positioning used by automotive navigation system. According to the specification of the GNSS receiver, the accuracy of position and velocity are 1.5m and 0.03m/s, respectively. In order to assess the accuracy of navigation solution calculated by the proposed algorithm, the reference data were collected by a post-processing of the data obtained from an Applanix's POS LV 520 system.

Table 1. Specification of on-board vehicle sensors

Sensor	Output range	Resolution	Unit
WSS	0 ~ 511.75	0.125	km/h
YRS	-40.95 ~ 40.95	0.01	deg/s
GS	-10.23 ~ 10.23	0.01	m/s^2

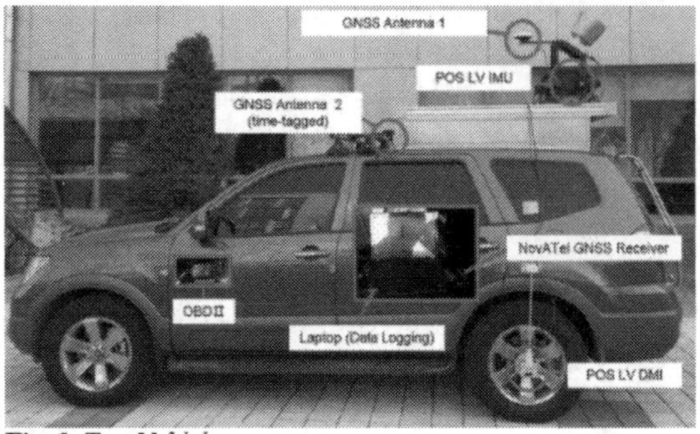

Fig. 2. Test Vehicle

The test trajectory for reference data is shown in Figure 3. The test trajectory covered various driving circumstance encountered during typical driving on urban roads with straight portions, turns, slopes, high speed, slow speeds, and jumping. The travelled distance of the trajectory is about 9.6km for 38 minutes. Figure 4 shows the velocity profile in the body frame with the maximum speed being about 15m/s. The number of tracked GNSS is more than five, as shown in Figure 5.

Fig. 3. Field test trajectory

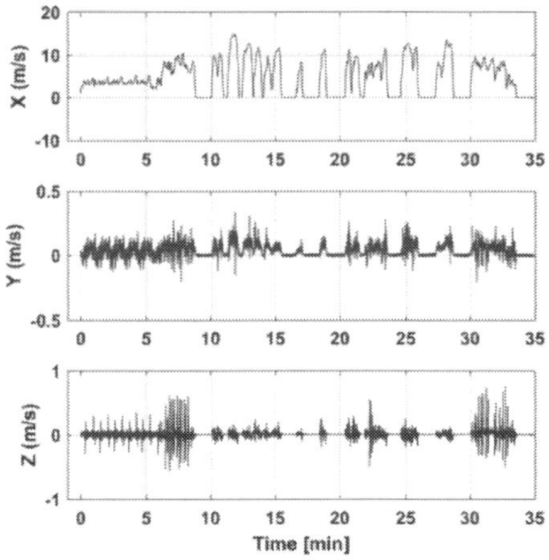

Fig. 4. Velocity in the body frane

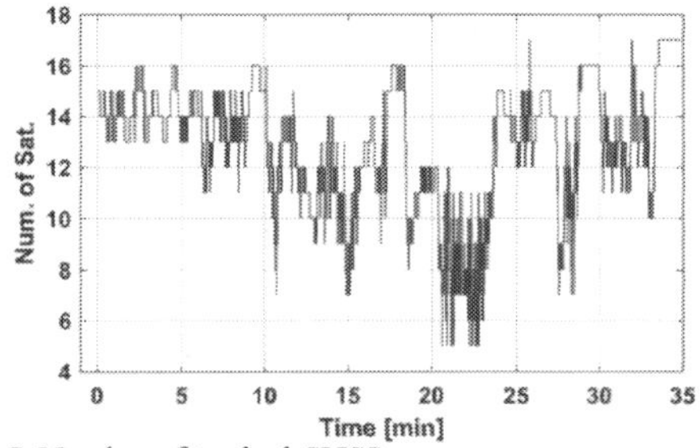

Fig. 5. Number of tracked GNSS

Table 2 summarize the statistics of the position error with respect to the reference data. It can be from Table 2 that the position error of the proposed algorithm is significantly decreased in comparison with the GNSS only solution. The standard deviation of position error along north and east direction is reduced by 70% and 43%, respectivly, from 2.36m and 1.91m for the GNSS only solution to 0.70m and 1.09m for the proposed algorithm. Also, a decrease of standard deviation of position error along down direction for the proposed algorithm is 61% as compared to the GNSS only solution. The magnitude of position error of proposed algorithm is compared with the GNSS-only solution as shown in Figure 6. As seen in Figure 5 and 6, the position error for GNSS-only solution is considerably affected by the number of tracked GNSS while aiding from the on-board sensors can provide a stable position during poor GNSS availability.

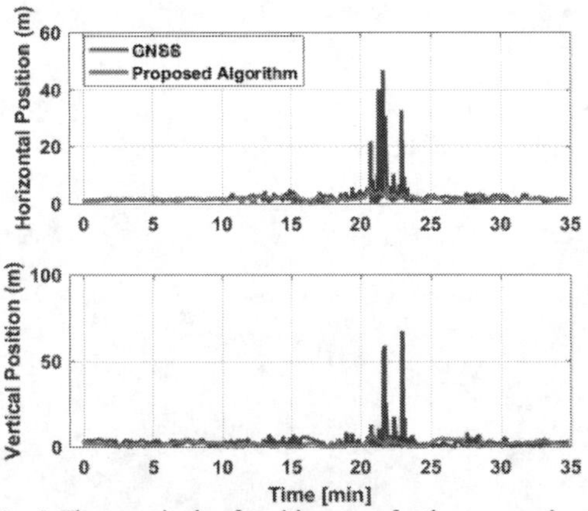

Fig. 6. The magnitude of position error for the proposed algorithm and the GNSS only solution

Table 2. The statistics of the postion error

	Type	Range	Mean	Standard Deviation
North (m)	Proposed algorithm	-1.20 ~ 5.62	0.61	0.70
	GNSS Only	-11.58 ~ 45.34	0.61	2.36
East (m)	Proposed algorithm	-2.78 ~ 5.20	1.13	1.09
	GNSS Only	-11.04 ~ 30.39	1.38	1.91
Down (m)	Proposed algorithm	-4.36 ~ 5.79	0.95	1.74
	GNSS Only	-67.10 ~ 17.12	-1.93	4.45

The statistics of the velocity error with respect to the reference data are given in Table 3. The magnitude of velocity error of proposed algorithm is compared with the GNSS-only solution is shown in Figure 7. Compared to the GNSS only solution, the velocity error of the proposed algorithm is decreased by using on-board vehicle sensors. Especially, the performance of horizontal velocity can be further improved by the proposed algorithm with respect to the GNSS only solution.

Table 3. The statistics of the velocity error

	Type	Range	Mean	Standard Deviation
North (m/s)	Proposed algorithm	-0.55 ~ 0.94	0	0.09
	GNSS Only	-1.45 ~ 2.20	0	0.10
East (m/s)	Proposed algorithm	-3.56 ~ 0.90	0	0.12
	GNSS Only	-3.77 ~ 1.43	0	0.12
Down (m/s)	Proposed algorithm	-1.45 ~ 1.34	0.04	0.12
	GNSS Only	-5.22 ~ 1.98	-0.01	0.16

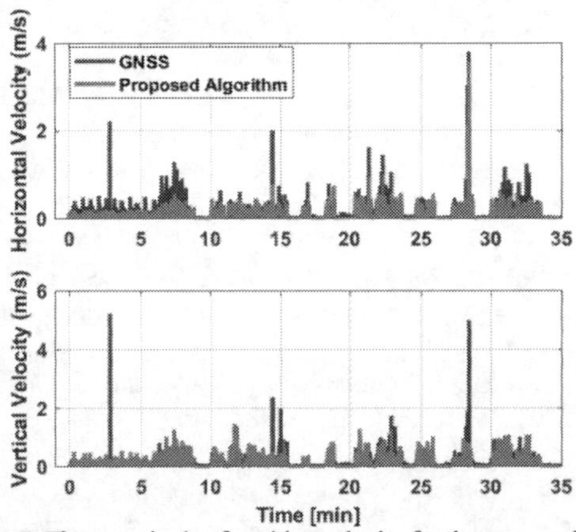

Fig. 7. The magnitude of position velocity for the proposed algorithm and the GNSS only solution

4 Conclusion

In this paper, GNSS and on-board vehicle sensors (two wheel speed sensors, a yaw rate sensor, and two gravity sensors) integrated vehicle positioning algorithm was developed to overcome the limitation of GNSS based technique. On-board sensors were applied for three dimensional dead reckoning to compute the navigation solutions without GNSS. And the GNSS/on-board vehicle sensors integration was implemented by EKF through a loosely coupled mode.

Performance was evaluated through tests carried out in real driving trajectory including various GNSS signals reception environments. The result indicates that the GNSS combined on-board vehicle sensors integration can enhance the positioning accuracy as compared with using only GNSS. Also, we found that GNSS/on-board vehicle sensors integration can provide a stable position during poor GNSS availability. Therefore, the proposed algorithm can be an alternative solution to compensate the limitation of the GNSS positioning technique, without the use of a low-cost inertial measurement unit.

Acknowledgements

This work was supported by the DGIST R&D Program of the Ministry of Science, ICT & Technology of Korea (18-NT-01).

References

1. K. Jo, K. Chu, and M. Sunwoo, *IEEE trans. Intell. Transp. Sys.*, 13, 1 (2012)
2. I. Skog, and P. Handel, *IEEE trans. Intell. Transp. Sys.*, **13**, 1 (2012)
3. X. Li, R. Jiang, X. Song, and B. Li, *Journal of Sensors*, 2017, 11 (2017)
4. D. Barbosa, A. Lopes, and R. E. Araujo, *IECON'16*, pp.1049-1054 (2016).

5. J. Kubo, T. Kindo, A. Ito, and S. Sugimoto, *ION GPS 1999*, pp.555-564 (1999).
6. P. Bonnifait, P. Bouron, D. Meizel, and P. Crubille, *Journal of Navigation*, **53**, 6 (2003).
7. J. Georgy, A. Noureldim, M.J. Korenberg, and M. M. Bayoumi, *IEEE Transaction on Vehicular Technology*, **59**, 2 (2010).
8. J. Gao, *Development of a precise GPS/INS/on-board vehicle sensors integrated vehicular positioning system* (2007).
9. P. Bonnifait, P. Bouron, P. Crubille, and D. Meizel, *2001 ICRA*, **2**, pp.1597-1602 (2001).
10. C.R. Carlson, *Estimation with applications for automobile dead reckoning and control* (2004).
11. U. Iqbal, *Multi-sensor data fusion for vehicular navigation applications* (2012).
12. S. Razaei, and R. Sengupta, *IEEE Transaction on Vehicular Technology*, **15**, 6 (2007).
13. K. Jo, K. Chu, and M. Sunwoo, *IEEE Transactions on Intelligent Transportation System*, **13**, 1 (2012).
14. E. Shin, *Estimation techniques for low-cost inertial navigation* (2005).

Navigation Performance Enhancement Using IMM Filtering for Time Varying Satellite Signal Quality

Dah-Jing Jwo *, *Shu-Ming* Chang and *Jen-Hsien* Lai

Department of Communications, Navigation and Control Engineering, National Taiwan Ocean University
2 Pei-Ning Rd., Keelung 202, Taiwan

Abstract. A novel scheme using fuzzy logic based interacting multiple model (IMM) unscented Kalman filter (UKF) is employed in which the Fuzzy Logic Adaptive System (FLAS) is utilized to address uncertainty of measurement noise, especially for the outlier types of multipath errors for the Global Positioning System (GPS) navigation processing. Multipath is known to be one of the dominant error sources, and multipath mitigation is crucial for improvement of the positioning accuracy. It is not an easy task to establish precise statistical characteristics of measurement noise in practical engineering applications. Based on the filter structural adaptation, the IMM nonlinear filtering provides an alternative for designing the adaptive filter in the GPS navigation processing for time varying satellite signal quality. The uncertainty of the noise can be described by a set of switching models using the multiple model estimation. An UKF employs a set of sigma points by deterministic sampling, which avoids the error caused by linearization as in an extended Kalman filter (EKF). For enhancing further system flexibility, the fuzzy logic system is introduced. The use of IMM with FLAS enables tuning of appropriate values for the measurement noise covariance so as to obtain improved estimation accuracy. Performance assessment will be carried out to show the effectiveness of the proposed approach for positioning improvement in GPS navigation processing.

1 Introduction

Multipath [1-4] is known to be one of the dominant error sources in high accuracy global navigation satellite systems (GNSS) positioning systems, such as the Global Positioning System (GPS)[5]. Since multipath errors are among uncorrelated errors that are not cancelled out during observation differencing, the performance of high precision GPS receivers are mostly limited by the multipath induced errors. Most of the existing multipath mitigation algorithms are designed for Gaussian noise. However, non-Gaussian noise is often encountered in many practical environments and their performances degrade dramatically in non-Gaussian cases. The extended Kalman filter (EKF) [5] has been shown to be a minimum mean square error estimator. Unfortunately, the fact that EKF highly depends on a predefined dynamics model forms a major drawback. For achieving good filtering results, the designers are required to have the complete *a priori* knowledge on both the dynamic process and measurement models, in addition to the assumption that both the process and measurement are corrupted by zero-mean Gaussian white sequences. Moreover, the calculation of the Jacobian matrices makes it difficult to implement, especially for the non-differentiable function.

The nonlinear filter is designed to give a preliminary estimation of the state. The mean square error criterion is limited to the assumption of linearity and Gaussianity. Multipath effects occur when GPS signals arrive at a receiver site via multiple paths due to reflections from nearby objects, such as the ground and water surfaces, buildings, vehicles, hills, trees, etc. Many multipath estimation algorithms have been studied to eliminate the positioning error caused by multipath. Although the particle filter (PF) [3] can deal with non-Gaussian, nonlinear system, it is computationally expensive for an online realization. The nonlinear filters considered in this research include the unscented Kalman filter (UKF)[7,8]. The UKF naturally suffers the same problem as the EKF. The uncertainty of the process noise and measurement noise will degrade the performance of UKF.

The adaptive Kalman filter [9,10] algorithm has been one of the strategies considered for estimating the state vector to prevent divergence problem due to modeling errors. An adaptive mechanism which dynamically identifies uncertainties or modeling errors can be adopted. To deal with the noise uncertainty and system nonlinearity simultaneously, the IMMUKF can be introduced. In the approach, these multiple models are developed to describe various dynamic behaviors. In each model an UKF is running, and the IMM algorithm makes uses of model probabilities to weight the inputs and output of a bank of parallel filters at each time instant.

* Corresponding author: djjwo@mail.ntou.edu.tw

The interacting multiple model (IMM) [11-14] algorithm has the configuration that runs in parallel several model-matched state estimation filters, which exchange information (interact) at each sampling time. The IMM algorithm has been originally applied to target tracking, and recently extended to navigation application. A model probability evaluator calculates the current probability of the vehicle being in each of the possible modes. A global estimate of the vehicle's state is computed using the latest mode probabilities. This algorithm carries out a soft-switching between the various modes by adjusting the probabilities of each mode, which are used as weightings in the combined global state estimate. The covariance matrix associated with this combined estimate takes into account the covariances of the mode-conditioned estimates as well as the differences between these estimates.

A fuzzy logic adaptive system (FLAS) [9,15] is added to the UKF innovation term to compensate for the non-Gaussianity of the whole system. The fuzzy logic reasoning system is based on the Mamdani type model. The fuzzy reasoning system is constructed for obtaining the suitable process noise according to the time-varying change in dynamics. By monitoring the innovation information, the FLAS is employed for dynamically adjusting the process noise based on the fuzzy rules so as to enhance the estimation accuracy and tracking capability. The FLAS approach is based on parametric adaptation, while the IMM approach is based on filter structural adaptation (model switching). The example on the GPS navigation processing based on the FLAS based adaptive IMMUKF (Fuzzy-IMMUKF) will be presented. The performance comparison will be demonstrated by using the proposed fuzzy-IMMUKF method as compared to the relatively conventional UKF and IMMUKF approaches.

The remaining of this paper is organized as follows. In Section 2, preliminary background on the multipath interference is reviewed. The interacting multiple model unscented Kalman filter is introduced in Section 3. Section 4 presents the fuzzy adaptive filter strategy. In Section 5, simulation experiments are carried out to evaluate the performance using the proposed fuzzy-IMMUKF as compared to the UKF and IMMUKF approaches. Conclusions are given in Section 6.

2 Multipath interference

Multipath [1-4] is the replica of direct signal caused by the reflection of buildings, hills and other obstacles. Multipath interference and non-line-of-sight (NLOS) reception are major sources of error for GNSS in an urban environment. It is one of the dominant error sources for high accuracy positioning systems due to the irrelevancy between different instants and the occurrence uncertainty along the observation period. In severe multipath environments, it may be possible that the LOS signal is obstructed completely and only the reflected signals are present.

Multipath signals are always delayed compared to line-of-sight signals because of the longer travel paths caused by the reflection. These multipath effects on the code phase measurements are most crucial, and the multipath error can reach up to a few tens of meters, or a couple of hundred. Unlike other error sources, multipath cannot be mitigated through differential processing, since it decorrelates spatially rapidly. The pseudorange errors caused by the multipath interference can be reduced significantly through carefully designed antenna, such as antenna siting, choke-ring antenna design. Receiver-based multipath mitigation techniques use modified discriminator designs, often with additional correlators, to improve the resolution of the signal correlation process.

The EKF is a useful algorithm for multipath estimation in Gaussian noises. However, it cannot be effectively used to cope with multipath estimation problem with non-Gaussian noises. The particle filter (PF) algorithm has been applied for multipath estimation in non-Gaussian noise environment. PF methods use the sequential importance sampling to characterize the posterior probability density function of multipath parameters. It involves the approximation of the posterior density function by a set of random samples taken from an importance density function. The selection of the density function is critical for PF's performance and the optimal one is usually hard to find in most cases. Furthermore, the problem of particle degeneracy also affects the PF's application in multipath estimation.

The unscented Kalman filter (UKF) made a Gaussian approximation with a limited number of points (sigma points) by using the UT. The deterministic sampling approach is used to capture the mean and covariance estimates with a minimal set of samples, and the posterior mean and covariance undergoing a nonlinear propagation can be calculated accurately at least to the second order.

3 The interacting multiple model unscented Kalman filter

The unscented Kalman filtering process model and measurement model are represented as :

$$\mathbf{x}_{k+1} = f(\mathbf{x}_k) + \mathbf{w}_k \tag{1}$$

$$\mathbf{z}_k = h(\mathbf{x}_k) + \mathrm{v}_k \tag{2}$$

where the state vector $\mathbf{x}_k \in \Re^n$, process noise vector $\mathrm{w}_k \in R^n$,measurement vector $\mathbf{z}_k \in \Re^m$, and measurement noise vector $\mathbf{v}_k \in \Re^m$ .The vectors $\mathbf{w}_k$ and $\mathbf{v}_k$ are zero mean Gaussian white sequences having zero cross-correlation with each other :

$$\mathbf{E}[\mathbf{w}_k \mathbf{w}_i^{\mathrm{T}}] = \begin{cases} \mathbf{Q}_k, & i = k \\ 0, & i \neq k \end{cases}; \quad \mathbf{E}[\mathbf{v}_k \mathbf{v}_i^{\mathrm{T}}] = \begin{cases} \mathbf{R}_k, & i = k \\ 0, & i \neq k \end{cases};$$

$$\mathbf{E}[\mathbf{w}_k \mathbf{v}_i^{\mathrm{T}}] = \mathbf{0} \qquad \textit{for all i and k} \tag{3}$$

where $\mathbf{Q}_k$ is the process noise covariance matrix, $\mathbf{R}_k$ is the measurement noise covariance matrix, $E[\cdot]$ represents expectation, and superscript "T'' denotes matrix transpose.

The IMM algorithm uses two or more models to describe the possible states in the working process. Let a general system for multiple models in discrete time be described by:

$$
\begin{aligned}
&x_1(k+1) = f(x_1(k)) + w_1(k) \\
&x_2(k+1) = f(x_2(k)) + w_2(k) \\
&\qquad\qquad \mathrm{M} \qquad\qquad\qquad\qquad (4) \\
&x_j(k+1) = f(x_j(k)) + w_j(k)
\end{aligned}
$$

Estimation of the system state is performed by effective weighted fusion, and the state variable (e.g., position, speed, etc.) can be corrected in real time. The adaptability can well overcome the problem of large single-model estimation error.

The unscented Kalman filter (UKF) is a nonlinear and distribution approximation method, which uses a finite number of sigma points to propagate the probability of state distribution through the nonlinear dynamics of system. Unscented Transform (UT) is the basic core of UKF method, which is a method to calculate the statistical characteristics of random variables after nonlinear transformation. UT transformation is based on prior information, and it is easier to approximate the probability density distribution of nonlinear function than to approximate its function. On the premise that the sampling mean and covariance are ensured, a set of Sigma points are selected. The nonlinear transformation is applied to each Sigma point in the sample, and the nonlinear transformation points are obtained by substituting into the nonlinear function.

The IMMUKF algorithm uses model probabilities to weight the input and output of parallel UKF at each time instant. The approach takes into account a set of models to represent the system behavior patterns or system model. The overall estimates is obtained by a combination of the estimates from the filters running in parallel based on the individual models that match the system modes. In each cycle, four major steps are involved: interaction, filtering, mode probability calculation, and combination[15].

3.1. Model interaction

For given states $\mathbf{x}^j_{k-1} = \mathbf{x}^j_{k-1|k-1}$ with corresponding covariances $\mathbf{P}^j_{k-1} = \mathbf{P}^j_{k-1|k-1}$ and mixing probabilities $\boldsymbol{\mu}^{i|j}_{k-1|k-1}$ for each model, , the initial condition for model j is:

$$\hat{\mathbf{x}}^{0j}_{k-1|k-1} = \sum_{i=1}^{r} \hat{\mathbf{x}}^{i}_{k-1|k-1}\boldsymbol{\mu}^{i|j}_{k-1|k-1}, \quad j = 1,2,...,r \tag{5}$$

with the covariance corresponding to the above is:

$$\mathbf{P}^{0j}_{k-1|k-1} = \sum_{i=1}^{r} \boldsymbol{\mu}^{i|j}_{k-1|k-1}\{\mathbf{P}^{i}_{k-1|k-1} + [\hat{\mathbf{x}}^{i}_{k-1|k-1} - \hat{\mathbf{x}}^{0j}_{k-1|k-1}][\hat{\mathbf{x}}^{i}_{k-1|k-1} - \hat{\mathbf{x}}^{0j}_{k-1|k-1}]^T\} \tag{6}$$

The model transition probabilities are related to Markov chain and are defined as:

$$\pi_{ij} = p\{M^j_k \mid M^i_{k-1}\} = \begin{bmatrix} \pi_{11} & \pi_{12} & \mathrm{K} & \pi_{1j} \\ \pi_{21} & \pi_{22} & \mathrm{K} & \pi_{2j} \\ \mathrm{M} & \mathrm{M} & \mathrm{O} & \mathrm{M} \\ \pi_{i1} & \pi_{i2} & \mathrm{K} & \pi_{ij} \end{bmatrix} \tag{7}$$

where $i, j = 1,2,..., r$, and r is the number of sub-models. Calculating the mixing probabilities with mode switching probability matrix π_{ij} and the Gaussian mixing probabilities are computed via the equations:

$$\boldsymbol{\mu}^{ij}_{k-1|k-1} = \frac{1}{\bar{\mathbf{c}}_j}\pi_{ij}\boldsymbol{\mu}^{i}_{k-1} \tag{8}$$

where $\bar{\mathbf{c}}_j$ is a normalization factor:

$$\bar{\mathbf{c}}_j = \sum_{i=1}^{r} \pi_{ij}\boldsymbol{\mu}^{i}_{k-1} \tag{9}$$

3.2 Model filtering using UKF

- ***Stage 1 in UKF loop***. The unscented transform creates $2n+1$ sigma vectors $\mathbf{X}$ and weighted points W . For state estimation at instant $k-1$, sigma points are generated according to

$$\begin{cases} \mathbf{X}^j_{0,k-1} = \hat{\mathbf{x}}^{0j}_{k-1} \\ \mathbf{X}^j_{i,k-1} = \hat{\mathbf{x}}^{0j}_{k-1} + (\sqrt{(n+\lambda)\mathbf{P}^{0j}_{k-1}})^T_i \\ \mathbf{X}^j_{i+n,k-1} = \hat{\mathbf{x}}^{0j}_{k-1} - (\sqrt{(n+\lambda)\mathbf{P}^{0j}_{k-1}})^T_i \end{cases}, \quad i = 1,...,n \tag{10}$$

where $(\sqrt{(n+\lambda)\mathbf{P}^{0j}_{k-1}})_i$ is the i th row (or column) of the matrix square root. $\sqrt{(n+\lambda)\mathbf{P}^{0j}_{k-1}}$ can be obtained from the lower-triangular matrix of the Cholesky factorization; $\lambda = \alpha^2(n+k) - n$ is a scaling parameter for controling the covariance matrix; α determines the spread of the sigma points and is usually set to a small positive (e.g., $1e-4 \le \alpha \le 1$) ; k is a secondly scaling parameter (usually set as 0); β is used to incorporate prior knowledge of the distribution of $\bar{\mathbf{x}}$ (When $\mathbf{x}$ is normally distributed, $\beta = 2$ is an optimal value); $W^{(m)}_i$ is the weight for the mean associated with the i th point; and $W^{(c)}_i$ is the weigh for the covariance associated with the i th point, given by

$$W^{(m)}_0 = \frac{\lambda}{(n+\lambda)} \tag{11a}$$

$$W^{(c)}_0 = W^{(m)}_0 + (1-\alpha^2+\beta) \tag{11b}$$

$$W^{(m)}_i = W^{(c)}_i = \frac{1}{2(n+\lambda)}, \quad i = 1,...,2n \tag{11c}$$

- ***Stage 2 in UKF loop***. Time update/prediction steps

$$\zeta^j_{i,k|k-1} = f_j(\mathbf{X}^j_{i,k-1}), \; i = 0,...,2n \tag{12}$$

$$\hat{\mathbf{x}}^j_{k|k-1} = \sum_{i=0}^{2n} W_i^{(m)} \zeta^j_{i,k|k-1} \tag{13}$$

$$\mathbf{P}^j_{k|k-1} = \sum_{i=0}^{2n} W_i^{(c)} [\zeta^j_{i,k|k-1} - \hat{\mathbf{x}}^j_{k|k-1}][\zeta^j_{i,k|k-1} - \hat{\mathbf{x}}^j_{k|k-1}]^T + \mathbf{Q}^j_{k-1} \tag{14}$$

$$\mathbf{Z}^j_{i,k|k-1} = h(\zeta^j_{i,k|k-1}) \tag{15}$$

$$\hat{\mathbf{z}}^j_{k|k-1} = \sum_{i=0}^{2n} W_i^{(m)} \mathbf{Z}^j_{i,k|k-1} \tag{16}$$

- ***Stage 3 in UKF loop***. Measurement update/ correction steps

$$\mathbf{P}^j_{zz} = \sum_{i=0}^{2n} W_i^{(c)} [\mathbf{Z}^j_{i,k|k-1} - \hat{\mathbf{z}}^j_{k|k-1}][\mathbf{Z}^j_{i,k|k-1} - \hat{\mathbf{z}}^j_{k|k-1}]^T + \mathbf{R}^j_k \tag{17}$$

$$\mathbf{P}^j_{xz} = \sum_{i=0}^{2n} W_i^{(c)} [\zeta^j_{i,k|k-1} - \hat{\mathbf{x}}^j_{k|k-1}][\mathbf{Z}^j_{i,k|k-1} - \hat{\mathbf{z}}^j_{k|k-1}]^T \tag{18}$$

$$\mathbf{K}^j_k = \mathbf{P}^j_{xz} (\mathbf{P}^j_{zz})^{-1} \tag{19}$$

$$\hat{\mathbf{x}}^j_{k|k} = \hat{\mathbf{x}}^j_{k|k-1} + \mathbf{K}^j_k \boldsymbol{\upsilon}^j_k \tag{20}$$

where

$$\boldsymbol{\upsilon}^j_k = \mathbf{z}_k - \hat{\mathbf{z}}^j_{k|k-1} \tag{21}$$

$$\mathbf{P}^j_{k|k} = \mathbf{P}^j_{k|k-1} - \mathbf{K}^j_k \mathbf{P}^j_{zz} \mathbf{K}^{jT}_k \tag{22}$$

The samples are propagated through true nonlinear equations so that the linearization is unnecessary and calculation of the Jacobian matrix is not required.

2.3 Model probabilities update

According to the model likelihood and model transition probability governed by the finite-state Markov chain, the model probability $\boldsymbol{\mu}^j_k$ is updated:

$$\boldsymbol{\mu}^j_k = \frac{1}{c} \Lambda^j_k \bar{\mathbf{c}}_j \tag{23}$$

where

$$c = \sum_{j=1}^{r} \bar{\mathbf{c}}_j \Lambda^j_k \tag{24}$$

and

$$\Lambda^j_k = \frac{1}{\sqrt{2\pi |\mathbf{P}^j_{zz}|}} \exp\left[-\frac{1}{2} \boldsymbol{\upsilon}^{jT}_k (\mathbf{P}^j_{zz})^{-1} \boldsymbol{\upsilon}^j_k\right] \tag{25}$$

2.4 Combination of model-individual estimates and covariances

The model-individual estimates and covariances are combined to overall estimates of state and covariance.

$$\hat{\mathbf{x}}_{k|k} = \sum_{j=1}^{r} \hat{\mathbf{x}}^j_{k|k} \boldsymbol{\mu}^j_k \tag{26}$$

$$\mathbf{P}_{k|k} = \sum_{j=1}^{r} \boldsymbol{\mu}^j_k \{\mathbf{P}^j_{k|k} + [\hat{\mathbf{x}}^j_{k|k} - \hat{\mathbf{x}}_{k|k}][\hat{\mathbf{x}}^j_{k|k} - \hat{\mathbf{x}}_{k|k}]^T\} \tag{27}$$

4 Fuzzy adaptive filter strategy

Fig. 1 shows the flow chart of the proposed fuzzy-IMMUKF implementation. The two blocks indicated by the dashed-line are the fuzzy logic adaptive systems for determining the value of process noise covariance. The rest represents the IMMUKF loop.

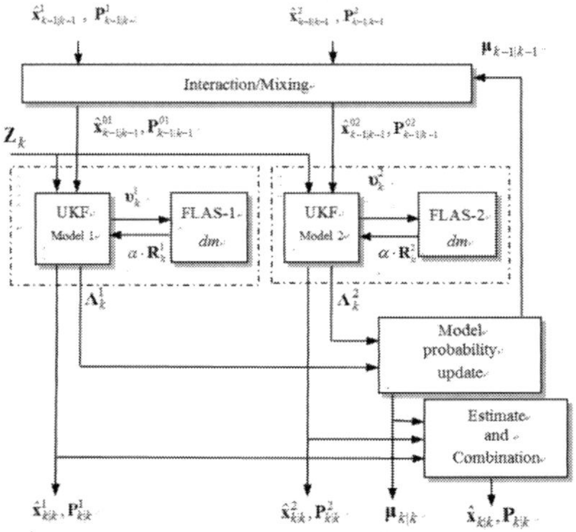

Fig. 1. Flow chart of the Fuzzy-IMMUKF.

4.1 The fuzzy logic adaptive system (FLAS)

Initially proposed by L.A. Zadeh in 1965, the fuzzy set theory provides a logical system to deal with the logic of human reasoning process, and can be used to design an intelligent system to resolve semantic analysis or descriptive language. As a result, the fuzzy system can be defined as using fuzzy set theory and fuzzy logic, and combined with the traditional control theory. That is especially useful for applying to a system where a mathematical model is difficult to establish.

A fuzzy system is used to detect the divergence and adapt the filter parameters of UKF. Mamdani proposed a fuzzy modeling approach to model nonlinear systems. The output is the weighted mean of the y:

$$y = \frac{\sum_{i=1}^{u} u_y(w_i) w_i}{\sum_{i=1}^{u} w_i} \tag{28}$$

where u represents the membership function, weights w_i is calculated by norm operator. The basic structure of the fuzzy system is shown in Fig. 2

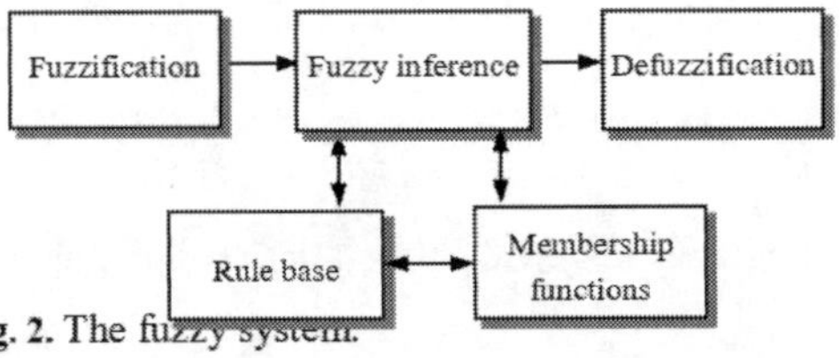

Fig. 2. The fuzzy system.

4.2 The fuzzy interacting multiple model unscented Kalman filter

A covariation matching technology is employed as the basis for adaption. The design of fuzzy inference system for real-time tuning of the measurement noise covariance is adopted according to the ratio of innovation covariance and the theoretical covariance, hence the accuracy and reliability of the filter are improved.

The calculation of UKF gain is rewritten as follows:

$$\mathbf{K}_k = \mathbf{P}_{xz}(\mathbf{P}_{zz})^{-1}$$

where

$$\mathbf{P}_{zz} = \sum_{i=0}^{2n} W_i^{(c)}[\mathbf{Z}_{i,k|k-1} - \hat{\mathbf{z}}_{k|k-1}][\mathbf{Z}_{i,k|k-1} - \hat{\mathbf{z}}_{k|k-1}]^T + \mathbf{R}'_k$$

The parameter referred to as the degree of matching (dm) is defined as follows:

$$dm = \frac{tr(C_{\upsilon_k})}{tr(\mathbf{P}_{zz})} \tag{29}$$

The innovation covariance matrix with length N is given by:

$$C_{\upsilon_k} = \frac{1}{N}\sum_{j=j_0}^{k} \upsilon_j \upsilon_j^T \tag{30}$$

The predicted residual is defined as the difference between the observed measurement of the filter and the predicted one, and is given by $\upsilon_k^j = \mathbf{z}_k - \hat{\mathbf{z}}_{k|k-1}^j$. In order to tune $\mathbf{R}_k$, the parameter $\mathbf{R}'_k = \xi \cdot \mathbf{R}_k$ is defined, and ξ is the measurement noise tunning factor. According to the above analysis, when $\mathbf{R}_k$ is appropriately tuned, dm sholud approach 1. If the strength of the measurement noise increases, dm should increase. For such case, $\mathbf{R}_k$ should be enlarged so as to bring dm back to 1. On the contrary, in the case that measurement noise decreases, dm should also decrease and $\mathbf{R}_k$ should be reduced so as to bring dm back to 1. When ξ=1 , it becomes the ordinary measurement noise covariance.

The input of the fuzzy controller is dm and the output is ξ . There are three fuzzy sets for the input, namely normal、large、small. The Sugeno type fuzzy logic system is employed, where the If-Then form consists of three rules for each of the two FLAS systems.

For the FLAS in Model 1

1. If dm is small Then $\xi = dm + 0.3$
2. If dm is normal Then $\xi = 1$
3. If dm is large Then $\xi = 2 * dm + 5$

For the FLAS in Model 2

1. If dm is small Then $\xi = dm + 0.5$
2. If dm is normal Then $\xi = 1$
3. If dm is large Then $\xi = 2 * dm + 20$

The membership functions are shown in Fig. 3

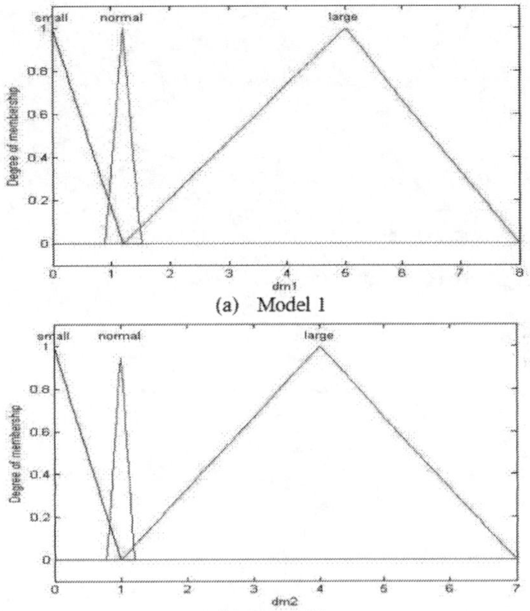

(a) Model 1

(b) Model 2

Fig. 3. Membership functions of the output fuzzy variable ξ for the two models in the IMM.

5 Simulation experiments and analysis

Simulation experiments have been carried out to evaluate the performance of the proposed approach in comparison with the conventional methods for GPS navigation processing. To validate the effectiveness of the proposed approach in time varying satellite signal quality, simulation is conducted for tuning the measurement noise covariance. The commercial software Satellite Navigation (SATNAV) Toolbox by GPSoft LLC was employed for generating the satellite positions and pseudoranges. The satellite constellation was simulated and the error sources corrupting GPS measurements include ionospheric delay, tropospheric delay, receiver noise and multipath. Assume that the differential GPS mode is used and most of the errors can be corrected, but the multipath and receiver thermal noise cannot be eliminated. The multipath interfences are added into the GPS pseudorange observation data during the vehicle moving. For testing the performance due to outlier type multipath interference, there are totally 5 durations where additional randomly generated bias errors are intentionally injected onto. Since the research focus on the mitigation of outlier type multipath errors, the influence of measurement noise $\mathbf{R}_k$ is relatively critical. A vehicle is designed to perform the uniform motion to reduce the impact on the $\mathbf{Q}_k$ caused by unmodelling system dynamic errors. The test trajectory for the simulated vehicle is shown as in Fig. 4. In the simulation, there are 8 GPS satellites available. The skyplot during the simulation time interval is shown as in Fig. 5.

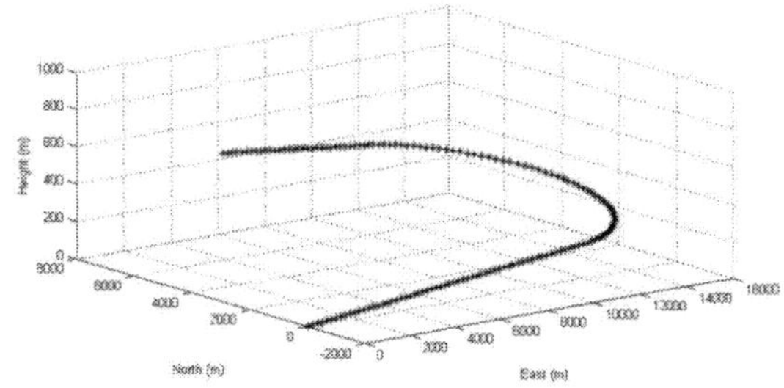

Fig. 4. Test trajectory for the simulated vehicle.

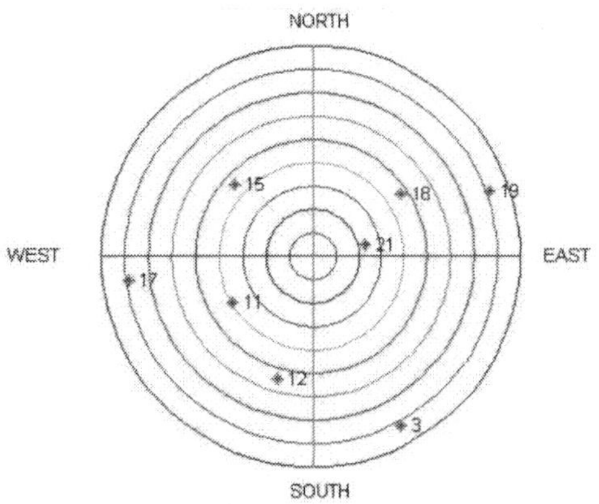

Fig. 5. The skyplot in the simulation.

5.1 Comparison for UKF and IMMUKF

GPS navigation accuracy comparsion for UKF and IMMUKF is shown in Fig. 6. Fig. 7 provides the model probabilty based on the IMMUKF method. The uncertainty of the noise can be described by a set of switching models, this modelling approach makes it possible to employ the multiple model estimation to deal with the problem of nonlinear filtering with noise uncertainty. The interaction multiple models used in this paper is employed for dealing with the measurement uncertainty by tuning the tuning $\mathbf{R}_k$.

Although it can be seen that the IMMUKF does provide improved accuracy than the UKF, however, it doesn't mitigate the multipath error remarkably.

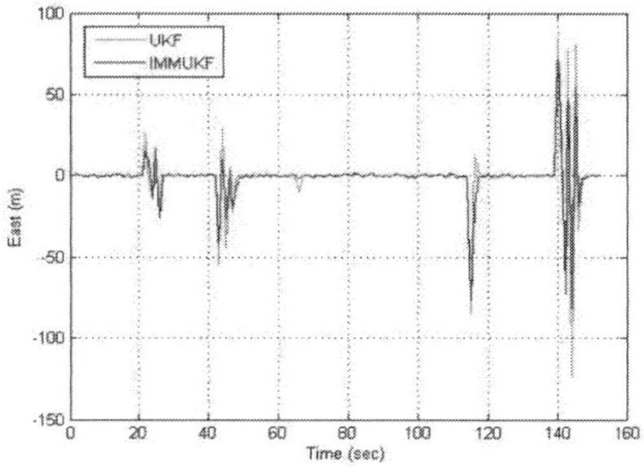

(a) East

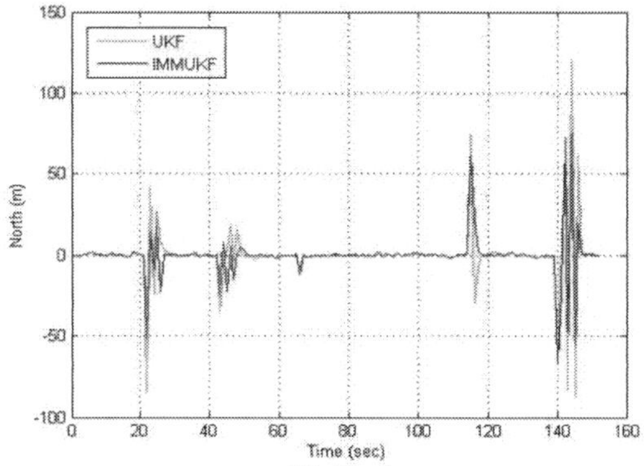

(b) North

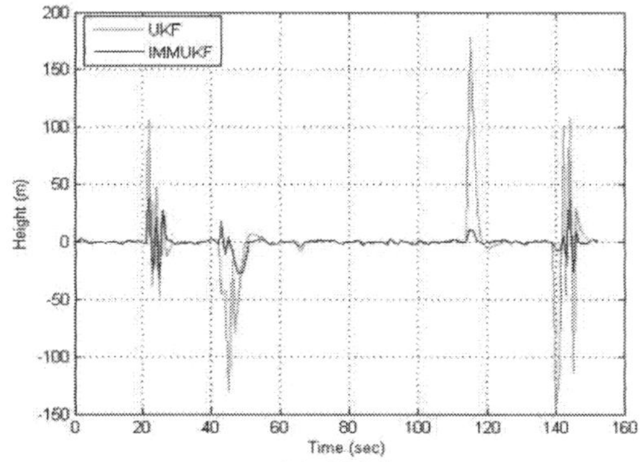

(c) Height

Fig. 6. Navigation accuracy comparsion for UKF and IMMUKF.

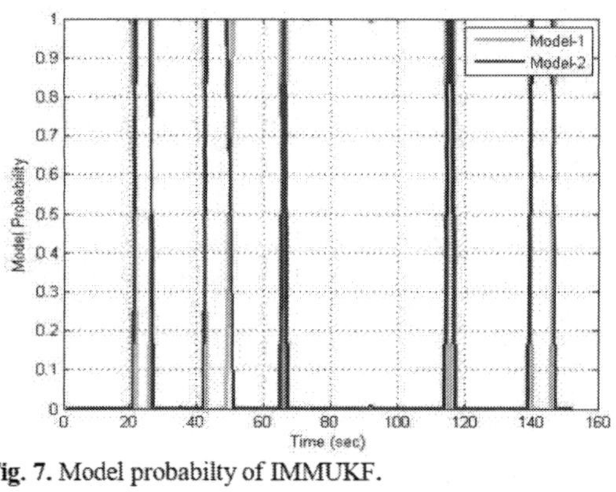

Fig. 7. Model probabilty of IMMUKF.

5.2 Further performance enhancement using Fuzzy-IMMUKF

Utilization of the fuzzy-IMMUKF is the other treatment for further performance enhancement. Positioning accuracy comparsion for IMMUKF and Fuzzy-IMMUKF is shown in Fig. 8. Fig. 9 shows the model probabilty of IMMUKF. For enhancing further system performance, the fuzzy logic system is introduced to timely adjust the measurement noise covariance according to the innovation. The use of IMM with FLAS enables tuning of an appropriate value for the measurement noise covariance so as to maintain good estimation accuracy. As can be seen form Fig. 8, the fuzzy-IMMUKF provides remarkable improvement as compared to the IMMUKF. Fig. 10 shows the error comparison of the three types of filters, while Fig. 11 shows comparsion of position RMS errors in meters for the three approaches.

6 Conclusions

This paper has presented a fuzzy logic based interacting multiple model unscented Kalman filter for GPS navigation processing for the outlier types of multipath errors. Multipath mitigation is crucial for improvement of the positioning accuracy. The conventional unscented Kalman filter does not possess the capability to monitor the change of parameters due to changes in measurement model. An interacting multiple-model based method is suggested to improve the unscented Kalman filter for navigation processing. The resulting IMMUKF exhibits superior navigation accuracy when compared with the classical UKF algorithm. The fuzzy system can be employed to enhance the IMMUKF performance. The fuzzy system is employed for dynamically adjusting the measurement noise covariance, which will be used in each of the parallel filters in the IMM architecture by monitoring the innovation information so as to provide further improvement in estimation accuracy. By monitoring the degree of matching between the estimated innovation covariance and the theoretical one such that the measurement noise covariance matrix is tuned in real time. These performance comparisons of UKF, IMMUKF and Fuzzy-IMMUKF have been carried out and the proposed Fuzzy-IMMUKF algorithm has demonstrated very promising results in navigational accuracy improvement.

Acknowledgements
Funding for this work was provided by the Ministry of Science and Technology of the Republic of China under grant number MOST 107-2221-E-019-025.

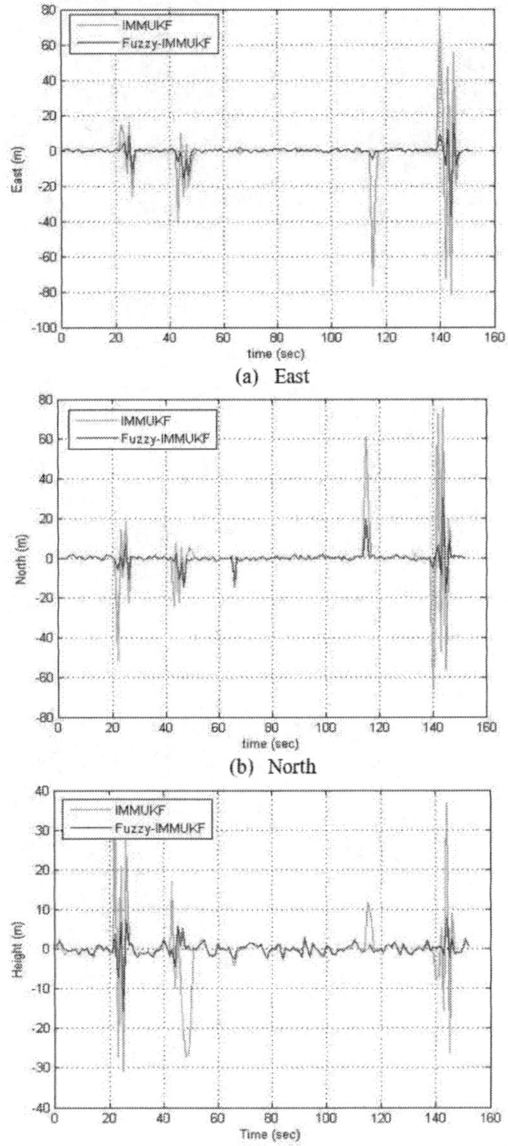

(c) Height

Fig. 8. Positioning accuracy comparsion for IMMUKF and fuzzy-IMMUKF.

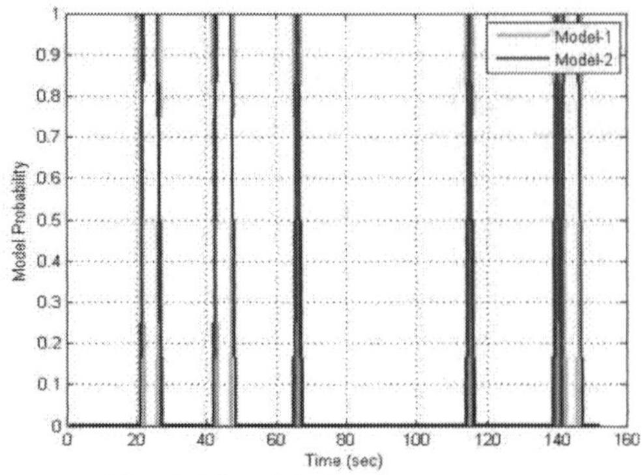

Fig. 9. Model probabilty of the fuzzy-IMMUKF.

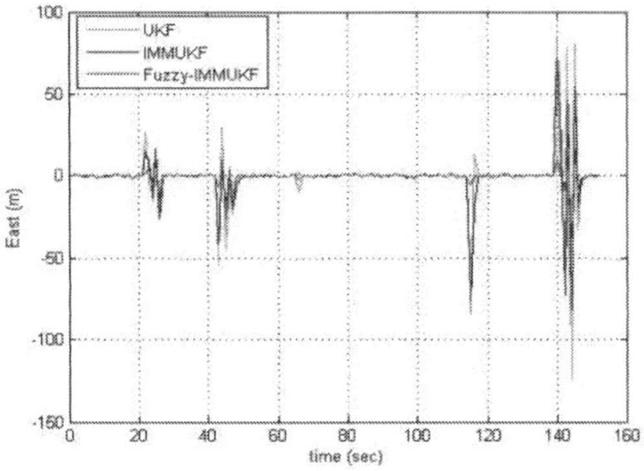

(a) East

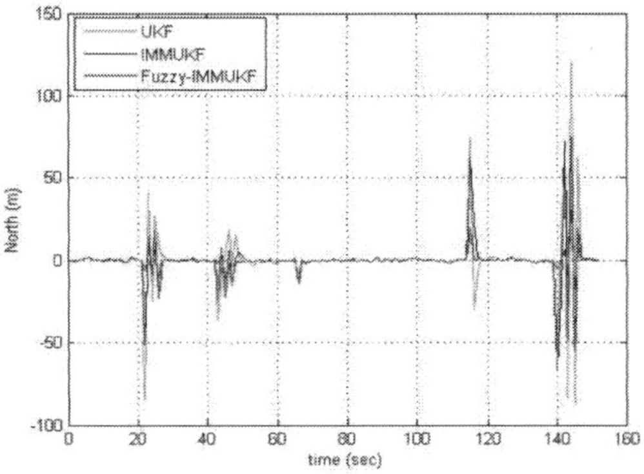

(b) North

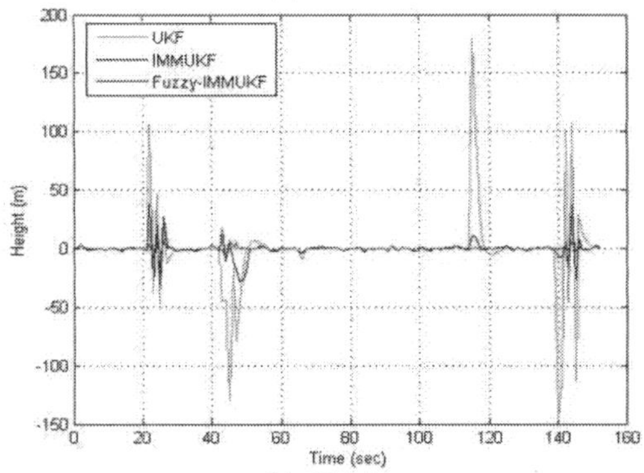

(c) Height

Fig. 10. Positioning accuracy comparsion for UKF, IMMUKF and Fuzzy-IMMUKF.

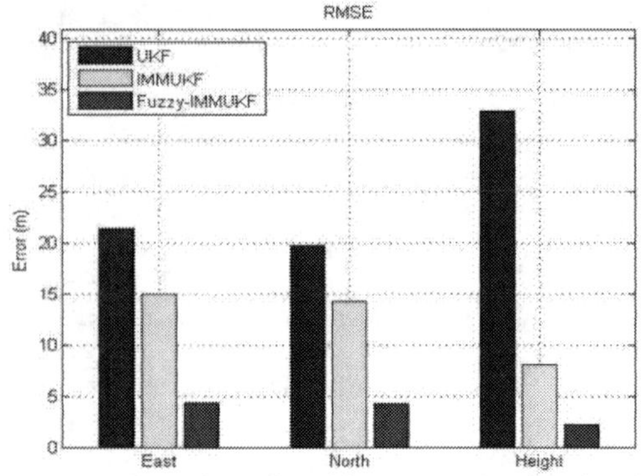

Fig. 11. Comparsion of position accuracies for the three approaches (RMS errors, in meters)

References

1. L. Cheng, H.Yue, G.Xie, M. F. Ren, Multipath Estimation Using an Intelligent Optimization Algorithm with Non-Gaussian Noise, Proceedings of the 23rd International Conference on Automation & Computing, UK (2017).
2. N. Sunderhauf, M. Obst, G. Wanielik and P. Protzel, Multipath Mitigation in GNSS-based Localization using Robust Optimization, Proc. of IEEE Intelligent Vehicles Symposium, 2012.
3. N.-S. Zheng, L.-S. Cai, H.-F. Bian, C. Lin, Hybrid particle filtering algorithm for GPS multipath mitigation, Transactions of Nonferrous Metals Society of China, Volume 24, Issue 5, May 2014, pp. 1554-1561.
4. S. Zair, S. L. Hegarat-Mascle and E. Seignez, Outlier Detection in GNSS Pseudo-Range/Doppler Measurements for Robust Localization, Sensors, **16**, 580, 22 pages (2016).
5. A. Pirsiavash, A. Broumandan and G. Lachapelle, Characterization of Signal Quality Monitoring Techniques for Multipath Detection in GNSS Applications, Sensors, 2017, **17**, 1579, 24 pages.
6. B. W. Parkinson, J. Spilker, P. Axelrad and P. Enge, *Global Positioning System: Theory and Applications*, Am. Inst. Aeronaut. Astronaut., Washington D. C., (1996)
7. E. A. Wan R. Van der Merwe, The unscented Kalman filter for nonlinear estimation, In Proc. of IEEE Symposium 2000 (AS-SPCC) (Lake Louise, Oct 2000).
8. D. J. Jwo and C. N. Lai, Unscented Kalman filter with nonlinear dynamic process modeling for GPS navigation, GPS Solutions, **12**, pp. 249-260 (2008).
9. H. X. Nie , J. Guan , H. W. Bian, Fuzzy Adaptive Kalman Filtering in INS/ GPS Integrated Navigation System, Ship Electronic Engineering,**Vol. 31** No.167 (2011)
10. A. H. Mohamed, K. P. Schwarz, Adaptive Kalman filtering for INS/GPS, Journal of Geodesy, **73**, 193-203 (1999)
11. G. Chen and M. Harigae, Using IMM Adaptive Estimator in GPS Positioning, SICE, pp. 25-27 (2001).

12. Y. Chong, K. Zhang and M. Lu, Exploring a Better IMM-UKF Fusion Algorithm Based on Current Statistical Model in Target Tracking, Journal of Northwestern Polytechnical University, Vol.**29**, No.6, December (2011).
13. R. C. Zang , P. Y. Cui , H. T. Cui ,Y. Jin, Integrated navigation algorithm based on IMM-UKF, Control Theory & Applications, Vol. **24**, No.4 (2007)
14. D. J. Jwo, F. C. Chung, K. L. Yu, GPS/INS Integration Accuracy Enhancement Using the Interacting Multiple Model Nonlinear Filters, Journal of Applied Research and Technology, **Vol. 11**, , pp.496-509 (2013)
15. C. H. Tseng, C.-W. Chang and D. J. Jwo, Fuzzy Adaptive Multiple Model Using Nonlinear Filter for Integrated Navigation Sensor Fusion, Sensors, **11**, 2090-2111 (2011)

Stereo visual-inertial odometry with an online calibration and its field testing

Jae Hyung Jung[1], *Sejong Heo*[2], and *Chan Gook Park*[1*]

[1]Dept. of Mechanical & Aerospace Engineering / Automation and Systems Research Institute, Seoul National University, Republic of Korea
[2]Hanwha Corporation/Defense, Republic of Korea

Abstract. In this paper, we present a visual-inertial odometry (VIO) with an online calibration using a stereo camera in planetary rover localization. We augment the state vector with extrinsic (rigid body transformation) and temporal (time-offset) parameters of a camera-IMU system in a framework of an extended Kalman filter. This is motivated by the fact that when fusing independent systems, it is practically crucial to obtain precise extrinsic and temporal parameters. Unlike the conventional calibration procedures, this method estimates both navigation and calibration states from naturally occurred visual point features during operation. We describe mathematical formulations of the proposed method, and it is evaluated through the author-collected dataset which is recorded by the commercially available visual-inertial sensor installed on the testing rover in the environment lack of vegetation and artificial objects. Our experimental results showed that 3D return position error as 1.54m of total 173m traveled and 10ms of time-offset with the online calibration, while 6.52m of return position error without the online calibration.

1 Introduction

Ego-motion estimation is one of the most crucial tasks for unmanned vehicles such as planetary rovers or autonomous driving cars to successfully carry out their missions. However, to deal with the absence or outage of GNSS signals, alternative navigation algorithms should be considered. For instance, NASA's Martian rovers are equipped with stereo cameras and localize itself by the vision-based navigation called visual odometry (VO) [1]. While VO suffers from the well-known error accumulation, visual-inertial odometry (VIO) decreases its rate by filling a gap between small baselined images using IMU readings [2]. A fusion of a camera and IMU is an attractive solution due to their complementary features.

Most of the visual-inertial fusion algorithms assume that output data from a camera and IMU is timely synchronized and the sensors are spatially well aligned. However, this causes significant estimation errors when time-delay of a camera is not negligible or a camera-IMU system is not well calibrated since the measurement model is linearized around the currently available estimate referenced at the camera frame. Even if a camera-IMU system is calibrated in advance, this cannot reflect uncertainties on calibration parameters to an estimator. In the worst case, calibration parameters could be changed due to external shocks.

Many efforts to deal with the above issue has been made. The authors of [3] showed that the cam-IMU extrinsic parameter, the scale factor, and the global gravity is observable with the global pose measurements.

Fig. 1. Testing rover mounted the visual-inertial sensor

However, the measurement model which assumes that images output global poses was somewhat unrealistic. Guo et al. in [4] proved that cam-IMU extrinsic parameter is observable using the proposed basis functions under the known depth (feature point) assumption. The work of [5] focused on the temporal calibration of a cam-IMU system. They theoretically showed that time-offset between cam-IMU system can be recovered, while practically implemented the online calibration algorithm in the extended Kalman filter (EKF) framework. Also in [6], camera intrinsics, as well as IMU intrinsics (misalignment, g-sensitivity) was modeled in the estimator.

In this paper, we exploit the theoretic results of [4,5] and formulate EKF-based VIO algorithm using feature point measurements obtained from the stereo camera. Specifically, we augment the state vector with the time-

* Corresponding author: chanpark@snu.ac.kr

offset and extrinsic parameter. Fig. 1 shows the testing rover equipped with the visual-inertial sensor to record the dataset which lacks artificial object and vegetation.

2 The filter description

The error state vector of the presented algorithm consists of the 15th order of IMU state, the calibration parameters: cam-IMU time-offset, extrinsic parameter and the sliding window pose/velocity as in Eq. (1).

$$\begin{aligned}\tilde{\mathbf{x}} &= \begin{bmatrix}\tilde{\mathbf{x}}_I^{\mathrm{T}} & \tilde{\mathbf{x}}_C^{\mathrm{T}} & \tilde{\mathbf{x}}_S^{\mathrm{T}}\end{bmatrix}^{\mathrm{T}} \\ \tilde{\mathbf{x}}_I &= \begin{bmatrix}\tilde{\boldsymbol{\theta}}_{GB}^{\mathrm{T}} & {}^G\tilde{\mathbf{p}}_B^{\mathrm{T}} & {}^G\tilde{\mathbf{v}}_B^{\mathrm{T}} & \tilde{\mathbf{b}}_a^{\mathrm{T}} & \tilde{\mathbf{b}}_g^{\mathrm{T}}\end{bmatrix}^{\mathrm{T}} \in \mathbb{R}^{15} \\ \tilde{\mathbf{x}}_C &= \begin{bmatrix}\tilde{\boldsymbol{\theta}}_{CB}^{\mathrm{T}} & {}^C\tilde{\mathbf{p}}_B^{\mathrm{T}} & t_d\end{bmatrix} \in \mathbb{R}^7 \\ \tilde{\mathbf{x}}_S &= \begin{bmatrix}\tilde{\boldsymbol{\theta}}_{GB_i}^{\mathrm{T}} & {}^G\tilde{\mathbf{p}}_{B_i}^{\mathrm{T}} & {}^G\tilde{\mathbf{v}}_{B_i}^{\mathrm{T}}\end{bmatrix} \in \mathbb{R}^{9N}\end{aligned} \tag{1}$$

In this expression, we denote the global frame as $\{G\}$, the camera frame as $\{C\}$, the body (IMU) frame as $\{B\}$, and the number of sliding window as N. Also, we define the error state as $\tilde{\mathbf{x}} = \mathbf{x} - \hat{\mathbf{x}}$ where $\hat{\mathbf{x}}$ means estimated value. For instance, $\tilde{\boldsymbol{\theta}}_{GB}$ is an attitude error expressed in a 3-dimensional vector, ${}^G\tilde{\mathbf{p}}_B$ and ${}^G\tilde{\mathbf{v}}_B$ are a position and velocity error expressed in $\{G\}$. Also, $\tilde{\boldsymbol{\theta}}_{CB}$ and ${}^C\tilde{\mathbf{p}}_B$ are extrinsic parameter error in a cam-IMU system, t_d is a cam-IMU time-offset due to latency in sensors defined as in [5]. Note that we include the sliding window velocity in the state vector since the measurement Jacobian matrix requires the current estimate of the velocity.

1.1 Prediction step

The IMU measurements are modeled as Eq. (3) with the zero-mean white Gaussian noise process (**n**), and the random walk process (**b**).

$$\begin{aligned}\mathbf{a}_m(t) &= \mathbf{R}_B^G(t)\left({}^G\mathbf{a}(t) - {}^G\mathbf{g}\right) + \mathbf{b}_a(t) + \mathbf{n}_a(t) \\ \mathbf{w}_m(t) &= \mathbf{w}_t(t) + \mathbf{b}_g(t) + \mathbf{n}_g(t)\end{aligned} \tag{3}$$

Where ${}^G\mathbf{a}(t)$ is the true acceleration of the sensing platform, ${}^G\mathbf{g}$ is the global gravity that is approximately $[0 \;\; 0 \;\; 9.81]^{\mathrm{T}}$ m/s^2 . The error-state continuous time propagation is as follow, while calibration-related states are assumed to be constant.

$$\begin{aligned}\dot{\tilde{\mathbf{x}}}_I(t) &= \mathbf{F}_I(t)\tilde{\mathbf{x}}_I(t) + \mathbf{G}_I(t)\mathbf{n}_I(t) \\ \mathbf{n}_I(t) &= \begin{bmatrix}\mathbf{n}_a^{\mathrm{T}}(t) & \mathbf{n}_g^{\mathrm{T}}(t) & \mathbf{n}_{wa}^{\mathrm{T}}(t) & \mathbf{n}_{wg}^{\mathrm{T}}(t)\end{bmatrix}^{\mathrm{T}} \\ \dot{\mathbf{b}}_a(t) &= \mathbf{n}_{wa} \\ \dot{\mathbf{b}}_g(t) &= \mathbf{n}_{wg}\end{aligned} \tag{4}$$

In Eq. (4), $\mathbf{n}_{wa}$ and $\mathbf{n}_{wg}$ are zero-mean white Gaussian noise processes. The nominal IMU state is integrated through the closed-form state-transition matrix derived in [7].

1.2 Calibration parameter error modeling

To deal with the calibration parameters of a cam-IMU system, their error state should be modeled in the measurement model. Note that the extrinsic parameter is observable under the point features [4], and the time-offset is also observable up to the time referenced at an IMU [5]. These motivate us to jointly estimate the parameters along with the navigation solution in a stereo vision scenario which provides reliable depth information.

In order to build constraints among multiple views for point features, sliding window poses/velocity should be augmented to the state vector. Propagating the current IMU state up to the time-offset (t_d), the sliding window state is as follow,

$$\tilde{\mathbf{x}}_{S_i} = \begin{bmatrix}\tilde{\boldsymbol{\theta}}_{GB_i}^{\mathrm{T}}(t+\hat{t}_d) & {}^G\tilde{\mathbf{p}}_{B_i}^{\mathrm{T}}(t+\hat{t}_d) & {}^G\tilde{\mathbf{v}}_{B_i}^{\mathrm{T}}(t+\hat{t}_d)\end{bmatrix}^{\mathrm{T}} \tag{5}$$

Accordingly, the Jacobian matrix with regard to the IMU state is

$$\tilde{\mathbf{x}}_{S_i} \approx \begin{bmatrix}\mathbf{I}_9 & \mathbf{0}_{9\times6} & \mathbf{0}_{9\times6} & \mathbf{J}_{t_d} & \mathbf{0}_9\end{bmatrix}\tilde{\mathbf{x}}_I(t+t_d) \tag{6}$$

Where $\mathbf{J}_{t_d}$ is the Jacobian related to the time-offset, and can be derived using 1st order approximation,

$$\mathbf{J}_{t_d} = \begin{bmatrix}\hat{\mathbf{R}}_B^G(t+\hat{t}_d)\left\{\mathbf{w}_m - \hat{\mathbf{b}}_g(t+\hat{t}_d)\right\} \\ {}^G\hat{\mathbf{v}}_B(t+\hat{t}_d) \\ \hat{\mathbf{R}}_B^G(t+\hat{t}_d)\left\{\mathbf{a}_m - \hat{\mathbf{b}}_a(t+\hat{t}_d)\right\} + {}^G\mathbf{g}\end{bmatrix} \in \mathbb{R}^9 \tag{7}$$

Assuming that a stereo camera is well calibrated in advance, the point feature measurement model is

$$\begin{aligned}\mathbf{z}(t) &= \begin{bmatrix}1/Z_L\,\mathbf{I}_2 & \mathbf{0}_2 \\ \mathbf{0}_2 & 1/Z_R\,\mathbf{I}_2\end{bmatrix}\begin{bmatrix}{}^{C_L}\mathbf{p}_f(1:2) \\ {}^{C_R}\mathbf{p}_f(1:2)\end{bmatrix} + \mathbf{n}_z \\ {}^{C_L}\mathbf{p}_f(t+t_d) &= \begin{bmatrix}X_L & Y_L & Z_L\end{bmatrix}^{\mathrm{T}} \\ {}^{C_R}\mathbf{p}_f(t+t_d) &= \begin{bmatrix}X_R & Y_R & Z_R\end{bmatrix}^{\mathrm{T}}\end{aligned} \tag{8}$$

with zero-mean white Gaussian noise process, $\mathbf{n}_z$. The linearized measurement model is given by,

$$\mathbf{r} = \mathbf{z}(t) - \hat{\mathbf{z}}(t+\hat{t}_d) \approx \mathbf{H}(t+\hat{t}_d)\tilde{\mathbf{x}}(t+\hat{t}_d) + \mathbf{n}_z \tag{9}$$

where **H** matrix is the measurement Jacobian matrix. Specifically, this matrix is computed from the left and right measurements,

$$\mathbf{H}(t+\hat{t}_d) = \left(\frac{\partial \mathbf{z}}{\partial {}^{C_L}\mathbf{p}_f}\frac{\partial {}^{C_L}\mathbf{p}_f}{\partial \mathbf{x}} + \frac{\partial \mathbf{z}}{\partial {}^{C_R}\mathbf{p}_f}\frac{\partial {}^{C_R}\mathbf{p}_f}{\partial \mathbf{x}}\right)_{t+\hat{t}_d} \tag{10}$$

To compute Eq. (10), the global pose is perturbed up to the 1st order Taylor series expansion with respect to the time-offset,

$$\mathbf{R}_B^G(t+t_d) \approx \mathbf{R}_B^G(t+\hat{t}_d) + \dot{\mathbf{R}}_B^G(t+\hat{t}_d)\tilde{t}_d$$
$${}^G\mathbf{p}_B(t+t_d) \approx {}^G\mathbf{p}_B(t+\hat{t}_d) + {}^G\mathbf{v}_B(t+\hat{t}_d)\tilde{t}_d \qquad (11)$$

The linearization in Eq. (11) enables us to model the time-offset in the measurement model.

3 Experimental results

The testing rover in Fig. 1 consists of Pioneer3-AT (rover platform), Xsens MTi-300 (IMU), ZED stereo camera, and the on-board computer for the purpose of data recording. While IMU outputs its data at 200Hz, the stereo camera gives 1280x720 grey images at 15Hz. Although both sensors are timestamped under the ROS environment, the nature of the separate system motivates us to estimate the time-offset. The initial guess of the extrinsic parameter was computed using Kalibr toolbox [8]. Also, a human pilot drove the testing rover returning to the starting point to quantify return position error. The typical environment of the site is shown in Fig. 2 which lacks artificial object and vegetation.

In what follows, we describe details of the vision front-end implementation and field testing results.

3.1 Vision front-end design

Features are provided to the estimator when either tracking fails or the number of tracks exceeds a user-defined maximum sliding window. To obtain reliable sets of feature tracks, we design a stereo feature tracker shown in Fig. 2 as similar to [9]. Assuming that the feature correspondence at t_{k-1} is obtained, features on the left image are tracked to the next time step t_k, then 8-point RANSAC eliminates outlier sets. Survived inliers on the left image are kept tracked to the right image. Again, 8-point RANSAC detects outliers between temporal right images at t_{k-1} and t_k. In the only case when the feature is successfully tracked both the temporal and static tracking, the feature is fed to the estimator. In contrast to a monocular case, the stereo features give scale information due to the baseline. Specifically, we triangulate feature points from the farthest two-view; for instance, the oldest frame in the left and the latest frame in the right before the multi-view triangulation. This strategy enables us to compute the feature depth, even the sensors are in static.

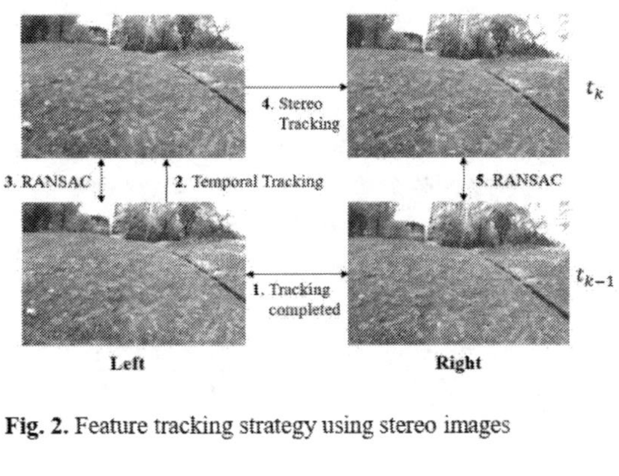

Fig. 2. Feature tracking strategy using stereo images

3.2 Field testing results

To test the presented VIO, the testing rover shown in Fig. 1 traveled the total distance of 173m for 224 seconds commanded by the human pilot. The testing site mainly consisted of soil with small rocks where typical images are shown in Fig .2. To compute an initial attitude with respect to the navigation frame (NED-frame), outputs of the accelerometer at the first 2 seconds were used. Also, the testing rover started from the static state; the initial velocity was set to zero.

To quantify the performance of the algorithm, we compare return position errors among three cases: "full calibration (td + extrinsic)", "partial calibration (only td)" and "no calibration". Table. 1 shows 3D return position of 3 cases in the Cartesian coordinate in which the starting point was $[0 \quad 0 \quad 0]^T \, m$. As expected the full calibration yields the best performance (2-norm) that is 76.4% error decrease when compared to the no calibration. It is interesting to note that the z-axis position of the partial calibration drifted up to -4.07m. We argue that this is due to the inaccurate extrinsic parameter that is computed beforehand. Also, Fig. 3 plots the entire estimated 2D trajectories of all cases. It is clearly seen in Fig. 3 that the no calibration largely drifts after the first 180 deg turning when compared the others.

Fig. 4 plots the estimated time-offset with its 3-sigma envelopes in the full calibration scenario. After quick convergence at the beginning, it converges to -10.3ms. Remind that the sampling time of images is 66.7ms (15Hz), thus the time-offset is not negligible.

Table 1. 3D return position errors for 3 cases

	No Calibration	Partial Calibration	Full Calibration
xyz Return position [m]	-0.8229; 3.3352; -5.5402	0.3627; 0.1956; -4.0725	-1.1922; 0.5711; -0.7856
2-norm [m]	6.52	4.09	1.54

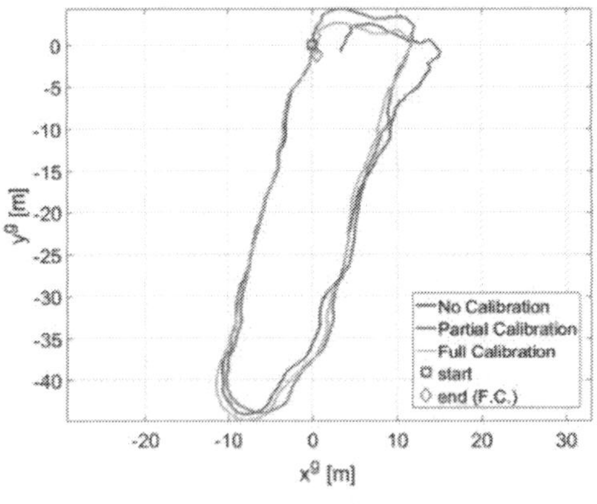

Fig. 3. Estimated 2D trajectory with the online calibration

 https://doi.org/10.1051/e3sconf/20199402005

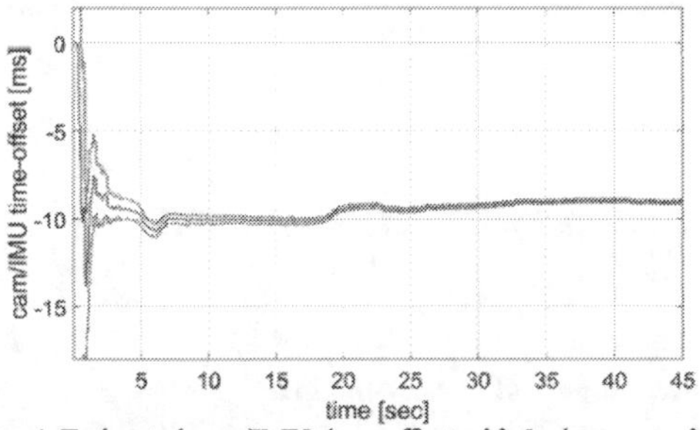

Fig. 4. Estimated cam/IMU time-offset with 3-sigma envelope

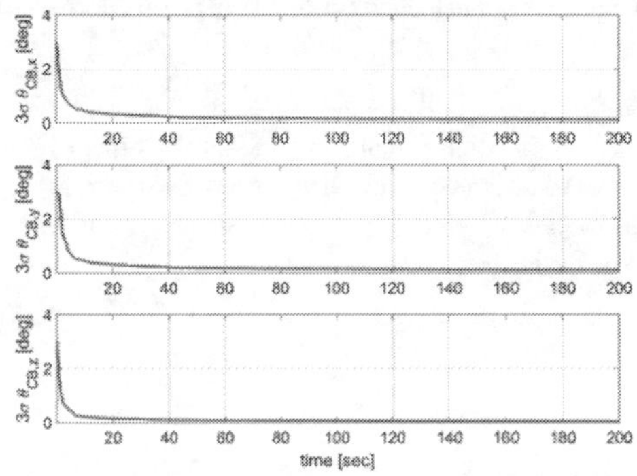

Fig. 5. Cam/IMU relative attitude 3-sigma envelopes

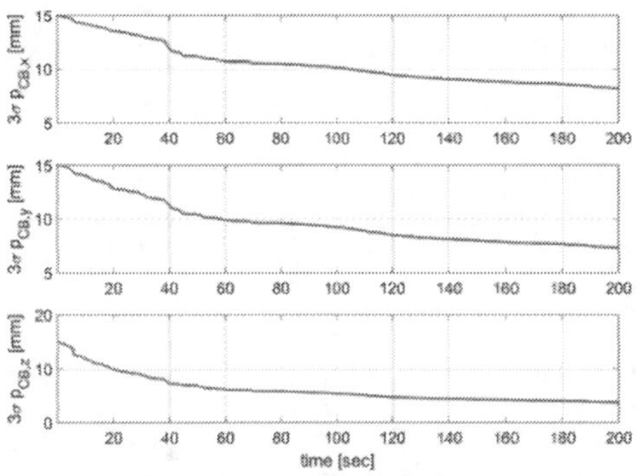

Fig. 6. Cam/IMU relative position 3-sigma envelopes

Fig. 5 and 6 show 3 standard deviations for the cam/IMU extrinsic parameter for each axis in the full calibration. We set the initial standard deviation as 1deg and 5mm respectively to cover the calibration uncertainty. Although we do not have the true value, the standard deviations are decreased as the filter is updated that is consistent results to the observability analysis in [4].

4 Conclusion

In this paper, we have presented the online calibration stereo VIO using naturally occurring point features in which the state vector is augmented by the time-offset and extrinsic parameters. To evaluate the presented VIO, the testing rover with the commercially available visual-inertial sensor recorded the dataset. Our experimental results have shown that when fusing independent sensors their extrinsic calibration is important; the online calibration method reduced the rover's return position error by 76.4% with respect to the no calibration method. Moreover, we experimentally showed that the time-offset and extrinsic parameter were observable under point features that is consistent with the observability analysis.

This work was supported by the Ministry of Science and ICT of the Republic of Korea through the Space Core Technology Development Program under Project NRF-2018M1A3A3A02 065722.

References

1. M. Maimone, Y. Cheng, L. Matthies, J. Field Roboticis, *Two years of visual odometry on the mars exploration rovers*, **24**, 3, 169-186 (2007)
2. D. Scaramuzza, F. Fraundorfer, IEEE robotics & automation magzine, *Visual odometry [tutorial]*, **18**, 4, 80-92 (2011)
3. J. Kelly, G. S. Sukhatme, Int. J. of Robotics Research, *Visual-inertial sensor fusion: Localization, mapping and sensor-to-sensor self-calibration*, **30**, 1, 56-79 (2011)
4. C. X. Guo, S. I. Roumeliotis, IEEE Int. Conf. on Robotics and Automation, *IMU-RGBD camera extrinsic calibration: Observability analysis and consistency improvement,* Proc. IEEE Int. Conf. on Robotics and Automation (2013)
5. M. Li and A. I. Mourikis, Int. J. of Robotics Research, *Online temporal calibration for camera–IMU systems: Theory and algorithms*, **33**, 7, 947-964 (2014)
6. M. Li, H. Yu, X. Zheng, A. I. Mourikis, *High-fidelity sensor modeling and self-calibration in vision-aided inertial navigation*, Proc. IEEE Int. Conf. on Robotics and Automation (2014)
7. M. Li, A. I. Mourikis, Int, J. of Robotics and Research, *High-precision, consistent EKF-based visual-inertial odometry*, **32**, 6, 690-711 (2013)
8. P. Furgale, J. Rehder, R. Siegwart, IEEE Int. Conf. On Intelligent Robots and Systems, *Unified temporal and spatial calibration for multi-sensor systems* (2013)
9. K. Sun, K. Mohtam B. Pfrommer, M. Watterson, S. Liu, Y. Mulgaonkar, C. J. Taylor, V. Kumar, IEEE Robotics and Automation Letters, *Robust stereo visual inertial odometry for fast autonomous flight*, **3**, 2, 965-972 (2018)

 https://doi.org/10.1051/e3sconf/20199402006

Performance analysis of GPS / Radar integrated navigation system

Gwang Hee Jo[1], *Jin Hyuk* Lee[1], *Jae Hee* Noh[1], *Ju Hyun* Lee[2], *Jae Min* Ahn[3], and *Sang Jeong* Lee[1,*],

[1]Department of Electronics Engineering, Chungnam National University, 34134 Daejeon, Korea
[2]Radio Navigation, Navcours, 34014 Daejeon, Korea
[3]Department of Radio and Information Communications Engineering, Chungnam National University, 34134 Daejeon, Korea

Abstract. GPS is used in various navigation fields. However, visibility is lowered in such an environment as urban canyon, and navigation performance deteriorates due to the visibility, multipath effect. So, in order to improve navigation performance in this environment, methods of integration with other sensors have been studied. In this paper, we use radar to measure the range of the landmark with known position. An integration algorithm is designed using GPS pseudorange and radar measurement.

1 Introduction

The Global Positioning System (GPS) transmits Pseudo Random Noise (PRN) codes using Code Division Multiple Access (CDMA). The PRN code is a ranging code used to measure the pseudorange between the satellite and the receiver. The pseudorange is calculated by the position vector of the satellite and the receiver, and the clock offset. Therefore, to solve for four variables, the receiver must receive at least four satellite signals [1].
When a receiver is located in urban canyon, satellite signals may be blocked by buildings or trees. When the number of visible satellites is insufficient, the position of the receiver can not be calculated as a general method. So we fix the altitude or receiver clock offset to reduce the number of variables we need to determine and get navigation solution. Alternatively, the position of the receiver is determined using sensors capable of providing navigation information such as an Inertial Navigation System (INS), dead-reckoning (DR), and altimeter [2-3].
In this paper, we use a radar to measure the range to a known landmark. Then, an integration algorithm is designed using GPS pseudorange and radar measurement. The simulation setup is as follows. We collect satellite signals using NI Universal Software Radio Peripheral (NI USRP). The radar signal is generated by randomly assuming the relative position of the detected landmark. Navigation performance will be shown as CEP and compared with navigation results using ublox.

2 Calculating Radar Target Position

The method of obtaining the azimuth angle and the elevation angle of the target is shown in Fig. 1. Elevation angle is the angle between xy-plane and radar.

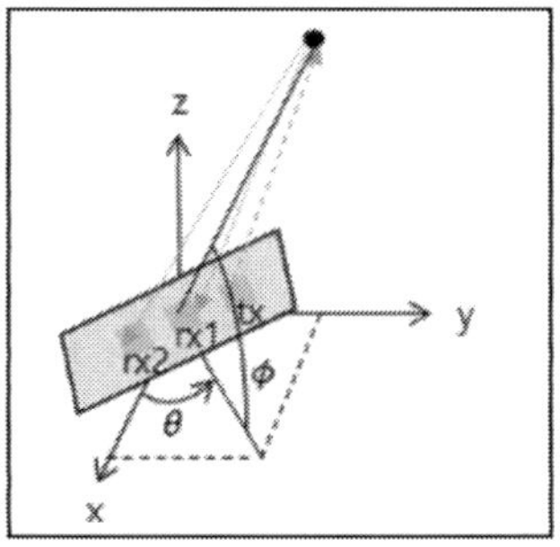

Fig. 1. Position recognition of three dimensional space target using radar

The method of calculating the azimuth angle of the target using two antennas is shown in Fig. 2.

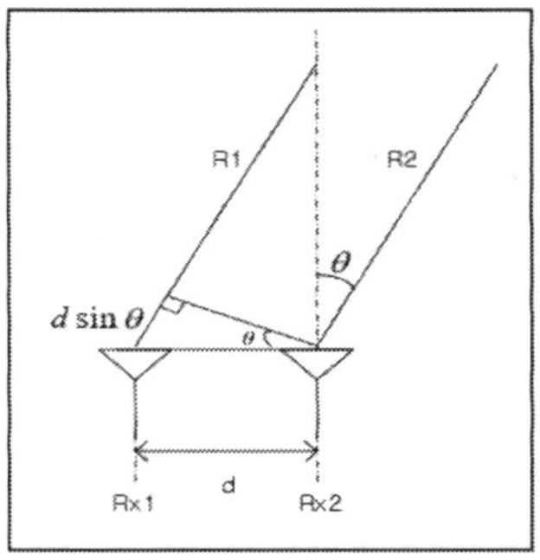

Fig. 2. Generating azimuth angle of a target

The reflected signal from the target arrives by moving R1 and R2 to the two antennas, which are separated by d cm. The distance between the antennas is in cm, so if the range

of the target is a few meters or tens of meters, it can be assumed that the signals arriving at the two antennas come in parallel.
The angle between the normal to the antenna and the target direction is θ . Then the distance difference between the two paths is $d\sin\theta$. The phase of the signal coming in through the two paths can be calculated using $\phi = ATAN(Q,I)$. The phases of the received signals are ϕ_1, ϕ_2, respectively. Then the phase difference of the two signals is $\phi_{diff} = \phi_1 - \phi_2$. The incident angle of the signal can be calculated as a phase difference and is expressed by the following equation [4]:

$$\theta = ASIN(\frac{\lambda\phi_{diff}}{2\pi d}). \tag{1}$$

We know the Azimuth angle, the elevation angle and the range, so we can calculate the relative position of the target.

3 GPS/Radar Integration

The pseudorange measurement for calculating user position (x_u, y_u, z_u) and clock offset (t_u) is

$$\rho_j = \|\mathbf{s}_j - \mathbf{u}\| + ct_u, \tag{2}$$

j is the satellite's index [1].
If we expand equation (2) by using satellite position, user position and clock offset, it is

$$\rho_j = \sqrt{(x_j - x_u)^2 + (y_j - y_u)^2 + (z_j - z_u)^2} + ct_u . \tag{3}$$

x_j, y_j, z_j is the jth satellite's position in three dimensions. Linearization of this equation results in

$$\rho_j = \hat{\rho}_j - \frac{x_j - \hat{x}_u}{\hat{r}_j}\Delta x_u - \frac{y_j - \hat{y}_u}{\hat{r}_j}\Delta y_u - \frac{z_j - \hat{z}_u}{\hat{r}_j}\Delta z_u + ct_u . \tag{4}$$

To simplify equation (4), we use the following equation:

$$\Delta\rho = \hat{\rho}_j - \rho_j \tag{5}$$

$$a_{xj} = \frac{x_j - \hat{x}_u}{\hat{r}_j}, a_{yj} = \frac{y_j - \hat{y}_u}{\hat{r}_j}, a_{zj} = \frac{z_j - \hat{z}_u}{\hat{r}_j}. \tag{6}$$

Then equation (4) becomes

$$\Delta\rho_j = a_{xj}\Delta x_u + a_{yj}\Delta y_u + a_{zj}\Delta z_u - ct_u . \tag{7}$$

The four satellite measurements are represented by

$$\Delta\boldsymbol{\rho}_{GPS} = H_{GPS}\Delta\mathbf{x}_{GPS} . \tag{8}$$

The vector and matrix are

$$\Delta\boldsymbol{\rho}_{GPS} = \begin{bmatrix} \Delta\rho_1 \\ \Delta\rho_2 \\ \Delta\rho_3 \\ \Delta\rho_4 \end{bmatrix}, \Delta\mathbf{x} = \begin{bmatrix} \Delta x_u \\ \Delta y_u \\ \Delta z_u \\ -c\Delta t_u \end{bmatrix}, \quad H_{GPS} = \begin{bmatrix} a_{x1} & a_{y1} & a_{z1} & 1 \\ a_{x2} & a_{y2} & a_{z2} & 1 \\ a_{x3} & a_{y3} & a_{z3} & 1 \\ a_{x4} & a_{y4} & a_{z4} & 1 \end{bmatrix}. \tag{9}$$

Radar range can be expressed as Eq. (8). The difference between radar and GPS is that the clock offset does not affect the radar range measurements. Therefore, the H matrix of Radar is given by

$$H_{Radar} = \begin{bmatrix} a_{x1} & a_{y1} & a_{z1} & 0 \\ a_{x2} & a_{y2} & a_{z2} & 0 \\ a_{x3} & a_{y3} & a_{z3} & 0 \\ a_{x4} & a_{y4} & a_{z4} & 0 \end{bmatrix}, \tag{10}$$

a_{xj}, a_{yj}, a_{zj} is defined in the same way as Eq. (6). Radar measurements are expressed as

$$\Delta\boldsymbol{\rho}_{Radar} = H_{Radar}\Delta\mathbf{x} . \tag{11}$$

We combine equation (8) and (11) to form

$$\begin{bmatrix} \Delta\boldsymbol{\rho}_{GPS} \\ \Delta\boldsymbol{\rho}_{Radar} \end{bmatrix} = \begin{bmatrix} H_{GPS} \\ H_{Radar} \end{bmatrix} \begin{bmatrix} \Delta x_u \\ \Delta y_u \\ \Delta z_u \\ -c\Delta t_u \end{bmatrix}. \tag{12}$$

We can use the least square method to navigate using equation (12).

4 Simulation

GPS signals were collected using NI USRP, and Radar transmit and receive signals were generated by Software. The radar was assumed to have a center frequency of 24 GHz and a bandwidth of 250 MHz. The landmark was set to one. Range and direction were defined as 58.2m, azimuth 314, elevation 26. Initially, navigation is performed using only four satellites. After 10 seconds, only 3 satellite signals were used and combined with Radar measurements. Navigation results are shown in Fig. 3. Navigation results using the measurements provided by the ublox receiver are shown in Fig. 4. This is the result of postprocessing using rtklibrary. Both navigation results use the Earth-Centered Earh-Fixed (ECEF) coordinate system.

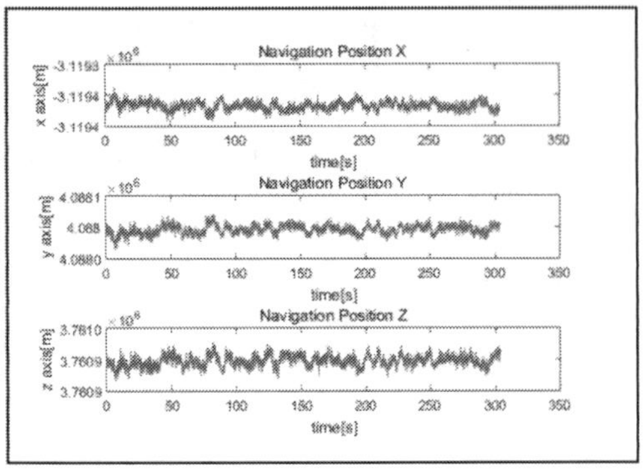

Fig. 3. Navigation results using GPS and Radar (ECEF)

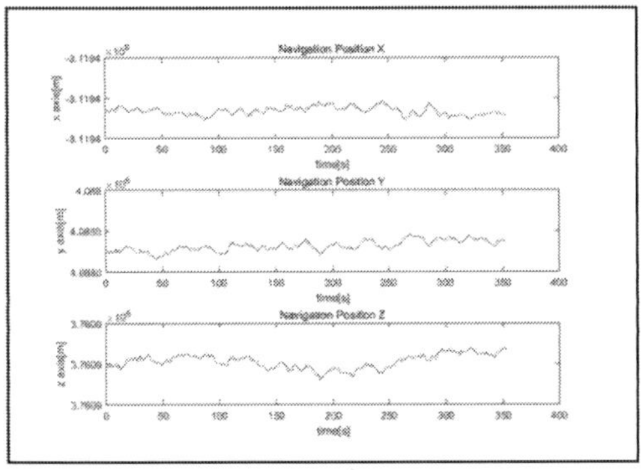

Fig. 4. Navigation results using ublox (ECEF)

The results of the two translations into the ENU coordinate system are shown in Fig. 5 and Fig. 6. When the visible satellite is not enough, the radar detects a landmark whose position is known and calculates a range. As a result, the receiver can navigate as if it received one more satellite signal. When radar is used as an assistant sensor, navigation performance deteriorates compared to postprocessing results using ublox receivers. However, since the CEP is 3.311 m, radar can be used as a navigation assistant sensor when the visible satellite is not enough.

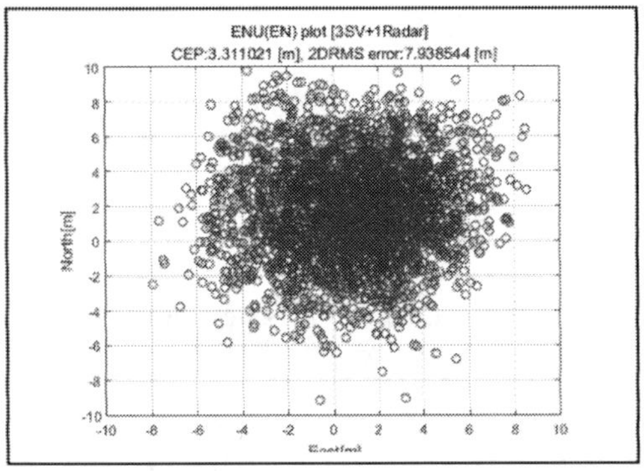

Fig. 5. Navigation results using GPS and Radar (ENU)

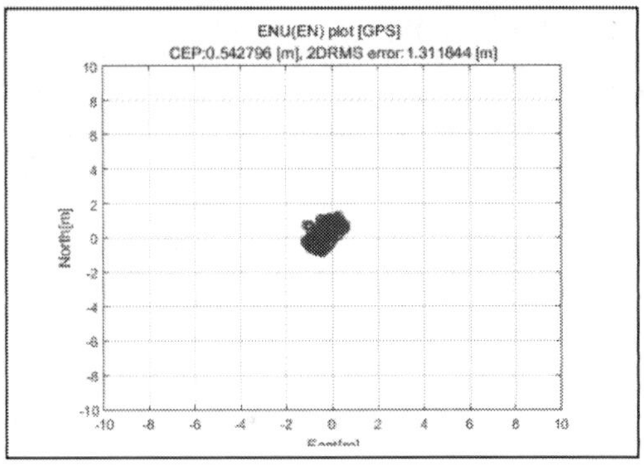

Fig. 6. Navigation results using ublox (ENU)

5 Conclusions

In this paper, we have designed an algorithm that integrates GPS and radar. When there were three visible satellites, we navigated using radar measurements. The results showed a CEP available for navigation. As further work, we will use the Kalman filter instead of the least square method, and consider how to compensate for the error in feedback.

Acknowledgments

This work has been supported partly by the National GNSS Research Center Program of Defense Acquisition Program Administration and the Agency for Defense Development and also supported by the Research Fund of Chungnam National University

References

1. E.D.Kaplan, C.J. Hegarty, *Understanding GPS* (2006)
2. D.B.Cox, Navigation, Jounal of the institute of Navigation, **25**, 2 (1978)
3. T.N.Upadhyay, S.Cotterill, A.W. Deaton, IEEE TRANSACTIONS ON Aerospace&Electronic Systems, **29**, 3 (1993)
4. H.K. Sim, M.A. Jung, The Journal of Korean Institute of Communications and Information Sciences, **40**, 07 (2015)

Error Analysis of PDR System Using Dual Foot-mounted IMU

Jae Hong Lee[1], *Hojin* Ju[2], and *Chan Gook* Park[1,2*]

[1]Dept. of Mechanical & Aerospace Engineering, Seoul National University, Seoul, 08826, Korea
[2]Automation and Systems Research Institute, Seoul National University, Seoul, 08826, Korea

Abstract. In this paper, we analyze the position errors of the pedestrian dead reckoning (PDR) system using foot-mounted IMU attached to each foot, and implement PDR system using dual foot-mounted IMU to reduce the analyzed error. The PDR system using foot-mounted IMU is generally based on an inertial navigation system (INS). To reduce bias and white noise errors, INS is combined with zero velocity update (ZUPT), which assumes that the pedestrian shoe velocity is zero at the stance phase. Although ZUPT could compensate the velocity and position, the heading drift still occurs. When analyzing the characteristics of the position error, the error shows a symmetrical characteristic. In order to reduce this error, the previous researches compensate for both positions by applying feet position constraints. The algorithm consists of applying a conventional PDR system to each foot and fusion algorithm combining both. The PDR system using foot-mounted IMU, one on each foot, is based on integration approach separately. The positions of both feet should be in a circle with a radius as step length during walking. The designed filter is constrained so that the position of both feet are in a circular boundary. The heading error that is symmetrically drifted is corrected by the position constraint when the pedestrian moves straight. Experimental results show the performance and usability of each previous algorithm to compensate for symmetric heading errors.

1 Introduction

As interest in indoor location service increases, various studies have been conducted on the technique of estimating the position of a pedestrian in real time. Among them, the pedestrian navigation system using the inertial measurement (IMU) -mounted on the shoes is being actively studied because it provides the high accuracy position even with the inertial sensor without any device is installed in advance.

Pedestrian positioning techniques are classified as a method using the infrastructure and method that are not. The method with the infrastructure to estimate the pedestrian position uses Wi-Fi, BLE or IMUs instead of using an infrastructure. The pedestrian dead reckoning (PDR) system based on the IMU has an advantage in that it can estimate the pedestrian position without needing prior information [1-9]. Since MEMS-IMU is compact, it has been used in PDR systems. However, since the measurement performance of the MEMS-IMU is poor, various studies have been conducted to improve the estimation error of a PDR system caused by sensor error. One of the PDR system using the IMU is parametric approach, which estimates the pedestrian position by accumulating the step length and direction of movement. This method is mainly used when the sensor is attached to the waist or held by hand [1-6]. The other PDR system is integration approach, which consists of INS, which is applied when the sensor is attached to the shoe [7-9]. Because it is based on INS, there is a disadvantage that error of integration approach accumulates due to sensor measurement error. To reduce estimate error by measurement errors, the INS is combined with zero-velocity update (ZUPT) at the stance phase. Foxlin proposed PDR system using the extended Kalman filter (EKF) to estimate and subtract errors with ZUPT during the stance phase. This algorithm uses the assumption that the velocity is zero when the shoe stuck to the ground. This approach is known as ZUPT-aided INS or INS-EKF-ZUPT.

Although the bias and white noise errors of the sensor can be reduced through integration approach, it can also be caused by the unexpected gait characteristics [10]. The heading error cannot be calibrated in the method of integration approach. In this paper, IMUs are attached to both feet and PDR system is performed. We analyze the characteristics of the estimated position error using the experimental results. Based on the results of the analysis, we applied the previous research to compensate position error to the PDR system. Experiments show that the characteristics of the analyzed position error are compensated by the prvious algorithm.

2 Methodology

2.1 Sensor

We use the MTw from xsens for data acquisition.

Table 1. Specification sensor mounted beside foot

	Gyro	Accelerometer

* Corresponding author: chanpark@snu.ac.kr

White noise	$0.05° / sec / \sqrt{Hz}$	$0.03g / \sqrt{Hz}$
Turn-on bias	$20° / hr$	-

Fig 1. Location of sensor on shoe

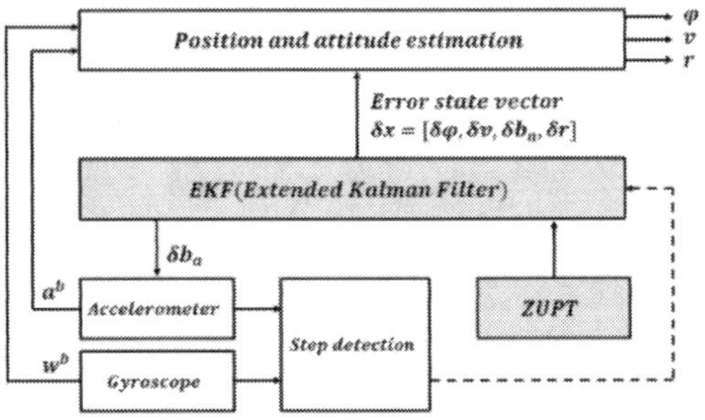

Fig 2. The PDR system with INS-EKF-ZUPT

The sensor specifications are summarized in Table 1. For the data analysis, the sampling rate of the sensor was set to the maximum value of 150 Hz. The sensors are attached to both shoes, as shown in Fig. 1.

2.2 Implementation of INS-EKF-ZUPT

The PDR system uses a foot-mounted IMU based on INS to estimate pedestrian position. INS uses angular rate and acceleration measured from IMU to calculate attitude, velocity, and position. Unfortunately, the INS is diverging because of bias and white noise. In general, EKF and ZUPT (zero velocity update) are combined in order to solve this problem. Assuming that the speed is zero when the bottom of the shoe is stacked on the ground, the estimation error can be reduced through ZUPT. Whenever it is determined that the shoe is stacked to the ground, the EKF updates the velocity measurements using the ZUPT. The error state in a general PDR system consists of nine or 15 error states. The 15 error states include gyro and accelerometer bias, attitude, position, and velocity error. In this paper, we used 12 error states in the INS-EKF-ZUPT system. The error states are expressed as follows:

$$\delta x = [\delta\varphi, \ \delta v, \ \delta b_a, \ \delta r] \quad (1)$$

which contains the errors of attitude ($\delta\phi$), velocity (δv), acceleration bias(δb_a), and position(δr).The state transition matrix is

$$\Phi = \begin{bmatrix} I_{3\times3} & 0 & 0 & 0 \\ S\cdot dt & I_{3\times3} & C_b^n & 0 \\ 0 & 0 & I_{3\times3} & 0 \\ 0 & I_{3\times3}\cdot dt & 0 & I_{3\times3} \end{bmatrix} \quad (2)$$

where C_b^n is the rotation matrix that transforms values from the body (b) to the navigation (n) frame, dt is the sampling time between two successive samples, and S is the skew-symmetric matrix for accelerations in the navigation frame. The velocity error is used for the error measurement update in EKF. The error measurement is $\hat{v}-[0 \ \ 0 \ \ 0]$, $\hat{v}$ is the estimated velocity and $[0 \ \ 0 \ \ 0]$ is the zero velocity, because the velocity of the foot is nearly zero during the stance phase. The measurement matrix is given as:

$$H = [0_3 \ \ I_3 \ \ 0_3 \ \ 0_3] \quad (3)$$

The block diagram of the algorithm used for the test is shown in Fig. 2. Stance phase detection is required in order to use ZUPT. The stance phase is the moment when the bottom of the shoe is attached to the ground in step motion. We have modified the stance phase detection method using the magnitude and variation of acceleration and angular rate. The reason for subtracting the gyro bias error from the state is that there is no way to calibrate them using a filter.

3. Error analysis about both feet

Using INS-EKF-ZUPT can reduce errors caused by sensors. Experiments with sensors attached to both feet show the error characteristics of both shoes. Fig. 1 shows the position of the sensor attached to the shoe for the experiment. The first experiment attached the sensor to the side and the second experiment attached the sensor to the shoe.

Fig. 3 (a) shows the results of the first experiment. The pedestrian moved about 32 [m] straight. The heading angle for the first five steps was averaged to match the initial moving direction. The bias was removed through the initial alignment for about 10 [sec] to minimize the error caused by the gyro bias. Equation (4) is the result of attitude error estimation by gyro bias after alignment. RW is the random walk of the gyro output, and σ_{align} is the standard deviation of the bias removed from the initial alignment. When moving about 32 [m], an heading error of 0.0097 [deg] occurs. If this is converted into position error, it becomes 0.0059 [m]. Since the estimated position error due to the gyro bias is smaller than the error mean shown in Table 2, it can be seen that an element other than the sensor error exists.

$$\delta\psi = \sigma_{align} \times t + RW \times \sqrt{t} = 0.0097[\text{deg}] \quad (4)$$

Red is the estimated trajectory by the sensor mounted on the left shoe and blue is the estimated trajectory by the sensor mounted on the right shoe. The tendency of the position error is symmetrical with the sensors attached to each shoe. Table 2 shows the error mean and standard deviations of the final position by each shoe. The mean error due to left foot is negative and the error due to right foot is positive, so each error is symmetric. The same experiment was carried out by attaching a sensor on the shoe. Fig 3.(b) and Table 3 show the experimental results. Similar to when the sensor is attached to the side, the position error appears symmetrically depending on the right and left shoes in which the sensor is attached. Comparing two experimental results, It can be inferred that position error has a symmetrical tendency according to the left and right shoe attached to the sensor, but depending on the mounting position of the sensor, the direction of drift may be different.

4. Applying dual foot-mounted PDR system

There is a PDR system in which an IMU is attached to both shoes as a method of compensating the position error analyzed in Section 3. In order to compensate the position error by the heading drift that is symmetrical form, the position of both shoes can be bounded through the constraints of each other. There are several prior studies, in which the basic concept is to use a constraint that the relative position of the two shoes is less than the maximum step length of the pedestrian. In Fig. 4, when the right foot is stepped, the estimated position due to heading drift exceeds the maximum step length (γ). At this time, it is possible to prevent the position error from diverging due to the heading drift by correcting the estimated position into the maximum step length [11-14].

4.1 Single foot-mounted IMU

In each foot, a PDR system is constructed by the INS-EKF-ZUPT method. Detailed algorithms are described in section 2. The PDR system operates independently on each foot.

4.2 Dual foot-mounted IMU

The estimated positions in each PDR system are combined in the stance phase. As shown in Fig. 4, when the left foot is in the stance phase and the right is in the swing phase, the position of the right foot is corrected. The conditions for correction are as follows:

$$d_k = norm(\hat{p}_k^l - \hat{p}_k^r) > \gamma \tag{5}$$

d_k is the relative position of both feet, $\hat{p}_k^i$ is the estimated position of the $i \in \{left, right\}$ side foot.

When the above condition is satisfied, the filter is updated with the position of the right foot considering the constraint.

One way to determine the measurements is to correct the position with the maximum step length (Method 1). The measurement is determined by Eq. (6). This method was proposed by G. V. Prateek [11, 12].

$$z_k^i = \frac{2}{d_k}((d_k - \gamma)\hat{p}_k^j + \gamma\hat{p}_k^i) \tag{6}$$

$i, j \in \{left, right\}$ and $i \neq j$ is satisfied.

The second method is to determine a measure that meets the minimum value of the cost function (Method 2). The measured value satisfying this is expressed as Eq. (8) This method was proposed by R. Girisha [13, 14].

$$J = \left\|\hat{p}_k^i - z_k^i\right\|_2^2 + \lambda\left(\left\|\hat{p}_k^i - \hat{p}_k^j\right\|_2^2 - \gamma^2\right) \tag{7}$$

$$z_k^i = \frac{1}{2d_k}((d_k + \gamma)\hat{p}_k^i + (d_k - \gamma)\hat{p}_k^j) \tag{8}$$

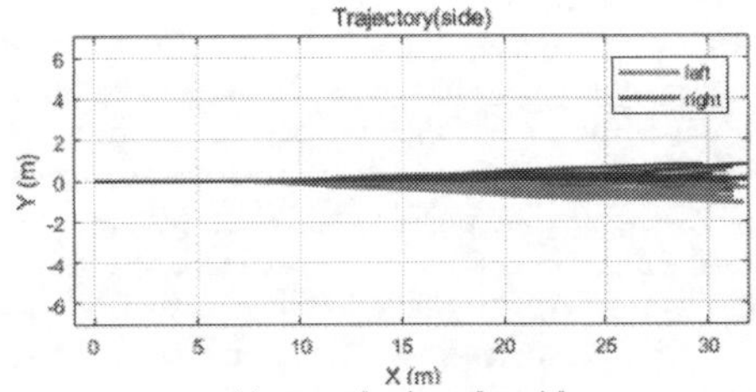

(a) Attached to the side

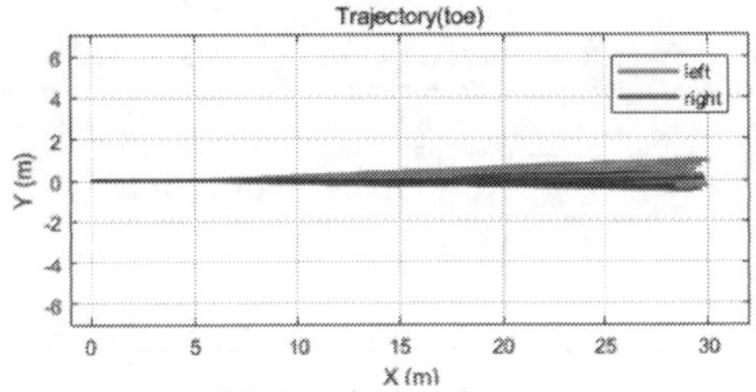

(b) Attached to the top

Fig 3. The estimated trajectory

Table 2. Y-axis position error (side)

	Mean [m]	σ [m]
Left	-0.4157	0.5484
Right	0.1688	0.3874

Table 3. Y-axis position error (top)

	Mean [m]	σ [m]
Left	0.4411	0.3804
Right	-0.0419	0.2675

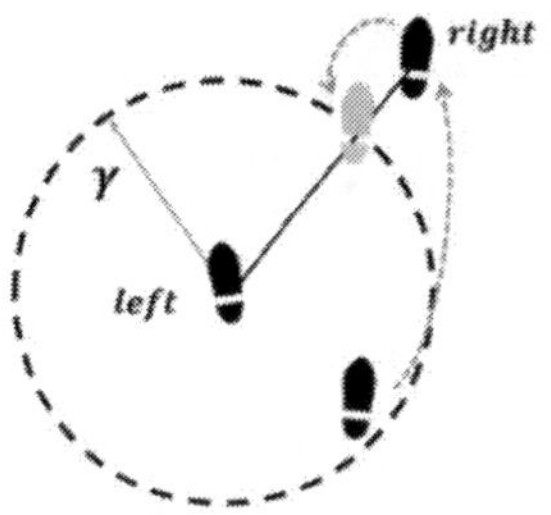

Fig 4. Movement of each foot and maximum step length

We define measurement matrix H as follows:

$$H = \begin{bmatrix} 0_3 & 0_3 & 0_3 & I_3 \end{bmatrix} \tag{9}$$

The algorithm of the previous study was applied to the data analyzed in Section 3. Table 4 shows the error mean for the end positions. It can be confirmed that the mean of the position error estimated from both feet becomes smaller when using the method 1 and 2. Fig. 4 shows the results of one experiment. The y-axis position is diverged, but dual foot-mounted IMU algorithm with method 1 and 2 make y-axis position is bounded.

However, fig. 4. (b) shows the limitation of the previous study. The position of both feet is compensated to midway through the constraint. If the symmetrical position error of both feet is not similar, and the degree of divergence of one foot is steeper, The position corrected by the filter is biased in the direction of the foot that is steeply diverging. Since the positional error of the left foot was more biased than the right foot, the corrected position was also biased downward without estimating it as a straight line (Fig 4.(b))

Table 4. Y-axis position error mean for each method

	Left	Right
None	-0.4157 [m]	0.1688 [m]
Method 1	-0.3414 [m]	0.0713 [m]
Method 2	-0.3505 [m]	0.0952 [m]

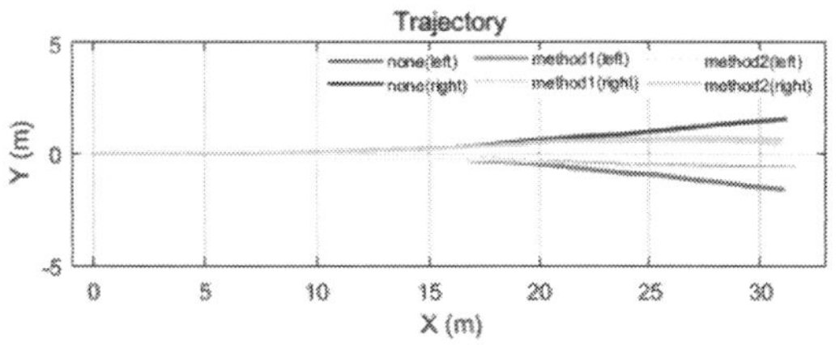

(a) Case 1

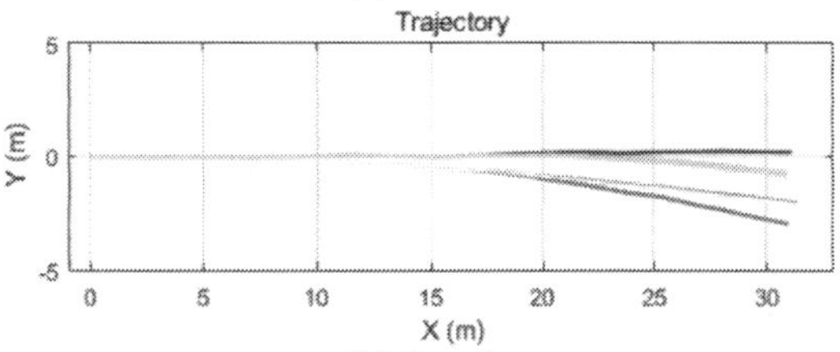

(b) Case 2

Fig 4. The estimated trajectory with each method

5 Conclusion

The purpose of this paper is to analyze the tendency of heading drift and to apply previous studies to reduce estimation error due to drift. To analyze the heading drift, IMU were attached to both feet and we collected data through several experiments. The analysis showed that both side heading drifts were symmetrical regardless of sensor location. To compensate for symmetric heading drift, previous studies use a constraint that the relative distance of the estimated position of each foot cannot be greater than the maximum step length. By using these constraints to compensate for position in the filter, the position is bounded. We confirmed that the method applied through experiment was valid and shown the limitation of previous studies

This work was supported by Institute for Information & communications Technology Promotion(IITP) grant funded by the Korea government(MSIT)(No. 2018-0-00781, Development of human enhancement fire helmet and fire suppression support system).

References

1. E. Foxlin, *IEEE Comput. Graph,* **25**, (2005)
2. S. Godha, G. Lachapelle, *Meas. Sci. Technol.*, **19** (2008)
3. R. F. Alonso, E. Z. Casanova, J. G. García-Bermejo, *J. Physical Agents*, 35–43 (2009)
4. A. R. Jiménez, F. Seco, J. C. Prieto, J. Guevara, *2010 7th Workshop on Positioning, Navigation and Communication*, 135-143 (2010)
5. M. S. Lee, C. Park, C. W. Shim, *Proc. 2012 Int. Meet. Inst. Navig*, 922–927 (2012)
6. H. Ju, et al., *Meas. Sci. Technol.*, **27**, (2015)
7. S. Y. Cho, and C. G. Park, *J. Navig.*, **59**, 135–153 (2006)
8. J. Kappi, S. Jari, and S. Jukka, *Proc. of the 14th Int. Technical Meeting of the Satellite Division of the Institute of Navigation*, 1369-1373 (2001)
9. B. Zhou, Q. Li, Q. Mao, W. Tu, and X. Zhang, *IEEE Trans. Hum. Mach. Syst*, 45, 562-574 (2015)
10. J. Nilsson, S. Isaac, and P. Händelm, *2013 Int. Conf. on Indoor Positioning and Indoor Navigation*, (2013)
11. J. O. Nilsson, et al., EURASIP J. Adv. Signal Processing, 164 (2013)
12. G. V. Prateek, R. Girisha, K. V. S. Hari, and P. Händel, *in Proceedings - International Conference on Intelligent Systems, Modelling and Simulation*, 208-213 (2013)
13. R. Girisha, G. V. Prateek, K. V. S. Hari, and P. Handel, *2014 International Conference on Signal Processing and Communications (SPCOM)*, 1-6 (2014)
14. W. Shi, Y. Wang, and Y. Wu, *Sensors*, **17** (2017)

OPTIMIZATION OF GROUND CONTROL POINT (GCP) AND INDEPENDENT CONTROL POINT (ICP) ON ORTHORECTIFICATION OF HIGH RESOLUTION SATELLITE IMAGERY

Teguh Hariyanto[1,*], *Akbar Kurniawan*[2], *Cherie Bhekti Pribadi*[1], *and Rizal Al Amin*[1]

[1]Geomatics Engineering Department, Faculty of Civil, Environment, and Geo Engineering, Institut Teknologi Sepuluh Nopember

Abstract. In the rapidly evolving technology era, various survey methods have been widely used one of them by remote sensing using satellite. It is known that the satellite image recording process is covered by rides (satellites) moving over the Earth's surface at hundreds of kilometers, causing satellite imagery to have geometric distortion. To reduce the effect of geometric distortion of objects on the image, geometric correction by orthorectification is done. Pleiades is a satellite of high resolution satellite image producer made by Airbus Defense & Space company. The resulting satellite imagery has a 0.5 meter spatial resolution. As a reference for the more detailed space utilization activities of space utilization arranged in the Regional Spatial Plans, Detailed Spatial Plans was created with the 1: 5000 scale map which has been governed by the Geospatial Information Agency. In the process of orthorectifying satellite imagery for this 1: 5000 scale map, ground control or Ground Control Point (GCP) is used for geometric correction and Digital Elevation Model (DEM) data. In this research, the optimal number of GCP usage for orthorectification process in Rational Function method is 21 GCP using 2nd order polynomial

Keywords : Orthorectification, Satellite Imagery, GCP, Rational Function, Polynomial.

I. INTRODUCTION

As a reference for more detailed space utilization activities of spatial activities regulated in the Spatial Plan, a Detailed Spatial Plan with a 1: 5.000 scale map has been prepared by the Geospatial Information Agency (BIG). Used on a scale of 1: 5,000, because on a scale map greater than or equal to 1: 5000, in addition to blocks, will also be drawn other elements such as channels and fences.

Pleiades is a satellite of high resolution satellite image producer made by Airbus Defense & Space company. The Pleiades satellite produces satellite imagery data in two modes, namely the panchromatic mode and the multispectral mode. Satellite images in the panchromatic mode have a spatial resolution of 0.5 meters with a band number of 1 band (panchromatic), while satellite images in multispectral mode have a spatial resolution of 2 meters with a band number of 4 bands (VNIR - Visible Near Infra Red). This satellite image has good specifications, so it is often used in survey planning and making thematic maps [4]. This satellite image is great for 1: 5.000 scale map with the required horizontal precision of 0.5-2.5m [1].

In the process of orthorectifying this satellite image, a ground control point or Ground Control Point (GCP) is used for geometric correction of x and y positions. This GCP has an important role to correct data and improve the overall image. The accuracy of ground control points depends on the type of GPS used and the number of point samples on the location and the time taken. For 1: 5,000 scale mapmaking, a static geodetic GPS receiver of static method with 30-45 minute observation [1] was used. For the addition of z position information, Digital Elevation Model (DEM) data was added. DEM was a digital data describing the geometry of the earth's surface shape or parts thereof which comprises the set of coordinate points of the sampling result from the surface of the earth with the algorithm defining the surface using the coordinate set. For 1: 5.000 scale mapmaking, DEM can be used with 5-10 meter vertical accuracy [1].

* Corresponding author: tgh_hary@yahoo.com

This study aims to examine the effect of the number of GCP with the uniform distribution pattern used in the image orthorectification process to the accuracy of the object analyzed by looking at the change of Independent Check Point position (ICP). It will also find out what the minimum GCP or limit on the process of orthorectification that entered the tolerance according to satellite image resolution and also will be sought GCP limitations so that the addition of GCP in the process of orthorectification does not affect the scale of the resulting image with respect to Root Mean Square Error (RMSE) which generated.

II. DATA AND STUDY AREAS

The location of this research was conducted in Lumajang Regency, East Java. The city coordinates are located at 112 ° 53 '- 113 ° 23' East Longitude and 7 ° 54 '- 8 ° 23' South Latitude. The research location in Lumajang City is one of the reasons for the orthorectification and not the usual rectification. Due to the relief form that varies from a height of 0-2000 meters.

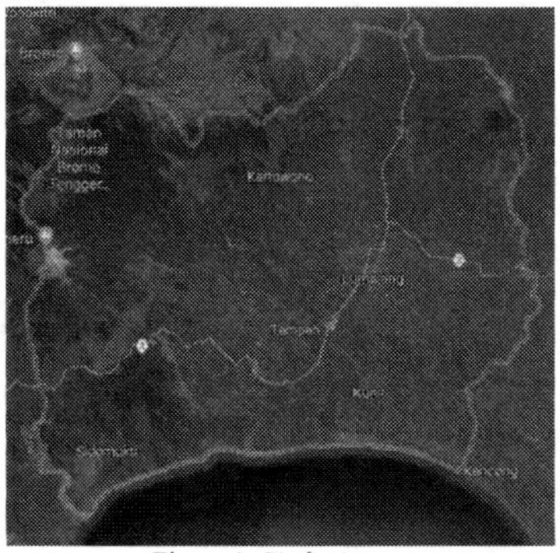

Figure 1. Study Area

The data used in this research, among others :

a. Satellite images of Pleiades 1-A scene 033 with 0.5x meter panchromatic accuracy and 2 meter multispectral keteitian in East Lumajang District.
b. DEM SRTM / X-SAR data from TerraSAR-X satellite with a relative accuracy of 6m and an absolute 16 meters lumajang district
c. Coordinate data of ground point amount 74 point measured by static methods for 30-45 minutes.

III. METHODS

In general, this research is conducted in five stages of research, namely the preparation stage consisting of problem identification process, literature study and data collection process, data processing stage, analysis phase and final stage in the form of report preparation.

Here is an explanation of the data processing stage:

First about data collection. The data required in this research is, satellite image data of Pleiades 1-A of East Lumajang Regency, TerraSAR-X DEM data, and GCP and ICP coordinate data obtained from field measurement.

Second, choose which GCP and ICP to use. In accordance to the desired distribution and RMSE values of GCP and ICP measurements.

Third, the design of the control point is divided into 22 different models based on the number of GCP and ICP entered. In this study, the authors used 74 coordinate measurement data.

Fourth, Ortortification is the process of geometric correction of satellite imagery or aerial photographs to correct the geometric error of an image derived from the influence of topography, sensor geometry and other errors. The method used in this research is Polinomial Rational Function. Rational function is a simple mathematical model that reflects the correlation between pixels and poisisi on the ground. The use of this model is used when it does not have the information necessary for a rigorous mathematical model, such as because; sensors of different models, geometric imagery has been processed, data providers have done the calculation of mathematical model and distributed in the image, or do not have the overall image (the result of the cut).

Rational function has 3 order polynomial with order 1 requiring at least 7 GCP, order 2 requires minimum 21 GCP, order 3 requires minimum 41 GCP. The following polynomial orde 1 [3, 7] equation is

$$x = \frac{(1\,X\,Y\,Z)(a0\ a1\ a2\ a3)^T}{(1\,X\,Y\,Z)(1\ b1\ b2\ b3)^T}\,.$$
$$y = \frac{(1\,X\,Y\,Z)(c0\ c1\ c2\ c3)^T}{(1\,X\,Y\,Z)(1\ d1\ d2\ d3)^T}\,. \quad (1)$$

where there are 7 parameters, including 4 in the numerator, and 3 and 1 constants in the denominator. In order to solve the Rational Function coefficient in this order of 3, then there are at least 7 control points (GCP) required. The following polynomial orde 2 [3, 7] equation is

$$x = \frac{(1\,X\,Y\,Z\,XY\,XZ\,YZ\,X^2Y^2\,Z^2)(a0\ a1\ a2\ a3 \cdots a9\ a10)^T}{(1\,X\,Y\,Z\,XY\,XZ\,YZ\,X^2Y^2\,Z^2)(1\ b1\ b2\ b3 \cdots b9\ b10)^T}$$
$$y = \frac{(1\,X\,Y\,Z\,XY\,XZ\,YZ\,X^2Y^2\,Z^2)(c0\ c1\ c2\ c3 \cdots c9\ c10)^T}{(1\,X\,Y\,Z\,XY\,XZ\,YZ\,X^2Y^2\,Z^2)(1\ d1\ d2\ d3 \cdots d9\ d10)^T} \quad (2)$$

where there are 19 parameters, including 10 in the numerator, and 9 and 1 constants in the denominator. In order to solve the Rational Function coefficients in this 2nd order, then there are at least 19 control points (GCP) required. The following polynomial orde 3 [3, 7] equation is

$$x = \frac{(1\,X\,Y\,Z \ldots YZ^2Z^3)(a0\ a1\ a2\ a3 \ldots a18\ a19)^T}{(1\,X\,Y\,Z \ldots YZ^2Z^3)(1\ b1\ b2\ b3 \ldots b18\ b19)^T}$$
$$y = \frac{(1\,X\,Y\,Z \ldots YZ^2Z^3)(c0\ c1\ c2\ c3 \ldots c18\ c19)^T}{(1\,X\,Y\,Z \ldots YZ^2Z^3)(1\ d1\ d2\ d3 \ldots d18\ d19)^T} \quad (3)$$

in which there are 39 parameters, including 20 in numerators, and 19 and 1 constants in the denominator. In order to solve the Rational Function coefficient in this order of 3, then there are at least 39 control points (GCP) required.

Fifth, The image has been orthorectificated if the Root Mean Square Error (RMSE) value less than equal to 0.25 meters. When that value has not been

 https://doi.org/10.1051/e3sconf/20199402008

reached, it returns to the octhorectification process using the next GCP model (GCP used increases).
Sixth, When the Mean Square Error (RMSE) GCP value meets the ≤ 2.5 meter requirement, the image has been orthorectificated. Then tested the geometric accuracy of the image with ICP coordinates. When the Mean Square Error (RMSE) ICP value does not meet ≤ 2.5 meters (map scale 1: 5000), then return to octhorectification process using the next GCP model (GCP used increases).
Seventh, When the Mean Square Error (RMSE) ICP value meets the ≤ 2.5 meter requirement, the image has been orthorectificated and can be used in scale of 1: 5000
Eight, If there is an unused image model (due to the use of the previous model), an orthorectification process remains to be performed. This step used to increase the number of GCP analyzes used with the maximum scale of maps that can be generated.
Then, Analysis of the effect of the number of GCPs with RMSE values done by looking at the RMSE GCP and ICP values displayed in image processing software. This value is related to how large the map scale can be made from the orthorectification image of the various given GCP variations. Planymetric precision analysis is divided into 3 parts order 1, 2, and 3 and each order is divided into classes 1, 2, and 3. Classification of GCP numbers with geometrically generated image scales divided to 3 classes 1, 2, and 3.
Analysis of image distance accuracy done by calculating the distance between GCP from the outermost side and comparing the results with the distance measurement results in the image. The resulting distance difference can be used to determine the RMSE value. T-Test Statistics test is used to find the distance error value allowed for the 1: 5000 scale map. In this research, 3 sample of the best orthorectification image distance from each polynomial order is used. Image analysis of orthorectified results is performed on 1 image with the best accuracy. Includes pixel analysis, analysis of aquatic objects, transformation analysis, and analysis of high objects. From the analysis, it can be determined how many points of GCP at what order orthorectification needed for optimization of 1: 5 scale scale map.

IV. RESULTS AND DISCUSSION

IV.1. RMSE Results Orthorectification

The Placement of GCP Point were located to represent terrain condition in order to increase the accuracy of RMSe. The process of orthorectification using the Rational Function method has 3 choices of polynomial order. 1st order (Nearest Neighbors) requires at least 7 GCP, 2nd Order (Bilinear Interpolation) requires a minimum of 19 GCP, and 3rd order (Cubic Convolution) requires a minimum of 39 GCP. Here is the distribution of 74 point measurement field.

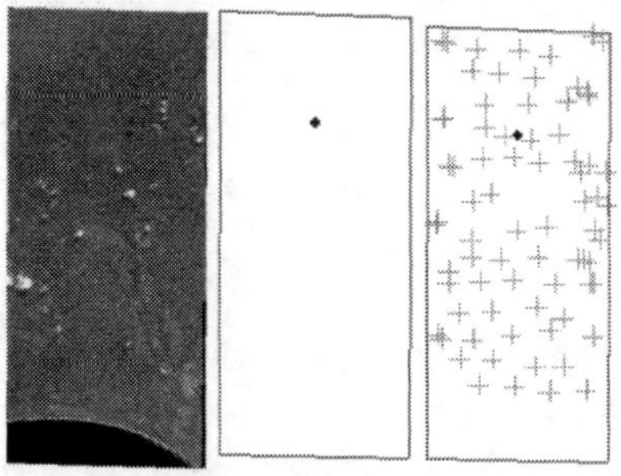

a) b) c)

Figure 1 a). High Resolution Image b). Image Area c). Output Measurement Point

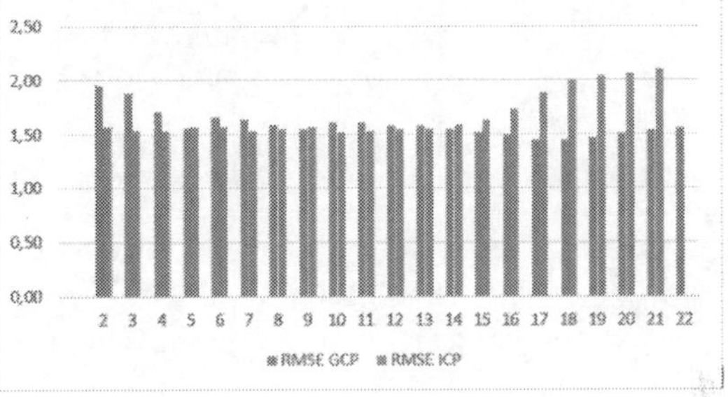

Figure 2. Graph of RMS Error GCP and ICP value of Orde 1 (in meters)

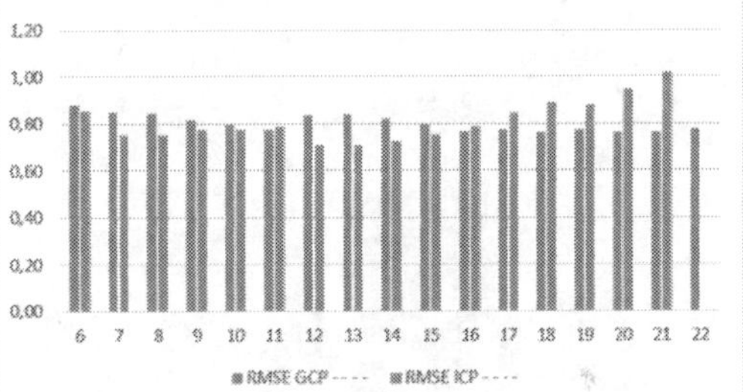

Figure 3. Graph of RMS Error GCP and ICP value of Orde 2 (in meters)

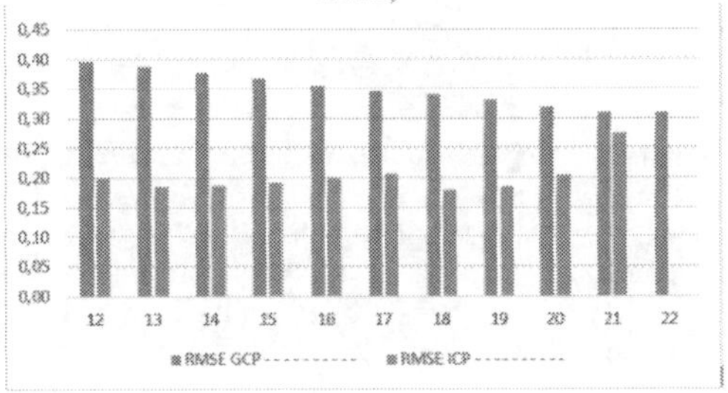

Figure 4. Graph of RMS Error GCP and ICP value of Orde 3 (in meters)

IV.2. Analysis of Distance Accuracy and Test of T-Test Statistics

In this approach, the distance analysis will only be performed on the best model of each order, ie at 1st order with the use of 9 GCP, 2nd Order with the use of 21 GCP, 3rd order with the use of 41 GCP.

Where

 https://doi.org/10.1051/e3sconf/20199402008

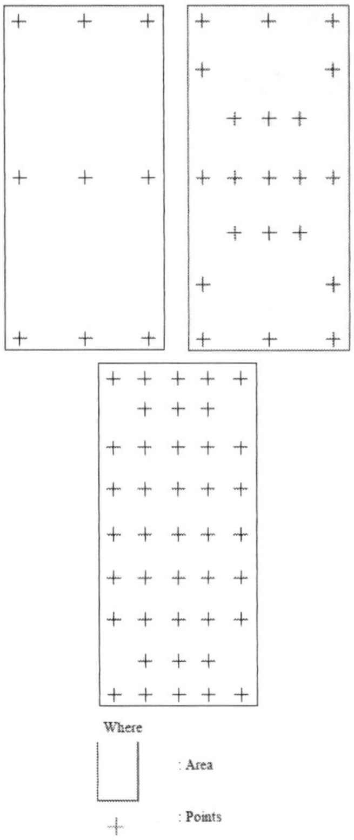

Figure 5. Point Distribution Point 9 GCP, 21 GCP, 41 GCP

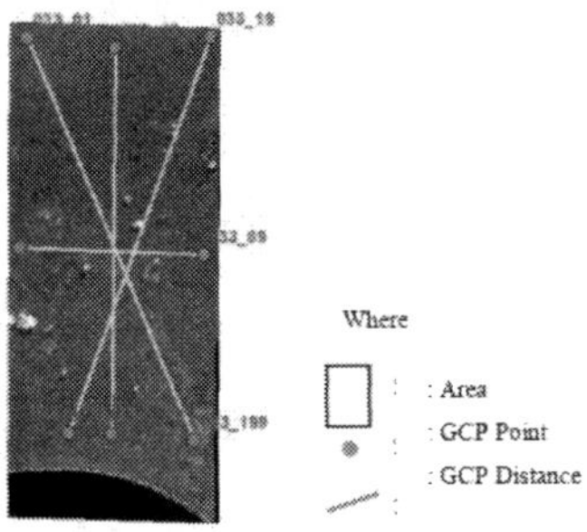

Figure 6. Sample Distance on distance accuracy test

If used α = 5% and degrees of freedom 2 (n = 3), then obtained:
tγ, 1 / 2α = t1, 0.05 = 4,303 (from the student t-test table). With two-sided test method is calculated:

X1 = μ - ((t1, 0.05 * σx) / √2) = μ - ((4,303 * 0.25) / √2) = μ - 0.761
X2 = μ + ((t1, 0.05 * σx) / √2) = μ + ((4,303 * 0.25) / √2) = μ + 0.761
If we use α = 10% and degrees of freedom 2 (n = 3), then we get:
tγ, 1 / 2α = t2, 0.05 = 2,290 (from the student t-test table). With two-sided test method is calculated:

X1 = μ - ((t1, 0.05 * σx) / √2) = μ - ((2,290 * 0.25) / √2) = μ - 0,516
X2 = μ + ((t1, 0.05 * σx) / √2) = μ + ((2,290 * 0.25) / √2) = μ + 0,516
Here is a sample test of distance from west of image (point 033_104) to east position of image (point 033_69) at α = 5% and α = 10%

Table 9 Test Results of t-test on Sample Distance west (point 033_104) to east (point 033_69) at α = 5%

Order	x	X_1	X2	Result
1st	18963.818	18962.217	18963.738	Accepted
2nd	18963.329	18962.217	18963.738	Rejected
3rd	18962.874	18962.217	18963.738	Rejected

Table 10 Results of t-test on Western Distance Samples (point 033_104) to East (point 033_69) at α = 10%

Order	x	X1	X2	Result
1st	18963.818	18962.461	18963.493	Rejected
2nd	18963.329	18962.461	18963.493	Accepted
3rd	18962.874	18962.461	18963.493	Accepted

From the calculations of 1st order, 2nd order, and 3rd order with α = 5%, there is 1 result that is beyond the measure which means Ho is rejected (Ha accepted) on the test of the west-to-east distance sample in 1st order. From the calculations of 1st order, 2nd order, and 3rd order with α = 10%, there is 1 result which is beyond measure which means Ho is rejected (Ha accepted) on testing of west to east sample in 1st order.
It can be concluded that although the best model for 1: 5000 scale map is available on 3rd order with 41 GCP usage, but for optimal quantity GCP use 2nd order with 21 GCP.

IV.3. Pixel Image Analysis Result Ortortification

In pixel image analysis ortorektifkasi results done on 2nd order with the use of GCP as much as 21 point order 2, which in the previous explanation found that the 2nd order with polynomial order 2 is the optimal model in the scale map 1: 5000. The following changes pixel size after the orthorectification process obtained from 5 sample point.

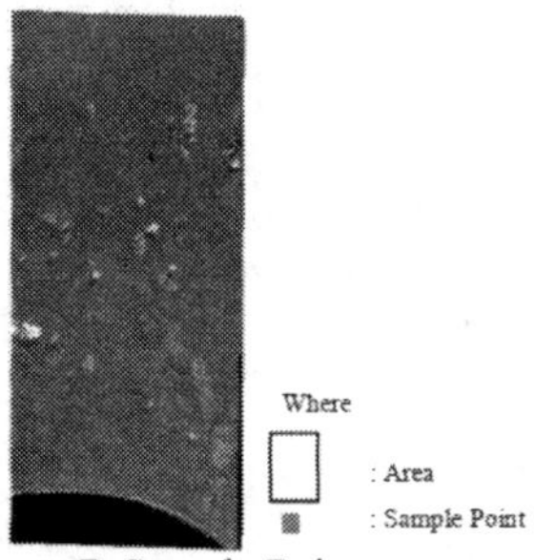

Figure 7. Sample Points Distribution

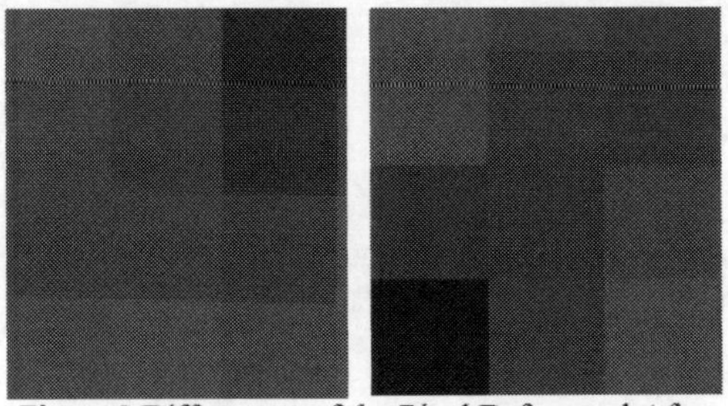

Figure 8 Differences of the Pixel Before and After Pixel Form

V. CONCLUSION

The conclusion from this research are :

a. In orthorectification process, so that RMSE GCP value $\leq$ 2.5m can be used amount of GCP as much as 8 GCP with polynomial of orde
b. In the process of orthorectification the addition of excessive amount of GCP does not alter the scale of the resulting map significantly. For order 1 orthorectification process, optimal GCP used is 9 GCP, 2nd order is 21 GCP, and order 3 is 41 GCP
c. Relation It is found that the order of polynomials used with the resulting image scale is in order 1 can be used for 1: 3000 - 1: 11000 scale map creation, order 2 can be used for 1: 1500 - 1: 5000 scale map creation, order 3 can be used to map scale $\leq$ 1: 1500. The scale varies depending on the accuracy class of the map used
d. Although the best model in geometric accuracy is found in 3rd order with the use of GCP as much as 41 points and using the order of polynomial 3. But for the scale map 1: 5000, simply use model 7 with the use of 21 GCP with the order polynomial 2.

References

[1] Geospatial Information Agency. 2015. Mapping Aspect for Detailed Spatial Plans. Cibinong

[2] K. D. R. Ma, and R. X. Li. 2003. "Rational Functions and Potential for Rigorous Sensor Model Recovery". American : Department of Civil and Environmental Engineering and Geo-detic Science, The Ohio State University, Columbus, OH 43210 (li.282@osu.edu).

[3] Tao, C.V., and Y. Hu, 2001a. 3-D reconstruction algorithms based on the rational function model, Proceedings of ISPRS Joint Workshop "High Resolution Mapping from Space" 2001, 19–21 September Hanover, Germany, unpaginated CD-ROM

[4] Tempfli, K. 1991. DTM and differential modelling. In : Proceedings ISPRS and OEEPE joint workshop on updating digital data by photogrammetric method. Oxford, England

[5] Th. Toutin a, R. Chénier, Y. Carbonneau. 2002. "3D Models for High Resolution Images: Examples with Quickbird, Ikonos And Eros". Canada : Canada Centre for Remote Sensing.

[6] Turker, M. and A. O. Ok. Tanpa Tahun. "Comparison Of Different Mathematical Models On The Accuracy Of The Orthorectification Of Aster Imagery". Ankara, Turkey: Hacettepe University.

[7] Whiteside, A. 1997. Recommended Standard Image Geometry Models, OpenGIS Web Site, URL : http://www.opengis.org/ipt/9702tf/UniversalImage/TaskForce.ppt

Windowing Design and Performance Assessment for Mitigation of Spectrum Leakage

Dah-Jing Jwo [1,*], *I-Hua* Wu [2] and *Yi* Chang[1]

[1] Department of Communications, Navigation and Control Engineering, National Taiwan Ocean University 2 Pei-Ning Rd., Keelung 202, Taiwan
[2] Bison Electronics, Inc., Neihu District, Taipei 114, Taiwan

Abstract. This paper investigates the windowing design and performance assessment for mitigation of spectral leakage. A pretreatment method to reduce the spectral leakage is developed. In addition to selecting appropriate window functions, the Welch method is introduced. Windowing is implemented by multiplying the input signal with a windowing function. The periodogram technique based on Welch method is capable of providing good resolution if data length samples are selected optimally. Windowing amplitude modulates the input signal so that the spectral leakage is evened out. Thus, windowing reduces the amplitude of the samples at the beginning and end of the window, altering leakage. The influence of various window functions on the Fourier transform spectrum of the signals was discussed, and the characteristics and functions of various window functions were explained. In addition, we compared the differences in the influence of different data lengths on spectral resolution and noise levels caused by the traditional power spectrum estimation and various window-function-based Welch power spectrum estimations.

1 Introduction

The spectrum analysis [1-4] is a critical concern in many military and civilian applications, such as performance test of electric power systems and communication systems, detection of mechanical vibration, testing the linearity of components.

Anti-jamming techniques [5,6] have been adopted to enhance the reliability and effectivity of Global Navigation Satellite System (GNSS). As a technique based upon Capon works and Neyman–Pearson theory, the amplitude domain processing (ADP) is an anti-jamming method to suppress multitone continuous wave, sweep continuous wave and narrowband interference without convergence problems, and therefore has been widely utilized to the GNSS receivers. Using ADP in frequency domain (FADP) will distort useful navigation signal while suppressing interference. FADP filter possesses superior performance, while induces some problems, such as the spectrum leakage of the frequency domain.

To relieve the performance deterioration, the spectral leakage suppression algorithms [6,7] for the DFT-based spectrum analysis is extensively studied, such as digital filtering, high-order spectral analysis, leakage compensation in frequency domain and weighting the time samples by a suitable window function. Window function method is the most widely used. However, window functions are varied and have different characteristics. How to choose suitable window function for different applications requires professional knowledge. Due to computer capacity and limitations on processing time, only limited time samples can actually be processed during spectrum analysis and data processing of signals, i.e., the original signals need to be cut off, which induces leakage errors. In spread spectrum system, frequency-domain interference suppression algorithms always use data windows to reduce the spectral leakage associated with truncation, and employ overlap to lessen the SNR degradation due to windowing.

Direct truncation equals rectangular window shaping. Rectangular time window has narrow main lobe and wide side lobe with small main lobe to side lobe ratio, which results in serious side lobe leakage. A method is proposed to mitigation the influence of spectral leakage of the Fourier transform spectrum by selecting appropriate window functions. Some windows with narrow side lobe, such as Blackman, Hanning, and Kaiser windows are usually employed in engineering instead of the rectangular one.

Periodogram is a method of estimating the autocorrelation of finite length of a signal, which possesses limited ability to produce accurate power spectrum estimation. The nonparametric Welch method [8,9] is an improvement on the periodogram spectrum estimation method where signal to noise ratio is high and reduces noise in the estimated power spectra for reducing the frequency resolution.

This paper is organized as follows. In Section 2, preliminary background on the Fourier transform is reviewed, including the discrete Fourier transform, and

* Corresponding author: djjwo@mail.ntou.edu.tw

the fast Fourier transform. The spectrum leakage is introduced in Section 3. In Section 4, windowing functions for spectrum leakage suppression is discussed. In Section 5, simulation experiments are carried out to evaluate the performance for various designs. Conclusions are given in Section 6.

2 Fourier transform

The Fourier transform is important in engineering, mathematics, and the physical sciences. The Fourier transform is a generalization of the complex Fourier series, defined by

$$F(\omega)=\int_{-\infty}^{\infty} f(t)e^{-j\omega t}dt \quad (1)$$

$$f(t)=\frac{1}{2\pi}\int_{-\infty}^{\infty} F(\omega)e^{j\omega t}d\omega \quad (2)$$

The discrete counterpart of the Fourier transform is the Discrete Fourier Transform (DFT). The DFT is ubiquitous in digital signal processing for the spectrum analysis, which can be efficiently realized by fast Fourier transform (FFT).

2.1 Discrete Fourier transform

The discrete Fourier transform converts a finite sequence of equally-spaced samples of a function into a same-length sequence of equally-spaced samples of the discrete-time Fourier transform (DTFT), which is a complex-valued function of frequency. DFT is the equivalent of the continuous Fourier Transform. DTFT is continuous (and periodic), and the DFT provides discrete samples of one cycle. If the original sequence is one cycle of a periodic function, the DFT provides all the non-zero values of one DTFT cycle. The DTFT foe the time domain signal $x[n]$ is given by:

$$X[\Omega]=DTF(x[n])=\sum_{-\infty}^{\infty}x[n]e^{-jn\Omega} \quad (3)$$

We could regard each sample $x[n]$ as windowing function

$$w_R[n]=\begin{cases}1\ ,\ n=0,1,2,L\ ,N-1\\ 0, \quad otherwise\end{cases} \quad (4)$$

Spectrum signal sample is

$$x_N[n]=x[n]w_R[n]=\begin{cases}1\ ,\ n=0,1,2,L\ ,N-1\\ 0, \quad otherwise\end{cases} \quad (5)$$

Here we definition signal N of $x_N[n]$ is complete signal. The DFT is the sampled Fourier Transform and therefore does not contain all frequencies forming an image, but only a set of samples which is large enough to fully describe the spatial domain image.

2.2 Fast Fourier transform

As the efficient calculation of DFT, the fast Fourier transform (FFT) has been widely used for many applications. The implementations of DFT usually employ efficient fast Fourier transform algorithms, so that the terms FFT and DFT are often used interchangeably. Table 1 provides comparison of workload for DFT and FFT.

Table 1. Comparison of workload for DFT and FFT.

N	DFT	FFT
2	4	1
4	16	4
8	64	12
16	256	32
32	1024	80
256	4096	192

3 Spectrum leakage

Spectral leakage is a problem that arises in the digital processing of signals. Signal in practical is always limited in time domain, namely truncated by time window, which results in spectrum leakage of signal. Leakage causes the signal levels to be reduced and redistributed over a broad frequency range, which is important for implementing digital signal processing properly.

The Fourier transform of a function of time, x(t) is a complex-valued function of frequency, and X(f) is referred to as a frequency spectrum. The flow charrt of the DFT calculation is shown as in Fig. 1. Direct truncation equals rectangular window shaping. Rectangular time window has narrow main lobe and wide side lobe with small main lobe to side lobe ratio, which results in serious side lobe leakage. Fig. 2 shows the discrete spectrum due to signal windowing truncation.

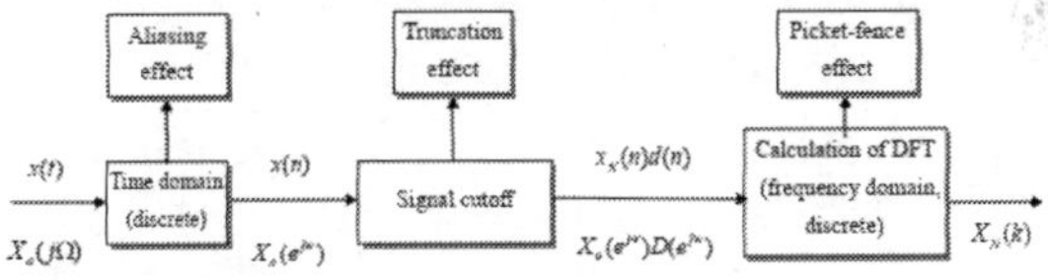

Fig. 1. Flow chart of the DFT calculation.

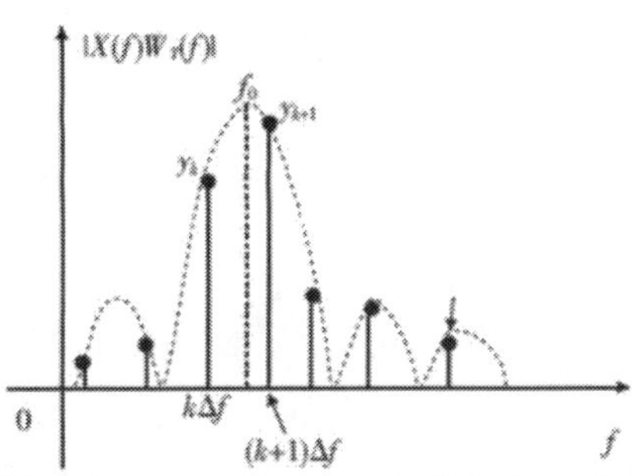

Fig. 2. Discrete spectrum due to signal windowing truncation.

 https://doi.org/10.1051/e3sconf/20199403001

3.1 Spectrum leakage suppression - periodic truncation

The sampling signal length is not integer multiple of the signal period length, and through the Fast Fourier transform (FFT), the sampling signal is going to make larger distortion, therefore it makes many unpredictable spurious components and spectral leakage in discrete spectrum. In conclusion, when signal period is T_0 and sampling period is T_s and sampling point is N, it is chosen to satisfy the relation

$$LT_0 / T_s = N \tag{6}$$

The FFT algorithm takes the small amount of captured data and repeats it, in order to perform the Fourier Transform and produce a frequency spectrum. In this case, the signal is periodic, and the resulting frequency spectrum will have no leakage. Since most of measured signals will possess non-periodic signals, the problem is how to minimize leakage in these cases. Figs. 3 and 4 show magnitude (in dB) of the DFT spectrum using a periodic and non-periodic truncation, respectively.

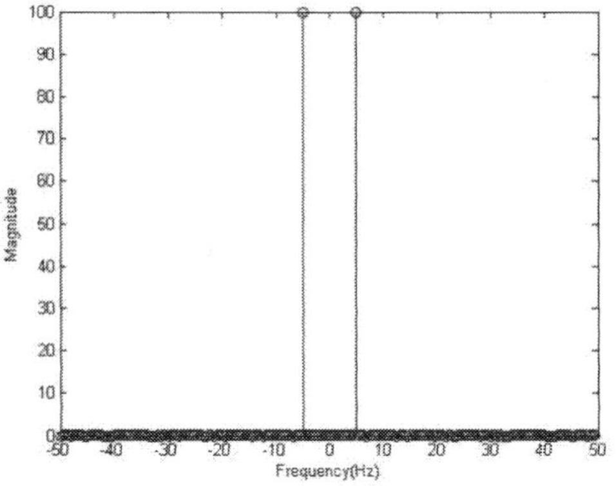

Fig. 3. Magnitude (in dB) of the DFT spectrum using a periodic truncation.

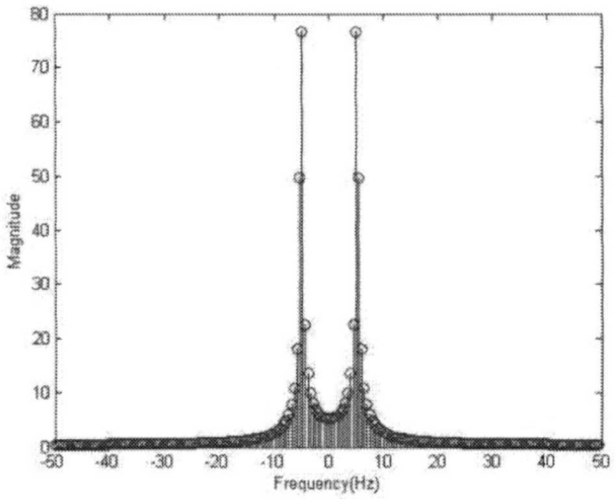

Fig. 4. Magnitude (in dB) of the DFT spectrum using a non-periodic truncation.

3.2 Spectrum leakage suppression - enlarging the data length in windowing function

Windowing is implemented by multiplying the input signal with a windowing function. Windowing amplitude modulates the input signal so that the spectral leakage is evened out. Thus, windowing reduces the amplitude of the samples at the beginning and end of the window, altering leakage. An input signal can be of any number of dimensions and can be complex. For complex-values a complex multiplication is required.

As data length increase, the rate of fluctuation in this is also increase. The variance of the periodogram is reduced by applying a window to the autocorrelation estimate to decrease the contribution of unreliable estimates to the periodogram. Increasing the width of window function is equivalent to enlarge the length of segment with large main lobe to side lobe ratio, which results in less side lobe leakage. Figs. 5 and 6 show the magnitude (in dB) of the DFT spectrum using a simple length-32 (N=32) and length-64 (N=64), truncation windows, respectively. The quality of the estimate increases as the length N of the data increase.

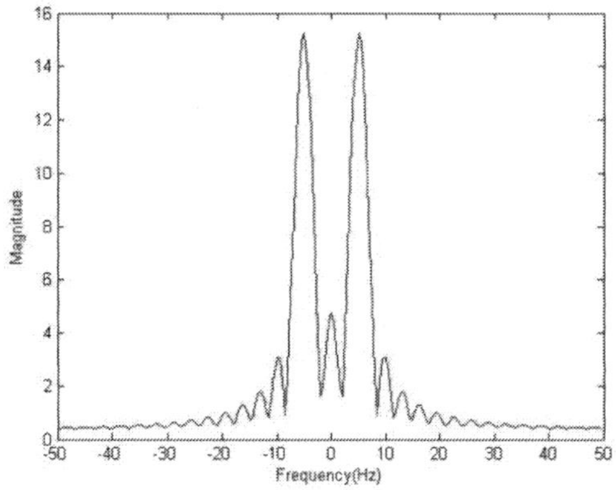

Fig. 5. Magnitude (in dB) of the DFT spectrum using a simple length-32 truncation window (N=32).

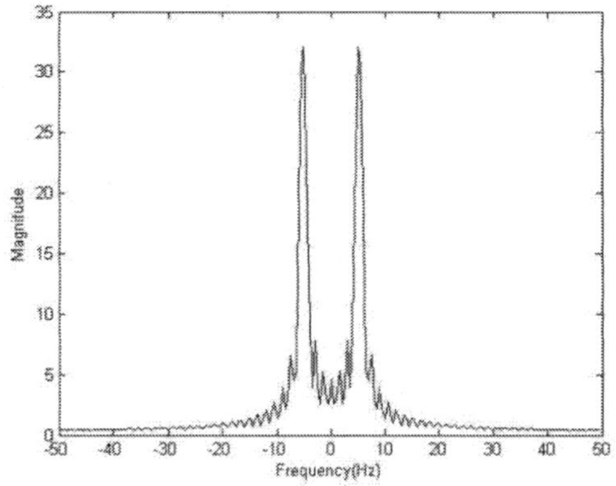

Fig. 6. Magnitude (in dB) of the DFT spectrum using a simple length-64 truncation window (N=64).

 https://doi.org/10.1051/e3sconf/20199403001

4 Windowing functions for spectrum leakage suppression

The method of windowing functions is most popular method for inhibition of spectral leakage. Windowing functions are also called tapering functions or apodization functions. Many different window functions have been developed for truncating and shaping a length-N signal segment for spectral analysis. It inhibits the spectral leakage by cutting the signal when the period is delay and two-side is continuous. There are many common windowing functions. The special techniques like window function and rectangular, Hanning, Blackman, and Kaiser window to extract the unwanted noise from the signal.

4.1 Rectangular window

A function that is constant inside the interval and zero elsewhere is called a rectangular window. Direct truncation equals rectangular window shaping. The simple truncation window has a periodic sinc DTFT. It has the narrowest main-lobe width, 2π/N at the -3 dB level and 4π/N between the two zeros surrounding the main lobe, of the common window functions, but also the largest side-lobe peak, at about -13 dB. The side-lobes also taper off relatively slowly. The truncation to a length $M-1$ is equivalent to multiplying the signal by a rectangular window. Expression of normal rectangular time window is defined as

$$w(n) = R_N(n)\begin{cases} 1 & 0 \le n \le N\text{-}1 \\ 0 & Otherwise \end{cases} \tag{7}$$

The frequency domain can be expressed as

$$W(e^{j\omega}) = \frac{\sin(\frac{\omega N}{2})}{\sin(\frac{\omega}{2})} e^{-j\omega(\frac{N-1}{2})} \tag{8}$$

Fig. 7 gives the time domain amplitude and magnitude spectrum with rectangular window. The rectangular window has good resolution characteristics for sinusoids of comparable strength.

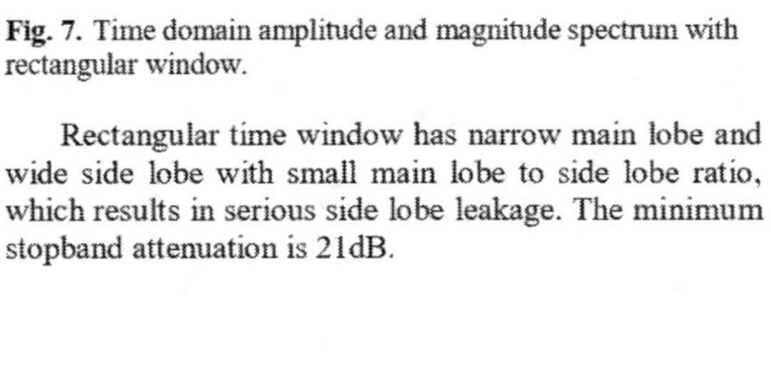

Fig. 7. Time domain amplitude and magnitude spectrum with rectangular window.

Rectangular time window has narrow main lobe and wide side lobe with small main lobe to side lobe ratio, which results in serious side lobe leakage. The minimum stopband attenuation is 21dB.

4.2 Blackman window

The Blackman method is used to reduce variance of the estimator. If we compare Blackman window with other windows there is better improvement in stopband attenuation. Blackman window has good characteristics for audio work. The Blackman window in time domain is defined as

$$w(n) = \left(0.42 - 0.5\cos\left(\frac{2\pi n}{N-1}\right) + 0.08\cos\left(\frac{4\pi n}{N-1}\right)\right)R_N(n) \tag{9}$$

The frequency domain is given by

$$W(e^{j\omega}) = 0.42W_R(\omega) - 0.25\left[W_R\left(\omega - \frac{2\pi}{N-1}\right) + W_R\left(\omega + \frac{2\pi}{N-1}\right)\right]$$
$$+0.04\left[W_R\left(\omega - \frac{4\pi}{N-1}\right) + W_R\left(\omega + \frac{4\pi}{N-1}\right)\right] \tag{10}$$

Fig. 8 shows the time domain amplitude and magnitude spectrum with Blackman window.

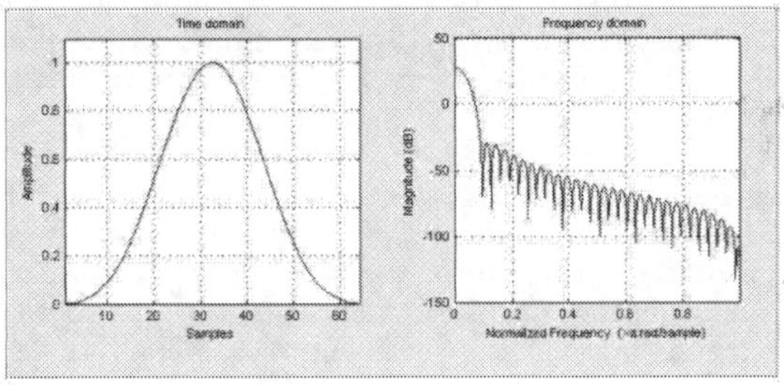

Fig. 8. Time domain amplitude and magnitude spectrum with Blackman window.

The maximum side lobe for the Blackman window is 57dB lower than main lobe, while which is three times as that of rectangular window, and the minimum stopband attenuation is 74dB.

4.3 Hanning window

The Hanning window (also called the Hanning window) is also known as a raised-cosine window due to its shape and form. The advantage of using Hanning Window method is that it reduces the side lobes. It has good frequency resolution over other window method like rectangular window. The Hann window takes the form:

$$w(n) = 0.5\left(1 - \cos\left(2\pi\frac{n}{N+1}\right)\right)R_N(n) \quad n = 1, 2, \Lambda, N \tag{11}$$

The frequency domain is defined as

$$W(e^{j\omega}) = 0.58W_R(\omega) - 0.25\left[W_R\left(\omega - \frac{2\pi}{N-1}\right) + W_R\left(\omega + \frac{2\pi}{N-1}\right)\right] \tag{12}$$

It has a main-lobe width considerably larger than the rectangular window, but the largest side-lobe peak is much lower, at about -31.5 dB. The side-lobes also taper off much faster. For a given length, this window is worse than the boxcar window at separating closely-spaced spectral components of similar magnitude, but better for identifying smaller-magnitude components at a greater distance from the larger components. It has a main-lobe width (about $3\pi/N$ at the -3 dB level and $8\pi/N$ between the two zeros surrounding the main lobe. Fig. 9 provides the time domain amplitude and magnitude spectrum with Hanning window.

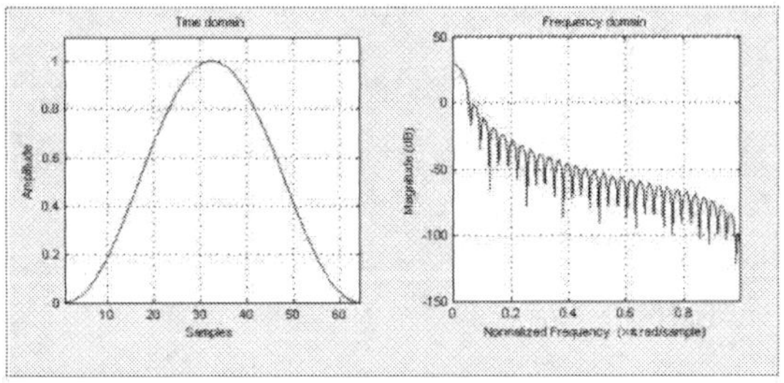

Fig. 9. Time domain amplitude and magnitude spectrum with Hanning window.

The Hamming window is use to minimize the maximum nearest side lobes, which has a form similar to the Hann window but with slightly different constants. Since it is composed of the same Fourier series harmonics as the Hann window, it has a similar main-lobe width, but the largest side-lobe peak is much lower, at about -42.5 dB. However, the side-lobes also taper off much more slowly than with the Hann window. For a given length, the Hamming window is better than the Hann windows at separating a small component relatively near to a large component, but worse than the Hann for identifying very small components at considerable frequency separation.

4.4 Kaiser window

The Kaiser window is a simple approximation of the DPSS window using Bessel functions, discovered by James Kaiser. As compared to the other window functions the Kaiser Window has maximum attenuation according to the given width of the main lobe. That is why it is also known as optimal window. The Kaiser Window function can be written:

$$w(n) = \frac{I_0\left[\beta\sqrt{1-\left(1-\frac{2n}{N-1}\right)^2}\right]}{I_0(\beta)} \qquad 0 \le n \le N-1 \qquad (13)$$

where $I_0(\beta)$ is the zero-th order modified Bessel function of the first kind. The variable parameter β determines the tradeoff between main lobe width and side lobe levels of the spectral leakage pattern.

$$\beta = \begin{cases} 0.1102(\alpha-8.7) & \alpha > 50 \\ 0.5482(\alpha-21)^{0.4} + 0.07886(\alpha-21) & 21 \le \alpha \le 50 \\ 0 & \alpha < 21 \end{cases} \qquad (14)$$

Fig. 10 gives the time domain amplitude and magnitude spectrum with Kaiser window.

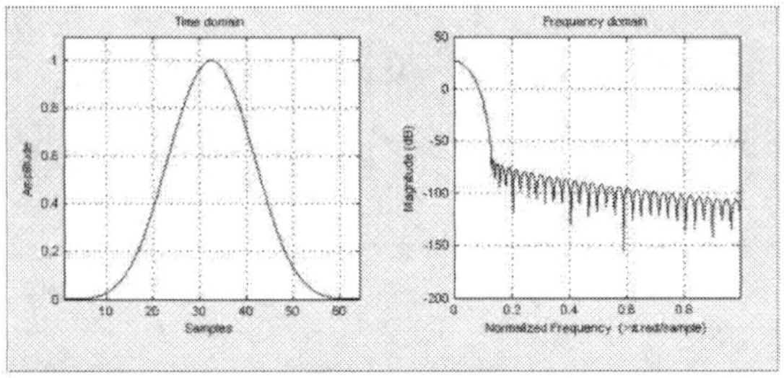

Fig. 10. Time domain amplitude and magnitude spectrum with Kaiser window.

4.5 The Welch method

The periodogram technique based on Welch method is capable of providing good resolution if data length samples are selected optimally. Welch's method is also called the periodogram method for estimating power spectra. The approach is carried out by dividing the time signal into successive blocks, forming the periodogram for each block, and averaging. As a non-parametric estimator of the power spectral density (PSD) of a random signal, the periodogram is not consistent due to the fact that its variance does not converge towards zero even when the length of the random signal is increased towards infinity. The Welch method is usually employed to overcome this problem, based on the following procedure: (1) split the random signal into segments; (2) estimate the PSD for each segment; and (3) average over these local estimates. The averaging reduces the variance of the estimated PSD. The Welch's method is a generalization using windowed overlapping segments.

A good resolution in power spectrum estimation (PSE) may be achieved by using optimum size of data sample. PSE has been performed using various windowing functions with the Welch method. Welch method is nonparametric method that include the periodogram that possesses the advantage of possible implementation using the fast Fourier Transform. In this section, the Welch method gives the result on power spectrum estimation with different windows. In DSP, Welch method is used to find the PSD of a signal with reducing the effect of noise.

A classical periodogram approach is an estimate of the spectral density of a signal, as shown in Fig. 11. Fig. 12 provides the flowchart of Welch method. An input signal can be of any number of dimensions and can be complex.

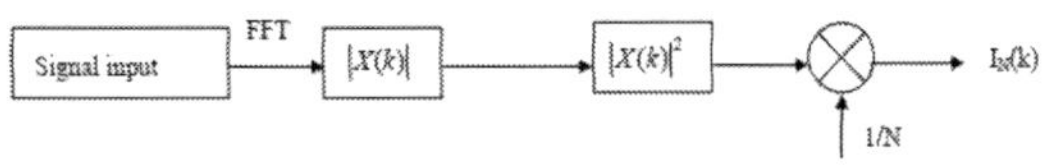

Fig. 11. Folw chart of the classical periodogram approach.

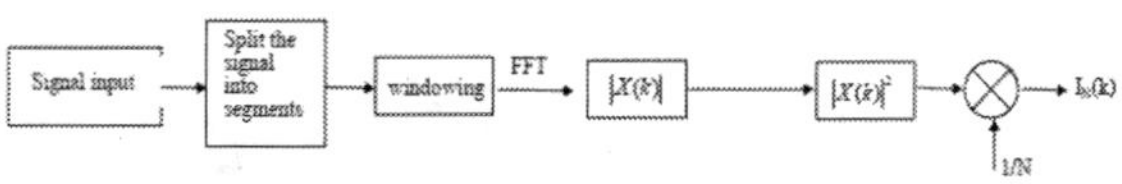

Fig. 12. Folw chart of the Welch method.

5 Results and Discussion

To investigate the capability of various window function for inhibition of spectral leakage, various windowing functions incorporated into the Welch power spectrum is carried out. Some results based on the numerical simulation are provided.

5.1 Spectra of a sine wave using various windowing functions

In the first test example, the continuous sinusoid signal $x(t) = \sin(2\pi ft)$, is employed, where $f = 5.2$ Hz, and the sampling frequency is $f_s = 100$ Hz, Truncate length N = 64. The rectangular window has admirable resolution characteristics for sinusoids of comparable strength.

The original time domain sinusoid signal and its magnitude spectrum are shown as in Fig. 13. Fig. 14 provides the rectangle windowed sinusoid and its magnitude spectrum. Figs. 15-17 provide the time domain signal and the corresponding magnitude spectra using the Blackman, Hanning, and Kaiser window, respectively.

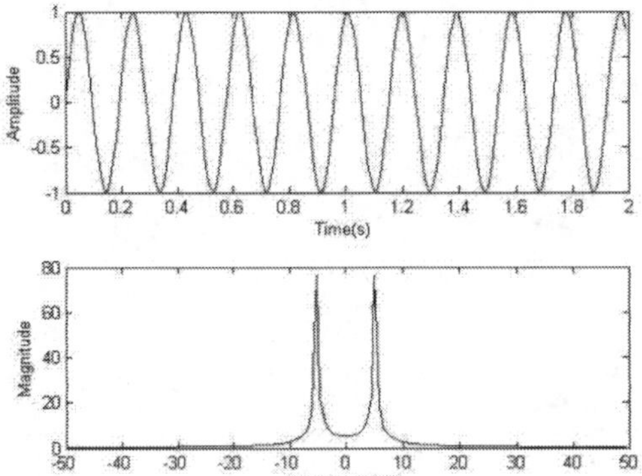

Fig. 13. Original time domain sinusoid signal and its magnitude spectrum.

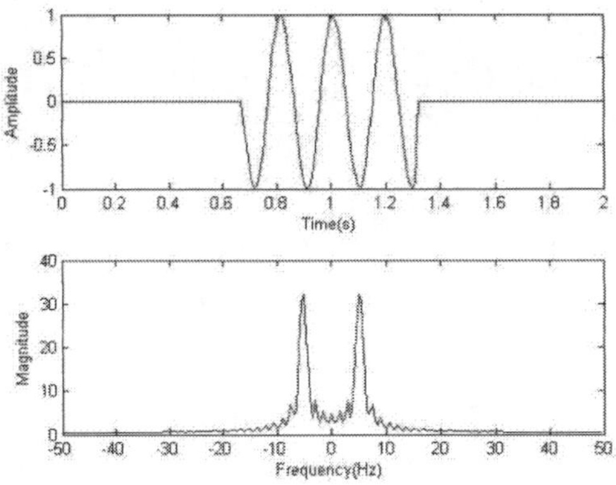

Fig. 14. The rectangle windowed sinusoid and its magnitude spectrum.

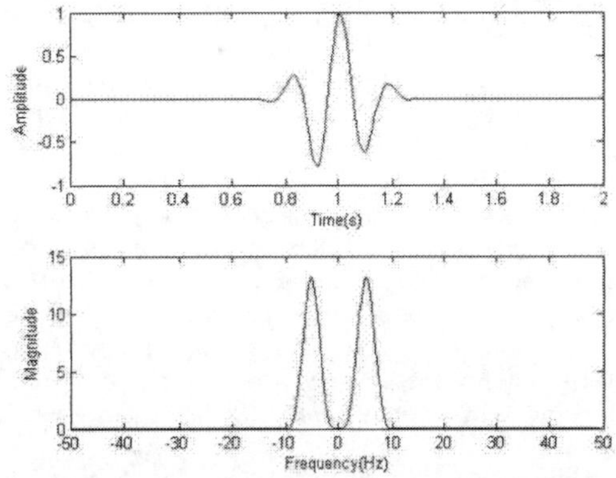

Fig. 15. Time domain signal with Blackman window and its magnitude spectrum.

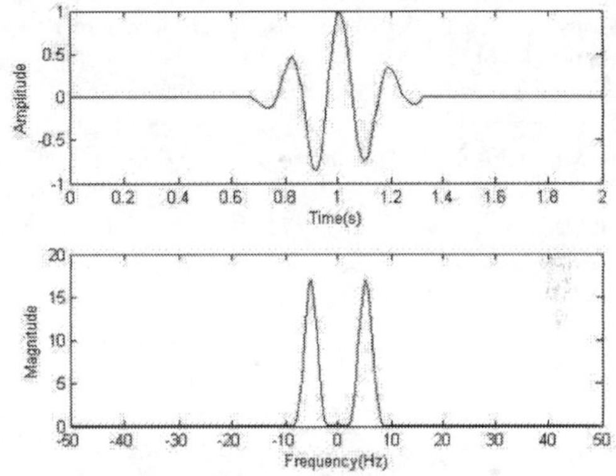

Fig. 16. Time domain signal with Hanning window and its magnitude spectrum.

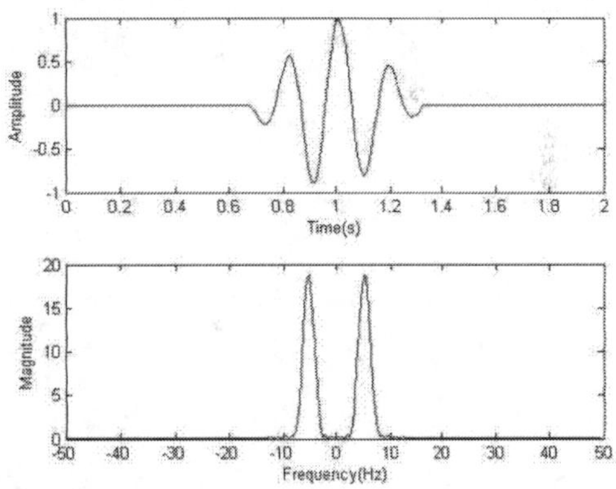

Fig. 17. Time domain signal with Kaiser window and its magnitude spectrum.

5.2 spectrum estimation using Welch method with various windowing functions

The simulation employed a signal is a sine signal with frequency 300Hz plus another sine signal with frequency 500Hz as the input. A Gaussian-white sequence is added into the signal, where the signal-to-noise ratio is 10dB. The sampling frequency is 3000Hz with the number of sampling points 3000. The data length of FFT is 512.

The characteristics of window function are analyzed from spectrum resolution and noise level. Simulation based on the periodogram method and then the Welch method using the rectangular, Blackman, Hanning window, and Kaiser windows (all with length 511) are performed for power spectrum estimation.

The selection and use of window function in Welch algorithm are analyzed. Power spectrum estimation using the periodogram is shown as in Fig. 18. Figs. 19-22 provide the power spectrum magnitude using Welch method with rectangular, Blackman, Hanning, and Kaiser windows, respectively. Comparison of Spectral estimation using various approaches is summarized in Table 2.

The rectangular window has the clear peak in the graph showing the power spectrum estimation. The spectral resolution of rectangular window and Kaiser window is higher, but the noise level near the signal frequency is higher. It is considered that both rectangular window and Kaiser window are suitable for high precision spectrum estimation of signals with high signal to noise ratio. Hanning window has better effect on spectrum leakage suppression, but the frequency resolution is relatively low, suitable for general frequency estimation of signals with low signal to noise ratio.

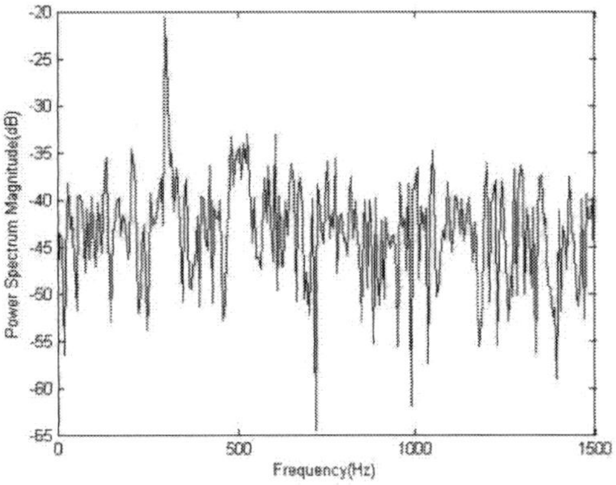

Fig. 18. Power spectrum estimation using the periodogram.

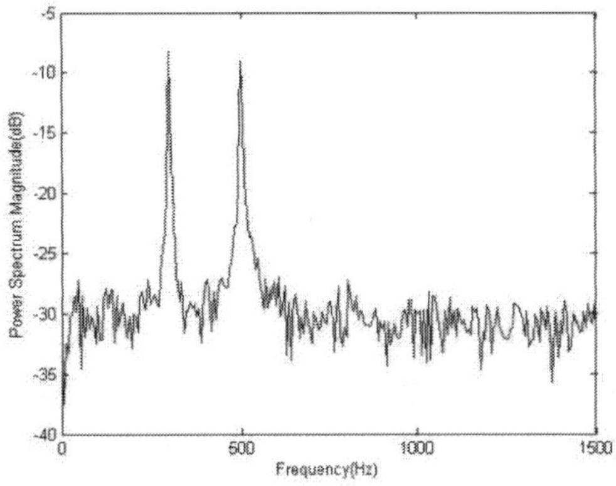

Fig. 19. Power spectrum magnitude using Welch method with rectangular window.

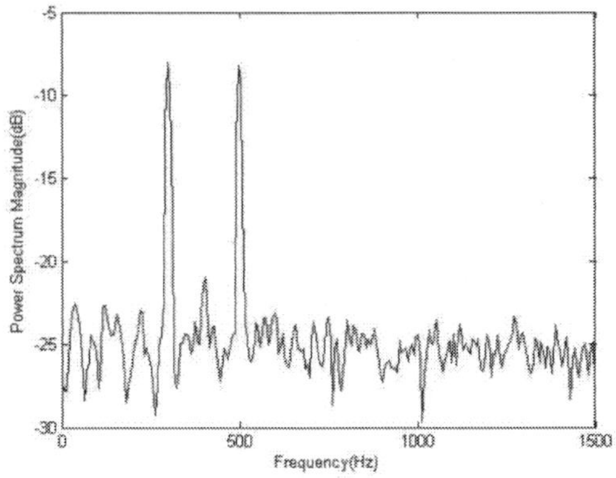

Fig. 20. Power spectrum magnitude using Welch method with Blackman window.

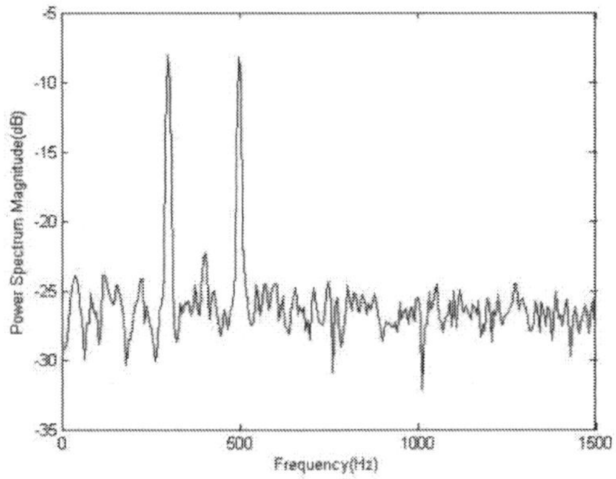

Fig. 21. Power spectrum magnitude using Welch method with Hanning window.

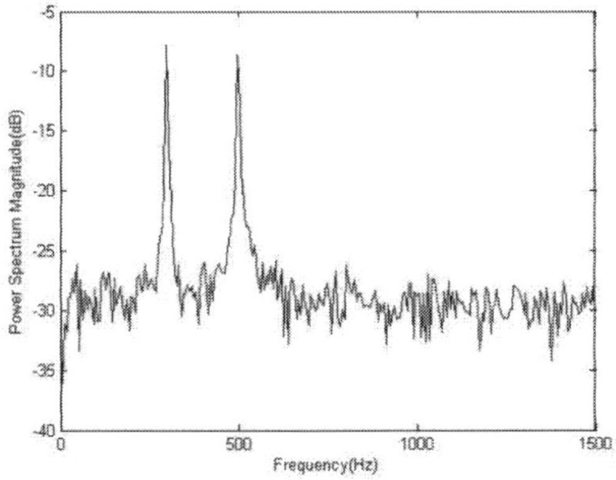

Fig. 22. Power spectrum magnitude using Welch method with Kaiser window.

6 Conclusions

This paper investigates the spectrum leakage suppression algorithm. The power spectrum estimation has been performed using various windowing functions with the Welch method.

Resolution is the ability to discriminate spectral feature and is a key concept on the analysis of spectral estimator performance. Estimation with low spectrum resolution causes the signal easily disturbed by the noise, leading to the failure of the detection. The performance of DFT method inherently suffers from the spectral leakage, which is caused by the non-coherent sampling in the practical acquisition system. The superiority on spectrum leakage suppression algorithm is verified by comparing with the traditional spectrum analysis based on the DFT with windowing. The quality of the estimate increases as the length N of the data increase.

Windowing amplitude modulates the input signal so that the spectral leakage is evened out. The windowing functions in this paper including the rectangular, Blackman, Hanning, and Kaiser windows have been employed to extract the unwanted noise from the signal. The effect of windowing functions on power spectral density is investigated by applying the Welch method. The Welch algorithm splits the random signal into segments before DFT to reduce the spectral leakage, which used a modified version of Bartlett method in which the portion of the series contributing to each periodogram are allowed to overlap. The Welch method gives the result on power spectrum estimation with different windowing functions in the window method to estimate the power spectral density of a signal, with less effect caused by noise.

Table 2. Comparison of Spectral estimation using various approaches.

Windowing function	**Average spectral error (Hz)**	**Average noise power (dB)**	**spectral leakage mean power (dB)**
Rectangular window	±1.3672	-29.4467	-23.4521
Blackman window	±2.4038	-25.1630	-25.9652
Hanning window	±2.8646	-26.1223	-26.2241
Kaiser window	±1.4625	-28.2806	-25.2102

Acknowledgements

Funding for this work was provided by the Ministry of Science and Technology of the Republic of China under grant number MOST 107-2221-E-019-025

References

1. C. L. Phillips and H. T. Nagle, *Digital Control System Analysis and Design*, **3d** ed. Upper Saddle River, NJ: Prentice Hall, (1996).
2. S. S. Soliman and M. D. Srinath, *Continuous and Discrete Signals and Systems*, **2d** ed. Upper Saddle River, NJ: Prentice Hall, (1997).
3. R. E. Ziemer, W. H. Tranter, and S. R. Fannin, Signals and System Continuous and Discrete, **4th** ed. (1998).
4. C. L. Phillips and H. T. Nagle, Digital Control System Analysis and Design, Upper Saddle River, NJ: Prentice Hall (1996).
5. T. Zhang, et. al, Effect of Frequency Domain Anti-Jamming Filter on Satellite Navigation Signal Tracking Performance, China Satellite Navigation Conference (CSNC, 2013), Lecture Notes in Electrical Engineering **243**, Chapter 46, J. Sun et al. (eds.), pp. 507-516.
6. J. Li, et. al, Effects of Spectrum Leakage on Frequency Domain Anti-jamming Performance, China Satellite Navigation Conference (CSNC, 2016), **Volume I**, Lecture Notes in Electrical Engineering **388**, pp.631-642.
7. Q. Wang, X. Yan, Y. Ren, Spectrum Leakage Suppression for Multi-Frequency Signal based on DFT, IEEE **13th** International Conference on Electronic Measurement & Instruments (2017).
8. P. D. Welch, The Use of Fast Fourier Transform for the Estimation of Power Spectra: A Method Based on Time Averaging Over Short Modified Periodograms, IEEE Trans. Audio Electroacoustic (1970).
9. H. R. Gupta, R. Mehra, Power Spectrum Estimation using Welch Method for Various Window Techniques, International Journal of Scientific Research Engineering & Technology (2013).

A New Method for converting Slant Ionospheric Delays to Vertical for SBAS Ionospheric corrections

Bongkwan Choi [1], *Deokhwa* Han[1], *Hwigyeom* Kim[2], and *Changdon* Kee [1,*]

[1] School of Mechanical and Aerospace Engineering and the SNU-IAMD, Seoul National University, Seoul, South Korea
[2] School of Computing, KAIST, Daejeon, South Korea

Abstract. SBAS gives ionospheric correction data to GNSS users for more accurate positioning. SBAS uses obliquity factor of thin shell model to convert slant ionospheric delays to vertical delays which is not precise especially at lower elevation angle. This paper suggests a new method for estimating the vertical delays which are needed for generating the ionospheric corrections. The new method uses Chapman profile assumption by which the vertical electron density distribution can be modeled. It is also assumed that Chapman profile's parameters are given and the vertical ionospheric delay can be linearly modeled. We divided ionosphere into multi-layer and mapped ionospheric vertical delays with a linear function. Converting vertical delays of each layer to slant delays, we can set a linear equation for the vertical ionospheric delay at IPP. We used IRI model to get information about ionosphere for simulation to verify our new method. Estimation error of vertical ionospheric delay at IPP was decreased about 40% in average when using our new method.

1 INTRODUCTION

Global Navigation Satellite System (GNSS) is a system by which a user can point the user's location. The user uses receiver to receive signals from GNSS satellite and can calculate the position using data of signals. However there are many errors in space, such as ionospheric error, tropospheric error, satellite clock/orbit error, which make inaccuracy of estimation of the user's location. A major error among them is the ionospheric error. To mitigate ionospheric errors in GNSS signal, the user can use ionospheric models such as Klobuchar or get information about ionospheric delay from a reference station. Satellite Based Augmentation System (SBAS) is also the way to reduce the error of ionosphere. SBAS generates correction data which helps user to locate user's position more precisely. One of the correction data is the ionospheric correction data. SBAS gives ionospheric correction data of Ionospheric Grid Point (IGP) and the user uses the information of IGP to calculate user's ionospheric delay. The correction data of ionospheric delay at IGP is generated with the slant ionospheric delays in signal between satellites and reference stations. Master stations of SBAS need vertical ionospheric delays at Ionospheric Pierce Point (IPP), instead of slant delays, to calculate ionospheric correction data at IGP. Each reference station can measure the slant ionospheric delays with dual frequency, but cannot get the vertical ionospheric delays directly. As a result, reference stations have to estimate the vertical ionospheric delay and SBAS uses obliquity factor of thin shell model to get vertical ionospheric delays. However, thin shell model has some limitations. First, thin shell model assumes that peak electron density height is constant. However the peak height is high at daytime and low at night time [1]. Furthermore thin shell model does not consider spatial characteristics of ionosphere. These factors occur errors in estimation of vertical ionospheric delay from slant ionospheric delay. In this paper, we suggested a new method for converting slant ionospheric delays to vertical ionospheric delay to mitigate the error of thin shell model.

2 Algorithm of the new method

In the new method we made several assumptions. First, we assumed that the variation of ionosphere is linear. We also assumed that the vertical electron density distribution follows Chapman profile [2]. Chapman profile is a model for electron density distribution of ionosphere. The function of Chapman profile is below.

$$n_e(\lambda,\phi,h)=\frac{N_0(\lambda,\phi)}{\sqrt{2\pi e}H}\exp\left(\frac{1}{2}(1-z-\exp(-z))\right)=N_0(\lambda,\phi)Chap(h) \tag{1}$$

$$z=\frac{h-h_0}{H} \tag{2}$$

$$\int Chap(h)=1 \tag{3}$$

n_e is electron density at height h, N_0 is the peak electron density, h_0 is the peak electron density altitude and H is the atmospheric scale height. The function of Chapman profile can be determined with two parameters h_0, H and we assumed that parameters of Chapman profile can be known at every point as a priory information.

* Corresponding author: kee@snu.ac.kr

Hoque suggested a method for estimating slant ionospheric delay in signal between a user and satellites with vertical ionospheric delay [3]. Fundamentally, the new method which is suggested in this paper started from the method in the paper of Hoque. The most different thing of the method of this paper from the Hoque's is that the process of the algorithm is inversed.

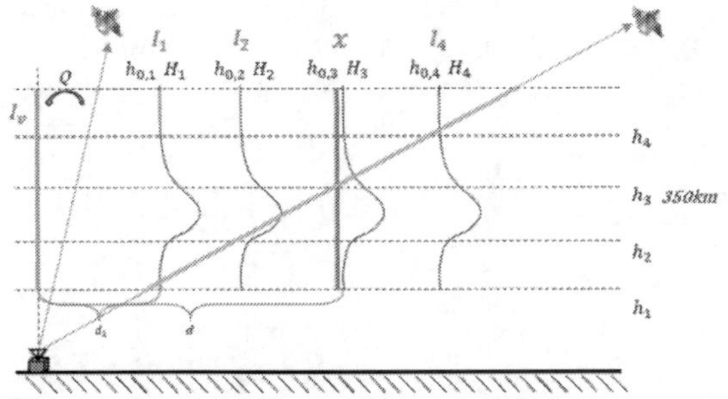

Figure 1. Conceptual figure of the new method

$$I_i = (x - I_v)\frac{d_i}{d} + I_v \tag{4}$$

$$I_{v,i} = I_i \times \int_{h_i}^{h_{i+1}} Chap(h_{0,i}, H_i, h)dh = I_i C_i \tag{5}$$

$$I_{slant} = \sum_{i=1}^{n} I_{v,i} \times Q_i \tag{6}$$

$$Q_i = \frac{1}{\sqrt{1 - \left(\frac{(h_{RX} + R_e)\cos(\mathrm{El})}{h_i + R_e}\right)^2}} \tag{7}$$

$$x = \frac{I_{slant} d - ((d - d_1)C_1Q_1 + (d - d_2)C_2Q_2 + \mathrm{L})I_v}{dC_3Q_3 + d_1C_1Q_1 + d_2C_2Q_2 + d_4C_4Q_4 + \mathrm{L}} \tag{8}$$

Our algorithm divided ionosphere into multi-shell. Figure 1 is a conceptual figure of the new method. First, we get vertical ionospheric delay at reference station from the slant delay of a satellite which has the highest elevation angle at the moment. When converting the slant delay to vertical delay, we use the obliquity factor of the thin shell model. It is acceptable idea because the error of the obliquity factor is negligible when the satellite has high elevation angle. I_i in the figure 1 means the vertical delay of ionosphere along the whole height at the point where line of sight (LOS) vector and the i'th shell meet. What we want to solve is vertical ionospheric delay at IPP, so we set it as an unknown character x. By assuming that the variation of ionosphere is linear, we can mapping the overall delay of the ionosphere as equation (4). Also we assumed that the distribution of vertical electron density follows the Chapman profile we can express the segment of whole ionospheric delay of i'th point as equation (5). If we multiply i'th obliquity factor of equation (7) to each segment and add them all, we can get slant ionospheric delay as a result like equation (6). Finally, by substituting equation (4), (5) into (6), we can solve the linear equation and get vertical ionospheric delay at IPP like equation (8). Obliquity factor in equation (7) can be obtained using geometric equations like the law of sines.

3 Verification of the new method

We verified the algorithm in the Korean region. We used reference stations of Korean Augmentation Satellite System (KASS) to get IPP data [4]. For ionosphere environment, we used IRI model. To verify our new method in various environment, we tested for 3 IPP data (2016.08.09 02h, 17h, 22h) in two different IRI model (2014.09.01 14h (UTC), 2011.10.23 14h (UTC)). We treated IRI model data as a true ionosphere environment. In this paper, it was assumed that electron of ionosphere exists from 100km to 2000km height. When obtaining the IPP data, we used broadcast (BRDC) as an ephemeris data to determine the orbit of global positioning system (GPS) satellites. Ionosphere was divided into every 5km height and this interval was used in the new method which is suggested in this paper.

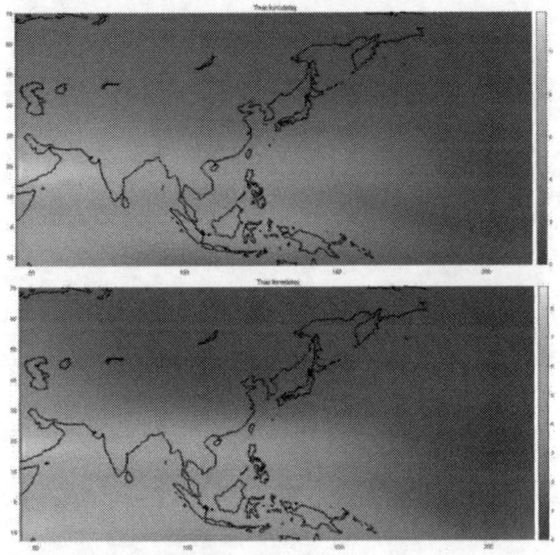

Figure 2 Ionospheric delay map
(up : 2014.09.01 14h(UTC), down : 2011.10.23 14h(UTC))

Figure 2 shows the vertical ionospheric delay of each IRI data. Because the time is 14h UTC, 23h for South Korea, activity around South Korea region is weak comparatively. Figure 3 and figure 4 show the result of estimation error of thin shell model and the new method. Circles in figures indicate IPPs and colors in the circle is degree of the error of each method.

As we can see in the figure 3, estimation error of thin shell model increases as IPPs are far from the Korean region where reference stations are. It means that estimation error at IPPs between the reference station and a satellite with a low elevation angle is high if the thin shell model is used. However, as we can see in the right-hand side of the figure 3, estimation error of IPPs with low elevation angle were mitigated if the new method is used. Besides overall error of estimation were mitigated.

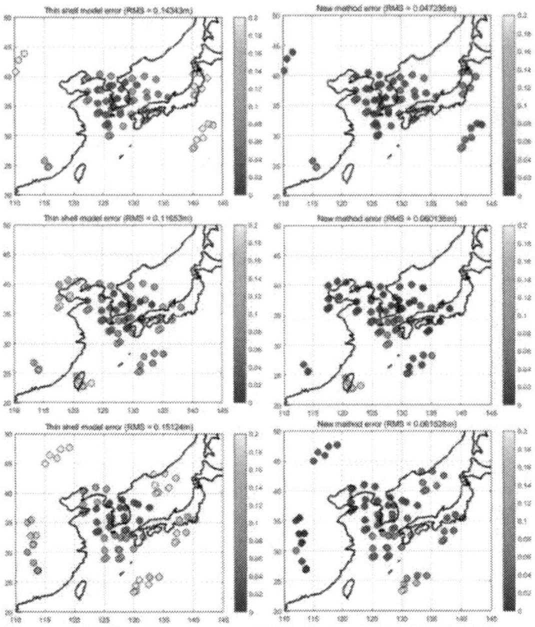

Figure 3 Estimation error at IPP (date : 2014.09.01 14h) (left : thin shell model , right : new method, up : 02h IPP data, middle : 17h IPP data, down : 22h IPP data)

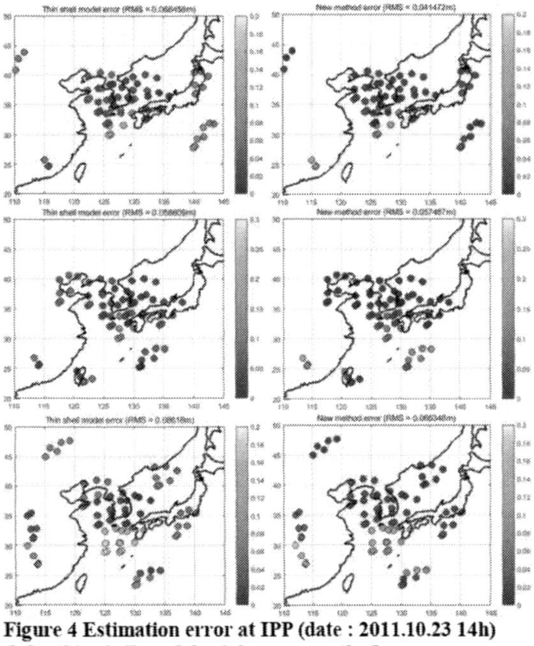

Figure 4 Estimation error at IPP (date : 2011.10.23 14h) (left : thin shell model , right : new method, up : 02h IPP data, middle : 17h IPP data, down : 22h IPP data)

Figure 4 shows that the estimation error is also decreased in another ionospheric environment when using the new method instead of the thin shell model. Comparing the IPPs which located at center of the map, we can see that estimation error is mitigated. It is because distance between the reference station and the satellite of IPPs at center is shorter than other IPP located at circumference. Variation of vertical ionospheric delay is can be treated linear in short distance. So estimation error of IPPs which have short distance can be more decreased when using the new method which assumed that variation of ionosphere is linear.

Table 1. Estimation error of each method (RMS)

IRI data	IPP data	Thin shell model error (m)	New method error (m)
2014.09.01 14h	02h	0.1434	0.0472
	17h	0.1165	0.0601
	22h	0.1512	0.0615
2011.10.23 14h	02h	0.0685	0.0415
	17h	0.0588	0.0575
	22h	0.0862	0.0663

Table 2. Percentage of mitigated error at IPP

IRI data	IPP data	Mitigated error (%)
2014.09.01 14h	02h	67.09
	17h	48.41
	22h	59.33
2011.10.23 14h	02h	39.41
	17h	2.21
	22h	23.09

Overall result of simulation is on table 1. In table 2, there are percentage points mitigated error at IPP. The percentage point indicates decreased error by using the new method over the error of thin shell model. As we can see in the table 1, estimation error was mitigated at all case. Besides the mitigated error was range from 2.2% to 67.1%. The average of mitigated error was about 40%.
The future work is to verify the new method in various ionosphere environment especially when the activity of ionosphere is severe. It is because when the ionosphere is severe, the assumption that ionosphere linear may occur the error more than in the weak ionosphere environment. However, with previous result, we verified that our new method works well in weak ionosphere environment.

4 Conclusion

In this paper we suggested the new method for converting slant ionospheric delay to vertical ionospheric delay at IPP. We used the Chapman profile which is model for vertical electron density distribution of ionosphere. Furthermore, with assumption that variation of ionosphere is linear and parameters of Chapman profile is given, the slant delay can be expressed in linear equation of vertical delay at IPP. Verification was performed with simulations which are consist of two IRI model sets and three IPP data sets. As a result, the estimation error at IPP was mitigated about 40% on average when using the new method instead of the thin shell model.

5 Acknowledgement

This research was supported by Basic Science Research Program through the National Research Foundation of Korea(NRF) funded by the Ministry of Science, ICT & Future Planning (No. NRF-2017M1A3A3A02016230), contracted through by the Institute of Advanced Aerospace Technology at Seoul National University. The Institute of Engineering Research at Seoul National University provided research facilities for this work.

6 Reference

[1] Hoque, M. M., and N. Jakowski. "A new global model for the ionospheric F2 peak height for radio wave propagation." *Annales Geophysicae*. Vol. 30. No. 5. Copernicus GmbH, 2012

[2] Feltens, J. "Chapman profile approach for 3-D global TEC representation." *IGS Presentation, in* (1998).

[3] Hoque, M. M., N. Jakowski, and J. Berdermann. "A new approach for mitigating ionospheric mapping function errors." *Proceedings ION GNSS*. 2014.

[4] Authié, T., Dall'Orso, M., Trilles, S., Choi, H., Kim, H., Lee, J., Lee, E., Nam, G., "Performances Monitoring and Analysis for KASS," *Proceedings of the 30th International Technical Meeting of The Satellite Division of the Institute of Navigation (ION GNSS+ 2017)*, Portland, Oregon, pp. 958-978, September 2017.

[5] Hoque, M. M., and N. Jakowski. "Mitigation of ionospheric mapping function error." *Proceedings of the ION GNSS+, Nashville/Tennessee/USA* (2013): 16-20.

Autonomous Base Station Placement for Localization of the GNSS Interference Source

Sun Young Kim[1,*], *Chang Ho* Kang[2], and *Chan Gook* Park[3]

[1]Mechanical and Aerospace Engineering and Automation and System Research Institute, Seoul National University, Gawnak-Gu, Seoul 08826, Republic of Korea
[2]BK21+ Transformative Training Program for Creative Mechanical and Aerospace Engineers, Seoul National University, Gawnak-Gu, Seoul 08826, Republic of Korea
[3]Mechanical and Aerospace Engineering and the Institute of Advanced Aerospace Technology, Seoul National University, Gawnak-Gu, Seoul 08826, Republic of Korea

Abstract. This paper presents the control strategy of autonomous base station placement for localization of the GNSS interference source. The proposed algorithm deals with the optimization of the base station trajectory for target motion analysis based on bearing only tracking problem. The control strategy of the proposed algorithm is designed to maximize a cost function which is generally a functional of the Fisher information matrix. Compared to the optimal control methods, the proposed algorithm is easy to be designed and implemented, and constraints of multiple base stations' trajectories can be effectively included. In addition, the proposed algorithm also considered target's dynamics that is both uncertain and random, and there are multiple base stations for observing the target. In order to verify the performance of the proposed algorithm, simulation was performed with dynamic target case in the 2D scenario. It is assumed that the base stations' networks have non-fully connected topology. According to the simulation results, it was confirmed that the proposed algorithm presents a flexible control strategy of autonomous multiple base stations' placement for bearing only target tracking system.

1 Introduction

In recent years, many researches have been conducted to guarantee the quality of satellite navigation system from various interference sources at home and abroad. Especially, importance of the related researches is increasing as South Korea was exposed to the attack of intentional interference source by North Korea several times under special circumstance. It is also necessary to study other types of countermeasures, assuming scenarios where it is impossible to use previous fixed base stations in special situations such as navigation warfare. Therefore, in this paper, we have studied the placements of the mobile stations in order to estimate the position of the interference source even navigation warfare. In this case, only the difference of angle (DOA) measurement is used instead of the differential received signal strength (DRSS) measurement used in the previous study [1, 2] in order to estimate the interference's position even in the presence of multiple moving interference sources. The DRSS measurement is difficult to apply for localization in the case of multiple signal sources because it is impossible to judge whether the received signal strength was obtained from which signal source. Using DOA measurements in the presence of multiple sources, both true and false values will be displayed together and the data association process is needed. However, using a filter such as a random finite set filter (RFSF), which is used in the multi-target tracking field, allows tracking of multiple sources without data association. Therefore, in this paper, the DOA measurement is used to estimate the position of a moving interference source using a mobile station, although the accuracy of the position estimation is somewhat lower than using other measurements. In order to improve the accuracy of position estimation, we have studied the placement of mobile stations. The placement performance of base stations was judged using estimation accuracy of the interference source's position and verified by simulation.

2 Base Station Arrangement

Studies on the placement of base stations should be considered first in order to precisely estimate the location of GNSS interference signal sources. Especially in an environment where conventional fixed base stations can not be used, as in the navigation warfare situation, it is more important to arrange base stations.

One important role of the base station is to monitor the navigation status and to guarantee the navigation quality by responding to the signal source through the detection and position estimation of the interference signal source.

The GNSS status monitoring is possible on the basis of a single reference station. However, placement studies

* Corresponding author: chanpark@snu.ac.kr

are more important because more than two reference stations are required for precise position estimation of the signal source and the position estimation performance is influenced by the reference station arrangement.

2.1. Network Topology

Arrangement used in the sensor network can be applied for the placement of multiple base stations for the positioning of GNSS interference signal sources. The deployment in the sensor network for location estimation can be largely divided into centralized and distributed (decentralized) deployments.

In general situations with no constraints, centralized deployment has the advantage of higher positional performance and effective location estimation. However, if all of the base stations are not available and only some of the base stations can be used, or if all of the existing fixed base stations become unavailable, such as navigation warfare, additional base station should be located for monitoring the status of GNSS and for estimating the position of the GNSS interference signal source. Thus, in this section, in order to maintain accurate estimation performance, the control strategy of base station replacement is explained.

2.2 Control Strategy

Since the operation of the base station in the emergency situation like the navigation warfare situation assumes that the existing fixed base station can not be used, the additional arrangement of the mobile station is considered. In this case, the number of available mobile station can be extended to N, and in the case where the fixed reference station arranged for the position estimation is available, the existing fixed reference station and the mobile reference station can be arranged together. When additional mobile reference stations were used, the estimation accuracy of DOA by measurement was analyzed on a Cramer-Rao lower bound (CRLB) basis.

The Cramer-Rao inequality lower bounds the covariance achievable by an unbiased estimator under two mild regularity conditions. Considering the unbiased estimate $\hat{p}$ for p, the Cramer-Rao bound states that

$$E\left[(\hat{p}-p)(\hat{p}-p)^T\right] \geq I^{-1}(p) = C(p) \tag{1}$$

where I is the Fisher information matrix. In general, if I is singular then no unbiased estimator for p exists with a finite variance.

2.3 DOA Based Localization and Placement

The measured value of angle (θ_i) shown in Figure 1 is given by

$$\hat{\theta}_i = \theta_i(p) + n_i = \arctan\left(\frac{y_p - y_{si}}{x_p - x_{si}}\right) + n_i \tag{2}$$

where the arctan is defined such that $\theta_i(p) \in [0, 2\pi)$ and the n_i is the measurement error. This error is assumed to be white Gaussian distribution with zero mean and variance $\sigma_\theta^2, i.e., n_i \sim N(0, \sigma_\theta^2)$.

Fisher information matrix $(I_\theta(p))$ for N number of base station around the target can be written as [3],

$$I_\theta(p) = \frac{1}{\sigma_\theta^2} \sum_{i=1}^{N} \frac{1}{r_i^2} \begin{bmatrix} \sin^2\theta_i & -\sin\theta_i \cos\theta_i \\ -\sin\theta_i \cos\theta_i & \cos^2\theta_i \end{bmatrix} \tag{3}$$

Especially, the Fisher information determinant for bearing-only localization can be given as,

$$\det(I_\theta(p)) = \frac{1}{\sigma_\theta^4} \sum_{S} \frac{\sin^2(\theta_j - \theta_i)}{r_j^2 r_i^2} \tag{4}$$

and

$$\det(I_\theta(p)) = \frac{1}{4\sigma_\theta^4}\left[\left(\sum_{i=1}^{N}\frac{1}{r_i^2}\right) - \left(\sum_{i=1}^{N}\frac{\cos 2\theta_i}{r_i^2}\right)^2 - \left(\sum_{i=1}^{N}\frac{\cos 2\theta_i}{r_i^2}\right)^2\right] \tag{5}$$

where $S = \{\{i, j\}\}$ is defined as the set of all combinations of i and j with $i, j \in \{1, \ldots, N\}$ and $j > i$, implying $|S| = \binom{N}{2}$. Here $|\cdot|$ indicates the number of combinations.

In Figure 1, the location of GNSS interference source is at $P(x_p, y_p)$ which is b distance away from the x-axis. N distance number of AOA sensors (one fixed at the origin, S_1) are the x-axis, separated by x distance from each other.

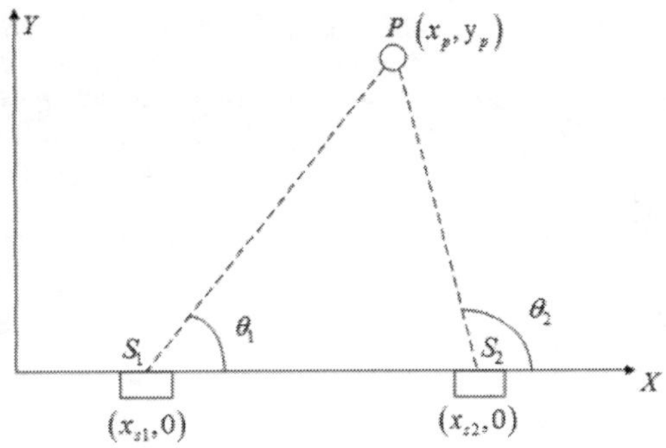

Fig. 1. Localization with two sensors (AOA) on x-axis.

The Fisher information determination for this case is

$$\det\left(I_\theta(p)\right) = \frac{1}{\sigma_\theta^4}\sum_{j=2}^{N}\sum_{i=0}^{j-2}\left\{\frac{b\left[j-(i+1)\right]x}{\left[(a-ix)^2+b^2\right]\left[(a-[j-1]x)^2+b^2\right]}\right\}^2 \tag{6}$$

where $(a,b)=(x_p,y_p)$. Translating Equation (4) into Cartesian coordinates and rearranging leads to Equation (6).

Consider that the target location is $P(x_p,y_p)$ and the position of the fixed sensor (S_1) and the line on which the second sensor to be placed is known as shown in Figure 1. The Fisher information determinant for this case is

$$\det\left(I_x(p)\right) = \frac{1}{\sigma_\theta^4}\left(\frac{-y_p x_{s2}}{(x_p^2+y_p^2)\left[(x_p-x_{s2})^2+y_p^2\right]}\right)^2 \tag{7}$$

By maximizing Equation (7) with respect to x_{s2}, it can be shown that, $\det\left(I_x(p)\right)$ maximizes when,

$$x_{s2} = \pm\sqrt{x_p^2+y_p^2} \tag{8}$$

Then the optimal distance between these two sensors is equal to the distance between the fixed sensor and the target ($\|S_1-S_2\|=\|S_1-P\|$).
By using results, the additional rearranged mobile station follows the triangular layout with target's location (GNSS interference source) and the available fixed base station.

3 Information-weighted Consensus Filter (ICF)

Due to high fault-tolerance and scalability to large networks in the GNSS quality monitoring system in the navigation warfare situation, consensus-based distributed algorithms are needed. One of the recent consensus algorithms is the information-weighted consensus filter which deals with the system with unknown cross correlation term in the covariance of state variables. The ICF is guaranteed to converge to the optimal centralized performance under certain reasonable conditions. In addition, the ICF also supports multiple consensus iterations at each time step to improve performance compared to other methods.

In general, the state variables' and measurement model are expressed by [4]

$$\mathbf{x}(t+1)=\mathbf{F}\mathbf{x}(t)+w(t) \tag{9}$$

$$\mathbf{z}_i(t)=\mathbf{H}_i(t)\mathbf{x}(t)+v_i(t) \tag{10}$$

where the system noise $w(t)$ and the measurement noise $v_i(t)$ are simplify modelled as white Gaussian noise with zero mean and variance $\mathbf{Q}$ and $\mathbf{R}_i$, respectively.

After obtaining the measurement $\mathbf{z}_i$ and the measurement information matrix $\mathbf{B}_i=\mathbf{R}_i^{-1}$ at each sensor i, the initial information matrix $\mathbf{V}_i^0$ and the initial matrix vector $\mathbf{v}_i^0$ are calculated as shown in (11) and (12), respectively.

$$\mathbf{V}_i^0=\frac{1}{N}\mathbf{W}_i^-(t)+\mathbf{H}_i^T\mathbf{B}_i\mathbf{H}_i \tag{11}$$

$$\mathbf{v}_i^0=\frac{1}{N}\mathbf{W}_i^-(t)\mathbf{x}_i^-(t)+\mathbf{H}_i^T\mathbf{B}_i\mathbf{z}_i \tag{12}$$

where N presents the number of sensors, $\mathbf{x}_i^-(t)$ represents the prior state estimate, and $\mathbf{W}_i^-(t)$ refers to the prior information matrix which can be calculated by the reciprocal of the covariance of the prior state estimate. The information matrix $\mathbf{V}_i$ and the matrix vector $\mathbf{v}_i$ of i -th node sensor independently perform an average consensus, repeating (13) and (14) from $k=1$ to $k=K$ (consensus iteration).

$$\mathbf{V}_i^k=\mathbf{V}_i^{k-1}+\varepsilon\sum_{j\in N_i}\left(\mathbf{V}_j^{k-1}-\mathbf{V}_i^{k-1}\right) \tag{13}$$

$$\mathbf{v}_i^k=\mathbf{v}_i^{k-1}+\varepsilon\sum_{j\in N_i}\left(\mathbf{v}_j^{k-1}-\mathbf{v}_i^{k-1}\right) \tag{14}$$

where j means all neighboring sensors which exchange information with connected sensors as in (13) and (14). ε is the rate parameter which should be chosen between 0 and $1/\Delta\max$, where $\Delta\max$ is the maximum number of connected sensors. The rest of detail explanation on the ICF is written in [4, 5].

The process of the ICF is given below.

Inputs: prior state estimate $\mathbf{x}^-(t)$, prior information matrix $\mathbf{W}^-(t)$, observation matrix $\mathbf{H}_i$, measurement $\mathbf{z}_i$, measurement information matrix $\mathbf{B}_i$, consensus rate parameter ε, state transition matrix $\mathbf{F}$, process covariance $\mathbf{Q}$.
Compute initial information matrix and vector

$$\mathbf{V}^0=\frac{1}{N}\mathbf{W}^-(t)+\mathbf{H}_i^T\mathbf{B}_i\mathbf{H}_i\ ,$$

$$\mathbf{v}^0=\frac{1}{N}\mathbf{W}^-(t)\mathbf{x}^-(t)+\mathbf{H}_i^T\mathbf{B}_i\mathbf{z}_i$$

Perform average consensus on $\mathbf{V}^0$ and $\mathbf{v}^0$ independently

 https://doi.org/10.1051/e3sconf/20199403003

for $k=1$ to K do

$$\mathbf{V}^k = \mathbf{V}^{k-1} + \varepsilon \sum_{j=1}^{N} \left(\mathbf{V}_j^{k-1} - \mathbf{V}^{k-1} \right),$$

$$\mathbf{v}^k = \mathbf{v}^{k-1} + \varepsilon \sum_{j=1}^{N} \left(\mathbf{v}_j^{k-1} - \mathbf{v}^{k-1} \right)$$

end

Compute a posteriori state estimate and information matrix for time t

$$\mathbf{x}^+(t) = \left(\mathbf{V}^k\right)^{-1} \mathbf{v}^k, \quad \mathbf{W}^+(t) = N\mathbf{V}^k$$

Predict a state estimate and information matrix for time $(t+1)$

$$\mathbf{x}^-(t+1) = \mathbf{F}\mathbf{x}^+(t),$$

$$\mathbf{W}^-(t+1) = \left(\mathbf{F}\left(\mathbf{W}^+(t)\right)^{-1} \mathbf{F}^T + \mathbf{Q} \right)^{-1}$$

Output: state estimate $\mathbf{x}^+(t)$, information matrix $\mathbf{W}^+(t)$

where $\mathbf{F} = \mathbf{I}$, $\mathbf{W}^-(t)$ can be calculated by the reciprocal of the covariance of the prior state estimate $\mathbf{x}^-(t)$, and N presents the number of fusion information.

4 Simulation Analysis

In this section, in order to verify the optimal replacement method explained in the section 2 and localization performance of the proposed algorithm compared to conventional method, simulation is performed and analyzed.

4.1 Simulation Conditions and Assumptions

The simulation conditions are as follows. First, it is assumed that there is no fully network connection between the sub base stations and the mobile stations (1-2, 1-3 connected). Observations are direction angles of the received signal and the connected fixed station is limited to less than two stations every time for additional placement of mobile stations. The measured field of view (FOV) of each station was set to 200 m width and 200 m height and the direction angle estimation error was set to 4 degrees. For the comparative analysis of the position estimation performance, the information-weighted consensus filter (ICF), the Kalman consensus filter (KCF) [6] and the generalized KCF (GKCF) [7] were selected.

4.2 Simulation Results

Figure 3 shows the results of the position estimation using each method, and Figure 4 indicates the filtering errors of the x-axis and y-axis, respectively. Table 1 presents the comparison on the position estimation error expressed by root mean square error (RMSE) and the computation time of the algorithm (relative time for one sequence), using each method.

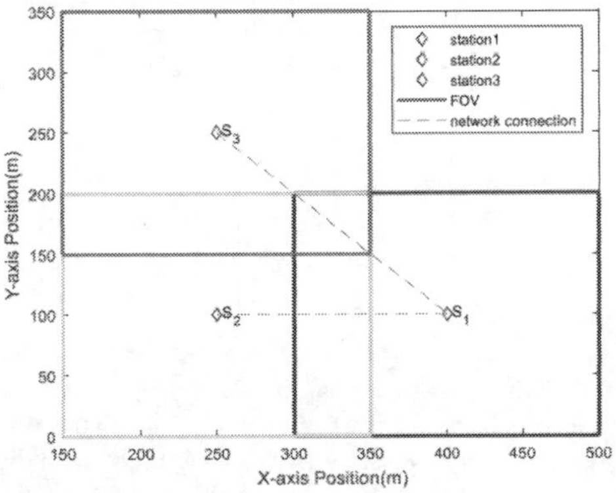

Fig. 2. Base station network and FOV.

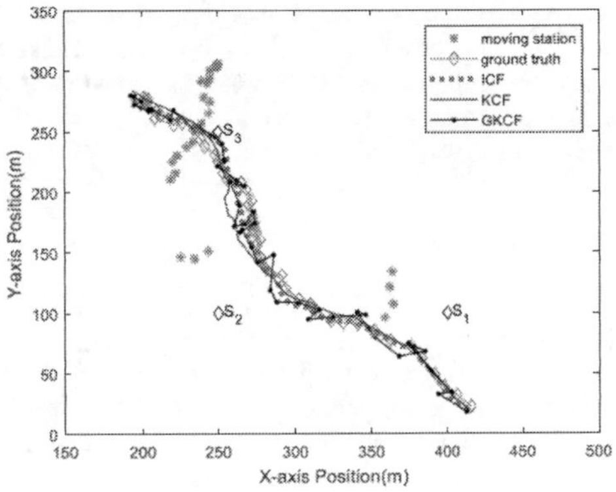

Fig. 3. Localization result.

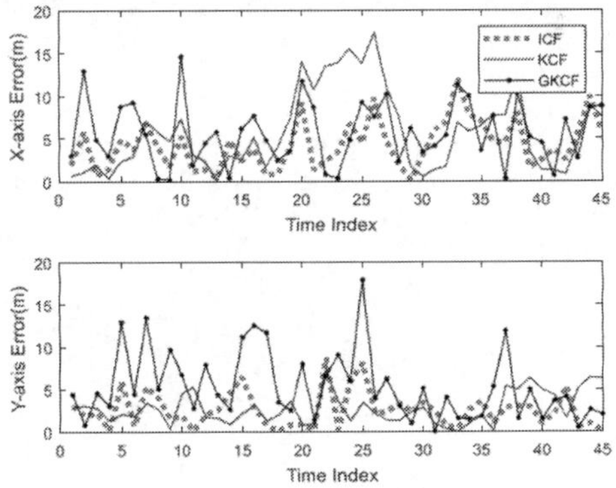

Fig. 4. Filtering error.

Table 1. Estimation error and computation time.

	RMSE(m)	Time(sec)
ICF	5.3735	0.0036
KCF	6.6564	0.0032
GKCF	8.8875	0.0038

From the simulation results, it is confirmed that the estimation performance of the ICF, which uses the information of each measurement as weight, is better than that of the GKCF and KCF. The computation time difference of each technique was small although the ICF performed consensus iteration (K = 20). If the quality of information fusion is not properly reflected as in the case of the GKCF, the performance is worse than the KCF. Also, it is confirmed that the position estimation performance can be improved by adding a mobile station in the case of the base stations are not fully connected as in the navigation warfare conditions.

5 Conclusion

The proposed algorithm deals with the optimization of the mobile station replacement with the fixed station for single target tracking effectively. In addition, this optimal placement method is applied to the ICF based localization method for tracking moving GNSS interference source. According to analysis results and simulation results, it is confirmed that triangular placement is the best arrangement type of mobile station and the proposed localization method has better performance compared to conventional methods in the distributed network situation which reflect the navigation warfare conditions.

This work has been supported by the National GNSS Research Center program of the Defense Acquisition Program Administration and Agency for Defense Development.

References

1. S.Y. Kim, C.H. Kang, C.G. Park, *ISGNSS 2015*, (2015)
2. S.Y. Kim, C.H. Kang, C.G. Park, K.H. Lee, M.J. Yu, *KIMST 2017* (2017). (in Korean)
3. Sanvidha C.K. Herath, Pubudu N. Pathirana, Sensors, **13** (2013)
4. A.T. Kamal, J.A. Farrell, A.K. Roy-Chowdhury, *2012 IEEE 51st Conf. Decision and Control*, Maui, HI, USA, pp. 2732-2737 (2012)
5. A.T. Kamel, J.A. Farrell, A.K. Roy-Chowdhury, IEEE Trans. Automat. Cont., **58** (2013)
6. R. Olfati-Saber, *Proceedings of the 48th IEEE Conference on Decision and Control and 28th Chinese Control Conference (CDC/CCC 2009)*, (2009)
7. A.T. Kamal, C. Ding, B. Song, J.A. Farrell, A.K. Roy-Chowdhury, *Proceedings of the 50th IEEE Conference on Decision and Control and European Control Conference (CDC/ECC 2011)*, (2011)

A Design of Anti-jamming Method Based on Spectrum Sensing and GNSS Software Defined Radio

Kwi Woo Park[1], *Min Joon* Lee[2], and *Chansik* Park[1,*]

[1]Chungbuk National University, Dept. of Electronics Eng., 28644 Cheongju, Republic of Korea
[2]Agency for Defense Development, 34186 Deajeon, Republic of Korea

Abstract. This paper presents result of new approach for anti-jamming using a method based on cognitive radio. To detect and get center frequency and bandwidth of jamming, a spectrum sensing based on multi-channel energy detector is implemented on the SDR. The SDR and a universal software radio peripheral is used to support real-time channel reconfiguration. And detected center frequency and bandwidth is used to select LO frequency to avoid jamming and receive GNSS signal. Then the receiver is reconfigured by the selected LO frequency. To verify the feasibility of the proposed anti-jamming process, position, carrier to noise ratio of each channel are measured using a test scenario that is consist of GPS and Beidou with a CW jamming. As a results, by switching of LO frequency, GNSS signal that is not affected by jamming can be received with the same performance as non-jamming.

1 Introduction

The GNSS signal is vulnerable to intentional and unintentional jamming, due to the extremely low receiving power of the satellite signal. To mitigate jamming, notch filter, pulse blocking, array antenna based nulling techniques were applied to many GNSS receivers [1]. However, when jamming mitigation method is used for GNSS receiver, signal power of the GNSS will be decreased. Sometimes, it may be efficient to receive GNSS signals in other bands that are not affected by jamming rather than when the jamming mitigation method was applied. The method can be realized using spectrum sensing and reconfigurable receiver based on SDR.

Recently, the GNSS software defined radio (SDR) has been widely used to develop and verify performance of GNSS signal processing algorithms for anti-jamming, multipath mitigation, multi-constellation and so on [2]. Because various algorithms can be applied easily in SDR without hardware modification. Furthermore, real-time operation of the SDR has been become possible with GPU-based signal processing. When the jamming is occurred in a GNSS band, the jamming status can be detected by spectrum sensing [3-4]. And the results are used to change channel of receiver to get other band signal which is not affected by jamming. This is an application of cognitive radio (CR) for GNSS anti-jamming. And we think this approach has been not attempted for GNSS anti-jamming.

This paper presents result of new approach for anti-jamming using a method based on cognitive radio. GNSS SDR is implemented using PC based on GPU and multi-core CPU. And a universal software radio peripheral is utilized as RF front-end. To detect jamming and check spectrum quality, a spectrum sensing based energy detector is implemented on the SDR. And estimated center frequency and bandwidth is used to select LO frequency for GNSS reception. To verify the feasibility of proposed method a test-bench was implemented. Using the test-bench, precision of position, carrier to noise ratio (C/N0) were observed on test scenario.

2 The SDR and spectrum sensing

2.1 Spectrum sensing

The concept of CR was proposed for efficient utilization of frequency in RF communication system [1-2]. When a primary user did not use a band, a secondary user can use the band for communication until that primary user re-use. To detect primary signal, the spectrum sensing technique is required for secondary user.

The energy detection (ED), matched filter, cyclostatio -nary, and so on are widely applied to spectrum sensing [3]. Among these technique, the energy detection is most suitable for the jamming signal detection of GNSS receiver that the jamming signal is assumed unknown signal. Because ED does not require prior information of jamming signal such as center frequency, bandwidth, modulation method, and so on.

$$H(t) = \begin{cases} h_1 & |s(f)|^2 > \lambda \\ h_0 & |s(f)|^2 \le \lambda \end{cases} \quad (1)$$

* Corresponding author: chansp@cbnu.ac.kr

The concept of ED is that state of band is divided into jamming or non-jamming by energy measurements of spectrum. The concept can be expressed in Eq. (1). Where, h_1 means that jamming exist on band f, h_0 means non-jamming. And λ is threshold.

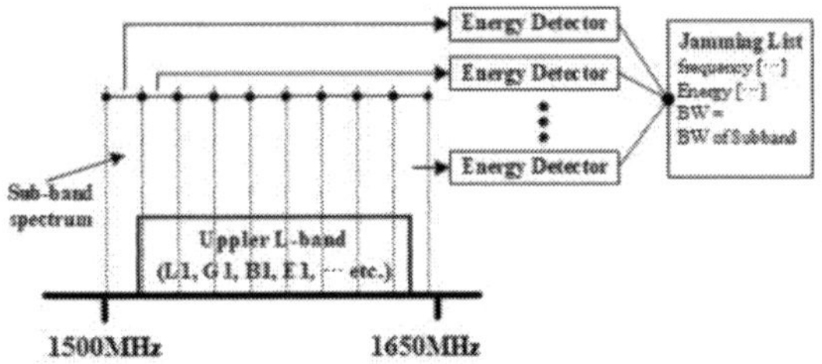

Fig.1. Multi-channel joint energy detector for GNSS receiver

The ED can be expand as multi-channel joint detection to detect jamming signal on wide-band spectrum for multi-channel receiver [4]. In the multi-channel joint method, an acquired wide-band spectrum is divided into several sub-band spectrum that size is smaller than original spectrum like figure 1. Then each sub-band spectrum is inputted to each energy detector. In the other research [4], each output of many energy detectors are combined some method such as OR rule.

In proposed anti-jamming process, each outputs are not integrated. Each output has center frequency and average of energy for sub-band spectrum. This information is useful to find frequency and bandwidth of the jamming signal. And the information is utilized to find another band that is not affected by jamming. In this method, accuracy of the estimated frequency and bandwidth of detected jamming signal will be depend on size of sub-band spectrum.

2.2 The implemented SDR software

In the receiver based on CR, channel flexibility is very important specification to change reception channel according to result of spectrum sensing in real-time. The SDR has been known that is most suitable for CR application. Because, most signal processing of the SDR is designed based on software using general purpose processor.

In our laboratory, a SDR has been designed and implemented to utilize development of anti-jamming, analysis of receiving environment, and multi-constellation positioning algorithms [5] since 2013. The SDR has been operated on high performance PC based on CPU and GPU. And the signal processing can be performed by parallel processing in real-time with 65 GNSS channels. The GUI of implemented SDR software is shown figure 2. Currently, GPS L1 C/A, Beidou B1I, B2I, GLONASS L1 and L2 signal can be received in our SDR. And navigation solution is determined by single GNSS measurements or all measurements of enabled-GNSS in SDR.

In this paper, the proposed anti-jamming process based on CR is implemented on the SDR to support channel reconfiguration. In the SDR, receiver channel can be switched using local oscillator (LO) frequency which is used to convert RF to intermediate frequency (IF). If the LO was changed, correlator, bit extractor, replica generator, and so on are auto adapted to receive GNSS signal that IF is changed. Then we can obtain useful results for performance analysis such as correlation output, C/N0, navigation solution, bit sequence, and so on from the SDR.

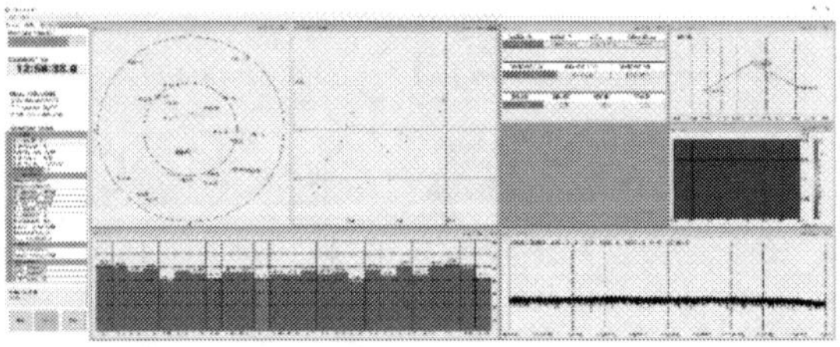

Fig. 2. GUI of implemented GNSS SDR

2.3 Reconfigurable RF front-end

By the implementing based on SDR approach, many signal processing module have been high flexibility. But because of most RF front-end will be fixed to fit a special band, implementation of CR-based receiver was difficult. Where, the RF front-end means a hardware part that down conversion, analog to digital conversion, and filtering such as image rejection is performed in the receiver.

Fortunately, a general purpose RF front-end with high flexibility was researched and developed along with the progress of SDR research and development. There is a Universal Software Radio Peripheral (USRP) that made by Ettus[6] as a typical general purpose RF front-end. The USRP can modify LO frequency of down converter, sampling rate of ADC, and gain of amplifier. In addition, the reception band can be changed without hardware modification. The reconfigurable parameters are set by function based on software such as USRP hardware driver (UHD) or GNURadio [6]. As the utilization of USRP and UHD, the implemented SDR software can get digital IF signal in real-time. And the reception channel of the SDR can be reconfigured in real-time.

3 A proposed method of anti-jamming

3.1 A process of anti-jamming based on CR

The concept of proposed anti-jamming is selection of LO frequency to reject bands that is occupied by jamming and to protect other GNSS bands that is not affected by jamming. For the proposed method to be realized, the information of the jamming must be measurable using the spectrum at the receiver. To do this, we added a spectrum acquisition and spectrum sensing to the anti-jamming process.

The GNSS services have been distributed and operating over a wide range of 500MHz bandwidth from GLONASS G1 (1602MHz) to GPS L5 (1175MHz). To scan all services requires a wide-band spectrum of 500MHz bandwidth. However, this spectrum cannot be obtained at once from a typical receiver. Because reception bandwidth of receiver should be limited to tens MHz. In this paper, sweeping the LO frequency and combining each spectrum were applied to obtain the wide-band spectrum. When each spectrum was combined, the overlap method was applied to improve accuracy of wide-spectrum [7]. The execution time and accuracy of implemented wide-band spectrum acquisition will be vary depending on the LO frequency sweep interval and the overlap ratio. The sweep interval is determined by sampling rate of receiver or reception bandwidth.

The spectrum sensing is performed based on multi-channel energy detection method mentioned in section 2. If the obtained wide-band spectrum includes one or more signal that have higher energy than threshold, by the spectrum sensing, number of sub-bands, the center frequency of each sub-band, and the average energy are measured. These information are considered to frequency bandwidth, and number of the jamming signals.

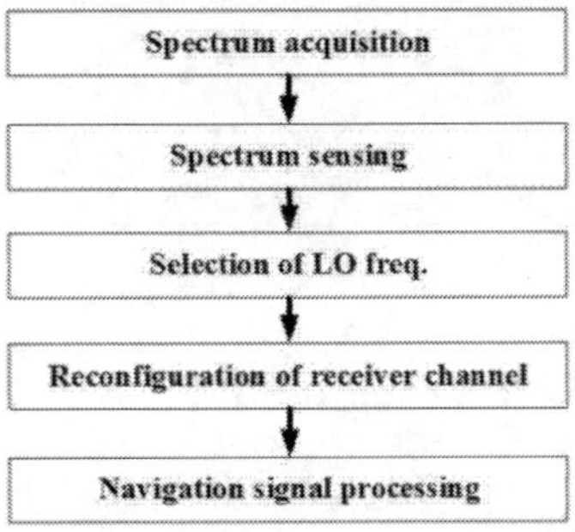

Fig. 3. Flow chart of proposed anti-jamming.

Based on the jamming information obtained from spectrum sensing, the LO frequency that can minimize the impact of jamming and receive GNSS signals can be selected by proposed method. Then receiver channel is reconfigured. The receiver performs signal processing operations for the available GNSS satellite signals in accordance with the reconstructed parameters. If more than four satellite signals are acquired, the navigation solution is also calculated. The proposed anti-jamming process can be summarized as shown in figure 4.

Using this method, the minimum power of the jamming signal that can be avoided is dependent on the performance of the spectrum sensing. Also, the maximum power of the jamming signal that can be avoided will be determined by the dynamic range of receiver. And in this process, the receiver must find the optimum LO frequency for continuous navigation. We propose a method to find the appropriate LO frequency using the LO frequency range model that determines which GNSS is available and the LO frequency range model that determines not to receive jamming signals.

3.2 Selection of LO frequency

Eq. (2) means range of LO frequency to receive GNSS signal. We get the LO frequency range using Eq. (2), when center frequency of GNSS signal and bandwidth was given. The signal information is known for anyone. In Eq. (2), f_{Gx} is center frequency of a GNSS signal, B_G is bandwidth of a GNSS signal, and B_R is bandwidth of receiver that is determined by sampling rate and pass band of filter. By the Eq. (2), if the LO frequency is included in range which is defined by a signal's frequency and bandwidth, the signal can be received.

$$\begin{aligned} f_{Gx}+B_{Gx}/2-B_R < f_{LO,Gx} < f_{Gx}-B_{Gx}/2 \\ f_{Gx}+B_{Gx}/2 < f_{LO,Gx} < f_{Gx}-B_{Gx}/2+B_R \end{aligned} \quad (2)$$

The LO frequency range model is applied to make a function that can output 1 or 0 according to probability of the GNSS reception. The function (W_{Gx}) can be shown Eq. (3). Where, Gx means name of GNSS service such as GPS, Beidou, GLONASS, and so no. hat of f_{LO} is selected LO frequency.

$$W_{G_x}(\hat{f}_{LO}) = \begin{cases} 1 & (\hat{f}_{LO} \in f_{LO,G_x}) \\ 0 & (\hat{f}_{LO} \notin f_{LO,G_x}) \end{cases} \quad (3)$$

If there are two or more GNSS were considered to select LO frequency, several W_{Gx} will be defined with its center frequency and bandwidth. Then all W_G are integrated by weighting sum. At this time, the weight values can be designed by a parameter of each GNSS system's performance such as error variance, visible number of satellites. And sum of weight values should be 1. If the weight values are determined by visible number of satellites of each GNSS, The product of integrated W_G and sum of all expected number of satellites means an estimation model for the number of satellites that can be received according to the LO frequency.

$$\begin{aligned} f_{LO,n} < f_{J,n}-(B_R+B_{J,n}/2) \ \ or \\ f_{LO,n} > f_{J,n}+(B_R+B_{J,n}/2) \end{aligned} \quad (4)$$

To reject jamming signal, a range of LO frequencies can be obtained by Eq. (4). Where, $f_{J,n}$ and $B_{J,n}$ are center frequency and bandwidth of nth jamming signal, respectively. And a function that outputs 1 or 0 according to the probability that the jamming signal is excluded is derived as shown in Eq. (5).

$$W_{J,n}(\hat{f}_{LO}) = \begin{cases} 0 & (\hat{f}_{LO} \in f_{LO,n}) \\ 1 & (\hat{f}_{LO} \notin f_{LO,n}) \end{cases} \quad (5)$$

When two or more jamming exists, all W_J be combined by OR rule to obtain a range of LO frequencies that do not receive all jamming signals.

$$f'_{LO} = mean(\arg\max[W(\mathrm{f}_{LO})]) \quad (6)$$

Finally, the production W_G and W_J is a function (W) that can find LO frequency to get GNSS signal and to reject jamming signal. When all LO frequency candidates

(f_{LO}) are inputted to W, The LO frequency that the highest value is calculated by the function is the optimal LO frequency. If there are two or more optimal LO, the final value is calculated by average.

4 Experiment

4.1 Test-bench

The test-bench was implemented using the LabSat, USRP, Signal generator, and a combiner. Figure 4 shows the implemented test-bench. We used the test-bench to verify the performance and validity of proposed anti-jamming based on CR.

To monitor performance changes as the LO frequency changes, repeated experiments with the same RF signal are required. The LabSat records live GNSS signal and then replay them as RF GNSS signals. Therefore, GNSS signals are supplied from LabSat. The jamming signals were generated using HSG-D2000A, a signal generator made by HP. This signal generator can generate signals such as CW, FM, and AM with power of -135dm to -15 dBm in 250 kHz to 2GHz.

The jamming signal and the GNSS signal are combined by the combiner, and the combined signal is entered into the USRP. USRP sends IF digital signals to PCs in real time, and SDR software receives these signals and performs GNSS signal processing. The proposed anti-jamming method is also implemented in this process.

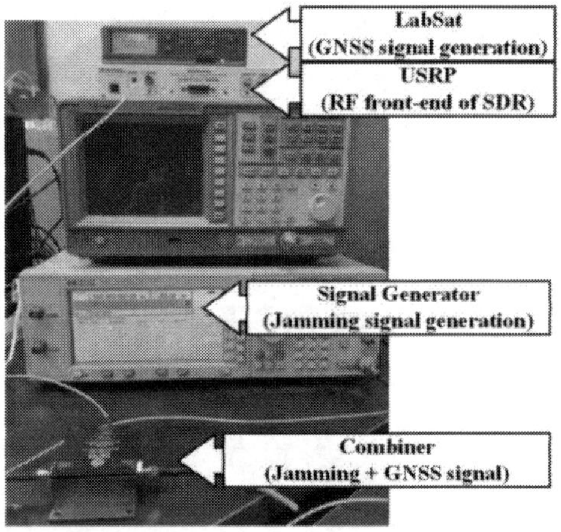

Fig. 4. A configuration of test-bench.

4.2 The result of a test scenario using GPS and Beidou with a jamming

A test scenario was defined using GPS L1 C/A, Beidou B1I and a single jamming signal. This scenario is used to confirm the validity of the proposed anti-jamming process. GPS L1 C/A exists at 1575.42 MHz and assumes approximately 2 MHz bandwidth. Beidou B1I exists at 1561.098 MHz and assumes approximately 4 MHz bandwidth. On the other hands, the jamming will be occurred in 1561.098 that is same to Beidou B1I signal.

The jamming method is CW type is used, and the signal power is set to 50dB jamming to signal ratio. It means that power of jamming signal is higher than noise power over 30dB. Directly affected by this jamming signal, the GNSS is not available.

The parameters of wide-band spectrum acquisition, spectrum sensing, and SDR are summarized in Table 1. The range of wide spectrum is set to 1540 to 1580MHz, and overlap ratio is 0.5. Because the sampling rate is 20MHz, bandwidth of receiver is determined as 10MHz. In this case, wide-band spectrum is obtained by the LO frequency sweep eight times and computation of narrow spectrum. A spectrum of 40MHz bandwidth is divided into 1MHz units to perform multi-channel energy detection.

Table. 1 The parameters for the test scenario

Parameter name	value
Range of spectrum[MHz]	1540 to 1580
Overlap ratio	0.5
Bandwidth of sub-band of ED[MHz]	1
Threshold of ED[dB]	-170
Sampling rate[MHz]	20
Quantization bit	16

The scenario was replayed for about three minutes. We tested three situations repeatedly when there was no jamming (Non-jamming), when jamming existed, when the anti-jamming method was applied (Anti-jamming turn on), and when anti jamming was not applied (Anti-jamming turn off).

First, we introduce the results of spectrum sensing. Figure 5 shows the results of spectrum sensing based on multi-channel energy detection when jamming is exist. Because 40MHz bandwidth is divided into 1MHz intervals, a total of 40 energy measurements can be obtained. Each energy measurement corresponds to the respective center frequency. The threshold value is -170 dB. As a result, a jamming signal was detected in the sub-band spectrum with a central frequency of 1560.5 MHz. At this point, the energy measurement is -160.7 dB, about 20 dB higher than the other sub-band spectrum, which is not affected by jamming. This result means that even 40 dB jamming to signal ratio can be found without false alarms.

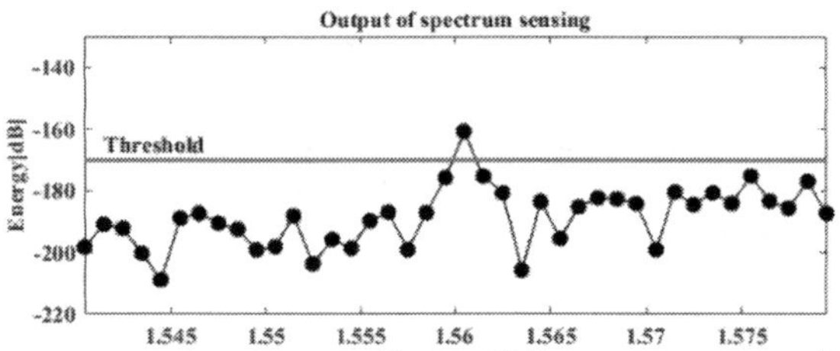

Fig. 5. A result of spectrum sensing

Figure 6 shows the appropriate LO frequency found based on the spectrum sensing results. In figure 6, red dot means that LO frequency is selected by proposed Eq. (6).

Where the y-axis is the output of function W, which means that it is capable of receiving GNSS signals. A value of 0.5 means that only one system of two systems, GPS and Beidou, can be received. And y value of different LO frequencies from 1572MHz to 1584MHz are equal. The average of these values is the final LO frequency, it is 1578 MHz.

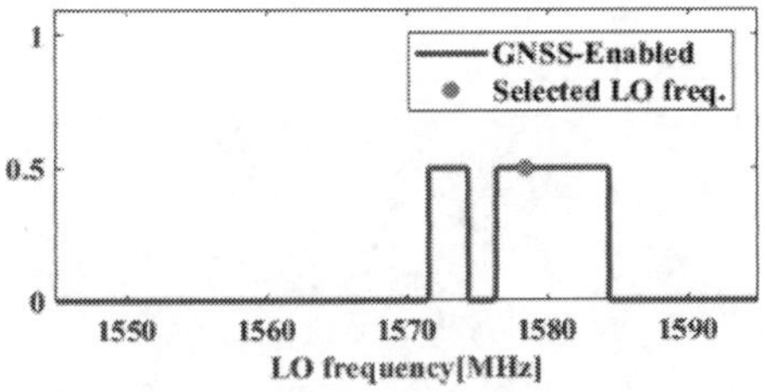

Fig. 6. A result of LO frequency selection

In non-jamming situations and situations where Anti-jamming does not apply, the LO frequency is set to 1568MHz. In this case, GPS and Beidou signals can be received simultaneously at 10 MHz bandwidth. Figure 7 shows that when there is no jamming, a total of 15 satellite signals are received by successfully receiving both GPS and Beidou. However, in the situation that jamming is occurred, keeping the LO frequency will make loss most satellites signal such as yellow bar in figure 7.

On the other hands, a case of that the selected LO frequency was applied to receiver channel by the proposed method can provide navigation solution using only GPS signal. This is because the LO frequency with only GNSS signals is properly found except for the band affected by jamming. As a result, 8 GPS satellite signals were received. At this time, C/N0s of each signal were only 0.3 dB different from the non-jamming situation. It is not possible to eliminate the jamming effect of a Beidou signal, but simply changing the LO frequency makes the GPS signal available.

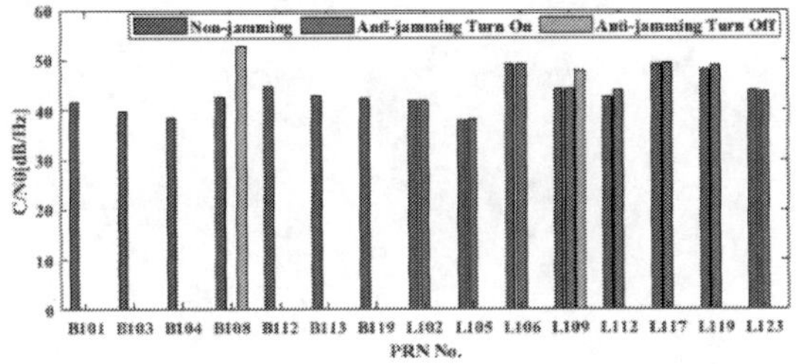

Fig. 7. C/N0 of all received signals for three situations: non-jamming, anti-jamming turn on or off

Table 2 summarizes the precision of navigation solution measured in each situation. The receiver position was calculated in the two situations of non-jamming and anti-jamming turn on. The precision is measured based on CEP. As a result, precision of non-jamming situation that GPS and Beidou is used to calculate position of receiver is 3.3m, and in the other case only GPS is used is 3.45m.

The CR-based anti-jamming that we proposed does not mitigate the jamming effect of Beidou. But just switching of LO frequency, GPS signal can be received with the same performance as non-jamming.

Table. 2 The position precision (CEP) in each situation

Situation	Precision [m]
Non-jamming(GPS/Beidou)	3.3
Anti-jamming On(Only GPS)	3.45
Anti-jamming Off	-

5 Conclusion

This paper presents result of anti-jamming based on CR. The process of anti-jamming is consist of 5 step such as spectrum acquisition, spectrum sensing, selection LO frequency, receiver channel reconfiguration, and navigation. The spectrum acquisition was implemented based on sweeping and overlap method, and the multi-channel energy detector is used for spectrum sensing.

The LO frequency selection method is proposed in this paper, the method can determined a LO frequency that GNSS can receive and jamming can reject. The receiver channel reconfiguration was implemented using SDR software and USRP. And the navigation signal processing for GPS, Beidou, and GLONASS be supported in SDR.

A test-bench was implemented using the LabSat, USRP, Signal generator, and a combiner. The proposed anti-jamming process was verified based on a test scenario using GPS and Beidou with a jamming signal. As a result of the experiments, the proposed method does not mitigate the jamming effect of attacked GNSS. But just switching of LO frequency, GNSS signal that is not affected by jamming can be received with the same performance as non-jamming.

Acknowledgments

This work has been supported by the National GNSS Research Center program of Defense Acquisition Program Administration and Agency for Defense Development.

References

1. Septentrionv, "Septentrio white paper GNSS Interference", www.septentrio.com, (2012)
2. S. Söderholm, M. Bhuiyan, S. Thombre, L. Ruotsalainen, & H. Kuusniemi, A multi-GNSS software-defined receiver: design, implementation, and performance benefits, Annals of Telecommunications, **71**, 399-410 (2016)
3. M. Ben R Z. Quan, S. Cui, A. Sayed & H. Poor, Optimal multiband joint detection for spectrum sensing in cognitive radio networks. IEEE Transactions on Signal Processing, **57**, 1128-1140 (2009)

4. T. Yucek, & H. Arslan, A survey of spectrum sensing algorithms for cognitive radio applications, IEEE communications surveys & tutorials, **11** (2009)
5. K. Park, J. Chae, S. Song, S. Son, S. Choi, & C. Park, A Performance Analysis of Multi-GNSS Receiver with Various Intermediate Frequency Plans Using Single RF Front-end, Journal of Position, Navigation, and Timing, **6**, 1-8 (2016)
6. Ettus research, USRP Hardware Driver and USRP Manual[Internet], cited 2018 Sep 12, available from: http://files.ettus.com/manual/index.html
7. W. Liu, O. Yaron, I. Moerman, S. Bouckaert, B. Jooris, Real-time wide-band spectrum sensing for cognitive radio, *In Communications and Vehicular Technology in the Benelux* (SCVT), 1-6 (2011)

Performance Analysis of Relative Positioning using GPS and BDS signals

Jae Hee Noh[1], *Sun Yong* Lee[2], *Deok Won* Lim[3], *Gwang Hee* Jo[1], *Jin Hyuk* Lee[1] and *Sang Jeong* Lee[1,*]

[1]Department of Electronics Engineering, Chungnam National University, Daejeon 305-806, Republic of Korea
[2]Navcours Co., Ltd., Daejeon 34014, Republic of Korea
[3]Satellite Navigation Team, Korea Aerospace Research Institute, Daejeon 305-806, Republic of Korea

Abstract. In general, the satellite signal received by GNSS receivers has errors such as satellite clock error, orbit error, ionospheric delay and tropospheric delay. In environments where high positioning accuracy is required, these error factors can be eliminated by using relative positioning using code measurements with carrier phase measurements. If relative positioning is performed using carrier phase measurements, it is possible to have positioning accuracy of cm level. In this paper, we analyse the positioning accuracy of relative positioning using the L1 signal of GPS and BDS. For this study, we collect GPS and BDS signal using two low-cost receivers. We also designed a software-based platform to perform the relative positioning. Finally, we analyse relative positioning accuracy for GPS/BDS integrated system as well as relative positioning accuracy for GPS and BDS.

1 Introduction

There have been reported a lot of researches on precision positioning using GNSS in many fields requiring accurate positioning information. In particular, many studies are being conducted to provide accurate positioning to improve the accuracy and reliability of Intelligent Transportation Systems(ITS) and autonomous vehicle technology. When the GNSS signal is transmitted from the satellite to the receiver, the positioning error occurs due to various factors. Satellite clock errors, orbit errors, ionospheric delay, tropospheric delay and multipath are the factors that make it difficult for a GNSS receiver to estimate an exact position. In case of absolute positioning, correction methods are used to reduce these errors. However, the accuracy of positioning is lower than that relative positioning using double-difference observations. When code measurements and carrier phase measurements are double differenced, those errors are removed. So, the precise relative positioning using double-difference observations is widely used in the fields that require the high accuracy of positioning. In the field of GNSS, there are many positioning studies using the integration of GPS and GLONASS. Precise relative positioning using BDS has been actively studied since BDS provided open services. Currently, GNSS that can observe the most the number of visible satellite for 24 hours in Korea is BDS. So, it is necessary to study precise relative positioning using BDS. BDS satellites transmit ranging signals based on Cod e Division Multiple Access(CDMA) principle, like GPS. BDS provides the similar parameter as GPS in order to caculate stellite position [1-2].

In this paper, we anlayse the perfromance of precise relative positioing of GPS-only, BDS-only and GPS/BDS integrated systme using GPS L1 signal and BDS B1 signal. For this study, we collect GPS L1 signal and BDS B1 signal using two u-blox EVK-M8T receivers and design software based platform to perform precise relative posisitoing.

2 Precise Relative Positioning

In section 2.1, we described the characteristic of the signal of BDS according to the three-phase development plan. In section 2.2, we described the method of precise relative positioing using GPS and BDS.

2.1 BDS Signal

BDS consist of the three-phase development plan. The Beidou-1 system provided the regional active service in 2000 using two GEO(Geostationary Orbit) satellites. The Beidou-2 system provides open service for the Asis-Pacific region by the end of 2012. The Beidou-2 constellation consists of three types of satellites: GEO, IGSO(Inclined Geosynchronous Orbit) and MEO (Medium Earth Orbit). The accuracy of positioning of the Beidou-2 system is optimized to 6 m. Table 1 summarizes Beidou-2 satellites in operation. By 2020, the Beidou-3 system will provide global service. When complete in 2020, it will have a constellation of 35 satellites to provide global coverage [3-4].

* Corresponding author: jhnoh3555@cnu.ac.kr

Table 1. Satus of Beiodu-2

PRN	Type	Launched Time
C01	GEO	2010/01/16
C02	GEO	2012/10/25
C03	GEO	2010/06/02
C04	GEO	2010/10/31
C05	GEO	2012/02/24
C06	IGSO	2010/07/31
C07	IGSO	2010/12/17
C08	IGSO	2011/04/09
C09	IGSO	2011/07/26
C10	IGSO	2011/12/01
C11	MEO	2012/04/29
C12	MEO	2012/04/29
C13	IGSO	2016/03/29
C14	MEO	2012/09/18
C17	GEO	2016/06/12

Currently, Beiodu-2 satellites transmit B1(1561.098 MHz) signal, B2(1207.140 MHz) signal and B3(1269.520 MHz) signal on channel I and channel Q. Channel I is used for civil services and channel Q is used for military purpose. When complete in 2020, Beidou-3 satellites transmit five signals. Beidou-3 satellites retain B1 and B3 signal. However, the B2 signal will have been replaced by three new signals, which are modernized signals in the B1C, B2a and B2b bands [3].

2.2 Precise Relative Positioning

2.2.1 GPS only & BDS only

The method of precise relative positioning uses the both double-difference code measurements and double-difference carrier phase measurements. When estimating the user position, it is possible to estimate an accurate position of cm-level using both code measurement and carrier phase measurement. In the short-baseline, the equation of double-difference code measurements and double-difference carrier phase measurements of GPS and BDS is Eq. (1-4) [5]. The equation of double-difference code measurements of GPS is

$$\lambda_{L1}\Delta\nabla\Phi^{ij}_{L1,ru} = \Delta\nabla\rho^{ij}_{L1,ru} + \lambda_{L1}\Delta\nabla N^{ij}_{L1,ru} + \Delta\nabla\epsilon^{ij}_{\Phi_{L1},ru}. \quad (1)$$

The equation of double-difference carrier measurements of GPS is

$$\lambda_{B1}\Delta\nabla\Phi^{ij}_{B1,ru} = \Delta\nabla\rho^{ij}_{B1,ru} + \lambda_{B1}\Delta\nabla N^{ij}_{B1,ru} + \Delta\nabla\epsilon^{ij}_{\Phi_{B1},ru}. \quad (2)$$

The equation of double-difference code measurements of BDS is

$$\Delta\nabla P^{ij}_{L1,ru} = \Delta\nabla\rho^{ij}_{L1,ru} + \Delta\nabla\epsilon^{ij}_{\Phi_{L1},ru}. \quad (3)$$

The equation of double-difference carrier measurements of BDS is

$$\Delta\nabla P^{ij}_{B1,ru} = \Delta\nabla\rho^{ij}_{B1,ru} + \Delta\nabla\epsilon^{ij}_{\Phi_{B1},ru}. \quad (4)$$

ϵ is residual errors, λ_{L1} is the length of the GPS L1 signal for one wavelength, λ_{B1} is the length of the BDS B1 signal for one wavelength. r and u denote the reference station and user, i and j is denote satellites. Eq. (5) is linear model using double-difference observations [5].

$$y = \begin{bmatrix} \rho_P \\ \rho_\Phi \end{bmatrix} = \begin{bmatrix} G_u(t) & 0 \\ G_u(t) & \lambda I_{n-1} \end{bmatrix} \begin{bmatrix} \tilde{x}(t) \\ N_u \end{bmatrix} + \epsilon \quad (5)$$

where $\tilde{x}(t)$ is unknown variables in linear model. The parameter of unknown variables includes the receiver position and the receiver clock error. Define $\tilde{x}(t)$ as

$$\tilde{x}(t) = [x \quad y \quad z \quad \delta t]. \quad (6)$$

2.2.2 GPS/BDS

Eq. (5-6) are the linear model of precise relative positioning for a single GNSS. In the GPS/BDS integrated system, there are five unknown variables because the receiver clock error for two GNSS are considered [5]. The linear model and unknown variables for the GPS/BDS integrated system are defined as

$$y = \begin{bmatrix} \rho_{P,L1} \\ \rho_{\Phi,L1} \\ \rho_{P,B1} \\ \rho_{\Phi,B1} \end{bmatrix} = \begin{bmatrix} G_{u,L1}(t) & 0 & 0 \\ G_{u,L1}(t) & \lambda_{L1} & 0 \\ G_{u,B1}(t) & 0 & 0 \\ G_{u,B1}(t) & 0 & \lambda_{B1} \end{bmatrix} \begin{bmatrix} \tilde{x}(t) \\ N_{u,L1} \\ N_{u,B1} \end{bmatrix} + \epsilon$$

$$\tilde{x}(t) = [x \quad y \quad z \quad \delta t_{GPS} \quad \delta t_{BDS}]. \quad (7)$$

 https://doi.org/10.1051/e3sconf/20199403005

3 Field Experiments

In this paper, we used the NovAtel GPS-703-GGG antenna and two u-blox EVK-M8T receivers to collect GPS L1 and BDS B1 signals in a zero-baseline environment. The elevation mask angle is 10°. Fig. 1 shows the configuration of the field experiment.

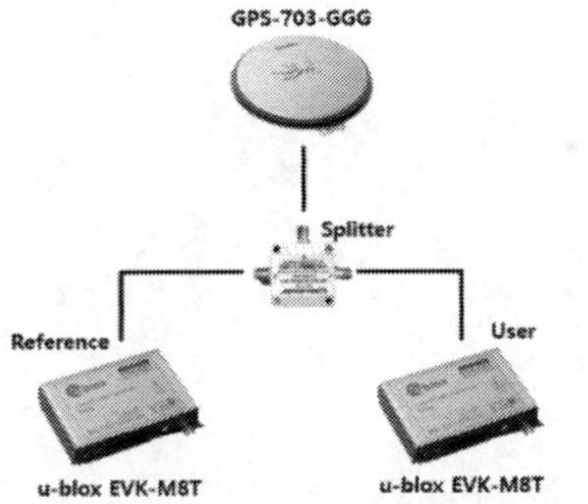

Fig. 1. Configuration of field experiment

We also designed software based platform to perform precise relative posisitoing of GPS-only, BDS-only and GPS/BDS integrated system. In section 3.1, we analyzed the visibility of GPS satellites and BDS satellites observed in the open sky for 24 hors. In section 3.2, based on results in section 3.1, we analyzed the accuracy of precise relative positiong when the number of visible satellite of GPS is the smallest. We also analyzed the accuracy of precise relative positiong when the number of visible satellite of BDS is the smallest.

3.1. Satellite's visibility

Fig. 2 shows the number of visible satellites of GPS and BDS observed for 24 hours in open sky. The elevation mask angle is 10°. For 24 hours, 6-12 GPS satellites can be observed and 11-14 BDS satellites can be observed. The result means that the number of visible satellites of BDS is more than that of visible satellite of GPS in Korea for 24 hours.

Fig. 3 shows the PDOP at 16:00 (UTC + 09) -17: 00 (UTC + 09) when the number of visible satellite of GPS is the smallest. Fig. 4 shows the PDOP at the time of 20:30 (UTC + 09) -21: 00 (UTC + 09) when the number of visible satellite of BDS is the smallest. In Fig. (3-4), PDOP decreases when the integration of GPS and BDS. It can be seen that the geometrical arrangement of satellites is better for GPS/BDS integrated system than single

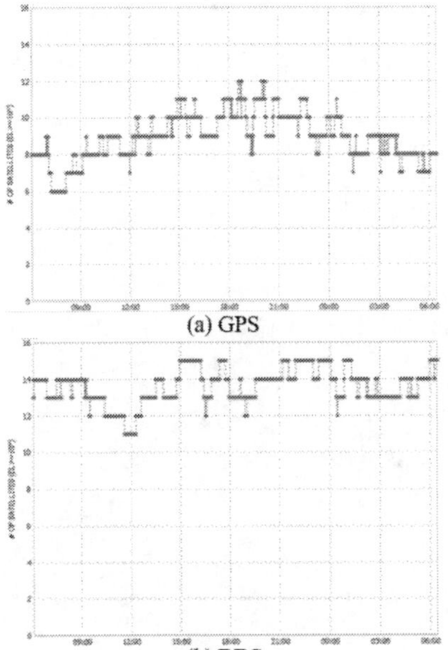

Fig. 2. The number of visible satellites of GPS and BDS for 24 hours

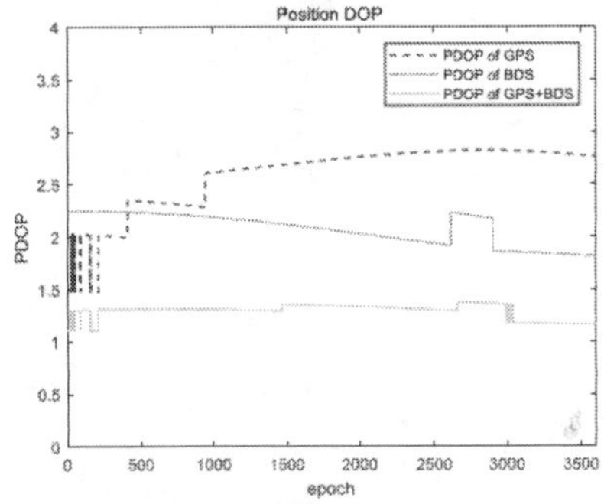

Fig. 3. PDOP at 16:00(UTC+09)-17:00(UTC+09)

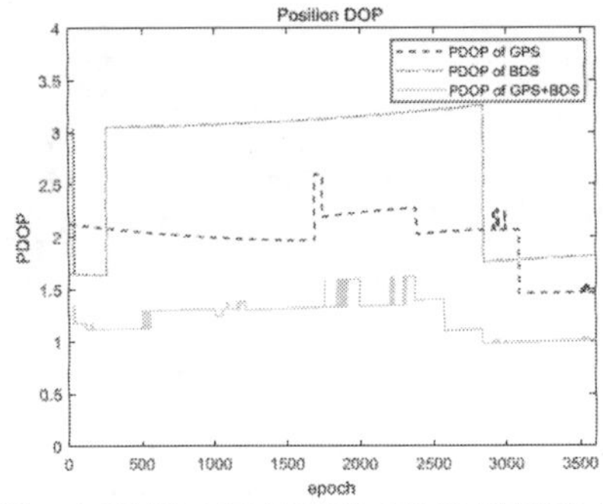

Fig. 4. PDOP at 20:30(UTC+09)-21:30(UTC+09)

3.2. Results of experiments

Fig. 5 shows the result of precise relative positioning of GPS-only, BDS-only and GPS / BDS integrated system at 16:00(UTC + 09)-17: 00(UTC + 09). At this time, the number of visible satellites of GPS is 6-7, and the number of visible satellites of BDS is 12-13.

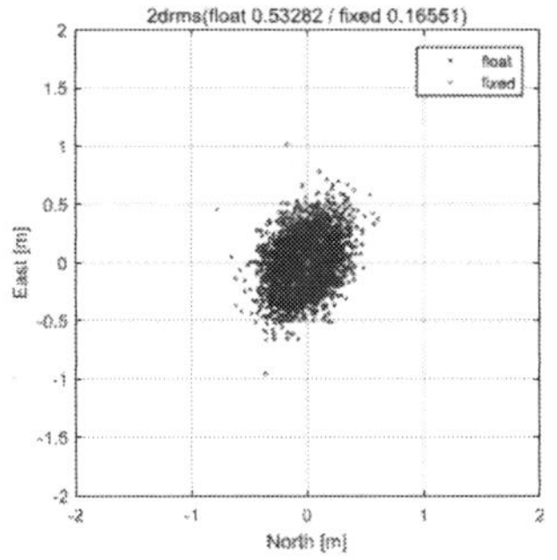

(a) GPS only

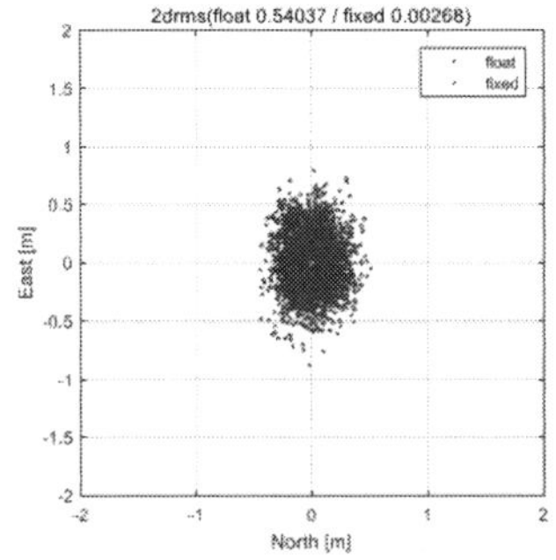

(b) BDS only

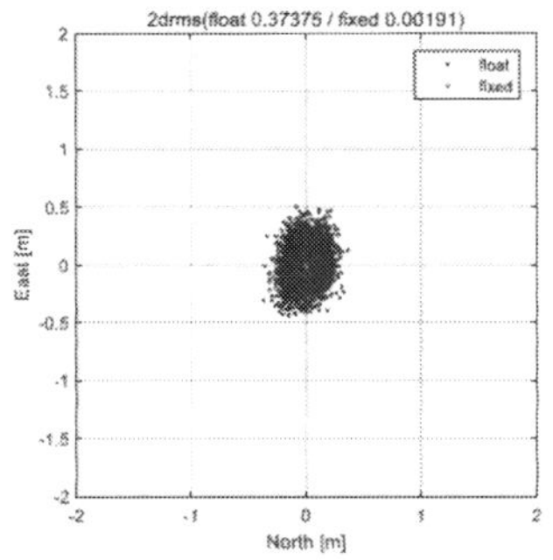

(c) GPS/BDS

Fig. 5. Results of precise relative positioing at 16 :00(UTC+09)-17 :00(UTC+09)

The fixed solution of BDS-only is 2.7 mm and the fixed solution of GPS/BDS integrated system is 1.9 mm. In the case of GPS-only, the fixed solution is 16.6 cm. Because it couldn't observe enough visible satellites for precise relative positioning at 16:00 (UTC + 09) -17: 00 (UTC + 09). The float solution of GPS-only and BDS-only is more than 45 cm. However, the float solution of GPS/BDS integrated system is 37 cm. This accuracy of positioning is below the maximum tolerance to distinguish the lane in the land traffic environment.

Fig. 6 shows the result of precise relative positioning of GPS-only, BDS-only and GPS / BDS integrated system at 20:30(UTC + 09)-21: 30(UTC + 09). At this time, the number of visible satellites of GPS is 8-10, and the number of visible satellites of BDS is 11-12.

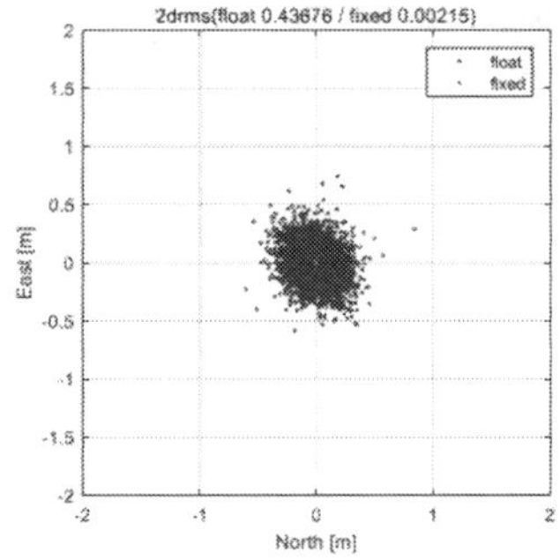

(a) GPS only

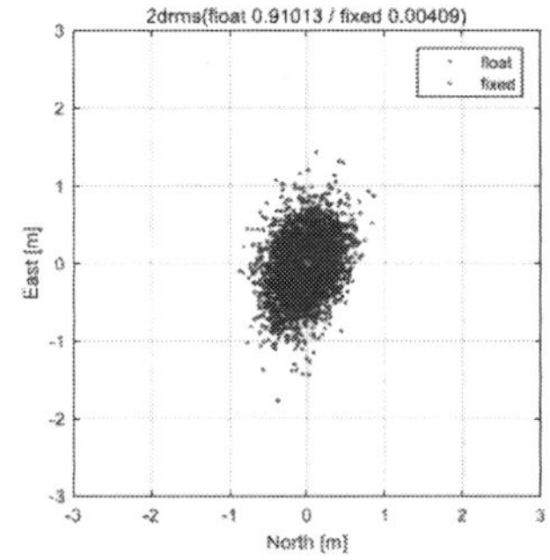

(b) BDS only

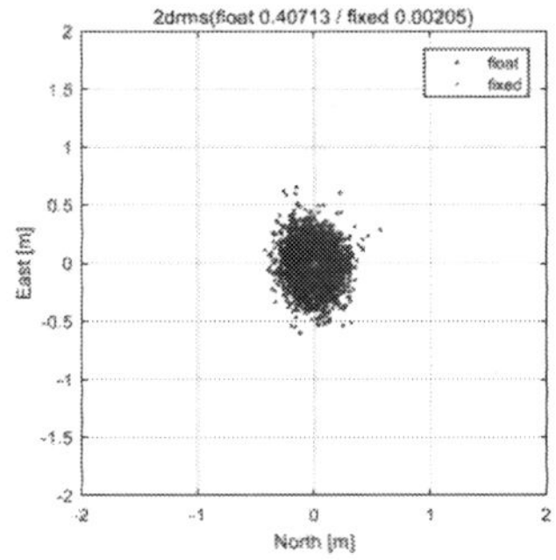

(c) GPS/BDS

Fig. 6. Results of precise relative positioing at 20 :30(UTC+09)-21 :30(UTC+09)

The fixed solution of GPS-only is 2.2 mm. The fixed solution of BDS-only is 4.1 mm. The fixed solution of GPS/BDS integrated system is 2.1 mm. In all cases, the accuracy of positioning is mm-level. The float solution of BDS-only is more than 45 cm. However, the float solution of GPS-only and GPS/BDS integrated system is below the maximum tolerance to distinguish the lane in the land traffic environment.

4 Conclusions

In this paper, we analyzed the accuracy of precise relative positioning of GPS-only, BDS-only and GPS/BDS integrated system using GPS L1 signal and BDS B1 signal. Currently, the number of visible satellites of GPS is 6-12 for 24 hours in Korea. and the number of visible satellites of BDS is 11-15 for 24 hours in Korea. It is possible to observe more BDS satellites than GPS satellites in Korea. When GPS and BDS are integrated, the number of satellites is increased, and the accuracy of positioing improves. As a result of precise relative positioing using GPS L1 signal and BDS B1 signal, the accuracy of positioing of GPS/BDS integrated system is more accurate than GPS-only and BDS-only. We analyzed the number of visible satellites of GPS and BDS in Korea for 24 hours and analyzed the performance of precise relative positioning. As a result, we can expect that BDS together with GPS is valuable for the research of precise positioining. However, it should be mentioned that the visibility of satellites can be not sufficient and evev worse multipath can occur in such an enviroment as urban canyon. So, it is necessary that analysis of the relative precision positioning using the GPS and BDS in the actual road environment.

Acknowledgments

This research was supported by a grant(18TLRP-C113269-03) from Transportation & Logistics Research Program funded by Ministry of Land, Infrastructure and Transport of Korean government.

References

1. Lee, J. M., Park, G. D., and Jeong, W. S., "Analysis of Positioning Accuracy for DGNSS-based Land Navigation Using GPS/BDS Navigation Satellite System," Transaction of KASE, **25**, 4, 422-429 (2017)
2. Son, M. H., Son, E. S., Lee, E. S., Heo, M. B., and Nam, G. W., "Configuration of Network Based GNSS Correction System for Land Transportation Navigation," Journal of the Korean Society for Aviation and Aeronautics, **21**, 4, 17-26 (2013)
3. Lu, X., "Construction and Development of Beidou Navigation Satellite System," in *Committee on the Peaceful Uses of Outer Space,* 61st session, Austria, Vienna (2018)
4. International GNSS Service (Dec 8, 2018) available from : http://mgex.igs.org/IGS_MGEX_Status_BDS.php M.
5. Teunissen, P., Montenbruck, O., *Springer Handbook of Global Navigation Satellite Systems*, Switzerland : Spring Intenational Publishing (2017)

A GPS multipath mitigation technique using correlators with variable chip spacing

Jin Hyuk Lee[1], *Deok Won* Lim[2], *Jae Hee Noh*[1], *Gwang Hee Jo*[1], *Chansik* Park[3], *Jae Min* Ahn[4] and *Sang Jeong* Lee[1,*]

[1]Chungnam National University, Department of Electronics Engineering, 34134 Daejeon, Korea
[2]Korea Aerospace Research Institute, Navigation R&D Division, 34133 Daejeon, Korea
[3]Chungbuk National University, Department of Electronics Engineering, 28644 Cheongju, Korea
[4]Chungnam National University, Department of Radio and Information Communications Engineering, 34134 Daejeon, Korea

Abstract. Various methods have been studied to mitigate the influence of multipath signals, representative methods focused the correlator structure are the Narrow Correlator and the Multipath Elimination Technique (MET). It is known that the MET has better performance than Narrow Correlator but it requires more complexity. In this paper, we propose a technique that has similar performance to the MET and it uses only three correlators like the Narrow Correlator. This technique switches the chip spacing of the correlators for each Predetection Integration Time (PIT) and applies it to the MET. For the performance analysis, we implemented a software platform and compared the code tracking error of the proposed technique with that of the Narrow Correlator and the MET.

1 Introduction

In urban GNSS navigation applications, the presence of multipath is a dominant source of performance degradation in the pseudorange measurement and the positioning. In order to mitigate the effect of the multipath signal, various techniques have been studied. Among them, the early studies were focused on designing the antenna or correlator structure. A well-known algorithm is Narrow Correlator, which reduces the chip space between early and late correlator in order to cut down the impact of multipath on the Delay Lock Loop (DLL) [1]. However, this algorithm suffers from high sensitivity to noise due to the broad RF bandwidth, and it cannot mitigate short delay multipath. And the other well-known algorithm is the MET, which estimate the error by calculating an intersection point from the slope of a correlation function [2]. And it is known that the MET has better positioning performance than that of the Narrow Correlator, although it requires more complexity due to the increased number of correlators.

In this paper, we propose a multipath mitigation technique which has similar performance to the MET by using only three correlators. This technique switches the chip spacing between correlators every PIT. So, this technique can serve as five or more correlators with only three correlators. In this paper, the proposed technique obtains five correlation values and then applies those values to the MET algorithm. In order to evaluate the validity of the proposed technique, we compared the code tracking error with the Narrow Correlator and the MET through computer simulation. From that, it can be checked that the proposed technique shows better performance than the Narrow Correlator using the same number of correlators. Also, it shows similar performance to the MET in a static environment, although it probably shows deteriorated performance due to a change in correlation value during PIT in a dynamic environment. Therefore, it can be expected that the proposed technique would be suitable for low receiver dynamics.

2 Multipath signal

GNSS receiver receive satellite navigation signals and calculates pseudoranges between the satellite and the receiver. After that, the receiver performs positioning using pseudoranges. However, satellite navigation signals incident on the receiver is not only a direct path signal but also signals reflected by obstacles. Signals reflected on the obstacles and incident on the receiver are called multipath signals. Figure 1 shows the direct path signal and the multipath signals incident on the receiver. The multipath signals have signal power attenuation, time delay, and phase delay compared to direct path signals. And these signals affect the code tracking loop in a receiver. When the direct path signal is received, the code discriminator on the code tracking loop is given in equation 1 [3].

$$D(\tau)=R(\tau+\tau_d)-R(\tau-\tau_d) \quad (1)$$

D is the discriminator output. R is the correlation function. τ_d is chip spacing between prompt correlator and early or late correlator. When a multipath signal is received, the code discriminator on the code tracking loop is given in equation 2 [3].

* Corresponding author: eesjl@cnu.ac.kr

$$D(\tau)=R(\tau+\tau_d)-R(\tau-\tau_d)+\alpha[R(\tau+\tau_d-\delta)-R(\tau-\tau_d-\delta)]\cos(\theta) \quad (2)$$

δ is relative chip delay between the direct path signal and the multipath signal. θ is relative phase between the direct path signal and the multipath signal. When the multipath signal is received, the discriminator output has an additional equation generated by the multiappath signal. The additional equation is a bias error in the code tracking loop. Therefore, in the pseudorange calculation, the receiver generates a bias error and increases the navigation error due to the influence of the multipath signal.

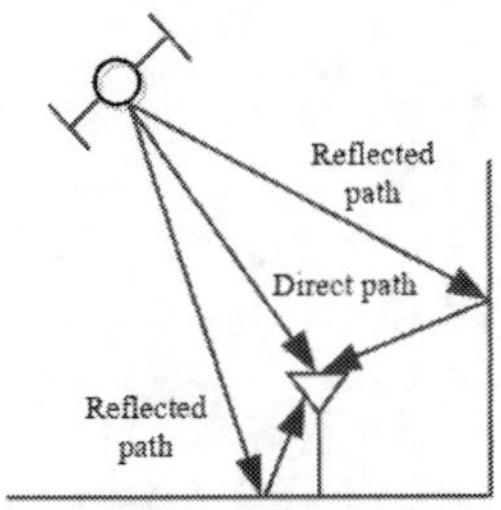

Fig. 1. Direct path and multipath signals.

3 Multipath elimination technique

3.1. Narrow Correlator

The Narrow Correlator has the simple structure with only three correlators. A typical receiver sets the chip space between the early correlator and the late correlator to 1.0 chip for signal tracking. The Narrow Correlator, unlike typical receivers, sets the chip space to less than 0.2 chip. By reducing the correlator chip space in this way, the pseudorange error caused by the multipath signal can be reduced. Figure 2 shows that the code phase error is reduced by reducing correlator spacing.

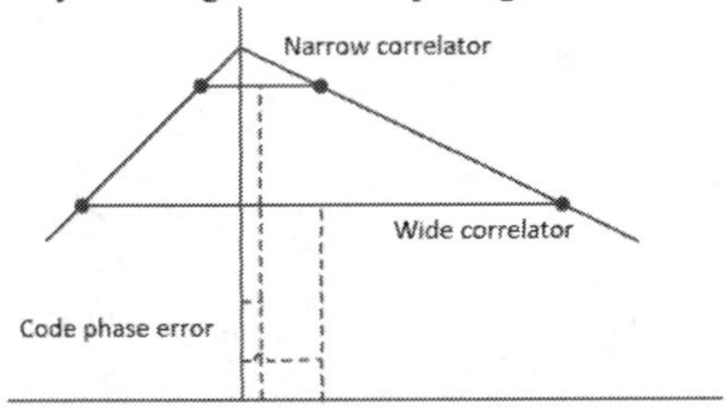

Fig. 2. Code phase error for the wide correlator and the narrow correlator.

3.2. Multipath Elimination Technique

The MET computes code phase error using slopes of the correlation function with five correlators. The arrangement of the correlator is two early correlators, one prompt correlator, and two late correlators. The two early correlation values are connected to form a line, and the two rate correlation values are also connected to form a line. Then calculate the x-coordinate of the intersection of the two lines. This x value is the code tracking error estimated by the MET and is shown in Equation 3. Figure 3 shows that concept of the MET.

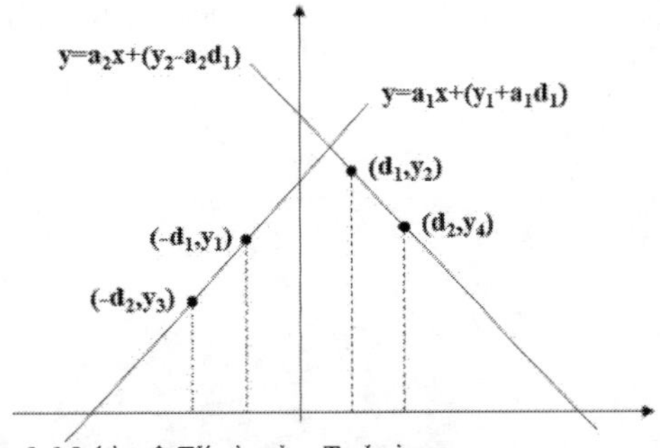

Fig. 3. Multipath Elimination Technique.

$$T=\frac{y_1-y_2+d/2(a_1+a_2)}{a_1-a_2} \quad (3)$$

y_1 and y_2 are the correlation values. d is the chip spacing of early correlator and late correlator. a_1 is the slope of the early correlators. a_2 is the slope of the late correlators. T is the code tracking error.

4 Proposed Technique

The proposed technique uses three correlators like the Narrow Correlator. This technique switches the chip space between correlators every PIT and stores correlation values. In detail, this technique uses two early correlators for the first PIT and two late correlators for the next PIT as shown if Figure 4. And then this technique applies these four stored correlation values to the MET.

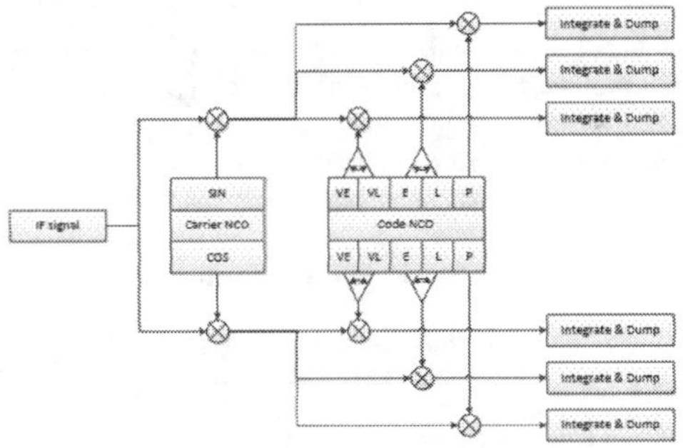

Fig. 4. Correlator structure of proposed technique.

5 Simulation

5.1 Simulation platform

By using the software based simulation platform, performance of multipath error mitigation techniques have been compared. The simulation platform is shown in Figure 5. The simulation platform consists of a signal generator and a signal receiver. The signal generator sets the scenarios and parameters, and then generates GPS signal and multipath signal. The signal receiver processes the IF signal generated by the signal generator and acquires and tracks the signal to find the code phase. At the signal acquisition part, the approximate signal code chip and Doppler frequency are found. At the signal tracking part, Frequency Lock Loop (FLL), Phase Lock Loop (PLL) and Delay Lock Loop (DLL) are equipped, and the multipath error mitigation technique is implemented in DLL. Code phase error can be obtained by subtracting the code phase from the signal receiver and the signal generator.

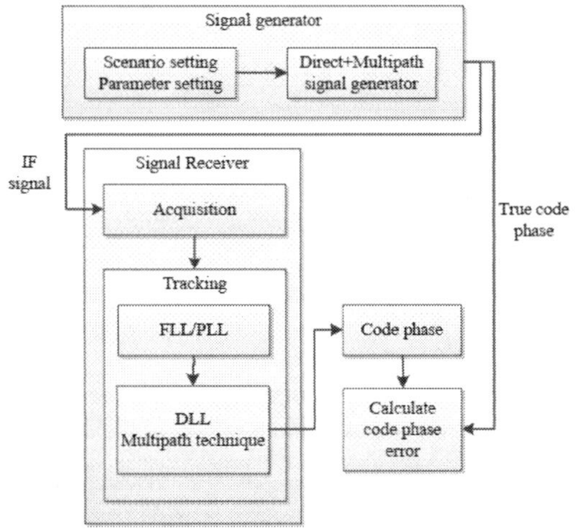

Fig. 5. The performance analysis platform of multipath mitigation techniques.

5.2 Simulation setup

In order to verify the effectiveness of the proposed technique, we implemented the Narrow Correlator, MET, and proposed technique, and then compared code tracking performance for those techniques. The dynamics of the receiver is static. The relative signal power, relative phase and relative chip delay of the direct path signal and the multipath signal are specified in the table 1.

Table 1. Simulation Setup.

Parameter	Setting
Relative amplitude	0.5
Relative phase	0, 180 [degree]
Relative chip delay	0 – 1.1 [chip]
Receiver dynamics	Static
Correlator chip space	0.05 [chip]

5.3 Results

Figure 6 shows the code phase errors according to the multipath delay of the tree techniques. From that, it can be checked that the proposed technique has better performance than the Narrow Correlator and has similar performance to the MET.

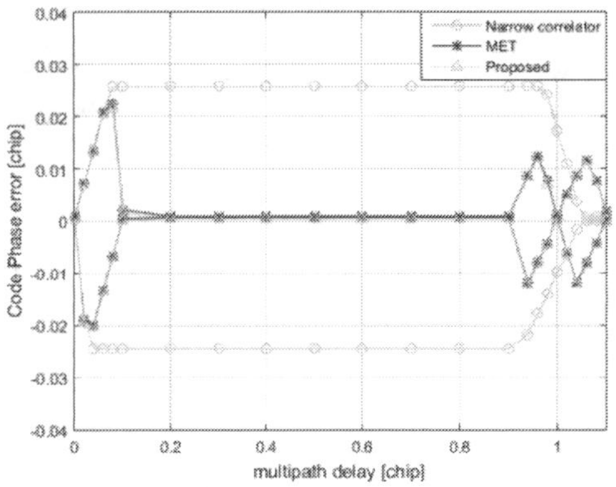

Fig. 6. Multipath error envelope.

6 Conclusions

In this paper, we propose a technique that has similar performance to the MET by using only three correlators like the Narrow Correlator. And we designed software platform to confirm the validity of the proposed technique. Based on the platform, we compared the code tracking error of the proposed technique with that of the Narrow Correlator and the MET. From the results, it can be confirmed that the proposed technique has better performance than the Narrow Correlator and has similar one to the MET by using only three correlators.

Acknowledgement

This work has been supported partly by the National GNSS Research Center Program of Defense Acquisition Program Administration and the Agency for Defense Development and also supported by the Research Fund of Chungnam National University

References

1. A. J. Van Dierendonck, P. Fenton, T. Ford, Theory and Performance of Narrow Correlator Spacing in a GPS Receiver, ION **39**, 3, pp.265-283 (1992)
2. B. Townsend, P. Fenton, A Practical Approach to the Reduction of Pseudorange Multipath Errors in A L1 GPS Receiver, *Proceedings of ION GPS-94*, pp. 143-148 (1994)
3. BW. Parkinson, P. Enge, P. Axelrad, JJ. Spilker Jr, *Global Positioning System: Theory and Applications Volume I* (American Institute of Aeronautics and astronautics, DC, Washington, 1996)

Performance of TPC based ranging signal for more than 2 services multiplexing

Seung Tae Kim[1], *Kap-Jin* Kim[2], Ki-Won Song[2], and *Jae Min* Ahn[1,*]

[1]Dept. of Radio Science and Information Communications Engineering, Chungnam National University, S. Korea
[2]Agency for Defence Development, S. Korea

Abstract. This paper presents signal structure and power efficiency performance for simultaneous transmission of Global Navigation Satellite System (GNSS) service signals based on Tiered Polyphase Code (TPC). For the simultaneous transmission of three or more service signals, the intermodulation terms addition and modification of the power allocations for the signal multiplexing are applied first to the spreading signal with the binary pseudorandom noise (PRN) code and a constant envelope signal is generated. Then, Zadoff-Chu sequence is applied as a secondary code to generate a multiplexed satellite navigation signal having a constant envelope characteristic. Simulation results show that power efficiency performance of more than 80% can be achieved in three service signal multiplexing.

1 Introduction

The use of Tiered Code (TC) using pseudo random noise (PRN) code of hierarchical structure is becoming popular as a method to facilitate signal acquisition in weak signal environment of Global Navigation Satellite System (GNSS) navigation signal. TC, which consists of a dual code structure of primary and secondary codes, is a binary PRN code in which both codes are combined to increase processing gain. Tiered Polyphase Code (TPC) structures have been proposed to reduce intra-system interference as well as increase processing gain by applying non-binary polyphase codes to the secondary codes. [1, 2]

On the other hand, with the proliferation of GNSS services, attempts have been made to simultaneously transmit more service signals using the same frequency band. Simultaneous transmission of three or more signals may degrade the power efficiency of the satellite high power amplifier. In order to minimize the degradation of power efficiency, various methods have been proposed to keep the envelope of the generated signal constant. [3] Most of the proposed methods are based on the assumption that the simultaneous transmission signals to be multiplexed have binary values. Therefore, when the simultaneous transmission is performed based on the TPC, the signal generation structure needs to be changed since the secondary code of the TPC is non-binary.

In this paper, we propose a signal generation structure that can maintain constant envelope characteristics when simultaneously transmitting three or more GNSS service signals based on TPC. Also, it is shown that the power efficiency of the amplifier is not different from the power efficiency of the binary signals during the amplification of the signal generated by the proposed method.

2 Generation of the multiplexed signal

In order to generate a transmission signal by multiplexing three or more signals based on TPC, signals to be multiplexed are defined as follows.

$$s_i(t) = d_i(t)C_{p,i}(t)C_s(t),\ i=1,\ \dots,\ N \qquad (1)$$

where N is the number of services to be multiplexed, $d_i(t)$ denotes a data signal of the i-th service, $C_{p,i}(t)$ denotes a primary code of the i-th service, $C_s(t)$ denotes the secondary code common to all services and is non-binary polyphase sequence.

In general, multiplexed and transmitted signals can be represented as functions of the signals for multiplexing. The signals multiplexed in the baseband are frequency shifted by the carrier signal and transmitted in the allocated frequency band. The following equation (2) shows this multiplexing process, where $f(s_i(t),\ i=1,\dots,N)$ is a function representing the signal multiplexing relationship in the baseband.

$$s(t) = \mathrm{Re}\{f(s_i(t),\ i=1,\dots,N)e^{j2\pi f_c t}\} \qquad (2)$$

where Re{ } denotes a function that extracts the real part of the argument and fc is the carrier frequency.

In (2), the power variation of the signal s(t) is directly related to the equivalent baseband signal component $f(s_i(t),\ i=1,\dots,N)$ since the carrier signal cannot contribute the envelope variation of the signal. To make the power variation constant, the multiplexing function in the baseband should generate constant envelope baseband signal.

* Corresponding author: jmahn@cnu.ac.kr

The baseband multiplexing function serves to synthesize the service signals to be multiplexed. In this process, since the secondary code Cs(t), which is commonly applied to all service signals, is included, signal components other than Cs(t) are synthesized to generate a multiplexed signal. This synthesis process can be modelled as follows.

$$f(s_i(t),\ i=1,\dots,N) = g(s_{b,i}(t),\ i=1,\dots,N)C_s(t) \qquad (3)$$

where, $g(s_{b,i}(t),\ i=1,\dots,N)$ is a baseband multiplexing function for synthesizing multiplexed signal with binary service signals spread by primary code, and $s_{b,i}(t)$ represents an i-th binary service signal and can be expressed as $s_{b,i}(t) = d_i(t)C_{p,i}(t),\ i=1,\ \dots,\ N$.

The power variation of the multiplexed signal can be obtained by taking the square of the absolute value of the result of equation (3) as follows

$$P(t) = |f(s_i(t),\ i=1,\dots,N)|^2$$
$$= |\ g(s_{b,i}(t),\ i=1,\dots,N)|^2\ |C_s(t)|^2 \qquad (4)$$

where $|C_s(t)|^2$ is constant since the secondary code $C_s(t)$ is a complex valued function drawn unit circle in the complex plane. Therefore $|\ g(s_{b,i}(t),\ i=1,\dots,N)|^2$ should be kept constant to make the multiplexed signal constant envelope.

Figure 1 shows the signal generator structure for generating multiplexed signal with constant envelope property where the signals for multiplexing are spread by TPC.

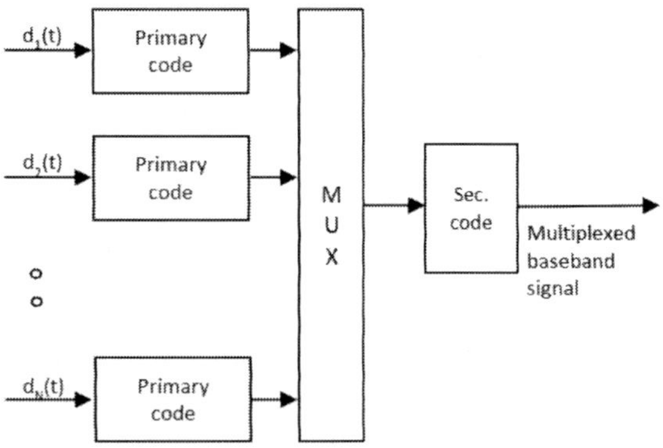

Fig. 1. Signal generator structure for TPC based signal multiplexing.

For the signal multiplexer in figure 1, there have been many research results achieving constant envelope characteristic for more than 3 binary signals multiplexing. By adding some intermodulation signals, they can achieve the constant envelope characteristics.

In this paper we add intermodulation terms and modify the gains of the signals to achieve the constant envelope characteristic of the multiplexed signal.

3 Power efficiency and constellation

The performance of the signal multiplexing can be measured by the power efficiency. The power efficiency is defined as the ratio of the sum of the signal powers at the multiplexed signal to the total signal power of the multiplexed signal. The total multiplexed signal power is the sum of the powers of signals and the powers in the intermodulation terms.

To evaluate the power efficiency of the multiplexed signal based on TPC spreading, we tried to find intermodulation terms and their weight. Also, to increase the power efficiency, we tried to modify the signal gains incorporated in the multiplexing process.

For a specific example, we tried to find a solution for the 3 signal multiplexing case. The baseline form of the multiplexed signal would be represented as follows

$$s_{mux}(t) = s_1(t) + s_2(t) + js_3(t) \qquad (5)$$

where $s_i(t),\ i=1,\ 2,\ 3$ is the signals for multiplexing and all of them are binary signals.

By numerical simulation, we have obtained the multiplexed signal form with constant envelope characteristic as follows

$$s_{mux}(t) = 0.8s_1(t) + 0.8s_2(t) + js_3(t)$$
$$- j0.64s_1(t)\ s_2(t)\ s_3(t) \qquad (6)$$

Figure 2 shows the constellation of the multiplexed signal with constant envelope property as shown in equation (6). By allowing the power allocation difference between signals for multiplexing up to 2 dB, the power efficiency of the multiplexed signal in equation (7) becomes 84.77%.

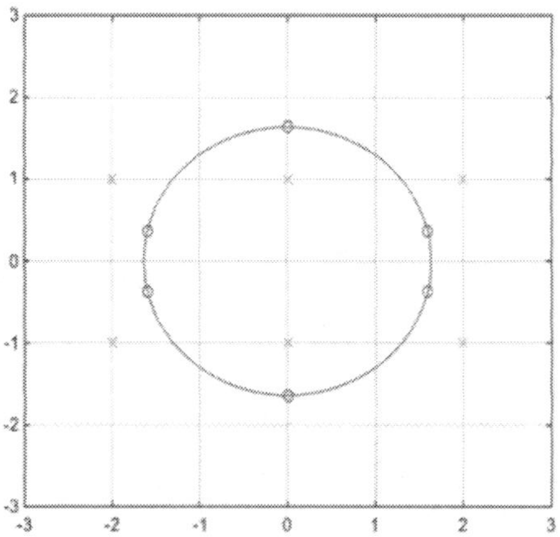

Fig. 2. Signal constellation of the multiplexed signal

The results given in equation (7) and figure 2 illustrate that there may be many difference results by changing the maximum value of the power allocation difference.

4 Conclusions

In this paper, we proposed a signal generator structure for TPC based signal multiplexing. Due to the polyphase structure of the TPC, legacy binary signal multiplexing schemes could not be applicable to the problem such that the proposed reordering of the multiplexing and spreading works well in the TPC case.

The numerical simulation results for the proposed signal multiplexer show that the power efficiency of the proposed scheme for 3 signal multiplexing case approaches 85% and can be higher value with power allocation modification.

To verify the validity of the proposed scheme, more numerical results for 3 or more signals multiplexing.

This work has been supported by the National GNSS Research Center Program of the Defense Acquisition Program Administration and the Agency for Defense Development.

References

1. J. Kim, J. Lee, D. Park, K.J. Kim, K.W. Song, S.J. Lee, J.M. Ahn, IET Elec. Lett. **50**, 218 (2014)
2. S.K. Han, J. Kim, J.K. Kim, A. Han, K.J. Kim, K.W. Kim, S.J. Lee, J.M. Ahn, IET Elec. Lett. **53**, 598 (2017)
3. Z. Yao, M. Lu, IEEE Sig. Proc. Mag. **34**, 16 (Sept. 2017)

Real-Time Orbit Determination of Korean Navigation Satellite System based on Multi-GNSS Precise Point Positioning

Gimin Kim[1,*], *Hyungjik* Oh[1,**], *Chandeok* Park[1,***], and *Seungmo* Seo[2,****]

[1]Department of Astronomy, Yonsei University, Seoul 03722, Republic of Korea
[2]Agency for Defense Development, Daejeon 34186, Republic of Korea

Abstract. This study proposes real-time orbit/clock determination of Korean Navigation Satellite System (KNSS), which employs the kinematic precise point positioning (PPP) solutions of multiple Global Navigation Satellite System (multi-GNSS) to compensate for receiver clock offset. Global visibility of KNSS satellites in terms of geometric coverage is first analyzed for the purpose of selecting optimal locations of KNSS monitoring stations among International GNSS Service (IGS) and Multi-GNSS Experiment (MGEX) network. While the receiver clock offset is obtained from multi-GNSS PPP clock solutions of real observation data, KNSS measurements are simulated from the dynamically propagated KNSS reference orbit and the receiver clock offset. The offset and drift of satellite clock are also generated based on two-state clock model considering atomic clock noise. Real-time orbit determination results are compared with an artificially generated true orbit, wihch show 0.4m and 0.5m of 3-dimensional root-mean-square (RMS) position errors for geostationary (GEO) and ellitically-inclined-geosynchronous-orbit (EIGSO) satellites, respectively. The overall results show that the real-time precise orbit determination of KNSS should be achievable in meter level by installing KNSS-compatible multi-GNSS receivers on the IGS and/or MGEX network. The overall process can be also used to verify integrity of KNSS monitoring stations.

1 Introduction

This study presents an alternative orbit determination (OD) of Korean Navigation Satellite System (KNSS), a regional navigation satellite system (RNSS) under development for covering Korea, in case communications with ground stations are not properly accessible. While inter-satellite ranging (ISR) was proposed for autonomous on-board orbit determination on the same environment [1, 2], the proposed algorithm uses existing GNSS infrastructure. The associated precise point positioning (PPP) techniques have been developed to find more precise navigation solutions by resolving carrier phase integer ambiguity with un-differenced observation in addition to implementing precise satellite orbit/clock data.

Introducing Multi-GNSS PPP of ground monitor stations to compensate for receiver clock bias and other metrological parameters, this paper presents experimental study of a new OD algorithm, and is organized as follows: in chapter 2, KNSS orbits are briefly introduced; in chapter 3, multi-GNSS PPP is conducted by observing from selected monitor stations of MGEX network; the overall process of KNSS OD simulation and its results are followed in chapter 4; finally, the summary and conclusion are given.

2 KNSS Orbits

KNSS (Table 1) is currently composed of 4 elliptical-inclined-geosynchronous-orbits (EIGSOs) and 3 geostationary Earth orbits (GEOs) satellites. Four EIGSO satellites with different right ascension of ascending node shares the same asymmetric 8-shaped ground tracks, so that at least two EIGSO satellites are observable from Korea. Three GEO satellites are located at the longitude of 128°E, 168°E, 88°E. The ground-track repeatability of EIGSO and GEO constrains the locations of monitoring stations to a certain region. Figure 1 shows the visibility of EIGSO satellites from ground locations with respect to 4 different cutoff elevation angles. The region near the central longitude of EIGSO shows 100% visibility. As a result, the receiver in the region could observe at least 4 KNSS signals from EIGSO and GEO satellites.

3 Multi-GNSS PPP

3.1 Constellation of Monitoring Stations based on KNSS Visibility

Due to the mixed combination of EIGSO and GEO, the combination monitor stations for KNSS must be located carefully. First, to reduce the total number of stations, the stations capable of observing KNSS with greater than 5° cutoff elevation angle are selected. Then, considering visibility of GEO satellites, the ground tracks of GEO2 in

*e-mail: orion12@yonsei.ac.kr
**e-mail: jayoh@yonsei.ac.kr
***e-mail: park.chandeok@yonsei.ac.kr
****e-mail: sms@add.re.kr

Table 1. Reference orbital elements of KNSS. Epoch is Jan 1, 2025 00:00:00.000 UTCG.

Orbital Element	GEO1	GEO2	GEO3	EIGSO1	EIGSO2	EIGSO3	EIGSO4
Semimajor axis (km)	42164	42164	42164	42164	42164	42164	42164
Eccentricity	0.000	0.000	0.000	0.075	0.075	0.075	0.075
Inclination (°)	0.000	0.000	0.000	43.0	43.0	43.0	43.0
Right Ascension of Ascending Node (°)	-	-	-	218	128	38	308
Argument of Perigee (°)	-	-	-	270	270	270	270
True Anomaly (°)	228.918	268.902	188.900	108.10	188.45	271.00	11.25

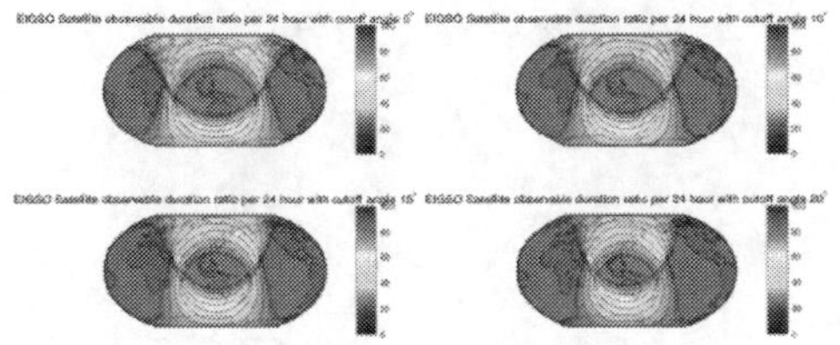

Figure 1. Global Visibility of KNSS EIGSO Satellite by the cut-off elevation angle 5°(top left), 10°(top right), 15°(bottom left) and 20°(bottom right). The contoured value shows the percentage of observable time with respect to 24 hour.

the far East and GEO3 in the far west are considered. Although these stations (No. 5, 8, 10, 12, 14 in Figure 2) barely observe the EIGSO satellites, position dilution of precision (PDOP) of the stations with respect to the GEO satellite could be improved with additional stations.

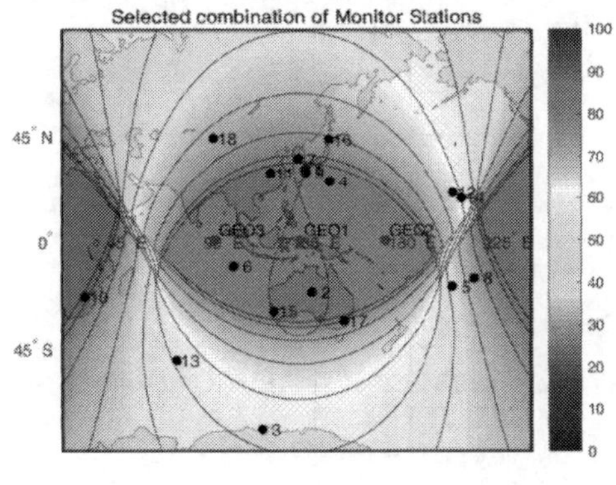

Figure 2. 18 monitor stations selected from IGS/MGEX Network. The contour and filled color represent observable duration of EIGSO in percentage when the cut-off elevation angle is set to 5°. The blue dots and blue line on the figure represent the ground-tracks of KNSS. Each number of the station corresponds to the number in Table 3.

3.2 Multi-GNSS PPP Processing

Real observation data of the stations in Figure 2 on the day of year (DoY) 1, 2018 are processed. Multi-GNSS PPP are performed by PPPH software [3] based on MATLAB. CODE solutions are used for precise GNSS satellite orbit and clock [4], and P1-C1 differential code bias (DCB) is applied. To reduce compatible measurements, code observables are smoothed by phase observables, cycle slips of which are detected by geometry-free combination on the preprocessing stage. Antenna phase offsets of satellites and receivers are corrected from IGS Antex file (IGS14.atx). Each observable is processed in adaptive Kalman filter, whose measurement weights depend on the evaluation at each update. Table 2 depicts the detailed parameters of PPP process.

Table 2. PPP filtering parameters

State	Initial Uncertainty	Process Covariance
Position	100 m	1.0 m^2/s
Receiver Clock	10^5 m	10^5 m^2/s
Trophosphere (ZTD)	0.5 m	10^{-9} m^2/s
Phase Ambiguities	2.0 m	1.0 m^2/s
System Time Difference	10.0 m	10^{-7} m^2/s

3.3 Multi-GNSS PPP Results

Table 3 shows the results of Multi-GNSS PPP using 18 stations. The position errors evaluated by comparing with CODE MGEX Final station solution show less than 10 cm overall. Up direction error shows larger than north and east direction except COCO, KOKV, TID1 and URUM station. The convergence time of PPP differs by each station, without any correlation of multi-GNSS. CKIS, GMSD, and URUM stations takes more than an hour for convergence.

Figure 3 presents a comparison between the PPP estimated receiver clock bias and CODE Clock solution. The RMS clock estimation error shows less than 20 cm for all stations. However, considering the long-term interval (5 min) of station clock product of CODE, the clock bias results cannot be analyzed.

4 KNSS Orbit Determination Simulation

4.1 Real-Time Orbit Determination Algorithm

Figure 4 shows the flowchart of KNSS simulation. Once measurements, site coordinates, antenna correction and

 https://doi.org/10.1051/e3sconf/20199403008

Table 3. PPP Results of 18 monitor stations on January 1, 2018. Letters on the third column shows GNSS availability (G: GPS, R: GLONASS, E: Galileo). The fourth and fifth column represent mean position errors and root-mean-square (RMS) position errors with respect to CODE daily final solution coordinates. N, E, and U represents North, East, and Up directions, respectively.

			Mean (cm)			RMS (cm)			
Site No.	Site	GNSS	N	E	U	N	E	U	Converg. *t* (minute)
1	AIRA	GR	0.0	0.7	-3.0	0.8	0.8	2.6	34.5
2	ALIC	GRE	-0.4	2.2	-2.8	1.1	4.3	4.8	12.5
3	CAS1	GRE	0.4	1.4	0.8	1.2	1.8	1.9	5.5
4	CCJ2	GR	0.2	-1.1	-3.0	0.6	1.1	4.3	50.5
5	CKIS	GRE	-0.6	-0.6	-1.3	0.7	1.6	3.5	101.5
6	COCO	GRE	-0.4	0.6	-1.6	1.0	4.6	2.2	21.0
7	DAEJ	GRE	-0.1	0.1	-3.8	1.3	0.8	3.1	18.5
8	FLRS	GR	1.4	0.3	-2.1	1.8	0.8	4.1	21.0
9	GMSD	GRE	0.3	-1.7	-3.8	0.4	1.2	3.9	82.0
10	HARB	GRE	0.1	1.3	-1.1	0.5	2.5	2.7	32.5
11	JFNG	GRE	0.0	0.4	-3.5	0.5	1.1	3.3	26.0
12	KOKV	GRE	0.5	-1.7	-2.2	0.5	3.8	2.3	13.0
13	KRGG	GRE	-0.8	1.5	0.7	0.8	-0.2	1.7	51.5
14	MKEA	GRE	0.3	-1.6	-6.1	1.1	6.5	9.2	17.5
15	PERT	GRE	-0.4	0.0	-2.5	0.8	1.1	2.5	17.0
16	STK2	GRE	-0.5	-0.7	-4.6	1.5	0.9	4.3	40.5
17	TID1	GRE	-0.8	0.5	-3.3	2.4	6.0	2.2	17.5
18	URUM	GRE	-0.7	-1.6	-1.5	0.6	2.2	1.5	89.5

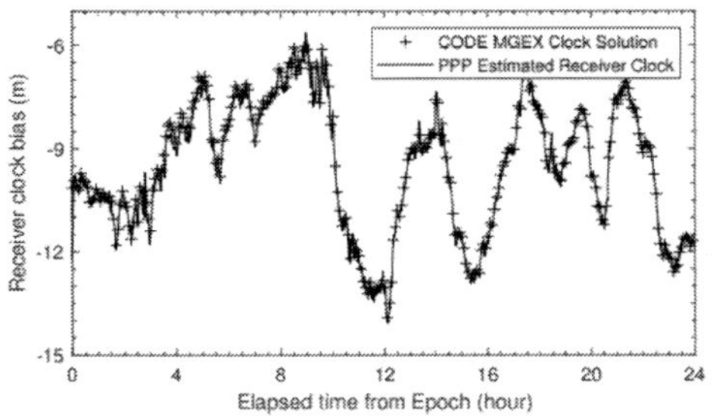

Figure 3. Estimated clock of AIRA station by PPP and 5 min-interval CODE MGEX Final Clock solution of AIRA station. The RMS errors from comparison between two clock biases show 17 cm.

station position which is known a priori are collected, measurement data is pre-processed in steps of cycle-slip detection and repair, outlier detection and carrier phase smoothing of code observable. Then, PPPH software performs PPP based on Kalman filter. The estimated receiver clock parameters and Zenith Total Delay (ZTD) are used simultaneously to make KNSS with Satellite *true* orbit and *true* clock parameters observable, where only undifferenced pseudo-range in ionosphere-free combination are used. The extended Kalman filter (EKF) is initiated with initial states as an inverse single position positioning (SPP) result in ionosphere-free code or by adding pre-defined 1 km position error for each of 3 axes when continuous SPP is unavailable. Once the filter is initialized, measurements of each station are collected, and the difference between computed or predicted measurements is obtained. In this simulation, the orbit and clock are evaluated simultaneously after state vectors are updated to confirm the orbital and clock error while running. The following assumptions apply for real-time orbit determination simulation.

- Receivers at all stations support the types of decryption and demodulation used by KNSS.
- Inter-system biases between KNSS and GPS are negligible.
- KNSS clock drift is constrained to a constant.
- Cut-off elevation angle at monitor stations is fixed to 5 deg.

4.2 Dynamic Model

The distinct characteristics of High-Earth-Orbit (HEO) satellites like EIGSO and GEO satellites justify low degree and low order aspherical geo-potential and necessitate larger third-body effects from the Sun and the Moon [10]. The atmospheric drag is negligible due to low air density in HEO. In this context, perturbations by Earth geopotential, third bodies, solar radiation pressure and relativistic dynamic correction are included in the dynamic model of KNSS satellites[equation (1)].

$$\ddot{\mathbf{r}} = \mathbf{a}_{geop} + \mathbf{a}_{body} + \mathbf{a}_{srp} + \mathbf{a}_{rel} \tag{1}$$

4.3 Clock Model

The two-state clock model [5] is implemented to generate and estimate the satellite clock bias. The clock state vector $\mathbf{x}^{clk}$ is composed of clock bias b_i (s) and clock drift d_i (s/s).

 https://doi.org/10.1051/e3sconf/20199403008

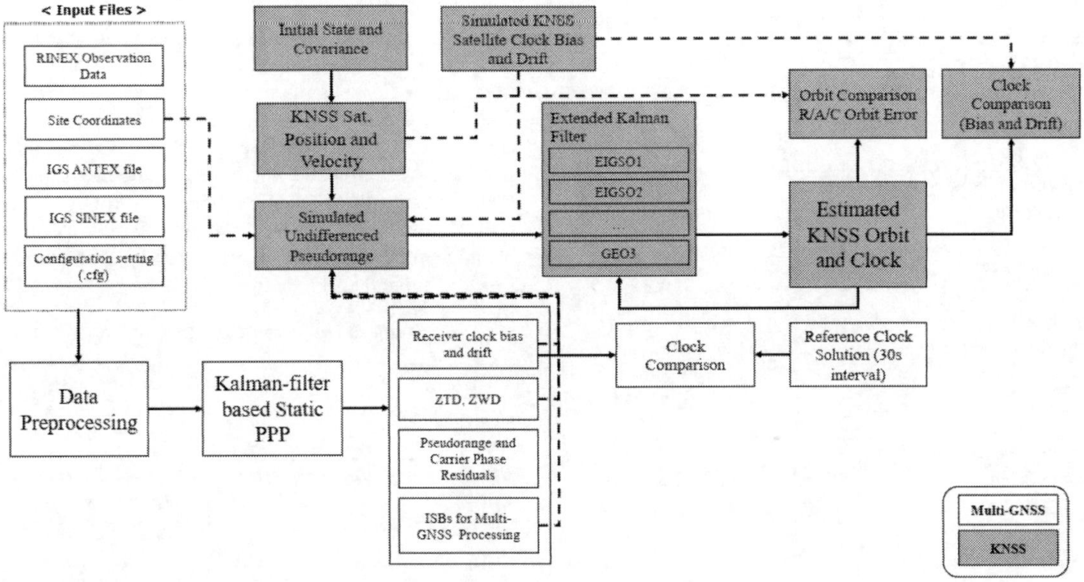

Figure 4. Flow chart representing the algorithm of KNSS OD simulation.

$$\mathbf{x}_k^{clk} = \begin{bmatrix} 1 & \tau \\ 0 & 1 \end{bmatrix} \mathbf{x}_{k-1}^{clk} + \begin{bmatrix} w_{1,k-1} \\ w_{2,k-1} \end{bmatrix}, \quad \mathbf{Q}^{clk} = \begin{bmatrix} q_1\tau + \frac{1}{3}q_2\tau^3 & \frac{1}{2}q_2\tau^2 \\ \frac{1}{2}q_2\tau^2 & q_2\tau \end{bmatrix} \tag{2}$$

Time interval τ of the above equation (2) refers to time step between adjacent epochs, which corresponds to 1 s in this study. w_1 and w_2 are defined as Gaussian random noise, with $w_1 \sim N(0, q_1)$ and $w_2 \sim N(0, q_2)$. In this clock model, the random walk frequency modulation (RWFM) of drift state results from accumulated Gaussian noise w_2, and the white frequency modulation (WFM) of bias state is due to accumulated Gaussian noise w_1. Here, q_1 and q_2 are the Allan variance of each process.

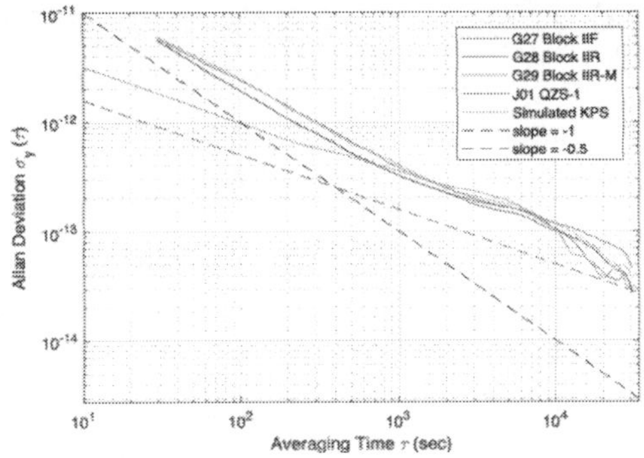

Figure 5. Allan deviation of simulated clock and other GNSS satellite clocks.

Figure 5 shows the simulated KNSS clock bias. The Allan deviations of GPS and QZSS satellite clocks are obtained by analyzing the clock bias with 30s-interval clock solutions of IGS. The Allan deviation also shows that the simulated clock bias and the drift match the real GNSS clock characteristics except the phase white noise on the $10^0 - 10^3$s averaging time. To account for these noises, additional measurement of the white noise is added to pseudorange measurement.

4.4 Condition of Simulation

Based on the PPP results, the KNSS simulation is conducted with parameters in Table 4. Fixed receiver coordinates are used for generating *true* pseudorange, while the non-stationary station position estimated from PPP is assigned to calculate the geometric distance between KNSS satellites and receiver. Measurement sampling rate is set as 1 Hz for satellite clock estimation. The estimated coordinates of monitor stations are considered as constants for 30 seconds. Consequently, KNSS measurements are modeled as the fixed station coordinates for 30 measurement updates. Receiver clock is assumed to be estimated with Gaussian random noise with 20cm of standard deviation.

5 Orbit Determination Results

5.1 Visibility

Figure 6 shows the station visibility of 6 - 14 in terms of PDOP for EIGSO satellites, which shows periodic visibility and PDOP as a result of the same ground-track characteristics. The minimum number of stations observe

Table 4. Models and parameters applied in Orbit Determination

Item	Model
Time and coordinate systems	
Time	GPS Time (GPST)
Inertial Frame	ICRF14
Earth-Fixed Frame	ITRF14
Observation model	
Pseudorange	Ionosphere-free combination
Sampling rate	1 Hz
Tropospheric delay	UNB3 with NMF [6]
Relativistic correction	Orbital eccentricity [7]
Additional Error	User Equivalent Range Error (UERE) + Receiver Clock = 0.36 m Gaussian [8]
Satellite dynamic model	
Geopotential	EGM2008 12 × 12 [9]
Solar radiation pressure	Spherical model+shadow function [10]
3rd-body	Moon and Sun (JPL-DE405)
Relativistic correction	Eq. of M. Correction [11]
Kalman filter setting	
Additional initial random error	1 km position error for each axes
Initial covariance (diagonal)	$[\mathbf{1}km, \mathbf{10}m/s, 5m, 10^{-3}m/s]^T$
Process noise	$10^{-6}m/\sqrt{s}, 10^{-9}m/\sqrt{s}, \mathbf{Q}_{clk}$
Measurement noise	UERE + Receiver clock

EIGSO1 satellite for 15 -17 hours from the epoch, where the maximum PDOP 10.11 occurs. Both GEO2 and GEO3 can be observed from 13 stations for 24 hours, while GEO1 can be observed from 11 stations. The PDOPs of GEO1, GEO2, and GEO3 are 7.942, 5.000 and 5.481 respectively.

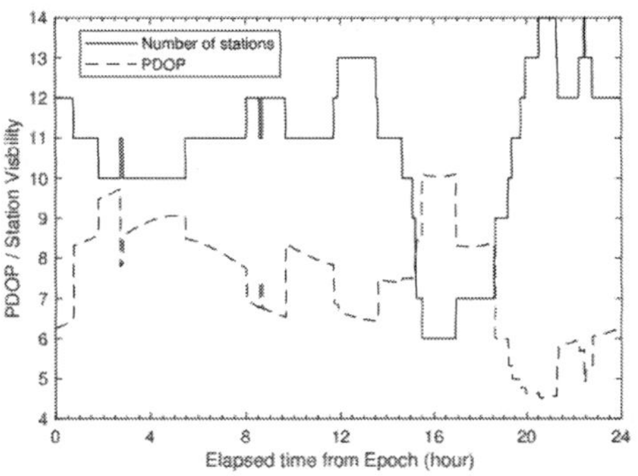

Figure 6. Station visibility of EIGSO1 with cutoff elevation angle 5°

5.2 OD Results

Orbit determination was validated by comparing the artificially generated *true* orbit and the estimated orbit from the filter. Table 5 shows the root-mean-square (RMS) of radial, along-track, cross-track, and 3-dimensional position errors of each KNSS satellite. RMS values are evaluated from about 2 hours after the epoch to the end of the day. It can be seen that the radial direction error is the most critical. Meanwhile, the orbit propagation originated from insufficient measurement did not occur by continuous visibility of more than 11 stations.

Table 5. Orbit determination RMS error

Satellite	Radial (m)	Along-track (m)	Cross-track (m)	3D (m)
EISGO1	0.422	0.041	0.039	0.426
EIGSO2	0.398	0.039	0.046	0.403
EIGSO3	0.282	0.045	0.041	0.289
EIGSO4	0.364	0.044	0.040	0.369
GEO1	0.372	0.041	0.032	0.375
GEO2	0.462	0.034	0.037	0.465
GEO3	0.369	0.038	0.029	0.372

5.3 Clock Estimation Results

Clock determination is validated by comparing the *true* clock and the estimated clock. Table 6 shows the root-mean-square (RMS) of clock bias estimation error of each satellite. The assumption of the PPP-residual receiver clock bias treated as Gaussian error does not correspond to the real clock. Therefore, the remaining systematic bias must be modeled more precisely to decrease the clock bias estimation error.

Table 6. Clock determination RMS error

Satellite	Clock bias (m)	Clock bias (ns)
EISGO1	0.420	1.401
EIGSO2	0.396	1.321
EIGSO3	0.281	0.939
EIGSO4	0.362	1.209
GEO1	0.369	1.231
GEO2	0.458	1.529
GEO3	0.366	1.222

6 Summary and Conclusion

An alternative real-time orbit determination of Korean Navigation Satellite System was proposed. The algorithm uses the KNSS navigation signal while users only have inaccurate KNSS clock or ephemeris. Adapting the multi-GNSS PPP for high precision receiver position and clock estimation, KNSS orbit as well as its clock has been successfully and precisely determined within 1 meter-level accuracy in simulation environment. Meanwhile, long-term stability of multi-GNSS PPP solution will remain as further work.

7 Acknowledgement

This study is conducted as a research part of national GNSS research center which is supported by agency for defense development (ADD) and defense acquisition program administration (DAPA).

References

[1] J. Choi, H. Oh, C. Park, S.Y. Park, International Journal of Aeronautical and Space Sciences, **18**,2, 327-333 (2017)

[2] K. Shin, H. Oh, S.Y. Park, C. Park, Journal of Astronomy and Space Sciences, **33**,1, 37-44, (2016)

[3] Bahadur, B., Nohutcu, M.,GPS Solutions, 22, 4, 113 (2018)

[4] L.Prange, R. Dach, S. Lutz, S. Schaer, A. Jäggi, *IAG 150 Years* (Springer, Cham, 2015) 767-773.

[5] L. Galleani, Metrologia **45**, 6, S175 (2008)

[6] R. Leandro, M.C. Santos, R.B. Langley, In Proceedings of ION NTM, **52**, 1, 564-73, (2006)

[7] N. Ashby, Living Reviews in relativity, **6(1)**,1 (2003)

[8] E.D. Kaplan, C. Hegarty, eds., *Understanding GPS/GNSS: principles and applications* (Artech House, 2017)

[9] N.K. Pavlis, S.A. Holmes, S.C. Kenyon, J.K. Factor, Journal of Geophysical Research: Solid Earth, **117**, B4 (2012)

[10] O. Montenbruck, and E. Gill, *Satellite orbits: models, methods and applications* (Springer Science & Business Media , 2012)

[11] G. Petit, B. Luzum, *IERS conventions (2010)* (Bureau international des poids et mesures, France, IERS-TN-36. 2010)

GNSS Array Antenna for Mitigating Multipath Errors in Urban Environment

Toshiaki Tsujii[1,*], *Kenta* Yonebayashi[2], *Takeshi* Fujiwara[3], and *Sohshi* Ohsawa[3]

[1]Department of Aerospace Engineering, Osaka Prefecture University, Sakai City, Osaka, Japan
[2]Department of Aerospace Engineering, Tokyo Metropolitan University, Hino City, Tokyo, Japan
[3]Aeronautical Technology Directorate, Japan Aerospace Exploration Agency, Mitaka City, Tokyo, Japan

Abstract. GNSS signal vulnerability has been a major concern especially for safety-of-life applications such as aircraft operations. Therefore, a GNSS array antenna technology was investigated focusing on beamforming to mitigate multipath errors in urban environment including airport surfaces. A commercial three-element GNSS antenna and RF-Front end were used to obtain digital IF data. The recorded In-phase/Quadrature IF data for three antennas were combined with proper weight to form beams towards satellites after so-called hardware biases were calibrated. Test results in multipath-rich environment demonstrated that 50-70% reduction of pseudorange errors due to multipath were possible if the beamforming algorithms were applied.

Introduction

Although GNSS has been widely used for navigation and positioning of various vehicles, its vulnerabilities to multipath, ionospheric anomalies, intentional and/or unintentional radio interference, etc. are big challenges especially for safety-of-life applications such as aircraft operations. Therefore, a GNSS array antenna technology was investigated focusing on beamforming to mitigate multipath errors in urban environment including airport surfaces. In this paper, a methodology to form beams to aimed satellites is introduced first. Then our test equipment including a commercial three-element GNSS antenna and a multi-input RF-Front end are shown. One of most important challenges for beamforming technique is to calibrate biases between antennas as well as front-ends. The bias calibration method and test results are shown next. Finally, multipath mitigation performance using antenna array with hardware biases calibrated will be demonstrated.

1 Array Antenna

In this section, the concept of array antenna is briefly introduced. A linear N-elements array is considered as shown in Fig. 1. When a satellite is observed in a direction of azimuth (φ) and zenith angle (θ), the received signal at the reference point is assumed as $E_0(t)$. Then received signal by the i-th element can be expressed as

$$E_i(t) = E_0(t - \tau_i) \quad (i = 1,2, \dots, N) \qquad (1).$$

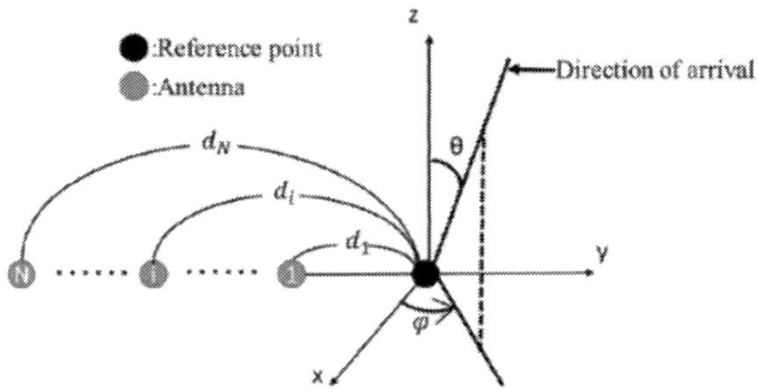

Fig. 1. N-element linear antenna array

In Eq. 1, τ_i is propagation delay with respect to the reference point, and given by

$$\tau_i = \frac{d_i \sin\theta \sin\varphi}{c} \qquad (2)$$

where d_i is distance of i-th element from the reference point, and c is speed of signal propagation. Therefore, Eq. (1) is expressed as

$$\begin{aligned} E_i(t) &= E_0(t - \tau_i) \\ &= E_0(t)\exp(-j2\pi f \tau_i) \\ &= E_0(t)\exp\left(-j2\pi f \frac{d_i \sin\theta \sin\varphi}{c}\right) \end{aligned}$$

* Corresponding author: tsujii@aero.osakafu-u.ac.jp

$$= E_0(t)\exp\left(-j2\pi\frac{d_i\sin\theta\sin\varphi}{\lambda}\right) \quad (3)$$

where f and λ are frequency and wavelenght of the signal, respectively. The purpose of array antenna in this research is to strengthen the signal of aimed satellite by adjusting phase delay at each antenna. The signal at i-th antenna ($E_i(t,\theta,\varphi) = E_i(t)$) is delayed by τ_i with respect to the signal at the reference point. To compensate this delay, the phase advance factor is multiplied as follows :

$$E_i(t,\theta,\varphi)\exp\left(\mathrm{j}2\pi\frac{d_i\sin\theta\sin\varphi}{\lambda}\right), \quad (i = 1,2,\cdots,\mathrm{N})\#(4).$$

The adjusted signals of N elements are summed and combined signal can be expressed as

$$E_{\mathrm{sum}}(t,\theta,\varphi) = \sum_{i=1}^{N} E_i(t,\theta,\varphi)\exp\left(\mathrm{j}2\pi\frac{d_i\sin\theta\sin\varphi}{\lambda}\right)\# = NE_0(t,\theta,\varphi) \quad (5).$$

The signal phases from (θ,φ) direction are adjusted to allign, and as a result the combined signal is amplified by N times.

An example gain pattern of a 6-element linear array antenna with half wavelength separation is shown in Fig. 2. Multipath error would be mitigated by directing the main lobe towards the aimed satellite.

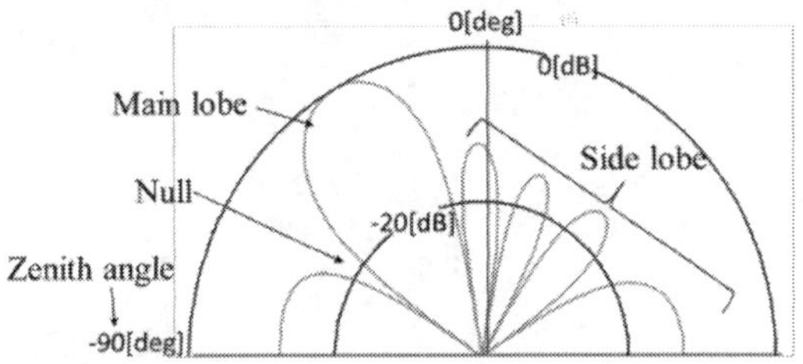

Fig. 2. Example gain pattern of a 6-elemnet linear array antenna

2 Beamforming Algorithms

In this research, a three-element antenna array was used and each antenna was connected to three RF front ends where a reference clock was commonly used. Intermediate frequency (IF) data for three antennas were collected by a PC as shown in Fig. 3. IF data consists of In-phase and Quadrature data, and they are combined to form a beam by using the following method. Fig. 4 illustrates the geometry of the array antenna and signal direction. Antenna 1 was defined as reference antenna, and the signal phases for other two antennas were adjusted to align to the reference antenna.

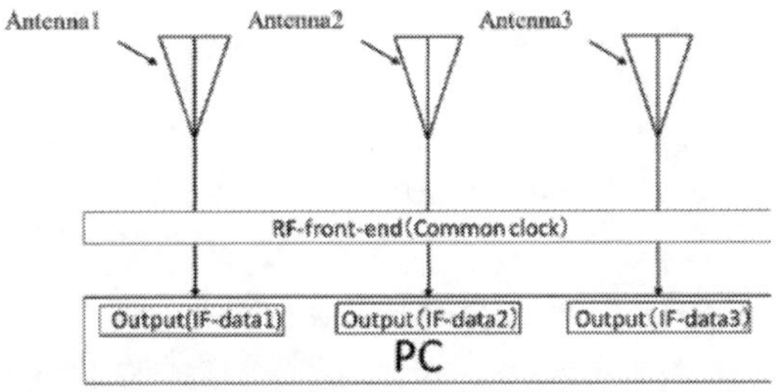

Fig. 3. IF data recording system for a three-element array antenna

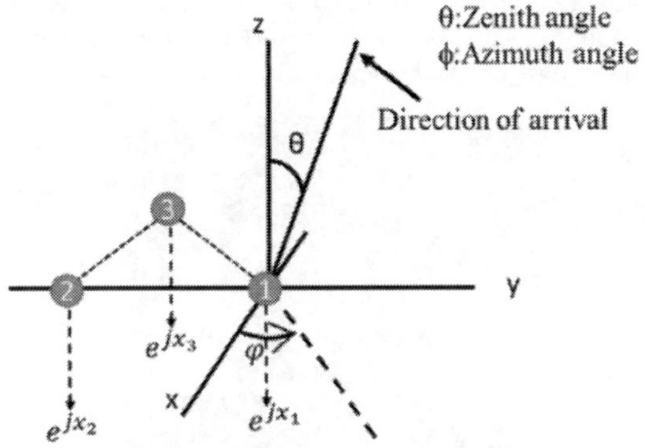

Fig.4. Geometry of 3-element antenna and signal direction

The signal from i-th antenna element can be expressed by the following equation.

$$e^{jx_i} = I_i + jQ_i \quad (6)$$

Now, phase differences between 2nd/3rd antennas and the reference antenna defined as δ_{21}, δ_{31}. Then the signal of second antenna is adjusted for its phase to align to the reference signal as follows:

$$e^{jx_2} \times e^{+j\delta_{21}}$$

$$\begin{aligned} &= (I_2 + jQ_2)(\cos\delta_{21} + j\sin\delta_{21}) \\ &= (I_2\cos\delta_{21} - Q_2\sin\delta_{21}) \\ &\quad + j(Q_2\cos\delta_{21} + I_2\sin\delta_{21}) \quad (7). \end{aligned}$$

Then the signal of third antenna is also adjusted as follows:

$$e^{jx_3} \times e^{+j\delta_{31}}$$

$$\begin{aligned} &= (I_3 + j3)(\cos\delta_{31} + j\sin\delta_{31}) \\ &= (I_3\cos\delta_{31} - Q_3\sin\delta_{31}) \\ &\quad + j(Q_3\cos\delta_{31} + I_3\sin\delta_{31}) \quad (8). \end{aligned}$$

Finally, three I/Q data are summed to obtain new I/Q data for a beam-formed signal according to the following equations.

$$I' = I_1 + (I_2 \cos\delta_{21} - Q_2 \sin\delta_{21}) + (I_3 \cos\delta_{31} - Q_3 \sin\delta_{31}) \quad (9)$$

$$Q' = Q_1 + (Q_2 \cos\delta_{21} + I_2 \sin\delta_{21}) + (Q_3 \cos\delta_{31} + I_3 \sin\delta_{31}) \quad (10)$$

3 Experiments and Results

3.1. Hardware bias calibration

In order to form proper directional beam, hardware biases due to antenna, antenna cable, RF front end have to be calibrated. In this research, the hardware biases were estimated by comparing carrier phases measured at antenna elements. Fig. 5 shows the three-element array antenna used for this experiment.

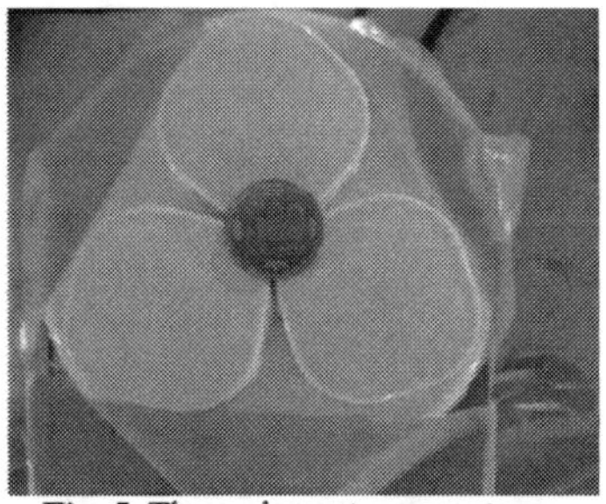

Fig. 5. Three-element array antenna

When carrier phase measurements for the first and i-th antenna are expressed by φ_1, φ_i , the hardware bias of the i-th antenna with respect to the first antenna (b_{i1}) can be calculated as follows

$$b_{i1} = \varphi_i - \varphi_1 - L_{i1} \quad (i = 2,3) \quad (11)$$

where L_{i1} is difference of geometrical distances between the satellite and i-th/first antennas calculated theoretically.

The hardware biases of antenna-2/3 relative to antenna-1 calculated by using carrier phase measurements of four satellites (G11, G17, G22 and G23) are shown in Fig. 6 and Fig. 7. The average of these biases are used for calibration.

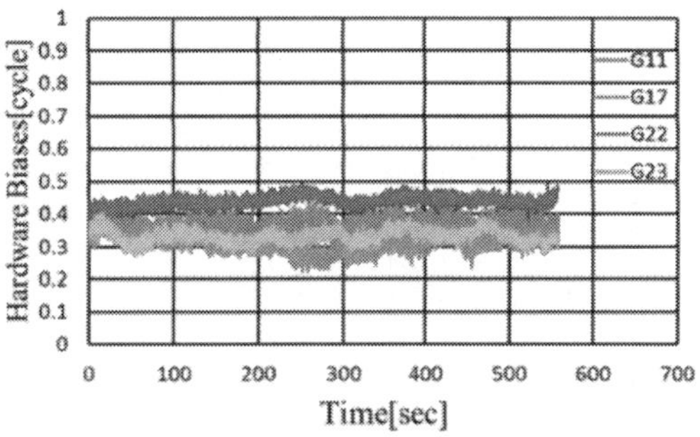

Fig. 6. Hardware bias of antenna-2 relative to antenna-1

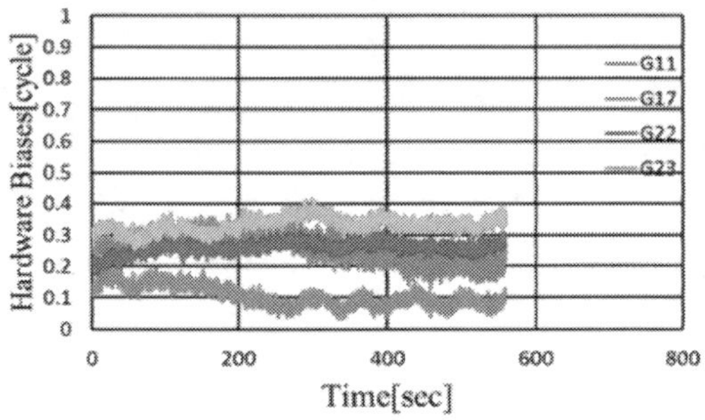

Fig. 7. Hardware bias of antenna-3 relative to antenna-1

In order to verify the efficacy of hardware bias calibration, theoretical calculation of received signal was compared with observation result. First, the expected signal strength variation before calibration was calculated (Fig. 8). The values at the right of color bar from -10 to +10 (dB) indicate increment/decrement from the signal strength received by single antenna. Although phase adjustment for beamforming was not conducted, a gain pattern was seen. This pattern seemed to be caused by uncalibrated hardware biases. On the other hand, Fig. 9 shows the observed signal strength variation where the values at the right of color bar indicate C/N_0 variation by a software receiver used for processing the IF data. The signals of satellites in eastern sky were weakened and strong correlation in signal strength variation can be seen between Fig. 8 and Fig. 9.

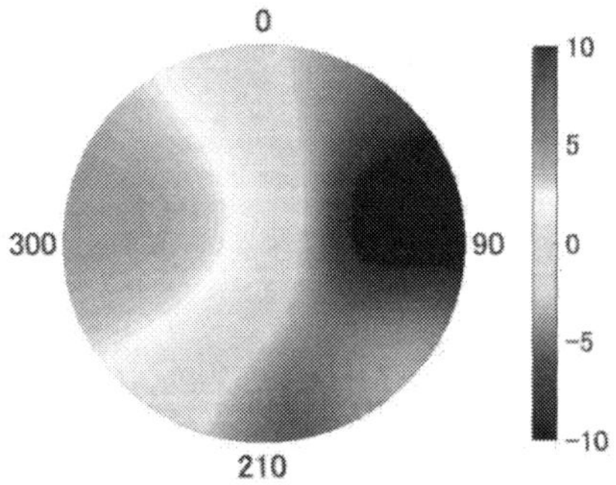

Fig. 8. Expected signal strength variation (biases NOT calibrated)

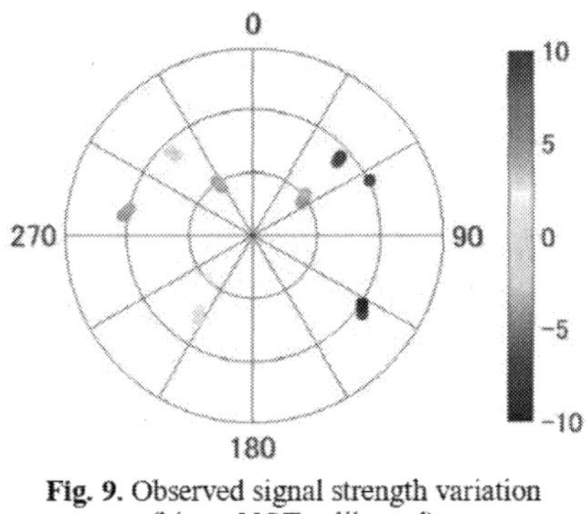

Fig. 9. Observed signal strength variation (biases NOT calibrated)

Next, the expected signal strength variation after calibration was calculated (Fig. 10). Since no beamforming adjustment was carried out, the signal from the zenith was strongest and unsymmetrical gain pattern was not seen as expected. Fig. 11 shows the observed signal strength variation after bias calibration. Compared to the results shown in Fig. 9, the signals of satellites in eastern sky were enhanced in this case and showed similar tendency to Fig. 10. These results show the efficacy of bias calibration and now it is ready to proceed to beam forming.

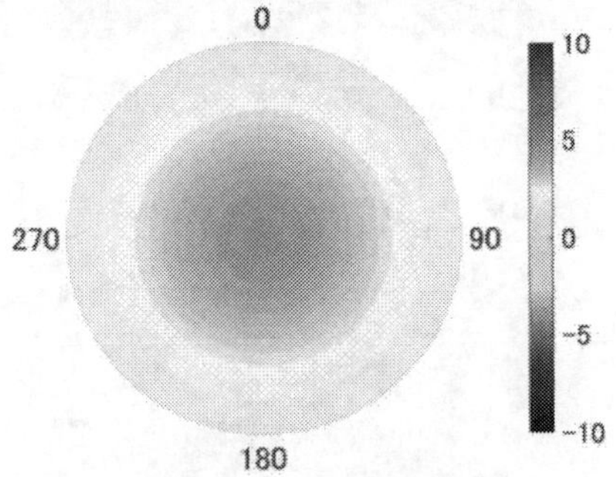

Fig. 10. Expected signal strength variation (biases calibrated)

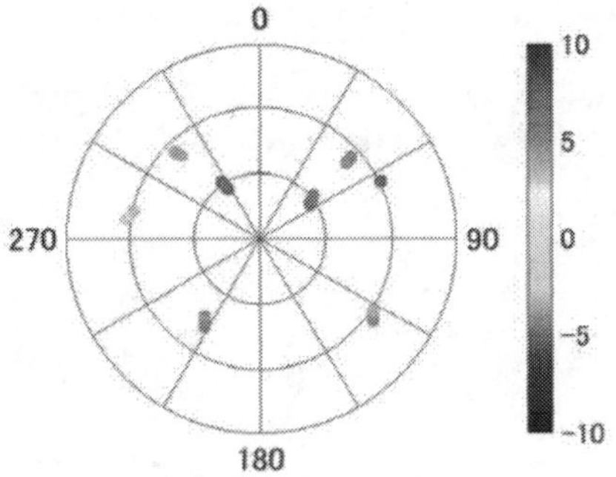

Fig. 11. Observed signal strength variation (biases calibrated)

3.2 Multipath mitigation testing

Before conducting multipath mitigation testing, GPS data were collected in open sky environment and hardware biases were estimated. Then test equipments were moved to multipath-rich environment. The satellite locations in the sky are shown in Fig. 12 while the map of test area is shown in Fig. 13. The GPS data were collected nearby four-story building and a large hunger for aircrafts.

Multipath effects were evaluated by taking difference between carrier phase and pseudorange (CMC, Code-minus-Carrier). Since multipath error on carrier phase is less than 1/4 of wavelength, CMC indicates the multipath error on pseudorange which reaches to tens of meters.

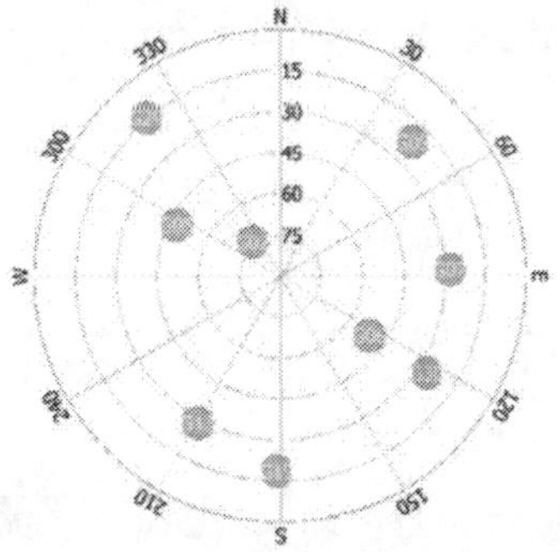

Fig. 12. Sky plot of GPS satellites

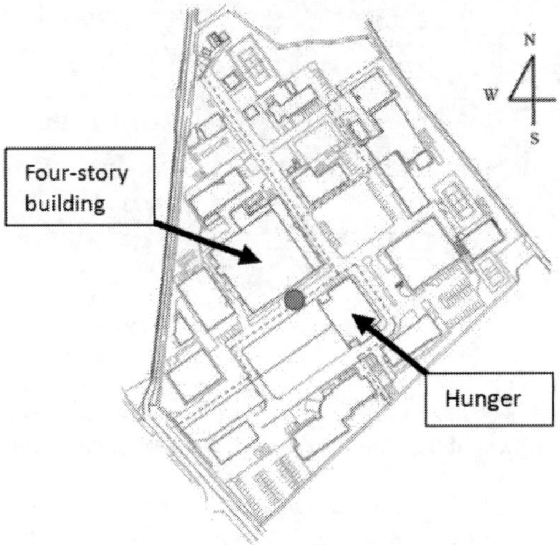

Fig. 13. Map of test area (● : Data logging point)

The variation of CMC for GPS02 satellite is shown in Fig. 14. Since carrier phase has ambiguity, only CMC variation from the initial time is shown. The CMC for three-element array antenna is indicated by orange line, while the CMC calculated by using a geodetic receiver with single antenna is shown by blue line. Multipath mitigation by the beam-formed array antenna can be seen. The CMC variations for other satellites (GPS06 and GPS13) are also shown in Fig. 15 and 16, respectively. The effect of beam forming can be seen for these satellites, too.

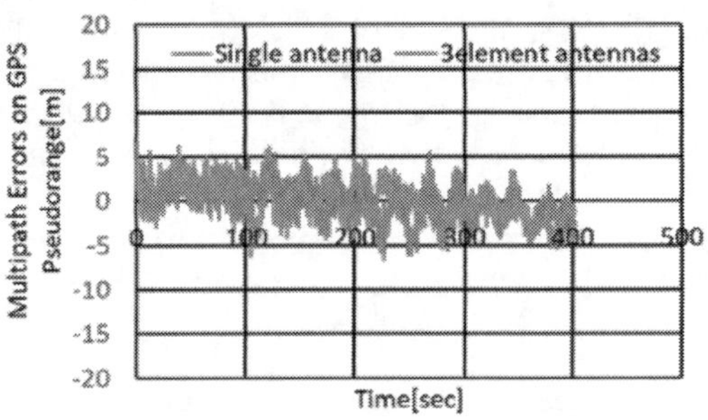

Fig. 14. Multipath error variation (G02)

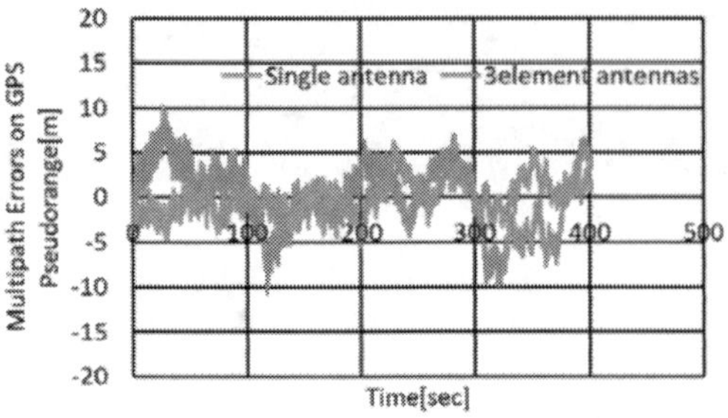

Fig. 15. Multipath error variation (G06)

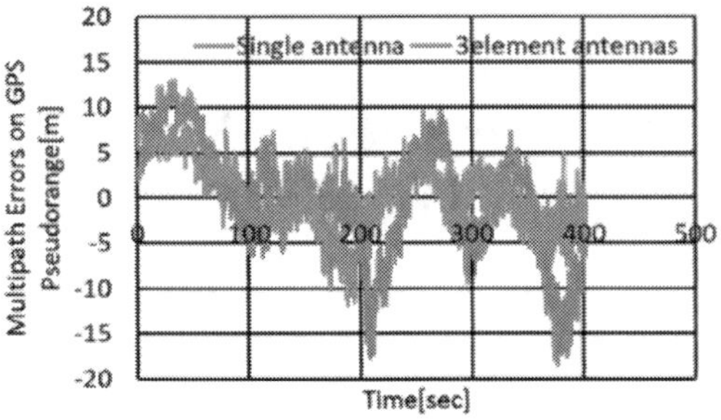

Fig. 16. Multipath error variation (G13)

Table 1 summarized the standard deviation (s.t.d) of CMC in this experiment. The first raw shows the s.t.d for an element of the array antenna (uncombed signal) while the second raw shows the s.t.d for the single geodetic antenna. The multipath error variations for two kinds of single antenna were similar. On the other hand, the CMC variation for the beam formed signal (in the third raw) showed smaller s.t.d, and therefore, a superior performance of array antenna for multipath mitigation was demonstrated.

Table 1 Standard deviation of pseudorange multipath error variation

standard deviation[m]	G02	G06	G13
3element antennas(non-synthetic)	3.41	4.66	6.77
Single antenna	2.44	4.50	6.04
3element antennas(synthetic)	1.88	1.91	3.95

Conclusion and Future Work

In this paper, the hardware bias calibration method by using carrier phase was validated. Then multipath mitigation experiment was conducted in the area surrounded by buildings. Test results demonstrated that 50-70% reduction of pseudorange errors due to multipath were able to be achieved if the beamforming algorithms were applied.

In the future work, the same algorithms will be applied to a seven-element array antenna (Fig. 17).

Fig. 17. Seven-element array antenna

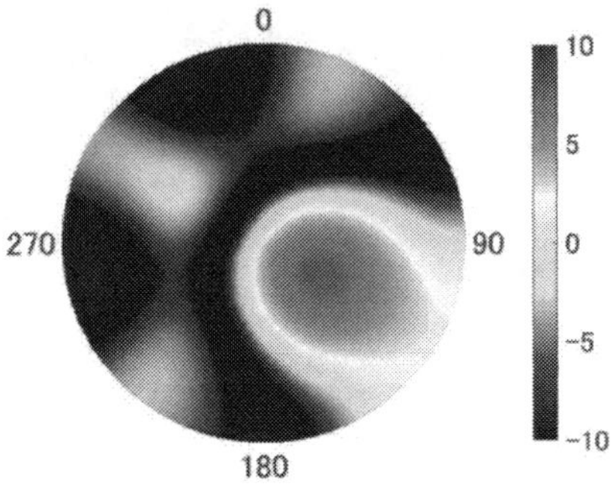

Fig. 18. Expected signal strength variation for seven-element array antenna

Due to the effect of many elements and smaller separation (9.5 cm) between elements, forming a sharper beam is possible (Fig. 18) and further multipath mitigation can be expected.

This work was supported by JSPS KAKENHI Grant Number JP16K06550.

References

1. Kikuma, Nobuyoshi., Adaptive Signal Processing by Array Antenna, Kagaku Gijutsu Shuppan, 2004.
2. Ung Suok Kim, Dennis Akos, Per Enge, Frederic Bastide, "Simulation and Validation of a GPS Antenna Array Concept for JPALS Application", ION GPS/GNSS 2003, 9-12 September 2003, Portland,OR p1852-1855.
3. Saeed Daneshmand, Negin Sokhandan, Mohammad Zaeri-Amirani and Gérard Lachapelle, " Precise Calibration of a GNSS Antenna Array for Adaptive Beamforming Applications", Sensors 2014, 14(6), 9669-9691

 https://doi.org/10.1051/e3sconf/20199403010

Identifying GNSS market in Indonesia before and the future

Heri Andreas[1,*] and *Sandy* Noveriansyah[2]

[1]Geodesy Research Division, Faculty of Earth Science and Technology, Institute of Technology Bandung, Indonesia
[2]Universitas Komputer (UNIKOM), Indonesia

Abstract. Global Navigation Satellite System (GNSS) is one of the best finding of the twenty century world technologies. It is satellite base positioning and timing system. A millimeter accuracy of 4D positions can be provided by this GNSS system, allowed us to measure the geodynamic with millimeter per year signal only, measure small deformation and even the change of pole of earth rotation. Not to mention the GNSS for navigation and transportation system, it helps a lot in such traffic management, tracking, controlling, etc. GNSS market has contributed huge amount of dollars in world's economy. Japan and America are two country of among others for biggest GNSS market so far. As for Indonesia, it is only part of 4% of Asia market in the early 2000. With such similar characteristic between Indonesia and Japan, especially relating to fast growing nation and the ring of fire, in this case market of GNSS in the future can be promising in Indonesia. This paper will highlight the GNSS market in Indonesia before and the future. We found that within ten to fifteen years the GNSS market in Indonesia will be the biggest around South East Asia and probably in Asia Pacific.

1 Introduction

The revolution in world scale positioning has begun as the satellite technology invented in the beginning of year 70. Global Navigation Satellite System (GNSS) has been played as remarkable tool for positioning and mapping with high accuracy can be achieved in the easiest way (Seeber [1], Abidin [2-3], Leick [4], Hofmann et. al. [5]). In everywhere and in anytime worldwide when signals from the satellites received by the receivers, in these cases the position in 3D or even 4D can be determined precisely (figure 1) and even with precision in the order of millimeter. Not to mention, the position can be also precisely determined "real-time" in the order of few centimeter by Real Time Kinematik (RTK) Method. The GNSS become a revolution in positioning on the 20th century.

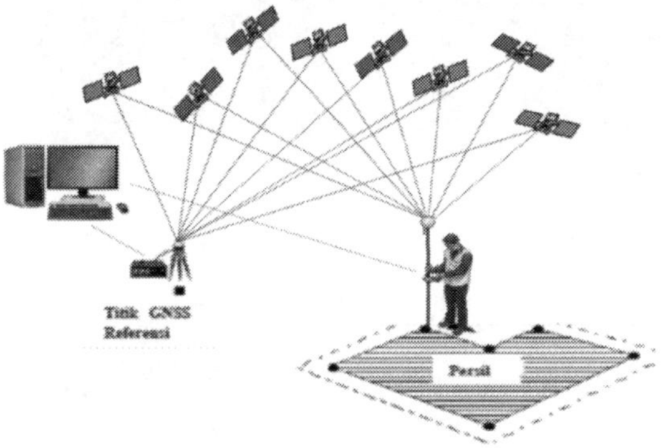

Fig. 1. Illustration of positioning using GNSS technology.

Global Positioning System (GPS) and Globalnaya navigatsionnaya sputnikovaya sistema (GLONASS) are GNSS product by US and Russia. For more than two decade they give all kind of services on positioning and timing. In the case of positioning they allowed us to measure the geodynamic with millimeter per year signal only, measure small deformation and even the change of pole of earth rotation. Not to mentioned their positioning services for survey and mapping and geodetic engineering. In the context of navigation, they helps a lot in such traffic management, tracking, controlling, etc. Figure 2 shows many multiuse of GNSS GPS GLONASS in variety of fields.

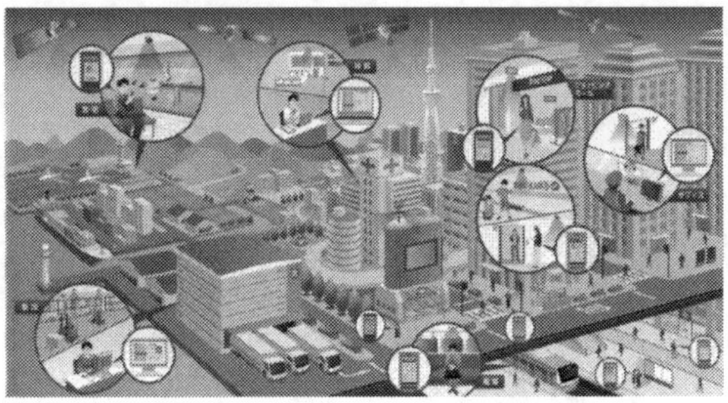

Source GPS World

Fig.2. Illustration of multiuse of GNSS (GPS and GLONASS) in variety of fields.

In the recent years, the GNSS is expanding when the BEIDOU or COMPAS has been launched by the China, the GALIEO by European Union, QZSS (Quasi Zenith Satellite System) by the Japan, etc. So, today it is not

*Corresponding author: heriandreas49@gmail.com

only GPS and GLONASS who existed and give services in positioning and timing, we have more. The additional satellite system is theoretically adding the value to others GNSS System since more satellite can be observed. Also with combination of geostationary and original prograde satellite of 12 hour period, the positioning will be more robust.

With such remarkable services in positioning and timing, GNSS market has contributed huge amount of dollars in world's economy. Japan and America are two country of among others for biggest GNSS market so far. As for Indonesia, it is only part of 4% of Asia market in the early 2000 (DOC [6]). With such similar characteristic between Indonesia and Japan, especially relating to fast growing nation and the ring of fire, in this case market of GNSS in the future can be promising in Indonesia. This paper will highlight the GNSS market in Indonesia before and the future.

2 World GNSS market

With such tremendous contribution to the world in context of application of positioning and timing (e.g. Navigation, transportation, survey and mapping etc. as mentioned) the GNSS market has given huge amount of dollar in world's economy like previously mentioned. The value of the world GNSS technology business in 2002 reached $ 9 billion with an annual increase of around $ 1 billion. This means that currently the value of the GNSS technology business is estimated linearly in more than $24 billion. On the other hand an estimation of $ 96 billion is given by GNSS market for present years (GPS World [7]). Global GNSS GPS receiver market by geography shows America and Asia Pacific (but mostly Japan) are the biggest market until today. It is 31.02% and 42.11%. Meanwhile 26.87% credit for Europe and Middle East (Businesswire.com [8]).

In 2016, the GPS receiver market in Asia Pacific (APAC) was valued at $1.52 billion. In the same year the GPS receiver market in Europe and Middle East (EMEA) is growing at a CAGR of 10.25%. The GPS Receiver market in Americas is expected to reach $2.26 billion by 2021 (Businesswire.com [8]).

Do not forget that we just talking about GPS receivers only. As explained above, In the recent years, the GNSS is expanding when the BEIDOU or COMPAS has been launched by the China, the GALIEO by European Union, QZSS (Quasi Zenith Satellite System) by the Japan, etc. Market of receiver is even more huge. Production of Receiver with has BEIDOU channel is growing rapidly. Previously we only familiar with TRIMBLE, LEICA, ASTECH, MAGELLAND and TOPCON, but now we have various brand like SOUTH, HI-TARGET, CHC, NAVCOM, COMNAV, STONEX, HEMISPHERE, UNISTRONG, etc.

Low cost GNSS receiver is also growing quite rapidly, and not to mentioned the handy type like Garmin, Magelland, etc. If we included this segment into economic value, in this case more billions dollar should be add.

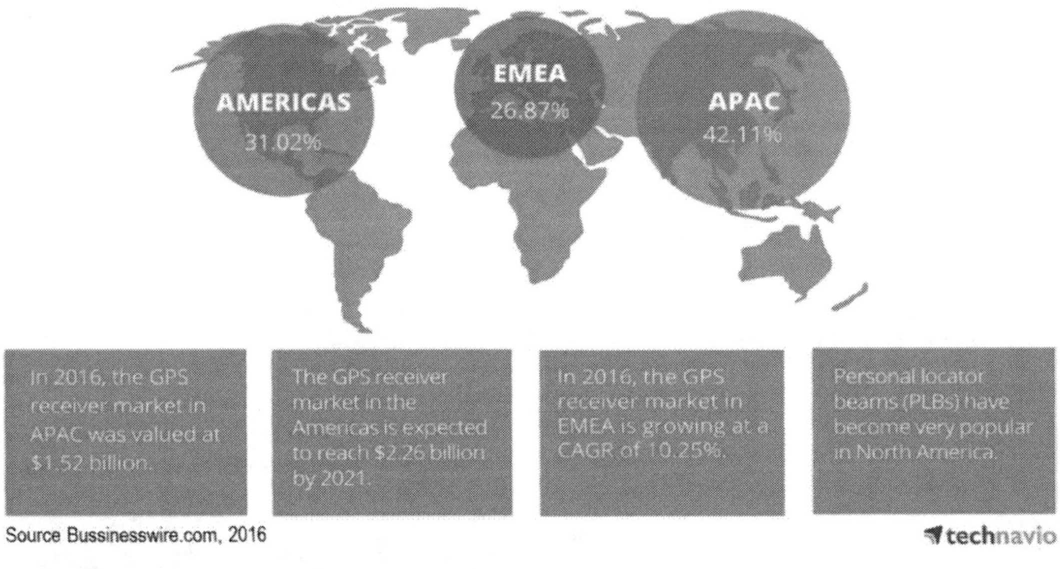

Fig.3. Map of world transaction on GNSS GPS Receiver by 2016. APAC own 42.11%, EMEA own 26.87% and AMERICAS own 31.02%. The future prediction conclude APAC will be the biggest market in the world [8].

China market and economic value of GNSS is still underestimated by calculation. It should be very huge in sales as well as the economic value. GNSS factories are growing rapidly in China. With such big country, the china market of GNSS in their own country will be the same or even bigger than Japan market. We mentioned again that Japan own 44% of world market in the early 2000. GNSS from China is now enter Africa and South America. We can easily found SOUTH Receiver, CHC, HI-TARGET in those continent and sub-continent.

 https://doi.org/10.1051/e3sconf/20199403010

3 GNSS market in Indonesia until today

GNSS market in Indonesia is still relatively small. Fields that are using GNSS technology such as navigation and LBS, transportation, survey and mapping and geodynamic study. Indonesia has only 200-300 CGNSS (Continous GNSS) while Japan has more than 1600. First GNSS receiver come to Indonesia was in 1989 and growing market started since 1994. Slowly but sure the market is growing toward positive direction. Roughly note the vendors have sold for more than 5000 geodetic type receiver so far (Geoprima Solution [9], Wisesa Berkah Bumi [10], and Asaba [11]). This is good news for the market.

First let's talk in detail the beginning the receiver come to Indonesia. It was demo in 1989. After demo the Government realize that GNSS is right tool to help problems of positioning in Indonesia. In 1994 a National Program creating Network Frame for Survey and Mapping executed with GPS. All Benchmark belong to primary and secondary of Network Frame measured by the geodetic type dual frequency receiver. Figure 4 show distribution of Benchmark.

After benchmark being established, another big project being established and indeed even earlier and that is high scale mapping. We used photogrammetry and remote sensing surveys beside conventional tachymetry survey. In order to accomplish the project, help from GPS is crucial. The ground control point for Photogrammetric and High Resolution Satellite Image Data comes from GPS measurements. Fix points of tachymetry is also comes from GPS. In this moment, purchasing of GPS receiver was quite remarkable. Figure 6 shows activities of GPS measurements in the fields.

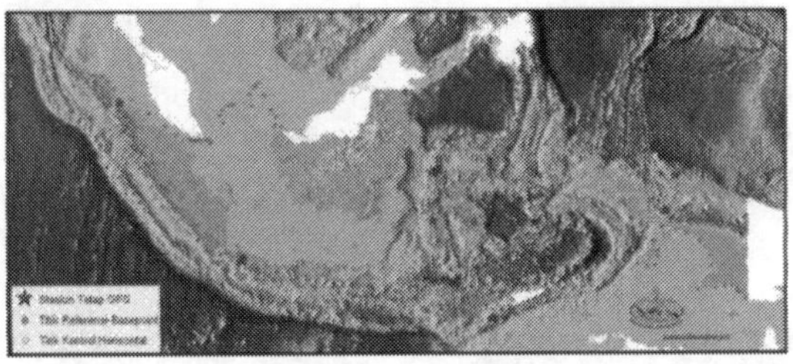

Fig.4. Distribution of benchmark belong to primary and secondary Indonesia Network Frame for survei and mapping (BIG [12])

Since Indonesia is very active tectonically, therefore GPS measurement for geodynamic and deformation is demanding and it started after 2004 Tsunami Earthquake in Aceh. The Government install CGNSS in many places. Approximately we have 200-300 CGNSS. The receiver put it on the stable benchmark. There are also CGNSS on tide gauge stations, on Buoy, etc. Figure 5 shows tectonic motion of Indonesia. This information is very much useful for earthquake and tsunami mitigation program and also for definition of semi dynamic datum. Today Indonesia has SRGI 2013 semi dynamic datum, replace DGN95 static datum.

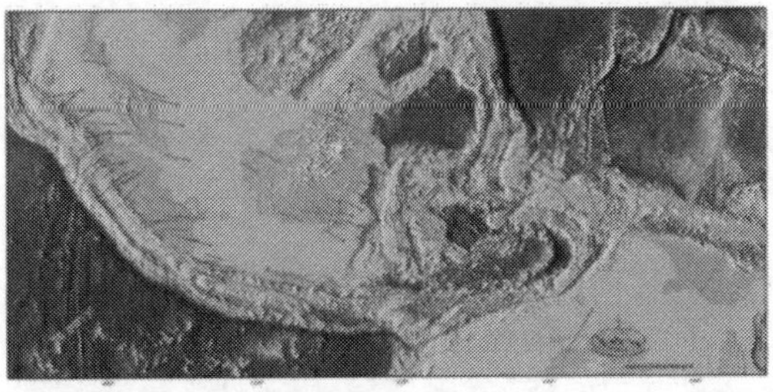

Fig.5. Tectonic motion of Indonesia regions derived from GNSS GPS measurements. The movement indicated by vector displacement (BIG [12])

Fig.6. Activities of GPS measurement in the field to support survey and mapping and others.

Another market of GNSS is on navigation and LBS using GPS handheld receiver, Integration of GPS with GIS (Geographic Information System) and also with the Smart City. Today the Smart Phone also capable on observing GPS satellite. Now we have many applications that is based on positioning and navigation and or LBS such as Google Map, WAZE, GOJEK, GRAB, UBER, etc. Other LBS (Location Base Services) is also available. Off course those all things adding the value of GNSS economy. Below is table 1 summarize the GNSS market in Indonesia until today.

Table 1. Summary of GNSS market in Indonesia until today

High precision positioning	Geodynamic and deformation monitoring, disaster mitigation, early warning
Survey and Mapping	Survey Network, Ground Control Point, Fix Points, etc.
Navigation and LBS	Tracking System, Google Map, WAZE, GOJEK, GRAB, etc.
Maritime	Batimetry, vessel navigation, etc.
Aviation	Flight Navigation, UAV positioning, etc.
Others	Military, GPS time transfer, agriculture, sport, recreation, etc.

 https://doi.org/10.1051/e3sconf/20199403010

4 Future GNSS in Indonesia

Trend of future GNSS applications in the world as well as in Indonesia can be seen in figure 7 below (gsa.europe.eu [13]). Indonesia becomes one of the fastest growing nations and quicker adaptation to the world's changing. The economic value of GNSS in the market will be tremendous. GNSS is expected to service many more fields in the future than today. The trend will be to LBS, Road and others (Surveying, Drones, Maritime, Aviation, Timing and Synchronization and Agriculture). The highest trend will be LBS. For countries with such disaster like Indonesia, the GNSS application for monitoring and disaster mitigation will also be future trend to accelerate.

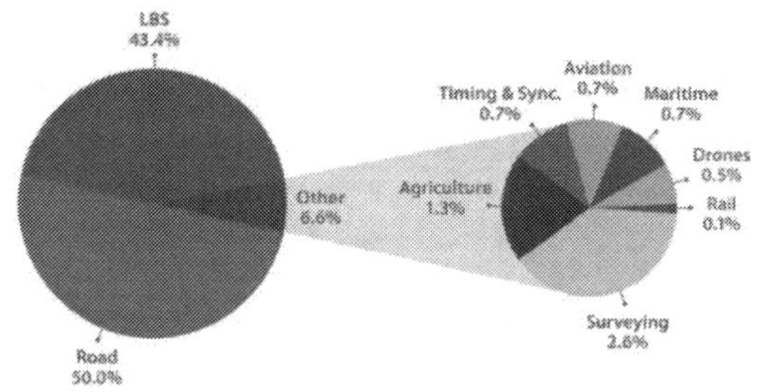

Fig.7. Trend of future GNSS application in the world [12]

With such similar characteristic between Indonesia and Japan, especially related to fast growing nation and the ring of fire, Indonesia will be one of the biggest market around South East Asia and even in Asia Pacific. Indeed the future prediction conclude APAC will be the biggest market in the world while Indonesia is belong to APAC. In another word Indonesia is also belong to the potential market for some reasons.

Indonesia is spatially bigger than Japan. If Indonesia applies GNSS in many fields, it is not impossible to defeat Japan and other countries. As noted earlier, Indonesia is still a 4.7% market share in South East Asia. This means that if Japan has reached 44%, then the deviation value is still very large as an opportunity.

The mandate of the Geospatial Information Act No. 4 of 2011 has opened up opportunities for surveys and mapping to high accuracy, which requires GNSS technology. The Indonesia Geospatial Agency (BIG) as a trustee institution must produce 1: 1000 maps of the entire territory of Indonesia, including the mapping of 80,000 villages (figure 8).

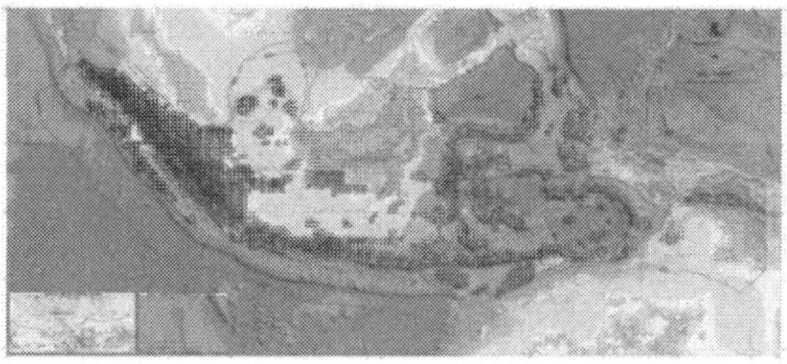

Fig.8. Fields to be survey for high scale high accuracy map in Indonesia including villages.

Disaster-laden Indonesia needs GNSS technology for disaster monitoring and mitigation. Indonesia is full of earthquakes, tsunamis, landslides, floods, etc. GNSS technology can be used as a module in modeling disaster phenomena, which in turn becomes an input for disaster mitigation models. Estimation of CGNSS for geodynamic study to be installed in Indonesia is 6000 (base on figuring 1600 at Japan). Not to mentioned for natural deformation purpose.

If we talking man made deformation (e.g. deformation on buildings, bridges, road, railways, platform oil and gas, DAM, etc.), prospect of GNSS to monitor man made deformation is very bright. Huge infrastructures is being developed today in all over Indonesia (figure 9). Today only few programs have been set up to monitor some bridges, platform oil and gas and DAM. Probably no program yet on monitoring building, road and railways. So, we can imagine the prospect in the future.

Fig.9. Indonesia is accelerating in development. Huge infrastructure is being developed.

Indonesia is one of the biggest archipelago country in the world. Located in the equator regions Indonesia is rich for natural resources such as forest (figure 10), fishing ground, farmland, mining, etc. Managing all resources need position as one basic parameters. So, we can imagine another prospect in the future for GNSS in Indonesia. One finest example in the future is precise farming. The others are delineation of forest boundary, calculate size of mining area, etc.

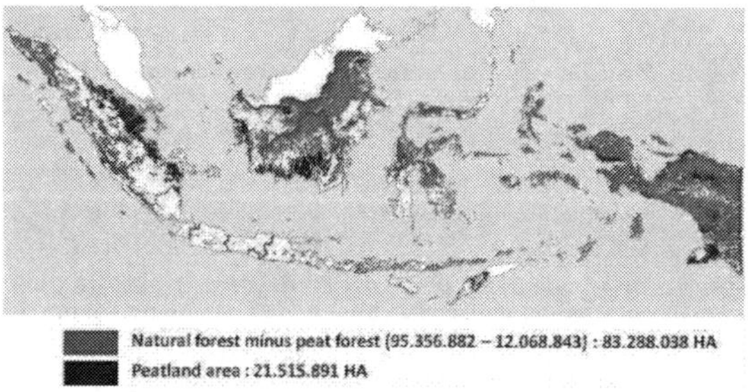

Fig.10. Map of forest (natural and peatland) in Indonesia

Land parcel in Indonesia consist of about 140 millions unit. Until today only 50 million is well define (e.g. certified). The rest we still need measurements. For about couple years ago, the RTK multi GNSS plays an important role in measuring land parcel in Indonesia. This RTK can speed up the measurement (Andreas [14]). Base on record from vendors (Geoprima Solution [9], Wisesa Berkah Bumi [10], and Asaba [11]), GNSS receiver selling reached more than 2000 unit in order to support land parcel measurements. In the future they estimate there will be more millions to sell. Land parcel certification expected to finish by 2025.

As for fleet managements system, navigation, tracking and controlling system, figure 11 show future of them in the world. Indonesia has the same future figure. As mentioned earlier in Indonesia now we have many applications that is based on positioning, navigation and LBS such as Google Map, WAZE, GOJEK, GRAB, UBER, etc.

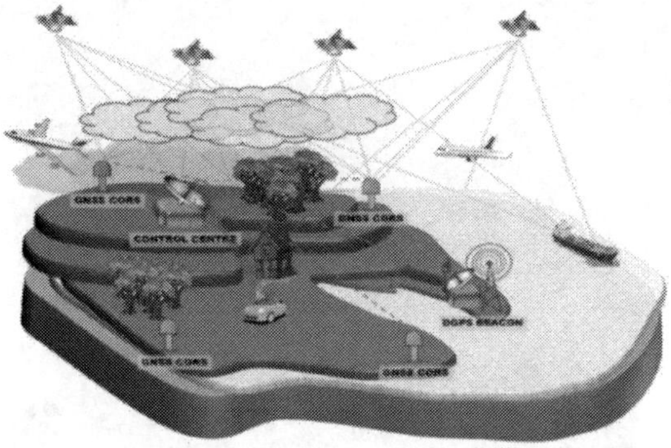

Source: MOSTI

Fig.11. GNSS infrastructures for fleet management system, navigation, controlling and LSB system.

Based on research on literature, interviewed and questionary the Goverment, the Experts, Academia, the Vendors, the variety of users, we found that within ten to fifteen years the GNSS market in Indonesia will be the biggest around South East Asia and probably in Asia Pacific. Below is table 2 summarizing the future GNSS market in Indonesia.

Table 2. Summary of GNSS future market in Indonesia

High precision positioning	Geodynamic and deformation monitoring, Infrastructure monitoring, disaster mitigation, early warning
Survey and Mapping	Survey Network, Ground Control Point, Fix Points, etc.
Navigation and LBS	Tracking, Fleet Management System, Google Map, WAZE, GOJEK, GRAB, etc.
Maritime	Batimetry, vessel navigation, surveillance, etc.
Aviation	Flight Navigation
Agriculture	Precise farming, Forrest management, etc.
Others	Military, GPS time transfer, agriculture, sport, recreation, etc.

5 Closing remarks

In everywhere and in anytime worldwide when signals from the GNSS satellites received by the receivers, in these cases the position in 3D or even 4D can be determined precisely and even with precision in the order of millimeter. Not to mention, the position can be also precisely determined "real-time" in the order of few centimeter by Real Time Kinematik (RTK) Method. The GNSS become a revolution in positioning on the 20th century.

For more than two decade the GNSS give all kind of services on positioning and time. In the case of positioning they allowed us to measure the geodynamic with millimeter per year signal only, measure small deformation and even the change of pole of earth rotation. Not to mentioned their positioning services for survey and mapping and geodetic engineering. In the context of navigation, they helps a lot in such traffic management, tracking, controlling, etc.

With such tremendous contribution to the world in context of application of positioning and timing, the GNSS market has given huge amount of dollar in world's economy. Global GNSS GPS receiver market by geography shows America and Asia Pacific (but mostly Japan) are the biggest market until today. It is 31.02% and 42.11%. Meanwhile 26.87% credit for Europe and Middle East. China market and economic value of GNSS in this country is still underestimated by calculation. It should be very huge in sales and in the economic value. GNSS factories are growing rapidly in China. With such big country, the china market of GNSS in their own country will be the same or even bigger than Japan market.

GNSS market in Indonesia is still relatively small as for today, nevertheless slowly but sure the market is growing toward positive direction. Based on research on literature, interviewed and questioner, we found that within ten to fifteen years the GNSS market in Indonesia will be the biggest around South East Asia and even in Asia Pacific.

Acknowledgements

Many thanks to students and surveyors who help us in distributing the questioner. Thanks also to people (expert, Academia, Government and bussinessman) who willing to interviewed.

References

1. Seeber, G., Satellite Geodesy: foundation, method, and applications, Walter de Gruyter, Berlin-New York, C7 (1993)
2. Abidin, H.Z., Penentuan Posisi dengan GPS dan Aplikasinya (PT. Pradnya Paramita, Jakarta, 1999)
3. Abidin, H.Z., Geodesi Satelit (Departemen Teknik Geodesi ITB, PT. Pradnya Paramita, Jakarta, 2001)
4. Leick A. GPS satellite surveying, 3rd edn Wiley, New York (2004)

https://doi.org/10.1051/e3sconf/20199403010

5. Hofmann-Wellenhof, B., Lichtenegger, H. and Walse, E., GNSS Global Navigation Satellite Systems: GPS, GLONASS, Galileo, and More. (Springer Verlag, Wien, 2007)
6. DOC, Sales Reporton the GPS Market (2008)
7. GPS World, News Report (2015)
8. Businesswire.com. Internet access May 2018 (2016)
9. Geoprima Solution Ltd. Interview and Questioner 2018 (2018)
10. Wisesa Berkah Bumi Ltd. Interview and Questioner 2018 (2018)
11. Asaba Indonesia Ltd. Interview and Questioner 2018 (2018)
12. BIG (Badan Informasi Geospasial). Presentation on the seminar Establishing New References System for Indonesia (SRGI 2013), Jakarta (2012)
13. Gsa.europe.eu, Internet access May 2018 (2018)
14. Andreas, H., 2017, Percepatan Pemetaan Persil Menggunakan Teknologi Mobile Base Station (MOBS) RTK MULTI GNSS dan RTPPP, Conference Proceeding FIT ISI CGISE Jogjakarta, Indonesia (2016)

The Potency of the Modernized GNSS Signals for Real-Time Kinematic Positioning

Dhota Pradipta[1], Heri Andreas[1], Dina A. Sarsito[1], and Hendy F. Suhandri[2]*

[1]Geodesy Research Group, Faculty of Earth Sciences and Technology, Institute of Technology, Bandung, Indonesia
[2]Coastal, Ocean and Maritime Engineering Research Group, Faculty of Earth Sciences and Technology, Institute of Technology, Bandung, Indonesia

Abstract. GNSS positioning has become popular in the past decade as an efficient method of precise and real-time positioning. It is relatively low cost and ease-of-use. Up to now, several parameters were defined to characterize the performance of real-time positioning: availability, precision, accuracy. This article evaluates the performance of signal linear combinations for real-time positioning, both for static as well as the kinematic positioning. This article starts with the investigation of linear combinations (LC) rising from the carrier frequencies of the GNSS systems. Some Linear Combination shows potential benefits in carrier phase integer ambiguity resolution, particularly utilizing the Galileo and Beidou signal phase carrier. For each system, a set of combinations was studied, analyzed, and then selected during the development of GNSS positioning method utilizing the Least-squares Ambiguity Decorrelation Adjustment (LAMBDA). Special signal selection can affect the estimated position and its standard deviation. To further analyze, the results obtained from data processing are compared with respect to baselines and signals. The ambiguity fixing rate is correlated with the baseline length and the method as well as the signals that were used. The analysis of the measurement noise level was first conducted to set a baseline for the real-time GNSS positioning application. According to the results and to assess the data quality and positioning performance of GNSS in respect with GPS (Global Positioning System), an experimental test has established using MGEX data. This research investigates the satellite visibilities, multipath, Signal to Noise Ratio (SNR), and positioning performance. It is shown that in every epoch, at least 8 satellites are visible. The SNR's are up to 60 dBHz, the code multipath residuals varies within ~1 m, while the phase residuals varies by about ~2 cm. hence the modernized GNSS signals have potencies to improves the RTK positioning.

1. Introduction

Satellite based navigation technology is continuously and rapidly growing in recent time. The Global Navigation Satellite System (GNSS) are Galileo System (GAL) and BeiDou System (BDS), which is developed and operated by European Union and China. Currently, GAL and BDS is entering the third phase of development that is expected to enhance the positioning performance will continue to the final phase on 2020 with global coverage of positioning and navigation system by a constellation of 35 satellites, which are consists of 5 Geostationary Earth Orbit (GEO) satellites, 3 Inclined Geosynchronous Orbit (IGSO) satellites and 27 Medium Earth Orbit (MEO) satellites [1]

Similar to GPS, GAL and BDS provides triple-frequency signal. Table I gives the frequencies and wavelengths of the signal from the GAL and the BDS as well as the GPS. Differs from GPS, BDS adopts the China Geodetic Coordinate System 2000 (CGCS2000) as the coordinate system and BeiDou navigation satellite system time (BDT) as the time system of BDS. GAL using Galileo Terrestrial Reference Frame (GTRF) and Galileo System Time (GST). CGCS2000 is a global, three-dimensional, right-handed, orthogonal, geocentric coordinate system which referred to ITRF97 (International Terrestrial Reference Frame 97) at the epoch 2000.0.

Table 1.1 Parameters of WGS84, CGS2000, GTRF ellipsoid

	WGS84	**CGCS2000**	**GTRF**
a (m)	6 378 137.000	6 378 137.000	6 378 137.000
f	1/298.257223563	1/298.257222101	1/298.257223563
GM (m^3s^{-2})	3.986005 E 14	3.986004418 E 14	3.986004418 E14
Ω (rad s^{-1})	7.292115 E-5	7.292115 E-5	7.292115 E-5

* Corresponding author: dhota@fitb.itb.ac.id

The ellipsoid used in CGCS2000 is slightly different from WGS84 (World Geodetic System 1984) as seen on Table II. Theoretically, the differences induced by those ellipsoids is within 1 millimeter in the equator [1]. BDT adopts seconds without any leap seconds as the international system of unit (SI). The BDT's start epoch was 00:00:00, 1 January 2006 of Universal Time Coordinated (UTC). In respect with GPS Time (GPT), BDT is 14 s ahead GPT (BDT = GPT + 14 s) [1].

Table 1.2 Frequencies and wavelength of GNSS signals (GPS, Galileo, and Beidou)

Satellite System	Signal	Carrier frequency (MHz)	Carrier wavelength (cm)
GPS	L1	1575.42	19.03
	L2	1227.60	24.42
	L5	1176.45	25.48
GAL	E1	1575.42	19.03
	E5a	1176.45	25.48
	E5b	1207.14	24.83
BDS	B1	1561.098	19.20
	B2	1207.14	24.83
	B3	1268.52	23.63

Several studies have been conducted in several areas, particularly in northern hemisphere. The combination of GPS, GAL, and BDS can increase the observation data quality as well as the positioning performance [1].

With a highly growth of infrastructure in Indonesia, the use of GNSS technology is inevitable, especially for the surveying and mapping purposes. Further research over GNSS data quality and positioning performance in Indonesia is needed. To assess the data quality and positioning performance GNSS in respect with GPS (Global Positioning System) over Indonesia, an experimental network had established using MGEX data. This research investigates the satellite visibilities, multipath, Signal to Noise Ratio (SNR), and the positioning performance.

2. Data Quality Assessment

In order to investigate the advantages of GNSS, the satellite visibilities were analysed. Better satellite visibilities lead a better geometry of satellites constellation, namely Dilution of Precision (DOP), which introduces to a better position accuracy and precision.

DOP can be divided into several terms, which are vertical DOP (VDOP), horizontal DOP (HDOP), position DOP (PDOP) and time DOP (TDOP). Those terms can be generalized by using Geometric DOP (GDOP) term. In order to achieve the highest position accuracy and precision (low DOP value), the satellites geometry is not supposed to clustered together in a single quadrant.

Fig. 2.1 shows the number of observed satellites for GPS, GAL, BDS, and combined systems with a cut off angle of 10°. It can be found that the satellite visibilities of GNSS combinations is more stable than the GPS. By using GNSS, at least 10 satellites can be observed for more than 80% of observation time., while the number of combined systems observed satellites is vary from 12 to 22 with an average of 14 satellites.

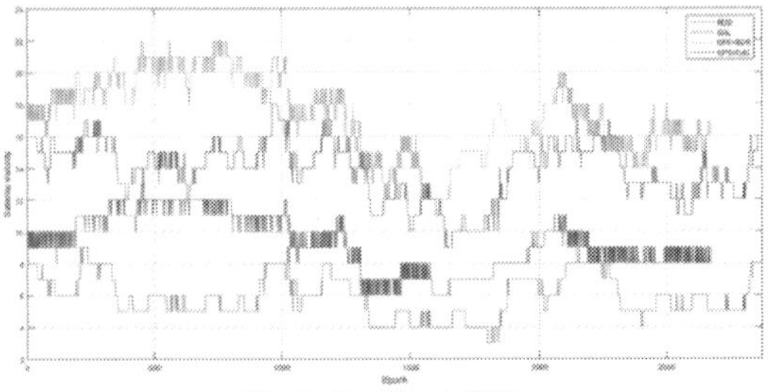

Fig. 2.1 Satellite visibility

2.1 Multipath

This section described the methods that used to assess the data quality of GNSS.

The multipath of GNSS can be investigate by applied the Multipath Combination (MPC) algorithm. The MPC can be expressed as [6]:

$$MP1 = P_1 - \frac{f_1^2+f_2^2}{f_1^2-f_2^2} B_1 + \frac{2f_2^2}{f_1^2-f_2^2} B_2 \quad (1)$$

$$MP2 = P_2 - \frac{2f_1^2}{f_1^2-f_2^2} B_1 + \frac{f_1^2+f_2^2}{f_1^2-f_2^2} B_2 \quad (2)$$

where P and L are the GNSS pseudorange and carrier phase range respectively and f is the frequency of the carrier phase. By using these combinations, the first order of ionospheric delay and geometric range from satellite and receiver are eliminated, while noise is assumed to be negligible due to the accuracy of the pseudorange observation.

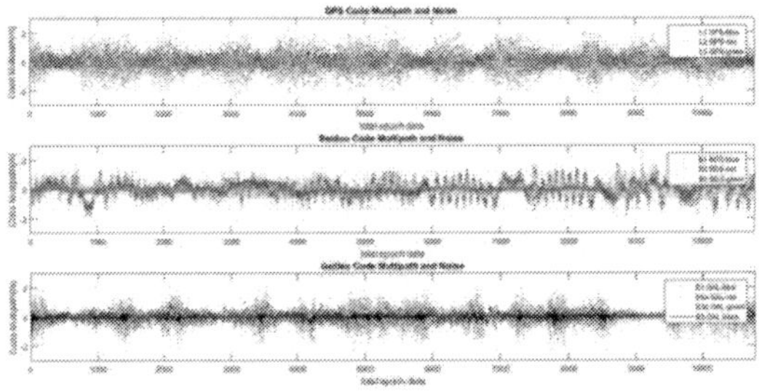

Fig. 2.2 Code Multipath for GNSS signals (GPS, Glonass, Galileo, and Beidou)

2.2 Signal to Noise (SNR) Ratio

Concerning satellite configuration, site-specific factors as well as atmospheric effects, the quality of GNSS observations may become inconsistent and affecting SNR. In addition, observation weighting plays a dominant role when GNSS receivers calculate positions by measuring pseudo-distances to transmitting satellites. A GNSS receiver performance mainly depends on the signal power in the receiver's tracking loops [2].

There are several methods to measure the GNSS signal strength. However, as the data sent by GNSS are through radio signals, it is a known fact that radio signals cannot maintain their strength for longer distances. The GNSS system employs phase modulation to superimpose data on the radio signals for better reception by the GNSS receiver and the manufacturers employ different algorithms to retrieve the data from the signals for offering the desired data.

All the factors correlating with the elevation angle of the transmitted GNSS signals like the SNR normally grow with increasing satellite elevation angle. SNR is usually expressed in decibels and it refers to the ratio of the signal power and noise power in a given bandwidth. Due to the fact that noise and signal are amplified in the same way, these ratios can be expressed as [3]:

$$\frac{C_{ant}}{N_{ant}} \approx \frac{S_{corr}}{N_{corr}} \approx S \qquad (3)$$

Signal to noise ratio can usually be found in the context of signal baseband of the modulated signal at correlator output (S_{corr}). The quality of a received GNSS signal is commonly described by carrier to noise ratio of the modulated carrier at the receiving antenna (C_{ant}). The system noise affects the signal quality and the noise and signal are amplified in the same way in the antenna (N_{ant}) and at the correlator output (N_{corr}). As the system noise is several magnitudes smaller than C_{ant} and S_{corr}, therefore the values are normally converted to decibels (dB) to represent a specific bandwidth, thus:

$$S(dB) = 10.\log_{10}(S) \quad \text{and} \qquad (4)$$

$$SNR(dB) = S/N \qquad (5)$$

Assuming the GNSS signal strength is S and the noise level is N, the basic formula to measure the GNSS signal strength is S/N. If the carrier waves facing obstructions, S will get affected by attenuation, because many signals have a very wide dynamic range and are expressed using the logarithmic decibel scale, signal and noise may be expressed in decibels (dB). Assuming the system noise (N_0) is several magnitudes smaller than the signal strength (S), the normalized signal quality is [3][4]:

$$SNR\ (dBHz) = S - N = 10.\log_{10}(S)(dB) - (N_0.B_L)(dBHz) \qquad (6)$$

The user should be careful when comparing different GNSS receivers, particularly for older models e.g. Trimble that provided the signal quality in "arbitrary manufacture unit" (AMU). AMU units are dependent and need to be converted by a conversion formula because the value can differ by up to 3 dB from the original value [4]. Different generations of GNSS satellites have inherently different signal strengths, which could cause different SNR values with nothing wrong at all.

Different GNSS receivers with the same antenna tracking the same satellite at the same time may provide different SNR values. These differences could be from band limitation or processing algorithms. In case of independent acquisition and tracking algorithms used by a receiver, the values could be considered to indicate the quality of the received signal when antenna and receiver type, design, and performance are neglected. Hence the SNR depends on the receiver bandwidth, signal acquisition and tracking parameter.

In order to analyze the behavior of SNR and code multipath/noise, all GNSS signals were processed. By using an epoch by epoch method, each epoch was processed to get SNR and code range residuals and then an averaging method was adapted to get mean values for the figures.

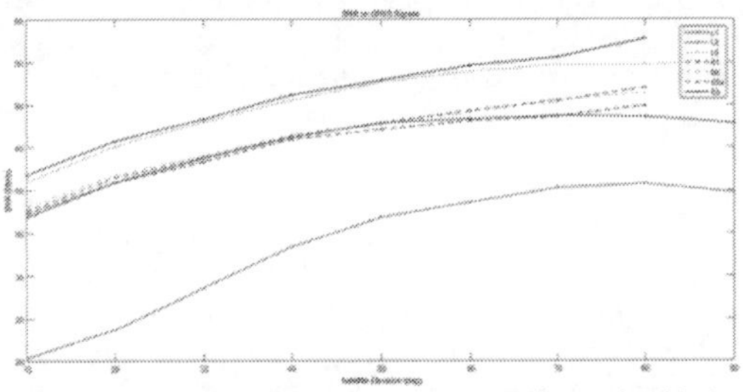

Fig. 2.3 SNR mean of GNSS signals (GPS, Galileo, and Beidou)

In case of the E1 Galileo signal, the SNR and the code multipath/noise residual seems to perform higher than the L1 GPS with up to 1-2 dBHz for signal strength and up to 0.1 m for residual difference, refer to figure 2.2 and 2.3. On the other hand, E5 Galileo performs best in SNR and code multipath/noise residuals at every station tested. When selecting promising signals for future real-time positioning, the combined E5 Galileo signal emerges as one of the alternatives (better than E5a) when using Galileo signals.

Because multipath errors are site-specific and particularly affect the code ranges, the use of E5 Galileo provides an advantage, as this signal shows a low multipath/noise residual behavior compared to all other GNSS signals. Moreover, due to its higher signal strength, the E5 Galileo signal is preferable for positioning because the signal is more resilient against outside interference than other GNSS signals and offers advantages to mitigate multipath/noise and ionospheric errors.

3. Performance Test

3.1 Relative Positioning

The performance of relative positioning was analyzed by using double difference (DD) positioning using carrier phase range that constructed by differencing two single difference (SD) observation. SD can be described as follows [6]:

$$\Delta L^{j}_{A,B} = \Delta \rho^{j}{}_{A,B} + d^{j}{}_{tropA,B} - d^{j}{}_{ionA,B} + c(dt - dT)^{j}{}_{A,B} + +ML^{j}{}_{A,B} + \lambda N^{j}{}_{A,B} + \vartheta L^{j}{}_{A,B} \quad (7)$$

where Δ is the difference between receivers A and B. The superscript -*j* is the observed satellite. The satellite clock error is eliminated by taking single difference between receivers that observed the same satellite, while the atmospheric biases like tropospheric and ionospheric may be eliminated depending to the length of the baseline. Multipath would be considered as a noise error that could not be eliminated.

The remaining receiver clock error is then eliminated by subtracting two single difference observation. Mathematically, a DD is defined as follows:

$$\nabla\Delta L^{jk}_{A,B} = \Delta \rho^{jk}{}_{A,B} + +ML^{jk}{}_{A,B} + \lambda N^{jk}{}_{A,B} + \vartheta L^{jk}{}_{A,B} \quad (8)$$

where the two satellites are denoted as he superscript-*j* and *k*. The atmospheric biases are negligible in Eq.8, however the noise error is multiplied up to two times with respect to SD.

By using MGEX data, we assumed that the precision of GAL and BDS are similar with GPS for all of the position components using DD method in kinematic solutions. The precision of the horizontal and vertical components is in cm level. The ambiguity fixing rate of GPS, BDS, GAL, and combined are more than 90% with the coordinate differences w.r.t. GPS solutions are in cm level (~2 cm)

3.2 Ionosphere Free Linear Combination

Several linear combinations could be introduced beside the standard L1/L2 GPS ionosphere-free linear combination [2][9]. Moreover, it is even possible to design useful triple frequency linear combinations from all frequencies in GNSS. As the ionospheric delay is dispersive, the phase observables delay of Φ_i can be related to the delay of Φ_j by the known ratio of wavelengths of the two observables:

$$i_j = (\lambda_j^2/\lambda_i^2) i_i \quad (9)$$

where the two observables are in order, $\lambda_j > \lambda_i$, and the ratio can be denoted as:

$$\frac{\lambda_j}{\lambda_i} = \frac{t}{n}, t > n \quad (10)$$

where both t and n are (positive) integers. Using the wavelength ratio, the ionosphere free linear combination ϕ_{ij} of two observables is obtained as:

$$E\{\phi_{ij}\} = \frac{t^2}{t^2-n^2} E\{\phi_i\} - \frac{n^2}{t^2-n^2} E\{\phi_j\} \quad (11)$$

Introducing the integer ambiguities N_i and N_j (11) can be detailed as:

$$E\{\phi_{ij}\} = \rho + \frac{t^2}{t^2-n^2}\lambda_i N_i - \frac{n^2}{t^2-n^2}\lambda_j N_j - \left(\frac{t^2}{t^2-n^2} - \frac{n^2}{t^2-n^2}\frac{t^2}{n^2}\right) i_i + e_{ij} \quad (12)$$

The range of observable ρ appears in the same way as in the original phase observation equation. Moreover, the ionospheric delays are eliminated $\left(\frac{t^2}{t^2-n^2} - \frac{n^2}{t^2-n^2}\frac{t^2}{n^2}\right) i_i \approx 0$, and a combined ambiguity term remains, which does not seem to be integer valued. However, using equation (12) with *t* and *n* integer, it is possible to rewrite the ambiguity term to be:

$$E\{\phi_{ij}\} = \rho + \frac{t^2}{t^2-n^2}\lambda_i \left(tN_i - nN_j\right) + e_{ij} = \rho + \lambda_{ij} N_{ij} + e_{ij} \quad (13)$$

where λ_{ij} denotes the artificial wavelength and N_{ij} the integer ambiguity of the ionosphere free combination and e_{ij} denotes multipath and noise values.

A consequence of taking the ionosphere-free linear combination is that the noise of the ionosphere-free observable is increased compared to the noise of the original phase observations. When it is assumed that two original observables are uncorrelated and have same precision $\sigma_{\Phi_i} = \sigma_{\Phi_j} = \sigma_\Phi$ in DD mode, the variance of LC follows:

$$D\{\phi_{ij}\} = \frac{t^4+n^4}{(t^2-n^2)^2}\sigma_\Phi^2 \quad (14)$$

where $D\{\phi_{ij}\}$ denotes the mathematical dispersion.

Denoting the greatest common divisor as c, we may write for the numerator and the denominator of the wavelength ratio $t = c \cdot t_c$ and $n = c \cdot n_c$, where $c \geq 1$.

3.3. Data Processing and methodology

Table 3.1 Data for data processing

Observation Data (RINEX) DOY (280, 2017)	CEBR-VILL IGS (35 km) GPS+GLO+GAL+BDS+SBAS
IGS data precise orbit file	IGS (pre)
Auxiliary data (updated using data from NGS)	antenna information file receiver information file satellite problem file noise model parameter file information coordinate file

The processing strategy was designed as follow:

- The following calculations were carried out using data from observation, i.e. 1 hour of observation Rinex data 1 second sampling rate. Calculations were also carried out with Glonass signals (if available) during similar observation

https://doi.org/10.1051/e3sconf/20199403011

periods in equal satellite geometry. Integer ambiguities are estimated and resolved on an epoch-by-epoch basis in kinematic positioning mode.

- The initial scenario assumes all the observations are processed in difference mode. Hence, the atmospheric errors and clock errors are taken into account. To create a scenario with different baseline, the data were sorted out by the stations to arrange the conditions required. As the local time and the location of the test are essentially affecting the results due to variations in the ionosphere and troposphere activity, calculations of the measurement effect on same time window sessions were performed.

- Mask angles of ten degrees were selected. The receiver noise level was neglected, and when required, IGS precise orbit corrections were used for reference. Tropospheric effects are also independent of frequency. And using a standard model correction.

- Furthermore, the observations were grouped in short-term observations (less than and equal to 60 minutes) for positioning for static(reference) and kinematic positioning.

- Additionally, since most observation data covers satellites with low elevation angles, observation to satellites which are below 10 degrees are removed to minimize the influence of errors in the data processing.

- The distance between base and rover was up to 40 kilometers.

- Ionosphere free linear combination and the MLAMBDA method was used to estimate the carrier phase ambiguities [5][8].

4. Results

Result from data processing shows that a combined signal (GPS+BDS and GPS+GAL) can be improved the resolution time when the GEO satellites is introduced for ambiguity fixing in case of obstruction problems.

Based on the results, it is shown that in every epoch, at least ten satellites of GNSS are visible. The SNR for BDS vary within 25-55 dBHz (figure 3) which is less power than other GNSS signals, the code multipath variation of all GNSS signals varies within ~1 m, while the phase residuals variation varies up to ~3 cm. In addition, a GNSS modernized signal has better precision compared with L1/L2 GPS, and the combined used of GPS+BDS and GPS+GAL improves the solutions on positioning, particularly on kinematic positioning.

Figure 4.1 and 4.2 shows the estimated kinematic position with GNSS data. To further analyze, the pseudorange and the carrier phase residuals obtained from observation are compared. The figure shows that there is similar accuracy up to 2 cm. According to the figure 4.1 and 4.2, all signals provides similar results position (about 2 cm of position deviation) to L1/L2 GPS solution as reference. However, the Galileo gives a smooth pattern of result. On the other hand, when combination signals were processed, a combination between GPS+BDS displays a slightly good trend with respect to L1/L2 GPS comparing with other combinations.

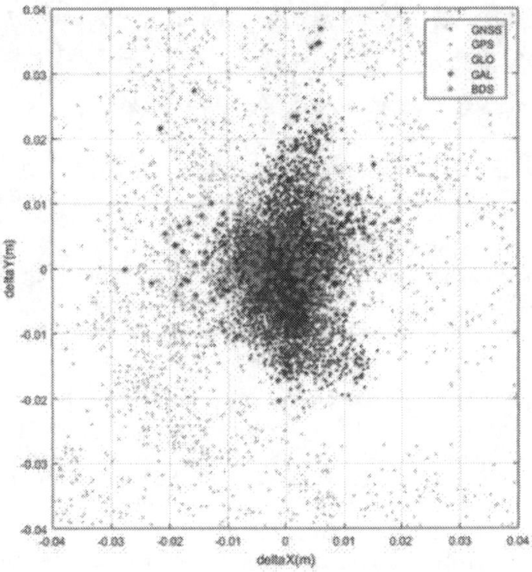

Fig. 4.1 Kinematic Solution from GNSS satelites with baseline up to 35 km (GPS, Glonass, Galileo, and Beidou)

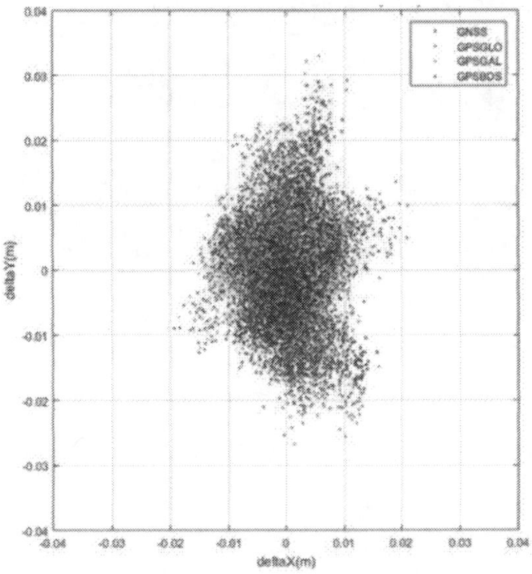

Fig. 4.2 Kinematic Solution from GNSS satellite combinations with baseline up to 35 km (GPS, Glonass, Galileo, and Beidou)

The residual level normally increases at the VILL-CEBR baseline with 35 km, as not all the ambiguities could not be fixed completely by utilized all satellites within observation time span. However, there is a systematic residual pattern in the code and phase residuals which indicates systematic noise that affected the position result (refer to figure 4.3 and 4.4).

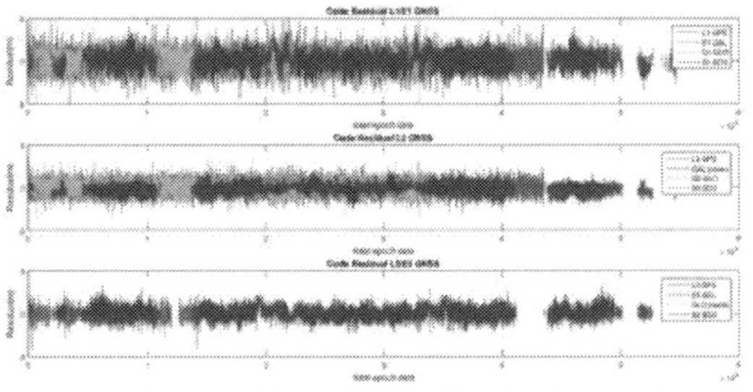

Fig. 4.3 Code Residual from GNSS satellite signals (GPS, Glonass, Galileo, and Beidou)

These characteristics can open the possibility of performing code-range measurements using modernized GNSS signals at the decimeter level and enable a better mitigation of multipath effects, particularly for signal combination with small code residuals.

Fig. 4.3 shows code residuals for all available satellites. By taking a large number of all satellite observations, the code multipath/noise residuals for L5 and E5 are smaller than L1/L2 GPS residuals. On average, the L5 and E5 provides ~1 m deviation. However, by using L5 and E5 signals are allowed more accurate combined code-and-carrier observable to mitigate ionospheric errors because it has the strongest signal strength of the modernized GNSS signals tested.

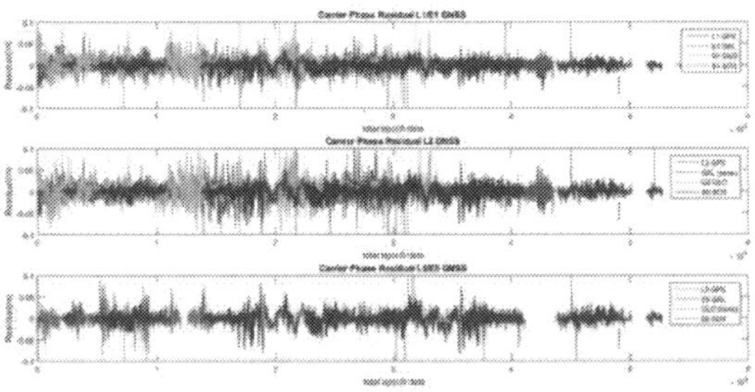

Fig. 4.4 Phase Residual from GNSS satellite signals (GPS, Glonass, Galileo, and Beidou)

Fig. 4.4 shows carrier-phase residual for medium baseline (35 km) from experiment test (MGEX data). Good solutions were possible due to several available signals and satellites. Hence, the utilization of GNSS data as combined signal. GPS, GAL, BDS, and its combination provides similar results that varies up to 5 cm for kinematic positioning.

the standard deviation of the coordinate time series shows interesting features (figure 4.5). The dual carrier phase combination, particularly from Galileo observable performs extremely well. It is mostly better (less than 2 cm) than the L1/L2 GPS standard deviation of ionosphere-free linear combination. On the other hand, the standard deviation of the L1/L5 GPS-LC and B1/B2 BDS-LC corresponds with the L1/L2 GPS pattern. A short time observation (at least 60 minutes) seems to be sufficient to resolve the ambiguity for kinematic positioning up to 40 km compared with the GNSS ionosphere free linear combination in case of the VILL-CEBR baseline with a length approx. 35 km. With a modernized GNSS system, the E1/E5 Galileo linear combination seems to perform much better than the other frequency combinations. However, when insufficient Galileo observations are not available (less than 5 satellites) the standard deviation becomes worse than L1/L2 GPS.

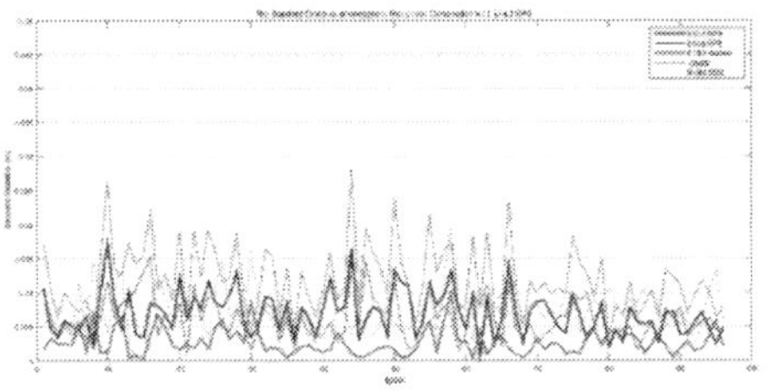

Fig. 4.5 Standard deviation from GNSS satellite combinations for baseline up to 35 km (GPS, Glonass, Galileo, and Beidou)

5. Conclusion

This research has been conducted to study the performance of the GNSS real time positioning technology introducing modernized signals on medium baseline, and by means of a free software application. Most of the investigated signal linear combinations are capable to deliver accurate, precise and consistent position solutions, although they perform differently in terms of noise, ionospheric content and ambiguity resolution ability. This research focuses on single baselines observed over short to medium periods.

Because multipath errors are site-specific the rover environment has to be chosen carefully. In case of evident multipath the E5 Galileo delivers an advantage compared to other signals due to its more multipath resistant codes which also goes in parallel with a higher received signal strength. Other unencrypted signals provide similar SNR-values with a difference of approximately 1-5 dBHz and range noise in zenith direction of up to 0.25 m. On the other hand, the GPS L2 signal in this research shows the lowest SNR value with differences up to 10 dBHz and zenith range noise up to 0.4 m.

The standard deviation of the position differences using GNSS dual frequency data of several minutes (up to 60 minutes) is very close to the L1/L2 GPS solution. Galileo and Beidou signals can be used as advanced substitute and simultaneously in case of insufficient or improper L2 GPS observations. Need to be taken into account, the results are of course affected by the number of available satellites, satellite geometry, and observation time spans.

Modernized GNSS signals deliver a potency to provide best performance in static and kinematic positioning. Compared to GPS L1/L2 a clear advantage to use Galileo and Beidou linear combination becomes apparent in order to reduce signal noise and multipath significantly with reveals biases up to a few centimeters (~2 cm). These offsets might be caused by un-modeled intersystem biases between GPS, Galileo, and Beidou signals.

References

[1] Hofmann-Wellenhof, B., Lichtenegger, E. Wasle. (2008). GNSS-Global Navigation Satellite Systems. Springer, Wien.

[2] Odijk, D. (2003). Ionosphere-Free Phase Combinations for Modernized GPS. Journal of Surveying Engineering Vol. 129. November

[3] Rost, C. and Wanninger, L. (2009). *Carrier Phase multipath mitigation based on GNSS signal quality measurements.* Journal of Applied Geodesy 3, de Gruyter, pp. 1-8. DOI 10.1515/JAG.2009.009.

[4] Amiri-Sikooci, A., Tiberius, C., C., J., M. (2007). Assessing Receiver Noise Using GPS Short Baseline Time Series. GPS Solution, Vol. 11. Pp21-35 DOI 10.1007/s10291-006-0026-8.

[5] Davaine, M. (2011). Code Bias and Multipath Estimation with Cascaded Kalman Filter. Thesis. Insitute for Communication and Navigation, Technische Universitaet Muenchen. Munich, November.

[6] Xu, G. (2007). GPS Theory, Algorithms and Application. Berlin: Springer.

[7] Joseph, A. and Petovello, M. (2010). Measuring GNSS Signal Strength. Inside GNSS. November, pp. 20-25.

[8] Teunissen, P. J. G., (1995). The Least-square Ambiguity Decorrelation Adjustment: A Method for Fast GPS Ambiguity Estimation. Journal Geodesy, vol.70.

[9] Richert, T., and N. El-Sheimy (2007). Optimal linear combinations of triple frequency carrier phase data from future global navigation satellite systems. GPS Solutions, Vol. 11, No. 1, pp. 11-19. DOI 10.1007/s10291-006-0024-x.

The Effect of TLS Radome on GNSS Precise Positioning

Dhota Pradipta[1], Dudy D. Wijaya[1], Heri Andreas[1], and Dina A. Sarsito[1]

[1]Geodesy Research Group, Faculty of Earth Sciences and Technology, Institute of Technology, Bandung, Indonesia.

Abstract. This article presents the results of a test carried out to check the usability of spherical TLS targets as GNSS antenna radomes (herein called TLS radomes). On different days, the survey was conducted using two GNSS antennas, one of them with a TLS radome. Measurements were made using 2 roof pillars on the rooftop as base-rover pillars with little obstruction. The measurements were carried out for approximately 1 hour in every scenario. The software used for data processing is MATLAB-based software and the raw data were processed using the double difference (DD) strategy to obtain optimal results. The results of the data processing indicated that the TLS radome has no significant influence on availability and accuracy of estimated position. The signals are slightly attenuated by the radome (1-2 dBHz) and the noise level is slightly increased but both effects are negligible for practical purposes. However, we found that the antenna should be calibrated with the TLS radome to clarify apparent minor phase center eccentricities (1-2 mm) and to reduce systematic effects with long periods (few minutes) and amplitudes up to about 5 mm which are likely due to phase center variations.

1. Introduction

Use The use of TLS targets is required for absolute orientation of point clouds obtained by laser scanning. It is particularly important for change monitoring where such targets can be used to establish the connection to a well-defined datum. The experiment presented herein is based on the idea of mounting a GNSS antenna inside a TLS target so that its position can be determined precisely while scanning. The spherical TLS target resembles an antenna radome. Therefore we will call it"TLS radome" within this report. The experiments were carried out at the rooftop for collecting the data. The purpose of the observations is to determine the effects of the TLS radome on the positioning. In particular we want to clarify

1. whether GNSS positioning is possible using the TLS radome (signal reception sufficient);
2. whether the TLS radome increases the noise level of the raw observations and the computed positions (P3 and P5), and lastly,
3. whether there are any systematic effects on the antenna phase center and phase center variation requiring calibration.

Two pillars were selected for use because they have little obstruction (P3, P5). Observations were carried out on 4 days and during periods with approximately equal satellite geometry.

For scenario 1 of the experiment, we used two NovAtel 702GG antennas, one without any modification and one mounted inside the TLS radome but without the top half of the radome. We put the GNSS antenna with the half open TLS radome on pillar P5 as a rover and the other one as base on pillar P3. Then, for scenario 2, data were collected using a closed TLS radome on P5 and the same antenna as before on P3. For scenario 3, we swapped the position of both devices such that the closed TLS radome was now on the base pillar located with fixed coordinates and the antenna without TLS radome is the rover. And lastly, we measured without any TLS radome and compared the results to those of the other scenarios.

The processing was carried out using in Matlab and the measurement data were taken from download in the rinex form. Satellite orbits were retrieved from the IGS server. Antenna phase center data were retrieved from NGS. In this article it is assumed that the reader has a basic understanding of GNSS and GNSS data processing.

2. GNSS Measurement

1.1. Measurement Equipment

Measurements were made using the same equipment and sites in the four scenarios with four days of measurement, as outlined below in table 2.1 and figure 2.1

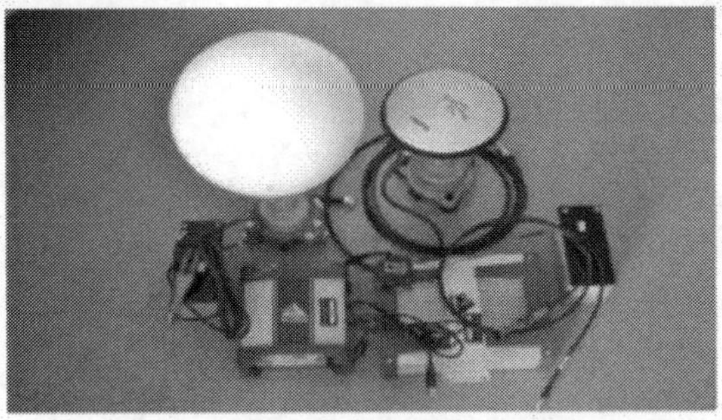

Figure 2.1 GNSS Equipment

Table 2.1. GPS Equipment dan sites used

Receiver	2 Receiver dual frequencies Novatel DL-V3 and SPAN SE-S
Antenna	2 Novatel antennas NOV702GG
Power Supply	2 batteries/Power supply
Site	2 Sites (P3 and P5)
Orientation	Antenna orientation approx. toward north
Data rate	1 second epoch data rate observation

2.2. Measurement scenarios

(Scenario 1) – open TLS Radome on Pillar 3

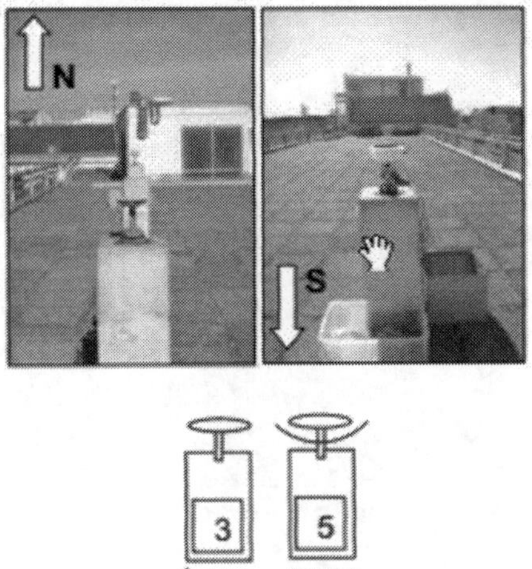

Figure 2.2 North – South view scenario 1

(Scenario 2) – Closed TLS Radome on Pillar 3

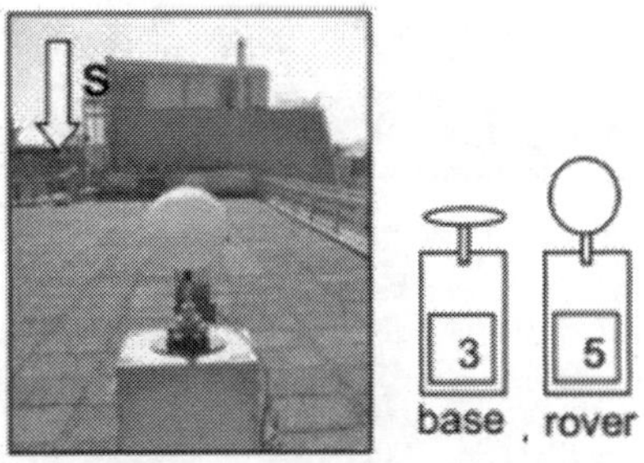

Figure 2.3 South view scenario 2

(Scenario 3) – Closed TLS Radome on Pillar 5

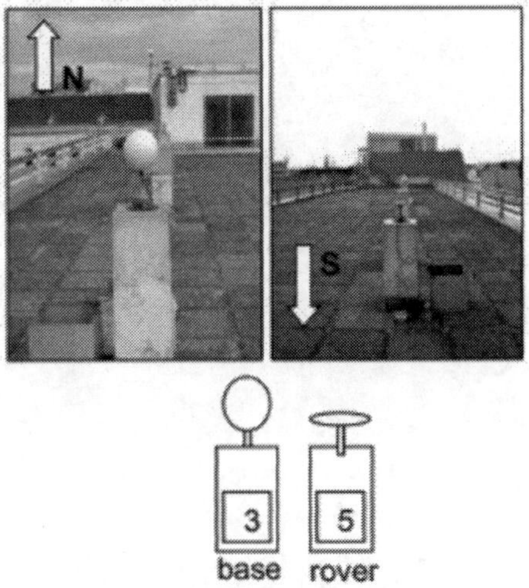

Figure 2.4 North – South view scenario 3

(Scenario 4)-Without TLS radome

Figure 2.5 North – South view scenario 4

The environment and obstruction view around the two points of observation are given in figures 2.6 and 2.7

Figure 2.6 Panoramic View of surrounding area sites

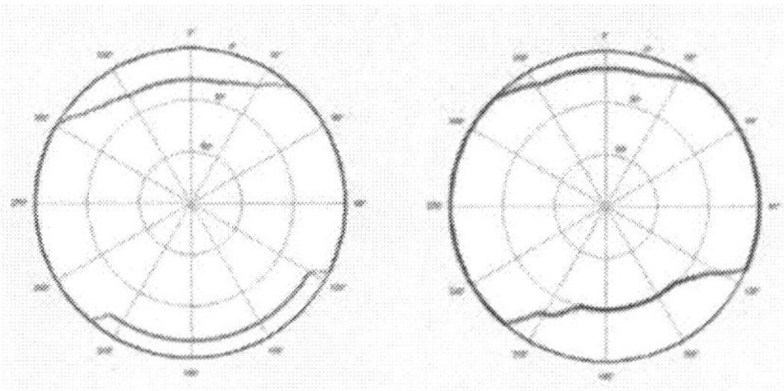

Figure 2.7 Obstruction view on Observation pillar 5 (right) and pillar 3 (left).

The measurement data and the required auxiliary data are as given in table 2.2.

Table 2.2 Data for data processing

Observation Data (RINEX) (PLAA = P3 fixed coordinate) PLAB = P5 coordinate)	DOY 089, DOY 090, DOY 093, DOY 094
IGS data Ultra rapid orbit file	igs16814.sp3, igs16815.sp3, igs16821.sp3, igs16836.sp3.
Auxiliary data (updated using data from NGS)	antenna information file receiver information file satellite problem file noise model parameter file information coordinate file

2.3. Data Processing and methodology

This article investigates the relative positioning performance. In general, the observed data from satellites can be defined as follows [1]:

$$P_i = \rho + d\rho + d_{trop} + d_{ion} + c(dt - dT) + MP_i + \vartheta P_1 \quad (1)$$

$$L_i = \rho + d\rho + d_{trop} - d_{ion} + c(dt - dT) + ML_i + \lambda_i N_i + \vartheta L_i \quad (2)$$

where P_i and L_i are pseudorange and carrier phase range on selected frequency (i =1,2), ρ is related to geometrical range from receiver to satellite, $d\rho$ is the orbital error, d_{trop} and d_{ion} are troposphere and ionosphere biases, c is the speed of light (299,729,458 m/s), dt and dT are time error of receiver and satellites, MP_i and ML_i are related to multipath error of pseudorange and carrier phase range, λ_i and N_i are related to wavelength and ambiguity number, while ϑP_i and ϑL_i are related to noise error.

Relative Positioning

The performance of relative positioning were analyzed by using double difference (DD) positioning using carrier phase range that constructed by differencing two single difference (SD) observation. SD can be described as follows:

$$\Delta L^j_{A,B} = \Delta\rho^j{}_{A,B} + d^j{}_{tropA,B} - d^j{}_{ionA,B} + c(dt - dT)^j{}_{A,B} + ML^j{}_{A,B} + \lambda N^j{}_{A,B} + \vartheta L^j{}_{A,B} \quad (3)$$

where Δ is the difference between receivers A and B. The superscript -j is the observed satellite. The satellite clock error is eliminated by taking single difference between receivers that observed the same satellite, while the atmospheric biases like tropospheric and ionospheric may be eliminated depending to the length of the baseline. Multipath would be considered as a noise error that could not be eliminated.

The remaining receiver clock error is then eliminated by subtracting two single difference observation. Mathematically, a DD is defined as follows [2] [6]:

$$\nabla\Delta L^{jk}_{A,B} = \Delta\rho^{jk}{}_{A,B} + +ML^{jk}{}_{A,B} + \lambda N^{jk}{}_{A,B} + \vartheta L^{jk}{}_{A,B} \quad (4)$$

where the two satellites are denoted as he superscript-j and k. The atmospheric biases are negligible in Eq. 3, however the noise error is multiplied up to two times with respect to SD. The processing strategy was designed as follow:

- The following calculations were carried out using data from observation, i.e. 1 hour of observation Rinex data 1 second sampling rate. Calculations were also carried out with Glonass signals (if available) during similar observation periods in equal satellite geometry. Integer ambiguities are estimated and resolved on an epoch-by-epoch basis in kinematic positioning mode.

- The initial scenario assumes all the observations are processed in difference mode. Hence, the atmospheric errors and clock errors are almost canceling. To create a scenario with different radome, the data were sorted out by the stations to arrange the conditions required. As the local time and the location of the test are essentially affecting the results due to variations in the ionosphere and troposphere activity, calculations of the measurement effect on same time window sessions were performed.

- Mask angles of ten degrees were selected. The receiver noise level was neglected, and when required, IGS precise orbit corrections were used. Tropospheric effects are also independent

https://doi.org/10.1051/e3sconf/20199403012

of frequency. Hence a Saastamoinen model was used as the standard model correction [3].

- Furthermore, the observations were grouped in short-term observations (less than and equal to 60 minutes) for positioning in particular to study with the impact of temporal variability for static and kinematic positioning.

- Additionally, since most observation data covers satellites with low elevation angles, observation to satellites which are below 10 degrees are removed to minimize the influence of errors in the data processing.

- The distance between base and rover was under 50 meters. By using this short baseline, the atmospheric errors are assumed to be eliminated.

- The LAMBDA ambiguity resolution search was used to estimate the carrier phase ambiguities [8]. The final solution was the combined (Forward + Backward filter).

3. Results

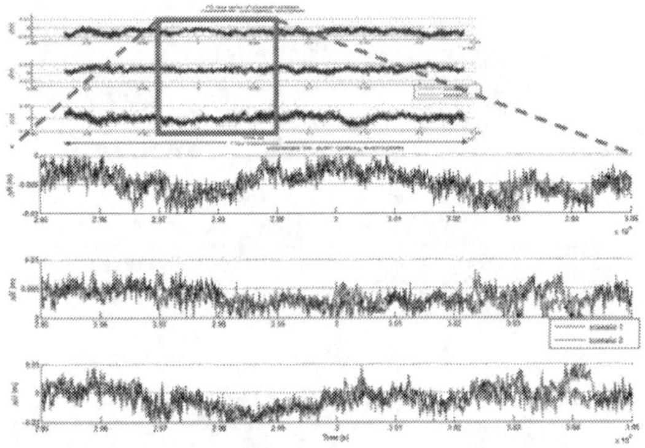

Figure 3.1 Comparison of the position between scenario 1 and 2 on pillar 5.

The results of the data processing show that both high- and low-frequency noise affects the estimated position. To further analyse, we compare the time series obtained for times with corresponding satellite distribution (figure 3.1 and 3.2).

Figure 3.1 shows the North-, East- and Up-coordinate variations as obtained from kinematic processing of the measurements from scenario 1 (black) and 2 (blue). The TLS radome was closed in scenario 2 but half open in scenario 1. The figure shows that there is slightly more high-frequency noise with closed TLS radome than using the half-open one. However, when computing the standard deviation of the kinematic coordinates, the low-frequency noise which is the effect of multipath interference and phase center variations dominates [5],[7],[9]. The level of these low-frequency components is not changed when the TLS radome is closed, see table 3.1. We conclude that there is no significant effect of the top half of the TLS target on the quality of the estimated position in case the position is determined from static processing of several minutes of data.

On the other hand, the time series exhibit equal noise level of both high- and low- frequency contributions before and after swapping the antennas i.e., for scenarios 2 and 3. This is expected. However, we also note that there is a mirrored systematic error pattern (figure 3.2). This is an indication of systematic errors due to unmodelled phase center variations. Since phase center variations of the employed Novatel GPS antennas were used we interpret this as an effect of the TLS radome on the phase center variations.

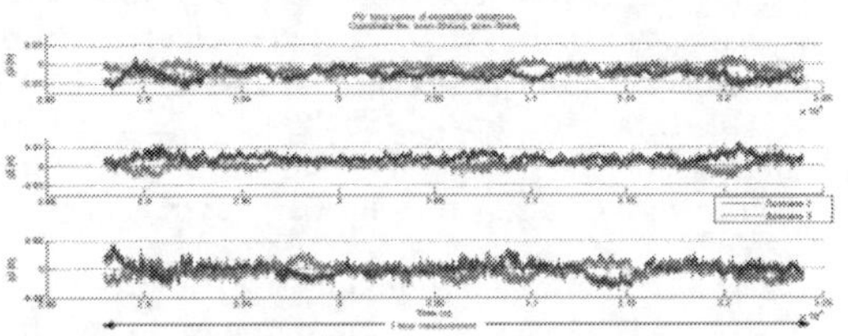

Figure 3.2. Comparison of the position between scenario 2 and 3 on pillar 5.

From figure 3.1, we know that there is no significant difference in noise level as well as systematic errors with half-open versus closed radome TLS, and also the median values differ by less than 1.0 mm (N, E) and 1.4 mm (U) (see table 3.2). This indicates that there this is a negligible effect of the top half of the TLS radome on noise and mean phase center.

From figure 3.2, we discovered that scenario 2 and 3 yield equal noise levels and but opposite sign of the systematic pattern. Any mean phase center difference Δp between antenna w/ and w/o TLS radome would cause a difference of magnitude $2|\Delta p|$ of the estimated coordinates before and after antenna swap. In this experiment (see table 3.2) the median values only differ by 1.6 mm (N), 3.5 mm (E), and 1.1 mm (U). So, the phase center eccentricity is most likely affected by less than 2 mm by the TLS radome.

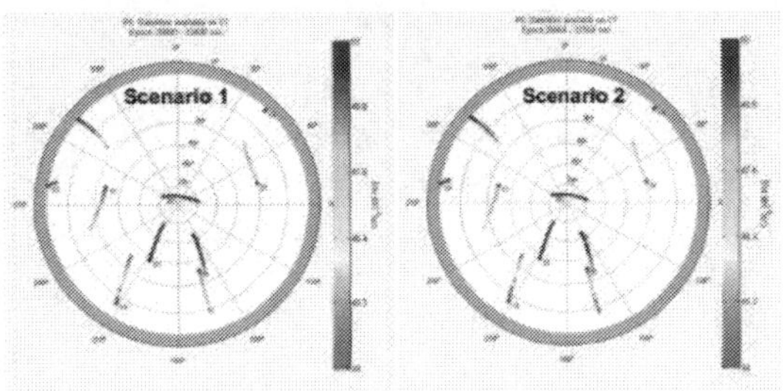

figure 3.3 The sky plot and signal strength of observation on pillar 5 (scenario 1 and 2)

https://doi.org/10.1051/e3sconf/20199403012

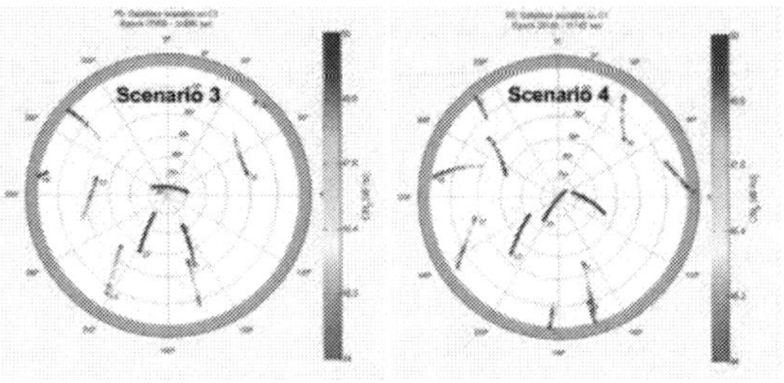

figure 3.4 The sky plot and signal strength of observation on pillar 5 (scenario 3 and 4)

Figure 3.3 and 3.4 indicate a change in signal strength of approximately 1-2 dBHz which is the effect of the TLS radome during the observation. This shows that there is a slight attenuation i.e., an effect on the signal strength, but the effect is small e.g. compared to the effect of satellite elevation on signal strength. So, the TLS radome does not attenuate signals strongly and thus not cause significant problems for GPS signal acquisition and tracking.

Figure 3.5 shows the residuals of individual raw observations. Again, the pattern corresponding to the different scenarios seems to be mirrored with an antenna swap (different colors for different scenarios, as before)

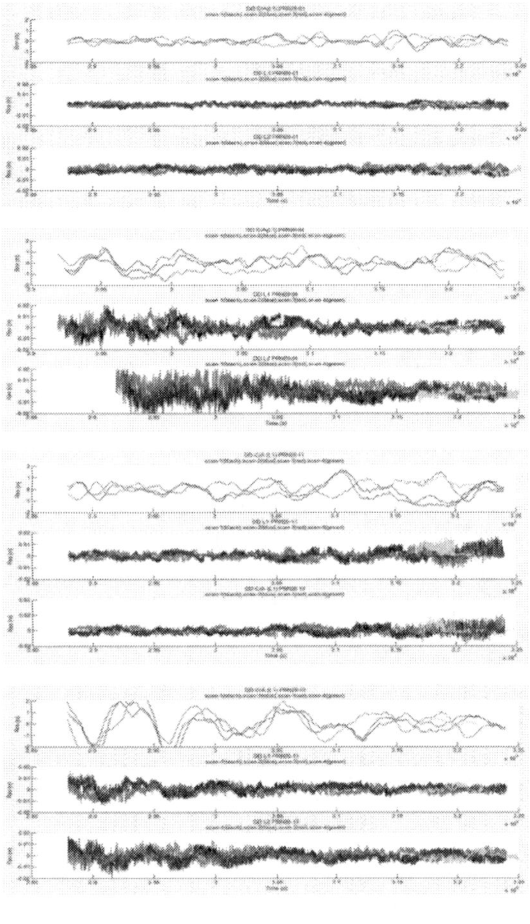

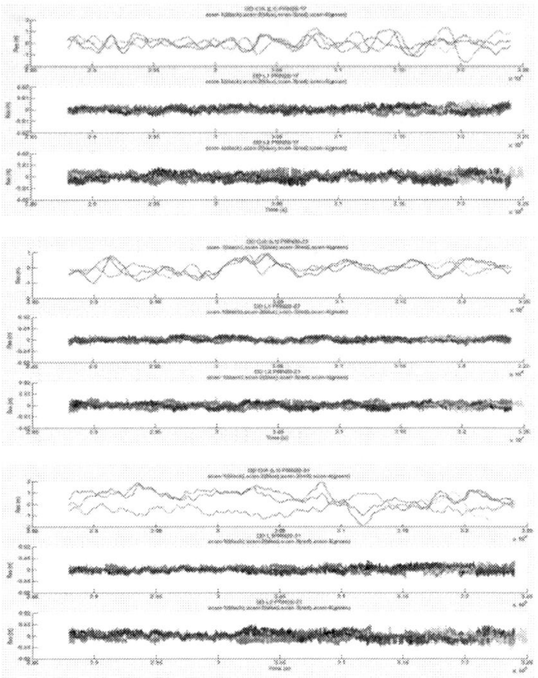

Figure 3.6 PRN residual on satellite 1, 4, 11, 13, 17, 23, and 31.

Key statistics of the estimated positions are given in tables 3.1 and 3.2.

Table 3.1 Statistic of kinematic coordinates of antenna on P5

Scenario	Mean difference w.r.t. given coordinates (mm)			Empirical standard deviation (mm)		
	ΔN	ΔE	ΔU	N	E	U
Scenario 1	3.1	4.4	-2.9	1.8	1.1	1.5
Scenario 2	2.4	4.7	-4.2	1.6	1.0	1.5
Scenario 3	1.0	0.9	-3.3	1.6	1.0	1.5
Scenario 4	3.8	3.4	-1.8	1.5	0.9	1.7

Table 3.2 Median coordinates of antenna on P5

Scenario	Median (m)			Difference of respective median w.r.t. scenario 2 (mm)		
	N	E	U	N	E	U
Scenario 1	4087003.1653	1200478.9254	4731808.9712	0.8	-0.2	1.4
Scenario 2	4087003.1645	1200478.9258	4731808.9698	0.0	0.0	0.0
Scenario 3	4087003.1629	1200478.9221	4731808.9709	-1.6	-3.5	1.1
Scenario 4	4087003.1659	1200478.9244	4731808.9723	1.4	-1.2	2.5

It can be seen from table 3.1, table 3.2 and figure 3.1, figure 3.2 that the precision is approximately equal for all different scenarios. In particular, is the standard deviation is 1.6 mm (N), 1.0 mm (E), and 1.5 mm (Up). However, the coordinates differ by up to 3.5 mm between the scenarios. Based on the respective empirical standard deviations, these differences are not significant. The duration of the test measurements is too short in order to clarify whether these differences are actually random deviations or are due to phase center eccentricities and systematic effects caused by the TLS radome. Even if they are systematic and due to the TLS radome the effects are small (less than 2 mm in mean phase center) and may be negligible for the intended application (if the effects are equal for all TLS radomes used within the network). However, it would be appropriate to carry out a proper antenna calibration using a TLS radome in order to further clarify this point.

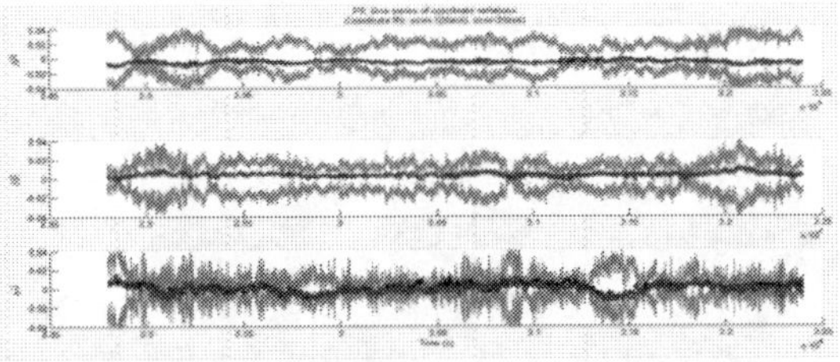

Figure 3.7 Variation of estimated coordinates of site P5

On figure 3.7, we assume that the measurements are normally distributed, that their errors are 0 on average, and that their variance is correctly given by the variance model used for post-processing the raw GPS observations. It means that most of the estimated coordinates (99.7%) should be within $\pm3\sigma$ of the true coordinates. Using the given coordinates as a reference and plotting the deviations of the estimated coordinates from the true ones (blue) and the respective $\pm3\sigma$ bounds about the true coordinates (red), we see in the figure that most of the time the estimated coordinates are within the error bounds and thus there is no need to further investigate the errors. It shows on figure 3.8 that on every scenario, the residuals of double difference are less than 2 cm.

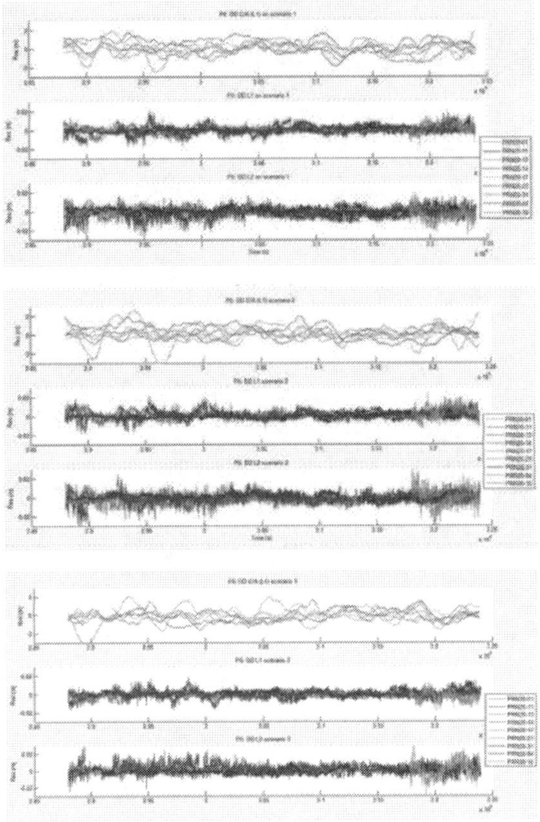

Figure 3.8 Time series of Double Difference Residuals from scenario 1, 2, and 3

4. Conclusion

The use of the TLS radome for GPS measurements slightly attenuates the signals (approximately 1-2 dBHz). However, this effect is small and does not impair the availability of GPS position solutions. GPS positioning is possible using this TLS radome and standard GPS data processing.

The precision obtained for kinematic positions in the different scenarios is about 1.6 mm (N), 1.0 mm (E), 1.5 mm (U) for all scenarios. Using the TLS radome does not significantly increase the noise level of the coordinates when processing data in static or short-term static mode (at least a few minutes of data).

We found mirrored systematic error patterns when swapping the antennas with and without TLS radome. The error patterns have a magnitude of up to 5 mm. The median coordinates over 1 hour changed by less than 4 mm between the scenarios. All this indicates that there may be a systematic effect of the TLS radome on mean phase center and on phase center variation on the mm-level. Given this order of magnitude, these effects would be negligible for the proposed application if the same TLS radome/GPS antenna were always used on the same network sites, the GPS antennas and radomes were always oriented equally, and GPS positions were derived from static or short-term static sessions only.

However, this may not be feasible from a practical point of view, and it is not possible to predict whether or not different TLS radomes would cause the same phase center eccentricities and variations as the radome used herein. Thus, we propose to calibrate 2-3 GPS antennas with TLS radome in oder to find out, whether these effects are actually systematic and predictable across different samples or not. The results of such a calibration (in particular: repeatability of parameters for the same antenna/radome, repeatability across antennas/radomes, order of magnitude of parameters) will allow selecting an appropriate site setup and data processing scheme.

Should the design of the TLS radome be changed, e.g. by selecting a different TLS target shape/size or material, or by coating the target for modified optical reflectivity, a test resembling scenario 2 and 3 of the experiments covered herein (i.e., static processing with antenna swap) should be carried out to quickly assess the impact. The corresponding data processing can be carried out using standard GPS post-processing software like Leica GeoOffice, Trimble Business Center, or others.

References

[1] Xu, G. (2007). GPS Theory, Algorithms and Application. Berlin: Springer.

[2] Kaplan, E. D. (1996). *Understanding GPS: Principles and Applications*. London: Artech House Boston.

[3] Amiri-Sikooci, A., Tiberius, C., C., J., M. (2007). Assessing Receiver Noise Using GPS Short Baseline Time Series. GPS Solution, Vol. 11. Pp21-35 DOI 10.1007/s10291-006-0026-8.

[4] Davaine, M. (2011). Code Bias and Multipath Estimation with Cascaded Kalman Filter. Thesis. Insitute for Communication and

Navigation, Technische Universitaet Muenchen. Munich, November.

[5] Dawidowicz, K. (2010). Antenna Phase center Variations Corrections in Processing of GPS Observations with the use of commercial Software. Technical Science. No 13, DOI 10.2478/v10022-010-0012-9.

[6] Hofmann-Wellenhof, B., Lichtenegger, E. Wasle. (2008). GNSS-Global Navigation Satellite Systems. Springer, Wien.

[7] Joseph, A. and Petovello, M. (2010). Measuring GNSS Signal Strength. Inside GNSS. November, pp. 20-25.

[8] Teunissen, P. J. G., (1995). The Least-square Ambiguity Decorrelation Adjustment: A Method for Fast GPS Ambiguity Estimation. Journal Geodesy, vol.70.

[9] Wu, J.T., S.C. Wu, G.A. Hajj, W.I. Bertiger, and S.M. Lichten. (1993). Effects of antenna orientation on GPS carrier phase. Manuscripta Geodaetica. Vol. 18. pp. 91-98.

Design of GPU Based Non-coherent Signal Tracking Module for Real-time GNSS SDR

Jong-Il Park[1,*], *Kwi Woo* Park[1], and *Chansik* Park[1]

[1]Dept. of Control and Robotics Eng. Chungbuk National University, South Korea

Abstract.
In this paper, we design and implement GPU-based non-coherent GPS signal tracking module for real-time SDR. When using CPU and GPU simultaneously, the signal tracking module should be designed considering the memory bottleneck between the two processors. The basic non-coherent module, which accumulates the 1msec correlation value 20 times, is changed to accumulate M(20/N) times of Nmsec units. From the experiments using real GPS signals, the computational performance of N=20 is improved by 80% compared to N=1. Therefore, the implemented SDR using notebook computer can tracks more channels simultaneously in the real time.

1 INTRODUCTION

In Global Navigation Satellite System(GNSS), Software Defined Radio(SDR) has replaced traditional receivers. Hard-wired analog components of traditional receivers are replaced with digital components in order to allow for greater flexibility. SDR allows a user to change the software to quickly modify how it operates, and better maintenance than traditional receivers [1-2]. Also, real-time GNSS SDR is possible as GPU and GPGPU performance is improved [1].

GNSS signal can be used anywhere in the world, however, GNSS signal is restricted from receiving if there are obstacles such as high buildings, wood and etc. [6]. To improve the performance of receiving GNSS signal, three methods are commonly adopted: 1) extended Kalman filter to signal tracking loop, 2) AGPS (Assisted GPS) and 3) non-coherent integration method for signal tracking and signal acquisition [3]. In this paper, the non-coherent integration method was used to improve the reception performance of GNSS SDR.

Non-coherent integration signal tracking module accumulates correlation values of 1msec GPS signals for integration time (T). As the integration time increases, the accuracy of measurements is increased, however, the loop filter in DLL (Delay Lock Loop) and PLL (Phase Lock Loop) should be redesigned to track the signal continuously. To extract GPS navigation bit, 20msec is maximum integration time. In GNSS SDR sudden changes in integration time makes tracking loop unstable, therefore, step by step changes are required. In this paper, 1, 2, 4, 5, 10, and 20msec integration times are used sequentially. After navigation bit extraction, the integration time is fixed to 20msec.

GPU-based non-coherent signal tracking module is implemented to support parallel processing with CUDA (Compute Unified Device Architecture). Computational efficiency of parallel processing using GPU is affected by 3 factors: 1) memory copy from CPU to GPU, 2) kernel call and operation time and 3) memory copy from GPU to CPU.

To compare the computational efficiency of the GPU-based signal tracking loop with 20msec integration time, the elapsed time of above 3 factors are measured. As main computational burden, memory bottleneck between CPU and GPU is analysed by changing the load balance. The 20msec IF data is divided into N(msec) x (20/N) to perform N parallel processing concurrently.

An experiment was conducted to compare the computational efficiency of GPU-based signal tracking loop by changing *N*.

2 Implementation of Non-coherent integration SDR using GPU

2.1 Characteristics of CUDA operations

The CUDA platform is a software layer that provides direct access to the GPU's virtual command set and parallel computation elements. The CUDA allow access to the memory and command sets of parallel computing elements of the GPU. If the calculations performed by the program are suitable for parallel processing operations, performance is improved by using GPU. Fig. 1 shows the parallel processing computation process of CUDA.

* whddlf915@naver.com

https://doi.org/10.1051/e3sconf/20199403013

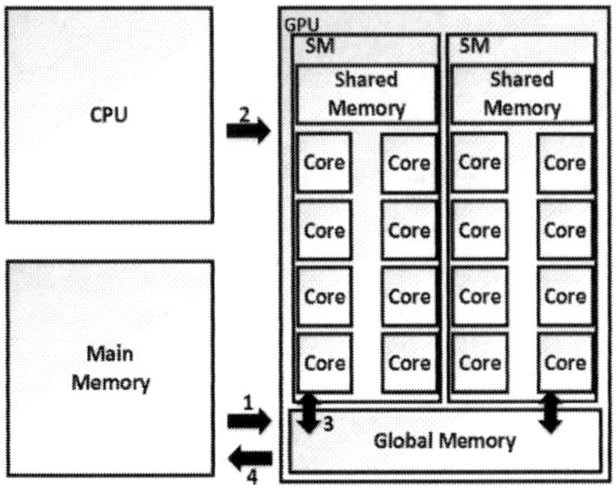

Fig. 1. Processing flow on CUDA

The CUDA processor operates in the order of the number shown in the arrow. First, data related to parallel computation is copied from main memory to global memory of GPU. Second, the CPU instructs the GPU process. Third, parallel operations are performed on the core of the GPU using data stored in the global memory. When parallel processing operations are performed, each Streaming Multi-processor(SM) in the GPU generates several blocks that perform parallel operations. Each block produces many threads that perform the operation in practice. The results are stored in the global memory after performing the procedure. Finally, copy the results stored in the global memory into the main memory.

2.2 Tracking structure of SDR

The SDR explained her is a real-time SDR based on GPU that is integrated into our lab Fig. 2. Shows the tracking loop behaviour of the implemented SDR. The white part operates on the CPU and the painted part operates on the GPU. The implemented SDR is a structure that tracks 1msec of IF signals. Copy received IF signal data to GPU, correlate with parallel computation, and store data back to CPU. Signal processing, such as PLL/DLL, bit extraction, and navigation, using correlation values from GPU. The tracking result is passed to the receiving part of the signal data for use in the next 1msec IF signal processing.

Fig. 3 shows the correlation part of Fig. 2. Correlator, which is mainly a repetitive operation, was implemented using CUDA. Correlator uses IF signal data and channel information stored in global memory of GPU. GPU generates blocks and threads, and blocks produce as many as the satellite number of successful signal acquisitions as IE, IP, IL, QE, QP and QL, which are correlated values of satellites. Each block has 1024 threads performing the operation, because the maximum number of threads that can be active on the GPU is 1024. The computation results of 1024 threads on each block are transferred to the shared memory, the shared memory is the memory shared within each block. Reason for storing computational results in shared memory is that data is sent to threads much faster

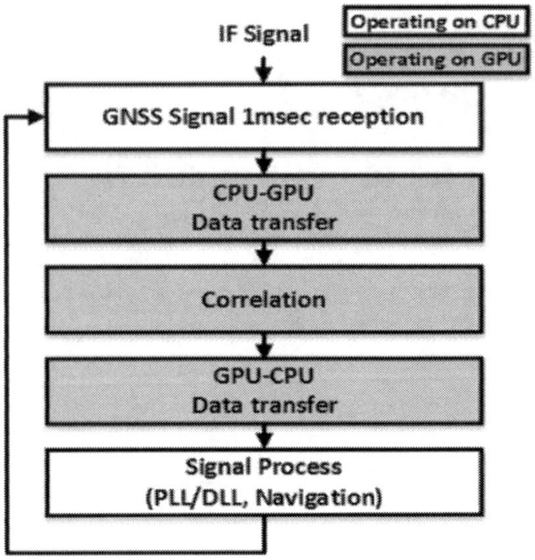

Fig. 2. Signal tracking processing

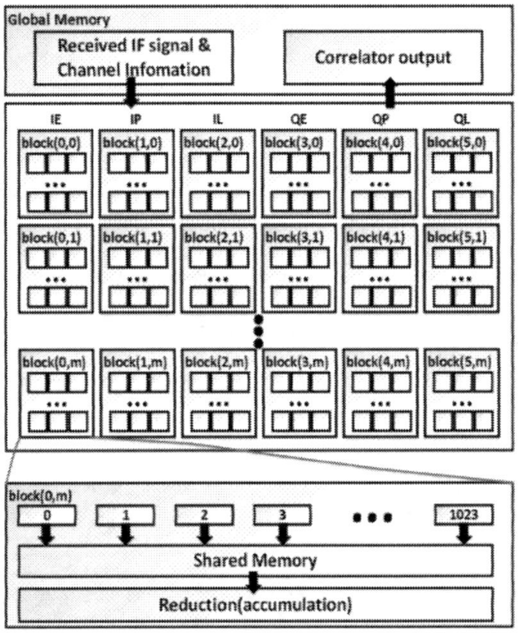

Fig. 3. Correlator implemented using CUDA

than global memory. After transfer to shared memory, add 1024 computational results to obtain correlation output. Add 1024 computational results by reduction method. The reduction method reduces the time complexity of $O(\log_2 n)$ that is faster than the existing $O(n)$. The correlation value obtained by adding 1024 computational results is sent to the global memory.

2.3 Non-coherent integration

Non-coherent integration is a method to integration correlation values to improve reception of receivers. The number set in integration time is an abbreviation of 20.

Because the GPS data transmission speed is 50 Bps and takes as much as 20msec per bit. When the integration time is *T*, *T* is defined as $T = \{1, 2, 4, 5, 10, 20\}$. If T is set to a number other than the abbreviation of 20, the data bit and the bit edge are unknown, so signal processing is not possible[3].

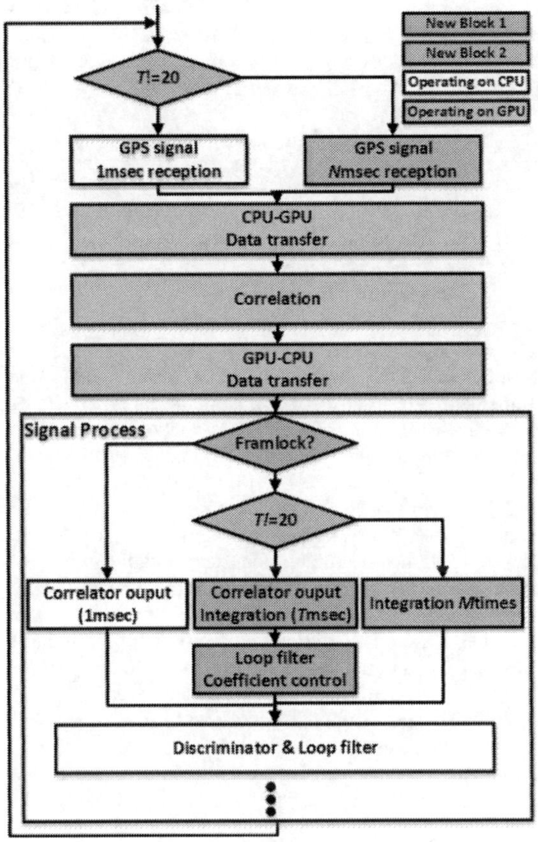

Fig. 4. Modified signal tracking processing

Fig. 4 shows the addition of non-correct integration using GPU in Fig. 2. New Block 1 is the part where non-coherent integration is added. Framelock of New Block 1 checks the start of the satellite signal's bit and whether the parity check of the satellite data have been completed. If the bit start point is ignored and integrated, the bit edge is unknown, so the data bit is unknown. If the Framelock is verified, integrate the output of the correlator by *T*msec. *T* increases to 20. Adjust the coefficient of the loop filter according to the *T* value. Depending on the *T*, the natural frequency and noise bandwidth of the loop filter change[2, 4].

2.4 Considering GPU operation non-coherent integration

Parallel processing operations are suitable for calculations where many data elements can run simultaneously in parallel. So we implemented correlator as CUDA. To use CUDA, data should be transferred from the CPU to the GPU. Number of times data is transferred from CPU to GPU should be reduced. It takes a lot of time to transfer data. Also, CUDA is most efficient in processing a lot of data with a lot of threads[5]. Therefore, to increase the efficiency of the CUDA, it is necessary to reduce the number of times data is transferred from the CPU to the GPU to the CPU and compute a lot of data at once.

Implement the structure shown in New Block 2 of Fig. 4 to compare the computational efficiency of the GPU. Comparison of the computational efficiency of GPU operates when *T*=20. When T=20, the length(*N*) of the IF signal data is changed. As the length of the IF signal data changes, the integration number(*M*) of non-corrections changes. *N*x*M* should be 20 to maintain the performance of the non-coherent integration *T*=20. As *N* changes, the number of times transferred from CPU to GPU and GPU to CPU changes, and the amount calculated at once by the GPU changes.

3 Experiment and Analysis

3.1 Experimental environment and purpose

Table 1 Laptop specification

OS	Windows 10 Home K 64-bit
CPU	Intel Core i7-7820HK
GPU	Geforce GTX 1080
Memory	DDR4-16GB
IDE	MS Visual Studio 2013, C++
CUDA version	Release 8.0

The experiment was conducted using the AORUS laptop. The specifications of the AORUS laptop are shown in Table 1. The specifications of the laptop, the OS is Windows 10, CPU is Intel Core i7-7820HK and GPU is GeForce GTX 1080. GPU has 2,560 cores, 1607MHz clock, 10Gbps memory clock, and 256bit memory bus. GPS signal data was obtained using an antenna installed on the roof of E10 of Chungbuk National University. The GPS signal's quantification bit is 16 bits and the sampling frequency is 25MHz.

Confirm the results of the two experiments using the signal received. The first experiment verifies the performance of the non-coherent integration method according to the *T* to verify feasibility of implementation. The performance of the non-coherent integration method is checked if the Doppler frequency, which is the output of the PLL, is properly tracked. The second experiment compares the computational time by adjusting the *N* and *M* of *N*x*M* in non-coherent Integration considering GPU operation. Compare the operation time of non-correct integration considering GPU operation and find the optimal *N*x*M*.

3.2 Validation of non-coherent integration implementation

Check the result of doppler frequency that is output when non-coherent integration is added to the Signal Process section of the signal tracking loop. Fig. 5 shows the Doppler frequency output as *T* changes. In the experiment, T was switched to 1, 2, 5 and 20, and as T increased, the variance of Doppler frequencies was reduced. Fig. 5 shows a continuous decrease in the Doppler frequency. This is because the satellite is moving. As a result, we added non-coherent integration to confirm that signal tracking performance is improved.

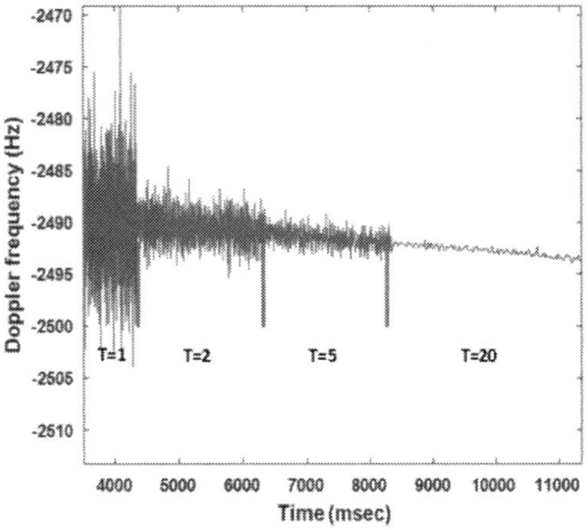

Fig. 5. GPS doppler frequency shift (GPS No. 12)

3.3 Comparison of computational time of non-coherent integration using GPU

The computational efficiency of GPU varies depending on number of data transfers and amount of data processing at a time. The operation time is checked by dividing three parts, the transfer time between CPU to GPU(A), kernel call and correlation operation time(B), and the transfer time GPU to GPU(C) in Table 2 and changing the *N*x*M*

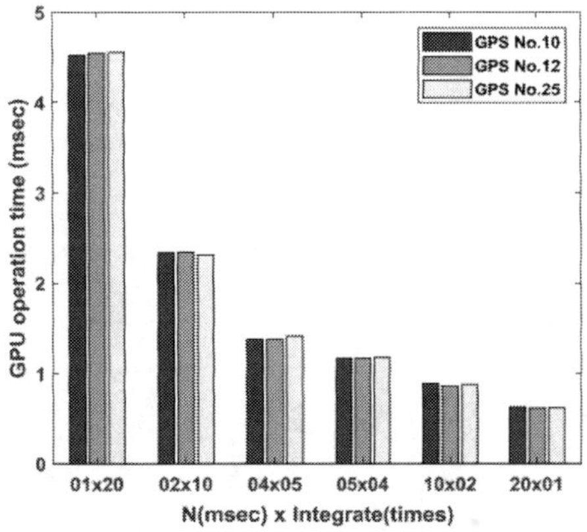

Fig. 6. CUDA operation time according to NxM

Fig. 6 shows the operating time of the CUDA for each satellite, changing the *N*x*M*, and Table 2 shows the operating time ratio for each part. Table 2 shows the ratio of operation time when *N*x*M* is 1x20. In all three parts, the operation time decreases as the size of N increasing. Compared to 1x20 and 20x1, the most time-reduced part is kernel call and operation time(B). It decreased by 90%. More than 80% of the operation time was reduced in all three parts. Fig 6. can be confirmed that the total operation time of GPU increases by N, which results in shorter processing time per 20 msec. The increasing the N in all three satellites, the shorter the time the GPU operates. When *N*x*M* is 20x1, its operation time is the shortest and its computational efficiency is the best.

Table 2. Operating time ratio in three parts

	1x20	2x10	4x5	5x4	10x2	20x1
A	1	0.52	0.32	0.27	0.21	0.17
B	1	0.51	0.30	0.25	0.18	0.11
C	1	0.50	0.31	0.32	0.21	0.14

4 Conclusion

Non-coherent integration of SDR using GPU was implemented to improve the computational efficiency of GPS signal tracking loops. Non-coherent integration reduced errors and improved tracking performance. Integration period of 20msec (*T*=20) gives the best tracking performance of the tracking loop. To evaluate the performance of GPU-based signal tracking module, the 1msec x 20times basic non-coherent module is changed to Nmsec x Mtimes module. By changing N, we compare the operation time of the three parts: 1) memory copy from CPU to GPU, 2) kernel call and operation time of GPU and 3) memory copy from GPU to CPU. In all three parts, the computation efficiency was improved as the size of N increased. From the experiments using real GPS signals, the computational performance of N=20 is improved by 80% compared to N=1. Therefore, the implemented SDR using notebook computer can tracks more channels simultaneously in the real time.

References

1. C.-H. Kang, S.-Y. Kim, J.-H. Yang, & C.-G. Park, Analysis of GPS signal acquisition algorithm for SDR, Institute of Control, Robotics and Systems(2011)
2. J. McGinthy, Captain, USAF, Global Navigation Satellite System Software Defined Radio, Air force Institute of Technology, Ohio(March 2010)
3. Nesreen I. Z., GNSS Receivers for Weak Signals, pp.28-37, (2006)
4. E. D. Kaplan, C. J. Hegarty, Understanding GPS/GNSS principles and applications, Third edition, Artech House, (2017)
5. NVIDIA, CUDA C Best Practices Guide, Design Guide, (October 2018)
6. K. H. Yoo, S. K. Sung, T. S. Kang, Y. J. Lee, E.-S. Lee, et al., Analysis of GPS+QZSS Availability at Uraban Canyon of Seoul , KSAS, (2008)

 https://doi.org/10.1051/e3sconf/20199403014

Determination of the relationship between Vietnam national coordinate reference system (VN-2000) and ITRS, WGS84 and PZ-90

Hoa Pham Thi[1*], *Dung* Nghiem Quoc[2], *Thu* Trinh Thi Hoai[1], *Huynh* Pham The[3] and *Nhung* Le Thi[1]

[a]Hanoi University of Natural Resources and Environment, Vietnam
[b] Department of Surveying, Mapping and Geoinformation of Vietnam, Vietnam
[c] Hanoi University of Mining and Geology, Vietnam

Abstract: In July 2000, Hanoi-72 reference system was replaced by the Vietnam reference system, namely as VN-2000 as an official geodetic background system in Vietnam. Ministry of Natural Resources and Environment of Vietnam has reported the transformation parameters between VN-2000 and WGS84. Nevertheless, there is a need to estimate a new transformation parameter set between VN-2000 and WGS84 because WGS84 has been updated. In addition, there is now a lack of an accurate published set of parameters for transformation from VN-2000 to not only the International Terrestrial Reference System ITRS but also PZ-90. In this study, coordinate transformation parameters between ITRS and VN-2000 are estimated through the use of a least square approach and the common points with known coordinates in both systems. These set of parameters was then deployed to determine the link between VN-2000 and WGS84 as well as PZ-90. The results denoted that the derived transformation parameters, on the basis of the results at the checkpoints, could generated station positions with the accuracy at several cm level for transformation from VN-2000 to the new realizations of ITRS, WGS84 and PZ90 and reversely. These achievements reveals that the set of parameters is great significance for many applications related to positioning in Vietnam.

Keywords: VN-2000, ITRS, ITRF, WGS84, PZ-90, coordinate transformation parameters

1.Introduction

In the era of globalization and modernization, Vietnam, a developing country, would adopts many scientific and technological achievements. In which the use of geospatial data generated by countries with the most advanced technology is extremely useful. However, these data sources are not in VN-2000 but in different coordinate systems. Thus, there is a need to convert spatial data in disparate sources to VN-2000 and and reversely.

With the Decree of the Vietnam Government No.83 dated December 12, Vietnam national coordinate reference system (VN-2000) became an became the official national reference system [1]. VN-2000 is static, or plate- fixed reference system, so its coordinates do not constantly change with time. The concept of a static datum, like VN-2000, has served Vietnam and many other countries well because it is easier to implement and maintain than dynamic coordinate systems. However, the dynamic one enables the change of positions on the earth to be tracked and modeled over time.

Ministry of Natural Resources and Environment of the Socialist Republic of Vietnam (Monre) has reported the transformation parameters between the VN-2000 and World Geodetic System 1984 (WGS84) [2]. Nevertheless, there is a need to estimate a new transformation parameter set between two systems because WGS84 has been updated.

Nowadays, the International Terrestrial Reference systems (ITRS) is more widely used than WGS84 [3]. However, there is now no means of transforming ITRF coordinate values to the local system. The lack of transformation parameters causes inconvenience to the Vietnamese geodetic community, especially the National GNSS CORS network is being established in Vietnam and will have been connected to the IGS network. Therefore, its stations will have accurate ITRF-based coordinates. Definitely, to meet regulatory requirements, data must be provided in the official datum. Therefore, it is necessary to have a readily available parameter sets for ITRF to VN-2000 transformations.

Along with the US GPS system using WGS84, the Russia Glonass system using the PZ- 90 reference system also could operate independently and promising more potential applications in Vietnam. However, the PZ-90, like ITRS, has no connection with VN-2000.

The shortage of official links between VN-2000 with three above-mentioned international reference systems will make VN-2000-based data not be able to integrate with international ones. Therefore, this study, as an interim method, aims to define the relationship between the ITRS and VN-2000 based the use of a least square approach and common points with known coordinates in both systems. Then, transformation parameters between the VN-2000 and the ITRS are used to determine the links between VN-2000 and not only WGS84 but also PZ-90.

2. Overview of VN-2000, WGS84, PZ-90 and ITRS

2.1 Overview of VN-2000

Since 1990, with the rapid development of satellite- based positioning technology in terms of accuracy and accessibility, Vietnam built new networks across the country and these networks was connected with older ones. Based on the data collection of networks across the country over time, from 1998 to 1999, the Viet nam General Department of Land Administration has deployed the project "Construction of the national coordinate system –VN-2000" [4]. The project was implemented 1999 and VN-2000 have been officially the Vietnam national reference system from July 2000 to date.

The classical VN-2000 datum is not geocentric. It is based on the ellipsoid which derived from fitting WGS84 reference ellipsoid to local geoid based on a least squares method [4]. VN-2000 is static, so there is no requirement for epoch of its coordinates. Further detailed information on the observation and adjustment of VN-2000 was described by [4].

2.2 Overview of ITRS

The ITRS is a system defined by the International Association of Geodesy and the International Astronomical Union and endorsed by the International Union of Geodesy and Geophysics [5]. The ITRS is geocentric and dynamic. The practical realization of ITRS is the International Terrestrial Reference Frame (ITRF). The ITRF was first published in 1988 and is the most precise earth-centered, earth-fixed coordinate fame currently available. It is maintained by the International Earth Rotation and Reference Systems Service and realized by an extensive global network of accurate coordinates derived from geodetic observations using GPS, Very Long Baseline Interferometry (VLBI), Satellite Laser Ranging (SLR), Lunar Laser Ranging (LLR) and Doppler Orbitography and Radiopositioning Integrated by Satellite (DORIS) [6]. To date, there are many ITRF realizations, for example, ITRF1992 [7], ITRF1996 [8], ITRF1997 [9], ITRF2000 [10], ITRF2005 [6], ITRF2008 [11] and most recently ITRF2014 [12]. Transformation parameters among ITRF products are availabe on the offical website [13].

The ITRF is a common standard which warrants interoperability between geospatial information systems. There are some main reasons for this. Firstly, most regional and global reference frames are today aligned or related to ITRF [5]. Secondly, many countries have redefined their geodetic systems to be compatible with ITRF [5]. Thirdly, all global satellite positioning systems can easily be used to coordinates in a recent ITRF [5]. Finally, all GNSS networks around the world can easily be expressed in the ITRF using IGS products [5]. As a consequence of these reasons, ITRF is becoming the most widely used international coordinate system. This calls for the production of a mathematical model of transformation from ITRF to VN-2000 and reversely. The availability of transformations between the two systems enables Vietnam users to enhance interoperability of geo-referenced datasets and services towards homogeneity of spatial data. More information on ITRS is available in [14].

2.3 Overview of WGS84 and PZ-90

The WGS84 and PZ-90 represent the system of geodetic parameters including fundamental geodetic constants, reference ellipsoid parameters, the Earth's gravity field parameters, geocentric coordinate system and transformation parameters to other reference systems.

WGS84 is a conventional Earth reference system established by the US Department of Defense (DoD), and used as the nominal system for GPS navigation [14]. The original WGS84 reference frame established in 1987, commonly known as WGS84 (Doppler), based on U.S. Navy Navigation Satellite System or TRANSIT (Doppler). It generated station coordinates with accuracies of about one meter. The others realizations of WGS84 based on GPS data, such as WGS84 (G730), WGS84 (G873), WGS84 (G1150), WGS84 (G1674), WGS84 (G1762), where the 'G' indicates these coordinates were obtained through GPS techniques and the number following the 'G' indicates the GPS week number when these coordinates were implemented in the precise GPS ephemeris estimation process [14]. The WGS84 (G730) reference frame are coincident with ITRF 92 at about 10-centimeter level [15]. However, the lastest G1762 realization adopted ITRF2008 coordinates for more than half of the reference stations and velocities of nearby sites for the others. Thus, ITRF2014, ITRF2008 and WGS84 (G1762) are in agreement at the centimeter level, provided conventional 0-transformation parameters. More information on WGS84 is available in [14].

The PZ-90 is a global system developed by Russia, similar to WGS84, and is a basis for geodetic support of the Global Navigation Satellite System (GLONASS). Up to now, the PZ 90 reference system has undergone two modernizations with corresponding versions of PZ 90.00, PZ-90.02 and PZ-90.11 [16]. In PZ-90.11 axes orientation, scale and origin are coincided to the similar ITRF parameters at the cm level. Detailed information on PZ-90 is available in the document [16].

WGS84, PZ-90 and ITRS were determined based on the same theoretical principles. However, there are small differences between the three's practical realizations that can be explained by discrepancy not only in the number, categories and distribution of input data but also in methodological differences [16]. Coordinate transformation between products of these references system are available in [14][16].

3. Coordinate transformation method

The most common used methodology to convert coordinate from one system to the other deploys a least square principle and known fundamental points, whose coordinates are known on both systems. However, in Vietnam, high accuracy VN-2000 and ITRF coordinates can be determined, but not WGS84 and PZ-90 coordinates [5]. Thus, this paper employs a least square method to deliver VN-2000 coordinates from an ITRF based computation system and then used relationship between ITRS and the others systems for estimation of parameters for coordinate transformation from WGS84 and PZ-90 to VN-2000.

3.1. ITRS to VN-2000 coordinate transformation method

Coordinates given with respect to VN-2000 are time independent. In contrast, coordinates given with respect to ITRF are time dependent. Conversely, the International Terrestrial Reference Frame (ITRF) is dynamic, its coordinates change as linear functions of time due to tectonic motion [17]. Therefore, the transformation approach between the two systems is to use a 14 - parameter transformation, which augment the original 7 parameters (three translations, three rotations, and one scale factor) with their time derivatives. This approach is currently applied in Australia to transform ITRF coordinates at the measurement epoch to Australian coordinate system (GDA94) which is a static datum fixed with ITRF92 at epoch 1994.0 [18]. It is also used in other countries and region such as Europe [19], United States, Canada, Mexico, Central America and the Caribbean Islands [20].

The general formulation to transform coordinates between two systems, say ITRF to VN-2000, is given according to the following equations [21]

$$X_{(2)} = T + (1+D)R^T X_{(1)}, \quad (1)$$

where $X_{(2)}$ is the vector of VN-2000-based coordinates, $X_{(1)}$ is the vector of ITRF-based coordinates; T is the vector translation components, D is the differential scale change, R is the matrix of differential rotation angles (expressed in radians) as follows [21]:

$$[A1]\; R^T = \begin{pmatrix} 1 & -R_3 & R_2 \\ R_3 & 1 & -R_1 \\ -R_2 & R_1 & 1 \end{pmatrix} \quad (2)$$

Because D is small quantity, we can neglect second-order terms. Equation (1) can be express as follows [22]:

$$\begin{pmatrix} X \\ Y \\ Z \end{pmatrix}_{(1)} = \begin{pmatrix} X \\ Y \\ Z \end{pmatrix}_{(1)} + \begin{pmatrix} T_1 \\ T_2 \\ T_3 \end{pmatrix}_{(1)} + D\begin{pmatrix} X \\ Y \\ Z \end{pmatrix}_{(1)} + \begin{pmatrix} 0 & -R_3 & R_2 \\ R_3 & 0 & -R_1 \\ R_2 & R_1 & 0 \end{pmatrix}\begin{pmatrix} X \\ Y \\ Z \end{pmatrix}_{(1)} \quad (3)$$

The seven transformation parameters, T1, T2, T3, R1, R2, R3 and D, change with time, thus, (1) can be expressed in other form as [21]:

$$\begin{bmatrix} X(t) \\ Y(t) \\ Z(t) \end{bmatrix}_{(2)} = \begin{bmatrix} X(t) \\ Y(t) \\ Z(t) \end{bmatrix}_{(1)} + \begin{bmatrix} T_1(t_0) + \dot{T}_1(t-t_0) \\ T_2(t_0) + \dot{T}_2(t-t_0) \\ T_3(t_0) + \dot{T}_3(t-t_0) \end{bmatrix}_{(1)} + (D(t_0) + \dot{D}(t-t_0))\begin{bmatrix} X(t) \\ Y(t) \\ Z(t) \end{bmatrix}_{(1)} + \tilde{R}\begin{bmatrix} X(t) \\ Y(t) \\ Z(t) \end{bmatrix}_{(1)}, \quad (4)$$

where t is computed epoch (yr), t_0 is the reference epoch (yr) of the transformation parameters and:

$$\tilde{R} = \begin{bmatrix} 0 & -(R3(t_0) + \dot{R}3.(t-t_0)) & R2(t_0) + \dot{R}2.(t-t_0) \\ R3(t_0) + \dot{R}3.(t-t_0) & 0 & -(R1(t_0) + \dot{R}1.(t-t_0)) \\ -(R2(t_0) + \dot{R}2.(t-t_0)) & R1(t_0) + \dot{R}1.(t-t_0) & 0 \end{bmatrix}$$

Differentiating Equation (1) with respect to time and eliminating the negligible terms it can be written [21]

$$\dot{X}_2 = \dot{X}_1 + \dot{T} + \dot{D}X_1 + D\dot{X}_1 + \dot{R}X_1 + R\dot{X}_1, \quad (5)$$

where $\dot{X}_2, \dot{X}_1, \dot{T}, \dot{D}, \dot{R}$ is the time derivatives of X_2, X_1, T, D, R, respectively.

Since D and R is very small, hence Equation (5) can be reduced to [21]:

$$\dot{X}_2 = \dot{X}_1 + \dot{T} + \dot{D}X_1 + \dot{R}X_1 \quad (6)$$

To estimate the fourteen- parameter similarity transformation between the two system, the coordinate differences between the ITRF and VN-2000 were treated as observations in the least squares solution of equations. Therefore, the identical points are used in a least squares process to define the relationship between the two systems. The above equations can be written as [21]:

$$X_2 = X_1 + T + DX_1 + RX_1 \Leftrightarrow X_2 = X_1 + A\theta, \quad (7)$$

$$\dot{X}_2 = \dot{X}_1 + \dot{T} + \dot{D}X_1 + \dot{R}X_1 \Leftrightarrow \dot{X}_2 = \dot{X}_1 + A\dot{\theta}, \quad (8)$$

with:

$$\theta = [T_1, T_2, T_3, D, R_1, R_2, R_3]$$

$$\dot{\theta} = [\dot{T}_1, \dot{T}_2, \dot{T}_3, \dot{D}, \dot{R}_1, \dot{R}_2, \dot{R}_3]$$

The least squares solutions are:

$$\theta = (A^T P_x A)^{-1} A^T P_x (X_2 - X_1), \quad (9)$$

$$\dot{\theta} = (A^T P_v A)^{-1} A^T P_v (\dot{X}_2 - \dot{X}_1), \quad (10)$$

where P_X and P_v are the weight matrix for station positions and velocities, respectively.

The statistical calculation a posterior variance of unit weight is determined as follows [21]:

$$s_{0X}^2 = ((A^T P_x - (X_2 - X_1))^{-1} . (A^T P_x - (X_2 - X_1))^{-1}) / n \quad (11)$$

where n is degrees of freedom.

The above mentioned principle derives parameters for a transformation between ITRF products and VN-2000 through the use of a least square approach and common points with known coordinates in both systems. The achievable accuracy of the transformation parameters is depended on the number, distribution and accuracy of the common points. It is necessary to obtain far more than the minimum number of common points because the redundant points will give an idea of the consistency of the derived transformation parameters. The accuracy of these parameters should be tested by comparing actual and transformed positions of check points.

The process of estimation coordinate transformation parameters between ITRF and VN-2000 consists of three steps following:

-Step 1: Identify stations at which coordinates are available in both the reference frames and velocities are available in ITRF

-Step2:Calculate appropriate coordinate transformation parameters

-Step 3:Assess the accuracy and reliability of the achieving transformation parameters based on using checkpoints as an independent check by comparing actual and transformed positions.

3.2. WGS84 and PZ-90 to VN-2000 coordinate transformation methods

As mentioned before, due to difficulty in determining WGS84 and PZ-90 coordinates with high accuracy in Vietnam, the paper proposed coordinate convertion from WGS84 and PZ-90 to VN-2000 based on relationship between ITRF and the three as the following formula:

VN-2000→WGS84=(VN-2000→ITRF)+(ITRF→ WGS84)

VN-2000→PZ-90 = (VN-2000→ITRF) + (ITRF→ PZ-90)

4. Input solution datasets

To define transformation from WGS84, PZ-90 and ITRF to VN-2000, data from two networks was collected. The first network belongs to the annual Asia Pacific Regional Geodetic Project (APRGP) GPS campaign, which are an important activity of the regional geodesy working group of the Permanent Committee on GIS Infrastructure for Asia and the Pacific Region (PCGIAP) [23,24]. This network consists of 7 -day observation sessions and have been undertaken from 1997 to 2016. The GPS data were processed using the Bernese GPS Software in a regional network together with selected IGS (International GNSS Service) sites [23]. The GPS solution was constrained to the ITRF2008 reference frame through adopting IGS08 coordinates on selected IGS reference sites and using the final IGS earth orientation parameters and ephemerides products[23].The second network is the Vietnamese marine one, which also consists of 7-day observation sessions and have been accomplished in 2016. Its GPS observation data were processed to deliver ITRF2005-based coordinates at epoch 2016.764 and VN-2000 coordinate values.

This research used data from a total of 21 stations within the two above mentioned networks, and their coordinates available in both ITRS and VN-2000 coordinate systems. Of these, ten well distributed common points in Vietnam, belonging to (APRGP) GPS campaign are used to compute transformation parameters between ITRS and VN-2000. Their ITRF2008-based coordinates and velocities were collected over a period of 4 years (*2011–2015*) [24, 25, 26,27]. Their VN-2000 coordinate values obtained by connecting them with other GPS local networks. The left eleven points belonging to the Vietnamese marine network was used as independent check points for assessing of achieved parameter accuracy.

The set of transfromation parameters between ITRS and VN-2000 was then deployed to determine the link between VN-2000 and WGS84 as well as PZ-90. The both networks were also employed to test parameters for transformation from WGS84 and PZ-90 to VN-2000.

The station positions are shown in Fig.1.

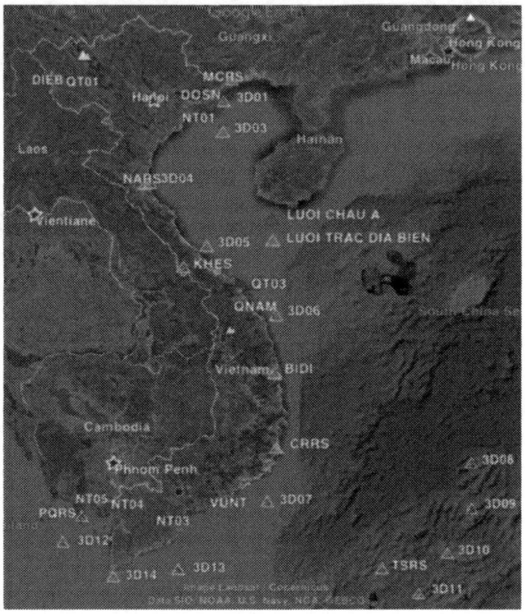

Fig.1 The position of 21 stations in two networks.

5. Results and discussion

5.1 Transfromation from ITRF to VN-2000

Originally, coordinates and velocities at 10 points in *APRGP*, known on the ITRF2008 and VN-2000, were used to determine the transformation parameters at epoch 2015.0. The defined parameters for transforming ITRF2008 to VN-2000 are shown in Table 1. The statistical a posterior variance of unit weight are 4.67 cm and 0.52cm/yr for original 7 parameters and their rates, respectively.

The transformation parameters between the other ITRF realizations denoted by $ITRF_{XY}$ and VN-2000 is determined according to the following formula:

ITRF$_{xy}$→VN2000=(*ITRF*$_{xy}$→*ITRF2008*)+(*ITRF2008*→*VN2000*)

The additional required information for propagating from $ITRF_{XY}$ to ITRF2008 to complete the transformation from $ITRF_{XY}$ to VN-2000 are published in the IERS Technical Notes and Annual Reports and available on the official ITRF webpage [13] . The final values of the 14 transformation parameters to transform coordinates given on the ITR_{XY} to the VN-2000 are presented in Table 1. Table 1 shows that two origins of systems have positive displacements on all the axes. The negative scale factor values indicate that the geometric shapes of the ITRF and VN-2000 are reduced when the scale factor is applied in conjunction with the other parameters for transforming coordinates from ITRF to VN-2000.

ITRF use the Geodetic Reference System 1980 (GRS80) as the reference ellipse to represent geographical coordinates whereas VN-2000 adopts the WGS84 reference ellipse that is slightly different to GRS80. However, the translations in table 3 are very significant and must be considered because the WGS84 reference ellipse in VN-2000 was best fit with local geoid. In general, these parameter values are not much different compared with the set of transformation parameters between WGS84 and VN-2000, and it is understood because WGS84 is regularly aligned to ITRF [5, 28].

Table 1. Transformation parameters from $ITRF_{XY}$ to VN-2000 at epoch 2015.0. Units are in m and $m.yr^{-1}$ for the translations and their rates, respectively, parts-per-billion (ppb) and $ppb.yr^{-1}$ for scale and its rate, respectively, and milli-arcseconds (mas) and $mas.yr^{-1}$ for the rotations and their rates, respectively.

T_1 $\dot{T}_1$	T_2 $\dot{T}_2$	T_3 $\dot{T}_3$	D $\dot{D}$	R_1 $\dot{R}_1$	R_2 $\dot{R}_2$	R_3 $\dot{R}_3$
ITRF2014						
193.9227	37.5110	110.6343	-7.51	-7.11	+20.08	+37.35
-0.0790	-0.0360	0.0188	0.16	-0.85	+1.33	-3.52
ITRF2008						
193.9211	37.5091	110.6319	-7.54	-7.11	+20.08	+37.35
-0.0790	-0.0360	0.0189	0.16	-0.85	+1.33	-3.52
ITRF2005						
193.9186	37.5100	110.6366	-8.48	-7.11	+20.08	+37.35
-0.0793	-0.0360	0.0189	0.16	-0.85	+1.33	-3.52
ITRF2000						
193.9215	193.9213	110.6694	-10.08	-7.11	+20.08	+37.35
-0.0791	-0.0361	0.0207	0.08	-0.85	+1.33	-3.52
ITRF97						
193.9148	193.9260	110.7131	-11.81	-7,11	+20,08	+36,99
-0.0791	-0.0355	0.0221	0.07	-0,85	+1,33	-3,54
ITRF96						
193.9148	193.9260	110.7131	-11.81	-7,11	+20,08	+36,99
-0.0791	-0.0355	0.0221	0.07	-0,85	+1,33	-3,54
ITRF94						
193.9148	193.9260	110.7131	-11.81	-7,11	+20,08	+36,99
-0.0791	-0.0355	0.0221	0.07	-0,85	+1,33	-3,54
ITRF93						
193,9871	193,9202	110,7065	-12,30	-3,75	24,41	36,60
-0,0762	-0,0359	0,0213	0,07	-0,74	1,52	-3,59
ITRF92						
193,9068	193,9240	110,7211	-11,10	-7,11	20,08	36,99
-0,0791	-0,0355	0,0221	0,07	-0,85	1,33	-3,54
ITRF91						
193,8948	193,9100	110,7271	-12,50	-7,11	20,08	36,99
-0,0791	-0,0355	0,0221	0,07	-0,85	1,33	-3,54
ITRF90						
193,4813	193,3275	112,2131	121,10	-7,11	20,08	36,39
-0,0791	-0,0355	0,0221	0,07	-0,85	1,33	-3,54
ITRF89						
193,5513	193,8435	112,6111	171,00	-8,61	20,08	36,39
-0,0791	-0,0355	0,0221	0,07	-0,85	1,33	-3,54
ITRF88						
193,8983	193,9185	110,7571	-17,95	-7,21	20,08	37,29
-0,0791	-0,0355	0,0221	0,07	-0,85	1,33	-3,54

The transformation is done in a single process, enabling $ITRF_{XY}$ data at any epoch (denoted as t) to be transformed to VN-2000 based on a 14-parameter transformation as the following two steps:

- Step 1: Calculate transformation parameters between $ITRF_{XY}$ and VN-2000 at Epoch t utilizing data in table 2
- Step 2: Calculate coordinates at Epoch t based on the achieved parameters.

Table 3 The differences between the computed and existing VN-2000 coordinates of checkpoints

Points	Diff. X (m)	Diff.Y (m)	Diff. Z (m)
3D01	+ 0.049	+0.011	+0.004
3D02	+0.040	+0.015	+0.008
3D03	+0.060	-0.076	-0.031
3D04	+0.058	-0.012	-0.003
3D05	+0.047	-0.037	-0.029
3D06	+0.028	-0.026	-0.035
3D07	+0.103	-0.142	-0.068
3D13	+0.088	-0.049	-0.045
3D14	+0.045	+0.093	-0.009
BIDI	+0.045	-0.052	-0.058
KHES	+0.040	-0.015	-0.025
Max Diff.	+0.103	+0.093	+0.008
Min Diff.	+0.028	-0.142	-0.068
Mean Diff.	+0.055	-0.026	-0.026
Standard Diff.	±0.059	±0.062	±0.035

To carry out the test of the computed transformation parameters, available ITRF2005 and VN-2000 coordinates of eleven points within marine networks that did not participate in the transformation solution were utilized. The 11 selected are 3D01, 3D02, 3D03, 3D04, 3D05, 3D07, 3D13, 3D14, BIDI and KHES. The test was directly performed using data in table 2 to transfer ITRF2005-based to VN-2000 coordinates. The differences between the VN-2000 values, after conversion, and the existing VN-2000 X, Y and Z values of independent test points are tabulated in Table 3.

These coordinate differences should ideally be zero. However, such results could never be achieved because of the effect of input data uncertainty. Data in table 3 indicates that transformation Z coordinates gave a better accuracy compared to the X and Y components. The standard deviation is approximate 6cm for X and Y whereas 3.5cm to Z. The coordinate difference is within 5 cm for 100% points in term of Z whereas 82.1% points in X and Y.

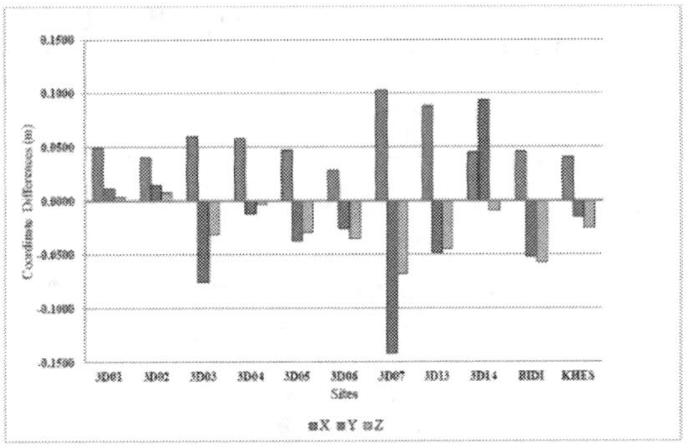

Fig 2. Coordinate Differences

The computed coordinate differences of checkpoints in Tables 3, represented in Fig.2 clearly reflects residuals for the eleven test points.

Fig.2 shows that the coordinate differences fluctuate for all coordinate components. The highest fluctuation is the Y coordinate difference, range from -14cm to 9cm, whereas X-component is the most stable. However, the difference is up to 10cm for X, but 7cm for Z.

The station, 3D07, has the highest differences between the computed and existing VN-2000 coordinates. It may be caused by its lower quality of observation, in comparision with the others sites.

5.2 Transformation from WGS84 to VN-2000

The parameters for transformation from the VN-2000 to the WGS84 were determined based on the coordinate transformation parameters between VN-2000 and ITRS as well as ITRF and WGS84 (shown in table 3).

Table 3. Coordinate transformation parameters between VN-2000 and WGS84

T_1 (mm)	T_2 (mm)	T_3 (mm)	D (10^{-9})	R_1 (mas)	R_2 (mas)	R_3 (mas)
WGS84 (G1762), epoch 2005.0						
194,7154	37,8661	110,4386	-2,2172	1,0920	7,0395	72,1838
WGS84 (1674), epoch 2005.0						
194,7114	37,8691	110,4426	-9,1172	1,3620	6,7695	72,5638
WGS84 (G1150), epoch 2001.0						
195,0293	38,01471	110,3792	-11,1682	4,7517	1,4456	86,6502
WGS84 (G873), epoch 1997.0						
195,3391	38,15302	110,3148	-13,0293	8,1414	-3,8783	100,7366
WGS84 (G730), epoch 1994.0						
195,5565	38,24353	110,2624	-13,9225	10,6837	-7,8713	111,3614
WGS84 (origin), epoch 1984						
196,2898	39,11956	110,2802	-96,1000	0,8579	-20,8810	139,7773

To evaluate the performance of these set of transformation parameters, station positions with respect to threre WGS84 reference frames, namely WGS84 (G1150), WGS84 (G1674) and WGS84 (G1762), were generated from two different ways. The first ways utilized the existing VN-2000 cooritantes and transformation parameters between VN-2000 and WGS84 that reprenseted in table 3. The last one employed the known ITRF cooritantes and transformation parameters between ITRF and WGS84 that indicated in [14,28]. The results showed that WGS84 based coordinates derived from VN-2000 coordinates is incoincide with corresponding quantities computed from the ITRF based coordinates. Statistical results shown in the table 4 reveals that the standard deviation of the coordinate difference between the two WGS84 derived coordinate values is the same level for all WGS84 reliazations in general. However, the standard deviation for WGS84 (G1674) and WGS84 (G1762) is small by comparision with WGS84 (G1150). The difference the standard deviation is at 1.5 cm and 2cm level for GPS marine and Asia Pacific network, respectively. That could be explained by the fact that WGS84 (G1150) was introduced in 2001 [14], which is quite far from the measuring epochs (2015 and 2016) of the two GPS networks by comparision with the two new successive products, WGS84 (G1674) and WGS84 (G1762) published in 2012 and 2013, respectively.

In addition, the data in table 4 also indicated that the difference between the two WGS84 coordinate values for the Asia Pacific network is large by comparision with GPS marine network. The difference were at ±1.5 to ± 2cm level in general. The standard deviation values were approximate ± 0.5dm, ± 1dm and ± 0.4dm for Z, Y and Z coodinates, respectively.

Table 4. The standard deviation between the two WGS84 coordinate values, one derived from ITRF coordinates and the other derived from VN-2000 coordinates

Networks	WGS84 products	Standard deviation			
		σ_X(m)	σ_Y (m)	σ_Z (m)	σ_{xyz} (m)
GPS marine network	WGS84 (G1150)	±0,0465	±0,1178	±0,0368	±0,0761
	WGS84 (G1674)	±0,0463	±0,0913	±0,0330	±0,0621
	WGS84 (G1762)	±0,0463	±0,0913	±0,0330	±0,0621
Asia Pacific Network	WGS84 (G1150)	±0,0550	±0,1629	±0,0468	±0,1029
	WGS84 (G1674)	±0,0503	±0,1206	±0,0362	±0,0783
	WGS84 (G1762)	±0,0503	±0,1206	±0,0362	±0,0783

This paper also investigated the difference between WGS84 coordinates determined from VN-2000 coordinates based on existing transformation parameters published in [2] and ITRF2008 coordintes that considered as WGS84 coordinates because ITRF 2008 is agreement with WGS84 (G1674) at epoch 2005.0 [28]. The results in table 5 showed that the standard deviation between the computed and the known WGS84 coordinates values is significant. The standard deviation values were approximate ± 4dm, ± 7dm and ± 3 dm for Z, Y and Z - axes, respectively. The standard deviation for position were at ± 5dm level that is quite large compared with the value of ± 0.07dm (shown in table 4). The huge difference reveals the new parameters outweight the existing ones published in [2] for transformation from VN-2000 to WGS84.

Table 5. The standard deviation between the WGS84 coordinates computed from VN-2000 coordinates based on existing transformation parameters and the known WGS84 coordinates

GPS marine Network	Standard deviation			
	σ_X(m)	σ_Y (m)	σ_Z (m)	σ_{xyz} (m)
GPS marine Network	±0,3960	±0,7158	±0,3167	±0,5065
Asia Pacific Network	±0,4483	±0,7057	±0,3510	±0,5235

5.3 Transformation from PZ-90 to VN-2000

The parameters for transformation from the VN-2000 to the WGS84 were determined based on the coordinate transformation parameters between VN-2000 and ITRS as well as ITRF and WGS84 (Table 6).

Similar to VN-2000 to WGS84 transformation, to evaluate the performance of these set of parameters, station positions with respect to PZ-90 reference frames, were yielded from two distinct solutions. The first deployed the available VN-2000 cooorditantes and transformation parameters between VN-2000 andPZ-90 that shown in table 6. The other one used existing ITRF coorditantes and transformation parameters between ITRF and PZ-90 that indicated in [16]. The results indicated that PZ-90 based coordinates derived from VN-2000 coordinates is incoincide with corresponding ones computed from the ITRF based coordinates. Statistical results shown in the table 7 reveals that the standard deviation of the coordinate differentiation between the two PZ-90 derived coordinate values is not the same level for all PZ- 90 versions. Th standard deviation for PZ-90.02 and PZ-90.11is small by comparision with PZ -90.00. The difference the standard deviation is at 1.3 cm and 4.5 cm level for GPS marine and Asia Pacific network, respectively.

Table 6. Coordinate transformation parameters between VN-2000 and PZ-90

T_1 (mm)	T_2 (mm)	T_3 (mm)	D (10^{-9})	R_1 (mas)	R_2 (mas)	R_3 (mas)
PZ 90.11, epoch 2010.0						
194,3132	37,6881	110,5373	-8,3285	-2,8942	13,4664	54,9538
PZ 90.02, epoch 2010.0						
193,9402	37,8741	110,7393	-16,3285	-0,5942	9,9264	59,1638
PZ 90.00, epoch 2002.0						
193,5202	38,0286	110,6000	-231,0905	3,9042	2,7766	213,1286

The data in table 7 also indicated that the discrepancy between the two PZ-90.00 coordinate values for the Asia Pacific network is large by comparision with GPS marine network. The standard deviation were at ± 1dm level for Asia Pacific network , but only were at ± 0.7dm level for GPS marine network . Conversely, the standard deviation for PZ-90.02 and PZ-90.11 coordinates for Asia Pacific network were slight smaller than GPS marine network. The standard deviation values ± 0.5dm, ± 1dm and ± 0.4dm for Z, Y and Z coodinates, respectively.

Table 7. The standard deviation between the two PZ – 90 coordinate values, one derived from ITRF coordinates and the other derived from VN-2000 coordinates

Networks	PZ–90 products	Standard deviation			
		σ_X(m)	σ_Y(m)	σ_Z (m)	σ_{xyz} (m)
GPS marine Network	PZ-90.00	±0,0445	±0,1049	±0,0342	±0,0687
	PZ-90.02 PZ-90.11	±0,0530	±0,0738	±0,0340	±0,0560
Asia Pacific Network	PZ-90.00	±0,0536	±0,1523	±0,0440	±0,0966
	PZ-90.02 PZ-90.11	±0,0488	±0,0707	±0,0271	±0,0520

6. Conclusion

A vital segment of a nation's positioning infrastructure is the determination and maintenance of transformations from widely used global reference frames to the national geodetic datum. In this study, 14 transformation parameters between ITRF products and VN-2000 have been estimated using 10 stations located in Vietnam of network in the (APRGP) GPS campaign. The outcome of this study indicate that these parameters can be used to transform ITRF to VN-2000 with accuracy of ±0.06m or better, they therefore meet most the demands for average level of data accuracy. However, it is not the final answer to the problem, but rather an interim solution. For higher-precision applications, a generation of better transformation parameters between these systems is required.

Because it is difficult for determining WGS84 and PZ-90 coordinates with a high level of accuracy so the parameters for transformation from the VN-2000 to the WGS84 and PZ-90 were determined based on the coordinate transformation parameters between VN-2000 and ITRS. The test results showed that transformation parameters, on the basis of the results at the checkpoints, could generated station positions with the accuracy at several cm level for transformation from VN-2000 to the new realizations of WGS84 and PZ90 and reversely.

The results of the link between VN-2000 and ITRS, WGS84 and PZ-90 meeted the demand of practical tasks with medium accuracy requirements. However, in the future, the accuracy of these parameters will be improved with the addition of more accurate GPS coordinates in both the ITRS and VN-2000.

Acknowledgments:
The work presented in this paper was supported by a research grant from the Natural Resources and Environment of the Socialist Republic of Vietnam.

REFERENCES

1. Decision on the use of Vietnam's national references and coordinate datumm, No: 83/2000/QD-TTg of Prime Minister of Vietnam.Vietnam Government. No: 83/2000/QD-TTg. (2000)

2. Decision on the use of coordinate transformation parameters between international coordinate system 1984 (WGS-84) and Vietnamese coordinate datum (VN-2000), No. 05/2007/ QD-BTNMT of Minister of Vietnamese Natuaral resources and environmental Ministry Vietnam, Minister of Vietnam Natuaral resources and environmental Ministry No. 05/2007/QD-BTNMT. (2007)

3. C. Boucher and Z. Antamimi (2001). ITRS, PZ-90 and WGS 84: current realizations and the related transformation parameters. Journal of Geodesy, **75**: 913-619.

4. G. Trần Bạch (2003). Introduction of Vietnam national reference and coordinate system (VN-2000). Department of Surveying, Mapping and Geoinformation of Vietnam, Vietnam

5. Z. Altamimi (2012), Role and importance of the International Terrestrial Reference Frame for sustainable development. Available on https://unstats.un.org/unsd/geoinfo/RCC/docs/rccap19/Side%20events/IAG-GGOS-ITRF-report2UNRRC-10Oct2012.pdf

6. Z. Altamimi, X. Collilieux, J. Legrand, B. Garayt and C. Boucher (2007). ITRF2005: A new release of the International Terrestrial Reference Frame based on time series of station positions and Earth Orientation Parameters. *J. Geophys. Res. Solid Earth*, **112,** B09401, doi:10.1029/2007JB00494

7. C. Boucher, Z. Altamimi and L. Duhem (1993). ITRF 92 and its associated velocity field, Technical Note

15. Paris, France,Central Bureau of the IERS, Observatoire de Paris.

8. C. Boucher, Z. Altamimi and P. Sillard (1998). Results and analysis of the ITRF96, Technical Note 24. Paris, France, Central Bureau of the IERS, Observatoire de Paris.
9. C. Boucher, Z. Altamimi and P. Sillard (1999). The 1997 International Terrestrial Reference Frame (ITRF97), Technical Note 27. Paris, France, Central Bureau of the IERS, Observatoire de Paris.
10. Z. Altamimi, P. Sillard and C. Boucher (2002). ITRF2000: A new release of the International Terrestrial Reference Frame for Earth science application. J. Geophys. Res. **107**(B10), 2214, doi:10.1029/2001JB000561.
11. Z. Altamimi, X. Collilieux, J. Legrand, L. Laurent (2011) ITRF2008: an improved solution of the international terrestrial reference frame. Journal of Geodesy, Vol. **85**(8), pp 457–473, doi:10.1007/s00190-011-0444-4
12. Z. Altamimi, R. Rebischung, L. Métivier and X. Collilieux (2016). ITRF2014: A new release of the International Terrestrial Reference Frame modeling nonlinear station motions, Journal of Geophysical Research. Journal of Geophysical Research, **121** (8): pp. 6109-6131, doi:10.1002/2016JB013098
13. http://lareg. ensg.ign.fr
14. Nga(2014). World geodetic System 1984. Its Definition and Relationships with Local Geodetic Systems.
15. S. Malys and J.A. Slater. Maintenance and Enhancement of the World Geodetic System 1984; Proceedings of ION GPS-94; Salt Lake City, Utah; September 1994.
16. http://eng.mil.ru/files/PZ-90.11_final-v8.pdf
17. Z. Altamimi, D. Angermann, D. Argus et al. (2001). The terrestrial reference frame and the dynamic Earth. Eos, Transactions, Am. Geophys. U., Vol. **82**(25): p. 273-279.
18. J. Dawson and A. Woods. ITRF to GDA94 coordinate transformations. Journal of Applied Geodesy, 4:189–199, 2010. doi:10.1515/JAG.2010.019.
19. C. Boucher, Z. Altamimi (1993). Specifications for reference frame fixing in the analysis of a EUREF GPS campaign. Available on http://etrs89.ensg.ign.fr/memo-V8.pdf.
20. S. Tomás (2014). Transformations between NAD83 (2011) and WGS84 (G1674). Available on https://www.ngs.noaa.gov/CORS/Articles/SolerWGS84(G1674)toNAD83(2011).pdf
21. B. Graeme et al (2014). *Reference Frames in Practice Manual, Commission 5 Working Group 5.2 Reference Frames*,FIG Guide 2014.
22. C. Jekeli (2016). *Geometric Reference Systems in Geodesy*. Division of Geodesy and Geospatial Science, School of Earth Sciences, Ohio State University
23. Project (APRGP) GPS Campaign 2013. Record 2014/34. Geoscience Australia: Canberra.
24. G. Hu (2012). Report on the Analysis of the Asia Pacifc Regional Geodetic Project (APRGP) GPS Campaign 2011. Record 2012/61. Geoscience Australia: Canberra.
25. G. Hu (2013). Report on the Analysis of the Asia Pacifc Regional Geodetic Project (APRGP) GPS Campaign 2012, Geoscience Australia.
26. G. Hu (2014). Report on the Analysis of the Asia Pacific Regional Geodetic
27. G. Hu (2016). Report on the Analysis of the Asia Pacific Regional Geodetic Project (APRGP) GPS Campaign 2015. Record 2016/20. Geoscience Australia, Canberra.
28. http://earth-info.nga.mil/GandG/sathtml

Integration of GNSS-IMU for increasing the observation accuracy in Condensed Areas (Infrastructure and Forest Canopies)

Mokhamad Nur Cahyadi[1] and *Irene* Rwabudandi[1]

[1]Geomatics Engineering Department, Institut Teknologi Sepuluh Nopember (ITS), Surabaya, Indonesia

Abstract. Position determination using satellite navigation system has grown significantly. It provides geo-spatial with global coverage called GNSS (Global Navigation System Satellite). GNSS satellites consists of GLONASS, GPS (Global positioning system) and Galileo.GPS is the most commonly used system and it is known to its capability to determine 3D position on the surface of the earth. In order to determine the position, a GPS receiver must be able to receive signals from at least four GPS satellites. However, the determination of position in condensed areas such as tunnels, area surrounded by high rise buildings, highly forested and in other closely-knit areas is not achieved because satellite signals cannot reach the receiver in the above-mentioned areas and also others where the signals are reflected before being received by a GPS receiver. In this paper, we present the algorithm to fuse GPS and the inertial measurement unit (IMU) to enable positioning in the above-mentioned Condensed Areas. The standard deviations of the two measurements show that GPS-IMU is better than GPS alone, the standard deviation when satellite outages occurred is - 4.57475 for GPS-IMU measurements and 0.218675 for GPS observations. We presented the results in graphics and it shows that GPS measurements are easily disturbed by external influence such as multipath but GPS-IMU graphic is continuous and robust. The advantages and disadvantages of GPS and INS are complementary and make them work together to enable the accurate measurements in the areas mentioned above. Integration of INS and GNSS can be classified into three types, loosely coupled Kalman filter, tightly coupled Kalman filters and ultra- tight coupled Kalman filter. In this research we used loosely coupled Kalman filter and tightly coupled Kalman filters to combine GPS and INS in one system.

1 Introduction

Nowadays, researchers have been recognized the advantages of combining the Global Navigation satellite system with the inertial navigation sensors. GNSS measurements encounters several errors due to the space segment, the user or receiver locations, signal propagation etc. [1]. The idea behind GNSS positioning is that at least four satellites must be visible in the horizon of the receiver. However, this conditions in not fulfilled in the extended GNSS signals denied environments such as in the tunnels, urban area with high rise buildings, in very dense forests and in other indoor environments. A further development is the INS (Inertial Navigation System) sensor application with acquisition data rate about 200 Hz, which the capability is greater than the GNSS data rate. The integration of GNSS and INS, has advantages in accuracy of measurement, especially in areas where satellite signals cannot be received by receiver.

Inertial Navigation System is defined as the sensor which represents sensitivity in the force and rotation. The force in this case is due to gravitational field of the earth, whereas the rotation in this case is due to rotation of the earth. This system consists of three main parts; the first part is gyroscope as the rotation sensor, the second part is accelerometer as the motion sensor and the third part is computer which is used to calculate the movement of vehicles [2]. Gyroscope and accelerometer observe continuously in position, velocity and attitude, in which the calculation is conducted in the specified reference frame with certain formula. An inertial navigation system determines components of the position, velocity and attitude by integrating acceleration and rotation which is occurred in the inertial reference system (such as body reference frame or global reference frame). The errors which is occurred in this sensor increases linearly as function of time. In reality, there are several applications of inertial navigation system, such as aircraft navigation, submarine, ships, and the strategic of the missile.

The Integration of the INS and GNSS have a such phenomenon which the INS sensor generates the position, velocity and attitude in faster rate than GNSS sensor. The INS sensor consists of triad accelerometer (for measuring acceleration rate), triad gyroscope (for measuring rotation rate) and a computer which is used to do calculation (Munguia, 2014). The calculation means integrate the position, velocity and attitude. Then the result of this calculation tuns out to be the output of INS sensor. So, the error that occurred in this process is due to position, velocity and attitude. The error is potentially unbounded.

* Corresponding author: cahyadi@geodesy.its.ac.id

On the other hand, GNSS receiver that generates position and velocity has bounded error. Actually, GNSS also can be used to observe the attitude. However, attitude measurement is more complicated, so INS sensor was chosen for attitude measurement. The output quality of the GNSS sensor has bounded error in position and velocity measurement. Moreover, it can be concluded that GNSS and INS sensor have complementary attributes. It means that position and velocity estimation from GNSS can also be used as the calibration process of the INS output (position, velocity and acceleration). The application of the INS is also important when the satellite outage of the GNSS occurs.

As described above, there are some weakness and strengths in GPS application, as well as INS application. GPS has a high accuracy in the determination of position in a long period of time. However, the GPS cannot work properly when located in areas where satellite signals cannot be received by a receiver. For example, in the areas surrounded by many high-rise buildings or measurements conducted in the tunnel. In this case, buildings cause multipath, so satellite signal is not directly received by the receiver. The signals are reflected by buildings and then received by a receiver. On the other hand, in the tunnel, receiver cannot receive satellite signals. The objective of this research is to Integrate GPS-IMU for Increasing the Observation Accuracy in Dense Areas, with respect to the error behavior of each system, and the relationship between the satellite outage and accuracy generated by each system.

2 Measurement Systems

The objective of this research is to combine GPS with IMU to enable positioning in the satellite's signals attenuation areas.

2.1 Inertial navigation Unit (IMU)

IMU is a sensitive device consists of three main parts; the first part is gyroscope as the rotation sensor, the second part is accelerometer as the motion sensor and the third part is computer which is used to calculate the movement of vehicles. Gyroscope and accelerometer observe continuously in position, velocity and attitude, in which the calculation is conducted in the specified reference frame with certain formula. A computer performs signal conditioning and temperature compensation, the accelerometer and gyroscope data outputs are velocities and angular rates via a serial interface Computer at a rate of 100HZ to 1000HZ [3].

2.2 Inertial Navigation System (INS)

The inertial navigation system principle stands for solving Newton's equations of the rotation of the earth, this has made possible by integrating the acceleration and angular rates sensed by IMU [3]. The following process is to initialize the inertial navigator with known position and velocity from GPS and aligned with respect to the vertical and true North. After the alignment, the inertial navigator has established a local level mathematical frame of reference called the navigation frame whose heading with respect to North in this case the orientation of IMU must be known.

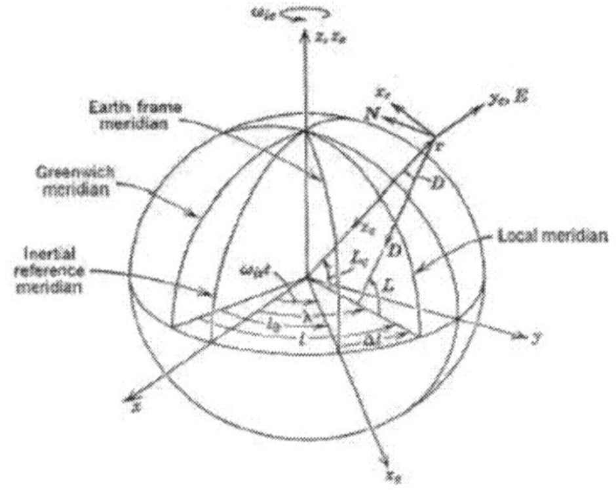

Fig. 1. Reference frames used in INS [3]

3 Results and Analysis

The objective of this study is to test and compare IMU-GNSS and GNSS alone measurements in dense area, we also compared the RMS errors of two systems and the relationship between the satellite outage and accuracy generated by each system. The data used was collected in Tainan near National Cheng Kung University. Both methods were evaluated with different solutions, forward and smoothing operation. Data post processing of GNSS solutions will also be compared with the integration of these two methods. Reference stations used in this research are three different reference stations.

In this research, two methods were compared to each other. The first method is GNSS only. In this method, two main processes, data post processing of GNSS solution are conducted by one process only. The first step is calculation of the GNSS post processing and the second step is integration of result of GNSS post processing with INS. The second method of integration navigation system is loosely coupled Kalman filter which is solved by Geopointer software. In this software, both two main steps of the calculation, which are GNSS post processing and integration of the GNSS- INS, are solved separately.

3.1 The Kalman filter process

The Kalman filter process is a mechanization which takes dynamic model of the system, measurement, deterministic input with the certain algorithm to blend all of the input parameter to get estimation [4]. This section will explain the basic concept of the linear Kalman filtering.

The equation can be explained in the following way. The is an (*nx1*) state vector, (*ti, ti-1*) is an (*nxn*) system transition matrix, *G* (*ti-1*) is an (nxs) noise input matrix, and *w* (*ti-1*) is an (*sx1*) white Gaussian noise (Bulut, Cavanaugh, & Bernal, 2010):

$$x(t_i) = \Phi(t_i, t_{i-1})x(t_{i-1}) + G(t_{i-1})w(t_{i-1}) \tag{1}$$

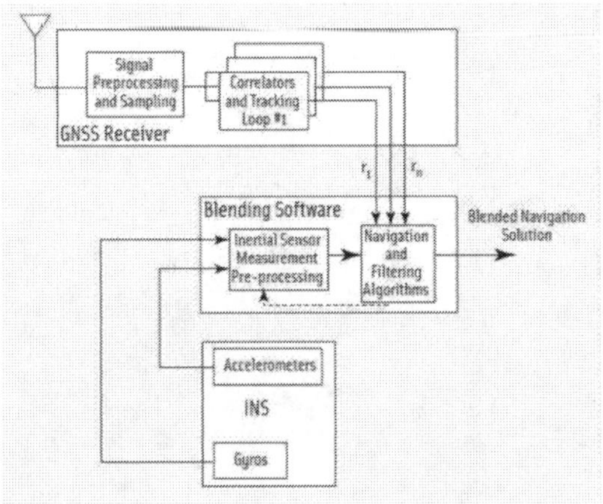

Fig. 2. The Kalman filter process

The non-linear observation is written as follows:

$$Z(t_i) = h[x(t_i), t_i] + v(t_i) \tag{2}$$

Where $Z(ti)$ is an $(mx1)$ measurement vector, $h[x(ti), ti)]$ is an $(mx1)$ non-linear measurement model vector, and $v(ti)$ is an $(mx1)$ white Gaussian measurement noise vector.

Kalman filter can be divided into several sequences in three steps, initial condition information, filter propagation, and filter update.

3.2 Kalman Filter Initial Condition Equations

The equation in this process can be written as follow:

$$\hat{X}(t_0) = E\{X(t_0)\} = \hat{X}_0$$
$$P(t_0) = E\left\{\left[X_0(t_0) - \hat{X}_0\right]\left[X_0(t_0) - \hat{X}_0\right]^T\right\} = P_0 \tag{3}$$

This is detailed by [5].

3.3 INS/GPS Integration

In this research, we use Geopointer to integrate GPS with INS.GPS data were collected separately with GPS-IMU data. This software is used to process GPS data to provide time, position and velocity, to process IMU/GPS integration data in the loosely coupled and tightly coupled integration, apply the extended Kalman filter (EKF) and smoothing in data processing to provide optimal navigation solutions including position, velocity and orientation, to provide functions for coordinates transformation, to provide graphical interface to display graphical navigation solutions and overlay map and finally it provides a textual editor interface to show and edit text.

The result of this research shows the comparison between GNSS and GNSS-IMU when satellite outage occurs. It's located in the area surrounded by many buildings and trees. Hence, GNSS receiver cannot obtain satellite signals in short of time. The error occurred before satellite signal outage in this area is multipath error, because of many high-rise buildings, it could be also seen from the DOP and VDOP value is 6.7. This phenomenon can be seen from the error of the GNSS solution only increased before satellite outage occurred. The value of rms error during satellite signal outage is getting worse. This condition shows that GNSS-IMU is 25 up to 45 times better compare to GNSS solution only. GNSS solution only has a problem when there is a loss of GPS signal or phase ambiguity from cycle slip. It could be seen from the figure after satellite signal outage during 45 seconds. The value of rms error requires more or less 4 seconds to become stable. It could be understood, because in the GNSS solution only, INS data cannot be used for ambiguity estimation. On the other hand, GNSS-IMU integration has a character of faster ambiguity estimation.

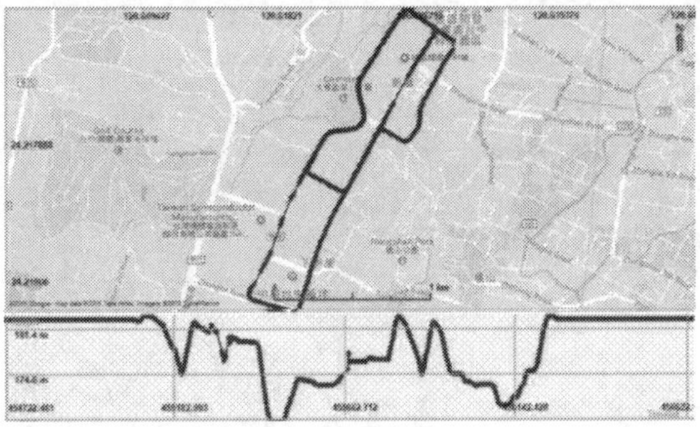

Fig. 3. GPS measurements trajectory

The figure above represents GPS measurements before being integrated with IMU, the trajectory is not continuous because the satellite outages occur several times. GPS recorded the data every single second. We computed the average time of the satellite outage and we found out that in 56 seconds GPS receiver was not recorded the data due to obstacles that surround the area.

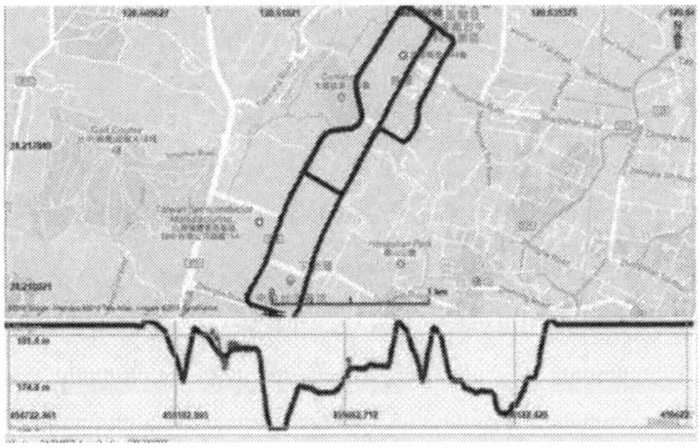

Fig. 4. GPS-IMU trajectory

The figure above shows the result of INS/GPS integration, GPS-IMU result shows that the system cannot be affected by external influences such as multipaths as shown in the figure 4 GPS-IMU makes a continuous, robust, and smooth trajectory and this made the system better than GPS measurements alone in figure 3, the trajectory is not continuous because of the occurrence of satellite outage. The standard deviations of the two measurements show that GPS-IMU is better than GPS alone, the standard deviation when satellite outages occurred is -4.57475 for GPS-IMU measurements and 0.218675 for GPS observations.

4 Conclusion

GNSS measurements encounter various errors when observing in an extended signal denied environment. The satellite outages affect the observation accuracy. However, INS/GPS integration is result in a very strong system that cannot be easily disturbed by satellite signals attenuation. In this paper we conclude that GPS-IMU system is far better than GPS system alone, this has proven by the comparison of RMS error of the two system. The RMS error of GPS system bigger than the RMS error of INS/GPS system and the trajectory graphics of the two systems show clearly that INS/GPS system is stronger than GPS alone.

References

1. Seeber, G. *Satellite Geodesy*. New York: Walter de Gruyter. (2003).
2. Munguia, R. *A GPS-aided Inertial Navigation System in Direct Configuration*. Journal of Applied Reasearch and Technology, 803-814. (2014).
3. Zhou, J., & Bolandhemmat, H. *Integrated INS/GPS Syatem for an Autonomous Mobile Vehicle.*
4. Bulut, Y., Cavanaugh, V. D., & Bernal, D. *Process and Measurement Noise Estimation for Kal,an Filtering*. Proceeding of the IMAC-XXVIII. (2010).
5. Suzdaleva, E. *Initial Condition for Kalman filtering: prior knowledge specification*. Proceeding of the 7th conference on 7th WSEAS International conference on systems Theory and scientific Computations, 45-49. (2007)

Latest GNSS signal in space developments – GPS, QZSS & the new Beidou 3 under examination

Steffen Thoelert[1,2]

[1]German Aerospace Center (DLR), Oberpfaffenhofen, 82234 Wessling, Germany
[2]Chair of Navigation, RWTH Aachen University, 52062 Aachen, Germany

Abstract. Nowadays one can use four global navigation satellite systems (GNSS). Two of them are complete constellations (GPS, Glonass) and two (Beidou, Galileo) are already usable and will be finish in the near future. Additionally satellite based augmentation systems (SBAS) like WAAS, EGNOS, GAGAN or QZSS complement the GNSS service. However, within all systems one can observe changes, modifications, and updates every year. This can be related to satellite renewables leading to signal property changes. Especially, for safety critical applications using GNSS, like advanced receiver autonomous integrity monitoring (ARAIM) or ground-based augmentation systems (GBAS) the new or changed signal properties are of high interest. With the help of detailed information about the signal deformation and the received signal power it is possible to calculate realistic error bounds and consequently realistic protection level for these kinds of safety critical applications. This paper presents an overview of the findings according new signals or signal configurations of GPS, Beidou and QZSS of the last two years. After a brief introduction of the measurement facility the paper will introduce basic analysis about the quality of the signal shape in spectral and modulation domain. Using our precise calibrated measurement facility, we will also present an analysis of the transmitted satellite signal power including estimates about the power sharing among individual signal components within each band. Considering the measured power in relation to the boresight angle of the satellite one can derive a cut through the antenna pattern of the satellite and can assess the antenna symmetry properties. Examples for different satellites will be presented. Finally, we will end with a conclusion regarding the considered signal developments and its impact on GNSS users.

1 Introduction

Global navigation satellite systems (GNSS) are used in thousands of applications all over the globe. Thus, it is not surprising that they are constantly modernized, supplemented and developed further. In the focus of this paper are the L-band signal transmissions of GPS, Beidou and QZSS. Changes in the signal transmission can vary from simple changes in signal power up to the entire signal structure or the frequency range. Even completely new signals can be added or signal components are turned off.

The Chinese Beidou navigations system (BDS) is one of the most rapidly growing satellite navigation systems of the last years. Started as a local navigation system, it is currently expanding into a global one with a launch frequency of approximately two satellites every two months. This development to a global system implies not only the expansion of the coverage but also a significant change of the transmitted signals and services to serve a wider range of applications and to achieve better compatibility to existing GNSS and consequently less implementation effort at manufacturer side, and therefore better competitiveness.

Approved information about all of the provided Beidou 3 signals and services are still not available. The paper will fill this lack of knowledge and the expectations in the navigation community e.g. collected and presented in [1] and the released interface control documents (ICDs) which have been published within the last 12 month.

While Beidou and QZSS have evolved over the past few years to their expansion plan, GPS has been a long established system. But even in a fully developed system, changes in the radiated signal can also be observed. This happened for instance in 2017 for all GPS-IIR-M satellites as reported in [7] and [12].

Usually common GNSS receivers are used for monitoring of signals. But typically they provide only information about the legacy signals for GPS for

 https://doi.org/10.1051/e3sconf/20199403016

instance L1 C/A and P(Y) pseudo code tracking. Neither information about the M-code nor the interplex signals are available from receiver measurements to assess e.g. for GPS the complete overview about the new power sharing of the IIR-M satellites.

Therefore, a special measurement facility is used to gather data for the analysis of the latest constellation updates. The German Space Operations Center (GSOC) of the German Aerospace Center (DLR) operates a 30 m dish antenna at its ground station in Weilheim (Germany). This antenna is regularly used by DLR's Institute of Communication and Navigation (IKN) for the analysis of GNSS signals [9]. The antenna provides a gain of about 50 dB and supports spectrum, inphase/quadrature (IQ), and calibrated power measurements covering the lower and upper L-Band. A detailed summary of the current measurement setup is given in Thoelert et al. (2013). Using such an instrument, the GNSS signals are raised above the noise floor and the gathered data provide a suitable basis for precise signal analysis.

2 GPS

GPS Block IIR-M and Block IIF satellites have the capability to redistribute transmit power between individual signal components. This so-called flex power can be used for increased protection against jamming and was already demonstrated in September 2010.

Since February 2017 GPS has changed the configuration of the transmit power of the L1 signal components (C/A-, P(Y)-, M-code) of the GPS IIR-M satellites [12]. Nearly at the same time, since January 2017, a geographically driven flex power mode is enabled on ten Block IIF satellites [7]. This is visible in carrier-to-noise density ratio observations of ground-based GPS receivers as well as differential code bias estimates between the L1 C/A- and P(Y)-code signals [6].

The signals of the GPS IIF satellites were also measured at the DLR ground station at Weilheim, Germany with a high gain antenna and a connected L-band measurement system. For the present work, L1/L2 signal spectra of GPS satellites have been obtained to highlight the presence or amplitude variation of different modulations in the course of flex power tests. These are complemented by in-phase and quadrature (IQ) measurements, which are the basis for the evaluation of the relative power distribution among individual signal components. Various calculation methods are described in detail in [12].

Figure 1 shows the L1 spectral flux density of the Block IIF satellite G065 with and without flex power mode. The blue curve recorded on 25 March 2018 at 10:34 UTC represents the nominal signal transmission including C/A-, P(Y)-, and M-code. The sharp peak at 1575.25 MHz represents the 1 MHz C/A-code whereas the smaller broader dome at the same center frequency is caused by the 10 MHz P(Y)- code. The BOC(10,5) binary offset carrier modulation of the M-code introduces the two lobes at 1565 and 1585 MHz.

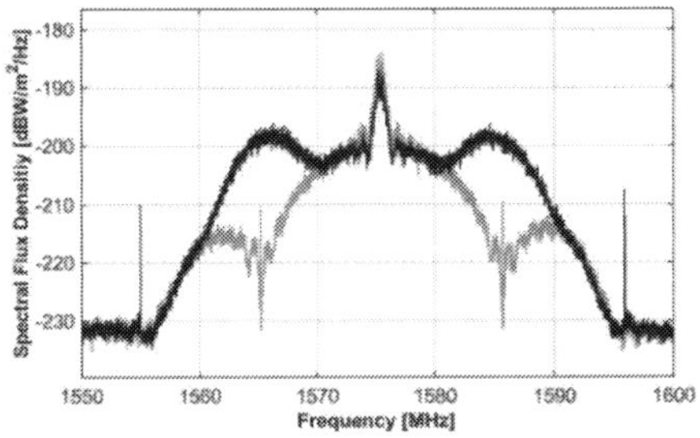

Figure 1 L1 spectral flux density of the GPS Block IIF satellite G065 (NAVSTAR 67) on 25 March 2018. Blue: nominal transmission including M-code at 10:34 UTC. Green: flex power mode without M-code transmission at 10:42 UTC

The green curve was acquired 5 minutes later after the switch to flex power mode. Obviously, the M-code lobes have disappeared and the smaller sidelobes of the P(Y)-code at 1560 and 1590 MHz become visible. Clearly, one can see that the C/A- code flux density is slightly increased. The question is, how was the power redistributed in this frequency band? Figure 2 depicts the equivalent isotropic radiated power (EIRP) measured over the complete frequency range from 1550 MHz until 1605 MHz. At the switch over from nominal to flex power mode the band power drops about 0.6 dB. Thus not the complete M-code power was transferred to the C/A-code. The reason for this might be a constraint regarding the constant envelope condition, which is a common goal for an effective power amplifier operation.

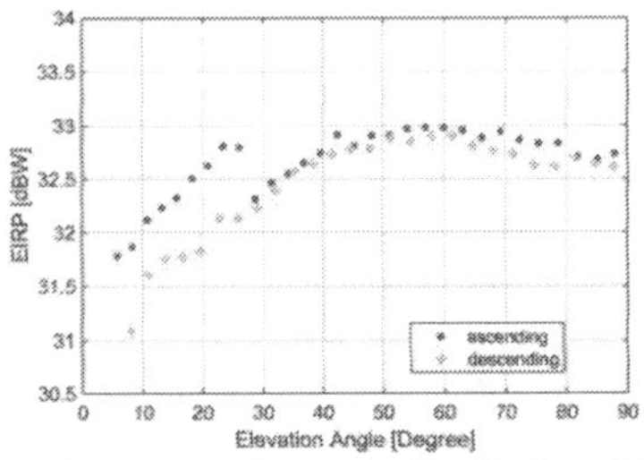

Figure 2 L1 Equivalent Isotropically Radiated Power (EIRP) of G065. 23 March 2018: nominal transmission including C/A-, P(Y)-, and M-code until approximately 27 degree elevation, then switch to flex power mode resulting in an EIRP reduction of about 0.6 dB

A different flex power setting was observed in April 2018. In contrast to the permanent installation of the geographically driven flex power mode described above, the configuration of the transmit power between the GPS components changed not only in L1 and also in L2 frequency band. Figure 3 and Figure 4 illustrate the change within the L1 band and L2 band based on calibrated spectral representations of the acquired data, respectively.

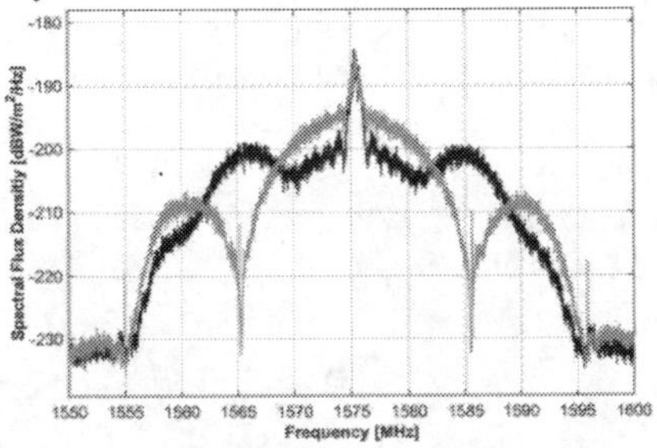

Figure 3 L1 spectral flux density of the GPS Block IIR-M satellite G055 (NAVSTAR 60). Blue: nominal transmission including M- code on May 11, 2018 at 05:06 UTC. Green: flex power mode without M-code transmission on April 17, 2018 at 09:01 UTC

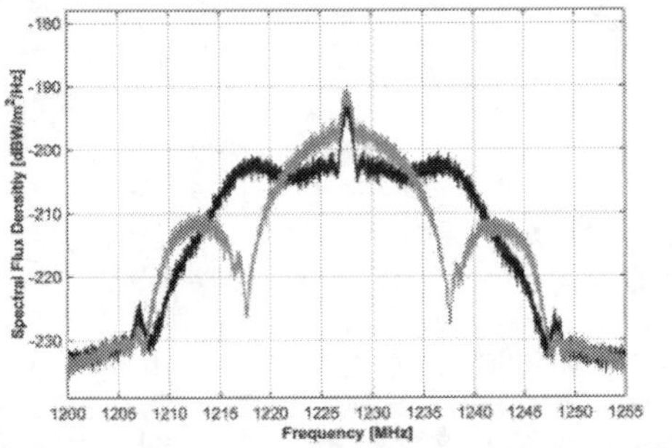

Figure 4 L2 spectral flux density of the GPS Block IIR-M satellite G055 (NAVSTAR 60). Blue: nominal transmission including M- code on May 11, 2018 at 05:07 UTC. Green: flex power mode without M-code transmission on April 17, 2018 at 09:02 UTC.

Similar to the first flex power mode the M-code has been switched off. But in contrast to the first flex power mode the focus of the redistribution of the power was obviously to increase the P(Y)-code instead of the C/A-code. While the power of the P(Y)-code have been increased by approximately 6 dB in L1 and 5 dB in L2 the C/A-code respectively L2C-code remain nearly constant.

Table 1 Transmit power changes due to flex power on 17 April 2018. Average values of G052 and G065 are given.

SVN	Mode	L1				L2			
		C/A	P(Y)	M	IM	L2C	P(Y)	M	IM
G052	Normal	35%	18%	30%	17%	25%	27%	23%	25%
	Flex II	32%	68%			23%	77%		
G065	Normal	31%	16%	34%	19%	30%	24%	25%	21%
	Flex II	31%	69%			29%	71%		

Consequences of these transmit power changes are not only the power variation itself, but also an influence on the pseudorage and consequently the resulting differential code bias (DCB). Further information about the observed flex power activities on GPS and the effect according the differential code bias can be found in [6].

3 Beidou 3

The Chinese Beidou navigations system (BDS) is one of the most rapidly growing satellite navigation systems of the last years. It starts 2000 with a demonstration phase with 3 geostationary test platforms. In a second step it has been expanded to a local navigation system with 16 space crafts in total [13]. In 2015 the Chinese have been started updating their system from a regional to a global one with the launch of their first Beidou 3 satellite. This development to a global system implies not only the expansion of the coverage but also a significant change of the provided signals and services to achieve better compatibility to existing GNSS and consequently less implementation effort at manufacturer side and therefore better competitiveness.

Until mid of 2017 the information about the Beidou 3 signals and services were very fragmentary. From official statements and information circulated in the navigation community draft overviews according to service type, frequency and spreading modulations were collected and presented in [1] and [8].

Within the last 10 month interface control documents (ICDs) regarding the new signal components B1C, B3I and B2a have been released, which provide detailed information about signal structure, modulation, coding, message types and structure etc.

The first satellite, which has been transmitting the new signals, was BDS I2-S. The transmission was started on August 10, 2015. Researcher from different research entities like JRC, Italy and DLR, Germany and from China as well as commercial company JAVAD GNSS observed and analyzed the signal of that particular satellite [2].

Based on their analysis they confirmed the presence of a time multiplexed binary offset carrier (TMBOC) signal and its power sharing between its individual components and an additional BOC(14,2) and a legacy B1I signal (Beidou phase 2) at L1-14 Mhz. The researchers at JAVAD GNSS have validated not only signals on L1 but also at E5a and E5b frequencies and gave a first impression on the signal strength which users can expect on ground. This first satellite transmitting the new Beidou 3 signal belongs to a group of test satellites for validation purposes [1] but with operational capability.

However, even at this time there are no complete information about the capabilities and the provided signals as well as services of the final Beidou 3 system and its satellites are available. Therefore, the DLR captured spectral and I-Q-data from the latest Beidou satellites to provide information about the currently transmitted signals of the Beidou 3 system. Figure 5 provides a spectral overview, recorded at our measurement facility at Weilheim, Germany on October 1, 2018.

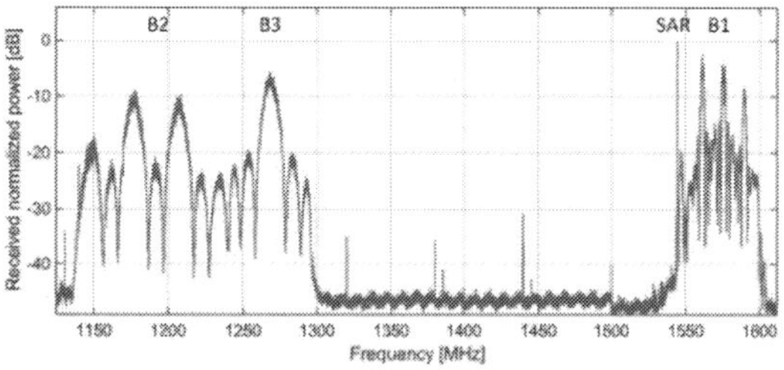

Figure 5 Power Spectra of Beidou 3 M13 captured October 1, 2018.

Based on the captured spectra one can see signal transmissions in B1, B2 and B3 band within the L-band. Clearly on can also observe a sharp peak at around 1544 MHz. This represents a signal of a search and rescue (SAR) transmitter. Further, analysis of the recorded IQ data show that the B1 signal contains transmissions of a BOC(1,1) data + pilot complemented by a BOC(6,1,4/33) in a QMBOC version which is in line with the published ICDs as expected. Furthermore BOC(14,2) components on I and Q channel were identified and the legacy B1I signal from Beidou 2.

Aside the identification about the provided signals of the new Beidou 3 satellites, the transmitted signal power is of interest for users. Especially, for the usability analysis of applications in areas with degraded receive signal strength it is important that there is still enough signal power remaining for receiver operation. Within the existing literature no information about the transmitted signal power can be found. Figure 6 shows the equivalent isotropic radiated power (EIRP) of two Beidou 3 satellites. The BDS- 3 M1-S is one satellite of the mentioned test satellite series labeled with the "-S" in the end and the other curve is obtained from a final Beidou 3 series, the BDS-3 M1. The EIRP is calculated using the calibrated sum over the complete B1 frequency band and the free space loss based on the geometric distance between satellite and ground station. The curves within the figure represent the full overflight of each satellite according the measurement station, separated by different markers in the ascending and descending part. This is helpful to assess the symmetry of the satellite antenna pattern. For a symmetric pattern the ascending and the descending curve has to be overlaid, which is the case for the BDS-3 M1 satellite. Regarding the BDS-3 M1-S satellite a pattern asymmetry is obviously.

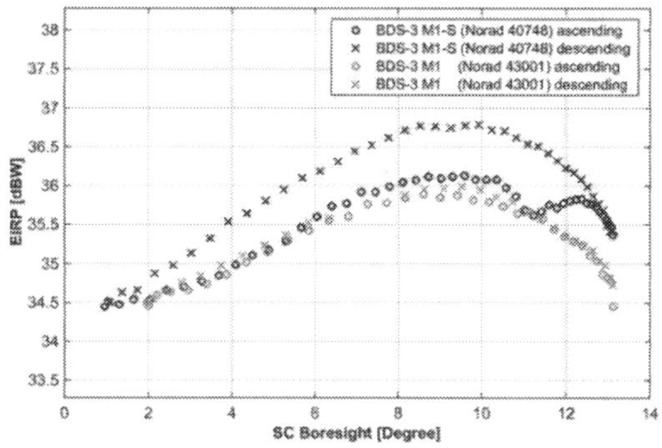

Figure 6 EIRP measurements of Beidou 3 satellites in the B1-band

Note that the pattern of the BDS-3 M1 is not necessarily fully symmetric. However, the measured cut through the satellite's pattern provide symmetry. The total transmit power within the B1 band is similar, just slightly higher for the M1-S considering the average over the complete path. QZSS

4 QZSS

The Japanese Quasi-Zenith Satellite System (QZSS) is a regional augmentation system to provide highly precise and stable positioning services in the Asia-Oceania region, which is compatible with GPS. The first QZS satellite "Michibiki" was launched in 2010. In June 2017 the second satellite QZS-2, or Michibiki-2, was launched and started transmitting signals since June 27. Followed by QZS-3 and QZS-4 in August and October the same year the planned constellation has been completed. All 4 satellites have been placed into inclined geosynchronous, elliptical orbits, which enable extended satellite visibility periods over Japan and are characteristic features for this regional navigation system.

Similar to Beidou 3 the Japanese QZSS experienced an update with the implementation of new signals since the launch of the QZS-2 satellite. Figure 7 show the spectral overview of transmitted signal within the L-band.

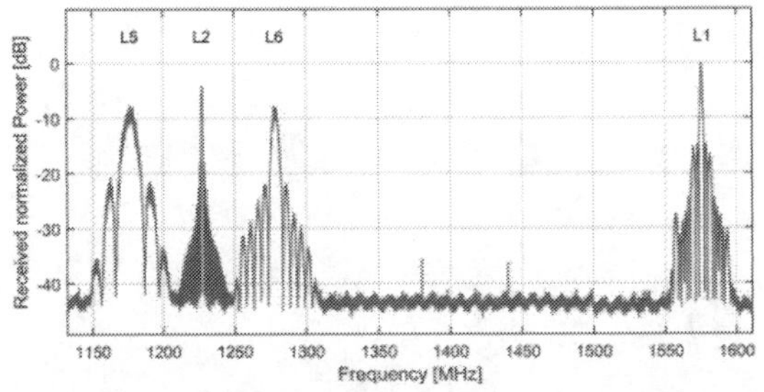

Figure 7 QSZ-2 L-band normalized power spectra recorded at Weilheim, Germany, on August 17, 2017.

A first measurement of the signals shows a good spectral shape, appropriate band filtering and no out- of-band unwanted spurious emissions of the satellite. For further analysis, we looked closer at each signal-band spectrum and the performed IQ-sample recordings.

Comparing the QZS-2 spectra to that of QZS-1, we see differences in the signal structure for the L1 frequency band. Figure 8 shows the L1 spectra of both satellites. The additional signal component at 6 x 1.023 MHz and 18 x 1.023 MHz can be clearly seen. This is the result of the new L1C-pilot modulation, which is based on the time-multiplexed binary offset carrier (TMBOC) modulation technique using a mixture of BOC(1,1) and BOC(6,1).

Other differences are present in the L5 and L6 band. More details can be found in [11] and [5]. Summarizing the new facts, within L5 an additional L5S signal has been transmitted by QZS-2 and the following spacecrafts, while in the L6 band a new component has been transmitted on the Q-component. On QSZ-2-4, an additional L6 signal component (Centimeter-Level Augmentation Message for Experiments, L6E) is implemented.

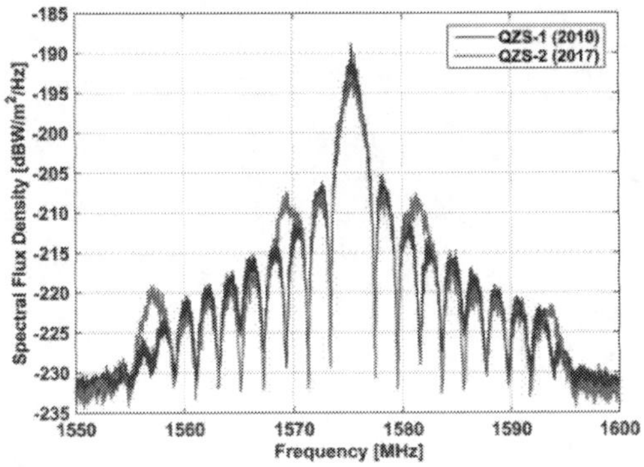

Figure 8 QZS-1 and QZS-2 L1 spectral flux density [Thoelert 2017].

5 Summary and Conclusion

The paper collected new as well as previously published information about signal in space developments of GPS, Beidou and QZSS over the last two years. We focused on flex power activities of GPS and the latest system implementations and updates of Beidou and QZSS. The presented examples show that signal changes respectively modifications can occur not only in the course of the implementation or modernization of a GNSS (like within Beidou and QZSS) but also within long-established systems, as described for the GPS signal power modifications in 2017 and 2018. The goal according the GPS activity can be just a test of the capability of the spacecrafts or to establish a new power sharing between the individual signal components within a frequency band for a more efficient energy consumption of the satellite payload, e.g. implemented for all GPS IIR-M satellites in 2017 [12]. Further aims can also be a system updates to provide more service variety, positioning accuracy or better compatibility with other system which may be able to relate to Beidou 3 or QZSS.

The presented examples for new or modified signals respectively signal power within the paper show that regular monitoring of the GNSS satellites could be beneficial to detect these changes and provide compensation if necessary. This is essential especially for safety-critical applications or for applications using prior knowledge of satellite properties, for instance in GNSS reflectometry applications like bi-static radar for calibration purposes. The presented events also indicate that modifications can be temporary or permanent.

References

1. Betz JW (2015) Engineering Satellite-Based Navigation and Timing. Wiley

2. Bravaro M, Curran J, Fortuny J (2015) First Signals of Beidou Phase 3 Acquired at Ispra, Italy. *GPS World*, Vol. **26** (9)

3. Cameron A (2015) New BeiDou TMBOC Signal Tracked; Similar to Future GPS L1C Structure. *GPS World*, Vol. **26** (10)

4. Steigenberger P, Thoelert S, Montenbruck O (2018a) GNSS satellite transmit power and its impact on orbit determination. *J Geod* **92**(6):609–624. https://doi.org/10.1007/s00190-017-1082-2

5. Steigenberger P, Thoelert S, Hauschild A, Montenbruck O, Langley R (2018b) Constellation completed: QZS-3 and QZS-4 join the Quasi-

Zenith Satellite System. *GPS World*, **29** (2), Page 43-48. ISSN 1048-5104

6. Steigenberger P, Thoelert S, Montenbruck O (2018c) GPS Flex power. *GPS Solutions* DOI: 10.1007/s10291-018-0797-8

7. Szilàgyi B, Bar-Sever Y, Bertiger W, Romans L (2017) New methodology and operational service for near- real-time calibration of GNSS inter-signal biases. In: ION GNSS+ 2017

8. Teunissen PJG and Montenbruck O (Eds.) (2017) *Springer Handbook of Global Navigation Satellite Systems*, Springer International Publishing, ISBN 978-3-319-42926-7, Page 1235

9. Thoelert S, Erker S, Meurer M (2009) *GNSS signal verifcation with a high-gain antenna—calibration strategies and high quality signal assessment.* In: Proc. ION ITM 2009, Institute of Navigation, Anaheim, California, USA, January 26–28, pp 289–300

10. Thoelert S, Furthner J, Meurer M (2013) *GNSS survey—Signal quality assessment of the latest GNSS satellites*. In: Proc. ION ITM 2013, Institute of Navigation, San Diego, California, USA, January 28–30, pp 608–615

11. Thoelert S, Hauschild A, Steigenberger P, Montenbruck O, Langley R (2017) Second QZSS signal on air. *GPS World*, Vol **28**(9), Page 10-14. ISSN 1048-5104

12. Thoelert S, Hauschild A, Steigenberger P, Langley R (2018) GPS IIR-M L1 transmit power redistribution: Analysis of GNSS receiver and high-gain antenna data. J Inst Navig DOI 10.1002/navi.250

13. Y. Yang (2017) *Chinese Navigation Satellite System. Springer Handbook of Global Navigation Satellite Systems.* Teunissen PJ and Montenbruck O, Eds. Springer International Publishing, Chap. 10, Page 280

Improving Detection Performance of Ionospheric Disturbances due to Earthquake by Optimization of Sequential Measurement Combination

Seonho Kang[1], Deokhwa Han[1], Junesol Song[2], Bugyeom Kim[1], Hyoungmin So[3], Gapjin Kim[3], Changdon Kee[1*]

[1]Mechanical and Aerospace Engineering, and the SNU-IAMD, Seoul National University, Seoul 08826, Korea

[2]Ecole Nationale de l'Aviation Civile (ENAC), Toulouse 31400, France

[3]Agency for Defense Development, Daejeon 305-600, Korea

Abstract. Energy generated from earthquake (EQ) is transferred to the ionosphere and results in co-seismic ionospheric disturbances (CID). CID can be observed in the ionospheric combination using L1, L2 frequency carrier phase. As ionospheric trend due to normal conditions such as elevation angle of satellites is generally larger than disturbances, a proper measure is required to extract disturbance signals. Derivative, or sequential combination, is a simple and effective way to remove the normal trend in the ionospheric delay. When using derivative, however, disturbance signals can often be obscured by noise due to its small amplitude. In order to reduce the noise while preserving the time rate of data, and thus to improve signal-to-noise ratio (SNR), we designed a new derivative method using optimization under a couple of assumptions. With simulation data, it is found that N, the number of epochs used for sequential combination, turned out to be the best when N=160 with maximum SNR. Finally, the proposed algorithm's SNR was compared to that of the previous study which also used derivative method. 120~260% improvements were observed for the proposed method compared to the conventional method.

1 Introduction

Global Navigation Satellite System (GNSS) measurement has various errors including satellite orbit error, satellite clock bias, receiver clock bias, ionospheric delay, tropospheric delay, multipath error, etc. As the ionospheric delay is proportional to the total electron content (TEC) from satellite to receiver, electron density in the ionosphere can be estimated using GNSS signal.

When earthquakes take place, the energy generated from the event is transferred to the atmosphere by ground-atmosphere coupling. Acoustic Gravity Wave (AGW) is responsible for the energy transfer, and with energy conservation and exponential decrease of air density with altitude, disturbance waves are magnified through propagation. This energy disturbs neutral particles in the ionosphere, which in turn disturb ions by momentum transfer [1, 2].

CID is comprised of several types. First type is induced by Rayleigh wave, the seismic wave on the ground which travels at 3.5km/s [3]. This CID is easily distinguishable from other types by its high speed. Second type is induced by direct acoustic wave from the ground source. Acoustic wave is generated from the abrupt vertical movement of the epicentre and moves upward and eventually reaches the ionosphere. The ionospheric disturbance by direct acoustic wave also shows horizontal movement, as the acoustic wave path is curved due to the variable temperature profile by altitude. There are also other types, including tsunami-induced gravity wave and ionospheric gravity wave that incur ionospheric disturbances. Among these various types of waves responsible for disturbances, CID by Rayleigh wave is the main interest in this study as it arrives first with dominant disturbance amplitudes.

In order to detect CID, normal trend needs to be removed. Generally, ionospheric delay measurement shows a U-shape along time series as a satellite rises and falls. This is mainly because ionospheric delay gets larger with low elevation angle, as signal travels longer path inside the ionosphere. There are other factors that contribute to the ionosphere such as diurnal change, seasonal change, solar activity, etc. However, these factors have long period (<1mHz) characteristics that their time rate is insubstantial compared to the main trend.

Several options are available to get rid of the normal trend. Commonly used are bandpass filter, moving average, and derivative. Among them, derivative is a relatively simple and intuitive method using linear combination of sequential measurements [4]. When there is CID, the derivative of ionospheric delay will be composed of three parts: the derivative of normal trend, noise, and CID. As ionospheric delay due to normal trend changes little for a short time, its derivative is quite small.

*Changdon Kee: kee@snu.ac.kr

Therefore, there remain noise and CID in the derivative of ionospheric delay.

If, however, CID amplitude is not big enough, chances are that CID would not stand out of the noise in the time series. Hence improving CID's SNR is a very important issue. Few studies, however, have focused on reducing the noise part of the derivative and thus improving the SNR of the signal. We propose a new method that deals with the issue which can enhance CID's SNR and improve detection performance.

2 Methodology

GPS L1, L2 carrier phase are denoted in the below. The GPS orbit error, multipath error and inter-frequency bias are assumed to be zero.

$$\phi_1 = d + B - b - I_1 + T + \lambda_1 N_1 + \epsilon_1$$

$$\phi_2 = d + B - b - I_2 + T + \lambda_2 N_2 + \epsilon_2 \quad (1)$$

Subscript 1 and 2 indicate L1, L2 frequency respectively. d is the distance between satellite to receiver, B receiver clock bias, b satellite clock bias, I ionospheric delay error, T tropospheric delay error, λ wavelengh of carrier phase, N ambiguity, and ϵ carrier phase noise. Ionospheric combination, or geometry-free combination can be derived in Eq(2).

$$\phi_{iono} = \frac{\phi_1-\phi_2}{\gamma-1} = I_1 + \frac{\lambda_1 N_1-\lambda_2 N_2}{\gamma-1} + \frac{\epsilon_1-\epsilon_2}{\gamma-1} \quad (2)$$

As the second term on the right side is a bias it disappears by taking derivative. In the end, the n-th derivative of ionopsheric combination is denoted as Eq(3).

$$\phi_{iono}^{(n)} = I_1^{(n)} + \frac{\epsilon_1^{(n)}-\epsilon_2^{(n)}}{\gamma-1} \quad (3)$$

CID is included in $I_1^{(n)}$. To derive the optimal sequential combination that can reduce the noise part, $\frac{\epsilon_1^{(n)}-\epsilon_2^{(n)}}{\gamma-1}$, while preserving $I_1^{(n)}$, two assumptions are adopted.

2.1 Assumptions

The first assumption is that the ionospheric delay can be approximated as linear for a short time. This assumption holds true as normal trends in the ionosphere have very long periods (>1000sec). As ionospheric delay by normal trend changes very slowly, it is nearly linear within a short time span.

The other assumption is that the noise in the ionospheric delay is Gaussian random. It means that there is no time correlation in the noise and it follows normal distribution. This assumption was adopted to simplify the calculation.

2.2 Minimum Noise Derivative (MND)

Ionospheric combination measurement can be denoted as follows. Notation is changed for concise expression.

$$f = g + v \quad (4)$$

where f is ionospheric combination, g true ionospheric delay, and v Gaussian noise with $v \sim N(0,\sigma^2)$. Now, Taylor series expansion for n sequential epochs are as follows.

$$f_{i+1} = f_i + hf_i' + O(h^2)$$

$$f_{i+2} = f_i + 2hf_i' + O(h^2)$$

$$\vdots$$

$$f_{i+n-1} = f_i + (n-1)hf_i' + O(h^2) \quad (5)$$

Here, the 2nd and higher order terms, $O(h^2)$, are zero in accordance with the first assumption. In order to get the derivative value at the i-th epoch, we will derive f_i' by linear combination of $f_i, f_{i+1}, \cdots, f_{i+n-1}$. Also, as this study deals with 1-sec interval data only, set h equal to 1.

$$a_1 f_{i+1} = a_1 f_i + f_i'$$

$$a_2 f_{i+2} = a_2 f_i + 2a_2 f_i'$$

$$\vdots$$

$$a_{n-1} f_{i+n-1} = a_{n-1} f_i + n a_{n-1} f_i' \quad (6)$$

By linear combination,

$$\begin{aligned} f_i' &= \frac{-[\Sigma_{k=1}^{n-1}(a_k)]f_i + \Sigma_{k=1}^{n-1}(a_k f_{i+k})}{\Sigma_{k=1}^{n-1}(k a_k)} \\ &= c_1 f_i + c_2 f_{i+1} + \cdots + c_n f_{i+n-1} \\ &= (c_1 g_i + c_2 g_{i+1} + \cdots + c_n g_{i+n-1}) \\ &\quad +(c_1 v_i + c_2 v_{i+1} + \cdots + c_n v_{i+n-1}) \\ &= g_i' + v_i' \end{aligned} \quad (7)$$

where g_i' is first derivative of ionospheric delay, and v_i' the derivative of noise at i-th epoch. The noise standard deviation (STD) of derivative, v'_i, is root square sum of its coefficients. That is,

$$v'_i \sim N\left(0, \sigma_{v'_i}\right) \ where \ \sigma_{v'_i} = \sqrt{\Sigma_{k=1}^{n} c_k^2} \quad (8)$$

Therefore, in order to minimize $\sigma_{v'_i}$, the square sum of sequential combination coefficients should be the minimum. Use zero gradient property at extreme values.

$$J = \Sigma c_i^2$$
$$= \frac{[\Sigma_{k=1}^{n-1}(a_k)]^2 + \Sigma_{k=1}^{n-1}(a_k^2)}{[\Sigma_{k=1}^{n-1}(ka_k)]^2}$$
$$= \frac{N}{D^2}$$

$$\frac{\partial J}{\partial a_i} = \frac{D^2\frac{\partial N}{\partial a_i} - 2ND\frac{\partial D}{\partial a_i}}{D^4} = 0 \quad (9)$$

where,

$$\frac{\partial N}{\partial a_i} = \frac{\partial}{\partial a_i}\{[\Sigma_{k=1}^{n-1}(a_k)]^2 + \Sigma_{k=1}^{n-1}(a_k^2)\}$$
$$= 2(\Sigma_{k=1}^{n-1} a_k + a_i) \quad (10)$$

$$\frac{\partial D}{\partial a_i} = \frac{\partial}{\partial a_i}\{\Sigma_{k=1}^{n-1}(ka_k)\} = i \quad (11)$$

With Eq(9-11) the following equation can be derived.

$$\frac{\Sigma_{k=1}^{n-1}(a_k) + a_1}{1} = \frac{\Sigma_{k=1}^{n-1}(a_k) + a_i}{i} \quad (i = 2,3, \dots, n-1) \quad (12)$$

Also, in the first row of Eq(7) it can be shown that the equation does not change even if the numerator and denominator are both divided by a_1. This means that f'_i is determined by relative size of $a_1, a_2, \dots, a_{n-1}$ and not by their absolute values. Therefore, as a pivot we can set a_1 equal to 1.

$$a_1 = 1 \quad (13)$$

Eq(12-13) have (n-1) equations in total and the number of unknowns, $a_1, a_2, \dots, a_{n-1}$, is also (n-1), which means that it is a solvable problem.

In the end, the sequential combination which minimizes noise level is,

$$f'_i = c_1 f_i + c_2 f_{i+1} + \dots + c_n f_{i+n-1} \quad (14)$$

where,

$$c_k = \frac{-6(n-1) + 12(k-1)}{(n-1)n(n+1)} \quad (k = 1,2, \dots, n)$$

Then STD of noise derivative, $\sigma_{v'_i}$ is

$$\sigma_{v'_i} = \sqrt{\frac{12}{(n-1)n(n+1)}}\sigma \quad (15)$$

Fig. 1 shows relative STD level by N, the number of epochs used for derivative. The y-axis is in log scale. As N increases, the noise level diminishes drastically. With N=100, for example, STD of derivative noise shrinks to 0.35% of its original noise STD, σ.

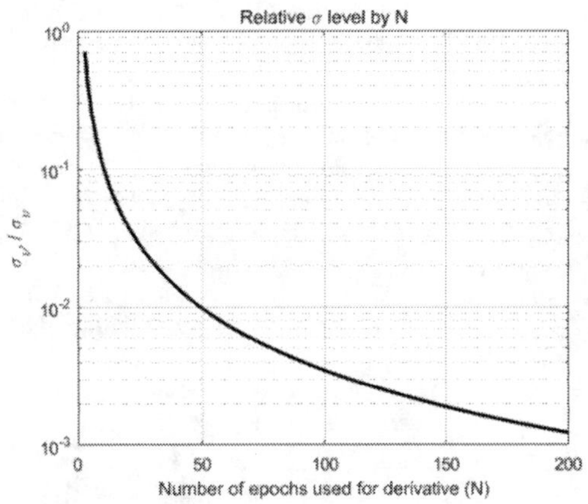

Fig. 1. Relative STD by N of the designed derivative method.

2.3 Derivative Level to Detect CID

Though normal condition trend changes slowly in the 1st derivative of ionospheric combination, it eventually makes an overall slant in time series. This is because unlike noise, normal trend accumulates with time for its low frequency. Hence, to completely remove the effect of normal trend, higher order derivatives are needed. We will use the 3rd derivative to detect CID as it contains no tendency in the normal condition. This is the same derivative level as the previous study [4].

2.4 N Selection by Simulation Data

SNR is widely used to indicate the relative amplitude of signal and ambient noise. It is defined as the ratio of signal variance to noise variance. This concept is important in CID detection as well, for SNR is closely related to detection. However, it is hard to calculated the variance of CID by Rayleigh wave as it lasts only for several minutes. Hence, here in this article we define SNR as the ratio of maximum absolute value of CID to STD of noise as shown in Eq(16). Here A indicates the maximum absolute value of CID by Rayleigh wave and σ_{noise} denotes STD of noise without CID.

$$\text{SNR} = \frac{A}{\sigma_{noise}} \quad (16)$$

While the designed derivative ensures the minimum noise level for its derivative, SNR of CID does not monotonically increase with N. This is because CID is not exactly linear for the time span N and induces error, which might curtail the peaks of CID in the derivative.

Therefore, we need to find the best N maximizing the SNR of CID.

Simulation data were used to find the best N. For data generation, CID was designed as a sine wave with amplitude 5 and period 225 sec. This period corresponds to the Airy phase of Rayleigh wave [5, 6]. Noise was modeled as Gaussian normal with STD value 1. For the ionospheric trend by elevation of satellites, 6 hr period sine wave with amplitude 10 was adopted. Here 6 hr period for normal trend is harsher than real trend, as typical normal trend has a 6 hr long U-shape, which can be approximated as one half of 12 hr period sine wave. Fig. 2 shows generated simulation data (black) and its pure CID (top, red). In the bottom plot, MND 3rd result with N=160 is drawn in red solid line. By using MND 3rd, CID is extracted with a sufficiently high SNR. Here SNR means the ratio of maximum absolute value in 2.8~3.2 hr to STD of 0.5~2.5 hr, as shown in the Fig. 2 bottom plot.

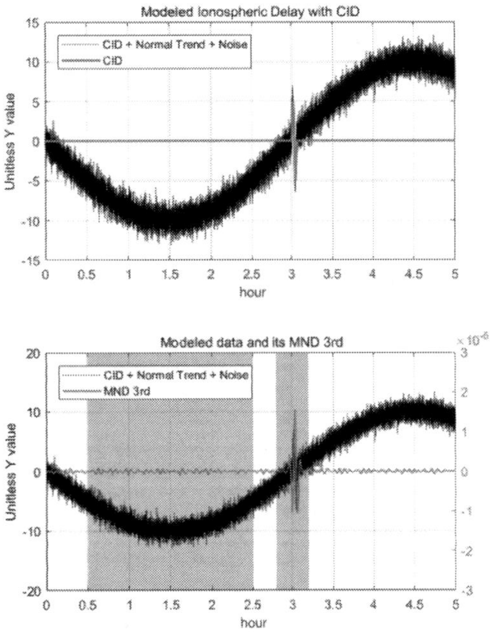

Fig. 2. Modeled ionospheric delay with CID (black), pure CID (top, red) and MND 3rd of modelled data (bottm, red). Shades represents the regions from which STD and maximum absolute value were calculated respectably.

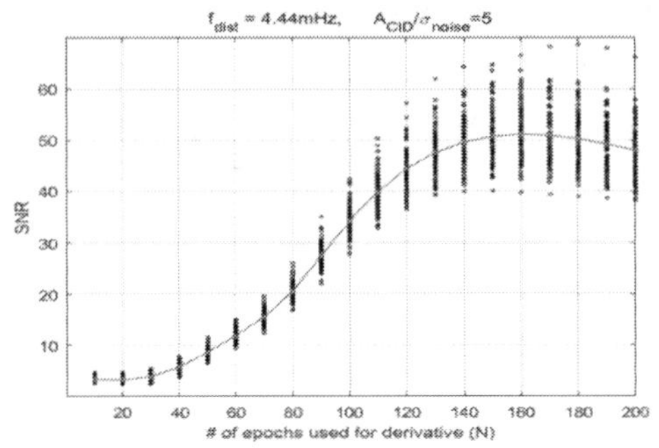

Fig. 3. SNR by N of simulation data. N=160 is the best option.

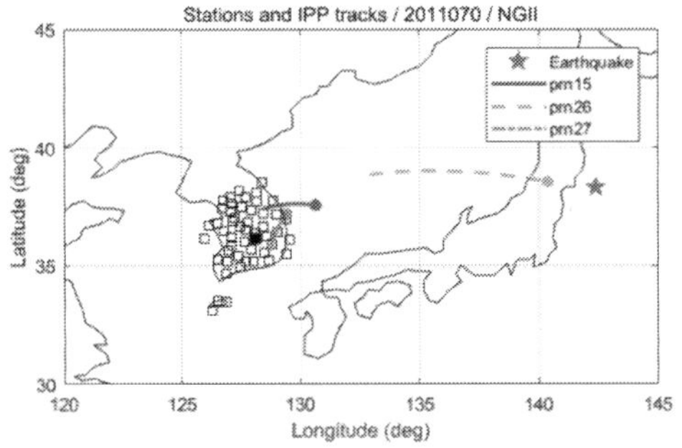

Fig. 4. Epicenter (red star), NGII stations (blank squares), and IPP tracks of KIMC (filled square) for 1 hour from EQ outbreak. IPPs move toward filled circles.

To find out the best N for CID detection, a numerical simulation with 100 iterations was performed. With N ranging from 5 to 200 with step size 5, SNR was computed for 100 different simulation data and averaged. Black dots in Fig. 3 represents the result of each data set with a particular N. Red solid line is the average value of 100 iterations. Consequently, N=160 turned out to be the best option to detect CID.

3 SNR Comparison with Previous Study

To analyze SNR performance of designed algorithm, 2011 Tohoku Earthquake data were used with National Geographic Information Institute (NGII) stations. The total number of stations are 44, and 3 GPS satellites are chosen for their proximity to the epicenter. In Fig. 4 red star denotes epicenter, black squares NGII stations, a filled square KIMC station of NGII. IPP tracks of prn 15,26,27 are drawn with respect to KIMC station.

CID by Rayleigh wave has 3.5km/s speed. It starts at 10 min after EQ from the ionospheric height above epicenter, and propagates as a circular wave [3]. CID by Rayleigh wave travels 4000 km for 20 min, and dissipates most of its energy at the end of propagation. Therefore, it is safe to say that CID, if detectable, will arrive within 10~30 min time span since EQ. Therefore, the amplitude of CID will be calculated as the largest absolute value in this region. STD of noise will be calculated from 1hr time window before EQ outbreak. In this way we can minimize the effect of elevation angle on noise and guarantee there is no CID in the region.

Previous study by Park used a derivative method called numerical 3rd order slant TEC derivatives to detect CID with 30-sec data [4]. As this method was based on 30-sec data, SNR with 1-sec data using this method shows less desirable results. Therefore, we will compare the SNR of 30-sec data using the previous study with that of 1-sec data using MND.

Fig. 5 shows examples of CID detection by each algorithm. Black line represents the result with the previous study, red with MND. Y axis was normalized by STD of 1 hr region before EQ. Maximum absolute value was extracted from the time span of [EQ+10min, EQ+30min], where CID by Rayleigh wave is expected to arrive. These two time regions are notated as shades in the figure. As the Y axis was normalized, maximum values in the plot represent SNR. These values are marked as hollow circles. As shown in Fig. 5, MND shows much improved SNR performance compared to the previous study results.

Table 1 is the statistics on average SNR for prn15, 26, and 27. MND showed 266%, 119%, and 226% improvements respectively.

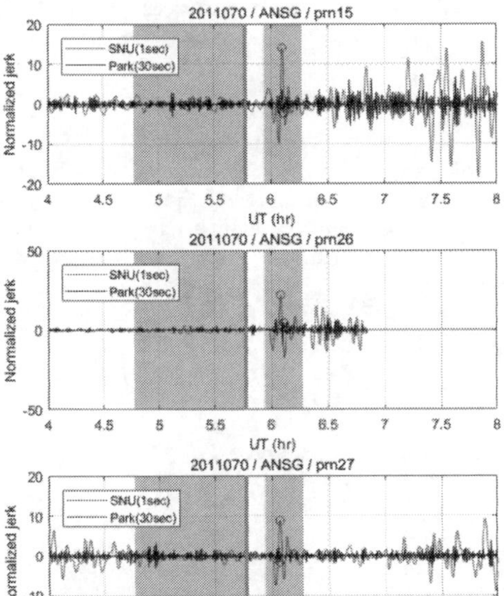

Fig. 5. SNR comparison between the previous study (Park, black) and the designed algorithm (red). Vertical magenta lines represent EQ outbreak. Refer to Fig.2 for the shaded regions. Each data was normalized by STD of the left shaded region.

Table 1. Mean SNR comparison of previous study and designed algorithm (NGII 44 stations)

prn	(a) SNR_{prev}	(b) SNR_{MND}	$\frac{(b)-(a)}{(a)}$
15	3.20	11.72	266 %
26	12.66	27.78	119 %
27	2.25	7.33	226 %

4 Conclusion

A new derivative method was proposed with 1-sec interval sequential measurement combination. Minimum noise level is guaranteed under the given assumptions for the algorithm, which enhances the SNR of CID. The 3rd derivative was chosen to remove the normal trend in the ionospheric delay measurements. To find out the best N that maximizes CID detection performance, simulation data was used and N=160 turned out to be the best option.

The SNR performance of the designed algorithm was compared with that of previous study and 120~260% improvements were observed.

Acknowledgments

This work has been supported by the program 'Satellite Navigation Augmentation to Improve Navigation Technology' of Agency for Defense Development, contracted through the SNU-IAMD. This research was supported (in part) by the Institute of Advanced Aerospace Technology at Seoul National University. The Institute of Engineering Research at Seoul National University provided research facilities for this work.

References

1. C. O. Hines, Internal atmospheric gravity waves at ionospheric heights, Canadian Journal of Physics, **38**(11), 1441-1481 (1960)
2. W. R. Peltier, and C. O. Hines, On the possible detection of tsunamis by a monitoring of the ionosphere, Journal of Geophysical Research, **81**(12), 1995-2000 (1976)
3. G. Occhipinti, L. Rolland, P. Lognonné, S. Watada, From Sumatra 2004 to Tohoku-Oki 2011: The systematic GPS detection of the ionospheric signature induced by tsunamigenic earthquakes. Journal of Geophysical Research: Space Physics, **118**(6), 3626-3636 (2013)
4. J. Park, D.A. Grejner-Brzezinska, R. R. von Frese, and Y. Morton, GPS discrimination of traveling ionospheric disturbances from underground nuclear explosions and earthquakes. Navigation: Journal of The Institute of Navigation, **61**(2), 125-134 (2014)
5. V. Ducic, J. Artru, and P. Lognonné, Ionospheric remote sensing of the Denali Earthquake Rayleigh surface waves. Geophysical Research Letters, **30**(18) (2003)
6. P. Lognonne, E. Clévédé, H. Kanamori, Computation of seismograms and atmospheric oscillations by normal-mode summation for a spherical earth model with realistic atmosphere. Geophysical Journal International, **135**(2), 388-406 (1998)

On the acceleration of land subsidence rate in Semarang City as detected from GPS surveys

Heri Andreas[1,*], *Hasanuddin* Zainal Abidin[1], *Irwan* Gumilar, *Teguh* Purnama Sidiq, *Dina* Anggreni Sarsito[1] and *Dhota* Pradipta [1]

[1]Geodesy Research Division, Faculty of Earth Science and Technology, Institute of Technology Bandung, Indonesia

Abstract. Land subsidence is not a new phenomenon for Semarang the capital city of Central Java Province with recent population of about 1.5 million. Some report said the subsidence in Semarang probably is occurring for more than 100 years. Geodetic surveys such as GPS Surveys can detect land subsidence accurately. Land subsidence in Semarang exhibits spatial and temporal variations with the typical average rates of about 3 to 10 cm/year until recently it seem the acceleration existed in some region of the city. This acceleration will increase the risk of negative consequences from the land subsidence. This paper present and discuss the acceleration of land subsidence in Semarang as detected from GPS Surveys. The surveys have been conducted in 2008, 2009, 2010, 2012, 2016 and 2017. From 2008 to 2012 the subsidence generally follow linier rates while from 2012 to 2017 seem they are accelerating. The northern eastern region of Semarang along the coastal area still exhibits relatively higher rates of subsidence along with acceleration in rates compare to others region. Ground water exploitation is suspected to be the causes of that land subsidence phenomenon in Semarang city

1 Introduction

Semarang is the capital city of Central Java Province, located in the northern coast of Java Island, Indonesia (see Figure 1). Size area of Semarang is about 37,367 hectares or 374 km2, with the population of about 1.55 million people in 2010 (BPS [1]). Geographical center of the city are -6°58' (latitude) and +110°25' (longitude). Topographically, Semarang consists of two major landscapes, namely lowlands and coastal areas in the north and hilly regions in the south. The northern part, comprising the city center, harbor, airport and railway stations, is relatively flat with topographical slopes ranging between 0° and 2°, and altitude between 0 and 3.5 m. The southern part includes slopes up to 45° and altitude up to about 350 m above sea level. The northern part has relatively higher population density and also has more industrial and business areas compared to the southern part. The land use of the southern part consists of residential housing, offices, retail, public use and open space areas.

Land subsidence is not a new phenomenon for Semarang the capital city of Central Java province with recent population of about 1.5 million. Some report said the subsidence in Semarang probably is occurring for more than 100 years. Based on the leveling surveys conducted by the Centre of Environmental Geology (GRDC [2]) from 1999 to 2003 it was found that relatively large subsidence was detected around northern place with the rates ranging from 1 to 17 cm/year. Results derived from GPS show that land subsidence has spatial and temporal variations. In general, subsidence rates in Semarang have an average rate of about 6 to 7 cm/year, with maximum rates that can go up to 14-19 cm/year at certain locations (Kuehn and Murdohardono [3], Lubis et. al [4], Abidin et. al [5]). The estimation based on the PS (Permanent Scatterer) InSAR technique also revealed that the areas close to the shoreline have subsidence rates of more than 8 cm/year (Murdohardono et al [6], Kuehn et al [7]).

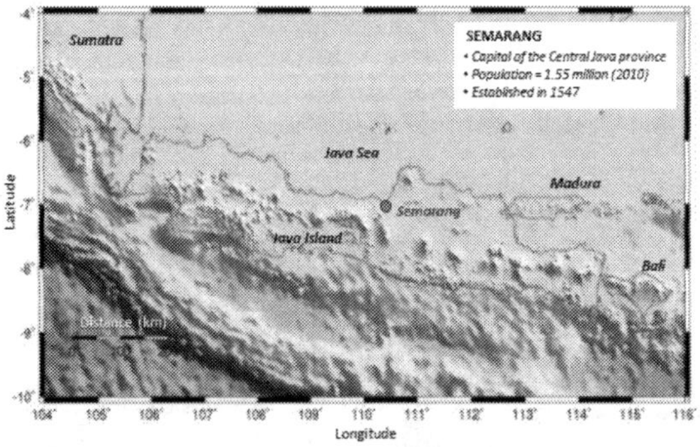

Fig. 1. Map of location of Semarang city, the capital city of Central Java province

If we see geology of Semarang, there are three main lithology, namely, volcanic rock, sedimentary rock, and alluvium deposits. According to Sukhyar [8], the basement of Semarang consists of Tertiary Clay stone of

*Corresponding author: heriandreas49@gmail.com

the Kalibiuk Formation. Overlying this formation is the Notopuro Formation which consists of Quaternary volcanic material. The two formations crop out in the southern part of the Semarang area. The northern part of Semarang is composed by very young alluvium with high compressibility. According to Barry [9] and Geological Research and Development Centre of Indonesia (GRDC) [2]), the alluvial deposits found in coastal areas of Semarang consist of beach, floodplain, tidal, near-shore, and alluvial fan deposits, as illustrated in Figure 2. Aquifers are found at depths ranging from 30 to 80 m in this alluvium. The northern part of the Semarang area is covered by Kali Garang deltaic alluvium up to a depth of 80 to 100 m in the coastal area. Several studies (Van Bemmelen [10], Marfai et.al [11]) have reported that in the period of 1695 to 1991, the shoreline of Semarang progresses relatively quick toward the sea, namely about 2 km in 2.5 centuries or about 8 m/year in average. Therefore it can be expected that a natural consolidation process is still occurring until now, causing also land subsidence in the northern part of Semarang.

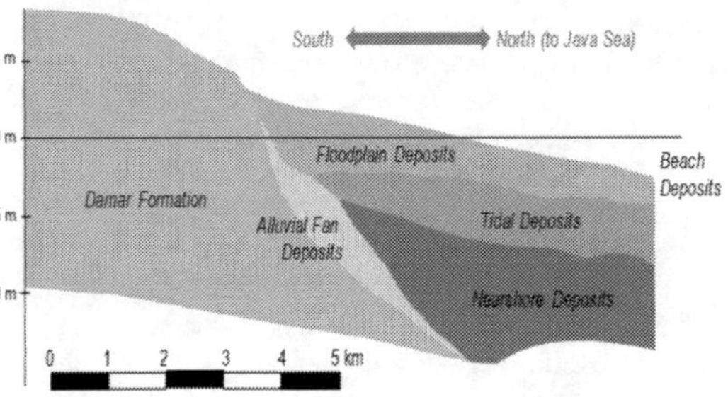

Fig.2. South to North cross section of Quaternary geological section East of Kaliwungu Semarang, after GRDC [2]

In spite of general trend of subsidence around the area of Semarang city, recent GPS surveys indicate the acceleration on its rate. This fact is very interesting especially for identification of the risks from negative impact of subsidence. Acceleration means more risks. So, this paper will present and discuss the acceleration of land subsidence in Semarang as detected from GPS Surveys. Hopefully our finding will be useful for the next steps of dealing with subsidence in the area.

2 Method

GPS (Global Positioning System) and InSAR (Interferometric Synthetic Aperture Radar) has been played as remarkable tool for monitoring land subsidence. As for GPS, this technology is best achievement so far for best positioning and mapping with high accuracy can be achieved in the easiest way (Seeber, [12], Abidin, [13-14], Hofmann et. al [15]). In everywhere and in anytime worldwide when signals from the satellites received by the receivers, in these cases the position in 3D or even 4D (like measuring land subsidence) can be determined precisely and even with precision in the order of millimeter.

To measure the land subsidence, the GPS surveys should be conducted repeatedly in each monitoring point in each session with observation to the satellite for about 10-12 hour. One station placed at stable area will be as reference station while others station located at suspected area as monitoring points or station. Figure 3 shows illustration of GPS surveys on monitoring land subsidence. Measurement can be done also continuously over points, but the cost will be relatively high. We even now have new approach of GPS extensometer, the combination of GPS and deep pile monitoring layers of subsidence.

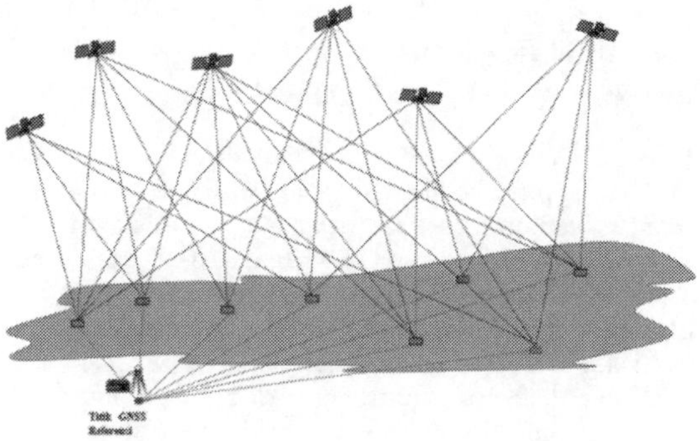

Fig.3. Illustration of GPS surveys for monitoring land subsidence. One point set up in stable area for reference while the others located on suspected area of subsidence

Figure 4 shows location of GPS surveys for monitoring land subsidence in Semarang area. Around 50 stations installed in suspected area of subsidence while the reference point set up at stable are in the southern part of Semarang city. In each point and each session we observed 10 hours. The surveys have been conducted in 2008, 2009, 2010, 2012, 2016 and 2017.

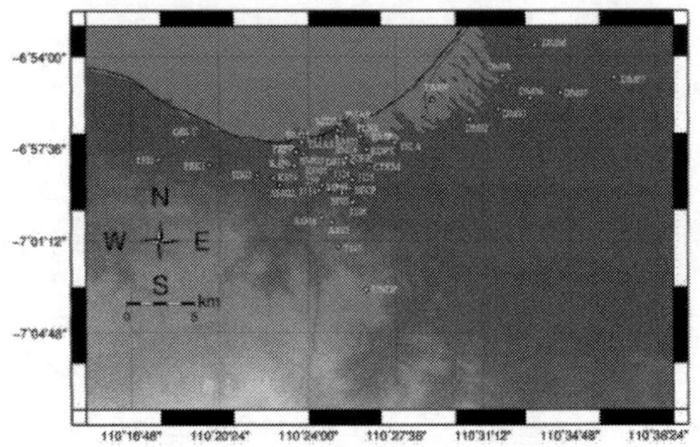

Fig.4. Location of GPS station for monitoring land subsidence in Semarang and the surrounding area.

Figures 5 show several documentations of measurements in the field. We use dual frequency geodetic type receiver Topcon GR3 and GR5 for most of the observations. In the early measurement we use Trimble 4000 SSE. Using the same type of receiver and also antenna type may reduce the error of antenna phase center and any other systematic error due to the device.

Fig.5. Documentation of GPS land subsidence monitoring point in Semarang and the surrounding area.

Table 1 shows the complete parameters observation strategy in order to monitor land subsidence by using GPS technology. As mentioned above we observe in each session each station for about 10-20 hour with observation rate of 30 second, we collect data from two frequency, we use specific antenna type to respond to the multipath potency, using mask angle 15 degree, etc.

Table 2 shows parameters taking into account for GPS data processing strategy in order to monitor land subsidence by using GPS technology. We use precise ephemeris to improve orbit accuracy, we estimate troposphere, we do linier combination to handle ionosphere biases, etc. Software for data processing is Bernese 5.2 (Beutler [16]). It is a scientific software that is good in handling most error and biases including resolving the phase ambiguity.

Table 1. Parameters observation strategy in order to monitor land subsidence by using GPS technology.

Parameters observation strategy	
Receiver	Geodetic Type dual frequency
Observation rate	30 seconds
Observation length	8-10 hour
Mask Angle	15 degree
Data collected	Code and Phase
Others data	Field condition

Table 2. Parameters processing strategy in order to monitor land subsidence by using GPS technology

Parameters processing strategy	
Orbit	Precise ephemeris
Atmospheric biases	Combination of dual frequency forionosphere and estimation for troposphere
Antenna	Phase center correction
Phase ambiguity	QIF strategy
Other biases and errors	Differencing and neglected

3 Results

Result of GPS data processing in every campaign so far; especially for the vertical component shows the accuracy mostly in several millimeters to maximum only reach 1 centimeter. These results proved the software is capable in reducing significantly the biases and errors on GPS data. Generally only the residual of troposphere effect and the noise on the signal those are still remains. With these accuracies we can confident to see the signal of deformation (e.g. subsidence) even in small value (e.g. several centimeters per year). Simply by comparing vertical position in each campaign in each monitoring point, the subsidence could reveal.

Figure 6 to 10 shows example of result on subsidence in several monitoring points out of 50 monitoring points in the field. From the figures we can see the graph of subsidence since 2008 up to 2016. It is clearly shown the pattern of acceleration of subsidence in almost all of the graphs. In detail, from 2008 to 2012 the subsidence generally follow linier trend while from 2012 to 2017 seem they are accelerating. The magnitude it shelf from 2008 to 2016 vary between 20 centimeter to 1.5 meter.

It is very interesting to analyze on how the subsidence is being accelerated. Something must drive the subsidence to accelerate. We assumed that it might be the anthropogenic causes like groundwater exploitation or natural causes like tectonic and natural compaction. Further on we can understand that the acceleration mean more risk to the impact from the subsidence on the area. We will discuss on the next chapter of all varieties causes of land subsidence in Semarang area. In many cases around the world, the groundwater exploitation plays an important role for land subsidence existence.

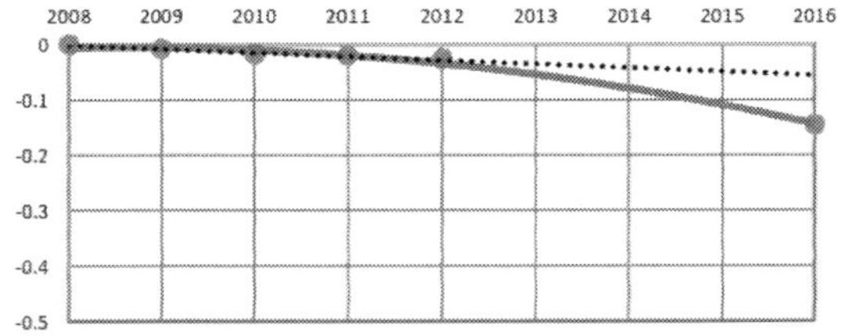

Fig. 6. Graph of land subsidence in station 1303 west northern Semarang from 2008-2016. Y axis shows magnitude in meter

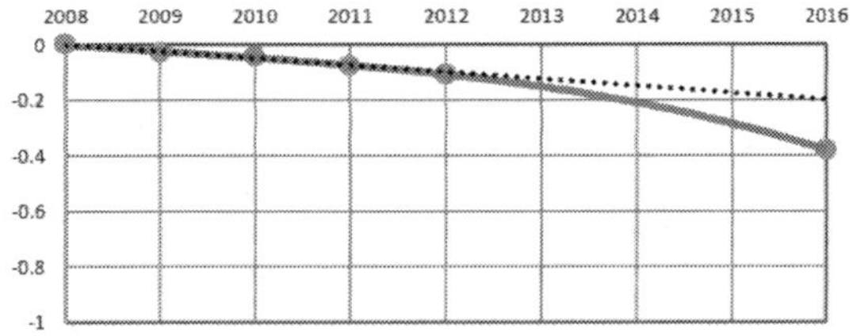

Fig.7. Graph of land subsidence in station QBLT west northern Semarang from 2008-2016. Y axis shows magnitude in meter

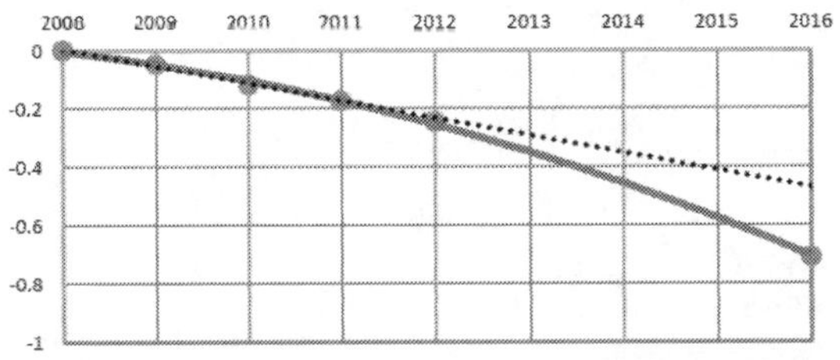

Fig.8. Graph of land subsidence in station BM05 northern Semarang from 2008-2016. Y axis show magnitude in meter

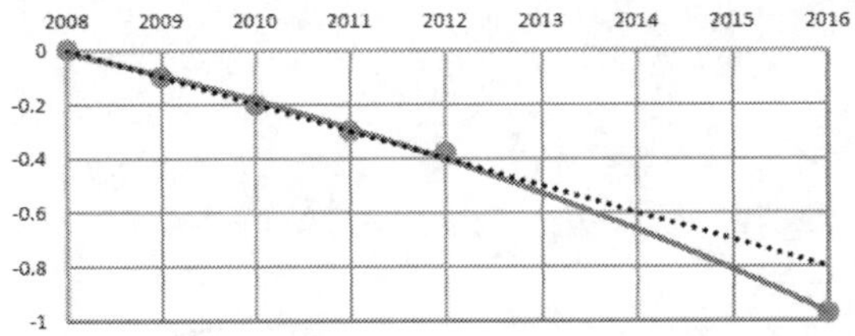

Fig.9. Graph of land subsidence in station RMPA northern eastern Semarang from 2008-2016. Y axis shows magnitude in meter

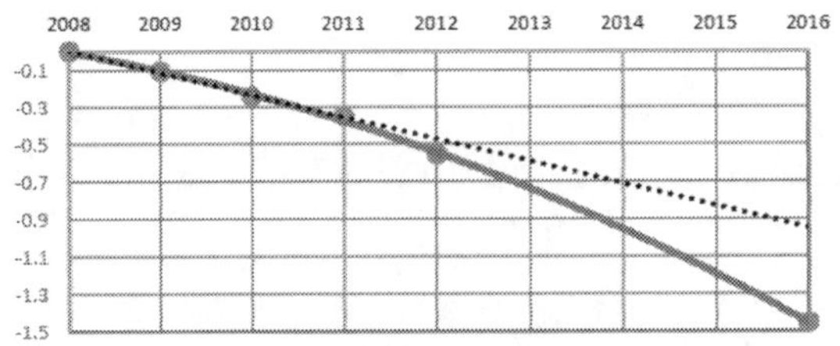

Fig.10. Graph of land subsidence in station SMG5 northern eastern Semarang from 2008-2016. Y axis shows magnitude in meter

Figure 11 shows map of information of subsidence characteristic in each stations over Semarang and the surrounding area. We can see most of the stations in northern eastern Semarang are experiencing acceleration in subsidence rates, meanwhile in central Semarang the subsidence is happening generally in the linear rate. Null subsidence is also recognize in the southern part of Semarang.

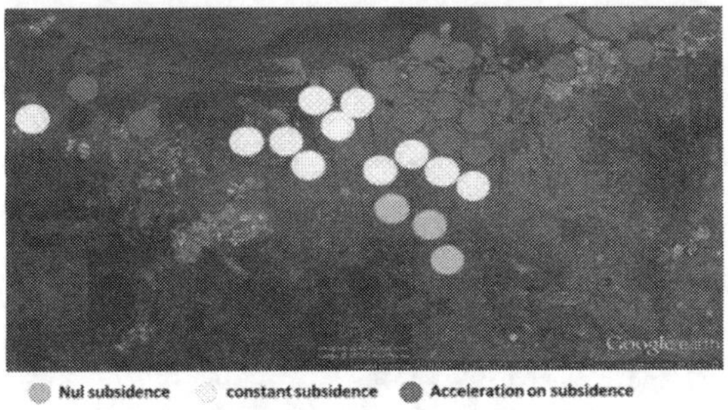

Fig.11. Map of information of subsidence characteristic in each station over Semarang and the surrounding area.

4 Discussions

The impact of land subsidence on the coastal area (e.g. in Semarang) can be seen in several forms, such as the wider expansion of (coastal) flooding areas, cracking of buildings and infrastructure and increased inland sea water intrusion. It also badly influences the quality and amenity of the living environment and life (e.g. health and sanitation condition) in the affected areas. The economic losses caused by land subsidence are enormous; since many buildings and infrastructure severely affected by this silent disaster of subsidence. Many houses, public utilities and a large number of populations are also exposed to this silent disaster. The corresponding maintenance cost is increasing every year. The living conditions of the affected population are deteriorating. The quality of their social and economic activity is consequently decreasing as well.

Figure 12 shows coastal flooding documentation in northern eastern part of Semarang city while figure 13 shows time series of high resolution satellite images around Tanjung Mas northern eastern of Semarang city from 2005 up to 2015. From the images we can see one place that is used to be land but now become the sea area. Indeed it is real view of disaster due to the occurring of land subsidence phenomenon.

Fig.12. Coastal flooding documentation in northern part of Semarang city due to land subsidence.

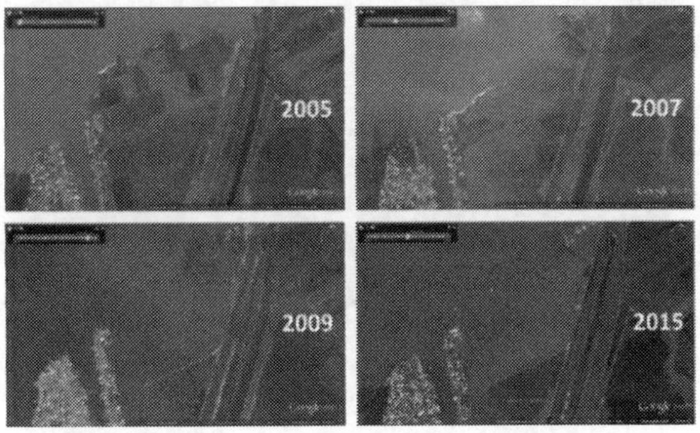

Fig.13. Time series of high resolution satellite images showing land loss to the sea due to land subsidence.

If indeed we have acceleration on the rate of subsidence, it would be mean that more severe disaster may be existed in the area. In this case we need to do better either mitigation or adaptation against the land subsidence. The beginning of the action is by understanding the causes of land subsidence.

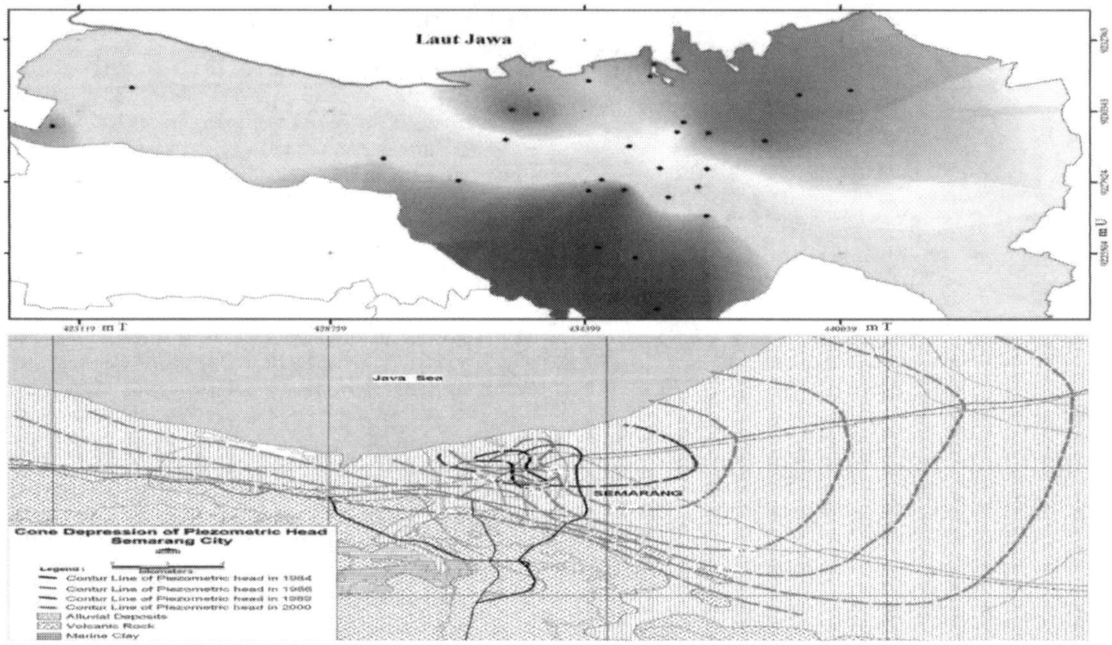

Fig.14. Maps correlation of land subsidence and water table decline in Semarang city. Generally we can see area where large subsidence existed correspond to significant declining of water table in confine aquifer.

There are several recognized causes such as natural compaction, loading of building, compaction of aquifer due to exploitation of groundwater, compaction of oil and gas reservoir due the exploitation and tectonic influence the subsidence. Many of publication conclude that the over exploitation of groundwater plays an important role on the subsidence (Holjer and Thomas [17], Rajiyowiryono [18], JICA [19]) and for the Semarang case it probably the same. Figure 14 and 15 each shows maps and graphs correlation of land subsidence and water table decline on the deep confine aquifer around Semarang city.

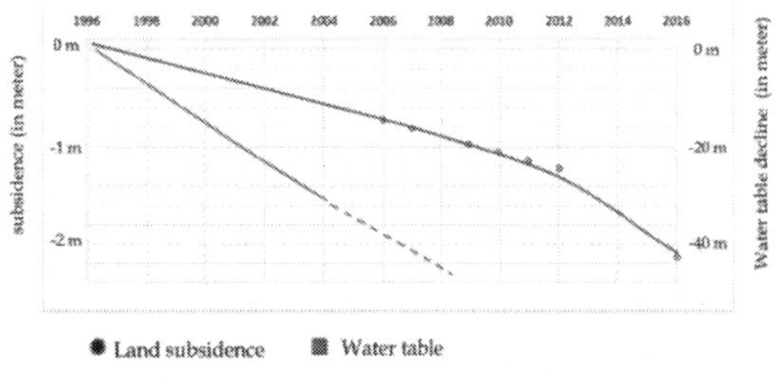

Fig.15. Graphs correlation of land subsidence and water table decline in Semarang city.

It seems that the subsidence is continuing as the water table is continuing to decline. The declining is due to increasing need of water for people and factories. As we know that northern eastern of Semarang is industrial area. Coincidently this place is the largest of subsidence area.

5 Conclusion

Land subsidence is not a new phenomenon for Semarang city. The rate in the recent year in fact is considerably quite significant with trend of acceleration. The impact of land subsidence in Semarang are obviously there and can be seen in several forms, such as the wider expansion of (coastal) flooding areas "rob", cracking of buildings and infrastructure and increased inland sea water intrusion. It also badly influences the quality and amenity of the living environment and life (e.g. health and sanitation condition) in the affected areas. Adaptation and mitigation are considered very important. Sometime in the future if less action taken in adaptation and mitigation, ecological disaster would be more and more serious. The sinking of Semarang through the sea is not weak hypothesis indeed.

We noticed people increased their house, and the local government elevated the road and the bridge, etc. regularly over less decade period as part of adaptation. We also noticed the central government built the dyke and pumping station. Nevertheless the adaptation is only made temporally since significant land subsidence keep coming and worsening by the sea level which is keep rising. As for the mitigation, until now we have seen lack of mitigation program, monitoring or even ineffective mitigation (mangrove program) in Semarang related to this subsidence issue. Indeed we have big homework on dealing with the subsidence in Semarang city. We need to start thinking on better water management in the area. It is quite obvious that groundwater exploitation play an important role on the subsidence. We need to manage the exploitation.

Simply if we show the Tokyo, Osaka, Shanghai cases, etc. where they successfully stop the groundwater exploitation, in other hand the land subsidence was also stopped. Off course it is not apple to apple comparison since subsurface properties are different, but from all the causes, we can only able to deal with the anthropogenic causes and that is the groundwater. We cannot stop the natural compaction and or even the tectonic if existed. It is worth to try on doing better water management.

As for last conclusion, monitoring is one very important thing on dealing with the land subsidence. How do we know that the land subsidence is accelerating or decreasing or stopping if none of monitoring is being taken?

Acknowledgements

Many thanks and appreciation to students from Institute of Technology Bandung and from Dipenogoro University who helped the investigation in the field, and especially to the local people in Semarang and nearby for kindly sharing the information and experience relating subsidence impacts

References

1. BPS, Website of the Badan Pusat Statistik (Statistics Indonesia), accessed date: 3 November 2011. http://www.bps.go.id/hasilSP2010/jateng/ (2011)
2. GRDC, Quaternary Geological Map of the Semarang Triangle, Jawa. Geological Research and Development Centre (GRDC), Bandung (1996)
3. Kuehn, F., Albiol, D., Cooksley, G., Duro, J., Granda, J., Haas, S., Hoffmann-Rothe, A and Murdohardono, D., Detection of land subsidence in Semarang, Indonesia, using stable point's network (SPN) technique. Environmental Earth Sciences, DOI 10.1007/s12665-009-0227-x (2009)
4. Lubis, A.M., Sato, T., Tomiyama, N., Isezaki, N and Yamanokuchi, T., Ground subsidence in Semarang-Indonesia investigated by ALOS–PALSAR satellite SAR interferometry, Journal of Asian Earth Sciences, 40, 5, 30 March, pp. 1079-1088 (2011)
5. Abidin, H.Z., R. Djaja, H. Andreas, M. Gamal, K. Hirose, Y. Maruyama, Capabilities and Constraints of Geodetic Techniques for Monitoring Land Subsidence in the Urban Areas of Indonesia, Geomatics Research Australia. No.81, December, pp. 45-58 (2004)
6. Murdohardono, D., Sudradjat, G.M., Wirakusumah, A.D., Kuhn, F and Mulyasari, F., Land Subsidence Analysis through Remote Sensing and Implementation on Municipality Level; Case Study: Semarang Municipality, Central Java Province, Indonesia. Paper presented at the BGR-GAI-CCOP Workshop on Management of Georisks, 23-25 June, Yogyakarta (2009)
7. Kuehn, F., Albiol, D., Cooksley, G., Duro, J., Granda, J., Haas, S., Hoffmann-Rothe, A and Murdohardono, D., Detection of land subsidence in Semarang, Indonesia, using stable point's network (SPN) technique. Environmental Earth Sciences, DOI 10.1007/s12665-009-0227-x (2009)
8. Sukhyar, R., Status and Progress of Urban Geology in Indonesia. Atlas and Urban Geology Vol. 14 : The Ground Beneath Our Feet: a Factor in Urban Planning, United Nations ESCAP (Economic and Social Commission for Asia and the Pacific), New York, pp. 335 – 340 (2003)
9. Barry, T., The Soft Soils of Semarang. Paper presented at the Seminar and Workshop of Polder Systems in Waterfront Cities, 27-28 September, Jakarta (2001)
10. Van Bemmelen, The Geology of Indonesia. Vol. IA, Government Printing Office, Martinus Nijhof, The Netherlands (1949)
11. Marfai, M.A., Almohamad, H., Dey, S., Susanto, B and King, L., Coastal dynamic and shoreline mapping: multi-sources spatial data analysis in Semarang Indonesia. Environmental Monitoring and Assessment, 142, pp. 297-308 (2008)
12. Seeber, G., Satellite Geodesy: foundation, method, and applications, Walter de Gruyter, Berlin-New York, C7 (1993)
13. Abidin, H.Z., Penentuan Posisi dengan GPS dan Aplikasinya (PT. Pradnya Paramita, Jakarta, 1999)
14. Abidin, H.Z., Geodesi Satelit (Departemen Teknik Geodesi ITB, PT. Pradnya Paramita, Jakarta, 2001)
15. Hofmann-Wellenhof, B., Lichtenegger, H. and Walse, E., GNSS Global Navigation Satellite Systems: GPS, GLONASS, Galileo, and More. (Springer Verlag, Wien, 2007)
16. Beutler, G., H. Bock, E. Brockmann, R. Dach, P. Fridez, W. Gurtner, U. Hugentobler, D.Ineichen, J. Johnson, M. Meindl, L. Mervant, M. Rothacher, S. Schaer, T. Springer, R.Weber. Bernese GPS software version 4.2. , University of Berne, 515 pp (2001)
17. Holzer and Thomas L., Land subsidence caused by groundwater withdrawal in Urban areas, GeoJournal 11.3 245-255. Reidel Publishing Company 1985 (1985)
18. Rajiyowiryono H., Groundwater and Land subsidence Monitoring along the North Coastal Plain of Java Island. CCOP Newsl 24(3):19 July-September (1999)
19. JICA, Lesson learns from land subsidence in Tokyo Japan. Presentation on "high Level Meeting on Subsidence". Balai Kota DKI Jakarta Indonesia 2014 (2014)

Study of Digital Elevation Model (DEM) Extraction using Stereo Radargrammetry TerraSAR-X in Madiun Area – Elevation Accuracy Improvement

Inggit L. Sari[1,*], *Rachmat* Maulana[1,*], *Haris* S. Dyatmika, *Agus* Suprijanto[1] *Rahmat* Arief[1] and *Shadiq* Ali[1]

[1]Remote Sensing Technology and Data Center, LAPAN, Pekayon, Jakarta, Indonesia

Abstract. High resolution images data from Terrasar-X are used to extract digital elevation model (DEM) using stereo radargrammetry in the attempt to achieve better resolution of terrain surface in Indonesia. As sample in this study, stereo pairs images from TerraSAR-X StripMap mode (~3m resolution) on Madiun city is used with difference of incidence angle around ~18.88 degree to extract the elevation of the area. Furthermore, field observation on the selected area will be used on elevation accuracy assessment. The digital surface elevation (DSM) generated by stereo radargrammetry in this study shows us high resolution with spatial pixel spacing 5.57 meter and elevation accuracy around ~4 meter.

1 Introduction

Synthetetic Aperature Radar (SAR) technology have been advanced through the years since its earliest day. This technology use radar as a means to observe the earth which means its not affected by clouds and time, in contrast to the optical remote sensing which affected by the clouds and only can works on day time when there's only sunlight.

On 2007, TerraSAR-X have been launched to the space carrying high frequency X band sensor, varying based on its imaging modes followed by TanDEM-X on 2010. TerraSAR-X resolution ranging around 1 m for its SpotLight mode to 40 m for Wide-ScanSAR mode. The most common mode on TerraSAR-X imagery is on its StripMap mode which have 3-meter resolution.[1]

Digital elevation model (DEM) is a digital representation of the Earth's relief that consist ordered array of elevations relative to a datum, and referenced to geographic coordinate. DEM can be distinguished by which representation on the elevation of earth surface, Digital surface model (DSM) is representing all feature on the earth surface like trees and houses while Digital Terrain model (DTM) representing the earth surface without all those features.

DEM has been a very important product on remote sensing imagery. The most used of DEM is on the process of orthorectification remote sensing image, be it as optical imagery or SAR imagery. Furthermore, its derivation can be applied on other area such as engineering works, agriculture, mining, or disaster management [2].

Stereo radargrammetry is traditional and mature approach on the elevation extraction from SAR imagery. The idea based on photogrammetry with its optical imagery while we use SAR imagery on its intensity (amplitude) to extract the elevation. As with the photogrammetry, stereo radargrammetry use two images (or more) with different incidence angles on the same area [3].

When a target is seen from different angles, the relief displacement on each SAR image will be different. The difference between the image coordinates of homologous points in a stereo pair is called parallax (leberl,1990). Each homologous point's parallax is relater to the corresponding ground target's height. When incidence angles of two sensors are constant, the target with larger parallax is higher than that with smaller parallax [4]. The optimized difference of this incident angle is ranging between 10° – 20° [5] or 15° – 25° [6].

The data we use is TerraSAR-X images which using X band on its mission. The elevation model we obtain will be a Digital Surface Model (DSM) which includes all features on earth surface as X band get backscattered at the top of any features on the earth surface.

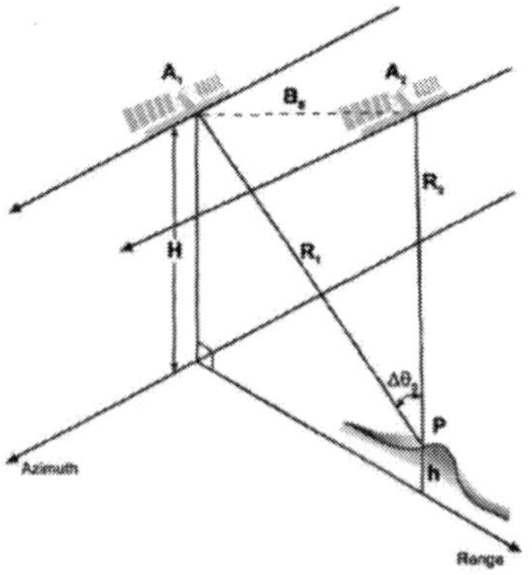

Fig. 1. Geometry of stereo-radargrammatry, A and H are the respective satellite position and altitude [7].

* Corresponding author: inggit.lolita@lapan.go.id, maularachmat@gmail.com

Table 1. Characteristic of TerraSAR-X images pairs.

	Image 1	Image 2
Sensor	TerraSAR-X	TerraSAR-X
Imaging Mode	StripMap	StripMap
Acquisition time	24/03/2018 22.22.10-22.22.18	10/04/2018 22.13.39-22.13.48
Product Type	SSC	SSC
Scene Centere Incidence Angle	28.765	47.653
Pass	Descending	Descending
Side Look	Right	Right
Polarization	HH	HH

2 Study Area and Processing

The study is carried out around Madiun City area, East Java. The characteristic of the surface relief of this area varies around agricultural lands, urban area, hills, and mountain. This elevation from this area ranges from 60 meters to 3265 meter while the maximum altitude is the peak of Lawu mountain.

Two TerraSAR-X images have been acquired on StripMap mode with HH polarization on Single-look Slant-range Complex (SSC). These images have same-side stereo pairs on descending orbits and have difference incidence angle of ~18.88° with 17 days acquisition interval.

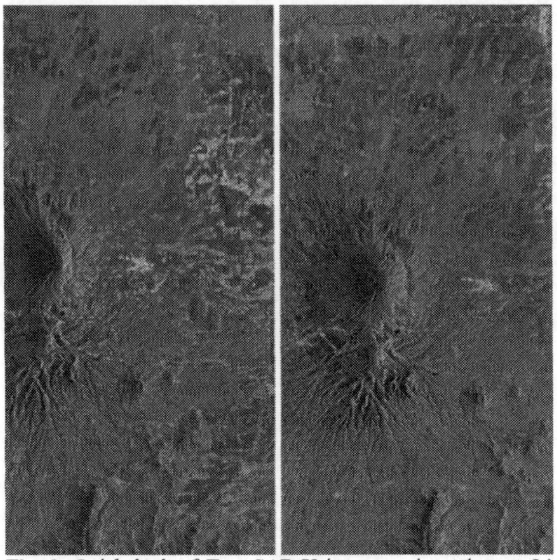

Fig. 2. Quick look of TerraSAR-X images pairs, taken at 24 March 2018 (left) and at 10 April 2018 (right).

The process of stereo radargrammetry is carried out automatically in order to achieve high precision and avoid manual interaction of the user. This is due to SAR images which are heavily distorted both radiometrically and geometrically by the terrain, such as shadow provided by slopes which facing away from the sensor. Furthermore, SAR images also contains random speckle noise which make the reduce the resolution or filter with the reference DEM to cope with this speckle noise [8].

The main idea of the stereo matching process is by retrieving a shift in pixel on range direction which is proportion.al to the topographic height. The shift then estimated by the means of co-registration between the two images using amplitude (intensity) cross correlation. This whole process is performed in pyramidal way as the estimating of initial shift is on the multi-looked ` then refining it iteration by iteration to obtain finer estimate.

Later on, these shifts are converted to height and geocoded into a map projection. The difference with basic geocoding procedure is that we applied the two antennae simultaneously in Range-Doppler equations. From there, we can obtain the height of each pixel and its location (Easting, Northing) in a given cartographic and geodetic reference system.

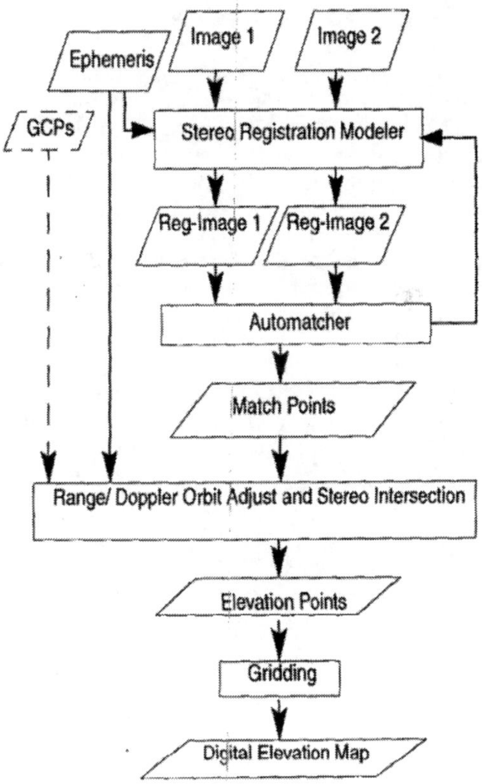

Fig. 3. Stereo radargrammetry processing flow chart [9].

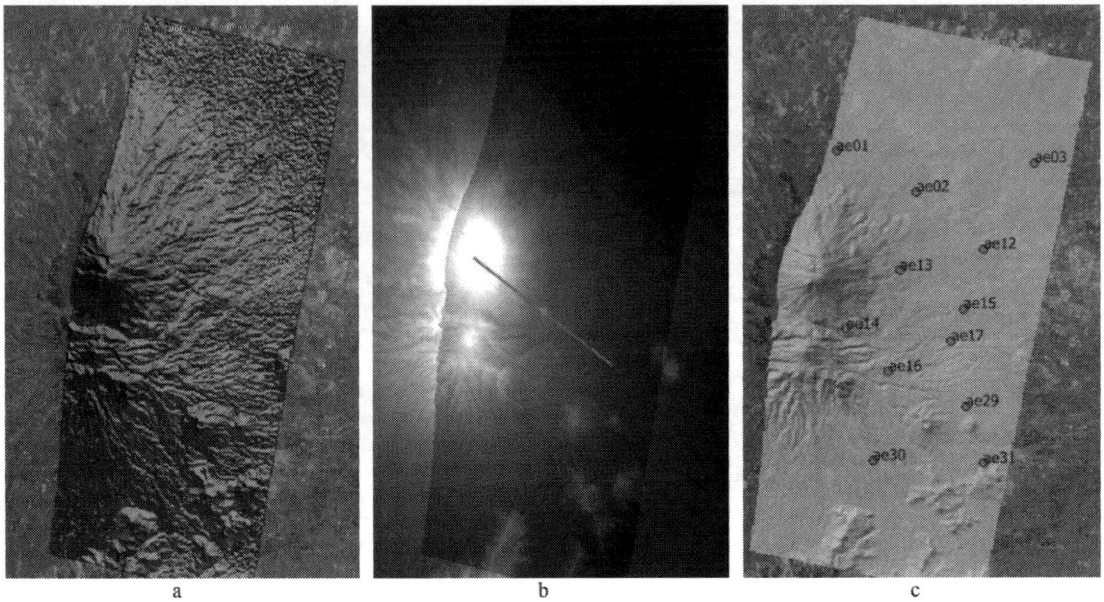

Fig. 4. (a) Result of DSM stereo radargrammetry TerraSAR-X, (b) Elevation profile line of DSM stereo and DEMNAS (c) Distribution points of GPS field observation.

3 Result and Discussion

The results of Digital Surface Model (DSM) created using stereo-radargrammetry in our area of study have high resolution with spatial pixel spacing around 5.57 meter. Furthermore, we carried out elevation accuracy measurement by comparing the elevation of the stereo DSM result to field elevation observation using GNSS GPS of Garmin Geo 7X with accuracy of 0.05 meter. We also evaluate the results of stereo DSM in our study to national digital elevation model (DEMNAS Indonesia) provided by Indonesia Geospatial Agency (BIG) by taking elevation profile of these two DEM. The DEMNAS is produced from DSM of IFSAR TerraSAR-X and ALOS-PALSAR with the accuracy improvement by processing addition of mass-points, spot-heights and break-line from topographic map using GMT-surface with tension 0.32[10].

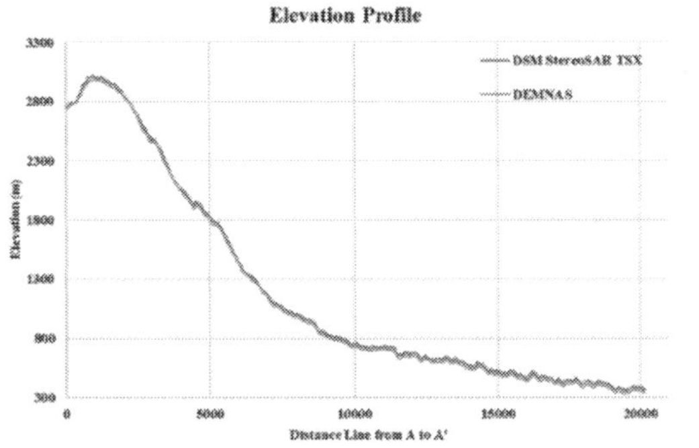

Fig. 5. Elevation profile between stereo radargrammetry DSM and DEMNAS, x-axis follow the red line on **Fig. 4**a with the elevation on the y-axis.

The elevation profile between the DSM stereo radargrammetry TerraSAR-X and DEMNAS can be seen at Fig. 5 where its elevation follows the red line on Fig. 4b. Based on both figures, the generated DSM has similar elevation profile with DEMNAS.

The elevation accuracy measurement of the DSM stereo radargarammetry TerraSAR-X using GPS field observation can be seen at Table 2 with respective points shown at Fig. 4c. The result from this measurement, we obtain the absolute mean height error of the DSM stereo radargrammetry is 3.676 meter and root mean square error is 4.018 meter with the standard deviation of error is 1.695 meter.

Table 2. Elevation accuracy measurement of stereo radargrammetry DSM with GPS field observation.

Code No.	GPS Height (m)	DSM Height (m)	Accuracy (m)
ae01	427.327	427.822	0.495
ae17	396.7880	390.772	6.016
ae02	300.5590	298.384	2.175
ae03	100.9570	105.676	4.719
ae31	249.4020	253.655	4.253
ae30	537.7290	542.123	4.394
ae29	357.1200	355.111	2.009
ae16	877.6850	879.378	1.693
ae15	388.4250	393.343	4.918
ae12	259.3960	264.910	5.514
ae13	647.8580	651.992	4.134
ae14	1321.6930	1317.897	3.796

4 Conclusion

Digital Surface Model (DSM) generation using TerraSAR-X imagery in StripMap mode at Single-look Slant-range Complex (SSC) have been generated using stereo radargrammetry. The generated DSM have spatial resolution of 5.57 meter with elevation accuracy around ~4 meter. This proves that TerraSAR-X images capable of generating digital surface model (DSM) in stereo radargrammetry and show good result from it.

The authors would like to thank Remote Sensing Technology and Data Center, Indonesian National Institute of Aeronatics and Space (LAPAN) for providing TerraSAR-X data and for the support from Ministry of Research, Technology and Higher Education of the Republic of Indonesia (KEMENRISTEKDIKTI) through Reseach Incentives of National Innovation System (INSINAS) 2018 program.

References

1. DLR (German Aerospace Center). Basic Product Specification Document. Vol. 53, no. 1.9, p. 126 (2013).
2. A. Nascetti. High resolution radargrammetry: development and implementation of an innovative image matching strategy (2013).
3. M. Crosetto, F. Pérez. Radargrammetry and SAR interferometry for DEM generation : validation and data fusion. *SAR Work. CEOS Comm. Earth Obs. Satell.*, no. 1, pp. 367–372 (2000).
4. T. Balz, X. He, L. Zhang, M. Liao. TerraSAR-X Stereo Radargrammetry for precise DEM generation in south-east asia. *Igarss 2014*, no. 1, pp. 1–5 (2014).
5. N. d'Ozouville, B. Deffontaines, J. Benveniste, U. Wegmüller, S. Violette, G. de Marsily. DEM generation using ASAR (ENVISAT) for addressing the lack of freshwater ecosystems management, Santa Cruz Island, Galapagos. *Remote Sens. Environ.*, vol. 112, no. 11, pp. 4131–4147 (2008).
6. S. D. Hennig, W. Koppe, N. Kiefl, J. Janoth. Digital Elevation Modeling Using Terrasar-X Stereo Pairs (2010).
7. T. Toutin, L. Gray. State-of-the-art of elevation extraction from satellite SAR data. *ISPRS J. Photogramm. Remote Sens.*, vol. 55, no. 1, pp. 13–33 (2000).
8. J. A. Ostrowski, P. Cheng. DEM Extraction from Stereo SAR Satellite Imagery. *Geosci. Remote Sens. Symp. 2000. Proceedings. IGARSS 2000. IEEE 2000 Int.*, vol. 5, no. 819, pp. 2176–2178 (2000).
9. M. Marra, K. E. Maurice, D. C. Ghiglia, H. G. Frick. Automated DEM extraction using RADARSAT ScanSAR stereo data. *IGARSS '98. Sens. Manag. Environ. 1998 IEEE Int. Geosci. Remote Sensing. Symp. Proceedings. (Cat. No.98CH36174)*, pp. 2351–2353 vol.5 (1998).
10. BIG (Indonesia Geospatial Information Agency). Seamless Digital Elevation Model (DEM) dan Batimetri Nasional. [Online]. Available: http://tides.big.go.id/DEMNAS/. [Accessed: 01-Sep-2018].

Time Series of Land subsidence rate on Coastal Demak Using GNSS CORS UDIP and DINSAR

B. D. Yuwono[1*], *S.* Subiyanto, *A. S.* Pratomo , *Najib* [2]

[1] Geodesy Department, Faculty of Engineering, Diponegoro University, Indonesia
[2] Geology Department, Faculty of Engineering, Diponegoro University, Indonesia

Abstract. Most of the studies land subsidence and impact have been done on the north coastal area of Java, especially Semarang and Demak. This landsubsidence has a very serious impact both in the infra structure, the economy and the environment. Techniques of observing landsubsidence using geodetic methods have been widely practiced. Geodetic technology is undergoing rapid development, especially in GNSS navigation satellite technology as well as satellite radar interferometry. Both have advantages and disadvantages of each. In this study will examine the application of DinSAR interferometric techniques and GNSS technology to predict the rate of land subsidence coastal of Demak regency. This paper also emphasize the role of GNSS and DinSAR application in deformation especially for landsubsidence monitoring.

1 Introduction

Coastal area in Sayung Demak is a very dynamic and have sufficient resource potential big, however, coastal areas are also areas that are very vulnerable to hazards such as flood and inundation land subsidence. The impact of disaster it will be more widespread if not handled properly. Rob floods have caused large loss due to inhibiting economic activity in the Regency Demak. More than 1200 houses flooded and hundreds of residents were forced relocated due to loss of settlement.[1] In this research DinSAR and GNSS measurement were conducted to indentify and analyze the trend of land subsidence.

SAR refers to the concept of RADAR using an active sensor that sends radio signals with pulses that bounce off the ground and move back to the sensor. Some of the advantages of using RADAR is that it is not limited by clouds or lack of sunlight. SAR as mentioned, a type of RADAR sensor called Synthetic Aperture Radar, which uses a synthetic antenna, made by a combination of stable data signals (Hanssen, 2001, pp. 10-11). The most effective way of monitoring ground subsidence can be conducted using dInSAR, GNSS and levelling is to first screen large areas for any movement using dInSAR.[2]

The principle of interferometry is to calculate phase differences between SAR images obtained at different times. Since this phase is a measure of distance, this, in theory, represents a change in the height of a point reflected by a signal [3].The problem of SAR image processing became more complex. The complexity is caused by different sources of error Phase comparison without any error correction will produce an inaccurate result, so the result is not realiable and unusable. Recently, different methods have been developed to exclude the error source from phase measurement and hence get much more accurate results. The application of SAR interferometry technology in this research is to monitor landsubsidence deformation. The source of phase error in SAR interferomteri is as follows, Impact of atmospheric change,The impact of orbital inconsistencies, multipath and Topography

1.1 SAR Interferometry

InSAR stands for SAR interferometry, the InSAR technique uses the measurement of phase change of signals (interference) between radar images. If there is a point on the surface of the earth moving there is a change in distance between the sensor and the point, it will produce the appropriate phase shift signal. The displacement in phase in the two SAR images measured at each point (pixels) is a phase difference and is known as an interferogram. The phase difference is calculated for each pixel. When InSAR is used to recognize and measure ground deformation, this process is referred to as the InSAR differential[4]. The general formation of differential Interferrograms shown in figure 1.

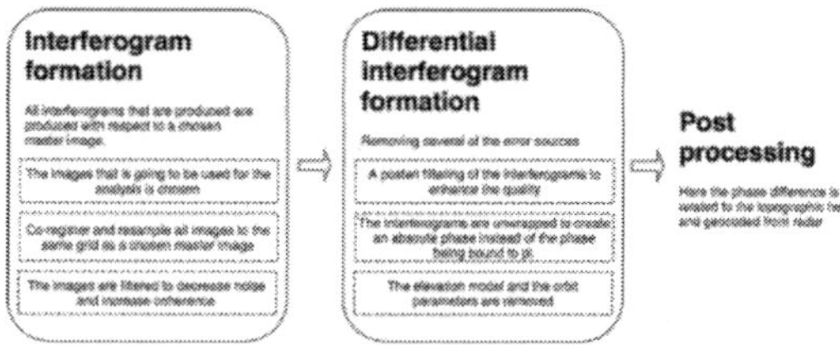

Fig. 1 General Formation of Differential Interferrograms[2]

* Corresponding author: bdyuwono92@gmail.com

1.2 GNSS Cors

Use of Global Navigation Satellite The GNSS system (GNSS) is increasing with accuracy reaches centimeters for relative position using the CORS station [5]. CORS applications include can be used for geoid modeling purposes (Wu et al., 2015) and for deformation purposes Dam [6].GNSS, like dInSAR, uses phase measurements from satellites. There are several types of GNSS measurements and many different systems included in GNSS terms, such as GPS, GLONASS, Galileo among others [7]

The most accurate type of measurement is the relative static position. Here there are several recipients used by being placed above the point where they are static during the session. To get a GNSS position, the receiver must get a selection to at least four different satellites, this is to get the four pseudorange data together so that it gets a 3D position and a clock error [7]. [8] describe in more detail about how GNSS measurements are performed in "GPS Satellite Surveys".

The GNSS CORS UDIP station was developed at the Diponegoro University Department of Geodesy in December 2012. The GNSS CORS UDIP installation is on the 3rd floor, while the server is in the laboratory Geodetic Department Measurement and Mapping,Faculty of Engineering, Diponegoro University. Installation / installation of the GNSS system [9] This CORS UDIP is based on needs survey needs, geodetic mathematical models, and digital signal processing. Description from the CORS UDIP GNSS station can be seen Figure 2.

Figure 2. Station GNSS CORS UDIP

2 Data and Method

We have been conducted several research investigations to this area study by field observations by (mapping the landsubsidence area, pictures, conduct GPS measurement and InSAR analysis). In this research there are two pairs of images were processed in two year 2016 and 2017. In this case, the subsidence is derived using differential method, and data SRTM was used for generating the DEM for the area. In the interferogram, the phase difference is described as the distance difference measured by the line of sight (LOS) radar and includes topography, orbit shifts, surface deformation and atmospheric effects[10]. The Sentinel Data were used shown in table 1, including data acquisition, polarisation and direction scanning.

Table 1. Sentinel Data

No	Time Period	Level	Acqui sition Mode	Pola risat ion	Direction Scanning
1.	14 November 2015	1.0	IW	VV	Descending
2.	8 November 2016	1.0	IW	VV	Descending
3.	24 February 2017	1.0	IW	VV	Descending
4.	15 November 2017	1.0	IW	VV	Descending

The next processing, we computed differential interferograms. (Digital Elevation Model (DEM) produced from the Shuttle Radar Topography Mission with about 90 × 90m2 spacing was used to remove the phase component due to the topography of the area.. Detail master and Slave image in each year were represented at table 2.

The GNSS data for this research of landsubsidence in Coastal Demak have been conducted on 2-8 may 2015, 23-26 april 2016,22-24 april 2017 and 7-8 may 2018. Bench Mark was installed in 6 Villages namely Sidodadi, Gemah, Tugu, Purwosari, Bedono and Timbulsloko which all of which are in the District Sayung.The GPS surveys exclusively used dual-frequency geodetic-type GPS receivers. The length of surveying sessions was in general between 6 to 7 hours. The data were observed with a 30 second interval with an elevation mask of 15 ^{0} The surveys of this research were mainly carried out by the staffs and students from the Department of Geodesy of Diponegoro University. GPS survey were conducted in 2018 shown in figure 3

Fig 3. GPS survey 2018 (Google Earth)

Table 2 Sentinel Data Aquisition

Data Sentinel 1 Aquisition year 2016								
Mst/Slv	Acquisition	Track	Orbit	Bperp (m)	Btemp (days)	Modeled Coherence	Height Ambg (m)	Delta fDC (Hz)
Master	14 November 2015	127	8599	0,00	0,00	1,00	∞	0,00
Slave	08 November 2016	127	13849	-12,11	360,00	0,66	1286,36	-1,55
Data Sentinel 1 Aquisition year 2017								
Master	24 Februari 2017	127	15414	0,00	0,00	1,00	∞	0,00
Slave	15 November 2017	127	19274	32,59	264,00	0,70	478,27	-7,33

3. Result and Discussion

(IW) Interferometric Wide , Single Look Complex (SLC). Deformation measurement will be conducted using Sentinel-1 images. An IW SLC Sentinel-1 scene covered approximately about 250 x 180 km and is consist of 3 swaths containing 9 bursts each. In this research, the DinSAR procedure is performed burst-wise over the interferograms, i.e., with a footprint of approximately 5 x 20 m in range and azimuth, respectively.The PSI products are the characteristic of deformation map and the time series of the deformation spanning the period from November 2015 to November 2016 and February to November 2017. The gathered deformation map was estimated over an area of approximately 35 km^2 in the northern sayung sub district, including some countryside areas. Result of Deformation DinSAR monitoring year 2015, 2016 and 2017 show figure 4.

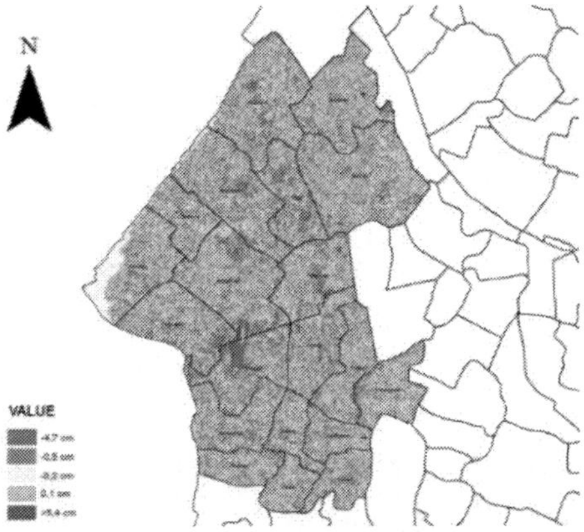

Fig 4. DinSAR 2015[11]

The further shown that land subsidence affects north parts of Sayung. This is particularly true for the northwestern districts of the city and situated north of the boundary at alluvial sediments. In the northern portion of the researched area, single points characterized by rapid subsidence are probably connected to tidal flood but have still to be checked in the field.

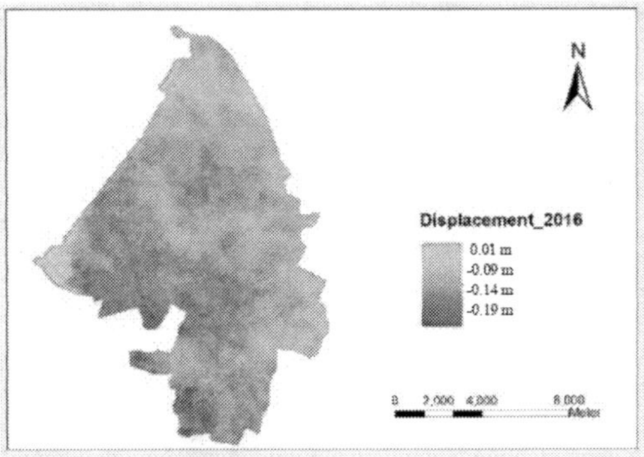

Fig 4. DinSAR 2016

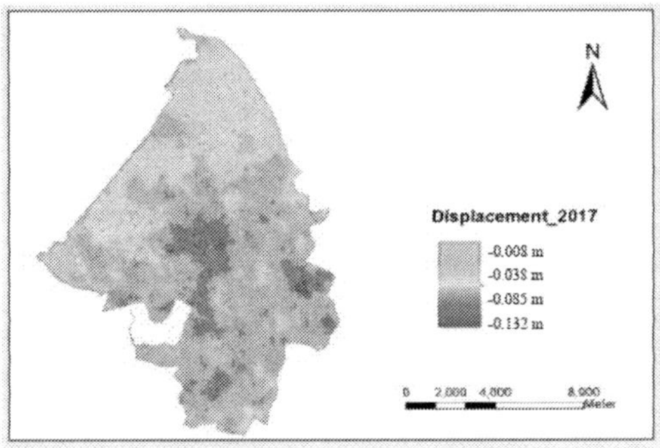

Fig 5 DinSAR 2017

Figure 4 and 5 shown widespread fringe patterns related to the slow deformation with a time lag of three years. The two interferometric methods determined similar results with small differences. The deformation fringes are to be verified in a future research article by advanced multitemporal DInSAR, and next research must be used by precise levelling measurements. Results from DInSAR processing shown in Figure 4 shown sayung district tend to subsided with a max value of 4.7. cm . The magnitude of the decline varies in every region of In Figure 4 shown the Phase unwrapping data, the next step is to change the phase to shift to determine the Los quantity. The result of the phase change process to the landsubsidece. DInSAR processing shown in Figure 5 show sayung district tend to subsided with a max value of 19.5cm in 2016. Figure 5.

DInSAR Sayung district. DinSAR ocessing year 2017 show sayung district having trend landsubsidence value of 13.2cm. The magnitude of the landsubsidence found in the middle of sayung district. Rekapitulation of min max value using DinSAR Processing in year 2016 – 2017 shown in table 3

Table 3 DinSAR Processing

Year	Sub District	Max	Min	Average	StdDevv
2016	Sayung	-0,195	0,010	-0,093	0,031
2017	Sayung	-0,132	0,055	-0,047	0,021

The gps data were processed using the GAMIT 10.6 [12]. The GPS data processing strategy uses CORS UDIP and UDIP9 IGS stations consisting of BAKO, CNMR, COCO, DARW,IISC,KAT1,PIMO,SOLO and XMIS. Several output file results such as h-files, summary files, and Q-file Gfiles, T-files, X-files, J-files, D-files, K-files, B-files from output results processing on gamit contains the most important files like h-files.
The result of gps data processing in 2018, there was postfit value< 0.5. from the results of these observations shows the existence of a fairly small cycle slips. The Wide lane value can be said to be very good because the WL value in the table above shows> 90%. Whereas the value of Narrow Lane can be said to be quite good because more show results> 80% where for NL values it is said to be good if> 80% for NL values that are <80% because of errors such as error in size, orbital errors and bad conditions atmosphere. Postfit nrms shonw in table 4.

Table 4 Posfit nrms and Phase Ambiquity 2018

Point	DOY	Postfit nrms				Ambiquity	
		Constrained		Loose			
		Free	Fix	Free	Fix	WL %	NL%
PRWS	128	0,18	0,18	0,177	0,180	89,9	65,7
GEMA	127	0,18	0,19	0,179	0,183	88,2	77,7
TUGU	127	0,18	0,18	0,178	0,183	86,9	76,1
TMBL	127	0,18	0,19	0,180	0,184	87,9	68,3
DADI	127	0,18	0,19	0,179	0,183	82,2	77,7
BDN1	128	0,18	0,18	0,176	0,180	89,3	65,7
BDN2	128	0,18	0,18	0,176	0,180	88,5	65,6
BDN3	128	0,18	0,18	0,177	0,181	87,8	67,8
BDN4	128	0,18	0,18	0,179	0,183	90,6	70,6

GLRED / GLOBK processing can be done after the GAMIT process that produces h-files which is the main requirement in processing GLOBK. The results obtained from this processing are 3D cartesian coordinates (X, Y, Z) and topocentric coordinates (N, E, U) with their respective deviation. To obtain the height value obtained from the difference between two high values of different epoch observations. List of topografi coordinat in 2018 can be seen in table 5
The standard deviations of GPS-derived relative ellipsoidal heights in 2018 from all surveys were in general better than 3mm – 4cm (see at Table 5). A few points have slightly larger standard deviations, due to the lack of observed data caused by the signal obstruction

Table 5 Coordinate Topocentric and Standart Dev 2018

Stn	n	e	u	mm	mm	mm
GMA	-770112,787	12212867,626	27,18	4,32	5,99	18,99
DDI	-764693,243	12215442,674	27,37	5,37	7,62	26,24
TBL	-767399,065	12213032,940	27,06	6,14	8,88	29,32
TGU	-768940,718	12213954,998	27,45	3,83	5,58	15,16
BN1	-770421,731	12209994,759	28,53	4,54	6,35	18,71
BN2	-771935,836	12208725,913	28,59	4,62	6,45	19,21
PWS	-772129,102	12210705,244	28,42	4,56	6,5	20,18
BN4	-770887,092	12208852,755	27,93	5,75	7,4	30,23
BN3	-771235,042	12209436,770	27,40	4,98	7,01	23,54

Analysis of Land Deformation period 2015-20108 period in the coastal area can be seen in Table 6. Results from GPS survye show that vertical displacement in Demak has spatial variations, ranging from 0.8 to 17,91 cm/year (see Table 6 and Figures 5). Midle region of Sayung district exhibits higher rates of subsidence compare to northern and southern region,

Table 6 Time Series of Landsubsidence

Station	2015-2016		2016-2017		2017-2018	
	Ddh_{12} (cm)	$nDdh_{12}$ (cm/year)	Ddh_{12} (cm)	$nDdh_{12}$ (cm/year)	Ddh_{12} (cm)	$nDdh_{12}$ (cm/year)
PRWS	-4,13	-4,11	-10,98	-10,92	-16.75	
WNSR	-8,09	-5,56				
SIDO	-11,88	-8,17				
GEMA	-12,26	-12,16	0,52	0,52	-17,2	-17,91
TUGU	-6,53	-6,49	-0,85	-0,85	-9,97	-10,35
TMBL	-11,74	-11,68	-4,77	-4,74	-5,17	-5,37
SURO	0,32	0,22				
DADI	2,62	2,60	-2,79	-2,77	-12,87	-13,36
BDN1			-11,88	-11,78		
BDN2					-16,24	-16,86
BDN3					-12,7	-13,26
BDN4					-4,06	-4,24

Several monitoring stations such as PWS, WNSR, SIDO, SURO, BDN1 was broken due to unstable due to road works / construction and even widening of the road. So It have to be installed in new location The new station is on BDN3 and BDN4.
Time series results shown that there is an increasing trend of land subsidence in the PRWS location. Whereas in the GEMA, TMBL, TUGU locations there were a variation in land subsidence in each year with different land subsidence rate of deformation.

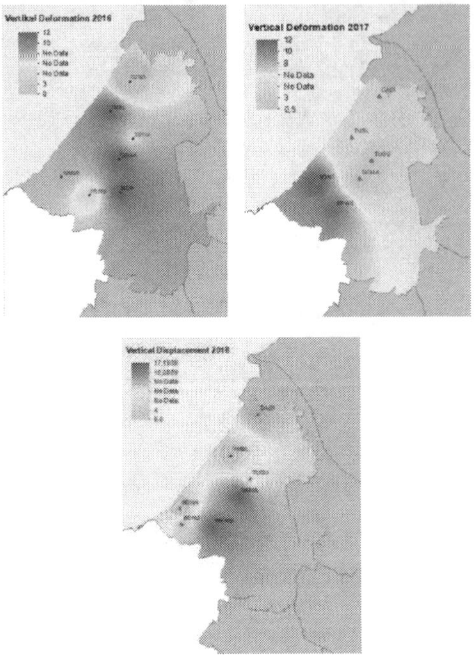

. **Fig 5** Land subsidence derived GPS survey 2015-2018

Mostly, the subsidence derived by two methods can be shown in table 6 extremly cannot be compared since it has quite different temporal and spasial coverage. The table show land subsidence interval observation from 2015 to 2018 , while interval of observation land subsidence for DinSAR from 2016 to 2017.

Table 6 Trend of Landsubsidence

Titik	**GNSS**		**DinSAR**	
	h16-17 (cm)	**h17-18 (cm)**	**h16 (cm)**	**h17 (cm)**
PRWS	-10,98	16,75	-11,40	-5,10
WNSR			-9,97	-5,10
SIDO			-10,77	-5,36
GEMA	-0.52	-17,20	-10,45	-3,29
TUGU	-0,85	-9,97	-10,27	-6,35
TMBL	-4,77	-5,17	-9,63	-3,21
SURO			-6,89	-6,00
DADI	-2,79	-12,87	-8,94	-2,36
BDN1	-11,88		-12,56	-0,55
BDN2		-16,24	-13,47	-1,36
BDNO			-13,31	-5,60
BDN3		-12,02	-11,20	-5,90
BDN4		-4,06	-9,60	-5,40

Closing Remark

One of the weakness of DinSAR Processing, is that the coherence is still quite low, this is due to temporal decorrelation, so there is quite a lot of data with adjacent temporal and baseline distances. For temporal distance data acquisition can be done every 6 months with a baseline distance = 150m. From the results shown there are still have low coherence due to temporal, atmospheric and noise decorrelation, it is necessary to increase the accuracy using the PS InSAR technique.
In this study we propose , It should be installed a stable BM for a long time and validate the DInSAR and GNSS analysis with leveling measurements, which aim to improve understanding of the characteristics of the geohazard process and enable a good correlation between methods.

4. Aknowledgment

This research was financially supported by Diponegoro, Indonesia through Riset Pengembangan dan Penerapan Grant 2018.
Special thanks to PT Adhi Mulia Interniagatama who installed GNSS CORS UDIP.

References

[1] Suryanti W A and Marfai A 2016 Analisis Multibahaya di Wilayah Pesisir Kabupaten Demak *J. BUMI Indones.* **5**, **Nomor 2**

[2] Östblom E 2017 Possibilities to make measurements of ground subsidence more effective , using dInSAR , GNSS and levelling

[3] Ferretti A, Prati C and Rocca F 2001 Permanent Scatterers in SAR Interferometry 39 8–20

[4] Ishwar S G and Kumar D 2017 Application of DInSAR in mine surface subsidence monitoring and prediction 112

[5] Haasdyk J, Roberts C and Janssen V 2010 Automated Monitoring of CORSnet-NSW using the Bernese Software Automated Monitoring of CORSnet-NSW using the Bernese Software 11–6

[6] Yuwono B D, Awaluddin M and Yusuf M A 2017 Geodetic Deformation Monitoring at Pendidikan Diponegoro Dam **040001**

[7] Hofmann-Wellenhof 2008 *GNSS* (SpringerWienNewYork)

[8] Alfred Leick, Lev Rapoport and Tatarnikov D *GPS Satellite Surveying* (Wiley)

[9] Yuwono B D, Awaluddin M and Widi H 2017 ANALISIS KECEPATAN PERGERAKAN STATION GNSS CORS UDIP (Velocity Rate Analysis GNSS Station CORS UDIP) *J. Ilm. Geomatika* **23 No.1 Me** 27–36

[10] Castañeda C, Pourthié N and Souyris J C 2011 Dedicated SAR interferometric analysis to detect subtle deformation in evaporite areas around Zaragoza, NE Spain *Int. J. Remote Sens.* **32** 1861–84

[11] Yuwono B D, Prasetyo Y and Islama L J F 2018 Investigation of Potential Landsubsidence using GNSS CORS UDIP and DinSAR, Sayung, Demak, Indonesia *IOP Conf. Ser. Earth Environ. Sci.* **123** 1–9

[12] Yuwono B D, Abidin H Z, Gumilar I, Andreas H, Awaluddin M, Haqqi K F and Khoirunisa R 2016 Preliminary survey and performance of land subsidence in North Semarang Demak *AIP Conf. Proc.* **1730** 1–12

Investigating the tectonic influence to the anthropogenic subsidence along northern coast of Java Island Indonesia using GNSS data sets

Heri Andreas[1,*], *Hasanuddin* Zainal Abidin[1], *Dina* Anggreni Sarsito[1], *Irwan* Meilano[1] and *Susilo*[2]

[1]Geodesy Research Division, Faculty of Earth Science and Technology, Institute of Technology Bandung, Indonesia
[2]Indonesia Geospatial Agency (Badan Informasi Geospasial), Indonesia

Abstract. Geodetic measurements (e.g. Spirit Leveling, GNSS and InSAR) have clearly measured the land subsidence in many parts along northern coast of Java Island Indonesia. The impacts from the subsidence (e.g. problems on infrastructures, wider expansion of flooding, tidal inundation, etc.) are significantly appeared in certain places and already concluded as ecological disaster. Since mostly the land subsidence are located in cities lying on sediment area like Jakarta, Pekalongan, Semarang, Demak, and Surabaya where consumption of groundwater is very huge, in this case the typical of subsidence might be categorize as anthropogenic land subsidence. Nevertheless in order to make sure this typical, in this case the investigation on the others factors like the tectonic influence is necessary (e.g. as key for appropriate of adaptation or mitigation from disaster).This paper will highlight the investigation by using GNSS dataset in order to see the tectonic influence to the anthropogenic subsidence along northern coast of Java Island. Our preliminary result shows relatively lack of tectonic influence to the anthropogenic subsidence around the investigated area.

1Introduction

Northern coast of Java lies along the Island of Java, the Island which is recorded as densest population in Indonesia. The straight length of the coastal is approximately reached 1000 kilometer. This area is one of the strategic places for our National development. Many of urban area including big cities like Jakarta, Bekasi, Cirebon, Tegal, Pekalongan, Semarang, and Surabaya lies along this area. More than 50% of people in Java Island living in the cities including the coastal city as mentioned here. Within the urban areas especially along the northern coast of Java, many of industrial area and trading area are being established. Others shape like farm land, fishpond, etc. lies also along the area. Many facilities can be found along the area such as big harbor (e.g. Tanjung Priok in Jakarta, Tanjung Mas in Semarang and Tanjung Perak in Surabaya). Toll road is also establishing along northern of Java Island. The toll road projected to connect the most western part of the Island (Merak) to the most eastern part (Banyuwangi). Until today the toll road segment from Merak to Surabaya is about to finished. This toll road is also belonging to the ASEAN highway. Within these infrastructures, the future development of urban area including the facilities in northern coast of Java will be very huge.

In spite of remarkable development, many places around northern coast of Java island are experiencing land subsidence with the rates vary from few centimeter to order of tens centimeter per year. According to some publications (e.g. Murdohardono and Tirtomihardjo [1], Murdohardono and Sudarsono [2], Rajiyowiryono [3], Abidin et. al [4-8], Koudogbo et. al [9], Ng, A.H.-M et.al [10], Chaussard et. al [11]) the yearly value of Jakarta's subsidence generally ranging from 1 to 10 centimeter per-year and may reach 20-26 centimeter in certain place, especially in northern part of Jakarta city for the recent years. Meanwhile, land subsidence in Bekasi is around 1-10 centimeter per year with large subsidence are happening in district of Cikarang and Downtown of Bekasi (Chaussard et. al [11]). Still according to Chaussard et. al [11] land subsidence around Pondok Bali area, Pamanukan area and pekalongan area are varying between 2 to10 centimeters per year for recent years. Further to the east we can see Land subsidence in Semarang and Demak ranging from 1 to 17 centimeter per-year (Marfai et. al [12], Murdohardono et. al [13], Kuehn et. al [14], Lubis et al [15], Chaussard.et. al [11], Andreas et al. [16]). Surabaya area are experiencing large subsidence with rate of about 1-5 centimeter per year. It is probably many other places in the northern coast of Java island are experiencing land subsidence but still unmeasured. Figure 1 shows map of land subsidence in Jakarta, Bekasi, Pondok Bali Blanakan, Pamanukan, Pekalongan, Semarang and Demak. As we can see geodetic measurements (e.g. Spirit Leveling, GNSS and InSAR) have clearly measured the land subsidence in the areas.

*Corresponding author: heriandreas49@gmail.com

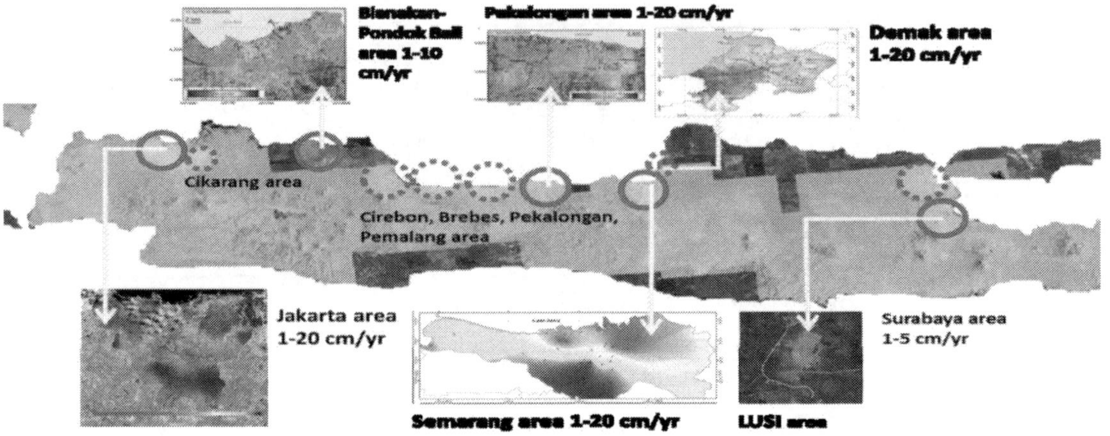

Fig. 1. Map shows many places around Java island are experiencing land subsidence (e.g. Jakarta, Pekalongan, Semarang, Demak, etc.) with the rates vary from few centimeter to order of tens to twenty centimeter per year.

The impact of land subsidence in Java Island especially around northern coast of the island can be seen in several forms, such as the wider expansion of (coastal) flooding areas, cracking of buildings and infrastructure, and increased inland sea water intrusion (Sutanta et. al [17], Mazzoti et. al [18], Andreas et. al [19-20]. It also badly influences the quality and amenity of the living environment and life (e.g. health and sanitation condition) in the affected areas. Some people indeed have been evacuated from their origin place. The place now become sea. The economic losses caused by land subsidence in Java Island are enormous; since many buildings and infrastructure severely affected and its collateral coastal flooding disasters in many places are located in the industrial zone, housing, farming, fish pond, etc. Off course a large number of populations are also exposed to this silent disaster. The corresponding maintenance cost is increasing every year. The living conditions of the affected population are deteriorating. The quality of social and economic activity is consequently decreasing as well. So, adaptation and mitigation are considered very important especially along northern coast of the Island. Sometime in the future if less action taken in adaptation and mitigation, ecological disaster would be more and more significant. Figure 2 shows the impacts of land subsidence along northern coast of Java Island which are already recognize among others which are probably believed still quietly unrevealed but it is there.

Question arises in regard to adaptation and mitigation is what would be the causes of the subsidence in the area. The tectonic is one of the suspected causes along with anthropogenic causes (e.g. ground water overexploitation). The question is very important for proper and effective mitigation or adaptation. As we can see the impact like damaging on infrastructures, wider area expansion of flood, etc. indeed they are formed a quite serious disaster now. If the tectonic play significant role, in this case the adaptation is more effective than mitigation. If the tectonic indeed is lack influencing, in this case we should focus to another causes and do better appropriate mitigation and or adaptation.

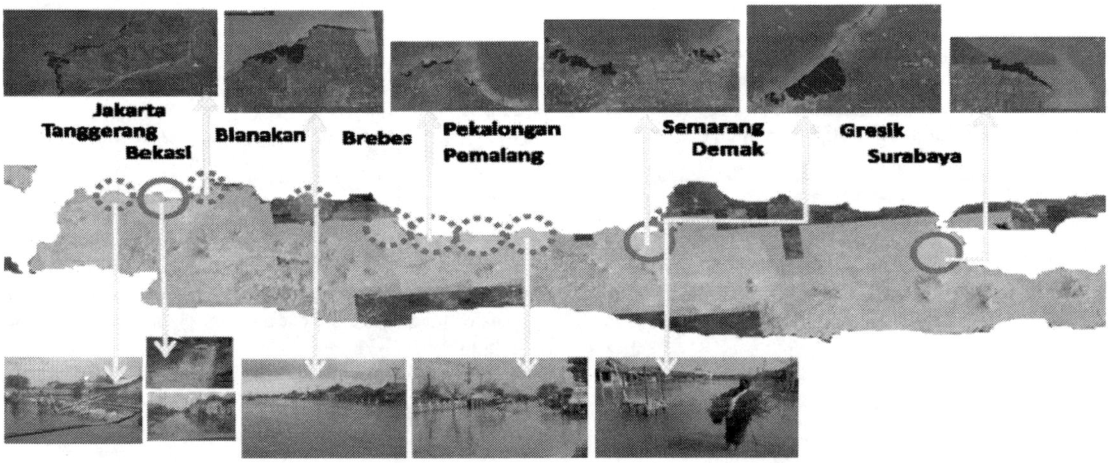

Fig.2. The impact of land subsidence in form of tidal inundation along northern coast of Java Island (e.g. Jakarta, Semarang, etc.)

https://doi.org/10.1051/e3sconf/20199404005

2 Method

When the plates meet each other there are mechanisms where one plate can subduct the other plate. The oceanic plate which has more weight is subducting the continental plate which has lighter weight. On the subduction zone there will part which are locked each other due to a friction and we call it seismogenic zone. As an oceanic plate is continuing to move and given a force, in this case the continental plate is experiencing deformation. As the consequences the fore arc basins is usually experiencing both uplift and submerge (subsidence) in certain part. The submerge mechanism we also call it tectonic subsidence. After sometime when the seismogenic zone reaches the maximum stress on the locked, latter on the locked can break and produce the earthquake (Hudnut [21], Bock et. al [22]). This moment we call it coseismic phase followed by postseismic. At these phases, the fore arc basin usually experiencing both uplift and subsidence in reverse.

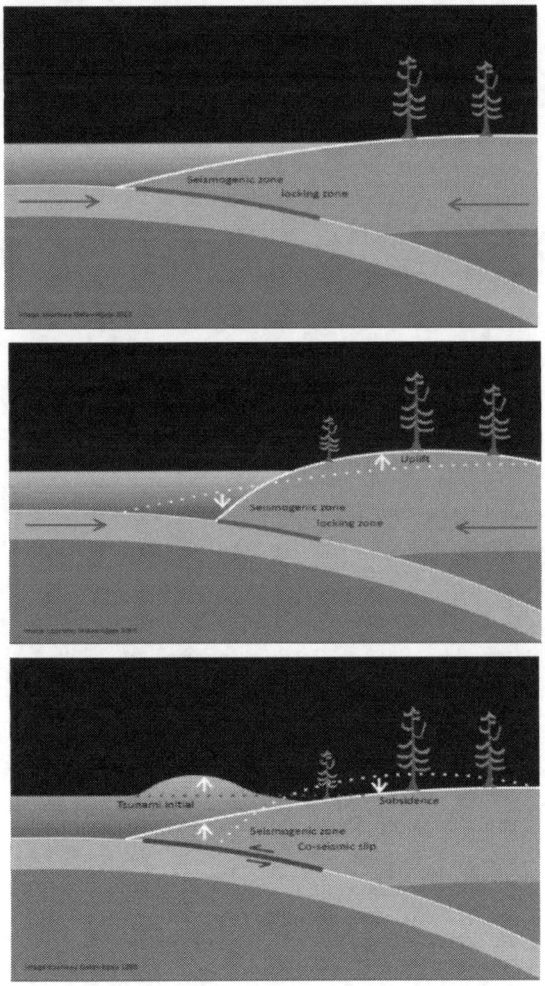

Fig.3. Illustration of uplift and submerge (subsidence) in the subduction zone.

Since basically the tectonic subsidence is a temporal variation on position at vertical component (e.g. Height), in this case measurement technology like GNSS GPS is one of the best tools to choose. We in this case choose GNSS GPS campaign and continuous for investigating the tectonic subsidence around northern coast of Java Island. The campaign mode means we regularly (e.g. monthly or yearly basis) measured the GPS satellites for about 12 to 48 hours, meanwhile continuous mode means we observe GPS satellite 24 hour a day and 7 in a week continuously. In this investigation luckily we have CORS network belong to BIG, our national geospatial agency that can be analyzed. At Java Island there are around 40 CORS station that can be used to analyze the tectonic subsidence of Java Island. Figure 4 shown illustrations of GNSS GPS surveys on investigating tectonic subsidence.

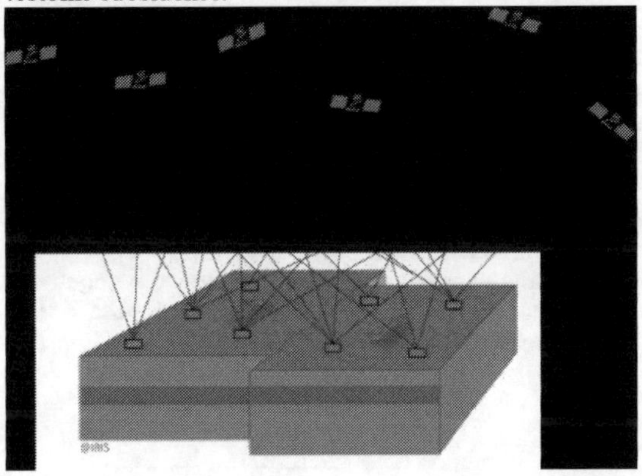

Fig.4. Method on investigating tectonic subsidence by using GNSS GPS. Monitoring point located in tectonic active area and it position especially the vertical components is investigation in time series.

Figure 5 shows documentation of Benchmark of CORS BIG in the field and also map of all Benchmark around Java Island. The Benchmark installed deeply on the ground for about one and a half meter. There are also Benchmark with steel pile attached to the ground below until 5-6 meter. The location arrange so they can see the movement of the plate. It mean it is very stable area, save from local movement like landslide or else.

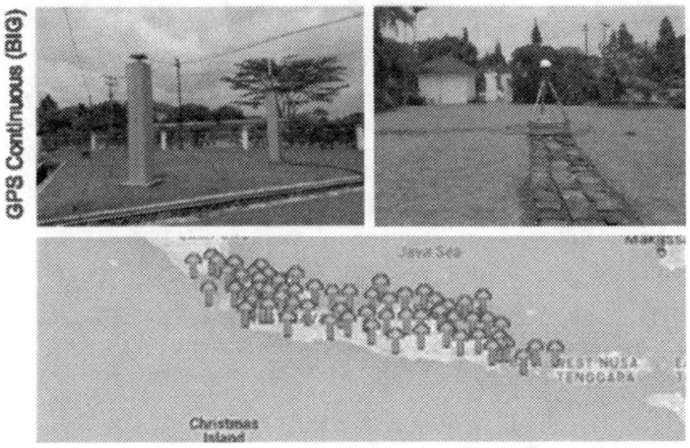

Fig.5. Documentation of Benchmark of CORS BIG and map of all location of Benchmark around Java Island.

Simply by comparing each height component position in a function of times (e.g time series), we can see whether the tectonic subsidence is there or generally not existed over northern coast of Java Island. For example if we found rate of 0.00 meters per year on the height component position changing, in this case no tectonic subsidence is existed. According to some publications, linier trend with very small magnitude (millimeter up to few centimeters per year) if existed may represent interseismic load from tectonic event (Hudnut [21], Bock et. al [22])

All of GNSS GPS data campaign and continuous taken for investigation tectonic subsidence on Java island were processed using scientific GPS software (e.g. Gamit Software) and completed with other scientific software as well (e.g. Bernese). This scientific software is commonly used for achieving the good accuracy level of relative coordinates from GPS surveyed data. All of errors and biases (e.g. Ionosphere, troposphere biases, cycle slip, phase ambiguity, antenna phase center bias, etc.) will be estimated or modeled and leaving the residual mostly only in few millimeter. Since the baseline from each combination of data will exceed typical of short baseline, in this case good handling of parameters errors and biases are crucial for high accuracy requirements especialy for vertical component. Table 1 and 2 each shows parameters of observation strategy and processing strategy.

Table 1. Parameters of observation strategy in order to monitor tectonic subsidence by using GPS technology.

Paremeters observation strategy	
Receiver	Geodetic Type dual frequency
Observation rate	30 seconds
Observation length	Continuously for CORS station and 48 hour for campaign measurements
Mask Angle	15 degree
Data collected	Code and Phase
Others data	Field condition, obstruction, etc.

Table 2. Parameters of processing strategy in order to monitor tectonic subsidence by using GPS technology

Parameters processing strategy	
Orbit and references	Precise ephemeris, Earth Rotation Parameters
Atmospheric biases	Combination of dual frequency for ionosphere and estimation for troposphere
Antenna	Phase center correction
Phase ambiguity	QIF strategy
Other biases and errors	Differencing and neglected

From comparing each height in a function of time is simply enough to see the tectonic subsidence if existed or not in that particular point. Nevertheless if we would like to see spatially for whole the Island on how is the tectonic subsidence characteristic looks alike then we need to do modeling. On this investigation we work with two models to explain about tectonic subsidence model on Java Island. The first model is simply the gridding model while the second one using mechanism of subduction process by elastic half space model (Okada model) (Okada et. al [23]).

Gridding is just simply geometric approach of interpolation. From all the GNSS GPS results we create grid sample and then followed by interpolation. We can use Krigging method for the interpolation or else. As a result of interpolation we visualize on map showing spatial distribution of any value of deformation.

Mechanism of subduction represent by elastic half space in general explanation is estimation of slip by forces on fault plane on subduction zone in three components U1 (slip sliding to each plate), U2 (slip perpendicular to the plate), U3 (opening) generate deformation on the surface. Figure 6 shows the illustration on slip by forces. On the figure we can see also dip angle of plate (δ), length of fault plane (L) wide of fault plane (W) and depth of fault centroid (d).

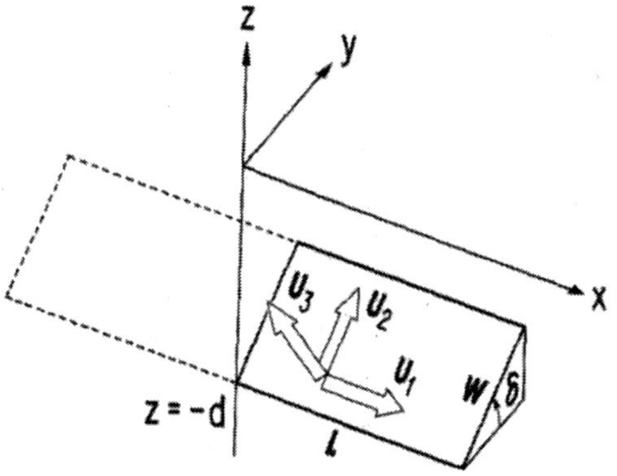

Fig.6. Mechanism of subduction represent by elastic half space. Basically explain the slip by forces on the fault plane.

Below we can see the equation 1 explaining mathematical processes on how slip by forces on fault plane on subduction zone in three components (uj) generate deformation on the surface (ui). We use strain as input parameters (ξ). As for the physical properties we input lame constant α and μ.

$$u_i = \frac{1}{F}\iint_{\Sigma} \Delta u_j \left[\lambda \delta_{jk} \frac{\partial u_i^n}{\partial \xi_n} + \mu\left(\frac{\partial u_i^j}{\partial \xi_k} + \frac{\partial u_i^k}{\partial \xi_j}\right)\right] \nu_k \, d\Sigma \quad (1)$$

On the process we do forward modeling calculation and we set up the fault plane base on historical mechanism of earthquake on the subduction zone in the southern of Java Island. We will first recognize segments of fault plane along west to east Java subduction zone.

https://doi.org/10.1051/e3sconf/20199404005

3 Results

After data processing we have more than thousands of height component coordinates solutions in each CORS BIG around Java Island (west, central and east), and plots each as time series. Data time span generally from 2011 until 2017 (five years). Meanwhile from around ten years of GPS campaign data, we also get the information of time series of height component coordinates solutions. Result of GPS data processing; especially for the vertical component shows the accuracy mostly in several millimeters to maximum only reach 1 centimeter. These results proved the software is capable on reducing significantly the biases and errors on GPS data. Generally only the residual of troposphere effect and the noise on the signal, those are still remains. With these accuracies we can confidently see the signal of deformation (e.g. tectonic subsidence) even in small value (e.g. only several millimeters per year).

Figure 7, 8 and 9 each shows time series of example processed data CORS BIG namely CSIT which is located in Situbondo east Java, CLUM located in Lumajang area East Java, and CMAG located in Magetan east Java for years 2011 to 2017. All of the graphs in those 3 stations shows relatively flat trend, with accuracy of few millimeter after removing some noise and outlier. These three locations are located on stable area with Benchmark design and construction established to hopefully represent plate motions explained before. So if there are signal of deformation on the station in height component (e.g. we have indication of gradient time series) it would represent uplift or tectonic subsidence. Turn out for all of the graphs including the rest which they are not showed here informed relatively flat trend or nearly zero gradients. As a conclusion, the flat trend on the graphs represents almost zero tectonic subsidence. Neverteles modeling is created to make sure the conclusion.

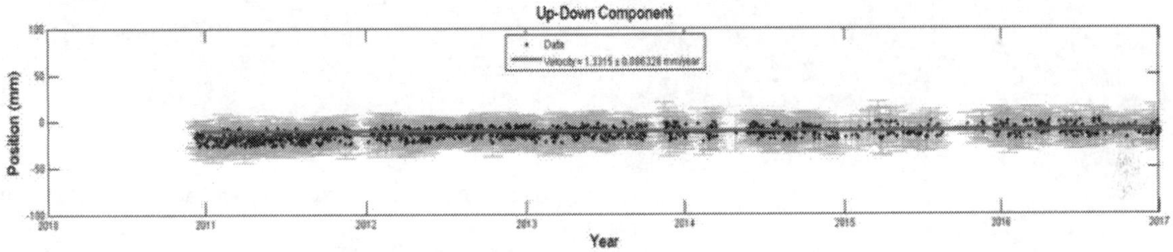

Fig.7. Ploted time series of vertical component/position of CORS BIG Station CSIT SitubondoEast Java from 2011 until 2017.

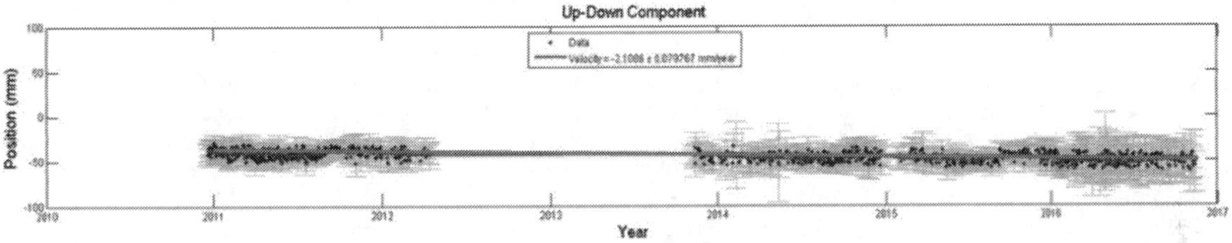

Fig.8. Ploted time series of vertical component/position of CORS BIG Station CLUMLumajangEast Java from 2011 until 2017.

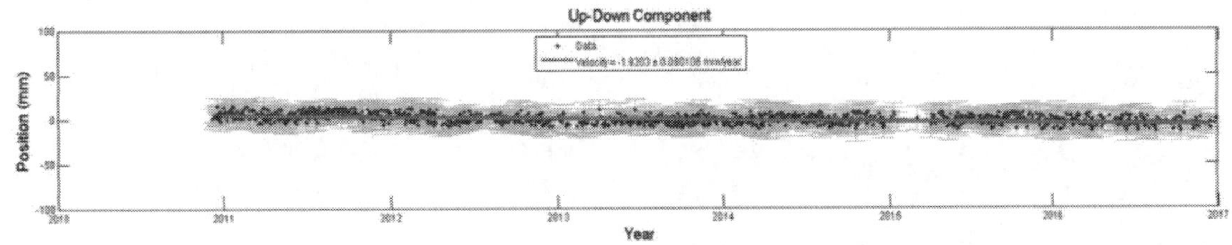

Fig.9. Ploted time series of vertical component/position of CORS BIG Station CMAG MagetanEast Java from 2011 until 2017.

As said on the method, we work with two models to explain about tectonic subsidence model on Java Island. The first model is simply the gridding model. Gridding is just simply geometric approach of interpolation. From all the GNSS GPS set results (rate per year on each height component) we create grid sample and then followed by interpolation. We use krigging method for the interpolation. More than 40 GNSS GPS points were included in the interpolation processes. As a result of interpolation we visualize on map showing spatial distribution of any value of deformation or zero value all over Java Island in a color range (figure 10). Blue indicate uplift, light yellow to bright orange indicate zero tectonic subsidence while dark orange indicate few millimeter of tectonic subsidence. For most of the Island seem zero tectonic subsidence are existed. Meanwhile there are few spot of tectonic subsidence even the values are relatively very small as we can say it belonging to zero tectonic subsidence as well. It is quite interesting to see on the map that there are several areas which are experiencing uplift (e.g. Southern part of west Java Island around Pelabuhan Ratu to the west until Ujung Kulon. If we talking forces from the subduction zone, it mean this areas have more energy accumulate compare to the other areas. As consequences this areas has more risk of earthquake disaster in the future.

As for the Jakarta area it is around 0.1-0.3 centimeter per year of negative value, for Blanakan area it is around 0.1-0.3 centimeter per year of negative value, for Pekalongan area it is around 0.1-0.3 centimeter per year of negative value, for Semarang and Demak it is around 0.1-0.5 centimeter per year of negative value, for Surabaya area it is around 0.0-0.01 centimeter per year of negative value. Generally almost no tectonic subsidence is taking places in all those areas.

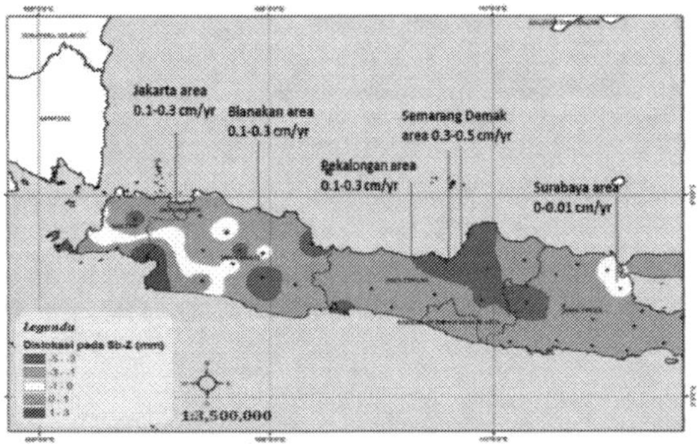

Fig.10. Map of tectonic subsidence and uplift on Java Island base on GNSS GPS data set gridding and interpolation.

The second model for investigation is elastic half space model Okada modeling. As mentioned on the method, we can see surface deformation from slip by the forces on the fault plane beneath the subduction zone. So we need to create the fault plane definition. We have choose four consequence of fault plane from west to east of java subduction zone (figure 11). This segmentation is based on historical evident, slab definition (Hanifa et.al [24], Hayes et. al [25]), etc. We recognize un-break segment below southern part of west Java and southern part of central Java while released segment was around Pangandaran area in 2006 and South of Banyuwangi area in 1994.

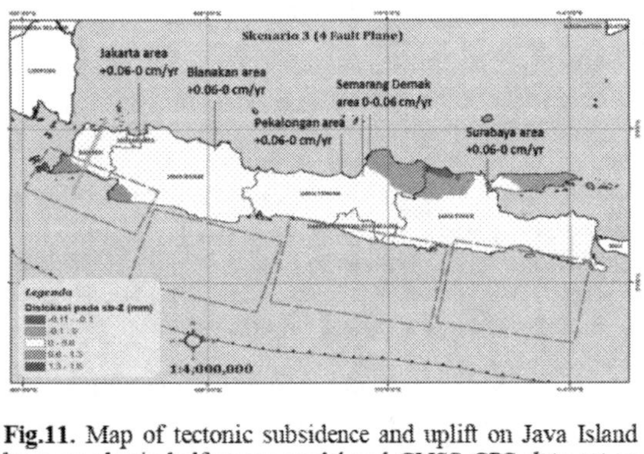

Fig.11. Map of tectonic subsidence and uplift on Java Island base on elastic half space model and GNSS GPS data set as input parameter.

Any value of deformation or zero value all over Java Island base on the Okada model is shown in a color range map (figure 11). Blue indicate uplift, light yellow to bright orange indicate zero tectonic subsidence while dark orange indicate few millimeter of tectonic subsidence. For most of the Island seem zero tectonic subsidence are existed. Meanwhile there are few spot of tectonic subsidence even the values are relatively very small and we can say it belonging to zero tectonic subsidence as well. It is quite interesting to see on the map that there are several areas which are experiencing uplift (e.g. southern part of west Java Island around Pelabuhan Ratu to the west until Ujung Kulon. We draw the cross section and make it on graph to show the uplift pattern (figure 12).

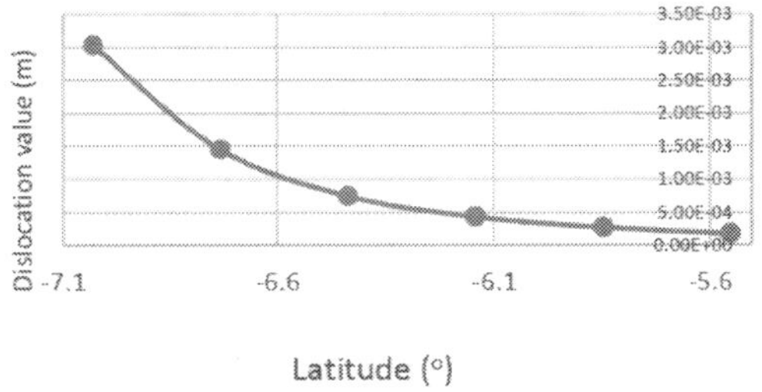

Fig.12. Graph of cross section around southern part of west of Java showing the uplift pattern.

As for the Jakarta area, Blanakan, Pekalongan, Semarang, Demak dan Surabaya it is around 0 centimeter per year of value. Generally almost no tectonic subsidence is taking places in all those areas. So base on two model and trend on the graphs on each CORS BIG station we may concluded the lack of tectonic subsidence influence the anthropogenic land subsidence along the northern coast of Java Island Indonesia.

Table 3 shows parameters that are used in elastic half space Okada modeling Java subduction including dip angle of plate (δ), length of fault plane (L) wide of fault plane (W) and depth of fault centroid (d).

Table 3. Parameters that are used in elastic half space Okada modeling Java subduction.

Parameter	Fault 1	Fault 2	Fault 3	Fault 4
Depth (km)	15-76	16-135	14-124	14-124
Dip (^{0})	8-38	8-47	8-48	9-48
Strike	239-315	256-298	265-294	265-294
Length (km)	380	400	300	300
Width (km)	200	260	260	260
Rake	-90	-80	-80	-80
Slip (cm/year)	6.7	6.7	6.7	6.7
Open	0	0	0	0

4 Discussions

Tectonic subsidence in Jakarta area, Blanakan, Pekalongan, Semarang, Demak and Surabaya is around 0 centimeter more less per year of value. Generally almost no tectonic subsidence is taking places in all those areas. Meanwhile antropogenic subsidence in Jakarta is around 1-20 centimeter per year, in Blanakan is around 1-10 centimeter per year, in Pekalongan is around 1-20 centimeter per year, Semarang and Demak is around 1-20 centimeter per year and in Surabaya is around 1-5 centimeter per year. We may concluded the lack of tectonic subsidence influence the anthropogenic land subsidence along the northern coast of Java Island Indonesia. If we calculate how many percent of contribution, the natural (e.g. tectonic subsidence) contribute less than 3% of total subsidence magnitude while anthropogenic subsidence contributes 80-90%.

So in order to choose appropriate mitigation and or adaptation we should pay more attention to the anthropogenic cause. We strongly believed that the exploitation of ground water is the main causes (Holjer and Thomas [26], Rajiyowiryono [3], Abidin et. al [27], JICA [28]). So, mitigation and or adaptation shoul start here. Many empirical example (Holjer and Thomas [26], JICA [28]), has prove that management of water (including groundwater) is best program of mitigation and or adaptation againts land subsidence.

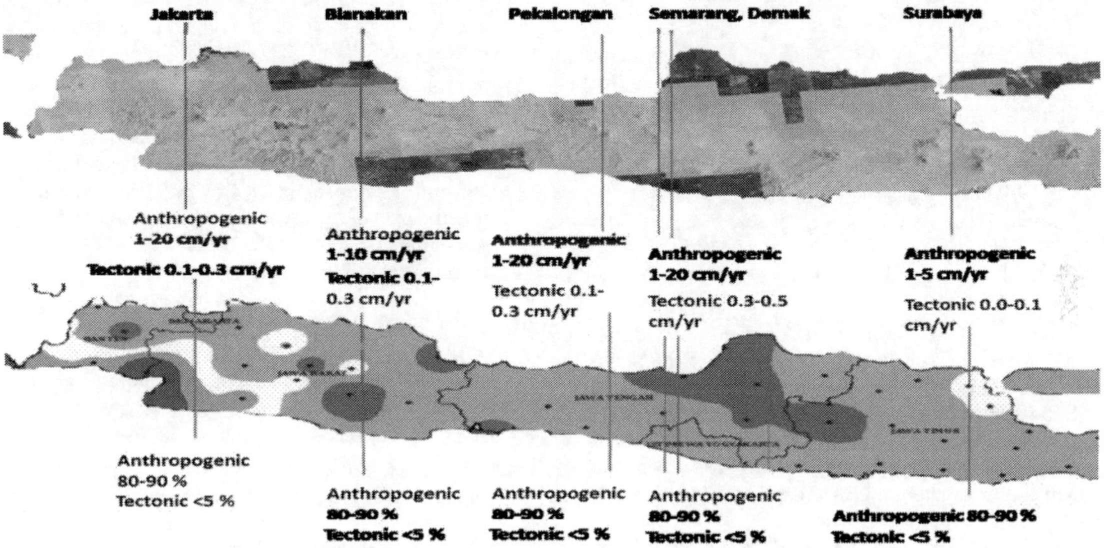

Fig.13. Comparation of land subsidence due to natural processes (e.g. tectonic, natural compaction) and due to antropogenic causes. For Jakarta and other urban places along northern coas of Java, the tectonic subsidence and natural compaction contribute less than 3% of total subsidence magnitude while anthropogenic subsidence contributes 80-90%.

5 Conclusion

In spite of remarkable development, many places around northern coast of Java island is experiencing land subsidence with the rates vary from few centimeter to order of tens to twenty centimeter per year. The impact of land subsidence in this area can be seen in several forms, such as the wider expansion of (coastal) flooding areas, cracking of buildings and infrastructure, and increased inland sea water intrusion. It also badly influences the quality and amenity of the living environment and life (e.g. health and sanitation condition) in the affected areas. Some people indeed have been evacuated from their origin place. The place now become sea. The economic losses caused by land subsidence are enormous

So, adaptation and mitigation are considered very important. Sometime in the future if less action is taken in adaptation and mitigation, ecological disaster would be more and more significant. As a key of adaptation and mitigation we should start from understanding the main causes. If we found it then we can kill it. That is the simple phrase. Some people said tectonic is the main causes while the other said groundwater exploitation is the main (anthropogenic causes).

Base on investigation by using GNSS GPS data set, gridding technique and elastic half space modeling we found the tectonic subsidence (and natural compaction) contribute less than 3% of total subsidence magnitude while anthropogenic subsidence contribute 80-90%. Tectonic subsidence in Jakarta area, Blanakan, Pekalongan, Semarang, Demak and Surabaya is around 0 centimeter more less per year of value while antropogenic subsidence in those areas is around 1-20 centimeter per year. Short story in order to choose appropriate mitigation and or adaptation we should pay more attention to the anthropogenic causes. We strongly believed that the exploitation of ground water is the main causes. We can neglect the tectonic causes. In Tokyo, Osaka, Shanghai, Bangkok, etc. when they stop taking the groudwater the subsidence is stopping.

Acknowledgements

Many thanks and appreciation to students from ITB, from Dipenogoro University and the surveyors who helped the investigation in the field, and especially to the local people along northern coast of Java Island for kindly sharing the information and experience relating subsidence impacts.

References

1. Murdohardono, D dan Tirtomihardjo, H., Penurunan tananh di Jakarta dan rencana pemantauannya, In: Proceedings of the 22nd annual convention of the indonesian association of geologists, Bandung, 6–9 December, pp 346–354 (1993)
2. Murdohardono, D and Sudarsono, U., Land subsidence monitoring system in Jakarta, In: Proceedings of symposium on Japan-Indonesia IDNDR Project: Volcanology, tectonics, flood and sediment hazards, Bandung, 21–23 September, pp 243–256 (1998)
3. Rajiyowiryono, H. Groundwater and Land subsidence Monitoring along the North Coastal Plain of Java Island (CCOP Newsl 24(3):19 July-September 1999)
4. Abidin, H. Z., R. Djaja, D. Darmawan, S. Hadi, A. Akbar, H. Rajiyowiryono, Y. Sudibyo, I. Meilano, M. A. Kusuma, J. Kahar, C. Subarya, Land Subsidence of Jakarta (Indonesia) and its Geodetic-Based Monitoring System, Natural Hazards. Journal of the International Society of the Prevention and Mitigation of Natural Hazards, Vol. 23, No. 2/3, March, pp. 365 – 387 (2001)
5. Abidin, H.Z., R. Djaja, H. Andreas, M. Gamal, K. Hirose, Y. Maruyama, Capabilities and Constraints of Geodetic Techniques for Monitoring Land Subsidence in the Urban Areas of Indonesia, Geomatics Research Australia. No.81, December, pp. 45-58 (2004)
6. Abidin, H.Z., Suitability of levelling, GPS and INSAR for monitoring land subsidence in urban areas of Indonesia, GIM Int 19(7):12–15 (2005)
7. Abidin, H.Z., H. Andreas, R. Djaja, D. Darmawan and M. Gamal, Land subsidence characteristics of Jakarta between 1997 and 2005, as estimated using GPS surveys, GPS Solutions, Springer Berlin / Heidelberg, Vol. 12, No. 1, pp. 23-32 (2008)
8. Abidin, H.Z., H. Andreas, I. Gumilar, Y. Fukuda, Y.E. Pohan, T. Deguchi, Land subsidence of Jakarta (Indonesia) and its relation with urban development, Natural Hazards, Volume 59, Issue 3, pp. 1753-1771 (2011)
9. Koudogbo, F. N., Duro, J., Arnaud, A., Bally, P., Abidin, H. Z., and Andreas, H., Combined X- and L-band PSI analyses for assessment of land subsidence in Jakarta, Proc. SPIE, Remote Sensing for Agriculture, Ecosystems, and Hydrology XIV, 8531, 853107, doi:10.1117/12.974821, 2012 (2012)
10. Ng, A.H.-M., L. Ge, X. Li, H.Z. Abidin, H. Andreas, K. Zhang, Mapping land subsidence in Jakarta, Indonesia using persistent scatterer interferometry (PSI) technique with ALOS PALSAR. Int. J. Appl. Earth Observ. Geoinf. 18, 232–242 (2012)
11. Chaussard Estelle, Amelung F, Abidin HZ, SanHoon Hong, Sinking cities in Indonesia: ALOS PALSAR detects rapid subsidence due to groundwater and gas extraction. Remote Sensing of Environment 128 (2013) 150 -161 http://dx.doi.org/10.1016/j.rse.2012.10.015
12. Marfai, M.A., Almohamad, H., Dey, S., Susanto, B and King, L., Coastal dynamic and shoreline mapping: multi-sources spatial data analysis in Semarang Indonesia. Environmental Monitoring and Assessment, 142, pp. 297-308 (2008)
13. Murdohardono, D., Sudradjat, G.M., Wirakusumah, A.D., Kuhn, F and Mulyasari, F., Land Subsidence Analysis through Remote Sensing and Implementation on Municipality Level; Case Study: Semarang Municipality, Central Java Province, Indonesia. Paper presented at the BGR-GAI-CCOP Workshop on Management of Georisks, 23-25 June, Yogyakarta (2009)
14. Kuehn, F., Albiol, D., Cooksley, G., Duro, J., Granda, J., Haas, S., Hoffmann-Rothe, A and Murdohardono, D., Detection of land subsidence in Semarang, Indonesia, using stable point's network (SPN) technique. Environmental Earth Sciences, DOI 10.1007/s12665-009-0227-x (2009)
15. Lubis, A.M., Sato, T., Tomiyama, N., Isezaki, N and Yamanokuchi, T., Ground subsidence in Semarang-Indonesia investigated by ALOS–PALSAR satellite SAR interferometry, Journal of Asian Earth Sciences, 40, 5, 30 March, pp. 1079-1088 (2011)
16. Andreas, H., Abidin, H.Z., I.Gumilar and Teguh, P.S.,Recent land subsidence in Semarang (Indonesia) as estimated using GPS Surveys. ISGNSS 2016 Conference Proceeding. Taiwan (2016)
17. Sutanta, H., Rachman. A., Sumaryo and Diyono, Predicting Land Use Affected by Land Subsidence in Semarang Based on Topographic Map of Scale 1:5.000 and Leveling Data. (Proceedings of the Map Asia 2005 Conference (in CDRom), Jakarta, 22-25 August 2005)
18. Mazzotti, S., Lambert, A., Van der Kooij, M., &Mainville, A., Impact of anthropogenic subsidence on relative sea-level rise in the Fraser River delta. Geology, 37(9), 771–774 (2009) http://dx.doi.org/10.1130/G25640A.1
19. Andreas, H., Abidin, H.Z., Gumilar, I., Sidiq, T.P., Yuwono, B, Adaptation and mitigation of land subsidence in Semarang, AIP Conference Proceeding 1857, 4987088 (2017)
20. Andreas, H., Zainal Abidin, H., Pradipta, D., Anggreni Sarsito, D., Gumilar, I, Insight look the subsidence impact to infrastructures in Jakarta and

Semarang area; Key for adaptation and mitigation. MATEC Web of Conference 147, 08001 (2018)

21. Hudnut K.W.,Earthquake Geodesy and Hazard Monitoring. U.S. National Report to IUGG 1991-1994. Rev.Geophys, vol 33 Suppl.,@ 1995 American Geophysical Union (1994)
22. Bock Y, Prawirodirdjo L, Genrich JF, Stevens CW, McCaffrey R, Subarya C, Puntodewo SSO, and Calais E, Crustal motion in Indonesia from global positioning system measurements. J Geophys Res 108(2367). doi:10.1029/2001JB000324 (2003)
23. Okada, Y., Surface deformation due to shear and tensile fault, Bulletin of Seismological Society of America (1985)
24. Hanifa, N. R., Sagiya, T., Kimata, F., Efendi, J., Abidin, H. Z. and Meilano, I., Interplate Coupling Model Off The Southwestern Coast of Java, Indonesia, Based on Continuous GPS Data in 2008-2010. Earth and Planetary Science Letters (2014)
25. Hayes, G. P., Wald, D. J., & Johnson, R. L., Slab1.0: A three-dimensional model of global subduction zone geometries,Journal of Geophysical Research: Solid Earth (2012)
26. Holzer and Thomas L., Land subsidence caused by groundwater withdrawal in Urban areas, GeoJournal 11.3 245-255. (Reidel Publishing Company 1985)
27. Abidin, H.Z., H. Andreas, M. Gamal, I. Gumilar, M. Napitupulu, Y. Fukuda, T. Deguchi, Y. Maruyama, E. Riawan, Land subsidence characteristics of the Jakarta Basin (Indonesia) and its relation with groundwater extraction and sea level rise, in Groundwater Response to Changing Climate, IAH Selected Papers on Hydrogeology No. 16, ed. by M. Taniguchi, I.P. Holman, chap. 10 (CRC Press, London, 2010a), pp. 113–130, ISBN: 978-0-415-54493-1 (2010a)
28. JICA, Lesson learn from land subsidence in Tokyo Japan. Presentation on "high Level Meeting on Subsidence". Balai Kota DKI Jakarta Indonesia 2014 (2014)

 https://doi.org/10.1051/e3sconf/20199404006

Sunda and Sumatra Block Motion in ITRF2008

Henri Kuncoro[1,*], *Irwan* Meilano[2], and *Susilo* Susilo[3]

[1]Geodesy Engineering, Institut Teknologi Nasional, Bandung, Indonesia
[2]Geodesy Research Group, Institut Teknologi Bandung, Bandung, Indonesia
[3]Badan Informasi Geospasial, Cibinong, Indonesia

Abstract. The Southeast Asia region is mostly surrounded by active subduction zones in which the Australian plate, the Indian plate, and the Philippine Sea plate submerges beneath the continental plates and blocks. The Sunda block covers the large part of the Southeast Asia region, which comprises of Indochina, the South China Sea, the northeastern part of Sumatra, Borneo, the northern part of Java, and the shallow seas in between. We collect the GPS data in the whole Southeast Asia region for the period from 1994 to 2016, and process the original carrier phase data of GPS using GAMIT/GLOBK 10.6 to obtain the velocity field in the International Terrestrial Reference Frame, ITRF2008. The velocity field thus obtained is utilized to update the Euler rotation parameters of the Sunda block in ITRF2008, and model the long-term slip rates between the adjacent plate and blocks. In this study, we model the Sunda block and the Sumatra block together with the Australian plate by using TDEFNODE. The estimated Euler pole parameters of the Sumatra and Sunda blocks are estimated as their locations at (37.4°S, 106.8°E) and (46.2°N, 89.4°W), respectively, and their angular velocities of 0.371°/Myr clockwise, and 0.327°/Myr counter clockwise, respectively. These parameters result in the slip rate of the Sumatra fault with magnitude of ~9 mm/yr.

1 Introduction

The Southeast Asia region is mostly surrounded by active subduction zones in which the Australian plate, the Indian plate, and the Philippine Sea plate submerges beneath the continental plates and blocks. The largest part of the area is called as the Sunda block which covers Indo-china, some part of Sumatra, Borneo, some part of Java, and the shallow seas located in between (Simons et al., 2007). In the north, the Sunda block is bounded by the collision zone between the Eurasian plate. In the west, the Indian plate subducts beneath the Sunda block. In the south, the Sunda block is bounded by the Sumatran fault and the Baribis-Kendeng fault in Java Island. In the east, the West Makassar block and the Philippine Sea plate is the boundary of the Sunda block. Hall and Morley (2004) suggested that the Sunda block presently moves as a coherent lithospheric block although its geological origin must not be monolithic. The interior of the Sunda block has been characterized by a very low seismicity consistent with strain rate lower than $\sim 7 \times 10^{-9}$ /yr estimated by Simons et al. (2007). By using high precision GPS measurements, the crustal motions can be accurately determined. Many GPS studies recently published have defined the Sunda block as an independent block (Bock et al., 2003; Simons et al., 2007). However, there are still significant discrepancies in the location of its boundaries and its rotation pole. The latest study of the Sunda block motion (Simons et al., 2007) yielded the Euler rotation parameters in the International Terrestrial Reference Frame, ITRF2000 (Altamimi et al., 2002). In this study, the GPS velocity field thus obtained is utilized to update the Euler rotation parameters of the Sunda block in ITRF2008.

2 Methodology

In this study, GNSS data from several sources for the period from 1994 through 2016 are used: 68 IPGSN stations for the period from January 2007 to the end of 2016, 28 International GNSS Service (IGS) stations for the period from January 2007 to December 2016, 7 SuGAr stations for the period from January 2002 through December 25, 2004 (before the Sumatra-Andaman Islands Earthquake, M9.1).

2.1 GNSS Data Processing Strategy

GNSS carrier phase observables from each station are used to estimate the 3-dimensional Cartesian coordinates and the integer phase ambiguities by applying loose constraints to the parameters: 6 orbital elements, semi-major axis, eccentricity, inclination, longitude of ascending node, argument of perigee, and mean anomaly are fixed and the Earth orientation parameters (pole position and rate and UT1 rate). The atmospheric zenith delay and its horizontal gradients at each station, the IGS elevation dependent antenna models, the ocean loading and solid Earth tides are given from the models. The GNSS stations were grouped into

* Corresponding author: henrikuncoro@itenas.ac.id

several networks with at least four overlapping tie stations to combine the individual network solutions. The maximum number of stations per network was set to 20. This step produced the RMS (root mean square of residuals per degree of freedom) of coordinate components for each station below 15 mm and the normalized RMS for all solutions are ~0.2.

The unconstrained parameters including the covariance matrices from GAMIT solutions were input into the GLOBK Kalman filter, which combines those loosely constrained parameters and applies uniform constraints to all parameters to derive final combined solutions in the reference frame ITRF2008 for the station coordinate estimates for each daily solution (Dong et al., 1998; Herring, 2015) and to estimate six components of a Helmert transformation (3 translation and 3 rotation). It has been done by using the stable stations in the list included in GAMIT software out of 28 IGS stations for each epoch. Basically, it was an iterative process, in which four iterations were used to eliminate bad stations and to calculate station weights for the reference frame stabilization (Nikolaidis, 2002). Each time series was cleaned using an outlier detection that excluded the outliers exceeding 95 % of confidence level (2 sigmas) and with uncertainties larger than 10 mm for the horizontal components and 20 mm for the vertical ones.

2.2 Time Series Analysis Method

In general, a time series of GNSS site coordinates consists of three major signals, inserseismic site velocities, seasonal variations, and earthquake-related signals including coseismic and postseismic deformation (Feng et al., 2015). The interseismic velocities can be described as a linear term before or even after earthquakes. The seasonal variations can be expressed by superposition of sinusoidal terms with constant amplitudes and may be attributed to some different sources such as gravitational excitation, thermal and hydrodynamics, local site errors, and model errors (Dong et al., 2002). Since the seasonal signals are modeled in the GAMIT solutions as the solid Earth tides and/or the atmospheric zenith delay to some extent, they should be already small. The largest impact of the seasonal signals exists in vertical component.

The coseismic signals can be represented by offsets in the time series. The postseismic deformation can be attributed to after slip, viscoelastic response, or poroelastic response (e.g. Feigl and Thatcher, 2006). Detailed studies are necessary to distinguish which source is dominant and it is beyond the scope of this study. Instead an exponential formula is used to represent postseismic deformation in the time series in order to quantify the pattern of postseismic processes, even though this formula cannot examine the driving mechanisms.

Some offsets are found in the time series obtained at the stations nearby significant earthquakes especially those of the IPGSN stations. At least two major earthquakes, the M7.0 Java Earthquake of 2 September 2009 and the M8.6 off the west coast of northern Sumatra Earthquake of 11 April 2012 affected the time series in the data period. Beside of these earthquakes, the possibility of ongoing postseismic deformation due to the M 7.7 Java Earthquake of 17 July 2006 was examined.

2.3 Time Series Analysis Method

The GNSS time series represent the motion of the Earth surface. This motion can be related to the kinematics of block rotation and the locking on the block-bounding faults. The motion of blocks can be described by Euler poles in spherical coordinates. An Euler vector in a spherical coordinate system $\mathbf{\Omega_i} = (\lambda_p, \varphi_p, \omega)$ gives the displacement at a surface observation point (λ, φ) caused by the rotation of a block i in the reference frame ITRF2008, where λ_p and φ_p are the longitude and latitude of the Euler pole, respectively and ω is its angular velocity. The horizontal velocity at a point in the i-th block is $\mathbf{V}_i = \mathbf{\Omega_i} \times \mathbf{X}$, where $\mathbf{X}$ is the vector pointing from the center of the Earth to the surface point (λ, φ). A geodetic inversion code, TDEFNODE is used to model simultaneously the block rotations, homogenous strain rates, and locking distributions on block-bounding faults (McCaffrey, 2009).

3 Results and Discussion

We carried out the kinematic modeling of the Sumatra block, the Sunda block, and the Australian plate using the GPS data from 1994 to 2016. These blocks are separated into several faults known as the Sumatran fault and the subduction fault along the Sumatra trench (the Sumatra subduction fault). The Sumatran fault is the boundary between the Sunda block and the Sumatra block, and running along the southwestern coast of Sumatra Island. The Sumatra subduction fault is the boundary between the Sumatra block and the Australian plate, where the activity of the interplate thrust earthquakes has been very high. I used the slab model from Hayes et al. (2012) to represent the Sumatra subduction fault. In order express the slab surface, several nodes were located every 200 km along the iso-depth contours of the slab model with 20 km depth interval. Coupling factors on these nodes are set to be free parameters except for the nodes on eastern and western edges where the coupling factors are set to be fully creeping considering the depth of the seismogenic zone in this area. In the inversion, the elastic deformation is calculated by integrating over small patches assumed in the regions between the nodes. Each small patch has a length of 10 km along strike direction and a width of 5 km along dip direction in this study. Smoothing of the locking is applied by imposing a damping factor of 5×10^{10} derived from the trade-off curve result.

The Sumatran fault has set to be full coupling from 0 km to the depth of 15 km and nine nodes along each iso-depth contour with an interval of 5 km are located based on the bending of the fault trace. The rest of boundaries are assumed to have no relative motion from one another, and to be fully creeping. In this first model,

I also add some slip vectors from several major earthquakes, the 2013 Sigli earthquake (M6.1), the 2008 northern Sumatra earthquake (M6.0), the 2007 southern Sumatra earthquake (M6.4), the 2009 southern Sumatra earthquake (M6.6), and the 1994 southern Sumatra earthquake (M6.9) that occurred on the Sumatran fault, and the 2004 Sumatra earthquake (M9.1), the 2010 northern Sumatra earthquake (M7.8), the 2005 northern Sumatra earthquake (M8.6), the 2007 and 2010 Mentawai earthquake (M7.9 and M7.8), and the 2007 southern Sumatra (M8.4) that occurred on the Sumatra subduction fault and the geological slip rates data along the Sumatran fault from some previous studies.

Figure 1 shows the fault slip rates decomposed into the fault-parallel and the fault-normal motions. The fault-normal convergence rates across the Sumatra trench increase from 46 mm/yr in the west to 54 mm/yr in the east. These estimates are generally similar with the previous study by McCaffrey (2009) who noted that the convergence rate at the Sumatra trench is likely to be 40-50 mm/yr. The fault-parallel velocities along the Sumatra trench show an increase from 18 mm/yr to 32 mm/yr from the east to the west. Right lateral slip rate is found along the Sumatran fault as ~9 mm/yr. These rates are slower than that predicted by Bradley et al (2017). Small compressions exist along the Sumatra fault at rates of 0.3 – 0.5 mm/yr. The locations of the Euler pole of the Sunda block estimated in this study and the previous ones are shown in Figure 2. The smallest uncertainty of the Euler pole parameters for the Sunda block is delivered in Simons's study. However, the uncertainty of the Euler pole parameters in this study are acceptable considering the reweighting that has been applied in this estimation.

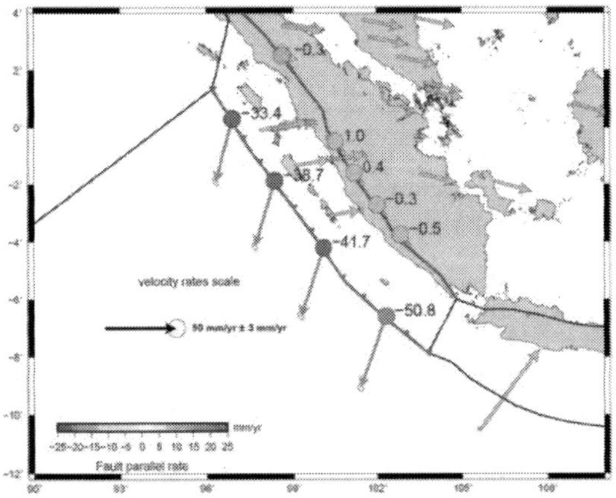

Fig. 1. Fault slip rates along the Sumatran fault and the Sumatra subducting fault. The fault parallel rates (right-lateral positive) are indicated by color in each circles. The numerical values near each colored circle indicate the trench/fault perpendicular slip rate (extension positive). Blue vectors show the slip vectors across the faults, indicating the motion of the hanging wall relative to the footwall. Red lines represent the faults where locking was assigned and the black lines are fully creeping boundaries. Orange vectors show the rotation vectors.

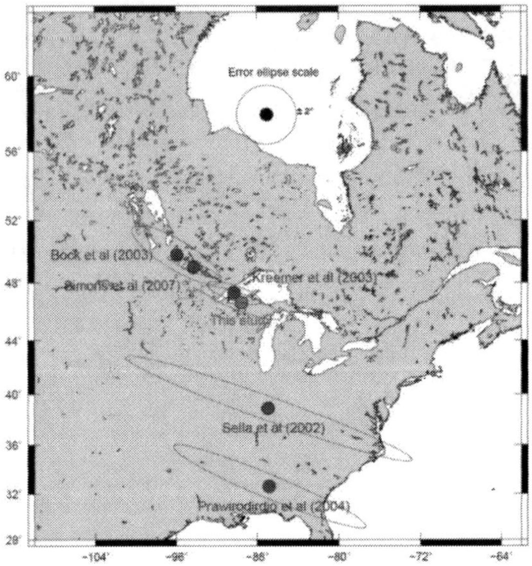

Fig. 2. Map showing the location of the Euler poles of the Sunda block estimated by the present and the previous studies together with the error ellipses.

4 Conclusion

The Euler pole parameters of the Sumatra and Sunda blocks are estimated showing the locations at (37.4°S, 106.8°E) and (46.2°N, 89.4°W), respectively, and their angular velocities of 0.371°/Myr clockwise, and 0.327°/Myr counter clockwise, respectively. These parameters result in the slip rate of the Sumatra fault with magnitude of ~9 mm/yr. The distribution of slip deficit rate on the Sumatra subduction fault is characterized by fully locking in the area between 97°E and 102°E in the depth range from 0 km to 60 km, which overlaps with the rupture area of the 1797 Sumatra earthquake (M8.4) and the 2007 Mentawai earthquake (M 8.4).

Acknowledgement

I thank to Dr. Wim Simons at Delft University of Technology for allowing me to use the GPS velocities in his study. The figures in this manuscript were prepared using Generic Mapping Tools (GMT) (Wessel and Smith, 1991).

References

[1] Altamimi, Z., P. Sillard, and C. Boucher, (2002). ITRF2000: A new release of the International Terrestrial Reference Frame for earth science applications, *J. Geophys. Res.*, **107**(B10), 2214, doi:10.1029/2001JB000561.

[2] Bock,Y., L. Prawirodirdjo, J. Genrich, C. Stevens, R. McCaffrey, C. Subarya, S. Puntodewo, and E. Calais, (2003). Crustal motion in Indonesia from

Global Positioning System measurements, *J. Geophys. Res.*, **108**(B8), 2367, doi:10.1029/2001JB000324.

[3] Bradley, K. E., L. Feng, E. M. Hill, D. H. Natawidjaja, and K. Sieh, (2017). Implications of the diffuse deformation of the Indian Ocean lithosphere for slip partitioning of oblique plate convergence in Sumatra, *J. Geophys. Res. Solid Earth*, **122**, 572–591, doi:10.1002/2016JB013549.

[4] Dong, D., Herring, T. and R. King, (1998). Estimating regional deformation from a combination of space and terrestrial geodetic data,*Journal of Geodesy*, **72**, 200-214,doi:10.1007/s001900050161.

[5] Dong, D., P. Fang, Y. Bock, M. K. Cheng, and S. Miyazaki, (2002). Anatomy of apparent seasonal variations from GPS-derived site position timeseries, *J. Geophys. Res.*, **107**(B4), 2075, doi:10.1029/2001JB000573.

[6] Feigl, K. L., and W. Thatcher, (2006). Geodetic observations of post-seismic transients in the context of the earthquake deformation cycle, *C. R. Geosci.*, **338**(14-15), 1012–1028, doi:10.1016/j.crte.2006.06.006.

[7] Feng, L., E. M. Hill, P. Banerjee, I. Hermawan, L. L. H. Tsang, D. H. Natawidjaja, B. W. Suwargadi, and K. Sieh, (2015). A unified GPS-based earthquake catalog for the Sumatran plate boundary between 2002 and 2013, *J. Geophys. Res. Solid Earth*, **120**, 3566–3598, doi:10.1002/2014JB011661.

[8] Hall, R. and Morley, C. K., (2004). Sundaland Basins, in Continent-Ocean Interactions Within East Asian Marginal Seas (eds P. Clift, W. Kuhnt, P. Wang and D. Hayes), *American Geophysical Union*, Washington, D. C., doi:10.1029/149GM04.

[9] Hayes, G. P., D. J. Wald, & Johnson, R. L., (2012). Slab1.0: A three-dimensional model of global subduction zone geometries, *J. Geophys. Res.*, **117**, B01302, doi:10.1029/2011JB008524.

[10] Herring, T. A., King, R.W., Floyd, M.A., and S.C. McClusky, (2015). Introduction to GAMIT/GLOBK Version 10.6, *Massachusetts Institute of Technology*, Cambridge.

[11] McCaffrey, R, (2009). *The tectonic framework of the Sumatran subduction zone, Annu. Rev. Earth Planet. Sci.*,**37**, 345–366.

[12] Nikolaidis, R., (2002). Observation of geodetic and seismic deformation with the Global Positioning System, *Ph.D. Thesis*, Univ. of California, San Diego, San Diego.

[13] Simons, W.J.F., Socquet, A., Vigny, C., Ambrosius, B.A.C., Abu, S.H., Promthong, C., Subarya, C., Sarsito, D.A., Matheussen, S., Morgan, P. and W. Spakman, (2007). A decade of GPS in Southeast Asia: Resolving Sundaland motion and boundaries, *J. Geophys. Res.*,**112**, B06420, doi:10.1029/2005JB003868.

[14] Wessel, P., and W. H. F. Smith, (1991). Free software helps map and display data, *Eos Trans. AGU*, **72**(41), 441, doi:10.1029/90EO00319.

Earthquake Monitoring Using Variometric GPS Data Processing

Mokhamad Nur Cahyadi, Ririn Wuri Rahayu, Buldan Muslim

Abstract. Variometric Approach for Standalone Engine Displacement Analysis (VADASE) is a technique used in seismology purposes using GPS measurements. VADASE is used to determine the small displacement from the earthquake. The VADASE L1 solution is using the klobuchar ionospheric model. In this study VADASE was used in earthquakes with magnitudes> 7 to> 9 righter scales. In the scale of the earthquake category> 9 used Indian Ocean earthquake of December 26, 2016 with the strength of 9.1 SR by using the closest SAMP station and the Japanese Tohoku earthquake of March 11, 2011 with a power of 9.1 SR using 4 different stations namely MIZU, KMSV, TSK2 and Knii . The earthquake category with a scale of> 8 SR is the offshore earthquake Bio Bio, Chile on February 27, 2010 with a power of 8.8 SR using 2 stations namely ANTC and SANT, the Bengkulu Indonesia earthquake on 12 September 2007 with a power of 8.4 SR using the SAMP station, an illaper earthquake, chile September 16 2015 with 8.3 SR using SANT station, and Tres Piscos earthquake - Mexico on September 8, 2017 with a power of 8.2 SR using IENG station. Earthquake with a strength of> 7 SR, namely the amberlay-New Zealand earthquake on November 13, 2016 with a strength of 7.8 SR using MRLL and WGTN stations, Puerto quello-chile earthquake on December 25, 2016 with a strength of 7.6 SR using COYQ station, Java sea earthquake -Indonesia on 8 August 2007 with 7.5 SR power using BAKO station and ayula mexico earthquake on 19 september 2017 with 7.1 SR power using INEG station. From the results of VADASE, the farthest distance from the epicenter to the observation station is 1100 km (INEG station) and the closest distance is 95 km (BAKO station). The highest speed is 0.12 m / s after 5 minutes from the earthquake in the earthquake Offshore Bio Bio-Chile 2010 uses the SANT station and the lowest speed is 0.006 m / s after 10 minutes from the earthquake in the 2007 Bengkulu earthquake using the SAMP station. Whereas in the other earthquakes was the 2011 Tohoku earthquake with a speed of 0.06 m / s after 1 minute using MIZU station, the amberley-New Zealand earthquake 2016 with a speed of 0.015 m / s after 1 minute using the MRLI satellite, Puerto quello- earthquake Chile 2016 with a speed of 0.025 m / s after 40 minutes using the COYQ satellite.

Keywords: VADASE, Earth quake, Deformation velocity

1 Preface

Variometrric Approach for Standalone Engine Displacement Analysis (VADASE) is a technique used in seismology purposes using GPS measurements. VADASE is used to determine the small displacement of the earthquake. The VADASE L1 solution is using the klobuchar ionospheric model. VADASE is proposed because it is an innovative strategy in GNSS data processing that uses the VADASE algorithm. VADASE is able to estimate in real time the speed and displacement in a global reference frame (ITRF), using introductory phase observation and high-speed broadcast products (1 Hz or more) (orbit, clock) collected by stand-alone GNSS receivers, achieving transfer accuracy in 1 -2 cm (usually better) for intervals of up to several minutes. VADASE can be used in real time even on the GNSS receiver board. VADASE can display time and waveform changes caused by earthquakes with accuracy can only be achieved with seismometers or with other 2 GNSS approaches such as Precise Point Positionong (PPP) and Differential Positioning (DP). In this study VADASE is used to monitor changes in velocity after an earthquake which is divided into several categories based on earthquake magnitude, namely strength> 9 SR, earthquake strength> 8 SR, and earthquake strength> 7 SR. By removing the nearest GPS station to the earthquake it can be used to determine the velocity of each earthquake to the nearest station. For earthquake category with magnitude> 9 SR using the Indian / Aceh oceanic earthquake in 2004 using the SAMP station, the Japanese Tohoku earthquake in 2011 using MIZU, KMSV, TSK2 and KGNI stations. For the earthquake category with magnitude> 8 SR, using Chile's Bio Bio earthquake in 2010 using ANTC station and SANT station, for the Bengkulu-Indonesia earthquake in 2007 using the SAMP station, for the 2015 Illapel-Chile earthquake using the SANT station, the Tres Picos earthquake -Mexico in 2017 using IENG station. Earthquake with a strength of> 7 SR using the Amberley earthquake. Vadase is used to determine the speed of displacement of x, y and z at the time of the earthquake.

2 Result and Discussion

2.1. Magnitude of earthquake >9 SR

2.1.1 Earthquake of Samudera Hindia / Aceh – Indonesia 2004 (9,1 SR)

* Corresponding author: cahyadi_geod@yahoo.com

The Indian Ocean earthquake struck in 26 December 2016 at 00:58:53 UTC, The quake which had the power of 9.1 SR was centered on 3,295°N – 95,982°E.

By using samp station data, the following velocity values are generated:

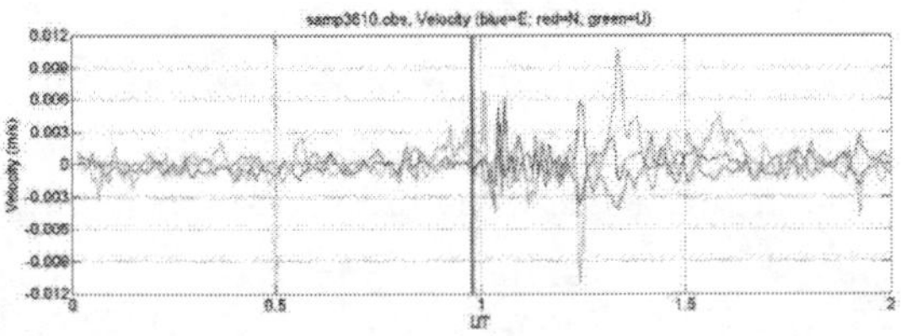

Fig. 1. Results values of Velocity station samp at 00 UTC – 02 UTC

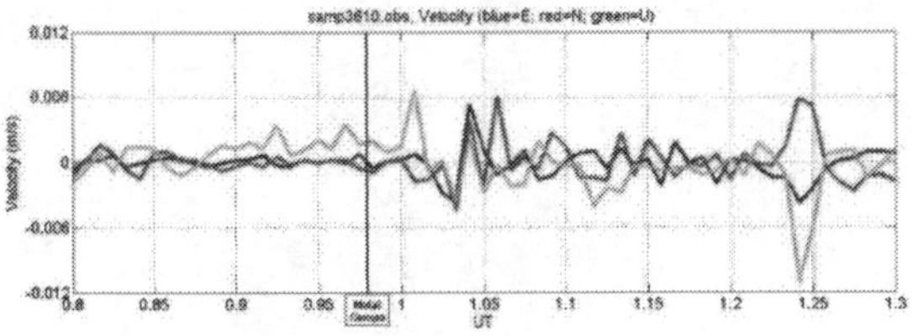

Fig. 2. Results values of Velocity station samp in CID

2.1.2 Earthquake Tohoku – Jepang 2011 (9,1 SR)

The Tohoku earthquake occurred on March 11, 2011 at 5:46:24 UTC. An earthquake centered on 38,297 ° N - 142,373 ° E with a depth of 29 km has a power of 9.1 SR.

In the case of the Tobuk earthquake, the GPS data used came from observations of 4 different stations. The GPS station used is:

- Station mizu, with distance from the epicenter ±142 km
- Station kmsv, with distance from the epicenter ±300 km
- Station tsk2, with distance from the epicenter ±310 km
- Station kgni, with distance from the epicenter ±385 km

The following are the results of variometric processing in the 2011 Tobok earthquake:

a) Station Mizu (distance from the epicenter ± 142 km)

Mizu station observation data in the event of an earthquake, only recorded until 05:59:30 UTC. This station began operating again on March 15, 2011.

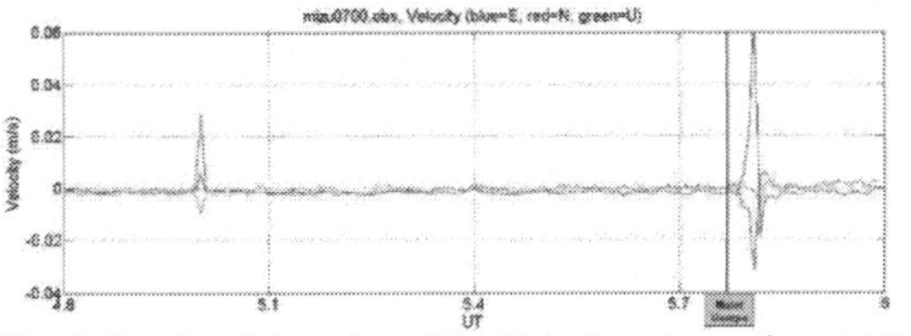

Fig. 3. Results of the value of the Velocity mizu station at 4.8 UTC - 6 UTC

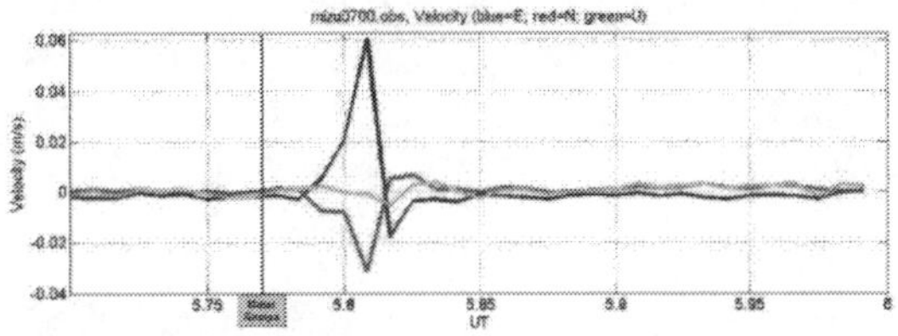

Fig. 4. Results of the value of the Velocity of the Mizu Station when the earthquake occurred

b) Station ksmv (distance from the epicenter ±300 km)

On the Ksmv station data at 5:50 p.m. to 8:58 p.m. is not available. So at that hour the resulting variometric value is equal to 0.

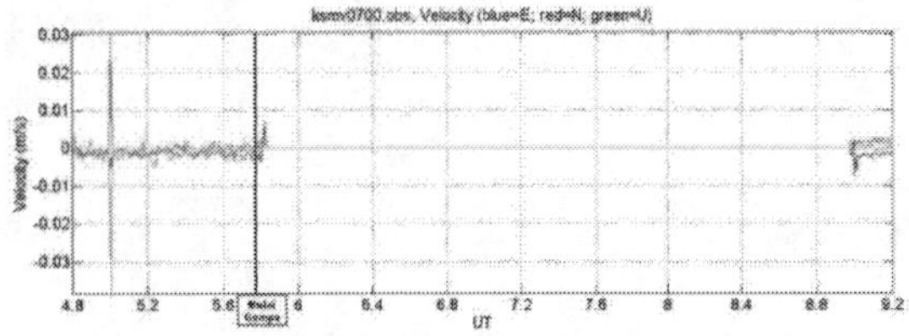

Fig. 5. Results of velocity of ksmv station at 4.8 UTC - 9.2 UTC

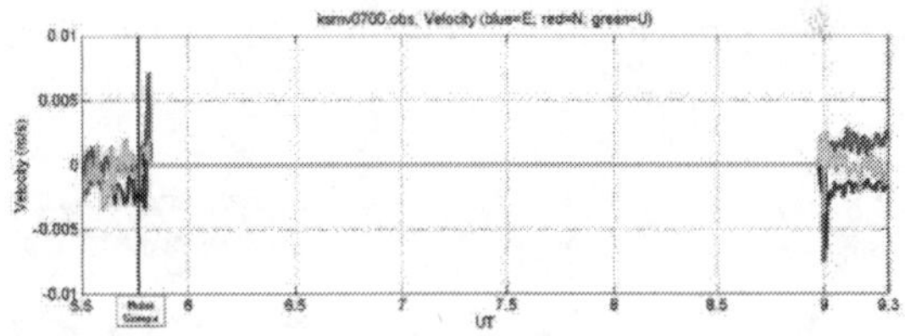

Fig. 6. Results of the value of Velocity ksmv station when an earthquake occurs

c) Station tsk2 (distance from the epicenter ±316 km)

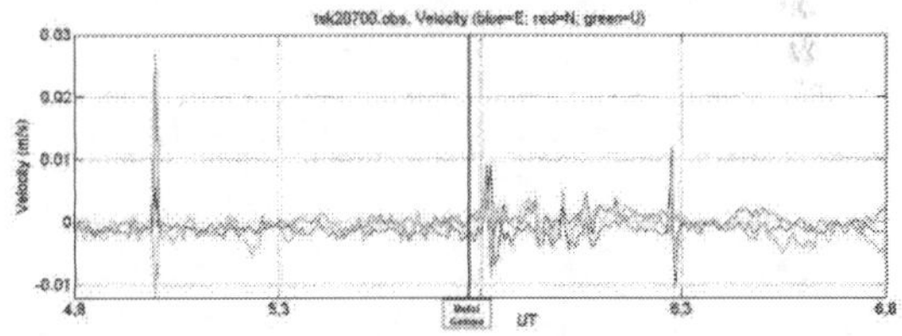

Fig. 7. Results of the value of Velocity tsk2 station at 4.8 UTC - 6.8 UTC

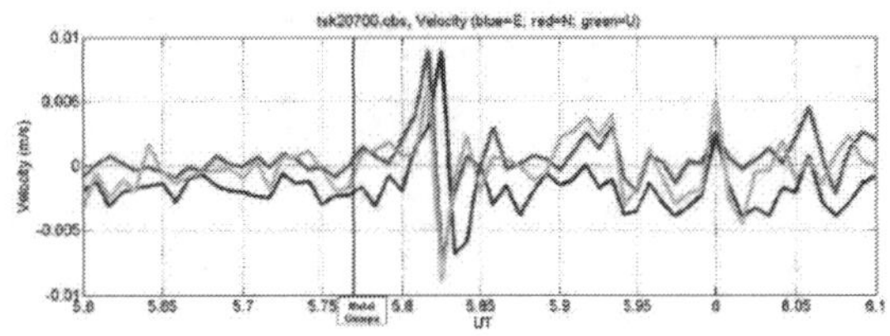

Fig. 8. Results of the value of Velocity tsk2 station when the earthquake occurred

d) Station kgni (distance from the epicenter ±385 km)

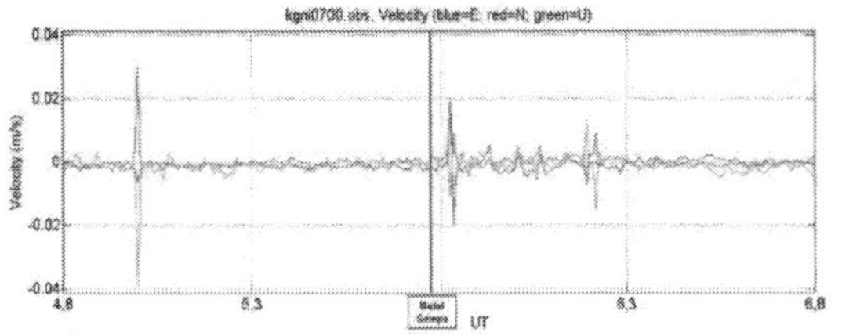

Fig. 9. The results of the value of the Velocity kgni station at 4.8 UTC - 6.8 UTC

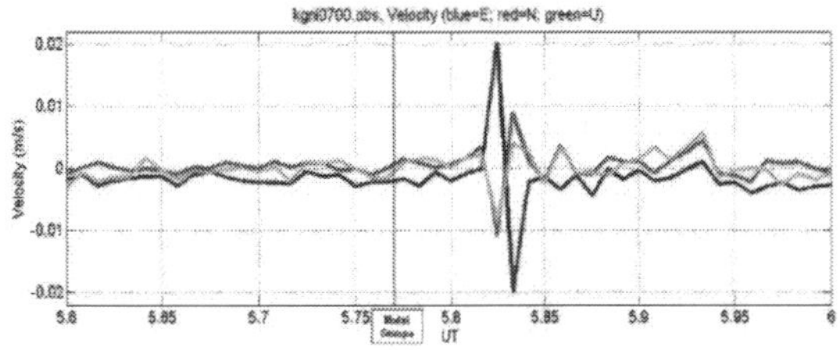

Fig. 10. The results of the value of the kg station Velocity when the earthquake occurred

2.2. Magnitude of earthquake >8 SR

2.2.1 Earthquake Offshore Bio Bio – Chile 2010 (8,8 SR)

An earthquake at Bio Bio Offshore, Chile occurred on February 27, 2010 at 6:34:11 UTC. An earthquake centered on 36.122 ° S - 72.889 ° W with a depth of 22.9 km has a power of 8.8 SR.

In the case of the above earthquake, the GPS data used came from observations of 2 different stations. The GPS station used is:

- Station antc, distance from the epicenter ±180 km
- Station sant, distance from the epicenter ±380 km

Here are the results of variometric processing in the 2010 Chile earthquake:

a) Station antc (distance from the epicenter ±180 km)

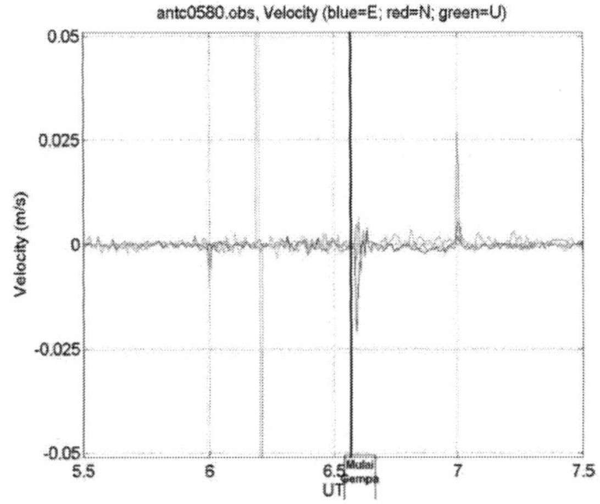

Fig. 11. Results of the value of the velocity of the antc station at 5.5 UTC - 7.5 UTC

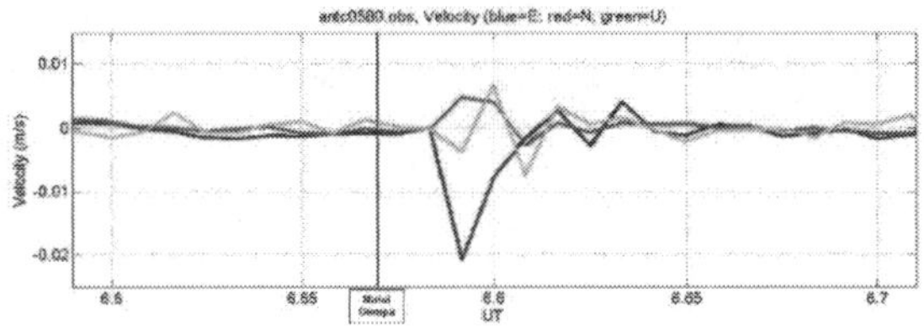

Fig. 12. Results of the value of the Velocity of the antc station when an earthquake occurs

b) Station sant (distance from the epicenter ±380 km)

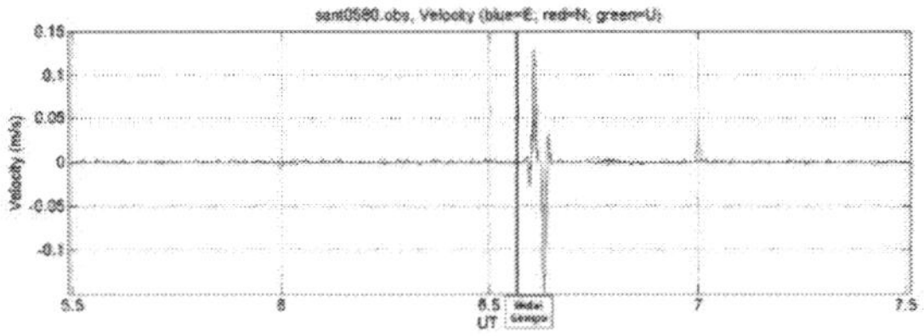

Fig. 13. Results of Velocity sant station at 5.5 UTC - 7.5 UTC

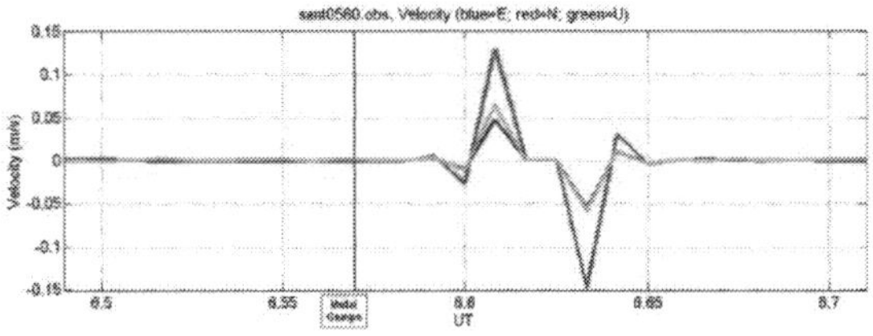

Fig. 14. Results of Velocity values of sant stations when an earthquake occurred

2.2.2 Earthquake Bengkulu – Indonesia 2007 (8,4 SR

Bengkulu Earthquake on 12 September 2007 at 11:10:26 UTC, the earthquake which has a power of 8.4 SR was centered at 4.438 ° S - 101.336 ° E with a depth of 34 Km.

By using samp station data, the following velocity values are generated:

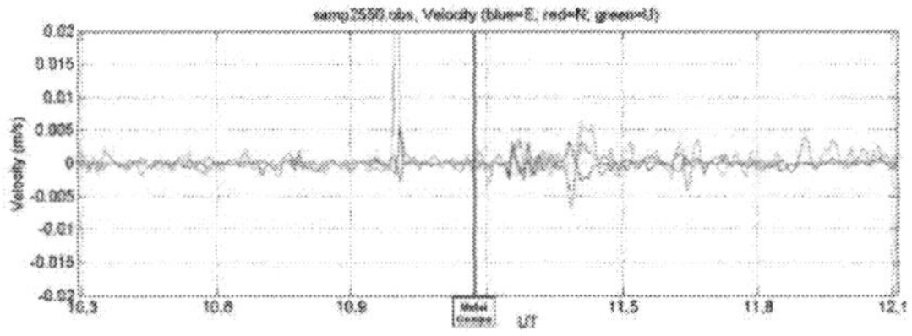

Fig. 15. Results of the Velocity samp station at 10.3 UTC - 12.1 UTC

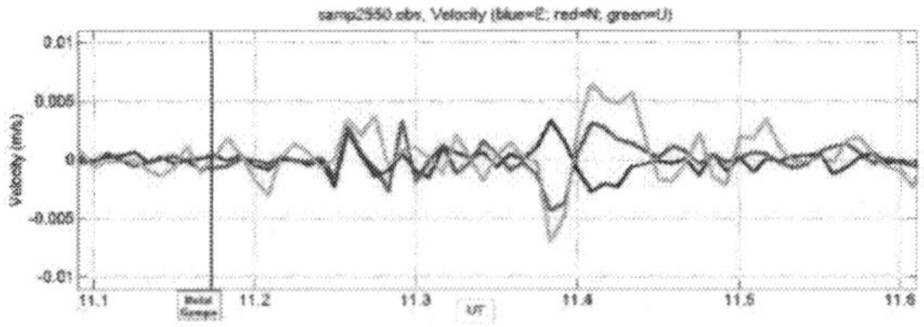

Fig. 16. Results the value of the Velocity station until the earthquake occurs

 https://doi.org/10.1051/e3sconf/20199404007

2.2.3 Earthquake Illapel – Chile 2015 (8,3 SR)

Illapel Earthquake, Chile on 16 September 2015 at 22:54:32 UTC, the 8.3 SR earthquake was centered at 31,573 ° S - 71,674 ° W with a depth of 22,4 Km.

By using sant station data, the velocity value is generated:

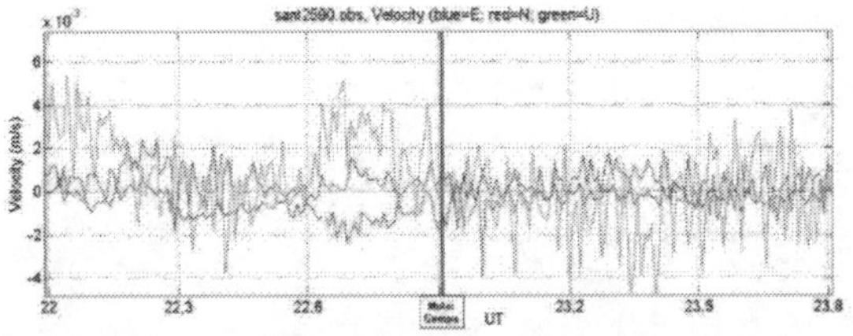

Fig. 17. Results of Velocity sant station at 22 UTC - 23.8 UTC

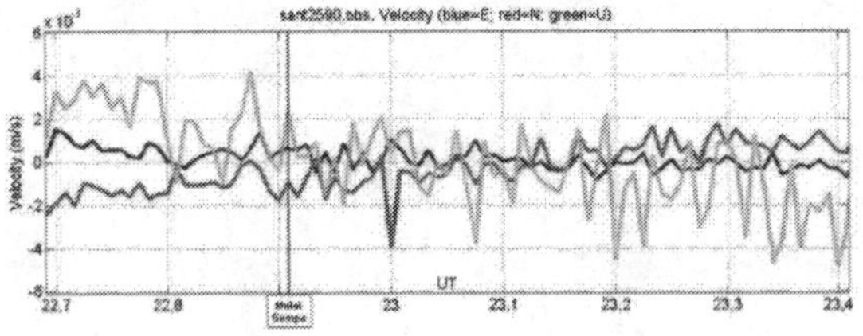

Fig. 18. Results of Velocity values of sant stations when an earthquake occurred

2.2.4 Earthquake Tres Picos – Mexico 2017 (8,2 SR)

Earthquake Tres Picos, Mexico on September 8, 2017 at 04:09:19 UTC, the 8.2 SR earthquake was centered at 15,022 ° N - 93,899 ° W with a depth of 47,4 Km.

By using ieng station data, the following velocity values are generated:

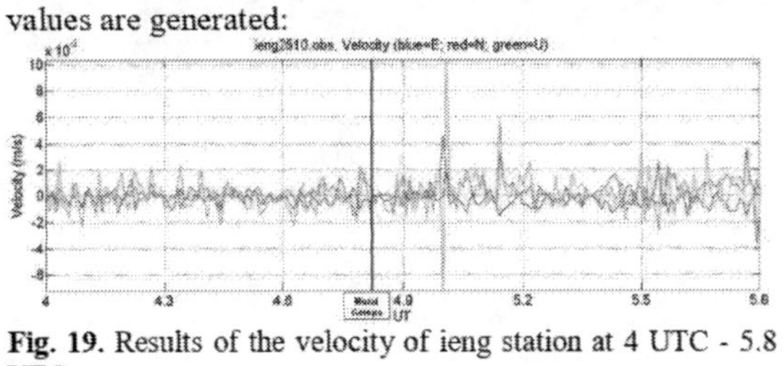

Fig. 19. Results of the velocity of ieng station at 4 UTC - 5.8 UTC

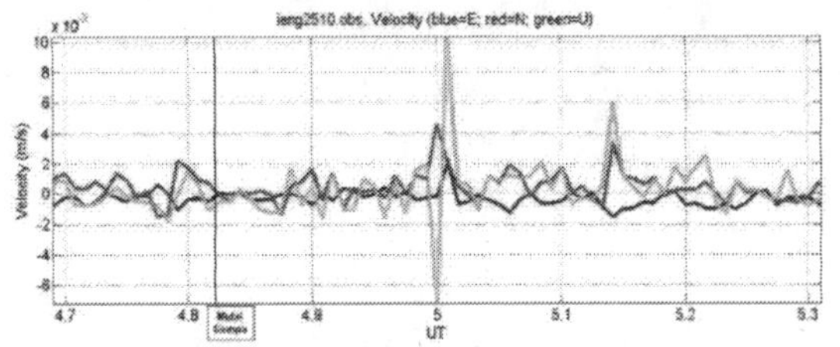

Fig. 20. Results of the velocity of the ieng station when the earthquake occurred

2.3. Magnitude of earthquake >7 SR

2.3.1 Earthquake Amberley – New Zealand 2016 (7,8 SR)

The earthquake in Amberley, New Zealand occurred on November 13, 2016 at 11:02:56 UTC. The earthquake centered on 42.737 ° S - 173.054 ° E with a depth of 15.1 km has a power of 7.8 SR.

In the case of the above earthquake, the GPS data used came from observations of 2 different stations. The GPS station used is:

- Station mrl1, distance from the epicenter ±140 km
- Station wgnt, distance from the epicenter ±210 km

Here are the results of variometric processing in the 2016 New Zealand earthquake:

a) Station mrl1 (distance from the epicenter ±140 km)

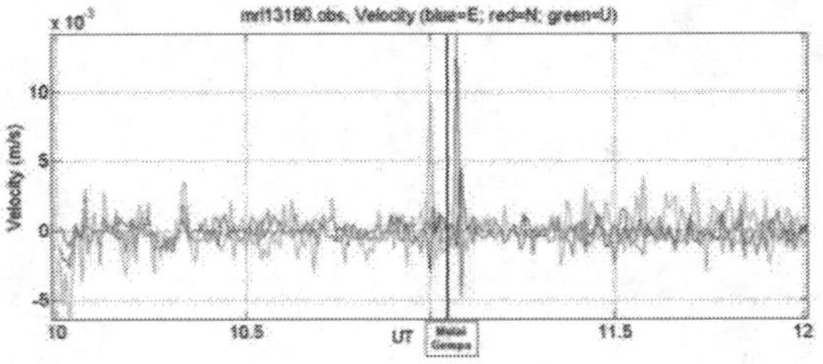

Fig. 21. The results of the Velocity station value are 1 to 10 UTC - 12 UTC

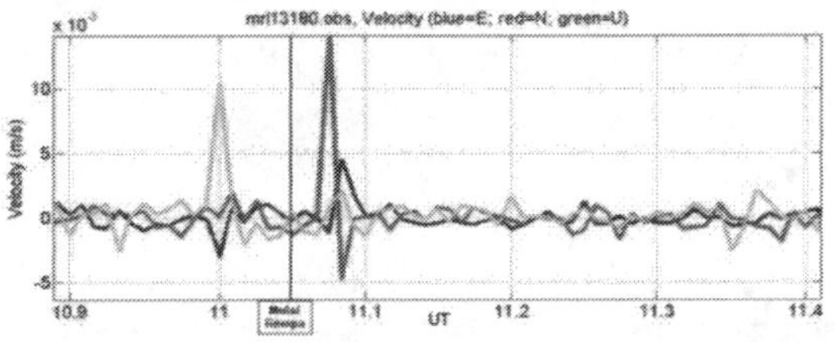

Fig. 22. Result of Velocity station mrl1 when earthquake occurred

b) Station wgtn (distance from the epicenter ±210 km)

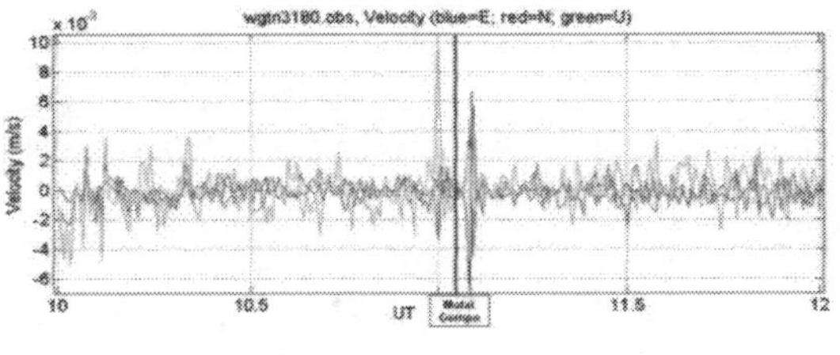

Fig. 23. Results of Velocity station values at 10 UTC - 12 UTC

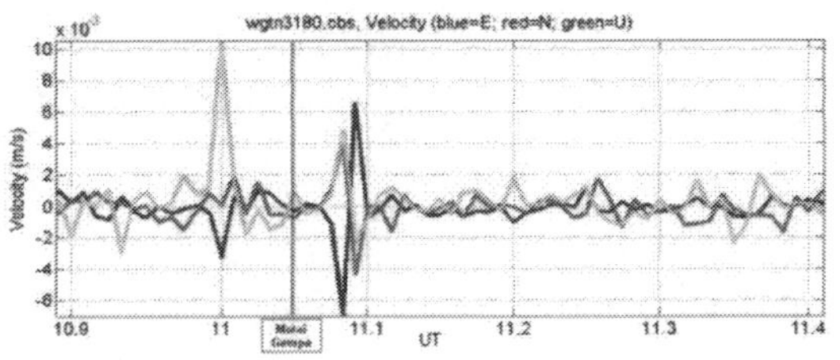

Fig. 24. Results of the value of Velocity wgtn station when an earthquake occurs

2.3.2 Earthquake Puerto Quello – Chile 2016 (7,6 SR)

Earthquake Puerto Quello, Chile on December 25, 2016 at 14:22:27 UTC, the earthquake with a magnitude of 7.6 SR was centered at 43.406 ° S - 73.941 ° W with a depth of 38 Km.

By using coyq station data, the following velocity values are generated :

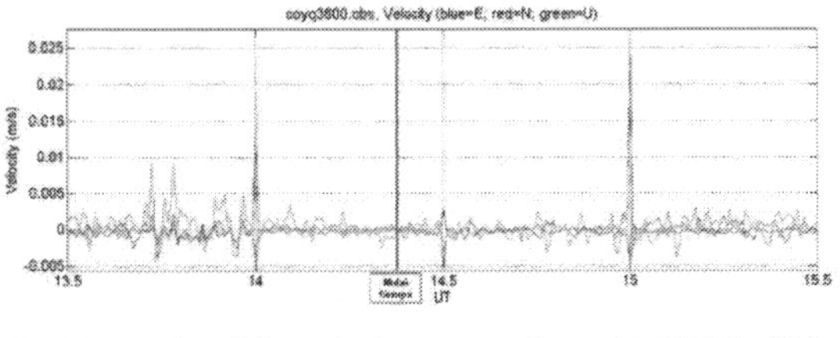

Fig. 25. Results of the Velocity coyq station at 13.5 UTC - 15.5 UTC

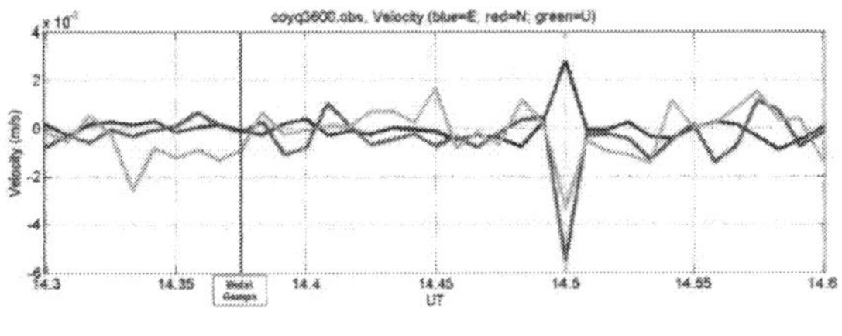

Fig. 26. Results of the value of Velocity coyg station when an earthquake occurs

2.3.3 Earthquake Laut Jawa – Indonesia 2007 (7,5 SR)

Earthquake in the Java Sea, Indonesia on August 8, 2007 at 5:05 p.m. UTC, The earthquake with a magnitude of 7.5 SR was centered at 5,859 ° S - 107,419 ° S with a depth of 280 Km.

By using the bako station data, the following velocity values are generated:

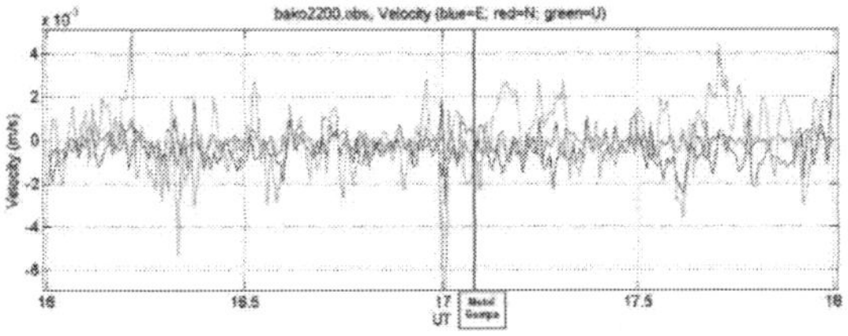

Fig. 27. Results of the value of Velocity bako station at 16 UTC - 18 UTC

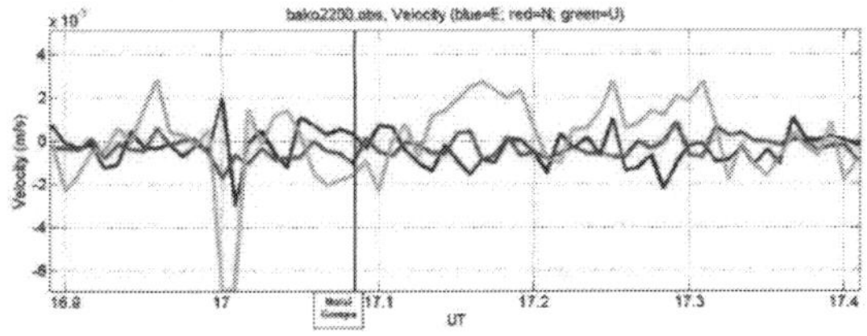

Fig. 28. Results of the value of the Velocity of the bako station when the earthquake occurred

2.3.4 Earthquake Ayula - Mexico 2017 (7,1 SR)

Earthquake in Ayutla, Mexico on September 19, 2017 at 18:14:38 UTC, the earthquake with a magnitude of 7.1 SR was centered at 18,550 ° N - 98,489 ° W with a depth of 48 Km.

By using the ineg station data, the following velocity values are generated:

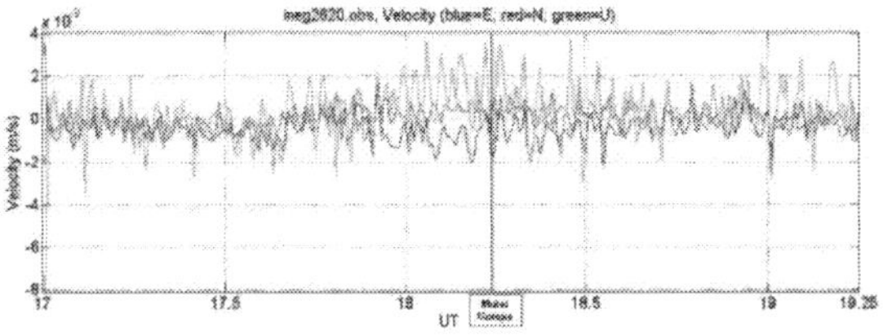

Fig. 29. The results of the Velocity ineg station at 17 UTC - 19.25 UTC

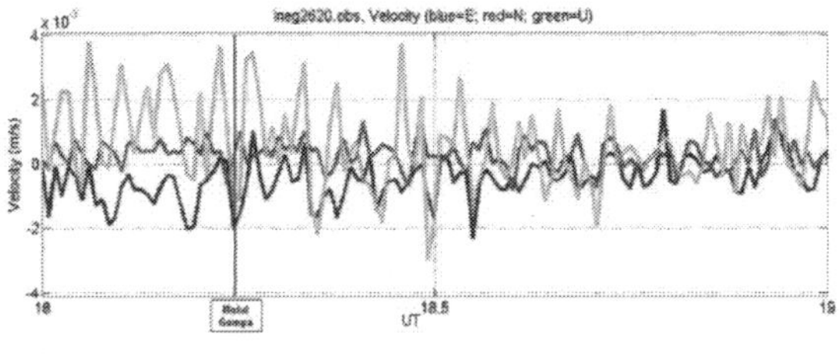

Fig. 30. Results of the velocity of the station ineg when the earthquake occurred

Earthquake Detection Table to GNSS Station

No	Stasiun	Jarak Epicenter ke stasiun (Km)	Delay waktu deteksi efek gempa ke stasiun GNSS (menit)
1	samp	± 835	10
2	mizu	± 142	1
3	kmsv	± 300	2
4	tsk2	± 310	3
5	kgni	± 385	3
6	antc	±180	1
7	sant	±380	2
8	samp	±940	12
9	sant	±198	5
10	ineg	±1100	10
11	mrl1	±140	1
12	wgtn	±210	1,2
13	coyq	±285	7
14	bako	±95	1

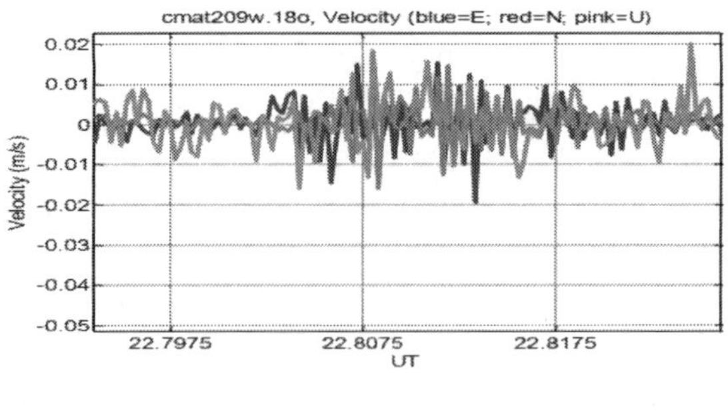

References

1. Branzanti, Mara. Software Defined receivers in GNSS scientific application: variometric approach to exploit GNSS-SDR phase observation. Geomatics workbooks n 12-FOSS4G Europe Como. (2015)
2. Benedetti, E. GNSS Seismology for the 2012 Mw = 6.1 Emilia Earthquacke: exploiting the VADASE algorithm. From PDF SRL-D-13-00094-esupp. (2012)
3. Fratarcangeli, Francesca. VADASE reliability and accuracy of real time displacement estimation: application to the central Italy 2016 eathquackes. Remote Sensing article. (2018)
4. Malia, Leonor Mendoza. Near Real-Time High-Rate GPS Data Analysis for Earthquacke and Tsunami Early Warning. Jerman. (2015)
5. Viiti, Alfonso & Augusto Mazzoni. Variometric approach for displacement analyss using Galileo data: first result. Geophysical research abstract vol. 19 EGU2017-5195. (2017)

WALANAE FAULT KINEMATIC DEDUCED FROM GEOMETRIC GEODETIC GNSS GPS MONITORING

Dina Anggreni Sarsito [1*], *Susilo* Susilo [2], *Alfend* Rudyawan [3], *Norman Arif* Muhammad[1] , *Heri* Andreas [1] and *Dhota* Pradipta[1]

[1] Geodesy Research Division, Faculty of Earth Science and Technology, Institute of Technology Bandung, Jl. Ganesha 10 Bandung 40132 – Indonesia
[2] Geospatial Information Agency, Jl. Raya Jakarta-Bogor KM.46, Cibinong 16911-Indonesia
[3] Geodynamic and Sedimentology Research Division, Faculty of Earth Science and Technology, Institute of Technology Bandung, Jl. Ganesha 10 Bandung 40132 – Indonesia

Abstract. The western Sulawesi region has the main structural boundary, the Palu Koro Fault which divides from Palu Bay at the northest part to Central Sulawesi and continues into the Bone Gulf in southest part. In the southern part of this region, namely the South Sulawesi Arm zone, there is a Walanae fault which is defined as a sinistral wrench with a NW-SE direction that divides the South Arm of Sulawesi. This fault in the northern part is expected to continue to the northwest intersecting the Makassar Strait and unite with Paternoster-Lupar (Kalimantan) sutures and at the southest ending in Flores thrust fault. Walanae fault system did not only have one strand but was divided into 4 parts, namely the northern East Walanae Fault with a slip rate of 6.634 mm/year and the southern part with a 7.097 mm/year of slip rate, as well as the northern part of West Walanae Fault with a slip rate of 4.528 mm/year and the southern part with a slip rate of 3.270 mm/year. The northern part of Walanae fault system has opening or spreading pattern occurs that is in harmony with the formation of Walanae depression. By using simple geometric modeling, we found the fault system have 2 strain partitions with dominant sinistral strike slip pattern at southern part and combination between left lateral strike slip with thrust fault pattern at northern part.

1 Introduction

The region of Eastern Indonesia is known to be an active tectonic region with high seismic activity which often has a negative impact in the form of material losses up to the loss of life after earthquakes hit the area. Sulawesi Island, which is located in this location, is in the western boundary between Eastern Indonesia and Sunda Blok which is relatively stable compare to the eastern area. This island is a result of triple junction convergence phenomena between Eurasian Continental-Sunda Block, Indo-Australian Plate and Pacific Ocean Plate, that creates several major faults across the island. Collision between Australian Craton Eastern Arc and Sunda Block Western Arc are dominated in Sulawesi and the region also divided into four different Mesozoic-Cenozoic stratigraphic provinces namely West-Southwest Sulawesi, East Sulawesi-Northon, North Sulawesi and Banggai Sula block [1, 2, 3, 4, 5, 6, 7, 8, 9, 10] . The Sulawesi western region has a main structural boundary, the Palu Koro Fault which divides from Palu Bay at the northest part to Central Sulawesi and continues into the Bone Gulf in the southest part. In the southern part of this region, namely the South Sulawesi Arm zone, there is a fault which is defined as a central wrench with a Northwest-Southeast direction that divides the South Arm of Sulawesi. This fault in the northern part is expected to continue to the northwest intersecting the Makassar Strait and unite with Paternoster-Lupar (Kalimantan) sutures and at the southest ending in Flores thrust fault.

The fault system kinematics have been studied geologically by [11, 12, 13, 14] but has never been done in the details of the geodetic method. This fault system consists of two parallel faults with Walanae depression separated it, namely the East Walane Fault and the West Walanae Fault. [14] mentioned that both faults formed at the end of the Middle Miocene with Bone Mountains as an eastern boundary and Western Divide Mountain as western boundary. [13] conclude that a sinistral strike slip motion of East Walanae Fault has played a major role in motion and geological structural developments nowadays. All of the above explanations are represented by Figure 1. Geodetic prior research using GNSS-GPS data from 1994 - 2009 by [15] estimated one slip-rate for the entire fault system by used 2 monitoring stations, namely is [east: 4.3 ± 0.6 mm / year, north: 2.0 ± 0.4 mm / year] with a sinistral / left lateral pattern and slip deficit of [east: 0.7 ± 0.3 mm / year, north: 0.2 ± 0.1 mm / year]. Thus, the Walanae fault system can be active with a total velocity of 5.1 ± 0.6 mm / year. To learn more details about the Walanae fault kinematics, the long observation data with GNSS-GPS with robust distribution stations are used in this paper. The validation of the geodetic results are from geological studies that have been carried out by previous researchers.

* Corresponding author: dsarsito@gd.itb.ac.id

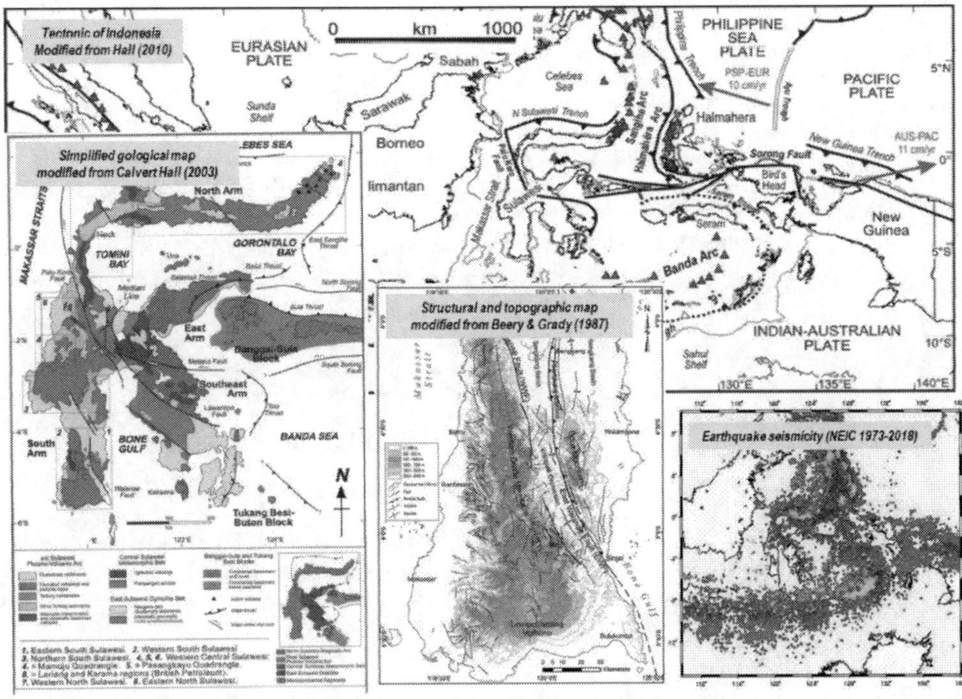

Fig 1. Tectonic of Indonesia modified from [8], Simplified feological map modified from [16], Structural and topographic map modified from [17] and Earthquake Seismicity from NEIC Catalogue (1973-2018)

2 Data and Method

<u>*GNSS-GPS Observation*</u>

The observation of GNSS-GPS in the South Arm of Sulawesi region was carried out using two methods, the first method is campaign or episodic type that carried out by the collaboration between Bakosurtanal (former) / BIG, ITB, DEOS-TU Delft and Paris ENS since GEODYSSEA Research Collaborations in 1994. This campaign type are done even though not routinely once per year for all stations in the area (UJPD, C018, C025, C026, C036 and C042). Another method we used in here is a continuous method that is managed by BIG using a fixed station measurement (CMAK and CPRE). Initially this deformation monitoring network design was dedicated to get a better understanding the kinematic pattern of the South Sulawesi Arm motion related to the need for deformation studies and the implementation of geodetic control network for mapping purposes. Furthermore, by using both episodic and continuous stations in the South Arm with a more complete and dispersed station distribution than the GNSS distribution from [15], it is expected that the Walanae fault pattern can be detected in more detail.

Data processing in this study uses GAMIT / GLOBK 10.6 GNSS processing using a multi-baseline tight constraint strategy for reference stations located outside the Eastern Indonesia zone and located in a relatively stable zone. The ITRF-2008 global terrestrial framework was mapped to obtain georeference and to obtain a local domination deformation pattern, a mapping was conducted by referring to the relatively stable Sunda Block Euler pole compared to the study area. The distribution of the observation station was originally designed to determine the rigid deformation pattern of the South Sulawesi Arm (euler pole position and rotational speed), then used for geometric initial detection of the Walanae fault movement which divides the South Arm with Northwest-Southeast direction. Since in this study two types of data were used, namely episodic and continuous, the strategy carried out would experience a slight difference in handling data for estimating survey solutions (campaign solution for episodic types), weekly solutions (weekly solution for continuous types) and time series analysis stages (time-series analysis) for estimating velocity values by correcting seismic effects of special earthquakes only for the type of continuous station using the equation of [18] as follows

$$y(t_i) = a + bt_i + c\sin(2\pi t_i) + d\cos(2\pi t_i) + e\sin(4\pi t_i) + f\cos(4\pi t_i) + \sum_{j=1}^{n_g} g_j H(t_i - T_{gj}) \sum_{j=1}^{n_h} h_j H(t_i - T_{hj})\, t_i + \textstyle\sum_{j=1}^{n_k} k_j exp(-(t_i - T_{kj})/\tau_j)\, H(t_i - T_{kj}) + v_i \qquad (1)$$

where t_i for $i = 1 \dots N$ is the epoch of the daily solution, H is the heaviside step function, coefficients a and b are the position and velocity rate of the station, coefficients c and d are annual periodic motions, coefficients e and f are semi-periodic annual motion, n_g is the number of offsets with magnitude g in the epoch T_g. Motion due to an earthquake is modeled as an exponential h and / or exponential decay with magnitude k in the epoch of earthquake T. The observation error v is assumed to be independent (not affect), identically distributed and random with error E (v) = 0. Furthermore, geometric deformation parameters are estimated using the results of the estimated diplacement vector or velocity vector of the above motion.

Geometric Deformation

To study the deformation pattern of a tectonic region, several models can be applied in order to quantify and analyze the displacement or deformation phenomena of the earth that are monitored using the GNSS-GPS geodetic method. The method of analysis in this study is a geometric method based only on observational geometric data through a simple representation of changes in the coordinates of the observation station with respect to a reference frame and homogeneous- isotropic strain parameters within a specified zone. The realization is through interpolation-extrapolation between stations without involving crustal physical parameters. From the difference between epochs for each station, we can obtain the displacement vector d (equation 2) or velocity rate v (equation 3).

$$d(n,e,u) = (n,e,u)_{tj} - (n,e,u)_{to} \quad (2)$$

$$v(n,e,u) = \frac{(n,e,u)_{tj}-(n,e,u)_{to}}{tj-to} \quad (3)$$

Where (n, e, u) are north, east and up displacement or velocity component, and t_o and t_j are the initial epoch and later epoch. From equation (2) or (3) it can derive translation T, rotation of R and dilation of D (equation (4)) deformation parameters.

$$v(n,e,u) = T + R + D \quad (4)$$

From equation (4), another deformation parameter can be described, namely Magnitude Translation T_M (equation (5)) which shows the translation magnitude in the horizontal direction and strain tensor (equation (6)) which shows the dilatation of ε_{mean} (equation (7)), pure strain ε_{pure} (equation (8)) and simple strain ε_{simple} (equation (9)) as follows

$$T_M = \left((v(n))^2 + (v(e))^2\right)^{0.5} \quad (5)$$

$$Strain\ Tensor = \begin{vmatrix} \frac{\partial v_n}{\partial n} & \frac{\partial v_e}{\partial n} \\ \frac{\partial v_n}{\partial e} & \frac{\partial v_e}{\partial ne} \end{vmatrix} = \begin{vmatrix} \varepsilon_{nn} & \varepsilon_{ne} \\ \varepsilon_{en} & \varepsilon_{ee} \end{vmatrix} \quad (6)$$

$$\varepsilon_{mean} = \frac{1}{2}(\varepsilon_{nn} + \varepsilon_{ee}) \quad (7)$$

$$\varepsilon_{pure} = \frac{1}{2}(\varepsilon_{nn} - \varepsilon_{ee}) \quad (8)$$

$$\varepsilon_{simple} = \frac{1}{2}(\varepsilon_{ne} + \varepsilon_{en}) \quad (9)$$

The above equations are then used for the geometric deformation analysis for the Walanae Fault System. The velocity rate used as the basis for the calculation is estimated in global terrestrial reference ITRF2008 to find out the consistency of the monitoring network. And to find out the deformation pattern more clearly, the velocity rate is estimated relatively to the recent Sunda Block Euler poles (51.991^0, -96.495^0, 0.291^0/My).

3 Result and Discussion

The velocity rate estimation results are divided into two part, for continuous CMAK and CPRE stations that have high reliability for the degree of solution accuracy in the ITRF2008 mapping for horizontal components namely postrms 0.003 m and 0.007 m for campaign type stations (UJPD, C018, C025 , C026, C036, C042). Figure (2 left) shows the magnitude of the velocity rate vector in the ITRF2008. From the distribution of observation stations, it can be seen that CMAK, UJPD and CPRE located in the western part of West Walanae Fault, have almost the same rate pattern (25.800 ± 0.24; -6.660 ± 0.18) mm / year, (24.720 ± 1.07; -7.630 ± 0.54) mm / year and (24.020 ± 0.17; -7.090 ± 0.29) mm / year where this indicates that the three stations are in the same region. In the Walanae Depression zone, there are three stations that also have almost the same rate stretching from north to south, namely C042, C036 and C025 with velocity rates(28.540 ± 2.06; -5.920 ± 1.60) mm / year, (28.040 ± 1.60; -5.090 ± 1.12) mm / year and (28.240 ± 1.87; -4.460 ± 1.35) mm / year. The rate of all station shows a tendency to be in the same region even though there is a slight velocity rate decreasing on the northern component of station C042 which is located northern part of C025 station in southernmost. For stations located in eastern part of the East Walanae Fault, they are C026 and C018 with velocity rate (34.890 ± 2.63; -4.190 ± 1.79) mm / year and (31.370 ± 1.87; -2.500 ± 1.35) mm / year indicating a faster velocity rate pattern compared to the stations located in Walanae Depression and in western part of West Walanae Fault. In general, it can be seen that for east-west velocity rate component, there is an increase in rate of the stations located in the western part of the South Arm to the station located on the left side of the South Arm. As for the north-south velocity components, there is generally a slowdown in the rate of motion for stations located in the northern part of the South Arm to the stations located in the southern part. A more detailed representation of the deformation pattern, the global regional effect is then eliminated by estimating the velocity rate with respect to the Sunda Block Euler Pole (Figure 2 right). Stations located in the western part of the South Arm, namely CMAK, UJPD and CPRE have velocity rate (1.815 ± 0.24; 5.037 ± 0.18) mm / year, (0.708 ± 1.07; 4.107 ± 0.54) mm / year and (-0.332 ± 0.17 ; 4.676 ± 0.29) mm / year shows a slight decrease in absolute rate from 5.354 mm / year in the southern part to 4.678 mm / year in the northern part. For stations located in Walanae Depression, namely C042, C036 and C025, they have velocity rate of (4.111 ± 2.06; 5.907 ± 1.60) mm / year, (3.671 ± 1.60; 6.792 ± 1.12) mm / year and (4.077 ± 1.87; 7.397 ± 1.35) mm / year, which shows the pattern of absolute velocity rate decrease from southern part to the northern part, with rate 8.446 mm / year to 7.197 mm / year. For C026 and C018 stations located at eastern part of East Walanae Fault, the velocity rate are (10.701 ± 2.63; 7.766 ± 1.79) mm / year and (7.375 ± 1.87; 9.425 ± 1.35) mm / year, that shows increasing rate pattern compare to the stations which are located in Walanae Depression and in western part of West Walanae Fault. This increasing rate show different pattern compare to the previous, from southern part to the northern part, we can see the absolute increasing rate are 11.967 mm / year to 13.222 mm / year.

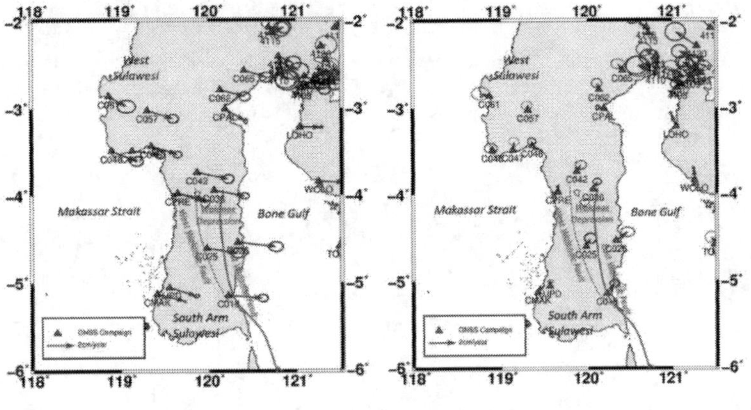

Fig. 2. Horizontal velocity rate of South Sulawesi Arm with respect to ITRF2008 (left) and Sunda Block – ITRF2008 (right)

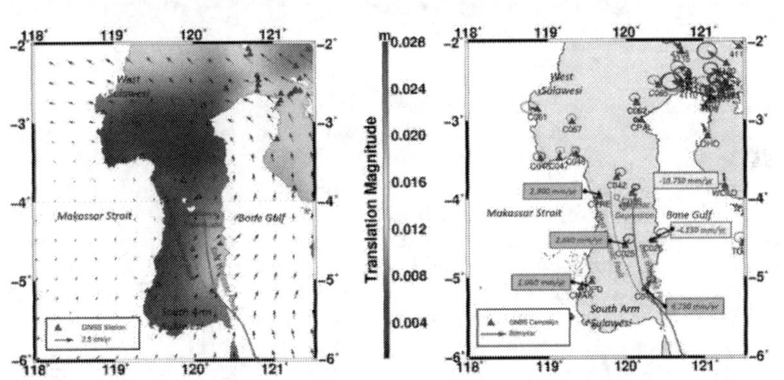

Fig. 3. Translation magnitude of horizontal velocity rate (left) and vertical velocity rate (right)

To get a clearer picture of the deformation pattern in the South Arm of Sulawesi, the horizontal velocity is described as translation magnitude (Figure 3 Left). The translation magnitude in this region ranges from 0.004 m to 0.016 m with the general pattern for the West Walane Fault region up to Walanae Depression have decreasing rate from the southern part which ranges from 0.008 m in the Makassar area to northern part up to 0.004 at the west-end of West Walanae Fault with a counter-clockwise rotation pattern for the entire South Arm. The dominance of rigid block rotation from the region above is very visible, and the velocity constraint in the northern part are estimated to be due to a collision with the Plutonic Arc Mountains in Central Sulawesi. For the eastern region of East Walanae Fault, namely Bone Mountain to the transition zone to the west at the Walanae Depression, the translation magnitude have increasing pattern from 0.008 m around Sinjai to 0.012 m in the East Sengkang Basin with counter clockwise rotation direction. The magnitude translation has gradually decrease northward to around 0.004 m in the Plutonic Arc Mountain region in Central Sulawesi. Translation magnitude generally increases from the western part of the West Walanae Fault to the eastern part of the East Walanae Fault, with a slight eastward turn in the Watampone area and looks back to the west approaching the Plutonic Arc Mountain region in the Sengkang anticline region. This indicates a long widening of the baseline dividing the east-west across Walanae Depression or showing the opening pattern. The vertical velocity rate from South Sulawesi Arm is shown in figure

3 right, where for the western part of West Walanae Fault increase vertical rate from 1.060 mm / year in the Makassar area to 2.900 mm / year in the Pare-pare area that located in the northern part. Whereas for the Walanae Depression and Bone Mountain areas located in the eastern part of the East Walanae Fault, have decreasing rate from the southern region around Sinjai with a vertical rate of 4.750 mm / year to the north, namely in the Walanae Depression area at 2.880 mm / year and East Sengkang Basin around -10,750 mm / year. This shows a difference in the increasing and decreasing patterns vertical velocity with the West Walanae Fault as a barrier, and the pattern of decline increasingly enlarges eastwards through East Walanae Fault.

Understanding the geometric pattern of deformation of the South Arm of Sulawesi is further described in Figure 4 which shows a pattern of dilation, simple shear and pure shear from the research zone. The pattern of dilatation in Figure 4 (left) shows a change of pattern that is very clearly trending north-south, namely from the region with very small dilatation approaching -0.2µs to 0.0 µs in the Plutonic Arc Mounting in the northern part, and ranging from 0.0 µs to 0.2 µs in the central region of the Sulawesi Arm which was passed by the Western Divide Mountain-Walanae Depression-Bone Mountain-East Sengkang Basin, each of which was accommodated by West Walanae Fault and East Walanae Fault. For the southernmost region of the Arm region, there is the largest dilatation pattern reaching 0.7 µs which is accommodated by Lompobattang Volcano mixed with interpolation effects due to limited data in the south. The dilatation pattern is seen to divide the Walanae Fault System into two parts, namely the northern part which has an intermediate rate and southern dilatation pattern which has a larger dilatation pattern.

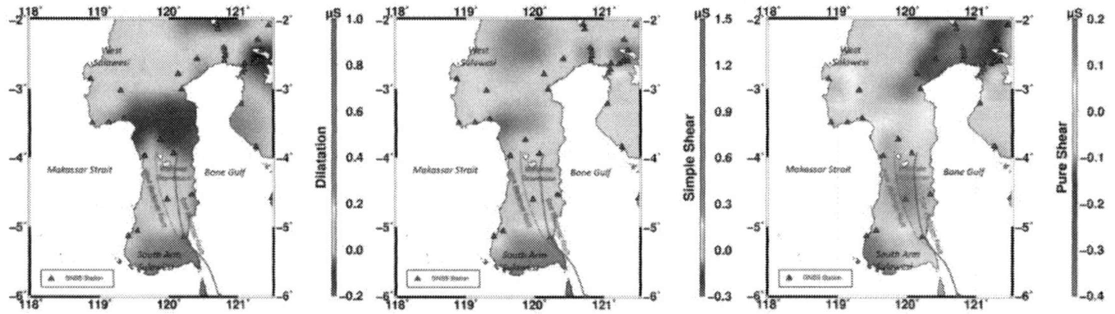

Fig. 4. Dilatation (left), simple shear (center) and pure shear (left) of South Sulawesi Arm

For the southernmost part of South Sulawesi Arm, the dominance of the high simple shear pattern (Figure 4 center) ranges from 0.3-1.3 µs and is divided into two parts pure shear pattern (Figure 4 right) which is between 0.1-0.2 µs in the Makassar region and -0.1-0.0 µs in the Bulukumba area with Lompobattang Volcano as the boundary. To the north of this region, changes in simple shear patterns can be seen that are almost homogeneous towards a minimum of 0.0 µs in the plutonic mountainous region. The change of pattern is seen to occur again separating the Walanae Fault System to the south with a high rate of simple shear and the northern part with a smaller simple shear. For the northern East Walanae Fault there is a change in the pattern in the northern part of Watampone, which is in the Sengkang East Basin that shrinks to the east, and in the northernmost part of the boundary this simple shear pattern is known to have Masupu Fault. This region's pure shear pattern shows a more varied pattern than simple shear. For northern Makassar, the pure shear pattern changes slightly up to 0.05 µs in Western Divide Mountain and decreases to 0.0 µs in the Bantimala area and then increases again in the area around Pare-pare. This increasing rate of pure shear did not take place because it subsequently decreased in the Plutonic Arc Mountains at northern part. As for the northern region of Bulukumba, the change in pattern has increased in the area of Walanae depression to 0.15 µs but has decreased in the easternmost region around Watampone. The value of pure shear in the Walanae Depression region has decreased again after collide with the Plutonic Arc Mountains. The change of pattern in pure shear is seen to separate the Walanae Fault System to the south with a small pure shear and the northern part with a larger pure shear, and a small pure shear pattern cutting in the east-west direction, where this indicates a widening process in Walanae Depression which is in line with the formation of the West Sengkang Basin in the eastern part of the South Arm.

https://doi.org/10.1051/e3sconf/20199404008

Fault	slip rate		slip deficit	
	E (mm/yr)	N (mm/yr)	E (mm/yr)	N (mm/yr)
east walane fault				
northern part	-7.030	-0.974	-17.250	12.894
southern part	-6.623	-0.368	-17.552	12.278
west walanae fault				
northern part	4.003	2.116	-28.363	9.709
southern part	2.263	2.360	-26.338	9.420

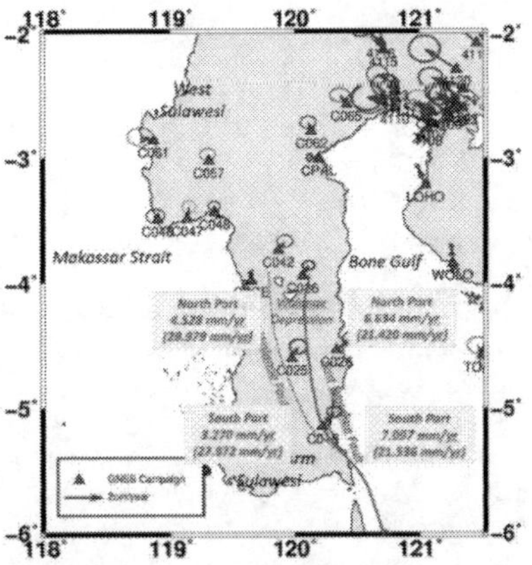

Fig. 5. Slip rate and slip deficit

Based on the dilation pattern, simple shear and pure shear described above, it can be seen that the Walanae Fault System can be divided into several strands, namely the northern and southern regions. By using a simple geometric modeling that is comparing the velocity rate of the station located in a different zone bounded by fault, we can estimate the slip rate of the fault and calculating the slip deficit based on the deficiency of the supposed rigid velocity of the Sunda Block on the station. Figure 5 shows the slip rate and slip deficit from the Walanae Fault System. The northern East Walanae Fault has an absolute slip rate of 6.634 mm / year with a slip deficit of 21.420 mm / year, and the southern part has a 7.097 mm / year of absolute slip rate with slip deficit of 21.536 mm / year. The northern part of West Walanae Fault has an absolute slip rate of 4.528 mm / year with a slip deficit of 29.979 mm / year and the southern part with an absolute slip rate of 3.270 mm / year and a deficit slip of 27,929 mm / year. The northern part of Walanae fault system has opening or spreading pattern occurs that is in harmony with the formation of Walanae depression and West Sengkang Basin at eastern part. By using simple geometric modeling, we found the fault system have 2 strain partitions with dominant sinistral strike slip pattern at southern part of Walanae Fault System (for both East and West Fault) and combination between sinistral / left lateral strike slip with thrust fault pattern at northen part of Walanae Fault System especially at East Walanae Fault. This is in line with the vertical movement of the fault system which indicates a graben pattern in the form of a surface drop in Walanae depression and a thrust fault positive (increasing) rate for the boundary area that limits this graben which is eastern part of the East Walanae Fault and in the western part of West Walanae Fault.

4 Conclusion

Walanae fault system did not only have one strand but was divided into 4 parts, namely the northern East Walanae Fault with a slip rate of 6.634 mm/year and the southern part with a 7.097 mm/year of slip rate, as well as the northern part of West Walanae Fault with a slip rate of 4.528 mm/year and the southern part with a slip rate of 3.270 mm/year. The northern part of Walanae fault system has opening or spreading pattern occurs that is in harmony with the formation of Walanae depression. By using simple geometric modeling, we found the fault system have 2 strain partitions with dominant sinistral strike slip pattern at southern part and combination between left lateral strike slip with thrust fault pattern at northern part. This is in line with the vertical movement of the fault system which indicates a graben pattern in the form of a surface drop in Walanae depression and a thrust fault positive (increasing) rate for the boundary area that limits this graben which is eastern part of the East Walanae Fault and in the western part of West Walanae Fault.

Deep appreciation and many thanks to Indonesian Geospatial Information Agency (BIG) and ITB for research collaboration. And deepest gratitude for Prof. C. Vigny, Dr. W.J.F. Simons, Prof. B. Sapiie and Prof. H.Z. Abidin, who provided knowledge to the author in the "state of the art" of geodynamic study using geodetic - technology and methods.

References

1. Hamilton, W. Tectonics of the Indonesian Region. U.S. Geological Survey Professional Paper 1078. (1979)
2. Yuwono, Y.S., Maury, R., Soeria-Atmadja, R., Bellon, H. Tertiary and Quaternary geodynamic evolution of South Sulawesi constraints from the study of volcanic units. Geologi Indonesia Jakarta 13, 32-48. (1988)
3. Coffield, D.Q., Bergman, S.C., Carrard, R.A., Guritno, N., Robinson, N.M., Talbot, J. Tectonic and stratigraphic evolution of the Kalosi PCS area and associated development of a Tertiary petroleum system, South Sulawesi, Indonesia. Proceedings of the Indonesian Petroleum Association 22 (1), 679-706. (1993)
4. Priadi, B., Polvé, M., Maury, R.G., Bellon, H., Soeria-Atmadja, R., Joron, J.L., Cotton, J. Tertiary and Quaternary magmatism in Central

Sulawesi: chronological and petrological constraints. Journal of Southeast Asian Earth Sciences 9 (1-2), 81-93. (1994)

5. Bergman, S.C., Coffield, D.Q., Talbot, J.P., Garrard, R.J. Tertiary tectonic and magmatic evolution of western Sulawesi and the Makassar Strait, Indonesia. Evidence for a Miocene continentecontinent collision. In: Hall, R., Blundell, D.J. (Eds.), Tectonic Evolution of SE Asia, Geological Society of London, Special Publications, vol. 106, pp. 391-430. (1996)
6. Polvé, M., Maury, R.C., Bellon, H., Rangin, C., Priadi, B., Yuwono, S., Joron, J.L., Soeria-Atmadja, R., Magmatic evolution of Sulawesi: constraints on the Cenozoic geodynamic history of the Sundaland active margin. Tectonophysics 272, 69-92. (1997)
7. Hall, R., Wilson, M.E.J.Neogene sutures in eastern Indonesia. Journal of Asian Earth Sciences 18, 781e808. (2000)
8. Hall, R.,. Cenozoic geological and plate tectonic evolution of SE Asia and the SW Pacific: computer-based reconstructions, model and animations. Journal of Asian Earth Sciences 20, 235-431. (2002))
9. Elburg, M., Foden, J.,. Geochemical response to varying tectonic settings: an example from Southern Sulawesi (Indonesia). Geochimica et Cosmochimica Acta 63, 1155-1172. (1999)
10. Jaya, A., and Nishikawa, O. Paleostress reconstruction from calcite twin and fault-slip data using the multiple inverse method in the East Walanae fault zone: implications for the Neogene contraction in South Sulawesi, Indonesia. Journal of Structural Geology, 34-49. (2013)
11. Van Bemmelen, R.W. The Geology of Indonesia, vol. 1a. Government Printing Office, The Hague, p. 732. (1949)
12. Van Leeuwen, T.M. The geology of southwest Sulawesi with special reference to the Biru area. In: Barber, A., Wiryosujono, S. (Eds.), The Geology and Tectonics of Eastern Indonesia. Geological Research and Development Centre, pp. 277-304. Special Publication 2. (1981)
13. Van Leeuwen, T.M., Susanto, E.S., Maryanto, S., Hadiwisastra, S., Sudijono, Muharjo. Tectonostratigraphic evolution of Cenozoic marginal basin and continental margin successions in the Bone Mountains, South Sulawesi, Indonesia.Journal of Asian Earth Sciences 38, 233-254. (2010)
14. Sukamto, R., Supriatna, S. The Geology of the Ujung Pandang, Benteng and Sinjai, Sulawesi. Geological Research and Development Centre, Bandung. Quadrangles Series, Scale 1: 250.000. (1982)
15. Sarsito, D.A. Pemodelan geometrik dan kinematik kawasan Sulawesi-Kalimantan Bagian Timur berdasarkan data GNSS-GPS dan Gayaberat Global , Disertasi, Institut Teknologi Bandung, Indonesia (2010)
16. Calvert, S.J., Hall, R. The Cenozoic geology of the Lariang and Karama regions, Western Sulawesi: new insight into the evolution of the Makassar Straits region. Proceedings of the Indonesian Petroleum Association 29, 501-557 (2003)
17. Berry, R.F., Grady, A.E. Mesoscopic structures produced by Plio-Pleistocene wrench faulting in South Sulawesi, Indonesia. Journal of Structural Geology 9, 563-571. (1987)
18. Nikolaidis, R. M. *Observation of geodetic and seismic deformation with the Global Positioning System*, Disertasi, University of California, San Diego (2002)

Climate Comfort Analysis for Tourism in Samosir District

Adhityo Haryadi[1], *Eko Kusratmoko*[2], *Asep Karsidi*[2]

[1]Student of Magister of Geography, Geography Department, Universitas Indonesia, Indonesia
[2]Lecturer of Magister of Geography, Geography Department, Universitas Indonesia, Indonesia

Abstract Tourism has become one of the sectors which are the mainstay source of foreign exchange in Indonesia. One of the region which has tourism potential is Samosir District at North Sumatra Province. Climatic conditions affect the tourist comfortability while doing the tourism activity. Studies on climate comfort in Toba Lake Region, especially in Samosir District have not been done. Way to determine the level of comfort associated with tourism activities are known to the Tourism Climate Index (TCI). This research aims to determine the level of climate comfort tourist destinations in Samosir District based on the value of TCI and knowing the relation between TCI value with the number of visits a tourist destination. Keyword: Climate, TCI, and Tourism

Introduction

The tourism sector is one of Indonesia's mainstays in generating foreign exchange. This is reinforced by the diversity of cultures and tribes that attract tourists to come. According to the Ministry of Tourism, in 2017 the tourism sector generates foreign exchange of US $ 17 billion (Gumelar, 2017). Not only natural attractions that become an attraction, but also the diversity of human beings which shows that Indonesia is rich in culture, ranging from tribes, races, and customs that have become unique and unique in the Indonesian tourism industry.

Comfort consists of psychological comfort and physical comfort. Psychic comfort namely psychological comfort (feeling safe, calm, happy, etc.) that is measured subjectively (qualitatively). Whereas physical comfort can be measured objectively (quantitatively); which includes spatial, visual, auditory and thermal comfort (Rilatupa, 2008). According to Lippsmeir (1994) the comfort limit for equatorial conditions is in the air temperature range of 22.5°C – 29°C with air humidity of 20 – 50%.

Samosir Regency has climate conditions will certainly support tourism activities. Tourists feel comfortable doing tourism activities in Samosir Regency. Samosir Regency is one of the districts in North Sumatra Province that has potential in the tourism sector. Samosir Regency which is supported by the existence of Lake Toba recorded an increase in the number of tourists from 2008 to 2013. In 2008 tourists amounted to 105,971, and continued to increase until 2013 tourists reached 149,414 (Tourism Office of Samosir Regency, 2014).

Mieczkowski (1985) has developed a measurement method as a climate comfort parameter with the Tourism Climate Index (TCI). TCI calculations use several climate variables that are relevant to tourism activities, namely: 1) air temperature, 2) air humidity, 3) rainfall, 4) duration of solar radiation, and 5) wind speed. This method is designed for climate comfort studies for tourism in Europe. Applying this method to tropical climate is still very lack. TCI is very helpful in identifying the comfort level of tourist destinations based on climate conditions.

The results of the analysis based on the TCI method can be useful as one of the information on the schedule of visits for tourists with a low level of climate risk in carrying out tourism activities in Samosir Regency. Some of the objectives in this study were to analyze the comfort level of climate in Lake Toba based on the Tourism Climate Index method, provide information for visitors about the right time for visitors to come to Samosir Regency, and analyze the influence of climate comfort level on the number of visitors in Samosir Regency.

Study area

The research was performed on the Samosir District (Fig.1). Astronomically, Samosir Regency is located at Latitude 20°24 '- 20°25'N and Longitude 98°21 '- 99°55'E. Its western position is located on the mainland of Sumatra, and its eastern part is on Samosir Island in the middle of Lake Toba. Samosir Regency which is in a tropical climate is very beneficial because it makes the region always illuminated by the sun throughout the year and has high rainfall during the rainy season so that it has fertile land and is overwhelmed by extraordinary nature. The average blowing wind is medium speed. The air temperature is not too low and not too high around 17 °C - 29 °C with an average humidity of 85%. The cool air temperature can certainly support the development of tourism.

The astronomical location of Samosir which is in a tropical climate causes Samosir to still have the influence of the moonson wind from Asia. This Asian moonson wind brings considerable rainfall. So that hydrologically, it has a large potential of water reserves. In addition, temperatures that are quite stable in the tropics cause the vegetation of tropical rainforests to thrive well.

* Adhityo Haryadi: adhityohar@yahoo.com

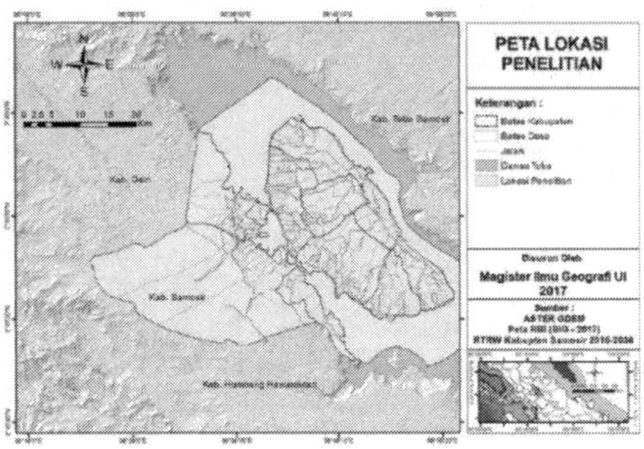

Figure 1. Maps of Research Location

Literature Review

Climate and Tourism

Climate is one of the important natural factors that is a concern for tourists. According to Aguiló et al. (2005) climate is one of the main drivers in international tourism, as most tourists look for opportunities to relax in the sun or snow. Tourists generally look for tourist attractions with climate conditions that are more comfortable and different compared to the conditions of the climate where they live. Each climate parameter has its own influence on tourists.

The use of climate information in the tourism sector is used by three main users, namely tourists, tourism developers and also government institutions. For tourists, weather forecasts in tourist destinations and weather conditions are very important for tourists. Then for tourism developers, existing climate information is useful for strategic planning for infrastructure development. As for government institutions, climate information is used to identify climate change risks and as a reference for future mitigation programs (Scoot and Lemieux, 2010).

Tourism Climate Index (TCI)

The concept of the Tourism Climate Index (TCI) was designed by Mieczkowski in 1985. The method and concept proposed by Mieczkowski aims to assess the implications of future climate change on the relative comfort level of visitors in an area, especially in tourism. Climate variables are combined into five parameters, three of which are independent and the other two are bioclimatic combinations. Climate variables used in TCI are maximum temperature, average temperature, minimum relative humidity, relative humidity, rainfall, duration of irradiation and wind speed. (Table 1).

Table 1. Parameters that use in TCI method

Sub-Indeks	**Climate variable by month**	**Impact of TCI index**	**weighting for TCI**
Daytime Comfort Index (CId)	Maximum temperature and minimum temperature	shows thermal comfort when maximum tourist activities occur	40 %
Daily Comfort Index (CIa)	average air temperature and average humidity	showing thermal comfort for 24 hours, including during sleep	10%
Rainfall	Percipitation	representing negative values related to outdoor activity	20%
Sunshine	Sun exposure	rated as a positive value in tourism, but can be negative because of the danger of sunburn and discomfort during hot conditions	20%
Wind	wind velocity average	variable that depends or has influence on temperature	10%

Effect of Climate on Tourism Visits

Tourism is one sector that is very vulnerable to climate change (Amelung et al. 2007, 8). The existence of climate change can result in a climate that was initially considered comfortable for tourists to become uncomfortable again, which has implications for the pattern of tourist visits to a tourism destination (Suwarto, 2011). The comfort of climate in tourism places is no longer obtained by tourists. So, these tourists will not come back to the tourist attraction.

Methods

In general, the tourism climate indices can be categorized to three categorized (Mieczkwoski, 1985). That index can be combined as Tourism Climate Index that combined of seven parameters, three of which independent and two in a bioclimatic combination:

$$TCI = 4\,CId + CIa + 2\,R + 2\,S + W \qquad (1)$$

Annotation:

TCI : Tourism Climate Index

CId : Daytime Comfort Index, consisting of maximum air temperature (°C) and the mean maximum relative humidity (%)

CIa : Daily Comfort Index, consisting of mean air temperature (°C) and the mean relative humidity (%)

R : Rainfall, precipitation (mm)

W : Wind, mean wind speed (m/s)

Data from each parameter obtained from globalwheater.com. The data used in this TCI is calculated on average per month then mapped using GIS.

This data is then made into a raster format with IDW tools. Each of these parameters is then calculated per month with the raster calculator tool with the TIC equation. In contrast to other climate indices, every contributing parameter is assessed. Because of a weighting factor (a value for TCI of 100), every factor can reach 5 points (Table 2.). The TCI value classification results are then mapped monthly, so that they can be analyzed further in relation to the number of visitors each month.

Table 2. Rating categories of the Tourism Climatic Index

TCI score	Category	Mapping category
90–100	Ideal	Excellent
80–89	Excellent	
70–79	Very good	Very good and good
60–69	Good	
50–59	Acceptable	Acceptable
40–49	Marginal	
30–39	Unfavourable	Unfavourable
20–29	Very unfavourable	
10–19	Extremely unfavourable	
< 10	Impossible	

(Mieczkowski 1985)

The climate comfort level of tourist destinations in Samosir Regency can be analyzed by looking at the results of TCI value calculations in 7 tourist objects using the climatic elements above. The monthly distribution chart of TCI values is used to help describe and compare TCI values at 7 tourist object. The relation between climate comfort level and number of visits to tourist destinations can be analyzed by looking at the correlation test results between the number of visits and TCI values. Data processing to see whether there is a correlation between the TCI value and the number of visitors is done by conducting a Spearman Rank correlation test.

Result

TCI index per month in Samosir District.

Based on the calculation of TCI values, the climate comfort value in Samosir Regency has a range of 67 - 85. The highest TCI value occurred in February. The TCI value range for this month ranges from 77 (Very Good) to 85 (Excellent). While the lowest is in March with a value range of TCI 67 to 75 (Good) (Fig. 2).

Changes in the value of TCI in Samosir Regency can't be separated from changes in climate patterns. The most easily identified from this climate pattern is rainfall patterns. Rainfall patterns in the Regency are affected by equatorial types. The pattern of changes in TCI values in several tourism destinations shows that there is a pattern similar to the pattern of rain (Fig.3). The rainfall pattern in Samosir Regency has two peaks (Tjasjono, 2003). The pattern showed an increase in February, then dropped to its lowest point in June, and again increased at its second peak in October (fig.4).

In general, Samosir District has a climate comfort level for tourism to go into comfortable conditions. Climate comfort in Samosir must be maintained by maintaining existing land use conditions. The development of tourism in Samosir District will be better directed at developing ecotourism that maintains its environmental conditions.

Correlation of TCI Value and Tourism Visits

Relation of climate comfort level to the number of visits to tourist destinations is seen by conducting a correlation test. Based on correlation calculations using the quantitative analysis method Spearman's Rho. The monthly distribution chart of TCI values is used to help describe and compare TCI values at 7 tourist object that are Air Terjun Efrata, Menara Pandang Tele, Aek Sipitudae, Batu Sawan, Aek Rangat, Pantai Pasir Putih Parbaba, and Pantai Situngkir. Distribution of 7 tourism destination served in (Fig. 4). Selected tourist attraction is a leading tourist attraction category.

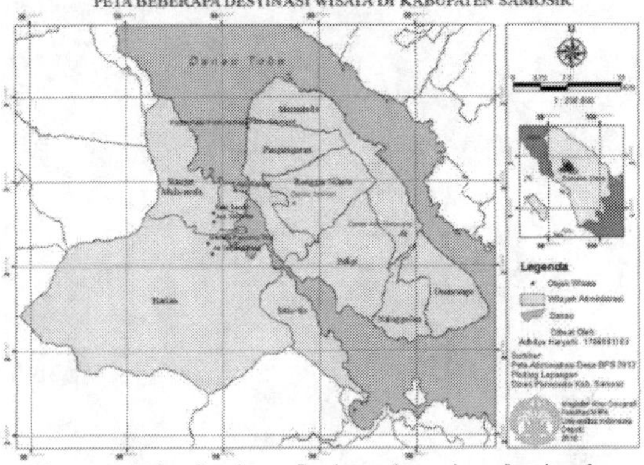

Figure 4. Distribution of selected tourism destination

Tourism destinations that have high visits are located on the edge of the national road and become the main road both to Samosir Island and to the one from Samosir Island. In addition, this attraction has attractions that can attract tourists. Changes in the number of visitors in each tourism destination can be seen in fig 5. The change follows the holiday season.

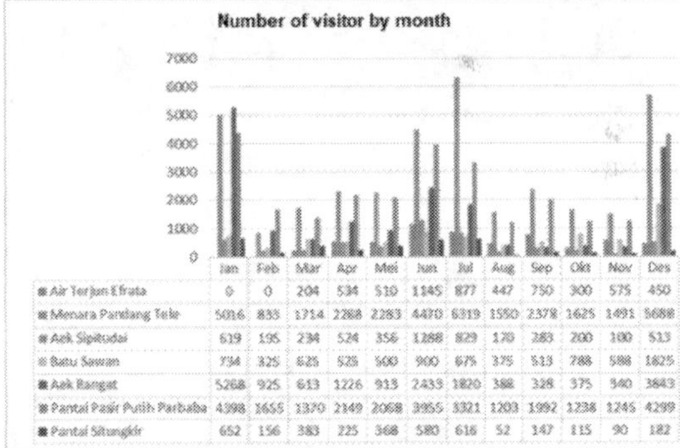

Figure 5. Number of visitors of selected tourist destination by month

The results of the correlation test between the number of visits and TCI values were conducted to determine whether there was a correlation between the level of comfort of the tourist destination area and the number of visitors who came to the tourist attraction. Based on the calculation of correlation using quantitative analysis method Spearman's Rho shows a significance value of 0.253, where this value is greater than the degree of trustworthiness = 0.05. So, if Sig. > 0.05 means there is no correlation between the number of visitors with TCI values at some points of tourism destinations (Tab.3).

 https://doi.org/10.1051/e3sconf/20199405001

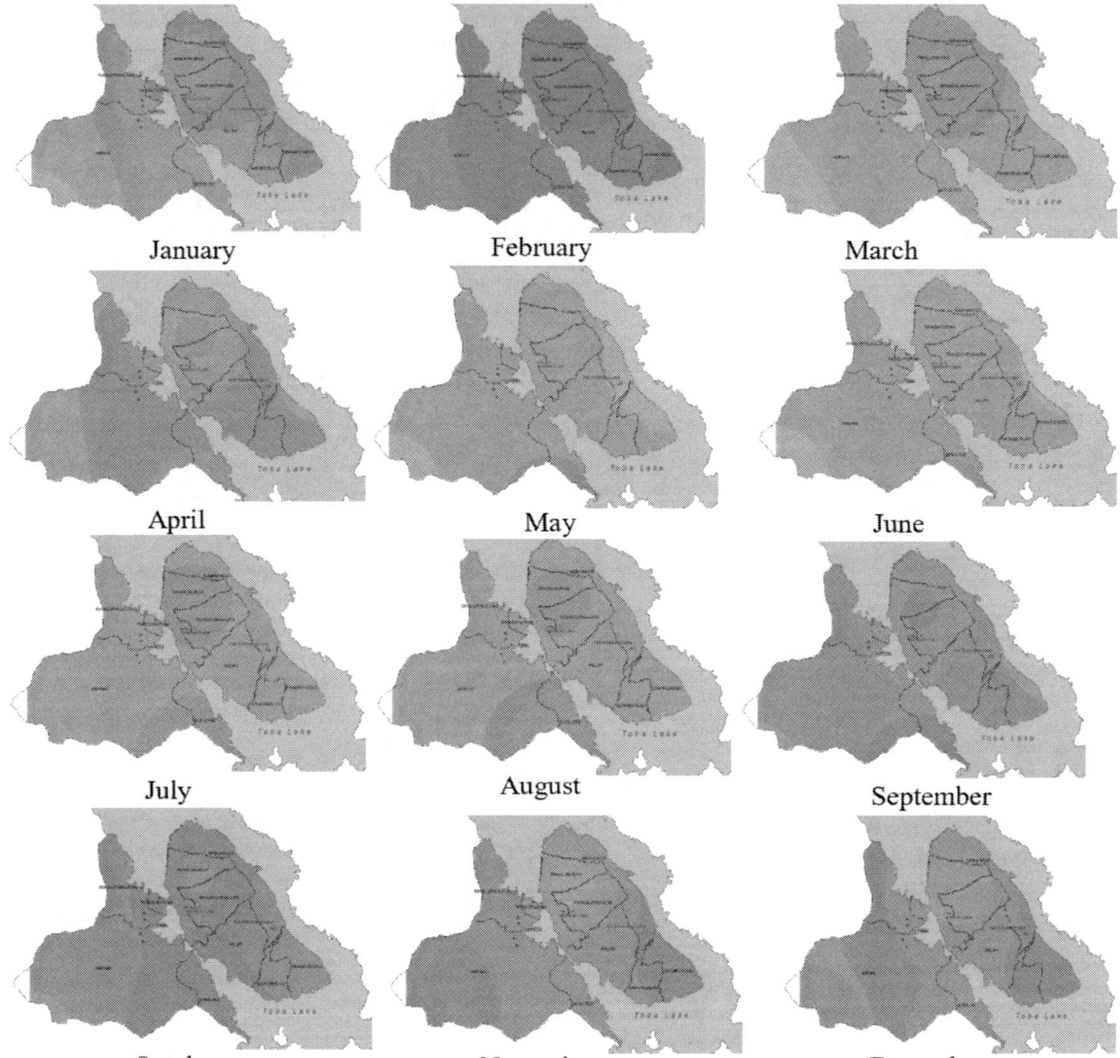

Figure 2. TCI Index by month in Samosir District.

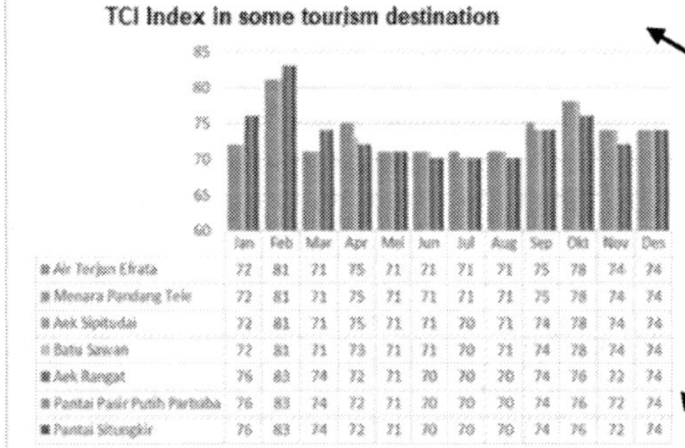

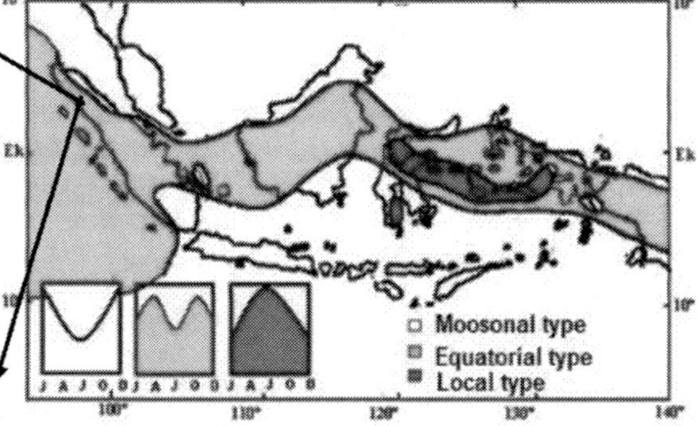

Figure 3. Spatial precipitation patterns in Indonesia and Samosir

https://doi.org/10.1051/e3sconf/20199405001

Table 3. Correlation between the number of visitor and TCI index.

Correlations[a]

			Jumlah Pengunjung	Nilai TCI
Spearman's rho	Jumlah Pengunjung	Correlation Coefficient	1.000	-.126
		Sig. (2-tailed)	.	.253
	Nilai TCI	Correlation Coefficient	-.126	1.000
		Sig. (2-tailed)	.253	.

a. Listwise N = 84

Conclusion

Based on the discussion above, it can be concluded several things to answer the objectives of this study, is:

1. The comfort value of climate in Samosir Regency has a range of 67 - 85. Variations in the range of values per month vary, one of which affects is the regional climate pattern in North Sumatra which is included in the equatorial rain pattern.
2. Based on the climate comfort index value map above, the right time to travel to Samosir Regency is in February.
3. There is no correlation between the number of visitors and TCI values at some tourism destination points.

Acknowledgement

Although climate comfort does not have a correlation with the number of visitors, it is still necessary to control exhaust emissions which will affect the increase in temperature and disruption to the amenities of tourists. The impact will further affect the cultural tourism attractions that are relied on by the local community through Batak culture.

To be able to advance tourism in Samosir Regency, the local government must be able to innovate tourism attractions in Samosir Regency, such as organizing cultural and culinary festivals in several existing tourist attractions. In addition, tourism promotion must be intensified as information for visitors to attract interest in visiting other tourism destinations. Factors supporting tourism such as supporting facilities and souvenir shops must also be reproduced.

Reference

1. Gumelar, G. *Ekonomi*. Retrieved from cnnindonesia: https://www.cnnindonesia.com/ekonomi/20171018180443-78-249279/kemenpar-klaim-pariwisata-jadi-kontributor-utama-devisa. (2017, October 19)
2. Kabupaten Samosir. *Geografis*. Retrieved from samosirkab.go.id: https://samosirkab.go.id/web/geografis/ (2014, April, 3)
3. Mieczkowski, Z. (1985). *The tourism climate index: A method for evaluating world climates for tourism*. - The Canadian Geographer 29: 220-233
4. Rilatupa, J. (2008). *Aspek Kenyamanan Termal Pada Pengkondisian Ruang Dalam*. Jurnal Sains dan Teknologi EMAS.
5. Scott, D. & Lemieux, C. (2010). *Weather and Climate Information for Tourism*. Procedia Environmental Sciences. 1, 146-183.
6. Suwarto, T. (2011). *Pengaruh Iklim dan Perubahannya Terhadap Destinasi* Pariwisata Pantai Pangandaran. Jurnal Perencanaan Wilayah dan Kota, 17-32.
7. Tjasjono. B., (2003). *Klimatologi*. Bandung : ITB

Variation of Precipitable Water Vapor derived from GNSS CORS Observations in Thailand

Paramee Meunram and Chalermchon Satirapod

Department of Survey Engineering, Faculty of Engineering, Chulalongkorn University,

Phyathai Road, Patumwan, Bangkok 10330, Thailand
e-mail: paramee.m44@gmail.com, chalermchon.s@chula.ac.th

Abstract: This research aims to study a distance variation of Precipitable Water Vapor (PWV) between CORS stations in Thailand using a Precise Point Positioning (PPP) technique. Nowadays, GNSS Continuously Operating Reference Stations (CORS) is not only used to obtain precise positioning applications but also plays an important role in meteorological applications. With a recent establishment of GNSS CORS around Thai region, the PWV can be accurately derived from these GNSS CORS data using the scientific Position and Navigation Data Analyst (PANDA) GNSS processing software. One-year period of GNSS CORS data collected between 1 January and 31 December 2016 are used in this study. The GNSS CORS data used in this study are gathered from various agencies, i.e. Chulalongkorn University, Department of Lands and Department of Public Works and Town & Country Planning. However, a coverage distance from each GNSS CORS station for PWV estimations is not precisely determined for Thai region. This information can help reduce expenses in an installation and maintenance of meteorology sensors at each GNSS CORS. Therefore, this paper focuses on determining the distance variation of PWV between GNSS CORS stations and the coverage distance from each CORS for PWV estimations. The result shows that the coverage distance from each CORS station at 74 km or less can provide accurate PWV in Thai region.

1. Introduction

Electromagnetic waves are transmitted from satellites when the waves travel through the atmosphere reflection and refraction make waves travel faster or slower. The atmosphere that affects this travelling wave is the ionosphere and the troposphere. In this study, the Troposphere which is the lowest layer of the atmosphere and above the earth's surface at 50 km. (Bernhard Hofmann-Wellenhof, 2007) It consists of two components; namely, about 10% of dry part and 90% of wet part of the refraction in the atmosphere. Both components result in the arrivals of the receiver slower than the actual travelling time because the measured distance is longer than it should be. We can apply the error due to the atmospheres and convert to Precipitable Water Vapor (PWV). The deviation of the wave passing through the atmosphere depends on several factors, such as the direction of the satellite and the receiver, the distance traveled by the wave, the temperature and the atmospheric pressure. There are two approaches to estimating the vertical deviation from the Zenith Total Delay (ZTD): Precise Point Positioning (PPP) and Baseline Networking. The application of the Global Navigation Satellite System (GNSS) in meteorology is another option that can be used. This information can help to reduce costs in an installation and maintenance of meteorology sensors at each GNSS CORS.

Previous studies in Thailand confirmed that the PWV values could be accurately derived from GNSS observations (Kitpracha et al., 2017; Satirapod et al., 2011; Suwantong et al, 2017). However, in the meteorological applications for Thailand, no coverage area of Precipitable Water Vapor was measured at each station. It can be used as a guideline for determinations and analyses of Precipitable Water Vapor in order to establish GNSS CORS network to be part of site location determinations in term of distance and coverage dependent.

This preliminary study, aims to study was study and analyze the horizontal distances that affected the changes of the errors due to the atmospheric effects and determine variations of PWV due to distance between GNSS CORSs and their coverage area from each CORS effecting the PWV estimations in order to assist reducing meteorological equipment installation costs at GNSS CORS ground and could applied in other water related applications such as agricultures, water management and weather prediction.

2. Observation Model

2.1 Precise Point Positioning (PPP)

PPP technique is a positioning method to computer a precise positioning solution to a level of few centimeter level of accuracy. The mathematic model of this positioning algorithm is determined by using an ionosphere-free combination for pseudorange and carrier phase GNSS observations to eliminate the first order of Ionosphere effects. The simplified PPP observation equation is shown as:

$$P_{L3} = \rho + c(dt - dT) + M(ZTD) + \varepsilon_p \quad (1)$$
$$\emptyset_{L3} = \rho + c(dt - dT) + M(ZTD) + N\lambda + \varepsilon_{\emptyset} \quad (2)$$

where P_{L3} and $\emptyset_{L3}$ are ionosphere free combination of pseudorange and carrier phase observations, respectively. ρ is geometry distance between a satellite and a receiver. dt and dT are a receiver clock error and a satellite clock error, respectively. c is the speed of light in a vacuum. N is defined as ionosphere free ambiguity. λ is ionosphere free wavelength. ZTD is tropospheric delay in zenith direction. ε_p and $\varepsilon_{\emptyset}$ are the multipath error and observation noise of ionosphere free combination observation. (Min Li, 2014) This paper focuses on ZTD value which is obtained from GNSS data using PPP technique. Therefore, ZTD can be converted to PWV. Additionally, in this PPP processing, the parameters to be determined are the distance between satellite and receiver (x, y, z), receiver clock error (dt) and ambiguity (N).

2.2 Tropospheric Delay

The troposphere is the atmospheric layer up to around km. from the earth surface. The troposphere is non-dispersive medium at GNSS carrier frequencies; which mean, the effects on the GNSS signal transmission are independent from its operating frequencies. The effect of troposphere on GNSS signals makes an extra delay in the measurement when the signal travels from the satellite to receiver. This delay depends on the temperature, pressure and humidity depending on station location and seasons. (Zong-qiu, Ai-gong, Xin-chao, & Ji-shan, 2012) Two major delays effected at the troposphere layer are often modeled as: the dry (hydrostatic) and the wet (non hydrostatic) components to define their refractivity.

PANDA is a GNSS data processing software to obtain a tropospheric delay at receiver's slant path delay (SPD) from a mapping function multiply by zenith total delay. The Mapping function is related to Zenith Hydrostatic Delay (ZHD) and Zenith Wet Delay (ZWD). The slant total delay can be written as:

$$SPD = ZTD \times Mf(E) = ZHD \times Mdry(E) + ZWD \times Mwet(E) \quad (3)$$

in which Mf is a total mapping function. $Mdry$ and $Mwet$ are mapping function for a dry part and wet part, respectively. E is elevation angle, in degree.

Any empirical tropospheric delay models have been established, including Saastamonien model (Saastamoinen, 1972) , hence, it is determined to applied Saastamonien model as the empirical model in this estimations (Kouba, 2015) to obtain the ZWD which is the one of the factors to specify its accuracy in GNSS positioning solution. This is due to the fact that the precision of ZWD was estimated; therefore, it is essential for high precision application, such as PPP. This study applied; several processing strategies to determine the tropospheric delay. Furthermore, the ZWD was calculated and can be used in numerical weather predictions as specified in the equation below.

$$ZWD = ZTD - ZHD \quad (4)$$

The most common method to describe the wet delay is through a combination of surface measured parameters (including water vapor pressure, or relative humidity, and temperature). Currently, many tropospheric models for mitigating the tropospheric delay are available such as Saastamonien model which can be expressed as:

$$ZHD = \frac{2.2768 \times Ps}{1 - 0.00266\cos(2\emptyset) - 0.00000028H} \quad (5)$$

where Ps is the pressure temperature (unit: millibar), $\emptyset$ is the station latitude (unit: radius) and H is the height of the station above the sea level (unit: meter).

Precipitation Water Vapor (PWV), retrieved from the national GNSS CORS network is used in weather forecastings. The PWV is the integrated amount of water vapor along the path between transmitting satellite and receiving antennas. The dimension quantity (π) depends on the mean temperature's weight of atmosphere and be calculated from the empirical model. (MICHAEL BEVIS, 1992)

$$PWV = \pi \times ZWD \quad (6)$$

The unit of PWV is millimeter (mm.) because the PWV content of this column equals the amount of water if all water vapor was condensed. The commonly used units are [kg/m2] reflecting the weight of the condensed water or [mm] if water is accumulated on the bottom of the column.(EUMeTrain, 2014)

$$\pi = \frac{10^6}{\rho w \times Rv(\frac{k3}{Tm} + k'2)} \quad (7)$$

in which π is a dimensionless constant of proportionality, Tm is mean of temperature and Tm was estimated Empirical Model by Global Mapping Function (GMF). ρw is the density of liquid water (999.97 kg./m^3). Rv is the constant of water vapor (461.525 JK^{-1}/kg^{-1}). $k3$ and $k'2$ are the physical constant derived by several laboratories with value 3739k^2/mb and 22.1 k/mb., respectively.

$$T_m = 70.2 + 0.72 \times T_s \quad (8)$$

In this study, the mean temperature (T_m) and surface pressure (T_s) are determined from Global Pressure and Temperature (GPT) model used to estimate mean of temperature and surface pressure (unit: kelvin) respectively. (see more information from this link: http://ggosatm.hg.tuwien.ac.at/DELAY/SOURCE/gpt.m.)

 https://doi.org/10.1051/e3sconf/20199405002

3. Methodology

3.1 PPP Processing

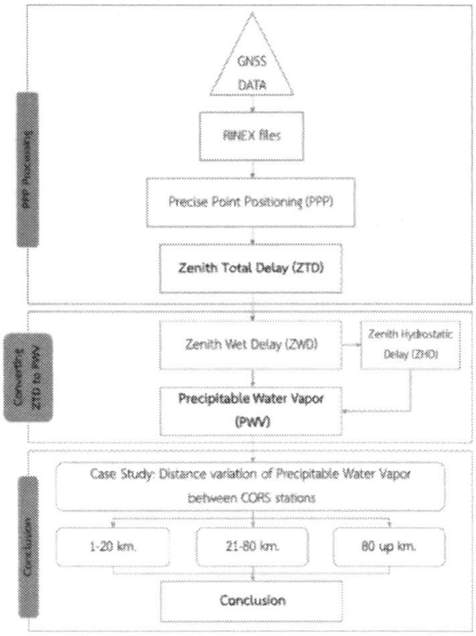

Fig. 1. Data processing step

In this paper, PPP technique is selected to calculate ZTD by PANDA software. The data processing steps are as followings. Firstly, observation data preparations, GNSS observation are obtained from 10 GNSS reference stations known as GNSS data; defined as Chulalongkorn University (CUUT), Ayutthaya (AYYA), Nakhon Nayok (OKRK), Nakornpatom (BLAN), Nonthaburi (PKKT) Samut Sakhon (KTBN), Saraburi (KKOI), Samut Prakan (BPLE), Bangkok (DTP9) and Nakhon Sawan (NKSW). These GNSS data is later regenerated using TEQC toolkit by UNAVCO to decimating observations in a RINEX file by the original sample interval is 1 second to decimated to 30-second interval observations. Secondly, PANDA software is originally developed by Wuhan University that has achieved their the advancement the world class. This PPP processing allows some settings to be included in the precise solution such as satellite orbit error, satellite clock offset, Phase Center Offset (PCO), Phase Center Variation (PCV) and solid earth tide & Ocean loading. (Kouba, 2015)

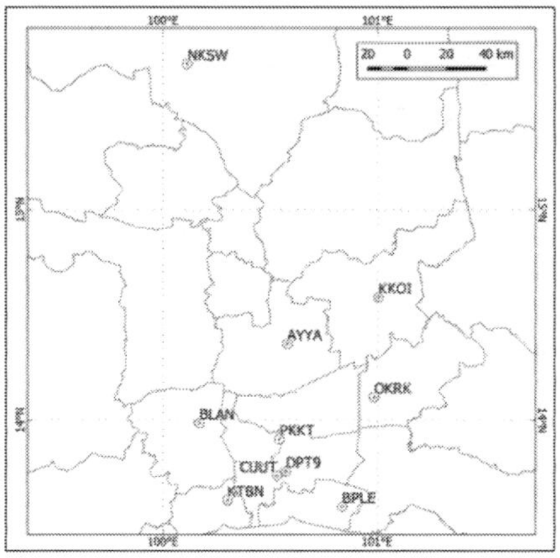

Fig. 2. Local distribution of GNSS Stations selected for this study. For these stations, we have collected GPS observation between January 1st and December 31st, 2016

3.2 Converting ZTD to PWV

The ZTD derived from PPP can be expressed in two components comprised of Zenith Hydrostatic Delay (ZHD) and a Zenith Wet Delay (ZWD). The ZHD can achieve better accuracy by obtaining some measurements from surface meteorological data. However, the ZWD is commonly used as an estimated parameter to obtain higher accuracy due to a high variation and can be transformed into PWV when a mean temperature (T_m) is realized. The ZWD can be expressed in terms of the ZTD and ZHD. (Bevis et al., 1992)

3.3 Data Analysis

The GNSS observation data and International GPS service (IGS) final products are used in this data analyses. The PANDA software calculates the double difference between GPS transmitter and receiver clock error. The Slant Path Delay is later computed into vertical precision or ZTD the previously determines results using PPP (as described in Section 3.2). ZTD observations are results provided from the GPS processing solution. ZTD had to be later converted to the PWV (as described in Equation 4). The results from the previous determination are summarized in standard deviation (S.D.) of PWV. The differences of PWV S.D. are compared with variations in distances due to distance variations of precipitable water vapor between GNSS CORSs could be provided to the best benefit in term of providing precipitable water vapor.

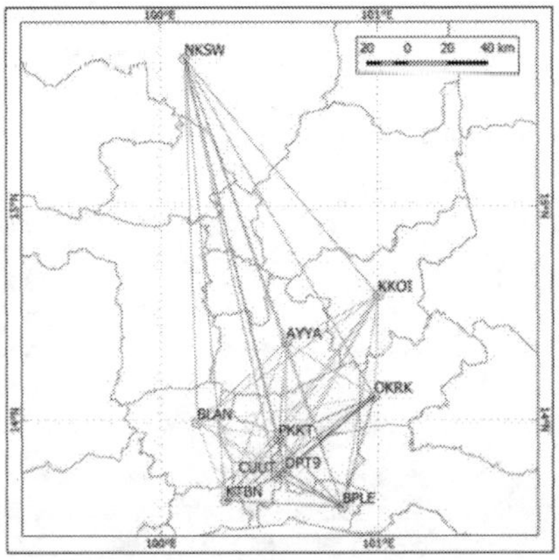

Fig 3. The all possible combinations of 10 stations.

4. Result

4.1 Variation of PWV

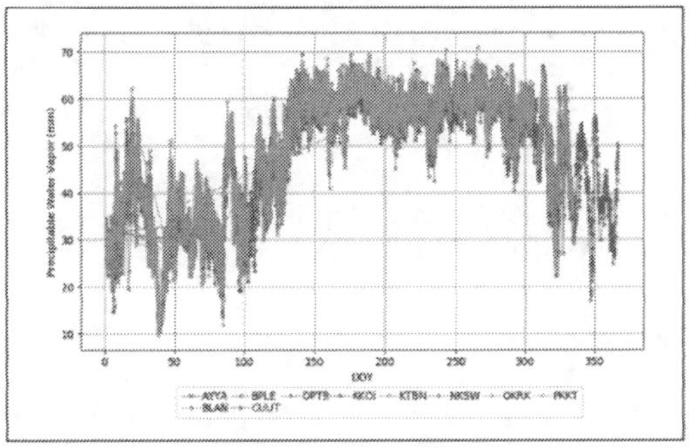

Fig. 4. Precipitable Water Vapor (PWV) in 2016

The scatter plot of the PPP-derived PWV time series between January and December in 2016 using IGS orbit and clock products from 10 stations is shown in Figure 4. The PPP-derived PWV time series are resampled at the interval of 2 hours. The results showed that the PWVs varied from 10 to 70 millimeters through this year. In Thailand, there are 3 seasons in a year: summer, rainy and winter. The summer period runs from mid-March to mid-May, with April and May the hottest months of the year. Consequently, the large amount of the PWVs continually increased from about 30 to 60 millimeters between DOY 100 to DOY 150 (see Figure 4). During this period of a year, the influence of changing season from northeast monsoon season to the southwest monsoon season which brings a large quantity of rainfall in this area. The rainy season runs from mid-May to mid-October. The amount of the PWVs in this period varied from about 50 to 70 millimeters and the winter season runs from mid-October to mid-March because of the northeast monsoon bringing relatively cool and dry condition to Thailand. Thus, the amount of PWVs decreased from 60 to 30 millimeters.

4.2 Determining the distance variation of PWV between GNSS CORS

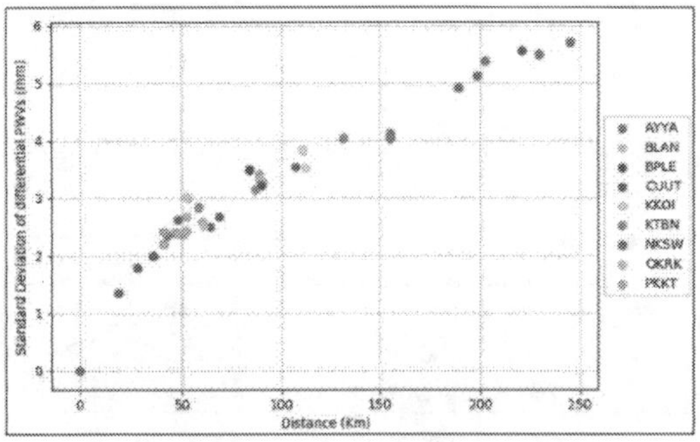

Fig. 5. Variations of SD of differential PWV and its corresponding distances between GNSS CORSs

In order to determine the coverage distance of the PWVs from each CORS stations, the PWVs from each station were compared at the same epoch. The number of all possible combinations of 10 stations are 45. Figure 5 displayed a comparison of variation between S.D. of differential PWVs and its distance, The S.D. of Differential PWVs (mm.) is compared with the GNSS referenced station distance (km.). The results show that S.D. of PWVs is increased when the distance changes. The PWV uses its S.D. to show the distribution of the computed PWV. The S.D. of PWVs in the atmosphere begins to change significantly at any distance. The results of the analysis show that:

- The first test case assigns the distance to be ranges from 1 km to 20 km. The averaged S.D. of PWV is approximately 2.20 mm.
- The second test case assigns the distance to be ranges from 21 km to 80 km. The S.D. is scattered, S.D. is higher than the first test case. Their averaged SD was 2.69 mm. The data on the amount of steam in the atmosphere between the stations start to be varies.
- The third test case assigns the distance to be ranged more than 80 km. The data spreads more when the distance between stations is in the same trend as for the second case. The data difference is approximately 4.3 mm.

This analysis could use CUUT; a reference station, as an example. It results that S.D. of differential PWVs (mm.) were compared to the distance of CORS for a whole year. The results are shown in Table 1 where each station which is compared with every other station with its relative distances and corresponding S.D. of its differential PWV, hence, the difference in variation in distances are provided. The figure 6, X-axis is Distance (km.) and the Y-axis is its corresponding Standard deviation of differential PWVs (mm.)

https://doi.org/10.1051/e3sconf/20199405002

Table 1. Distance from the reference station **(CUUT)**

Stations		**Distance (km.)**	**S.D.**
CUUT (Reference Station)	DPT9	5	2.36
	PKKT	19	1.35
	KTBN	28	1.79
	BPLE	36	2.00
	BLAN	48	2.62
	OKRK	64	2.49
	AYYA	69	2.67
	KKOI	107	3.55
	NKSW	221	5.56

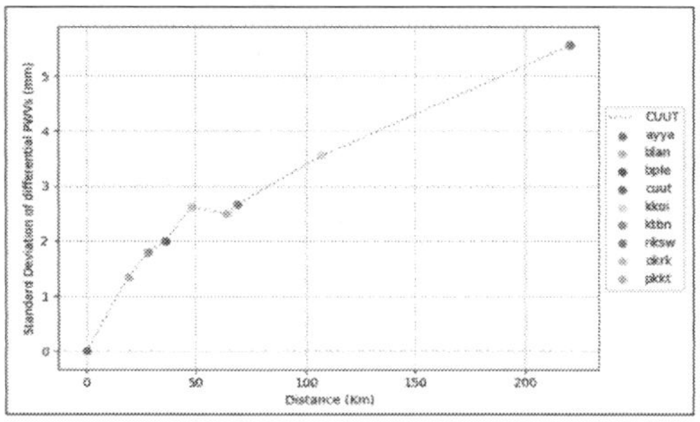

Fig. 6. S.D. of differential PWVs (mm.) of CUUT station

In the computation step, Linear Regression Analysis was used for approving the equation to determined its suitable for the analysis. The distances between GNSS CORS should not exceed 74 km. in Thailand. The result of this study obtained from polynomial equation that is

y = 0.00008*x2+0.03988*x+0.47367

The reason for 74 is the answer to this study because the differential of PWVs between CORS should not exceed its difference of to 3 mm. (Haan, 2006) and is in-lined with the substation results from the above where x is the GNSS CORS distance and y is the difference of PWV. In the case, when the differences of PWV (in term of y) as 3, the result of distance (in term of x) is approximately 74. It could be confirmed as the answer of this study that distance should not exceed 74 km. for GNSS CORS's establishment in Thailand. Furthermore, this polynomial equation is defined at 95% confident level at the R-squared test which means the factor 2 of its standard deviations which considered enough for the desired reliability.

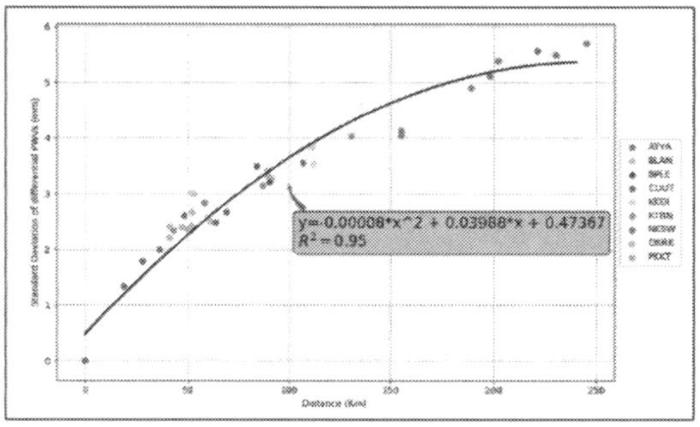

Fig. 7. A 2nd order polynomial trendline was used to illustrate the relationship between the S.D. of the differential PWVs between stations.

5. Conclusion

This study determines the distance between GNSS CORS that affects the PWV estimations in central part of Thailand. It found that the relationship of the distance between the GNSS CORS and the PWV's distribution can be expressed as quadratic polynomial equation. The polynomial equation could be expressed as $y = 0.00008 * x^2 + 0.03988 * x + 0.47367$, where the acceptable PWV component should not be greater than 3 mm. (or $y \leq 3$). The distance between each reference stations is 74.47 km as, determined; hence, the distance between the station in central part of Thailand should be within 74 km.

References

1. Bevis, M., Businger, S., Herring, T. A., Rocken, C., Anthes, R. A., and Ware, R. H. (1992) GPS Meteorology - Remote-sensing of atmospheric water-vapor using the global positioning system. *Journal of Geophysical Research-Atmospheres,* **97**(D14), 15787-15801.
2. Bernhard Hofmann-Wellenhof, H. L. (2007) GNSS – Global Navigation Satellite Systems. In SpringerWienNewYork.
3. Haan, S. d. (2006) *National/regional operational procedures of gps water vapour networks and agreed international procedures.*
4. Kitpracha, C., Promchot, D., Srestasathiern, P. and Satirapod, C. (2017) Precise Tropospheric Delay Map of Thailand using GNSS Precise Point Positioning Technique, *International Journal of Geoinformatics*, **13**(2), 17-21.
5. Kouba, J. (2015) A Guide to Using the IGS Products. International GNSS Service (IGS).
6. Michael bevis, S. B. (1992) GPS Meteorology' Remote Sensing of Atmospheric Water Vapor Using the Global Positioning System. *Journal of geophysical research,,* **97**.
7. Min Li, L. Q. (2014) Precise Point Positioning Using PANDA Software Package. GNSS Research Center,Wuhan University.

8. Wu (1993) Effects of antenna orientation on GPS carrier phase. *Manuscripta Geodaetica*, 91-98.
9. Saastamoinen, J. (1972) Atmospheric Correction for the Troposphere and Stratosphere in Radio Ranging Satellites. In S. W. Chovitz, *Geophysical Monograph Series*. doi:https://doi.org/10.1029/GM015p0247
10. Satirapod C., Anonglekha S., Choi Y-Sand Lee H-K (2011) Performance Assessment of GPS-Sensed Precipitable Water Vapor in Thailand Using IGS Ultra-rapid Orbits, *Engineering Journal*, **15**(1), 1-8.
11. Suwantong, R., Srestasathiern, P., Satirapod, C., Chuang, S. and Kitpracha, C. (2017) Mean atmospheric temperature model estimation for GNSS meteorology Using AIRS and AMSU data, Engineering and Applied Science Research, **44**(1), 46-52.
12. Zong-qiu, X., Ai-gong, X., Xin-chao, and Ji-shan, L. (2012) Research on the Correlation of Troposphere Delay Parameters in GPS. *Advances in Information Sciences & Service Sciences*.

Apply GNSS-Reflectometry Technique for wind retrieval in typhoon condition

Hwa Chien[1], *Quang-Huy Lu*[1], *Wen-Hao* Yeh[2]

[1]Institute of Hydrological & Oceanic Sciences, National Central University, Taiwan

[2]National Space Organization (NSPO), Taiwan

Abstract. Global Navigation Satellite System-Reflectometry (GNSS-R) is an innovative Earth observation technique that exploits signal from satellite constellations after reflection on the Earth surface. The GNSS-R techniques is also known to have the potential of mapping the surface wind speed up to 70 m/s, and thus provide a promising solution. Abundant real-time data of the typhoon surface wind speed will play the crucial role on the improvement of typhoon intensification forecasting. The aim of present study is to investigate the influences of high wind speed and the corresponding giant waves during typhoon to the GNSS-R wind speed retrieval algorithms. The Mean Square Slope that altered by the complex wave directionality is discussed. Finally, the uncertainties of wind speed retrieval with respect to the influences of wave directionality is assessed. The level 1 product from the GNSS-R receiver is a map of GPS signal power scattered from the sea surface, as a 2D function of delay and Doppler frequency, which is known as a Delay-Doppler Map, or DDM. Based on Zavorotny-Voronovich model, the DDMs are simulated from the Directional Mean Square Slope (DMSS) that obtained from the combination of capillary wave spectra and gravity wave spectra. The gravity wave spectra were calculated using a 3rd generation numerical wave model that driven by the Dujuan typhoon (2015) wind fields with super-fine resolution. The complexity of directional wave spectrum, such as extreme spatial heterogeneity, bimodal spectra and varying directional spreading alter the DMSS and DDM. Various observables, e.g. – DDM Average (DDMA), and Leading Edge Slope (LES) are then applied to the simulated DDM. Regression-based wind retrievals are developed for each individual observable using empirical geophysical model functions. The wind speed retrieval in case of Dujuan typhoon are compared with the target data uncertainty assessment.
Key word: GNSS-R, DDM, Typhoon, Sea Surface Wind speed, Z-V Model, Wave Directional Spectrum

1 INTRODUCTION

The GPS signal is reflected from the surface of the ocean, and processed to obtain information about the scattering surface. The receiver used to process these reflections essentially performs similar operations to those of an ordinary GPS receiver for positioning. The main difference is that the receiver deals with the signal scattered by the ocean surface, and not with a direct signal. The output of the processing also changes from a pseudo range measurement to a map of scattered power. For classical GPS positioning, the received signal is normally equal to the transmitted one, but delayed and shifted in frequency due to the Doppler Effect. For GNSS-R, the received signal is the result of the reflection of the incident GPS signal from the sea surface, which in principle distorts the incident signal according to its impulse response.
The final product from the GPS-R receiver is a map of GPS signal power scattered from the sea surface, as a 2D function of delay and Doppler frequency, which is known as a Delay-Doppler Map, or DDM. The generation of DDMs from UK-DMC datasets has been carried out using the Daaxa software, developed by Scott Gleason [Gleason et al. (2005), Gleason (2006)]. Details of the software and the way it works can be found in [Gleason (2006)].
The estimation of sea state parameters is mainly based on the theory of wind-wave. So there is still a huge uncertainty estimating the sea state under very high wind speed condition, especially in Typhoon cases when the sea surface roughness changes dramatically. Successful acquisition of in situ wave measurements within a Tropical Cyclone (TC) is a difficult task. The conditions to be sampled, high winds and large waves, are energetic and often lead to the failure and destruction of instruments and platforms. Consequently, measurements of winds and waves in TCs remain rare.
Based on different quantities derived from the DDMs by NASA's Cyclone Global Navigation Satellite System (CYGNSS), five wind speed retrieval algorithms are developed. Each of these observable is introduced as a means of extracting wind speed information from the DDMs. Regression-based wind retrievals are developed for each individual observable using empirical geophysical model functions. The wind speed retrieval in case of Dujuan typhoon from those observables is

 https://doi.org/10.1051/e3sconf/20199405003

compared to data from numerical model to verify the algorithm.

2 THEORY

2.1 Sea Surface Roughness

The mean square slope (MSS) of sea surface is defined as the variance of surface slope, which is a key parameter in understanding the air–sea interactions and ocean remote sensing. Air–sea fluxes of mass, momentum, and heat as well as radar scattering are believed to be significantly correlated with MSS. Many factors including wind speed, wave state, air– sea temperature difference, and intensity of sea surfactant films have impacts on the MSS.

The analysis of the source function balance leads to the conclusion that the dimensionless wavenumber spectrum, B(k), is functionally dependent on the dimensionless wind speed, u_*/c. Hwang and Wang in 2004 report an analysis of wave spectrum measurements in the ocean focusing on the wavenumber band between 1 and 300 rad/m. This analysis produces a power-law function for $B(\frac{u_*}{c};k)$:

$$B\left(\frac{u_*}{c};k\right) = A(k)\left(\frac{u_*}{c}\right)^{a(k)} \quad (1)$$

Because c and k are related by the wave dispersion relation $c^2 = \left(\frac{g}{k}\right) + \tau k$ in deep water, where g is the gravitational acceleration and τ is the ratio of surface tension and fluid density, $B(\frac{u_*}{c};k)$ can be written as $B(u_*;k)$, which is a convenient parameterization function of the ocean surface roughness spectrum.

The results of A and a are tabulated in Hwang (2005) as lookup tables to facilitate the computation of $B(u_*;k)$. Hwang (2008) further simplifies the computational procedure by developing analytical functions for three wavenumber branches: $0 < k \le k_1$, $k_1 < k \le k_2$, and $k_2 < k \le \infty$, where k1 = 1.5 and k2 =300 rad/m

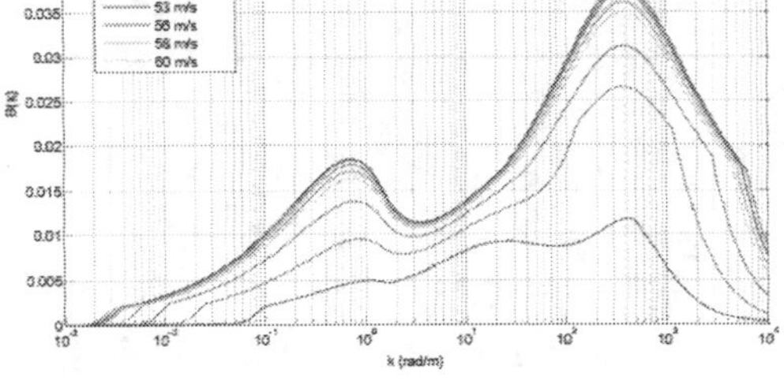

Figure 1. Wavenumber spectrum combined from low to high-wind conditions, by Paul Hwang (RoughSpecPack2015)

Figure 1 illustrated the variation of wavenumber spectrum over the large range of wavenumber coverage, calculated for different wind speed levels. The computed spectrum increases monotonically with U10 up to 50m/s and then decreases for U10 > 50m/s. It is recognized that there is still considerable uncertainty in the ocean surface drag coefficient in high wind.

An essential method to obtain the MSS is the integration of wave spectrum, which is defined as (Phillips 1977):

$$s^2 = \int_0^\infty k^2 F(k)dk \quad (2)$$

Where $F(k)$ is the wavenumber spectrum of ocean waves.

With the dispersion relationship of surface wave, equation (2) can be transformed into the integration of the frequency spectrum of the surface wave, F(f), which is the spectrum simulated using SWAN model. It can be rewritten as:

$$s^2 = \int_0^\infty \frac{(2\pi f)^4}{g^2} F(f)df \quad (3)$$

Where f is the frequency.

The mean-square slope integrated from the spectral peak wavenumber kp to an arbitrary upper-bound wavenumber ku is denoted by:

$$s^2(k_u) = \int_{k_p}^{k_u} k^2 F(k)dk \quad (4)$$

By varying U10 from 2 to 50m/s and ku from 1 to 104 rad/s, a dataset of $s^2(k_u)$ as a function of U10 and ku is created (Hwang 2013). The wind speed dependence deviates from the empirical linear relationship over the wide range of wind speeds and can be written as:

$$s^2(k_u) = b_2(k_u)U_{10}^2 + b_1(k_u)U_{10} + b_0(k_u) \quad (5)$$

Least square fitting procedure is applied to compute $b_2(k_u)$, $b_1(k_u)$, and $b_0(k_u)$ for wind sea and mixed sea conditions, as shown in Hwang 2013. Then, this above empirical equation can be used to calculate the MSS of an arbitrary wavenumber band of the ocean surface roughness.

2.2 The Zavarotny-Voronovich Model for DDM Simulation

The theoretical model commonly used to simulate DDMs, based on the theory formulated by [Zavorotny and Voronovich (2000)], and hereafter referred to as the Zavorotny-Voronovich (Z-V) model. This model describes the average scattering of GNSS signals from the sea surface, using a specific ElectroMagnetic (EM) approximation called Geometrical Optics (GO). The expression for the average scattered GPS power as a function of the delay and Doppler frequency, under the GO limit is the following:

$$\langle P(\tau, f_D)\rangle = T_i^2 \int\int_S \frac{1}{4\pi R_0^2 R_T^2} D^2(\boldsymbol{r})\Lambda^2(\frac{\delta\tau}{\tau_c})S^2\left(\frac{\delta f_D}{T_i}\right)\sigma_o(\boldsymbol{r})d^2r \quad (6)$$

where S is the scattering surface, and r is the point on the scattering surface; Ti is the coherent integration time (chosen equal to 1 ms for UK-DMC data); 1/4πR20R2T represents the attenuation due to path losses, as R0 and RT are respectively the transmitter and receiver range from the scattering point; D (r) is the footprint function of the receiving antenna in terms of complex amplitudes, and D2 is the power antenna footprint; Λ(...)· S (...) is the Woodward Ambiguity Function or WAF (χ (...)) of pseudorandom C/A sequences; σ0 (r) is the bistatic Normalized Radar Cross Section (NRCS).

The NRCS is obtained using the GO approximation, resulting in the following mathematical expression:

$$\sigma_0(\boldsymbol{r}) = \frac{\pi|\Re|^2 q^4}{q_z^4} f_q\left(\frac{-q_\perp}{q_z}\right) \quad (7)$$

It depends on the Fresnel reflection coefficient $\Re$, and on the Probability Density Function (PDF) fq () of the sea surface slopes, defined as s = −q⊥/qz = [−qx/qz, −qy/qz]. The vector q = [qx, qy, qz] is known as the scattering vector, namely the vector obtained as the sum of the unitary vector pointing from the scattering point towards the transmitter, and the unitary vector pointing from the scattering point towards the receiver. This vector plays a crucial role, as it represents the ideal orientation that the tangent to the scattering point considered should have for the power to be scattered exactly towards the receiver.
Equation (7) for the NRCS does not specify a PDF of slopes and therefore is valid for any slope statistical distribution [Zavorotny and Voronovich (2000)]. In our case, we consider a gaussian PDF of the sea surface slopes, which also takes into account the wave direction [Germain et al. (2004)]. Its expression is as follows:

$$f_q\left(\frac{-q_\perp}{q_z}\right) = 1/2\pi\det(\boldsymbol{M})exp\left[-\left(\frac{1}{2}\boldsymbol{q}_\perp^t\boldsymbol{M}^{-1}\boldsymbol{q}_\perp\right)\right] \quad (8)$$

$$\boldsymbol{M} = \begin{bmatrix} cos(\phi) & -sin(\phi) \\ sin(\phi) & cos(\phi) \end{bmatrix} \begin{bmatrix} \sigma_{up}^2 & 0 \\ 0 & \sigma_{cross}^2 \end{bmatrix} \begin{bmatrix} cos(\phi) & sin(\phi) \\ -sin(\phi) & cos(\phi) \end{bmatrix}$$

where σ_{up}^2 and σ_{cross}^2 are respectively the Directional Mean Square Slopes (DMSS) along the major and minor axes of the 2D gaussian PDF, and φ is the Principal Wave Slope Direction (PWSD), namely the angle between the x-axis and the major axis of the PDF, clockwise. For brevity we call these two parameters the DMSS and PWSD. For wind generated waves, the DMSS can be thought as the MSS upwind and crosswind, and the PWSD as the angle defining the direction of the wind waves.
These three parameters are extremely important as they entirely characterize the Gaussian PDF of the sea surface slopes, and therefore they represent the sea surface roughness parameters in the Z-V model. The 2D elliptical shape characterizing the Gaussian PDF reduces in amplitude for larger DMSS and decreases more slowly when moving away from the SP, consistent with the expected behavior of the scattered power for rougher seas. A rotation of such elliptical shape can be also noticed for changing ϕ values, indicating a change in the direction the waves are travelling.

3 WIND SPEED RETRIEVAL – CONSIDER THE SWELL CONTRIBUTION TO DIRECTIONAL MSS

The realistic ocean is the combination of wave types, especially in typhoon case. In which, swell contributes a very important affect to the totally ocean sea surface roughness. This chapter will verify the retrieved algorithm in case of the combination of mean square slope in both low and high frequencies. The approach detail is shown in Figure 2

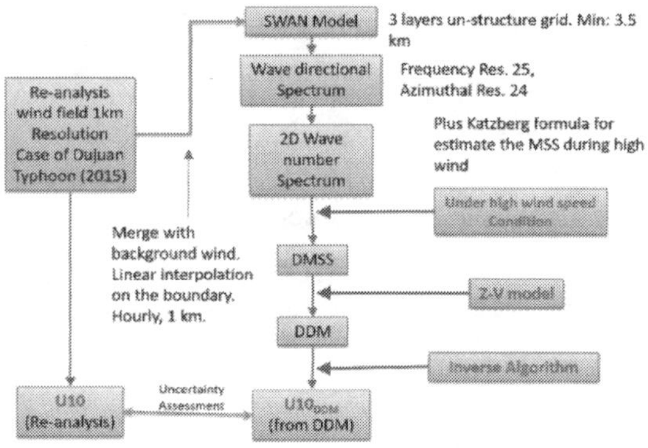

Figure 2. Wind speed retrieval approach – Consider the Swell contribution

3.1 The fully range of MSS in frequency

To verify the retrieved algorithm, the wave directional spectrum simulated from SWAN model using 3 layers unstructured grid has been used. The upwind and crosswind mean square slope, also the wave direction are calculated from spectrum that represented the ocean sea surface roughness effected by waves. For estimate the MSS during high wind, Katzberg formula has been added. The total MSS in full range of frequency is the combination of low and high wind MSS. The direction and MSS then are used as input for Z-V model to simulate DDM. The retrieved wind speed algorithm is applied to DDM to estimate wind speed using observables. After that, the retrieved wind speed will be compared to re-analysis wind field 1km resolution (Figure 3) to estimate the uncertainty assessment.

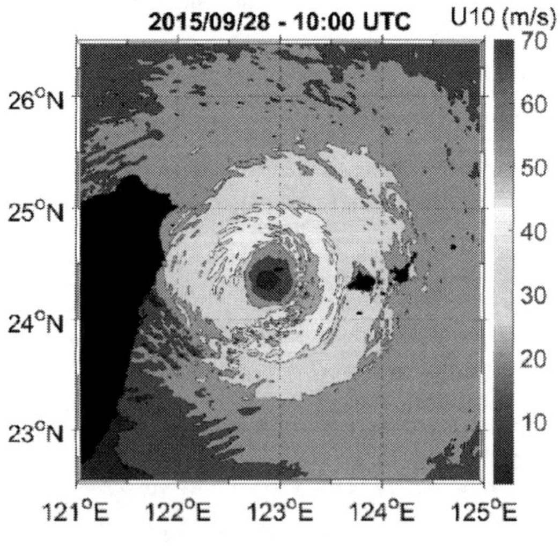

Figure 3. Wind field 1km resolution (10h – 2015/09/28)
A method to obtain the MSS is the integration of wave spectrum, which is defined as (Phillips 1977):

$$s^2 = \int_0^\infty k^2 F(k)dk \quad (9)$$

Where $F(k)$ is the wavenumber spectrum of ocean waves.

With the dispersion relationship of surface wave, equation (9) can be transformed into the integration of the frequency spectrum of the surface wave, F(f), which is the spectrum simulated using SWAN model. It can be rewritten as:

$$s^2 = \int_0^{\infty} \frac{(2\pi f)^4}{g^2} F(f) df \qquad (10)$$

Where f is the frequency. DMSS can be calculated using (10), then combine to high frequency DMSS by Paul Hwang model to get the full range of MSS. The total MSS is shown in figure 4.

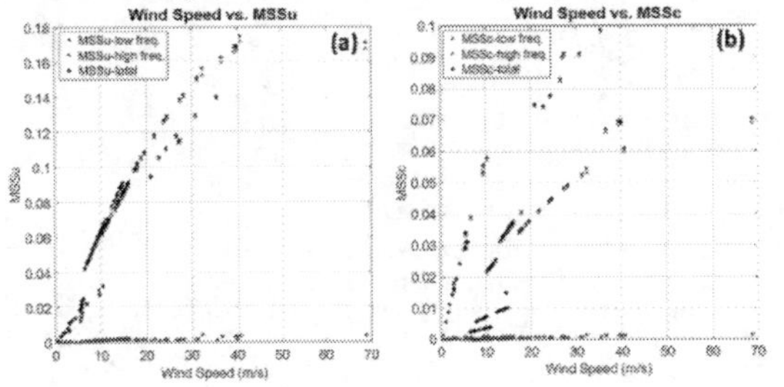

Figure 4. The variation of MSS upwind (a) and crosswind (b) in vertical axis with the increasing of wind speed (horizontal axis)

Figure 4 shows the variation of MSS upwind and crosswind with the increasing of wind speed. The black dots represents total MSS, which is the combination of MSS in low and high frequencies. The development of DMSS during typhoon is in Figure 5. It shows the corresponding between MSS and wind field from typhoon eye to faraway, and between both sizes of the typhoon. The values of DMSS calculated by roughness spectrum are much higher than DMSS from wave model, which means effect of swell is considered in DMSS calculation. Those estimated DMSS then are used as the input parameter to simulate DDMs using Z-V model.

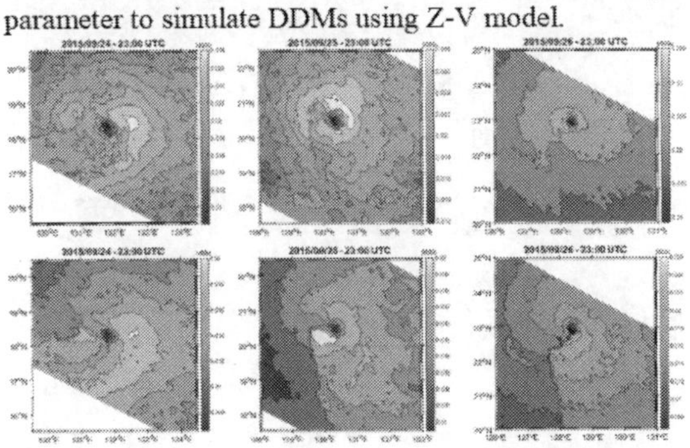

Figure 5. The variation of MSS during Dujuan typhoon

3.2 Estimated Wind Speed and Uncertainty Assessment

The direction extracted from wave spectrum and Directional Mean Square Slope in full range of frequency are used as the input parameter for Z-V model to simulated Delay-Doppler Map (an example of Z-V DDM is shown in Figure 6).

A bulk of DDM have been simulated for 11204 data point over the domain, start from 6am 2015/09/23 to 7pm 2015/09/28. The retrieved wind speed algorithm (mentioned in beginning of section 2.3) is applied to all those DDMs to estimate the wind speed during Dujuan typhoon time.

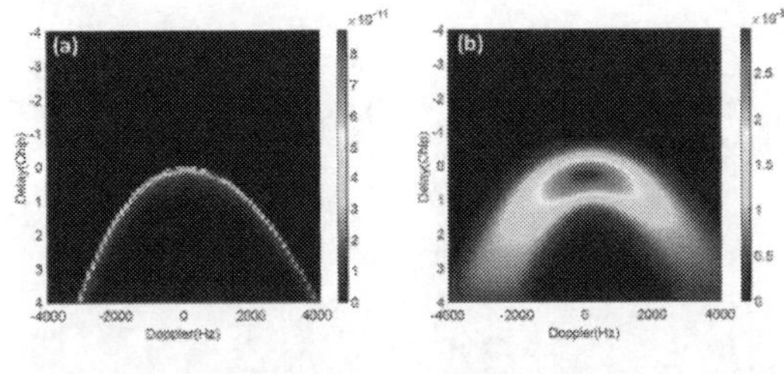

Figure 6. Simulated Z-V DDM in cases without Woodward Ambiguity Function (WAF) (a) and with WAF (b). The resolution is 128 (Delay) x 64 (Doppler frequency). Waves travelling assumed along the x-direction ($\phi = 0$)

At 23.980N, 123.160E, the wind speed at this point reaches to 69m/s in 10h – 2015/09/28. Estimated wind speeds from both two observables, DDMA and TES are all match the reference wind speed. Root mean square error (RMSE) of estimated wind speed from DDMA is 1.4689 m/s and RMSE of estimated wind speed from TES is 1.4018 m/s which is quite acceptable. The highest retrieved wind speed at this location reach over 70 m/s which mean the wind speed retrieve method is completely suitable for typhoon wind speed condition.

After applying GMFs for all 11204 data points, the estimated wind field has been re-constructed in simulated domain, then compare to re-analysis wind field 1km resolution. The details can be seen in Figure 7, where the parallelogram domain represents the re-constructed wind field.

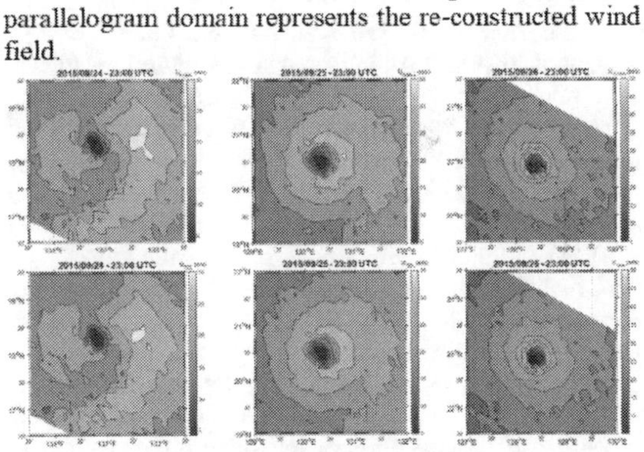

Figure 7. Comparison between 2 wind field

The uncertainties assessment between reference wind field and estimated wind is shown in figure 8 to visualize the range and other characteristics of responses for a large group. The central mark indicates the median; the bottom and the top edges of the box indicate the 25th and 75th percentiles, respectively. The whiskers extend to the most extreme data points not considered outliers, and the outliers are plot individually using the '+' symbol. Wind data is divided into six groups: 0 – 10 m/s, 10 – 20 m/s, 20 – 30 m/s, 30 – 40 m/s, 40 – 50 m/s, and over 50 m/s. Group of 50 – 60 m/s and 60 – 70 m/s (and higher value) are merged to one group because of the limited number of samples. Each group is represented by the middle values of the groups (7.04, 13.59, 24.2, 35.49, 45.60, 59.66 m/s). When the wind increases, the deviation of estimated wind speed rises respectively. The box plot of the first 4 groups is comparatively short suggest that overall wind speed in those groups have a high level of agreement with each other. It means the combination DMSS method seems stable for low and middle range wind speeds. The box plot of group 5 is comparatively tall which means wind speed values in this group are diverse or maybe due to lack of data in this group and worthy further investigation in that group. However, the method also works quite well for high range of wind speed.

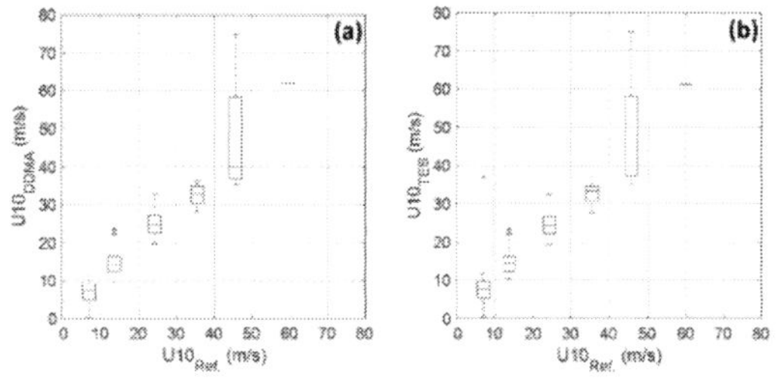

Figure 8. The uncertainties of retrieved wind speed using 2 observables DDMA (a) and TES (b) compared to reference wind speed (horizontal axis). On each box, the central mark indicates the median; the bottom and the top edges of the box indicate the 25th and 75th percentiles, respectively. The whiskers extend to the most extreme data points not considered outliers, and the outliers are plot individually using the '+' symbol.

6. CONCLUSIONS

The aim of the study is to assess the GNSS-R inverse algorithms for high wind speed conditions (storm condition). The 1 km re-analysised wind field of Dujuan Typhoon is used as input to drive the sea surface wave and roughness for DDM simulation. In the simulating case, as the retrieved wind speed reached to 70 m/s, the algorithm still works well. But real field data, especially at higher wind speed condition are needed for the validation.

Observables approach is processed. Two observables are derived from GNSS-R Delay-Doppler Maps (DDMs). Regression-based wind retrievals are developed for each individual observable using empirical geophysical model functions. The wind speed retrieval in case of Dujuan typhoon from those observables show good agreement with the data from numerical model. TES observable gives better results of wind speed retrieval than DDMA in idealized DDM.

The combination DMSS method that consider swell contribution can work in high wind condition, especially in typhoon to estimate wind speed. Further study is needed to test the statistic approach for real wind data. The expectation is to simulate the ocean wave surface based on roughness spectra in high wind, and then develop the algorithm with more realistic DDMs.

REFERENCES

[1] Antonio Rius et al, "Sea surface state measured using GPS reflected signals", GEOPHYSICAL RESEARCH LETTERS, VOL. 29, NO. 23, 2122, doi:10.1029/2002GL015524, 2002.

[2] Attila Komjathy et al, "Retrieval of Ocean Surface Wind Speed and Wind Direction Using Reflected GPS Signals", American Meteorological Society 2004.

[3] B.Arguillat et al, "Measurements of the wavenumber-frequency spectrum of wall pressure fluctuations under turbulent flows", 11th AIAA/CEAS Aeroacoustics Conference (26th AIAA Aeroacoustics Conference) 23 - 25 May 2005, Monterey, California.

[4] Binglan Wang, Lili Song and Wenchao Chen, "Drag Coefficient during Strong Typhoons", Hindawi Publishing Corporation Advances in Meteorology Volume 2013, Article ID 650971.

[5] B. S. Gohil, Rajesh Sikhakolli, and Rishi Kumar Gangwar, "Development of Geophysical Model Functions for Oceansat-2 Scatterometer", IEEE GEOSCIENCE AND REMOTE SENSING LETTERS, VOL. 10, NO. 2, MARCH 2013.

[6] Charles Cox and Walter Munk, "Measurement of the Roughness of the Sea Surface from Photographs of the Sun's Glitter", JOURNAL OF THE OPTICAL SOCIETY OF AMERICA, VOLUME 44, NUMBER 11, NOVEMBER, 1954.

[7] Chen Li and Weimin Huang, "SIMULATING GNSS-R DELAY-DOPPLER MAP OF OIL SLICKED SEA SURFACES UNDER GENERAL SCENARIOS", Progress In Electromagnetics Research B, Vol. 48, 61–76, 2013.

[8] Chen Li and Weimin Huang, "An Algorithm for Sea-Surface Wind Field Retrieval From GNSS-R Delay-Doppler Map", IEEE GEOSCIENCE AND REMOTE SENSING LETTERS, VOL. 11, NO. 12, DECEMBER 2014.

[9] Christine P. Gommenginger, "TOWARDS LONG-TERM SUSTAINABLE OBSERVATIONS OF OCEAN WIND AND WAVES WITH GNSS SIGNALS OF OPPORTUNITY".

[10] Donald E. Barrick, "Rough Surface Scattering Based on the Specular Point Theory", IEEE TRANSACTIONS ON ANTENNAS AND PROPAGATION, VOL. AP-16, NO. 4, JULY 1968.

[11] E. Cardellach et al, "GNSS-R ground-based and airborne campaigns for ocean, land, ice, and snow techniques: Application to the GOLD-RTR data sets", RADIO SCIENCE, VOL. 46, RS0C04, doi:10.1029/2011RS004683, 2011.

[12] Gary A. Mastin et al, "Fourier Synthesis of Ocean Scenes", 0272-1716/87/0300-0016-01.00 1987 IEEE.

[13] Giuseppe Foti et al, "Spaceborne GNSS reflectometry for ocean winds: First results from the UK TechDemoSat-1 mission", Geophysical Research Letters 10.1002/2015GL064204.

[14] Gary S. Brown et al, "The Wind-Speed Measurement Capability of Spaceborne Radar Altimeters", IEEE JOURNAL OF OCEANIC ENGINEERING, VOL. OE-6, NO. 2, APRIL 1981.

[15] Hasselmann et al, "Directional Wave Spectra Observed During JONSWAP 1973", Journal of Physical Oceanography.

[16] Hugo Carreno-Luengo et al, "GNSS-R Derived Centimetric Sea Topography: An Airborne Experiment Demonstration", IEEE JOURNAL OF SELECTED TOPICS IN APPLIED EARTH OBSERVATIONS AND REMOTE SENSING, VOL. 6, NO. 3, JUNE 2013.

[17] H. Hersbach, "An improved C-band scatterometer ocean geophysical model function: CMOD5", JOURNAL OF GEOPHYSICAL RESEARCH, VOL. 112, C03006, doi:10.1029/2006JC003743, 2007.

[18] H. K. Johnson et al, "On the Dependence of Sea Surface Roughness on Wind Waves", JOURNAL OF PHYSICAL OCEANOGRAPHY, VOLUME 28.

[19] James L. Garrison et al, "Effect of sea roughness on bistatically scattered range coded signals from the Global Positioning System", GEOPHYSICAL RESEARCH LETTERS, VOL. 25, NO.13, PAGES 2257-2260, JULY 1, 1998.

[20] Juan Fernando Marchán-Hernández, "An Efficient Algorithm to the Simulation of Delay–Doppler Maps of Reflected Global Navigation Satellite System Signals", IEEE TRANSACTIONS ON GEOSCIENCE AND REMOTE SENSING, VOL. 47, NO. 8, AUGUST 2009.

Zenith Wet Delay (ZWD) Seasonal Correlation with Rainfall in Cikapundung River Discharge, North Bandung Region, Indonesia

Wedyanto Kuntjoro[1], *D.D. Wijaya*[1], *A. Pramansyah*[1], *Z.A.J. Tanuwijaya*[1], *and Dhota Pradipta*[1]

[1]Geodesy Research Group, Faculty of Earth Sciences and Technology, Institute of Technology, Bandung, Indonesia

Abstract. In a GPS survey study, the biases produced by the ionosphere and troposphere layers are known as ionospheric biases and troposphere bias. The distance deviation due to the slowing travel time of GPS signals in troposphere is commonly referred to as Zenith Tropospheric Delay (ZTD). The magnitude of this ZTD can also be used to characterize and analyze the troposphere conditions around the GPS observation area. This can be done by separating the wet delay component from ZTD, so as to obtain Zenith Wet Delay (ZWD) and dry component so as to obtain Zenith Hydrostatic Delay (ZHD). The total moisture content in the troposphere (precipitable water vapor, PWV) of an area can be estimated based on the bias characteristics of zenith wet delay (ZWD). The ZWD pattern is very important in the study of atmospheric water cycles which are associated with rainfall patterns and flood events. The methods used in the research include preliminary data processing and estimation of ZTD value using RTKLIB 2.4.2. This article analyzes the correlation between ZWD, rainfall and Cikapundung river discharge in the North Bandung Region (KBU), based on the daily average data in the 2011-2015 observation period. Based on the reconstruction of harmonic components, it was found that the seasonal pattern of river discharge is correlating with the seasonal pattern of rainfall and moisture content in the troposphere. The pattern of the three variables is strongly influenced by the Asian and Australian Monsoon exchanges phenomena. Linear correlation between ZWD and river discharge exhibits clear results, which is based on the Pearson correlation value is 88.84% with a 95% confidence level using t-student statistic. Based on cross-spectrum analysis, the three variables are dominated by the seasonal cycle of one-year monsoon (annual) and the six-month cycle phenomenon (semi-annual).

1. Introduction

The Cikapundung watershed starts from the upstream area in the north mountainous zone of Bandung into Citarum river as a part of the fluvial system. This system can be divided into three zones: production zones, transfer zones, and deposition zones [1]. The production zone is defined in the Lembang drainage basin (Cikapundung upstream watershed), where the entire river network in this basin at the Maribaya estuary. The transfer zone is defined starting from the Maribaya estuary (A) to Dago Curug (E), where the riverbed is closed by the basal layer. The deposition zone is defined from Dago waterfall to Citarum, which rivers flow on the alluvial base of pyroclastic sediments of the Sunda volcanic complex and lake sediments.

2. Data and Method

The data used in this study are: (1) Zenith wet delay (ZWD), at the ITB GPS-Continuous station (6° 53 '29,501 "LS, 107° 36' 43,229" BT) which has an elevation of 816,517 m with period of data collection from 2011-2015. (2) Daily debit of the Cikapundung river at Maribaya station (6° 50 '11,000 "LS, 107° 39' 23,500" BT) with an elevation of 1091 m from 1971-2016 discharge data observation. The Daily debit data obtained from West Java Province of PSDA. (3) BMKG Lembang station daily rainfall data (6° 49 '35,600" LS, 107° 37' 3,600 "BT), has an elevation of 1275 m with the 1977-2012 rainfall observation period. The location of the three observation stations (A, B, C) can be seen in Figure-1. The series of daily average times of ZWD and Cikapundung Maribaya river discharge for the 2011-2015 period can be seen in Figure-2.

To see the seasonal correlation between ZWD and river discharge, we calculate an averaging estimation of ZWD and river watershed from 2011-2015 data based on the reconstruction of seven dominant harmonic components. Then, the harmonic average pattern of river discharge from the period 2011-2015 (5 years) is then compared with the long period of 1971-2016 (46 years) normal harmonic average pattern. For Lembang rainfall data, because daily data is only available until 2012, only the normal harmonic average is reconstructed for the period 1977-2012 (36 years).

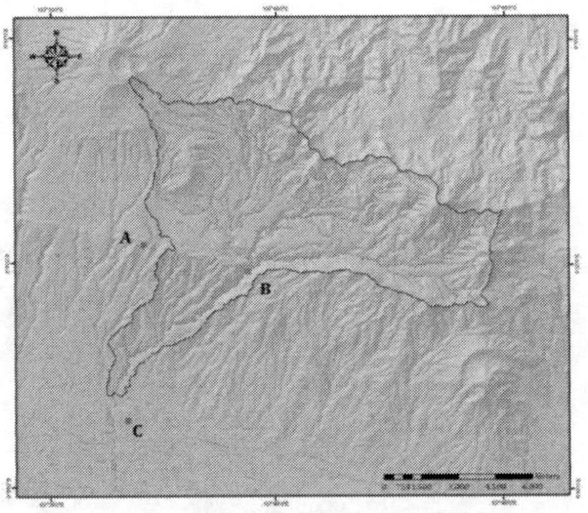

Fig. 1 Site location A. Lembang, B. Cikapundung-maribaya, and C. ITB-CORS

To measure the strength and linear relationship between ZWD and river discharge in the time domain, statistical tests were performed with Pearson Correlation. The linear correlation between harmonic components of the two variables mean was carried out in the frequency domain based on Cross Spectrum Analysis and Coherence.

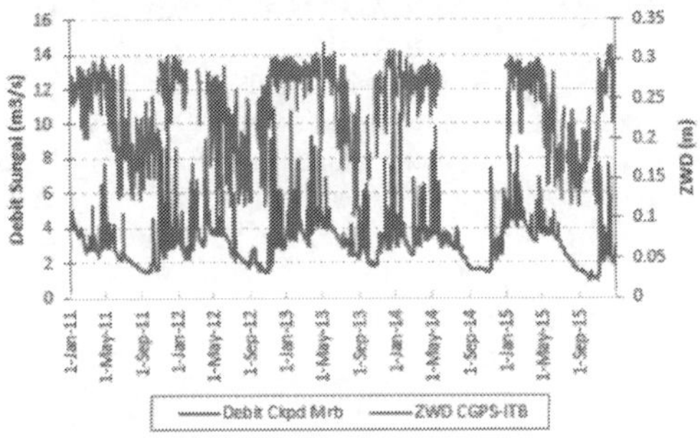

Fig. 2 Daily mean ZWD in ITB-CORS (b) and Maribaya station (r).

3. Results

Based on the data extraction of ZTD and ZHD from the ITB-CGPS results within 5 years observation (2011-2015) with interval epcoh of 30 seconds, ZWD data were obtained. The daily ZWD averaging process was carried out, i.e. 2880 total epochs. Based on the ZWD chart, there are some empty data, especially in 2014, indicating that there is no GPS measurement. The process of averaging ZWD in the daily database was done from Cikapundung river discharge data in the format of daily average data (the average of three times of manual observation from river water levels, at 07.00, 12.00 and 17.00 Indonesia Time). The average of debit represents daytime discharge conditions, hence the daily debit that obtained reduces the fluctuating value at night, while the daily ZWD data is the average result of day and night for 24 hours. ZWD charts and daily river discharge can be seen in Figure-2. The River debit data was estimated based on water level data through a rating curve. The daily debit of the Cikapundung River measured at Maribaya Station is an outlet discharge from the Cikapundung upstream watershed, covering all the rainfall patterns that caught by the Lembang Drainage Basin, hence all surface water flowing in river canals in this basin estuary into Maribaya's floodgate. Due to the unavailability of completed daily rainfall data within the Cikapundung Hulu watershed, the characteristic of the daily rainfall pattern that falls into the Lembang Basin was approached by rainfall data at the Lembang station which is located not far from the watershed area boundary (Figure-1).

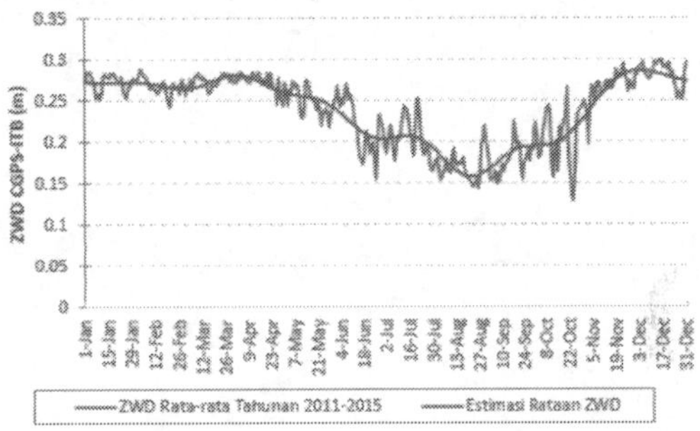

Fig. 3 Annual mean ZWD(b) and harmonic pattern reconstruction.

To obtain seasonal characteristics of ZWD, river discharge and rainfall, an annual cross-process is carried out on each corresponding date. For the Cikapundung Maribaya river discharge data, the seasonal pattern was obtained from averaging of 46 years observation (1971-2016), and the seasonal pattern of Lembang rainfall based on averaging of 36 years observation (1977-2012). As for the ZWD seasonal pattern, because the data is still limited to 30 years, the seasonal pattern obtained is only based on the average results over a period of 5 years (2011-2015). The seasonal pattern of ZWD and mean estimation can be seen in Figure-3.

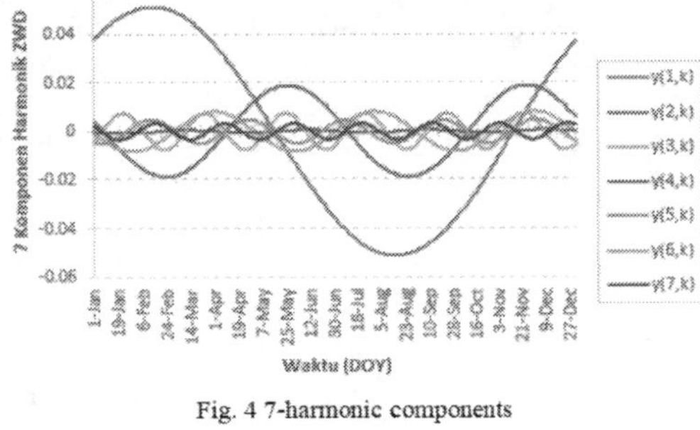

Fig. 4 7-harmonic components

The Harmonic Analysis method was carried out to estimate the average pattern of ZWD seasonal characters. By using the seven most dominant harmonic components, the estimated seasonal mean of ZWD can be reconstructed (Figure-3). The seven ZWD harmonic components that were successfully extracted can be seen in Figure-4. Using the same method, a seasonal average pattern for river discharge and rainfall was obtained. Especially for the river discharge, the estimated seasonal pattern was carried out both on the population scale (1971-2016 period) and the sample scale (2011-2016 period).

The average seasonal characteristics of the Cikapundung-Maribaya discharge pattern that are closer to the population conditions are shown by the 46-year average results (1971-2016), compared to the 5-year sample average results (2011-2015). Therefore, the seasonal characteristics of the average ZWD are more appropriate than the average discharge based on longer observations. In the graphical relationship between ZWD and river discharge on the sample scale, it appears to be a harmony between the two, especially around September to October (Figure-5).

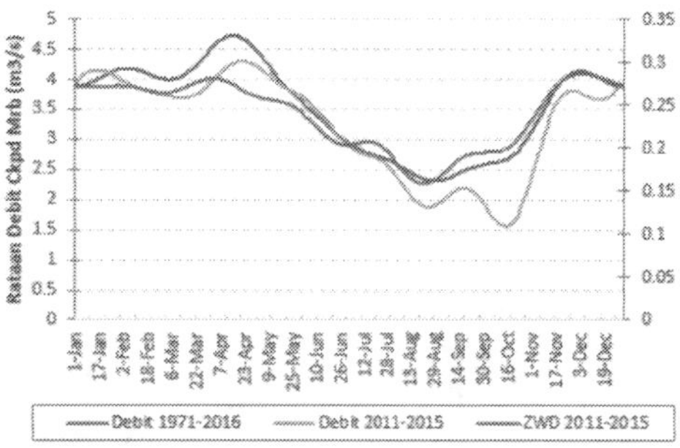

Fig. 5 Seasonal pattern ZWD and Cikapundung watershed

The most important results obtained from ZWD reconstruction are about seasonal character patterns, where the pattern of water vapor content in the troposphere of the North Bandung region is controlled by the dynamics of the monsoon wind circulation. Based on Figure-5 it can be seen that the average pattern of ZWD is closer to the average pattern of river discharge based on population averages. The closeness of the linear correlation value between the average ZWD and the average population discharge and the average sample discharge can be expressed by the correlation coefficient or determination of R2 coefficient, which have a value of 0.8956 and 0.7893. It means, almost 90% of the sample ZWD correlates with the average population discharge compared to the average sample discharge which only correlates around 79%, because the special conditions of the sample have been eliminated. The relationship between the two quantities is very strong at the 95% significance level.

ZWD measurement is very important in the study of the hydrological cycle, because the ZWD value can estimate the value of PWV (precipitable water vapor), which is about the potential of water vapor in the troposphere that can be transformed into water precipitation in the earth's surface, especially in the form of rainfall (Rakhecha & Singh, 2009). Because rainfall is a climatic element between the tropospheric moisture content and river discharge as surface water flow, the discussion is divided into two parts. First, about the response of river discharge to rainfall (Figure-6). Second, about the rainfall response to the accumulation of water vapor in the troposphere (Figure-7).

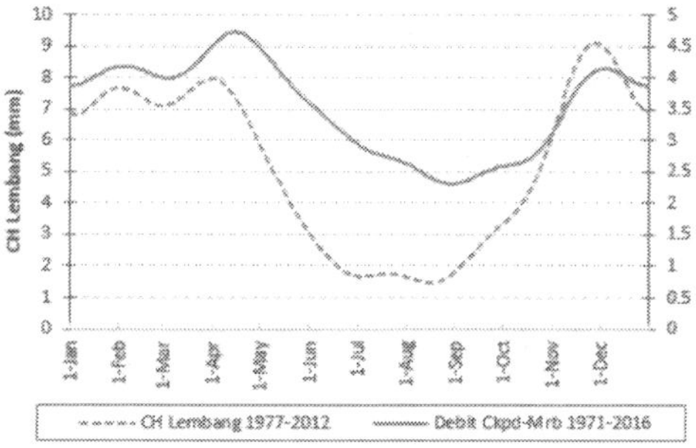

Fig. 6 Seasonal pattern ZWD 2011-2015 and seasonal debit 1971 - 2016

The measured discharge at Maribaya Station is from the Upper Cikapundung watershed which is a rain catchment area with an area of 74.881 km^2. Based on the average of the river discharge, the largest discharge occurred in April and the smallest discharge occurred in August. In general, the maximum discharge occurs at the peak of the rainy season and minimum discharge occurs at the peak of the dry season. Based on the normal nature of rainfall at Lembang station, the peak of rain occurs twice a year, namely in November (Asian Monsoon) and April (Australian Monsoon), where rainfall generated by the Asian Monsoon is greater than the Australian Monsoon.

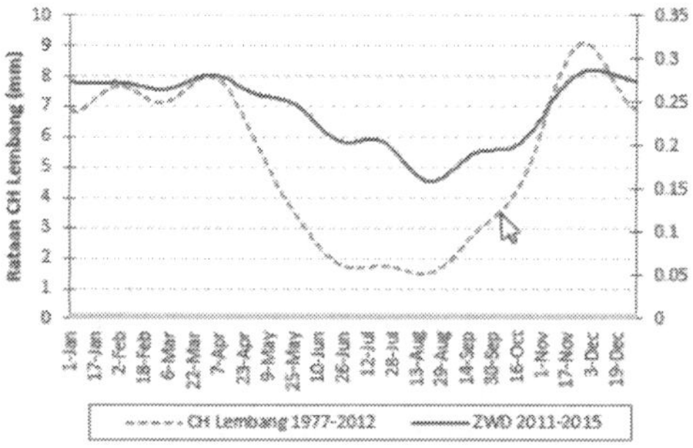

Fig. 7 Seasonal ZWD 2011-2015 and river debit (1971-2016)

The increase of delay in discharge responds related with the increase in the rainfall curve in the interval of several days to one week. This means, the overflow of river discharge waiting the land filling time by rainwater until reaches saturation. When the soil is saturated, rainwater will flow on the surface of the earth as runoff and then run into the river channels and increase the discharge quantity. Therefore, the peak of Cikapundung discharge occurs in the first week of April, after the peak of the second rainy season at the end of March. Although the peak of the rainy season occurs around the third week of November, the peak does not occur at the end of November because more rainfall is saturate to the soil. When a monsoon break occurs, the rate of discharge recession is not as deep as the rate of decline in rainfall because percolation of water in the soil takes longer. After a minor post-Monsoon discharge recession around the end of December and early January, discharge increases again due to Australian Monsoon rainfall and reaches its peak annual discharge after the land is saturated with Asian Monsoon rainfall. River discharge also responds to delay in the peak events of the Australian Monsoon (Figure-6).

Rainfall response to accumulation of water vapor in the troposphere. Based on the graph of rainfall and ZWD average (Figure-7), the maximum and minimum rainfall peaks appear in phase with the maximum and minimum conditions of ZWD. Because ZWD is related to PWV (precipitable water vapor), according to the graph it appears that rainfall is part of the realization of the total content of water vapor in the troposphere. Not all tropospheric moisture content is condensed further into cloud drops and becomes rainfall, because the rain clouds are formed random to space and time, the rainfall recorded at one Lembang station point does not represent the character of the whole bulk rain falling in the rain catchment area of the Lembang Basin. As the atmosphere is open, the condition of the total moisture content above the Lembang rainfall station and above the CGPS-ITB device is still assumed not significantly different. The horizontal distance between the two stations is around 7 km with a height difference of around 458.5 m.

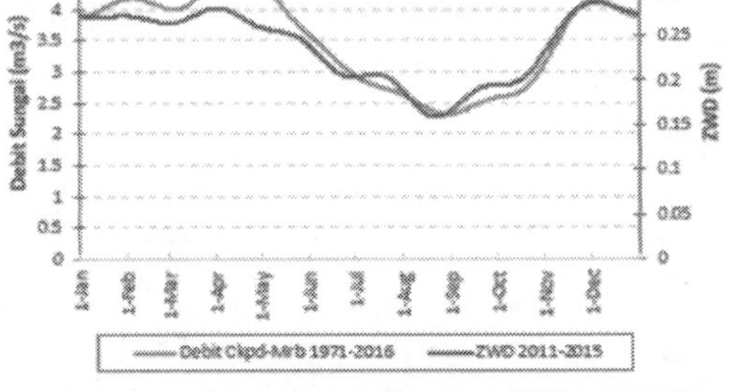

Fig. 8 Seasonal ZWD 2011-2015 and rainfall (1977-2012)

The water vapor content in the troposphere comes from the evaporation process of the ocean and the earth's surface by solar radiation. Therefore, seasonal fluctuations are controlled by variations in earth-sun distance and projections of the movement of the sun above the earth's surface in one year of revolution. This condition starts the dry season around the Lembang station which peaks around mid-August coincides with the minimum tropospheric water vapor condition.

Within one year there are two peaks of water accumulation (ZWD) and rainfall formed by two different monsoon mechanisms. The two peaks occur in November and April, where between the two peaks there is a decrease in rainfall (monsoon break), which is in the range from January to February. The rainy season in Java generally occurs when the sun's pseudo position is in the southern hemisphere, between the Equinox Autumnal (September 22) and Vernal Equinox (March 20). The North Bandung region experiences the peak of the first rainy season in mid-November, where the peak of the rain occurs before the sun reaches the southern turning point (Winter Solstice) on December 21th and before the earth reaches its closest distance to the sun on January 3rd (perihelion). The peak of the second rainy season occurs in the first week of April after the sun moves north past the equator. The first rainy season is generated by the westerlies of the Asian Monsoon, while the first rainy season is generated by the Australian Monsoon easterlies. Low pressure belts (monsoon troughs) migrate in the north-south direction and control winds that undergo a process of convergence in the intertropical convergence zone which accumulates water vapor in the troposphere and generates rainfall. This low-pressure belt migration follows the apparent movement of the sun that crosses Java twice a year. The peak of the rainy season does not occur when the sun is above the North Bandung horizon, which is in early October or early March, but occurs after the sun has passed the two months. This means that monsoon rainfall is not generated spontaneously through a pure convection mechanism, so the wind speed factor that lifts the air mass and the quantity of water vapor that condensed in the troposphere becomes very decisive.

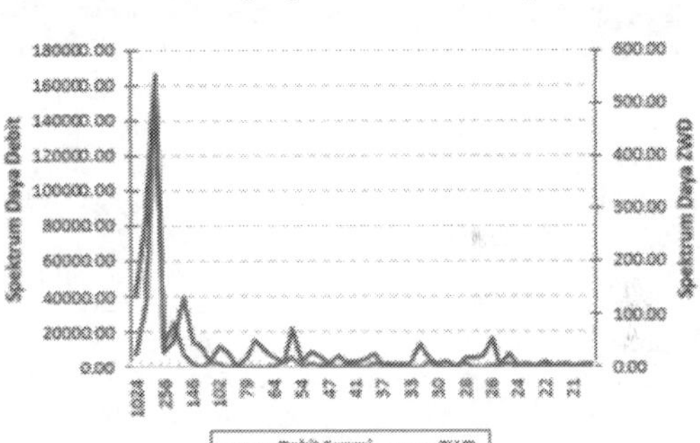

Fig. 9 ZWD power spectrum and Cikapundung debit

The peak of the first rainy season (November) occurs when the sun's projection has moved far south of Java, when the island is crossed by winds originating from Asia, where wind movements are controlled by temperature differences between the Asian region in the north and the Indian Ocean in the south. Winds that enter the Javanese land carry abundant water vapor which is supplied especially by the Java Sea when undergoing radiative heating. The abundance of water vapor from the Java Sea and Karimata Strait is caused by the shallow Sundaland Craton warming. In general, the sea surface temperature of these shallow waters is higher than the temperature of the deeper Indian Ocean.

It appears that monsoon rainfall in the North Bandung region is largely determined by the trade wind speed factor. Rainfall in this region is more a product of interaction between the trade winds that carry water vapor and local topographic factors, therefore rainfall in the Bandung Basin area is known as local type rainfall. The tropospheric moisture content and rainfall at the peak of the first rainy season are relatively higher than the second rainy season, because the supply of water vapor from the warming of the Sunda Shelf is more abundant than originating from the Indian Ocean.

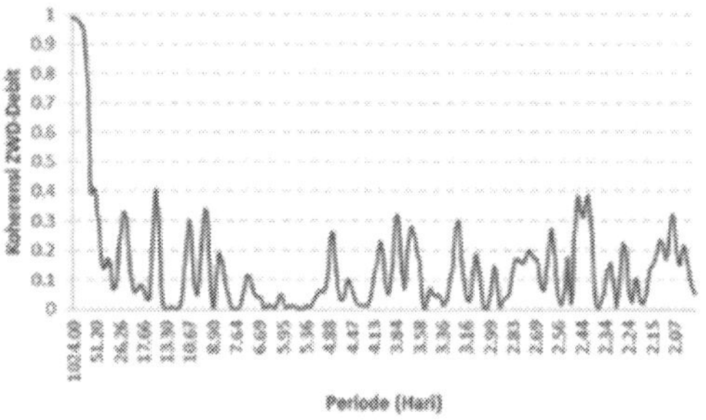

Fig. 10 ZWD coherence

Based on the graph of ZWD and river discharge (Figure-8) in general, the temporal patterns of the two quantities appear to be more correlated than rainfall, except in the second rainy season there appears to be an amplification of the discharge when the soil has reached saturation. Thus, ZWD can potentially be a good predictor of river hydrology systems rather than rainfall. Because the measured discharge at a river outlet includes all rainfall that falls on the watershed area instead of measured rainfall only on one observation station. The area of a watershed covers the area of the atmosphere above it and all possible events of condensation and precipitation that occur that fall into the watershed area.

Based on the ZWD power spectrum and river discharge (Figure-9), the two quantities are dominated by the components of the one-year monsoon cycle (11.22 monthly), while the discharge contains an intermediate component (6.70 monthly). Because the two spectra are processed based on a daily database that is limited to a data sample of only five years (2011-2015), the seasonal signals fall in the low-resolution spectral area. Meanwhile, based on the 46-year data range (1971-2016) several other important cycles can emerge with more accurate period values. With a longer daily data range, we obtained river discharge cycles 11.91 (annual), 6.02 (semi-annual), 4.0 monthly in respectively. These three cycles are the main rainfall generators which generate seasonal patterns of rainfall and river discharge in the North Bandung area (Tanuwijaya et al., 2018). Not every rainfall station in Java has a semi-annual and 4-month component, especially at stations located in coastal areas (Tanuwijaya & Liong, 2002)

Because the length of ZWD data is still limited, it cannot be confirmed about the existence of the mid-year and 4-month cycles of the moisture content in the troposphere. However, for a one-year dominant cycle, it can be confirmed that there are relatively no phase differences between the seasonal patterns of ZWD and river discharge, as visually shown by the temporal pattern of both (Figure-8). Both quantities have the same dominant spectrum period value of 341.33 daily (Figure-9), the coherence value or linear correlation in the frequency domain is close to 1 namely 0.985 (Figure-10), and the cycle phase difference value is close to zero which is 0.0084 (Fig. 11).

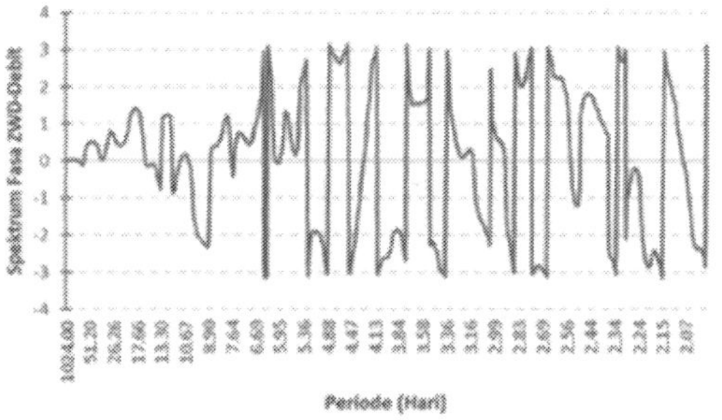

Fig. 11 ZWD phase spectrum

4. Conclusions

The amount of ZWD in the CGPS-ITB data for the period 2011-2015 is between 10-35 cm/year. The mean values of harmonic from ZWD daily correspondent with the harmonic mean of the daily average Cikapundung river discharge at Maribaya station, even though the horizontal distance and the height difference of the two stations are about 7 km and 458.5 m respectively. The sample ZWD average (2011-2015) correlates with the average debit based on a long-range data (1971-2016) compared to the average debit based on the sample data in the same year (2011-2015), the correlation around 90 % and 78%. Due to the data continuous, ZWD has the potential to be an excellent predictor of river hydrology systems compared to rainfall data from a single station.

Concerning with rainfall and river discharge, ZWD as the quantity associated with the moisture content of the troposphere in the North Bandung region which controlled by the exchange dynamics of Asian Monsoon and Australian Monsoon. The three data have the same one-year cycle (annual) component as the most dominant component. Daily ZWD data in the 5-year sample range (2011-2015) have not been able to generate semi-annual and 4-monthly cycles, as can be seen in rainfall data and river discharge.

References

[1] Bohm, J., and H. Schuh eds. (2013). Atmospheric Effects in Space Geodesy. Berlin: Springer-Verlag.

[2] Charlton, R. 2008. Fundamentals of Fluvial Geomorphology. New York: Routledge.

[3] Kuntjoro, W. (1999). New Approaches of Tropospheric Delay Determination Using GPS Observation. Doctor Science Thesis, Earth and Planetary Science Division, Kyoto University.

[4] Rakhecha, P.R. and V.P. Singh (2009). Applied Hydrometeorology. Springer.

[5] Shelton, M.L. (2009). Hydroclimatology, Perspectives and Applications. Cambridge: Cambridge University Press.

[6] Tanuwijaya, Z.A.J. dan T.H. Liong (2002). Analisis faktor dan spektral frekuensi anomali curah hujan Pulau Jawa. Prosiding Seminar Nasional Statistika, IPB, Bogor, 28 September.

[7] Tanuwijaya, Z.A.J, Hendarmawan, A. Sudradjat, dan W. Kuntjoro (2018). Karakteristik musiman debit sungai Cikapundung di Kawasan Bandung Utara, Jawa Barat. Bulletin of Scientific Contributions, Vol. 16, No. 1, 39-46, April.

[8] Wijaya, D.D. (2009). Atmospheric Correction Formulae for Space Geodetic Techniques. Doctorate of Technical Sciences, the Faculty of Technical Mathematics and Technical Physics, the Graz University of Technology.

Analysis of Total Electron Content (TEC) Near Real Time Using Dual Frequency GPS Data (Study Case: Surabaya)

Mokhamad Nur Cahyadi, Almas Nandityo Rahadyan, and Buldan Muslim

Abstract. Ionosphere is part of the atmospheric layer located between 50 to 1000 km above the earth's surface which consists of electrons that can influence the propagation of electromagnetic waves in the form of additional time in signal propagation, this depends on Total Electron Content (TEC) in the ionosphere and frequency GPS signal. In high positioning precision with GPS, the effect of the ionosphere must be estimated so that ionospheric correction can be determined to eliminate the influence of the ionosphere on GPS observation. Determination of ionospheric correction can be done by calculating the TEC value using dual frequency GPS data from reference stations or models. In making the TEC model, a polynomial function is used for certain hours. The processing results show that the maximum TEC value occurs at noon at 2:00 p.m. WIB for February 13, 2018 with a value of 35,510 TECU and the minimum TEC value occurs in the morning at 05.00 WIB for February 7, 2018 with a value of 2,138 TECU. The TEC model spatially shows the red color in the area of Surabaya and its surroundings for the highest TEC values during the day around 13.00 WIB to 16.00 WIB.

Keywords: Ionosfer, TEC, TEC Model

1 Preface

Ionosphere is part of the atmosphere layer which is located between 50 to 1000 km above the earth's surface. Ionospheres contain electrons that can affect the propagation of electromagnetic waves in the form of additional travel time in signal propagation, this depends on Total Electron Content (TEC) in the ionosphere and GPS signal frequency.

The biggest ionospheric effect is on the speed of the signal, which will directly affect the value of the distance from the observer to the satellite. The ionosphere will slow down the pseudorange (the size of the distance becomes longer) and accelerate the phase (the size of the distance becomes shorter), with the same distance bias (in length units). The magnitude of the distance bias is because the ionospheric effect will depend on the concentration of electrons along the signal path and the frequency of the signal in question. While the concentration of electrons alone will depend on several factors, especially solar activity and the earth's magnetic field.

TEC is the number of electrons in a 1m2 cross section of vertical (cylindrical) columns along the signal path in the ionosphere. the effect of TEC on signals is the signal from GPS satellites that through the ionosphere will experience a delay time because it is affected by free electrons in the ionosphere.

The ionosphere is an important source of distance and range error values for Global Positioning System (GPS) users who require high accuracy measurements. Determination of ionospheric correction can be done by calculating the TEC value using dual frequency GPS data from reference stations or models.

In this research, the analysis of the ionospheric TEC value in Surabaya in near real time is carried out using the daily TEC computation method of two frequency GPS data and spatial TEC depictions are carried out in Surabaya and its surroundings. This is done to provide information on the characteristics of the TEC in Surabaya in near real time

2 Method

The location of the study was located in the Surabaya area at coordinates 07° 09 '- 07° 21' LS and 112° 36 '- 112° 54' BT.

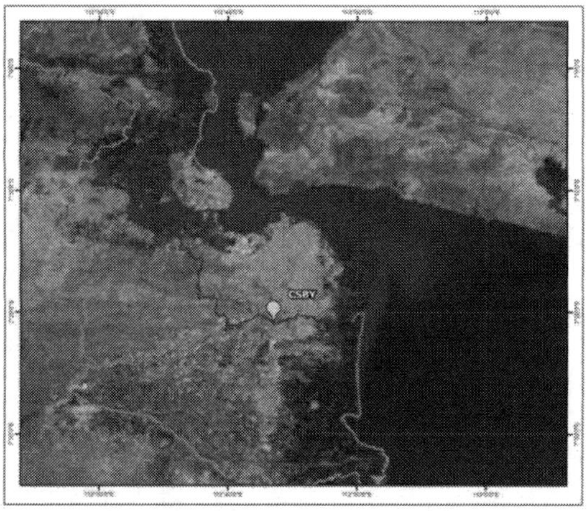

Fig. 1. Research Location (BIG, 2017)

* Corresponding author: cahyadi_geod@yahoo.com

https://doi.org/10.1051/e3sconf/20199405005

Perform data processing RINEX format observation uses the rdrnx.f program to get the time and value of the STEC value from the observation station. Determination of the STEC value in accordance with the satellite that has an orbit within the territory of Indonesia where the results are adjusted to the IPP data that has been determined. In STEC calculations also carried out correction of satellite bias, receiver bias. In determining the STEC value obtained by the formula:

$$STEC = TEC_{observasi} - bias_{satelit} - bias_{receiver} \quad (1)$$

The satellite orbit position that has been obtained from processing using the rdeph.f program on the Gfortran application then continues processing to determine the position of Ionospheric Pierce Points (IPP) using the Matlab application. From the position of Ionospheric Pierce Point (IPP) that has been obtained, the location at the ionospheric point can be known.

VTEC calculation for the mapping function to get the VTEC value in the Surabaya area, with the formula:

$$\begin{bmatrix} STEC^1 \\ STEC^2 \\ \cdots \\ STEC^n \end{bmatrix}^T = [a_0 + a_1 + a_3 + b_1 + b_2] \cdot \begin{bmatrix} m^1 & m^2 & & m^n \\ m^1\theta^1 & m^1\theta^1 & & m^n\theta^1 \\ m^1\theta^{1^2} & m^1\theta^{1^2} & & m^n\theta^2 \\ m^1\theta^{1^3} & m^1\theta^{1^3} & \cdots & m^n\theta^3 \\ m^1\lambda^1 & m^1\lambda^1 & & m^n\lambda^1 \\ m^1\lambda^{1^2} & m^1\lambda^{1^2} & & m^n\lambda^2 \end{bmatrix} \quad (2)$$

$$VTEC = a_0 + a_1\theta^1 + a_2\theta^2 + a_3\theta^3 + b_1\lambda^1 + b_2\lambda^2 \quad (3)$$

The description of the VTEC model is done by limiting the Surabaya area and its surroundings by presenting a table of corresponding VTEC values of the VTEC value that has been obtained.

The analysis is carried out on the graph of changes in the TEC value and the characteristics of the TEC values in daily. As well as an analysis of the model of the VTEC value of the Surabaya area and its surroundings.

3 Analysis and Discussion

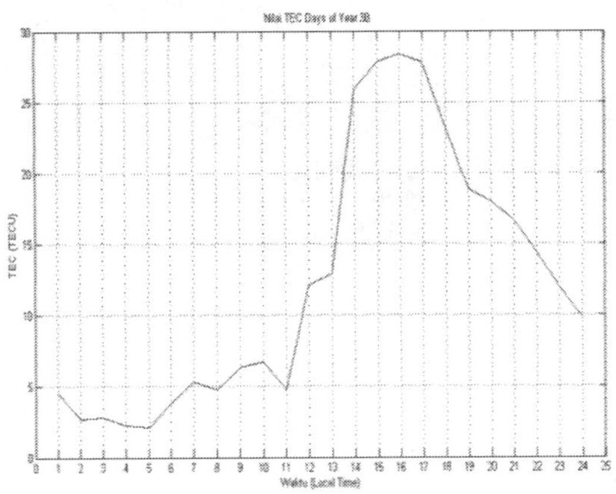

Fig. 2. TEC Value Chart for First Day

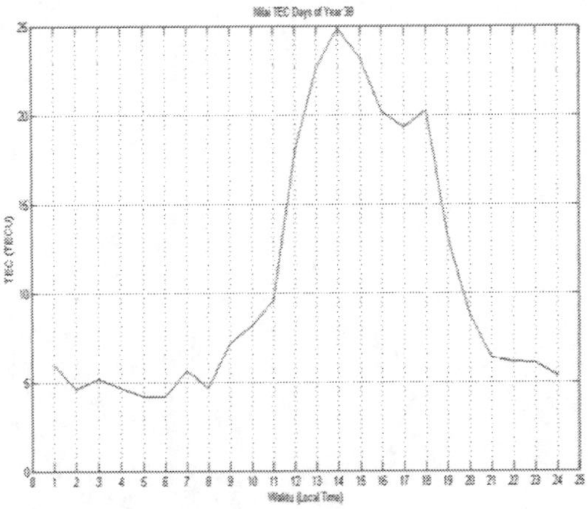

Fig. 3. TEC Value Chart for Second Day

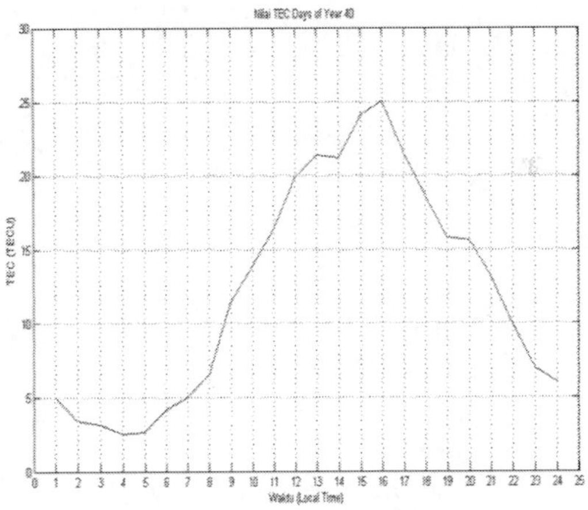

Fig. 4. TEC Value Chart for Third Day

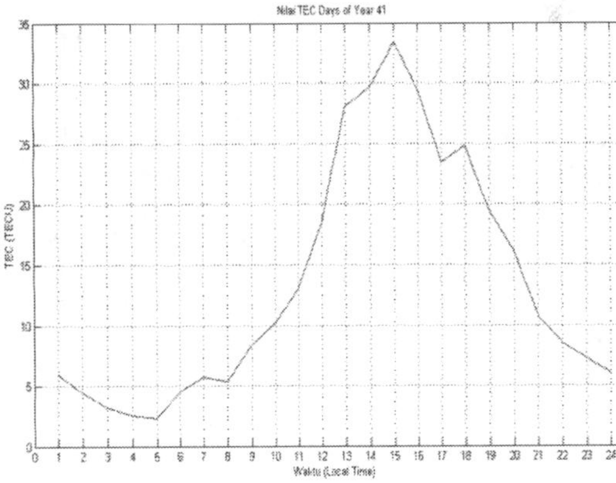

Fig. 5. TEC Value Chart for Fourth Day

Based on Figure 2 to Figure 8, the TEC value is obtained for the maximum and minimum values on 7 February 2018 to 13 February 2018 with the details in the table 3.

https://doi.org/10.1051/e3sconf/20199405005

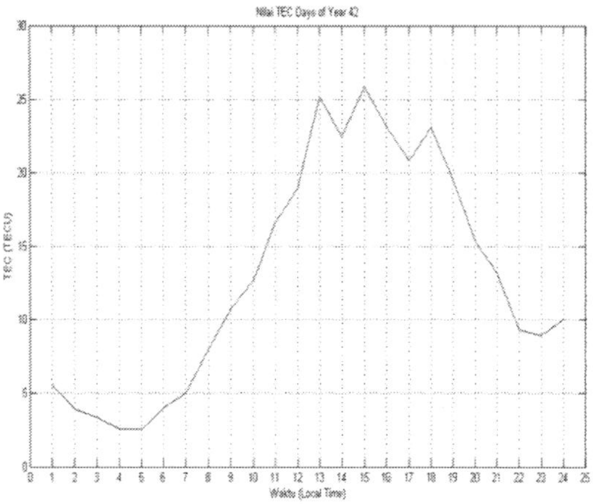

Fig. 6. TEC Value Chart for Fifth Day

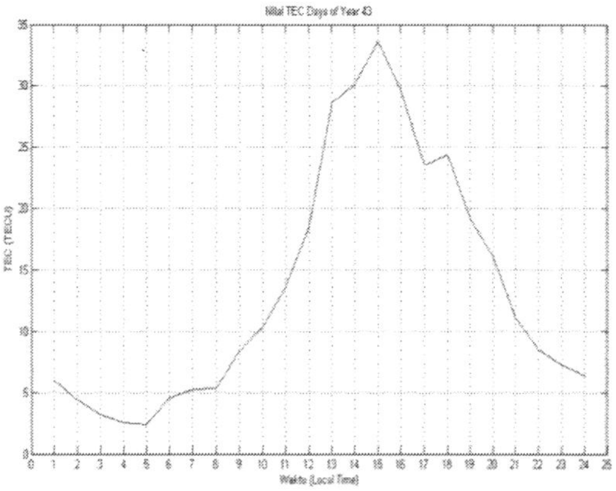

Fig. 7. TEC Value Chart for Sixth Day

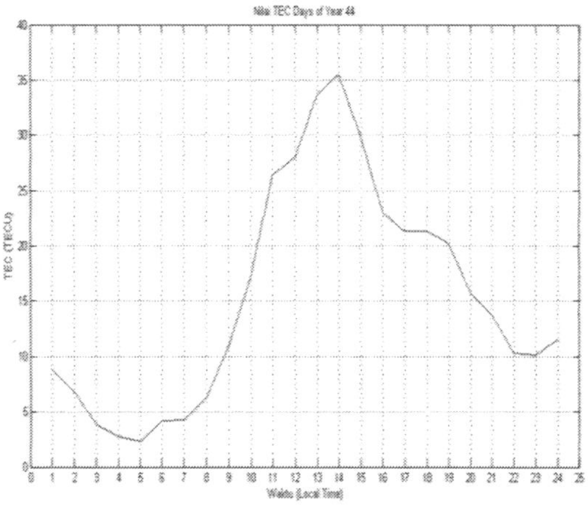

Fig. 8. TEC Value Chart for Sevent Day

Based on the TEC values obtained, shows that the TEC value has increased during the day where this is caused by the influence of the sun which causes the number of electrons to increase. While the minimum TEC value occurs at night due to weak solar activity so that the number of electrons weakens.

Table 3. Maximum and Minimum TEC values on 7 February 2018 to 13 February 2018

Date	O'clock	Value ofTEC (TECU)
7 Februari 2018	16.00 WIB	28,394
	05.00 WIB	2,138
8 Februari 2018	14.00 WIB	24,889
	05.00 WIB	4,166
9 Februari 2018	16.00 WIB	25,031
	04.00 WIB	2,552
10 Februari 2018	13.00 WIB	33,395
	05.00 WIB	2,337
11 Februari 2018	15.00 WIB	25,880
	04.00 WIB	2,529
12 Februari 2018	15.00 WIB	33,636
	05.00 WIB	2,400
13 Februari 2018	14.00 WIB	35,510
	05.00 WIB	2,319

3.1. Analysis of the Total Value Front Content (TEC) Model of the TEC Value Model at 2:00 p.m.

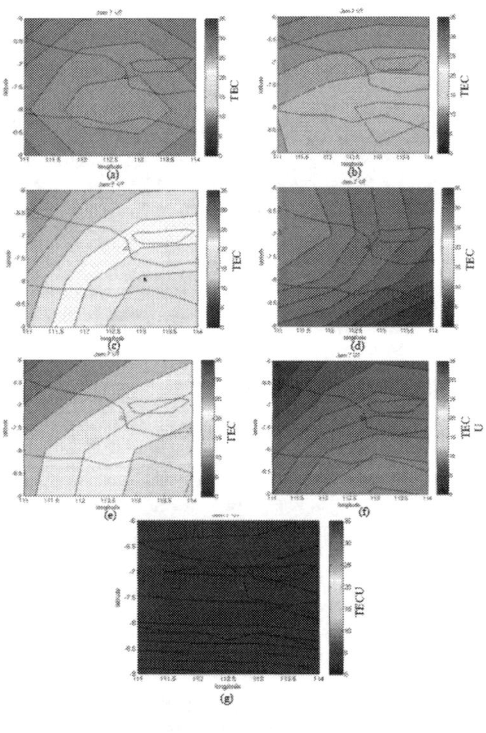

Fig. 9. TEC Value Model at 14.00 WIB (02.00 pm)

In Figure 9 is a TEC model for 14.00 WIB from 7 February 2018 to 13 February 2018. It is known that the largest TEC value occurred on 13 February 2018 so that the 9g area of Surabaya and its surroundings is red. For figures 9a to 9f experience a state of increasing the value of TEC so that the Surabaya area and its surroundings experience a change to red.

 https://doi.org/10.1051/e3sconf/20199405005

4 Conclusion

Based on data processing and analysis conducted, the authors can draw conclusions in this study as follows:

1. The maximum TEC value occurs on February 13, 2018 with a value of 35,510 TECU at 14.00 WIB. While the minimum TEC value occurs on 7 February 2018 with a value of 2,138 TECU at 5.00 WIB.
2. The Model TEC movement for 14.00 WIB shows a high TEC value, this can be seen in the red area of Surabaya and its surroundings.

References

1. Muslim, B. Pemodelan TEC Ionosfer Di Atas Sumatra Dan Sekitarnya Mendekati Real Time Dari Data GPS NTUS. Bandung: Pusat Pemanfaatan Sains Antariksa, LAPAN. (2009)
2. Rizal, Mochammad. Analisa Nilai TEC (Total Electron Content) pada Lapisan Ionosfer Dengan Menggunakan Data Pengamatan Gps Dua Frekuensi. Surabaya: Jurusan Teknik Geomatika Institut Teknologi Sepuluh Nopember. (2009)

AUTHOR INDEX

AUTHOR INDEX

EDP Sciences – Web of Conferences
17, Avenue du Hoggar
Parc d'Activité de Courtabouf
BP 112
F-91944 Les Ulis Cedex A
France

CURRAN ASSOCIATES INC.
proceedings.com

ISBN 978-1-5108-8619-3